CHRISTIAN
ROMAN EMPIRE
SERIES

Vol. 12

THE ECCLESIASTICAL HISTORY

OF

SOZOMEN

*A HISTORY OF THE CHURCH
FROM AD 324 TO AD 425*

Translated by
Edward Walford

Evolution Publishing
Merchantville NJ
2018

This translation originally published by
Henry G. Bohn, London
1855

This edition ©2018 by Evolution Publishing
Merchantville, New Jersey.

Printed in the United States of America

ISBN 978-1-935228-15-8

TABLE OF CONTENTS

Preface to the 2018 Edition xi
Bibliography and Further Reading xv
Prefatory Remarks by Valesius Concerning the Life and Writings of Sozomen xix
Memoir of Sozomen xxiii

Address to the Emperor Theodosius by Salamanes Hermias Sozomen,
    and proposal for an Ecclesiastical History xxv

The Ecclesiastical History of Sozomen

BOOK I
Chapter I: Concerning the Jewish nation — Authors to whom Sozomen was indebted 3
Chapter II: Of the bishops of the large towns in the reign of Constantine,
    and how from fear of Licinius, Christianity was professed in secret
    in the East as far as Libya, while in the West, through the favor of Constantine,
    it was openly professed 7
Chapter III: By the vision of the cross, and by the appearance of Christ, Constantine
    is led to embrace Christianity. He receives religious instruction from our brethren 8
Chapter IV: Constantine commands the sign of the cross to be carried before him
    in battle. 9
Chapter V: Refutation of the assertion that Constantine embraced Christianity
    in consequence of the death of his son Crispus 10
Chapter VI: Constantine the Great causes Christianity to be preached
    throughout the world 11
Chapter VII: Concerning the dispute between Constantine and Licinius,
    his brother-in-law, about the Christians. Defeat and death of Licinius 13
Chapter VIII: Constantine legalizes the profession of the Christian religion, constructs
    religious edifices, and performs other deeds for the public welfare 14
Chapter IX: Constantine enacts a law in favor of the clergy and of those
    who preserve their virginity 16
Chapter X: Concerning the great confessors of the faith who flourished
    at this period 18
Chapter XI: Account of Saint Spyridion, his modesty and tranquility 18
Chapter XII: On the manners and customs of the monks. Their origin and founders 20
Chapter XIII: Antony the Great and Saint Paul 22
Chapter XIV: Account of Saint Ammon and Eutychius of Olympus 24
Chapter XV: The Arian heresy, its origin, its progress, and the contention
    which it occasioned among the bishops 27
Chapter XVI: Constantine, having heard of the strive of the bishops and the
    difference of opinion concerning the Passover, is greatly troubled, and sends
    Hosius, a Spaniard, bishop of Cordova, to Alexandria to settle these disputes 29
Chapter XVII: Of the council convened at Nicæa on account of Arius 30
Chapter XVIII: Two philosophers are converted to the faith by the simplicity
    of two old men with whom they held a disputation 32
Chapter XIX: The emperor harangues the assembled synod 33
Chapter XX: After giving audience to both parties, the emperor condemns
    the followers of Arius to exile 34

Chapter XXI: The decrees of the Council. The condemnation of Arius. His books are to be burned. Certain of the archierarchy differ from the Synod. The Passover 35
Chapter XXII: Acesius, Bishop of the Novatians, is summoned by the emperor to be present at the first synod 36
Chapter XXIII: Canons appointed by the Council. Paphnutius, a certain confessor of the faith, restrains the Council from forming a canon enjoining celibacy to all who would have the priesthood honored 37
Chapter XXIV: Concerning Meletius, the ordinations made by him, and the just enactments of the holy Council 38
Chapter XXV: Honor paid to the bishops by the emperor 38

BOOK II
Chapter I: The discovery of the Cross and of the Holy Nails 41
Chapter II: Concerning Helena, the mother of the emperor. She visited Jerusalem, built temples in that city, and performed other godly works. Her death 43
Chapter III: Temples built by Constantine. The city called by his name. The temple dedicated to Michael the Archangel 44
Chapter IV: Constantine the Great abolishes superstition and builds a temple 46
Chapter V: Constantine destroys the places dedicated to the idols, and persuades the people to embrace Christianity 48
Chapter VI: Under Constantine the name of Christ is spread throughout the world ... 49
Chapter VII: How the Iberians received the faith of Christ 50
Chapter VIII: How the Armenians and Persians embraced Christianity 52
Chapter IX: Sapor, king of Persia, is excited against the Christians. Symeon, bishop of Persia, and Usthazanes, a eunuch, suffer the agony of martyrdom 53
Chapter X: Christians slain by Sapor in Persia 55
Chapter XI: Pusicius, superintendant of the Artisans of Sapor 56
Chapter XII: Martyrdom of Tarbula, the sister of Symeon 57
Chapter XIII: Martyrdom of Saint Acepsimus and of his companions 57
Chapter XIV: Conduct and Martyrdom of Milles the bishop. The multitude of bishops slain in Persian by Sapor, besides obscure individuals 58
Chapter XV: Constantine writes to Sapor to stay the persecution of the Christians 59
Chapter XVI: Eusebius and Theognis, who at the Council of Nicæa, had assented to the writings of Arius, are reinstated in their own bishoprics 60
Chapter XVII: On the death of Alexander, bishop of Alexandria, Athanasius is elected in his stead. Details concerning his youth and education, and his friend Antony the Great 62
Chapter XVIII: The Arians and Meletians confer celebrity on Athanasius. Concerning Eusebius, and his request to admit the Arians to communion. Concerning the term consubstantial. Contest between Eusebius Pamphilus and Eustathius, bishop of Antioch 64
Chapter XIX: Synod of Antioch. Unjust deposition of Eustathius. Euphronius elected in his stead. Constantine the Great writes to the Synod and to Eusebius Pamphilus, who refuses the bishopric of Antioch 65
Chapter XX: Concerning Maximus, who succeeded Macarius in the bishopric of Jerusalem 66
Chapter XXI: The Meletians and Arians agree in sentiment. Eusebius and Theognis relapse into the errors of Arius 67
Chapter XXII: Machinations of the Arians and Meletians against Saint Athanasius 68
Chapter XXIII: Calumny respecting Saint Athanasius and the hand of Arsenius 70
Chapter XXIV: Some Indian nations are converted to Christianity through the instrumentality of two captives, Frumentius and Edesius 71

Chapter XXV: Council of Tyre. Illegal deposition of Saint Athanasius 73
Chapter XXVI: Erection of a temple by Constantine the Great at Golgotha
in Jerusalem. Its dedication... 77
Chapter XXVII: Concerning the presbyter by whom Constantine was persuaded
to recall Arius and Euzoius from exile. The written confession of faith
propounded by Arius, and the reception of this latter by the Synod
assembled at Jerusalem.. 77
Chapter XXVIII: Letter from the emperor Constantine to the Synod of Tyre.
Exile of Saint Athanasius through the machinations of the Arian faction 80
Chapter XXIX: Alexander, bishop of Constantinople. His refusal to admit
Arius into communion. Death of Arius 82
Chapter XXX: Account given by the great Athanasius of the death of Arius 83
Chapter XXXI: Events which transpired in Alexandria after the death of Arius.
Letter of Constantine the Great 84
Chapter XXXII: Constantine enacts a law against all heresies and prohibits
the people from assembling in any place by the Catholic Church, and thus
the greater number of heresies disappear 85
Chapter XXXIII: Marcellus, bishop of Ancyra. His heresy and deposition 86
Chapter XXXIV: Death of Constantine the Great. He receives the rite of baptism
in his last moments, and is buried in the temple of the Holy Apostles 87

BOOK III
Chapter I: After the death of Constantine the Great, the adherents
of Eusebius and Theognis renew the controversy concerning the faith
established at Nicæa 89
Chapter II: Return of the great Athanasius from exile. Letter of Constantine
Cæsar, son of Constantine the Great. Machinations of the Arians against
Athanasius. Acacius. War between Constantine and Constans 90
Chapter III: Paul, bishop of Constantinople. Heresy of Macedonius 91
Chapter IV: A sedition was excited on the ordination of Paul 92
Chapter V: Council of Antioch. Deposition of Athanasius. Installation of Gregory.
Two formularies of faith 93
Chapter VI: Eusebius, surnamed Emesius. Gregory accepts the bishopric
of Alexandria. Athanasius seeks refuge in Rome 95
Chapter VII: Bishops of Rome and of Constantinople. Restoration of Paul
after the death of Eusebius. Death of Hermogenes, a general of the army 96
Chapter VIII: Arrival of the eastern archbishops at Rome. Letter of Julius, bishop
of Rome. By means of the letters of Julius, Paul and Athanasius are reinstated
in their own bishoprics. Letters from the archbishops of the east to Julius 98
Chapter IX: Election of Paul and Athanasius. Macedonius is invested
with the government of the church of Constantinople 99
Chapter X: The bishop of Rome writes to the bishops of the east in favor of Athanasius,
and they send a deputation to Rome to justify their proceedings. This deputation
is dismissed by Constans Cæsar 100
Chapter XI: The Long Formulary and the enactments issued by the Council
of Sardica. Julius, bishop of Rome, and Hosius, bishop of Spain, deposed
by the bishops of the east 101
Chapter XII: Deposition in their turn of the eastern bishops by the bishops of the west,
who compile a formulary of faith 103
Chapter XIII: After the council, a separation takes place between the eastern
and the western churches. The church of the west adheres to the faith of
the Nicæan Council, while that of the east is disturbed by doctrinal
disputes and discussions 104

Chapter XIV: Of the holy men who flourished about this time in Egypt namely
Antony, the two Macariuses, Heraclius, Cronius, Paphnutius, Putubastes,
Arsinius, Serapion, Piturion, Pachomius, Apollonius, Anuphus, Hilarion,
and many others 105
Chapter XV: Didymus the Blind, and Ætius the Heretic 111
Chapter XVI: Concerning the piety of Saint Ephraim 112
Chapter XVII: Transactions of that period, and progress of the Christian
doctrine through the joint efforts of emperors and archbishops 115
Chapter XVIII: Concerning the doctrines held by the sons of Constantine.
Distinction between the terms "Homousian" and "Homœosian."
Constantius is led to abandon the true faith 116
Chapter XIX: Further particulars concerning the term "consubstantial."
Council of Arminum 117
Chapter XX: Return and re-installation of Athanasius. Archbishops of Antioch.
Question put by Constantius to Athanasius. Hymns of praise to God 118
Chapter XXI: Letter of Constantius to the Egyptians in behalf of Athanasius.
Synod of Jerusalem 120
Chapter XXII: Epistle written by the Synod of Jerusalem in favor of Athanasius 121
Chapter XXIII: Valens and Ursacius, who belonged to the Arian faction,
confess to the bishop of Rome that Athanasius had been unjustly deposed 122
Chapter XXIV: Letter of conciliation from Valens and Ursacius to the Great
Athanasius. Restoration of the other eastern bishops. Ejection of
Macedonius and accession of Paul 123

BOOK IV

Chapter I: Death of Constans Cæsar. Occurrences which took place in Rome 125
Chapter II: Constantius again ejects Athanasius, and banishes the Homousians.
Death of Paul, Bishop of Constantinople. Macedonius, his usurpation
and evil deeds 125
Chapter III: Martyrdom of the holy Martyrius and Marcian 126
Chapter IV: Military enterprises of Constantius in Illyria, and details
concerning Vetranio and Magnentius. Gallus receives the title of Cæsar,
and is sent to the east 127
Chapter V: Cyril succeeds Maximus in the sacerdotal office, and the sign of the cross,
surpassing the sun in splendor, again appears in the heavens, and is visible
during several days 127
Chapter VI: Photinus, bishop of Sirmium, his heresy, and the council convened
at Sirmium in opposition thereto. Three formularies of faith 128
Chapter VII: Death of the tyrants Magnentius and Silvanus. Sedition of the Jews
in Palestine. Gallus Cæsar is slain 130
Chapter VIII: Arrival of Constantius at Rome. A council is held in Italy. Account of
what happened to Athanasius the Great through the machinations of the Arians 131
Chapter IX: Council of Milan. Banishment of Athanasius 132
Chapter X: Divers machinations of the Arians against Athanasius and his
escape from various dangers through divine interposition. Evil deeds
perpetrated by George in Egypt after the expulsion of Athanasius 134
Chapter XI: Liberius, bishop of Rome, and the cause of his being exiled
by Constantius. Felix, his successor 136
Chapter XII: Ætius the Syrian, and Eudoxius the successor of Leontius
in the bishopric of Antioch. Concerning the term "consubstantial" 138
Chapter XIII: Innovations of Eudoxius censured in a letter written by George,
bishop of Laodicea. Deputation from the Council of Ancyra to Constantius 139
Chapter XIV: Letter of the Emperor Constantius against Eudoxius
and his partisans 140

Chapter XV: The emperor Constantius repairs to Sirmium, recalls Liberius and restores him to the church of Rome. Felix is associated with him in the government of that church 141

Chapter XVI: The emperor purposed, on account of the heresy of Ætius, to convene a council at Nicomedia, but as an earthquake took place in that city, the council was first convened at Nicæa and afterwards at Arminum and Seleucia. Account of Arsacius the Confessor 143

Chapter XVII: Proceedings of the Council of Arminum 146

Chapter XVIII: Letter from the council convened at Arminum to the emperor Constantius ... 148

Chapter XIX: Concerning the deputies of the council and the emperor's letter. Machinations of Ursacius and Valens. Exile of the archbishops. Concerning the Synod at Nicæa 150

Chapter XX: Events which took place in the eastern churches. Marathonius, Eleusius of Cyzicus, and Macedonius expel those who maintain the term "consubstantial." Concerning the church of the Novatians. The Novatians enter into communion with the orthodox 152

Chapter XXI: Proceedings of Macedonius in Mantinia. Removal of the remains of Constantine the Great. Julian becomes Cæsar 154

Chapter XXII: Council of Seleucia 155

Chapter XXIII: Acacius and Ætius. How the deputies of the two councils of Arminum and of Seleucia were led by the emperor to accept the same doctrines 159

Chapter XXIV: Formulary of the council of Arminum approved by the Acacians. List of the deposed archbishops, and the causes of their condemnation 160

Chapter XXV: Causes of the deposition of Cyril, bishop of Jerusalem. Mutual dissensions among the bishops. Meletius is ordained by the Arians, and supplants Eustathius in the bishopric of Sebaste 163

Chapter XXVI: Death of Macedonius, bishop of Constantinople. Eudoxius and Acacius strenuously seek the abolition of the formularies of faith set forth at Nicæa and at Arminum. Troubles which thence arose in the church 165

Chapter XXVII: Macedonius, after his rejection from his bishopric, blasphemes against the Holy Ghost. Propagation of his heresy through the instrumentality of Marathonius and others 166

Chapter XXVIII: The Arians, under the impression that the holy Meletius upheld their sentiments, translate him from Sebaste to Antioch. On his preaching the orthodox doctrines, he is deposed, and his bishopric transferred to Euzoius 167

Chapter XXIX: The partisans of Acacius excite fresh commotions, strive to abolish the term "consubstantial," and favor the heresy of Arius 168

Chapter XXX: George, bishop of Antioch, and the bishop of Jerusalem after the deposition of Cyril, Three bishops successively succeed to his bishopric. Restoration of Cyril to the church at Jerusalem 169

BOOK V

Chapter I: Apostasy of Julian. Death of the emperor Constantius 171

Chapter II: Education and life of Julian, and his accession to the empire 172

Chapter III: Julian, on his accession to the throne, sought to suppress Christianity and to promote paganism 176

Chapter IV: Julian persecutes the inhabitants of Cæsarea. Bold fidelity of Maris, bishop of Chalcedon 178

Chapter V: Julian restores liberty to the Christians in order to excite further troubles in the Church. His evil treatment of Christians 179

Chapter VI: Athanasius, after having been seven years concealed in the house of a holy virgin, re-appears in public, and enters the church of Alexandria 181

Chapter VII: Violent death of George, the result of certain occurrences in the temple of Mithra. Letter of Julian on the subject 182

Chapter VIII: Concerning Theodore, the keep of the sacred vases of Antioch. How Julian, the uncle of the emperor, having violated the sacred vases, falls prey to worms and corruption 183
Chapter IX: Martyrdom of the saints Eusebius, Nestabis, and Zeno in the city of Gaza 184
Chapter X: Concerning Saint Hilarion and the virgins of Helenopolis. Martyrdom of Mark, bishop of Arethusa 185
Chapter XI: Martyrdom of Macedonius, of Theodulis, of Tatian, of Busiris, and of Eupsychus 187
Chapter XII: Concerning Lucifer and Eusebius, bishops of the west. Eusebius with Athanasius the Great and other bishops hold a council at Alexandria, and confirm the faith established at Nicæa 189
Chapter XIII: Concerning Paulinus and Meletius, Archbishops of Antioch. Dispute between Eusebius and Lucifer. Eusebius and Hilarius defend the Nicene faith 190
Chapter XIV: Dissension between the partisans of Macedonius and those of Acacius 191
Chapter XV: Athanasius is again banished. Concerning Eleusius, bishop of Cyzicus, and Titus, bishop of Bostra. Ancestors of the author 192
Chapter XVI: Efforts of Julian to establish paganism and abolish Christianity. His epistle to some of the pagan high priests 194
Chapter XVII: Julian resorts to artifice rather than open violence against the Christians. The sign of the cross ceases to be used as a standard. The soldiery invited to offer sacrifice 197
Chapter XVIII: Christians prohibited by the emperor from studying polite literature. Resistance of Basil the Great, Gregory the Theologian and Apollinarius to this decree 198
Chapter XIX: Work written by Julian entitled "Aversion to Beards." Daphne, a suburb of Antioch. Translation of the Remains of Babylas, the priestly martyr 200
Chapter XX: In consequence of the circumstances attending the translation of these relics, many of the Christians are ill-treated. Theodore the Confessor. Temple of Apollo at Daphne destroyed by fire from heaven 202
Chapter XXI: Of the statue of Christ in the city of Paneades. Fountain of Emmaus in which Christ washed his feet. Concerning the tree which worshiped Christ in Egypt 203
Chapter XXII: From aversion to the Christians, Julian grants permission to the Jews to rebuild the Temple at Jerusalem. Their attempt is frustrated by fire from heaven, and by the appearance of the sign of the Cross on their garments 205

BOOK VI
Chapter I: Expedition of Julian against the Persians, and his miserable end. Letter written by Libanus, describing his death 207
Chapter II: Visions of the Emperor's death seen by various individuals. Calamities which Julian entailed upon the Romans 209
Chapter III: Accession of the Emperor Jovian 212
Chapter IV: Troubles again arise in the churches. Council of Antioch in which the Nicene faith is confirmed. Letter of the Council to Jovian 213
Chapter V: The great Athanasius obtains the favor of the emperor and is re-appointed over the churches of Egypt. Vision of the great Antony 214
Chapter VI: Death of Jovian, accession of Valentinian, and association of his brother Valens in the government 216
Chapter VII: Troubles again arise in the churches, and the council of Lampsacus is held. Meletius, bishop of Antioch, and other orthodox bishops are ejected from their churches by the Arians 217
Chapter VIII: Revolt and extraordinary death of Procopius. Eleusius, bishop of Cyzicus, and Eunomius the heretic 219

TABLE OF CONTENTS

Chapter IX: Sufferings of those who maintained the Nicene faith.
Agelius, bishop of the Novatians 220
Chapter X: Concerning Valentinian the Younger and Gratian. Persecution excited by Valens. The Homousians, being persecuted by the Arians and Macedonians, send an embassy to Rome 220
Chapter XI: The Confession of Eustathius, Silvanus, and Theophilus, the deputies of the Macedonians, to Liberius, bishop of Rome 222
Chapter XII: Councils of Sicily and of Tyane. Renewed persecution of the orthodox. Exile and return of Athanasius 223
Chapter XIII: Demophilus elected bishop of Constantinople by the Arians, and Evagrius by the orthodox. Account of the persecutions which ensued 225
Chapter XIV: Eighty orthodox priests put to death by Valens 226
Chapter XV: Disputes between Eusebius, bishop of Cæsarea, and Basil the Great, concerning the church of Cæsarea 226
Chapter XVI: Basil succeeds Eusebius in the bishopric of Cappadocia, and speaks with great freedom in the presence of Valens 227
Chapter XVII: Friendship of Basil and of Gregory the Theologian. They maintain the Nicene doctrines 229
Chapter XVIII: Persecution of Christians at Antioch on the Orontes. The people assemble near the church of the Apostle Thomas at Edessa 229
Chapter XIX: Death of the great Athanasius. His bishopric transferred to Lucius the Arian. Peter, the successor of Athanasius, seeks refuge in Rome 230
Chapter XX: Persecution of the Egyptian monks and of the disciples of Saint Antony. Miracles wrought by them 231
Chapter XXI: List of the places in which the Nicene doctrines were preached. Faith manifested by the Scythians 233
Chapter XXII: Debate concerning the nature of the Holy Ghost. It is decided that He is to be considered consubstantial with the Father and the Son 234
Chapter XXIII: Death of Liberius, bishop of Rome. He is succeeded by Damasus and Ursinus. Orthodox doctrines prevail throughout the west, except at Milan. Synod held at Rome, by which Auxentius is deposed 235
Chapter XXIV: Concerning Saint Ambrose and his elevation to the archbishopric. The Novatians of Phrygia and the Passover 237
Chapter XXV: Concerning Apollinarius. Father and son of that name. Vitalius, the presbyter. Relapse into heresy 239
Chapter XXVI: Eunomius and Ætius, their life and doctrines. Opinions first broached by them concerning the rite of baptism 241
Chapter XXVII: Account given by Gregory the Theologian of Apollinarius and Eunomius in a letter to Nectarius. The heresy of Eunomius is opposed by the monks of that period 243
Chapter XXVIII: Of the holy men who flourished at this period in Egypt 245
Chapter XXIX: Concerning the monks of Thebaïs 246
Chapter XXX: Monks of Scetis 250
Chapter XXXI: Concerning the monasteries of Nitria. Monasteries called cells 252
Chapter XXXII: Monks of Palestine 253
Chapter XXXIII: Monks of Syria 254
Chapter XXXIV: Monks of Edessa, monks of Galatia and Cappadocia 255
Chapter XXXV: The wooden tripod on which were indicated the first letters composing the name of him who was to succeed to the throne. Destruction of the pagan philosophers 257
Chapter XXXVI: Expedition against the Sarmatians. Death of the emperor Valentinian in Gaul. Valentinian the Younger. Persecution of the priests. Oration of the philosopher Themistius 258

Chapter XXXVII: Concerning the barbarians beyond the Danube, and their conversion to Christianity. Ulphilas and Athanaricus. Cause of Arianism being embraced by the Goths.. 259

Chapter XXXVIII: Concerning Mavia, queen of the Saracens. War and subsequent peace between the Saracens and Rome. Details concerning the Ishmaelites and the Saracens, and their conversion to Christianity............................... 262

Chapter XXXIX: Peter, having returned from Rome, supersedes Lucius in the government of the churches of Egypt. Expedition of Valens against the Scythians.. 264

Chapter XL: Saint Isaac the Monk predicts the death of Valens. Valens is defeated. His death 265

BOOK VII

Chapter I: Mavia assists the Romans against the barbarians. Gratian leaves to everyone full liberty of opinion 267

Chapter II: Theodosius is associated with Gratian in the government of the empire. Arianism prevails throughout the eastern churches except that of Jerusalem. Council of Antioch 267

Chapter III: Concerning Saint Meletius and Paulinus, bishops of Antioch. Their oath respecting the bishopric.. 268

Chapter IV: Reign of Theodosius the Great. He is baptized by Ascholius, bishop of Thessalonica 269

Chapter V: Gregory the Theologian receives from Theodosius the government of the churches. Expulsion of Demophilus and of all who deny that the Son is consubstantial with the Father 270

Chapter VI: Intrigues of the Arians. Eloquence of Eunomius. Boldness of Saint Amphilochius.. 271

Chapter VII: Concerning the second holy general council, and the place and the cause of its convention. Abdication of Gregory the Theologian............ 273

Chapter VIII: Election of Nectarius to the bishopric of Constantinople. His birth-place and education 274

Chapter IX: Decrees of the second general council. Maximus, the cynical philosopher 276

Chapter X: Concerning Martyrius of Cilicia. Translation of the remains of Saint Paul the confessor, and Meletius, bishop of Antioch 277

Chapter XI: Ordination of Flavian as bishop of Antioch, and subsequent occurrences 278

Chapter XII: Project of Theodosius to unite all the different forms of religion into one. Agelius and Sisinius. The Novatians. Those who reject the term "consubstantial" are ejected from the churches.. 279

Chapter XIII: Tyranny of Maximus. Concerning the empress Justina and Saint Ambrosius. Death of the emperor Gratian.. 281

Chapter XIV: Birth of Honorius. Theodosius leaves Arcadius at Constantinople and proceeds to Italy. Succession of the Novatian and other patriarchs. Audacity of the Arians. Triumph of Theodosius 282

Chapter XV: Flavian and Evagrius, bishops of Antioch. Demolition of idolatrous temples 283

Chapter XVI: In what manner and from what cause the functions of the presbyter, appointed to preside over the imposition of penance, were abolished. Dissertation on the mode of imposing penance.............................. 286

Chapter XVII: Banishment of Eunomius by Theodosius the Great. Heresies of his successor, Theophronius, of Eutychus, and of Dorotheus. Division among the Arians.. 288

Chapter XVIII: Another heresy originated by the Novatians. Digression concerning the festival of Easter 290

Chapter XIX: Dissertation on the various customs prevalent among different churches and nations.. 292

Chapter XX: Extension of the Christian religion. Demolition of Temples.
   Inundation of the Nile 294
Chapter XXI: Discovery of the head of the precursor of our Lord 295
Chapter XXII: Death of Valentinian. Tyranny of Eugenius.
   Prophecy of John, a monk of Thebaïs 297
Chapter XXIII: Exaction of the tribute in Antioch. Demolition of the statues
   of the emperor. Embassy headed by Flavian the archbishop 298
Chapter XXIV: Victory of Theodosius over Eugenius 299
Chapter XXV: Intrepid bearing of Saint Ambrose in the presence of the
   emperor. Massacre at Thessalonica 300
Chapter XXVI: Saint Donatus, Bishop of Eurœa, and Theotimus,
   archbishop of Scythia 302
Chapter XXVII: Particular account of Saint Epiphanius, bishop of Cyprus 303
Chapter XXVIII: Virtues of Acacius, bishop of Berœa, of Zeno and of Ajax 304
Chapter XXIX: Discovery of the remains of the prophets Habakkuk
   and Micha. Death of the emperor Theodosius the Great 305

BOOK VIII
Chapter I: Successors of Theodosius the Great. Rufinus, the prætorian
   prefect, is slain. Primates of the principal cities. Disputes among
   the heretics. Account of Sisinius, bishop of the Novatians 307
Chapter II: Conduct and wisdom of the great John Chrysostom.
   His promotion to the bishopric of Constantinople 309
Chapter III: Promotion of John to the bishopric. He re-establishes discipline
   in the churches. Deputation to Rome 312
Chapter IV: Enterprise of Gaïnas, the Goth. Evils which he perpetrated 312
Chapter V: Public discourses of John concerning the Macedonian woman,
   and the conversion of bread into stone 315
Chapter VI: Proceedings of John in Asia and Phrygia. Heraclides, bishop
   of Ephesus, and Gerontius, bishop of Nicomedia 316
Chapter VII: Concerning Eutropius, chief of the eunuchs, and the law
   enacted by him. Murmurs against John 318
Chapter VIII: Hymns against Arianism introduced by John.
   Effects of his public ministrations 318
Chapter IX: Serapion the archdeacon and Saint Olympia.
   Complaints of the clergy against John 320
Chapter X: Severian, bishop of Gabales, and Antiochus, bishop of Ptolemais.
   Dispute between Serapion and Severian. Reconciliation effected
   by the empress 321
Chapter XI: Question agitated in Egypt as to whether God has a corporeal
   form. Theophilus, bishop of Alexandria. Books of Origen 322
Chapter XII: Enmity of Theophilus against four brothers, called "the great" 323
Chapter XIII: The monks repair to John. Hostility of Theophilus against John 324
Chapter XIV: Perversity of Theophilus. Arrival of Saint Epiphanius
   at Constantinople. He excites the people of that city against John 325
Chapter XV: The son of the empress and the holy Epiphanius. Conference
   between the "great brothers" and Epiphanius, and the return of this
   latter to Cyprus. Epiphanius and John 327
Chapter XVI: Dispute between the empress and John. Arrival of Theophilus
   from Egypt. Cyrinus, bishop of Chalcedonia 328
Chapter XVII: Council held by Theophilus and the enemies of John. John is
   summoned to attend, but on his refusal, is deposed by Theophilus 329
Chapter XVIII: Sedition of the people against Theophilus and members of his
   council. Re-installation of John in the bishopric 331

Chapter XIX: Perversity of Theophilus. Enmity between the Egyptians and the citizens of Constantinople. Departure of Theophilus. Nilammon the Ascetic 332
Chapter XX: The statue of the empress. Public teaching of John. Convocation of another synod against John. His deposition 334
Chapter XXI: Calamities suffered by the people after the expulsion of John. Machinations against his life 335
Chapter XXII: Unlawful expulsion of John from his bishopric. Conflagration of the church by fire from heaven. Exile of John to Cucusum 336
Chapter XXIII: Arsacius appointed to supplant John in the bishopric. Persecution of the followers of John 337
Chapter XXIV: Eutropius the Reader, and the blessed Olympiade, and the presbyter Tigris are persecuted on account of their attachment to John 338
Chapter XXV: Troubles in the church followed by disturbances in the state. Stilicho, the general of Honorius 340
Chapter XXVI: Two epistles from Innocent, the Pope of Rome, of which one was addressed to John Chrysostom, and the other to the clergy of Constantinople 341
Chapter XXVII: Death of the empress Eudoxia. Death of Arsacius. History of Atticus the Patriarch 344
Chapter XXVIII: Efforts of Innocent, bishop of Rome, to convene a council, and procure the recall of John. Death of John Chrysostom 345

BOOK IX

Chapter I: Death of Arcadius. Accession of Theodosius the Younger. Piety, virtue, virginity, and good works of the princess Pulcheria 347
Chapter II: Discovery of the remains of the Forty Holy Martyrs 348
Chapter III: The virtues and piety of Pulcheria and of her sisters 351
Chapter IV: Truce with Persia. Honorius and Stilicho. Transactions in Rome and Dalmatia 351
Chapter V: Numerous nations take up arms against the Romans, of whom some are, through the providence of God, dispersed, and others brought to terms of amity 352
Chapter VI: Alaric, king of the Goths. Siege of Rome 353
Chapter VII: Deputation sent to Alaric by Innocent, bishop of Rome. Jovius, prefect of Italy. Embassy despatched to the emperor 354
Chapter VIII: Rebellion of Attalus, and how he eventually craves forgiveness at the feet of Honorius 355
Chapter IX: Presumptuous expectations entertained by the pagans and Arians concerning Attalus. Alaric, by a stratagem, obtains possession of Rome 357
Chapter X: Virtue of a Roman Lady 358
Chapter XI: Many instances of rebellion and usurpation occur in the west. The favor of God manifested towards Honorius by the defeat and death of the tyrants 358
Chapter XII: Theodosiolus and Lagodius. The Vandals and Suevi. Death of Alanicus. Retreat of the tyrants Constantine and Constans 359
Chapter XIII: Concerning Gerontius, Maximus, and the troops of Honorius. Defeat of Gerontius. He and his wife perish together 360
Chapter XIV: Defeat and death of Edovicus 361
Chapter XV: Constantine throws aside the emblems of imperial power, and is ordained as presbyter. His death. Death of the other tyrants who had conspired against Honorius 362
Chapter XVI: Favor of God manifested towards the emperor Honorius. Death of Honorius. His successors. Peace established throughout the world 362
Chapter XVII: Discovery of the remains of Zechariah the Prophet, and of Stephen the Proto-Martyr 363

Index 365

PREFACE TO THE 2018 EDITION

When reading the history of Salamanes Hermias Sozomen, one steps back to an era that will seem quite alien to most modern readers. Yet, for others of a more religious bent, it may feel very familiar. It is a time when the great civilized world was shaken to its core; when things which seemed invincible and immortal proved startlingly vulnerable and eminently mortal; when great cities fell and political dynasties crumbled; when religious movements rose, and men of the cross did battle as fiercely as men of the sword.

Providing an account of events during the momentous years between AD 324 and 425, the first few books of Sozomen's history cover the period when the power of the Christian Roman Empire was at its peak. By Book VII, however, the Empire is tottering, and names like Constantine and Valentinian are beginning to be replaced by Stilicho and Arbogastes. By Book IX, the Eternal City—Rome—has been sacked. It was said by Henri Valois (called "Valesius" in the present text) in his *Memoir* below that Sozomen intended his history to extend down to AD 439. The work that we have ends abruptly after the death of the Western emperor Honorius, even cutting off in mid-chapter after promising to describe the relics of Saint Stephen the proto-martyr and never doing so. It is commonly thought that Sozomen passed away in Constantinople in the late 440s. If true, it means that he died as the fortunes of the Empire were approaching a nadir as imperial provinces became barbarian kingdoms, and the Huns encroached on the Danube frontier at will, demanding heavy tributes from the impotent court in Constantinople. It is not unreasonable to posit that Sozomen may have given up writing his history in his old age out of sheer despair. He must have known by the time of his death that the Roman Empire would never be the same as it was during his youth.

Sozomen's history is often criticized as being merely derivative of a similar work of ecclesiastical history written by his contemporary, Socrates Scholasticus. Indeed, the reader will notice numerous notes alluding to this connection throughout the text. In his *Library* (or *Bibliotheca*) of the 9th century AD, Saint Photius of Constantinople says that the style of Sozomen's work is "better than that of Socrates, from whom he differs in certain particulars."[1] Writing in the 17th century, Valesius agrees, saying in the prefatory remarks below that Sozomen made use of a style, "most agreeable to a writer of ecclesiastical affairs." Gibbon termed Sozomen "more curious" than Socrates, at least with regard to particulars of the life of Saint Athanasius which takes up a sizable portion of the history.[2]

Among more recent historians, Rohrbacher posits that Sozomen's reason for writing such a similar work was not merely to amend factual errors found in Socrates, but more importantly, "to correct broader stylistic and thematic flaws that he sees in Socrates' work."[3] This seems a logical conclusion.

Beyond attempting a more classicizing style than that of Socrates, Sozomen also added considerable data from his own resources. Given his parentage as a child of "Bethelia, a populous town near Gaza,"[4] it is no surprise that Sozomen has much to say about ecclesiastical and political affairs on the eastern frontier. Regarding Sozomen's contribution to our knowledge of relations between the Roman Empire and the Arabs, Shahid considers his account to be, "most trustworthy, based as it is on sound written and oral tradition."[5] Sozomen also gives us considerable detail about the rise of monasticism, particularly in Egypt, and focuses with frequency on the lives of individual holy men and women, being unusually fair when calling out the virtues of those belonging to heretical sects. Regarding the inclusion of these *vitae* as capsule biographies within the larger work, Urbainczyk says that Sozomen, in contrast to Socrates, provides, "vastly more information on specific Christians....He mentions more individuals and gives more details about these individuals....Given that there are very few such tales in Socrates' work, Sozomen clearly felt that he was correcting a serious omission in his predecessor."[6]

Perhaps the most important section of Sozomen's work is the fragmentary ninth book. It is here that Sozomen largely untethers himself from Socrates as his primary source, and delves into the alarming political affairs of the Western empire. He provides good coverage of the crisis in the early fifth century when the aggrieved Alaric and his Goths roamed at will through Italy, eventually sacking Rome. It is believed that his principal source for this section is the lost historical work of Olympiodorus of Thebes which exists today only as a summary provided by Saint Photius in his 9th century *Library*. As for the East, he provides invaluable information on the life and reign of the Empress Saint Pulcheria, regent for Theodosius II, as well as a descriptive first-hand account of the procession of the relics of the Forty Martyrs of Sebaste in Constantinople. As mentioned above, the work seems to terminate abruptly in mid-chapter for reasons that are subject to conjecture, but are ultimately unknowable.

Sozomen's overall value to the study of this period is considerable. Writing in the *Catholic Encyclopedia* (1913), Patrick J. Healy sums up Sozomen's contribution aptly: "The history as a whole is fairly comprehensive, and though his treatment of affairs in the Western Church is not full, his pages abound in facts not available elsewhere and in documentary references of the highest importance."[7]

Preface to the 2018 Edition

This edition of Sozomen's *Ecclesiastical History* has been prepared using the 1855 translation of Edward Walford, as published in Bohn's Ecclesiastical Library. The reasons for choosing this particular English version over the 1890 version by Chester D. Hartranft published in the *Select Library of Nicene and Post-Nicene Fathers* are three. First, modern reproductions of the latter are quite common. Second, the editor felt that the footnoting in the Bohn version was generally more informative, and the more antique sources referred to by Walford are now quite easily accessible online. And third, in the opinion of the editor, Walford's more elegant style of English is better suited to an author like Sozomen who was praised in antiquity for the quality of his language. That said, I would refer the interested reader to Hartranft's scholarly introduction to his translation of Sozomen which includes an admirably comprehensive analysis of the text, biography of Sozomen drawn from the history, summary of the manuscript tradition, listing of the translations, and historical literature review.[8]

For this new edition, we have retained the footnotes of the 1855 Bohn translation, as mentioned above, supplementing them with occasional new notes which may be easily identified. The actual text of the translation is practically unchanged, save for a few very obvious typographical errors which we have corrected. To help with text flow for modern readers, we have swapped out the myriad upon myriads of semi-colons in favor of periods and commas where possible. We have also added new paragraphs in appropriate places to help break up particularly large blocks of text.

—*Anthony P. Schiavo, Jr.*
Merchantville, NJ
January 2018

NOTES

1. See *The Library of Photius* as translated by Freese [1920], page 28.
2. See *Decline and Fall of the Roman Empire*, Chapter XXI, footnote 97.
3. See *The Historians of Late Antiquity*, page 123.
4. Book V, Chapter XV of the present volume.
5. See *Byzantium and the Arabs in the Fourth Century*, page 277.
6. "Observations on the Differences between the Church Histories of Socrates and Sozomen," in *Historia*, page 364.
7. See the *Catholic Encyclopedia* (1913), entry for "Salminius Hermias Sozomen."
8. See the Bibliography and Recommended Further Reading below for additional English translations of Sozomen.

BIBLIOGRAPHY AND FURTHER READING

Ammianus Marcellinus. Walter Hamilton (transl.) 1986. *The Later Roman Empire*. Penguin Classics: New York.
Apostolic Constitutions. Alexander Roberts and James Donaldson (eds.) 1886. *The Ante-Nicene Christian Library: Translation of the Writings of the Fathers down to AD 325. Volume 7: Fathers of the Third and Fourth Centuries: Lactantius, Venantius, Asterius, Victorinus, Dionysius, Apostolic Teaching and Constitutions, Homiy and Liturgy*. T&T Clark: Edinburgh.
Athanasius. Philip Schaff and Henry Wace (eds.) 1903. *A Select Library of Nicene and Post-Nicene Fathers of the Christian Church, Volume 4: Saint Athanasius: Select Works and Letters*. Charles Scribner's Sons: New York.
Athanasius. Robert T. Meyer (transl.) 1950. *The Life of Saint Anthony*. Newman Press: New York, NY.
Augustine. Philip Schaff and Henry Wace (eds.) 1994. *A Select Library of Nicene and Post-Nicene Fathers of the Christian Church, First Series, Volume 4: St. Augustin: The Writings against the Manichaeans and against the Donatists*. Hendrickson Publishers: Peabody, MA.
Augustine. Philip Schaff (ed.) 1994. *A Select Library of Nicene and Post-Nicene Fathers of the Christian Church, First Series, Volume 2: St. Augustin: City of God and Christian Doctrine*. Hendrickson Publishers: Peabody, MA.
Ayer, Joseph Cullen. 1970 [1913]. *A Source Book for Ancient Church History: From the Apostolic Age to the Close of the Conciliar Period*. AMS Press: New York.
Baronius, Caesare. 1738. *Annales Ecclesiastici*. Typis Leonardi Venturini: Lucca, Italy.
Basil the Great. Philip Schaff and Henry Wace (eds.) 1895. *A Select Library of Nicene and Post-Nicene Fathers of the Christian Church, Second Series, Volume 8: St. Basil: Letters and Select Works*. Parker and Company: Oxford and London.
Bordeaux Pilgrim. Aubrey Stewart (transl.) 1887. *Itinerary from Bordeaux to Jerusalem*. Palestine Pilgrims' Text Society: London.
Brock, S. P. 1977. "A Letter Attributed to Cyril of Jerusalem on the Rebuilding of the Temple," In *Bulletin of the School of Oriental and African Studies, University of London*, Vol. 40:2.
Bull, George. 1851. *Defensio Fidei Nicænæ: A Defence of the Nicene Creed out of the Extant Writings of the Catholick Doctors Who Flourished During the Three First Centuries of the Christian Church. Vol. 1*. John Henry Parker: Oxford.
Bury, J. B. 1923. *History of the Later Roman Empire from the Death of Theodosius I to the Death of Justinian. Volumes I and II*. MacMillan and Company: London.
Catholic Church 2003. *Catechism of the Catholic Church: With Modifications from the Editio Typica*. Doubleday: New York.
Cave, William. 1840. *Lives of the Most Eminent Fathers of the Church that Flourished in the First Four Centuries, Volume II*. T. Tegg: London.
Chestnut, Glenn F. 1986. *The First Christian Histories: Eusebius, Socrates, Sozomen, Theodoret, and Evagrius, Second Edition*. Mercer University Press: Macon, GA.
Cicero. Andrew Peabody (transl.) 1886. *Tusculan Disputations*. Little, Brown & Co.: Boston.
Codex Canonum Ecclesiæ Universæ. The Cannons of the First Four General Councils of the Church and Those of the Early Local Greek Synods. William Lambert (ed.) 1870. R. D. Dickson: London.

Dunn, Geoffrey D. 2010. "Innocent, Alaric, and Honorius: Church and State in Early Fifth-Century Rome," in Luckensmeyer, *Studies of Religion and Politics in the Early Christian Centuries*. Saint Pauls Publications: Strathfield, Australia.

Eusebius Pamphilus. Anonymous (transl.) 2008 [1846]. *The Life of the Blessed Emperor Constantine*. Evolution Publishing: Merchantville, NJ.

Ferguson, Everett (ed.) 1998. *Encyclopedia of Early Christianity, Second Edition*. Garland Publishing: New York.

Gregory Nazianzen. Philip Schaff and Henry Wace (eds.) 1894. *A Select Library of Nicene and Post-Nicene Fathers of the Christian Church, Second Series, Volume 7: S. Cyril of Jerusalem, S. Gregory Nazianzen*. Parker and Company: Oxford and London.

Gregory of Nyssa. Philip Schaff and Henry Wace (eds.) 1893. *A Select Library of Nicene and Post-Nicene Fathers of the Christian Church, Second Series, Volume 5: Gregory of Nyssa: Dogmatic Treatises etc*. Parker and Company: Oxford and London.

Greer, Rowan A. 1979. *Origen: An Exhortation to Martyrdom, Prayer and Selected Works*. Paulist Press: New York.

Greer, Rowan A. and Margaret Mary Mitchell. 2007. *The "Belly-Myther" of Endor: Interpretations of 1 Kingdoms 28 in the Early Church*. Society of Biblical Literature: Atlanta.

Herbermann, Charles G., et al. 1913. *The Catholic Encyclopedia: An International Work of Reference on the Constitution, Doctrine, Discipline, and Hisotry of the Catholic Church*. The Encyclopedia Press: New York. Electronic edition available at: http://www.newadvent.org/cathen/

Herodotus. Henry Clay (transl.) 1904. *The Histories of Herodotus*. D. Appleton and Company: New York.

Hunter, Sylvester J. 1898. *Outlines of Dogmatic Theology*. Longmans, Green and Co.: London.

Irenaeus. Alexander Roberts and James Donaldson (eds.) 1869. *The Ante-Nicene Christian Library: Translation of the Writings of the Fathers down to AD 325. Volume 1: The Apostolic Fathers, Justin Martyr, Iranaeus*. T&T Clark: Edinburgh.

James, M. R. (transl.) 2004 [1924]. *The New Testament Apocrypha*. Apocryphile Press: Berkeley, CA.

Jerome. Philip Schaff and Henry Wace (eds.) 1912. *A Select Library of Nicene and Post-Nicene Fathers of the Christian Church, Second Series, Volume 6: Saint Jerome, Letters and Select Works*. Charles Scribner's Sons: New York.

John Cassian. Philip Schaff and Henry Wace (eds.) 1894. *A Select Library of Nicene and Post-Nicene Fathers of the Christian Church, Second Series, Volume 11: Sulpitius Severus, Vincent of Lerins. John Cassian*. Charles Scribner's Sons: New York.

John Chrysostom. Philip Schaff (ed.) 1908. *A Select Library of Nicene and Post-Nicene Fathers of the Christian Church, Volume 9: Saint Chrysostom: On the Priesthood; Ascetic Treatises; Select Homilies; Homilies on the Statues*. Charles Scribner's Sons: New York.

John Chrysostom. Philip Schaff and Henry Wace (eds.) 1905. *A Select Library of Nicene and Post-Nicene Fathers of the Christian Church, Volume 13: Saint Chrysostom: Homilies on Galatians, Ephesians, Philippians, Colossians, Thessalonians, Timothy, Titus and Philemon*. Charles Scribner's Sons: New York.

John Chrysostom. Graham Neville (transl.) 1996. *Six Books on the Priesthood*. Saint Vladimir's Seminary Press: Crestwood, NY.

Julian. Emily Wilmer Cave Wright (transl.) 1913. *The Works of the Emperor Julian*. Harvard University Press: Cambridge, MA.

King, C. W. 1888. *Julian the Emperor, Containing Gregory Nazianzen's Two Invectives and Libanius' Monody with Julian's Extant Theosophical Works*. George Bell and Sons: London.

Lactantius. Anthony Bowen and Peter Garnsey (transl.) 2003. *The Divine Institutes*. Liverpool University Press: Liverpool, UK.

Livy. Canon Roberts (transl.) 1912. *History of Rome*, Volume 1. E. P. Dutton and Co.: New York.

Novak, Ralph Martin. 2001. *Christianity and the Roman Empire: Background Texts*. Trinity Press International: Harrisburg, PA.

Olympiodorus. Christopher Chaffin (transl.) 1993. *Olympiodorus of Thebes and the Sack of Rome: A Study of the Historikoi Logoi with Translated Fragments, Commentary and Additional Material*. E. Mellen Press: Lampeter, UK.

Palanque, J. R., G. Brady, P. de LaBriolle, G. de Pinval and L. Brehier. 1949. *The Church in the Christian Roman Empire*. Volumes 1 and 2. Burns Oates & Washbourne: London.

Palladius. Herbert Moore (transl.) 1921. *The Dialogue of Palladius on the Life of Saint John Chrysostom*. Society for Promoting Christian Knowledge: London.

Palladius. W. K. Lowther Clarke (transl.) 1918. *The Lausic History*. The Macmillian Company: London.

Peter the Martyr. Alexander Roberts and James Donaldson (eds.) 1869. *The Ante-Nicene Christian Library: Translation of the Writings of the Fathers down to AD 325. Volume 14: The Writings of Methodius, Alexander of Lycopolis and Peter of Alexandria, and Several Fragments*. T&T Clark: Edinburgh.

Pharr, Clyde. 2001. *The Theodosian Code and Novels and the Sirmondian Constitutions*. The Lawbook Exchange: Union City, NJ.

Photius. J. H. Freese (transl.) 1920. *The Library of Photius*. Society for Promoting Christian Knowledge: London.

Plutarch. Bernadotte Perin (transl.) 1926. *Plutarch's Lives*. Harvard University Press. Cambridge, MA.

Procopius. H. B. Dewing (transl.) 1954. *Buildings*. Harvard University Press. Cambridge, MA.

Procopius. H. B. Dewing (transl.) 1916. *History of the Wars: The Vandalic War. Book III*. Harvard University Press. Cambridge, MA.

Prudentius. Eagan, Sr. M. Clement (transl.) 1962. *The Poems of Prudentius*. Catholic University of America Press: Washington, DC.

Rohrbacher, David. 2002. *The Historians of Late Antiquity*. Routledge: London.

Rufinus of Aquileia. Philip R. Amidon (transl.) 1997. *The Church History of Rufinus of Aquileia: Books 10 and 11*. Oxford University Press: Oxford, UK.

Shahid, Irfan 1985. *Byzantium and the Arabs in the Fourth Century*. Dumbarton Oaks Research Library and Collection: Washington, DC.

Smith, Kyle (transl.) 2013. *The Martyrdom and History of Blessed Simeon Bar Sabba'e*. Gorgias Press: Piscataway, NJ.

Smith, William (ed.) 1843. *Dictionary of Greek and Roman Antiquities*. American Book Company: New York.

Smith, William (ed.) 1870. *Dictionary of Greek and Roman Biography and Mythology, Volume 3*. Little, Brown, and Company, Boston, MA.

Socrates Scholasticus. Edward Walford (putative transl.) 1853. *The Ecclesiastical History of Socrates, Surnamed Scholasticus, or the Advocate*. Henry G. Bohn: London.

Socrates Scholasticus. Philip Schaff and Henry Wace (eds.) 1890. *A Select Library of Nicene and Post-Nicene Fathers of the Christian Church, Second Series, Volume 2: Socrates, Sozomenus: Church Histories*. The Christian Literature Company: New York.

Sophocles. Ezra Pound (transl.) 1957. *The Women of Trachis*. New Direction Books: New York.

Sozomen. Edward Walford (transl.) 1855. *The Ecclesiastical History of Sozomen, Comprising a History of the Church from AD 324 through AD 440*. Henry G. Bohn: London.

Sozomen. Philip Schaff and Henry Wace (eds.) 1890. *A Select Library of Nicene and Post-Nicene Fathers of the Christian Church, Second Series, Volume 2: Socrates, Sozomenus: Church Histories*. The Christian Literature Company: New York.

Sulipitius Severus. Philip Schaff and Henry Wace (ed.) 1894. *A Select Library of Nicene and Post-Nicene Fathers of the Christian Church, Second Series, Volume 11: Sulpitius Severus, Vincent of Lerins. John Cassian*. Charles Scribner's Sons: New York.

Tacitus. Michael Grant (transl.) 1956. *The Annals of Imperial Rome*. Penguin: New York.

Tertullian. Alexander Roberts and James Donaldson (eds.) 1869. *The Ante-Nicene Christian Library: Translation of the Writings of the Fathers down to AD 325. Volume 11: The Writings of Tertullian, Volume 1*. T&T Clark: Edinburgh.

Theodoret. Schaff, Philip and Henry Wace (eds.) 1892. *A Select Library of Nicene and Post-Nicene Fathers of the Christian Church, Second Series, Volume 3: Theodoret, Jerome, Gennadius, Rufinus: Historical Writings, etc.* The Christian Literature Company: New York.

Urbainczyk, Theresa. 1997. "Observations on the Differences between the Church Histories of Socrates and Sozomen," in *Historia: Zeitschrift für Alte Geschichte*, pages 355-373.

Waterworth, James 1898. *The Canons and Decrees of the Sacred and Oecumenical Council of Trent*. C. Dolman: London.

Yarnold, Edward. 2000. *Cyril of Jerusalem*. Routledge: London.

Zosimus. Ronald T. Ridley (transl.) 1982. *New History*. Australian Association for Byzantine Studies: Melbourne, Australia.

PREFATORY REMARKS BY VALESIUS CONCERNING THE LIFE AND WRITINGS OF SOZOMEN

Hermias Sozomen practiced the law at Constantinople, at the same time with Socrates. His ancestors were not mean. They were originally natives of Palestine, being inhabitants of a village near Gaza, called Bethelia. This village was very populous in times past, and had most stately and ancient churches. But the most glorious structure of them all was the Pantheon, situated on an artificial hill, which was the tower as it were of Bethelia, as Sozomen relates in Chapter XV of his fifth book.

The grandfather of Hermias Sozomen was born in that village, and first converted to the Christian faith by Hilarion the monk. For when Alaphion, an inhabitant of the same village, was possessed with a devil, and the Jews and physicians, attempting to cure him, could do him no good by their enchantments, Hilarion by a bare invocation of the name of God cast out the devil. Sozomen's grandfather, and Alaphion himself, amazed at this miracle, with their whole families embraced the Christian religion.

The grandfather of Sozomen was eminent for his expositions of the Sacred Scriptures, being a person endowed with a polite wit and an acuteness of understanding, and besides, he was well skilled in literature. Therefore he was highly esteemed by the Christians inhabiting Gaza, Ascalon, and the places adjacent, as being useful and necessary for the propagating of religion, and could easily unloose the knots of the Sacred Scriptures. But Alaphion's descendants excelled others in their sanctity of life, in kindness to the indigent, and in other virtues, and they were the first that built churches and monasteries there, as Sozomen says in the passage above cited, where he also adds that some holy persons of Alaphion's family were surviving even in his own days, with whom he himself conversed when very young and concerning whom he promises to speak more afterwards. Most probably he means Salamanes, Phuscon, Malchio, and Crispio, brothers, concerning whom he speaks in Chapter XXXVII of his sixth book. For he there says that these brethren, instructed in the monastic discipline by Hilarion, were, during the empire of Valens, eminent in the monasteries of Palestine, that they lived near Bethelia, a village in the country of the Gazites, and were descendants of a noble family in those parts. He mentions the same persons in the 15th chapter of book VIII, where he says that Crispio was Epiphanius's archdeacon. It is evident, therefore, that the brothers were of Alaphion's family. Alaphion, too, was related to Sozomen's grandfather, as we may conjecture, first, because the grandfather of Sozomen is said to have been converted (together with his whole family) to the Christian religion, upon account of Alaphion's wonderful cure, whom Hilarion had healed by calling on the name of Almighty God. Secondly, this conjecture is confirmed by what Sozomen relates, *viz.* that when he was very young, he conversed familiarly with the aged monks that were of Alaphion's family. And, lastly, from the fact that Sozomen took his name from those persons who were either the sons or grandchildren of Alaphion. For he was called Salamanes Hermias Sozomenus (as Photius declares in his Bibliotheca) from the name of that Salamanes who, as we observed before, was the brother of Phuscon, Malchio, and Crispio. Wherefore Nicephorus and others are mistaken in supposing that Sozomen had the surname of Salaminius because he was born at Salamis, a city of Cyprus. But we have before shown from Sozomen's own testimony, that he was not born in Cyprus, but in Palestine. For his grandfather was not only a Palestinian, as is above said, but Sozomen himself was also educated in Palestine, in the bosom (so to say) of those monks who were of Alaphion's family.

From this education Sozomen seems to have imbibed that most ardent love of a monastic life and discipline which he declares in so many places of his history. Hence it is, that in his books he is not content to relate who were the fathers and founders of monastic philosophy, but he also carefully relates their successors and disciples who followed this way of life both in Egypt, Syria, and Palestine, and also in Pontus, Armenia, and Osdroëna. Hence also it is that in the twelfth chapter of the first book of his history, he has proposed to be read (in the beginning as it were) that gorgeous account of the monastic philosophy. For he supposed that he should have been ungrateful had he not after this manner at least made a return of thanks to those in whose familiarity he had lived and from whom, when he was a youth, he had received such eminent examples of a good conversation, as he himself intimates, in the opening of his first book.

It is inferred that Sozomen was educated at Gaza, not only from the passage above mentioned, but also from Chapter XXVIII of his seventh book, where Sozomen says that he himself had seen Zeno, bishop of Majuma, for this Majuma is a sea-port belonging to the Gazites. After this Sozomen applied himself to the profession of the law. He was a student of the civil law at Berytus, a city of Phœnicia, not far distant from his own country, where there was a famous school of civil law. But he practiced the law at Constantinople, as himself asserts in Book II, Chapter III. And yet he seems not to have been very much employed in pleading of causes, for at the same time that he was an advocate in Constantinople, he wrote his *Ecclesiastical History*, as may be concluded from his own words in the last-mentioned passage. Before he wrote his nine books of ecclesiastical history, Sozomen composed a *Breviary of Ecclesiastical Affairs*, from our Savior's ascension to the deposition of Licinius. This work was comprised in two books, as himself bears witness in the opening of his first book, but these two books are now lost.

In the composure of his *History*, Sozomen has made use of a style neither too low nor too high but one between both, as is most agreeable to a writer of ecclesiastical affairs. Photius prefers Sozomen's style to that of Socrates, and we agree with him in his criticism. But though Sozomen is superior in the elegance of his expression, yet Socrates excels him in judgment. For Socrates judges incomparably well, both of men and also of ecclesiastical business and affairs, and there is nothing in his works but what is grave and serious, nothing that can be expunged as superfluous. But on the contrary, some passages occur in Sozomen that are trivial and childish. Of this sort is his digression in his first book concerning the building of the city Hemona, and concerning the Argonauts, who carried the ship Argo on their shoulders some furlongs, and also his description of Daphne without the walls of the city Antioch, in Chapter XIX of his sixth book, to which we must add that observation of his concerning the beauty of the body, where he treats of that virgin with whom the blessed Athanasius absconded a long while. Lastly, his ninth book contains little else besides warlike events, which ought to have no place in an ecclesiastical history.

Sozomen's style, however, is not without its faults. For the periods of his sentences are only joined together by the particles δέ and τέ, than which there is nothing more troublesome. Should any one attentively read the epistle in which Sozomen dedicates his work to Theodosius junior [see page xxv below], he will find it true that Sozomen was no great orator.

It remains, that we inquire which of these two authors, Socrates or Sozomen, wrote first, and which of them borrowed, or rather stole, from the other. Certainly, in regard both of them wrote almost the same things of the same transactions, inasmuch as they both began at the same beginning, and concluded their history at the same point, (both beginning from the reign of Constantine, and ending at the seventeenth consulate of Theodosius junior,) it must needs be true, that one of them robbed the other's desk. This sort of theft was committed by many of the Grecian writers. But which was the plagiary, Socrates or Sozomen, it is hard to say, in regard both of them lived in the same times, and both wrote their history in the empire of Theodosius junior. Therefore, in the disquisition of this question, we must make use of conjecture. Let us therefore see upon which of them falls the suspicion of theft. Indeed this is my sentiment, I suppose that the inferior does frequently steal from the superior, and the junior from the senior. But Sozomen is in my judgment far inferior to Socrates, and he betook himself to writing his history when he was younger than Socrates. For he wrote it whilst he was yet an advocate, as I observed before. Now, the profession of the advocates amongst the Romans was not perpetual, but temporary. Lastly, he that adds something to the other, and sometimes amends the other, seems to have written last. But Sozomen now and then adds some passages to Socrates, and in some places dissents from him, as Photius has observed, and we have hinted in our annotations. Sozomen therefore seems to have written last. And this is the opinion of almost all modern writers, who place Socrates before Sozomen. So Bellarmine in his book *De Scriptoribus Ecclesiasticis*, who is followed by Mirceus, Labbreus, and Vossius. Amongst the ancients, Cassiodorus, Photius, and Nicephorus name Socrates in the first place. So also Theodorus Lector recounts them in his epistle which he prefixed to his Tripartite History.

Thus far concerning Sozomen.

MEMOIR OF SOZOMEN

Little more than cursory allusions to Sozomen occur in the works of contemporary writers, and the materials for a memoir of his life are therefore at best but few and scanty. We should, in fact, be destitute of almost all knowledge as to his birth, education, mode of life, and private history, had not some information on these points been furnished by himself. In the work before us, the only one which has caused his name to be handed down to posterity, he draws aside the curtain which would otherwise have concealed his origin and parentage, and makes known to us a portion of his family history. He tells us (Book V, Chapter XV) that his grandfather was a native of Palestine, and of Pagan parentage, that he, with all his family, was converted to Christianity on witnessing a miracle wrought by Saint Hilarion, and that being possessed of great mental endowments, he afterwards became eminently useful to the men of Gaza and Ascalon by his extraordinary power in expounding the most obscure passages of Holy Writ.

Our author himself seems to have been born about the beginning of the fifth century. He tells us that in his youth some of the founders of monasticism in Palestine were still living, although they had reached a very advanced period of life, and that he had enjoyed opportunities of intercourse with them. To this circumstance may probably be attributed the tone of reverential admiration in which Sozomen invariably speaks of the ascetic inhabitants of the desert.

The education of Sozomen was conducted with a view to the legal profession, and he studied for some years at Berytus, then noted for its school of law. He afterwards established himself at Constantinople and, it has been conjectured, held some office at the court of Theodosius the Younger. He is reputed to have possessed some skill in the law, but it is certain that he never attained any eminence in his profession. It is only in the character of an historian that he has rendered himself conspicuous. His first work was an abridgment of Ecclesiastical History, from the ascension of our Lord to the deposition of Licinius (AD 324), but this is not extant.

The work before us seems to have been commenced about the year 443. It embraces a period of 117 years, namely, from AD 323 to AD 439. It is generally admitted to have suffered many alterations and mutilations, and this may in some measure serve to account for the frequent inaccuracies in point both of narrative and of chronology which pervade the nine books of which it is composed. It is evident, from the very abrupt termination of this history, that it is but a fragmentary portion of a larger work. The precise object of Sozomen in undertaking to write this history is not apparent, as exactly the same ground had previously been gone over by Socrates, if we except the ninth book of the former, which is almost entirely devoted to the political history of the times. The learned Photius prefers the style of Sozomen to that of Socrates, yet Sozomen frequently evinces great deficiency in point of judgment, and on many occasions enlarges upon details which are altogether omitted by Socrates, as unworthy of the dignity of ecclesiastical history. To us, there is manifest advantage in possessing these separate chronicles of the same events. Facts which might perhaps have been doubted, if not rejected, had they rested upon the sole authority of a single writer, are admitted as unquestionable when authenticated by the combined testimony of Socrates, of Sozomen, and of Theodoret. And, indeed, the very discrepancies which, on several minor points, are discernible in the histories of these writers, are not without their use, inasmuch as they tend to the removal of all suspicion of connivance or collusion.

ADDRESS TO THE EMPEROR THEODOSIUS BY SALAMANES HERMIAS SOZOMEN, AND PROPOSAL FOR AN ECCLESIASTICAL HISTORY

The popular saying is, that the former emperors were zealous about some useful matter or other: such as were fond of ornaments, cared for the royal purple, the crown, and the like; those who were studious of letters, composed some mythical work or treatise capable of fascinating its readers; those who were practised in war, sought to send the weapon straight to the mark, to hit wild beasts, to hurl the spear, or to leap upon the horse. Every one who was devoted to a craft which was pleasing to the rulers announced himself at the palace. One brings a precious stone not easily susceptible of polish. Another undertakes to prepare a more brilliant color than the purple robe. One dedicates a poem or treatise. Another introduces an expert and strange fashion of armor.

It is considered the greatest and a regal thing for the ruler of the whole people to possess at least one of the homely virtues. But no such great estimate has been made of piety which is, after all, the true ornament of the empire. Thou, however, O most powerful Emperor Theodosius,[1] hast in a word, by God's help, cultivated every virtue. Girt with the purple robe and crown, a symbol of your dignity to onlookers, you wear within always that true ornament of sovereignty, piety and philanthropy. Whence it happens that poets and writers, and the greater part of your officers as well as the rest of your subjects, concern themselves on every occasion with you and your deeds. And when you preside as ruler of contests and judge of discourses, you are not robbed of your accuracy by any artificial sound and form, but you award the prize sincerely, observing whether the diction is suitable to the design of the composition, so also with respect to the form of words, divisions, order, unity, phraseology, construction, arguments, thought, and narrative. You recompense the speakers with your favorable judgment and applause, as well as with golden images, erection of statues, gifts, and every kind of honor. You show greater personal favor toward the speakers than the ancient Cretans did toward the much-sung Homer, or the Alevadæ did to Simonides, or Dionysius the tyrant of Sicily to Plato the companion of Socrates, or Philip the Macedonian to Theopompus the historian, or the Emperor Severus to Oppianus who related in verse the kinds, nature, and catching of fish. For after the Cretans had rewarded Homer with a thousand *nummi,* they inscribed the amount of the gift on a public column as if to boast of their excessive munificence. The

Alevadæ, Dionysius, and Philip were not more reserved than the Cretans, who boasted of their modest and philosophical government, but quickly imitated their column, so that they might not be inferior in their donative. But when Severus bestowed upon Oppianus a golden gift for each line of his moderate verse, he so astonished everybody with his liberality, that the poems of Oppianus are popularly called golden words to this day. Such were the donations of former lovers of learning and discourses.

But you, O Emperor, surpass any of the ancients in your liberality to letters, and you seem to me to do this not unreasonably. For while you strive to conquer all by your virtues, you also conduct your own affairs successfully, according to your thorough knowledge of the story of those ancient affairs, so prosperously directed by the Greeks and Romans. Rumor says that during the day, you take military and bodily exercise and arrange affairs of state by giving judicial decisions and by making note of what is necessary and by observation, both in public and private, of the things which ought to be done, and at night that you busy yourself with books. It is a saying, that there serves you for the study of these works, a lamp which causes the oil to flow automatically into the wick by means of some mechanism, so that not one of the servants in the palace should be compelled to be taxed with your labors, and to do violence to nature by fighting against sleep. Thus you are humane and gentle, both to those near and to all, since you imitate the Heavenly King who is your pattern in that He loves to send rain and causes the sun to rise on the just and unjust, as well as to furnish other blessings ungrudgingly.

As is natural, I hear also that by your various learning, you are no less familiar with the nature of stones, and the virtues of roots, and forces of remedies, than Solomon, the wisest son of David, while you excel him in virtue. For Solomon became the slave of his pleasures and did not preserve to the end that piety which had been for him the source of prosperity and wisdom. But thou, most powerful Emperor, because you set your restraining reason in array against levity, art not only an autocrat of men but also of the passions of soul and body, as one would naturally suppose.

And this, too, ought to be remarked: I understand that you conquer the desire for all food and drink, neither the sweeter figs, to speak poetically, nor any other kind of fruit in its season, can take you prisoner except the little that you touch and taste after you have returned thanks to the Maker of all things. You are wont to vanquish thirst, stifling heat, and cold by your daily exercise, so that you seem to have self-control as a second nature. Lately, as is well known, you were anxious to visit the city of Heraclea in Pontus and to restore it, prostrated by time, and you took the way in the summer season through Bithynia. When the sun about midday was very fiery, one of the body-guard saw you heated with much sweat and clouds of dust and, as if to do you a favor, he anticipatingly offered to you a bowl which reflected brilliantly the rays of the sun. He poured in some sweet drink and added cold water thereto. But you, most powerful Emperor, received it and praised the man for his good will, and you made it obvious that you would soon reward him for his well-wrought deed with royal munificence. But when all the soldiers were wondering with open mouth at the dish, and were counting him blessed who should drink, you, O noble Emperor, returned the drink to him and commanded him to use it in whatever way he pleased. So that it seems to me that Alexander, the son of Philip, was surpassed by your virtue, of whom it is reputed by his admirers that while he with the Macedonians was passing through a waterless place, an anxious soldier found water, drew it, and offered it to Alexander. He would not drink it but poured out the draught. Therefore, in a word, it is appropriate to call you, according to Homer, more regal than the kings who preceded you. For we have heard of some who acquired nothing worthy of admiration, and others who adorned their reign with scarcely one or two deeds. But thou, O most powerful Emperor, hast gathered together all the virtues and hast excelled every one in piety, philanthropy, courage, prudence, justice, munificence, and a magnanimity befitting royal dignity.

And every age will boast of your rule as alone unstained and pure from murder, beyond all governments that ever existed. You teach your subjects to pursue serious things with pleasure, so that they show zeal for you and public affairs, with good will and respect.

So that for all these reasons, it has appeared to me, as a writer of ecclesiastical history, necessary to address myself to you. For to whom can I do this more appropriately, since I am about to relate the virtue of many devoted men, and the events of the Catholic Church, and since her conflicts with so many enemies lead me to your threshhold and that of your fathers? Come, you who knows all things and possesses every virtue especially that of piety, which the Divine Word says is the beginning of wisdom, receive from me this writing and marshal its facts and purify it by your labors out of your accurate knowledge, whether by addition or elimination. For whatever course may seem pleasing to you, that will be wholly advantageous and brilliant for the readers, nor shall any one put a hand to it after your approval.

My history begins with the third consulate of the Cæsars Crispus and Constantine, and stretches to your seventeenth consulship.[2] I deemed it proper to divide the whole work into nine parts. The first and second books will embrace the ecclesiastical affairs under Constantine. The third and fourth, those under his sons. The fifth and sixth, those under Julian, the cousin of the sons of the great Constantine, and Jovian, and, further, of Valentinian and Valens. The seventh and eighth books, O most powerful Emperor, will open up the affairs under the brothers Gratian and Valentinian, until the proclamation of Theodosius, your divine grandfather, as far as your celebrated father Arcadius, together with your uncle, the most pious and godly Honorius, received the paternal government and shared in the regulation of the Roman world. The ninth book I have devoted to your Christ-loving and most innocent majesty, which may God always preserve in unbroken good will, triumphing greatly over enemies, and having all things under your feet and transmitting the holy empire to your sons' sons with the approbation of Christ, through whom and with whom, be glory to God, and the Father, with the Holy Spirit forever. Amen.

NOTES

1. *Note to the 2018 edition:* Sozomen here addresses Theodosius II, the Roman emperor in Constantinople who ruled until AD 450. He was the son of Arcadius and the grandson of Theodosius I.
2. *Note to the 2018 edition:* Here Sozomen marks the proposed limits of his history, from AD 324 through AD 439. As is mentioned in the Preface above, however, the extant history ends abruptly about the year AD 425.

THE ECCLESIASTICAL HISTORY
OF SOZOMEN

BOOK I

CHAPTER I
CONCERNING THE JEWISH NATION — AUTHORS TO WHOM SOZOMEN WAS INDEBTED

My mind has been often exercised in inquiring how it is that other men are ready to believe in the word of God, while the Jews are so incredulous,[1] although it was to them that instruction concerning the things of God was, from the beginning, imparted by the prophets, who likewise made them acquainted with the events attendant upon the coming of Christ before they came to pass.[2] Besides, Abraham, the head of their nation and of the circumcision, was accounted worthy to be an eye-witness, and the host of the Son of God.[3] And Isaac, his son, was honored as the type of the sacrifice on the cross, for he was led bound to the altar by his father and, as accurate students of the Sacred Scriptures affirm, the sufferings of Christ came to pass in like manner. Jacob predicted that the hope of the nations would be in Christ, which prediction is now accomplished, and he likewise foretold the time of Christ's appearance when he said, "The princes of the Hebrews of the tribe of Judah, the chiefs of the tribe shall fail."[4] This clearly referred to the reign of Herod, for this king was, on his father's side, an Idumean, and on his mother's an Arabian, and the government of the Jewish nation was delivered to him by Augustus Caesar and the Roman senate. And besides, among the other prophets, some declared beforehand the birth of Christ, his ineffable conception, his family, his country, and the continuance after his birth of his mother's virginity.[5] Some predicted his divine and wonderful actions, while others foretold his sufferings, his resurrection from the dead, his ascension into the heavens, and the signs by which each of these events was accompanied. But if any be ignorant of these facts, it is not difficult to obtain information by referring to the sacred books.

Josephus, the son of Matthias,[6] who was a priest, and moreover held in the highest repute by the Jews and Romans, may likewise be regarded as a notable witness to the truth concerning Christ,[7] for impressed, no doubt, by the wonderful works wrought by our Lord, and the truthfulness of his doctrines, this writer evidently shrinks from calling him a man, but openly calls him Christ, and records that he was condemned to the death of the cross, and appeared alive again the third day. Nor was he ignorant of numberless other wonderful predictions accomplished in Christ, and uttered by the holy prophets. He further testifies that many, both Jews and Greeks, followed after Christ and continued in his love, and that the people who bear his name had never lost their corporate existence. It appears to me that in bearing witness to these things, he loudly proclaims as the truth implied by the works that Christ is God. It appears, too, that, being struck by the lustre of our Lord's miracles, he was led to steer a middle course, and did not vilify those who believed in him but, on the contrary, rather coincided in opinion with them.[8]

When I reflect on these things, I am seized with profound astonishment at the fact that Christianity was not, in the first place, embraced by the Hebrews prior to its reception by any other nation. It is true, indeed, that the sibyl and certain oracles foretold what was about to happen to Christ,[9] yet all the Greeks must not on that account be accused of unbelief. These prophecies were, for the most part, written in verse, and were intelligible only to the few who by their erudition were able to understand more important truths than those commonly taught to the people. It was, as appears to me, by a Providence from above directing the harmonious sequence of events, that truth was declared, not by the prophets only, but also in part by men of other nations. It was, in fact, as if a musician, in order to elicit some rare melody, were to strike a supernumerary chord, or attach an additional chord to his instrument.

Having now shown that the Hebrews, although in the possession of numerous and most distinct prophecies concerning the coming of Christ, were less willing than the Greeks to embrace the faith that is in him, let what has been said on the subject suffice. Yet let it by no means be, hence accounted contrary to reason that the church should have been mainly built up by the conversion of other nations, for in the first place, it is evident that in divine and great affairs, God delights to bring to pass changes in a marvellous manner, and then, be it remembered, it was by the exercise of no common virtues that those who, at the very beginning, were at the head of religious affairs, maintained their influence. If they did not, indeed, possess resplendent gifts of eloquence, nor the power of convincing their hearers by means of mathematical demonstration, yet they accomplished the work they had undertaken. They gave up their property, neglected their kindred, were stretched upon a cross and, as if endowed with bodies not their own, suffered divers excruciating tortures.[10] Neither seduced by the adulation of the rulers and people of any city, nor terrified by their menaces, they clearly evidenced by their conduct that they were supported in the struggle by the hope of a high reward. So that they, in fact, needed not to resort to verbal arguments, for without any effort on their part, their very deeds constrained the inhabitants of every city and of every house to give credit to their testimony, even before they knew wherein it consisted.

Since then so divine and marvellous a change has taken place in the circumstances of men, that ancient superstitions and national laws have fallen into contempt. Since many of the most celebrated writers among the Greeks have tasked their powers of eloquence in describing the Calydonian boar, the bull of Marathon, and other similar prodigies which have had a real or imaginary existence, why should not I rise above myself, and write a history of the Church? For I am persuaded that as the topic is not the achievements of men, it may appear almost incredible that such a history should be written by me. But, with God, nothing is impossible.

I at first felt strongly inclined to trace the course of events from the very commencement, but on reflecting that similar records of the past, up to their own time, had been compiled by the learned Clemens[11] and Hegesippus,[12] successors of the apostles, by Africanus[13] the historian, and by Eusebius surnamed Pamphilus,[14] a man intimately acquainted with the Sacred Scriptures and the writings of the Greek poets and historians, I merely drew up an epitome in two books of all that is recorded to have happened to the churches, from the ascension of Christ to the deposition of Licinius.[15] Now, however, by the help of God, I will endeavor to relate the sequel of the history.

I shall record the transactions with which I have been connected, and also those concerning which I have been informed by persons who, from their own observation or otherwise, were well acquainted with them. And I shall embrace the history of our own and the preceding generation. But I have sought for records of events of earlier date amongst the established laws appertaining to religion, amongst the proceedings of the synods of the period, amongst the novelties that arose, and in the epistles of kings and priests. Some of these documents are preserved in palaces and churches, and others are dispersed, and in the possession of the learned. I thought seriously at one time of transcribing the whole, but on further reflection I deemed it better, on account of the prolixity of the documents, to give merely a brief synopsis of their contents. Yet whenever controverted topics are introduced, I will readily transcribe freely from any work that may tend to the elucidation of truth.

If anyone who is ignorant of past events should conclude my history to be false because he meets with conflicting statements in other writings, let him know that since the dogmas of Arius[16] and other more recent hypotheses have been broached, the rulers of the churches, differing in opinion among themselves, have transmitted in writing their own peculiar views for the benefit of their respective followers. And further, be it remembered, these rulers convened councils and issued what decrees they pleased, often condemning unheard those whose creed was dissimilar to their own, and striving to their utmost to induce the reigning prince and nobles of the time to side with them. Intent upon maintaining the orthodoxy of their own dogmas, the partisans of each sect respectively formed a collection of such epistles as favored their own heresy, omitting all documents of a contrary tendency. Such are the obstacles by which we are beset in our endeavors to arrive at a conclusion on this subject! Still, as it is requisite in order to maintain historical accuracy to pay the strictest attention to the means of eliciting truth, I felt myself bound to examine all writings of this class with great diligence.

Let not an impertinent or malignant spirit be imputed to me, for having dwelt upon the disputes of ecclesiastics among themselves, concerning the primacy and the pre-eminence of their own sect. In the first place, as I have already said, an historian ought to regard everything as secondary in importance to truth, and moreover, the purity of the doctrine of the Catholic Church is evidenced by the fact of its being the most powerful, for often has it been tested by the attacks of opinionists of antagonistic dogmas. Yet, the disposal of the lot being of God, the Catholic Church has maintained its own ascendancy, has re-assumed its own power, and has led all the churches and the people to the reception of its own truth.

I have had to deliberate whether I ought to confine myself to the recital of events connected with the church under the Roman government; but it seemed more advisable to include, as far as possible, the record of transactions relative to religion among the Persians and barbarians. Nor is it foreign to ecclesiastical history to introduce in this work an account of those who were the fathers and originators of what is denominated monachism, and of their immediate successors, whose celebrity is well known to us either by observation or report. For I would neither be considered ungracious,[17] and willing to consign their virtue to oblivion, nor yet be thought ignorant of their history, but I would wish to leave behind me such a record of their manner of life that others, led by their example, might attain to a blessed and happy end. As the work proceeds, these subjects shall, therefore, meet with due attention.

I now, in full reliance upon the help and propitiousness of God, proceed to the narrative of events. So here closes the introduction to the work.

NOTES

1. δύσπιστος. On this word Valesius remarks that Sozomen was a great imitator of the style of Xenophon, and that he commences his work in almost the very words of the latter, in his *Cyropædia*.
2. Compare Eusebius, *Ecclesiastical History*, Book I, Chapter 4.
3. Alluding to the occasion on which Abraham entertained three angels, and interceded on behalf of Sodom and Gomorrah. See Genesis 18, and especially verses 2 and 3.
4. Alluding to the dying words of Jacob, Genesis 49:10, "The sceptre shall not depart from Judah, nor a lawgiver from between his feet, until Shiloh come."
5. Isaiah, 7:14, foretells that "a virgin shall conceive and bear a son," but he does not declare, in

words, the perpetual virginity of the mother of God. The Catholic Church, however, infers the doctrine from certain types in the Old Testament, such as that of "the bush which burnt with fire, and was not consumed" (See Exodus 3:2).
6. Otherwise written Mattathias.
7. See Josephus, *Jewish Antiquities,* Book XVIII, Chapter 4. *Note to the 2018 edition:* Sozomen here refers to the Testimonium Flavianum. For a full discussion, see "Eusebius and the Testimonium Flavianum" in *Catholic Biblical Quarterly,* Vol. 61:2, page 305–322.
8. See the observations prefixed to Whiston's Josephus.
9. He alludes to the wide-spread belief in a coming Savior or Conqueror, so prevalent during the reign of Augustus. See among other passages, Virgil, Eclogue IV. *Note to the 2018 edition:* Sozomen mentions this again with regard to Constantine's oration. See Constantine's *Oration to the Assembly of the Saints,* Chapter 18 and 19. See also Augustine's *City of God,* Book XVIII, Chapter 23.
10. See Cave's *Lives of the Apostles and Primitive Fathers, passim.*
11. Valesius considers this Clemens to have been the same Clement who was bishop of Rome, and the author of the Epistle to the Corinthians which bears his name, and of some books entitled *Recognitiones,* which were translated by Rufinus.
12. See the *Life of Eusebius* prefixed to his *Ecclesiastical History,* and note on Socrates, *Ecclesiastical History,* Book I, Chapter 1.
13. *Note to the 2018 edition*: Fragments of Hegesippus's works were preserved by Eusebius Pamphilus in his *Ecclesiastical History*. He is known to have been active in the late 2nd century AD. See Ferguson: *Encyclopedia of Early Christianity,* page 515.
14. *Note to the 2018 edition:* Sozomen here refers to Sextus Julius Africanus, a Christian writer from the 3rd century AD whose works survive in fragments only. He influenced later Christian historians including Eusebius Pamphilus. See Ferguson: *Encyclopedia of Early Christianity,* page 644.
15. See Memoir of Sozomen prefixed to this volume. These books are not now extant.
16. For an account of Arianism, see Socrates, *Ecclesiastical History,* Book I, Chapters 5–9.
17. Valesius thinks that it is to be inferred from this passage that Sozomen was a monk himself.

CHAPTER II

OF THE BISHOPS OF THE LARGE TOWNS IN THE REIGN OF CONSTANTINE, AND HOW FROM FEAR OF LICINIUS, CHRISTIANITY WAS PROFESSED IN SECRET IN THE EAST AS FAR AS LIBYA, WHILE IN THE WEST, THROUGH THE FAVOR OF CONSTANTINE, IT WAS OPENLY PROFESSED

AD 324 — During the consulate of Constantine Caesar and Crispus Caesar, Silvester governed the church of Rome, Alexander that of Alexandria, and Macarius that of Jerusalem. No one since Romanus[1] had been appointed over the church of Antioch on the Orontes, for the persecution, it appears, had prevented the ceremony of ordination from taking place. The bishops assembled at Nicæa were, however, so sensible of the purity of the life and doctrines of Eustathius, that they adjudged him worthy to fill the apostolic throne. He was then bishop of Berœa, a place in the neighborhood. They, therefore, translated him to Antioch.[2]

The Christians of the East, as far as Libya on the borders of Egypt, did not dare to meet openly as a church, for Licinius had withdrawn his favor from them, but the Christians of the West, the Greeks, the Macedonians, and the Illyrians, met for worship in safety through the protection of Constantine, who was then at the head of the Roman empire.[3]

NOTES

1. Who this Romanus was is uncertain, as his name does not occur in the catalogue of bishops of Antioch according to Jerome and Nicephorus. In one catalogue, however, in the Florentine Library, his name occurs next before that of Cyril.
2. Compare Socrates, *Ecclesiastical History,* Book I, Chapters 13 and 24.
3. For an account of the treatment of the Christians by Licinius, and the war between Constantine and Licinius on their account, see Socrates, *Ecclesiastical History,* Book I, Chapters 3, and 4. *Note to the 2018 edition:* See also, Eusebius Pamphilus's account in *The Life of the Blessed Emperor Constantine,* Book II, Chapters 1–18.

CHAPTER III

BY THE VISION OF THE CROSS, AND BY THE APPEARANCE OF CHRIST, CONSTANTINE IS LED TO EMBRACE CHRISTIANITY. HE RECEIVES RELIGIOUS INSTRUCTION FROM OUR BRETHREN

We have been informed that Constantine was led to honor the Christian religion by the concurrence of several different events, particularly by the appearance of a sign from heaven. When he first formed the resolution of entering into a war against Maxentius, he was beset with doubts as to the means of carrying on his military operations, and as to the quarter whence he could look for assistance. In the midst of his perplexity, he saw in a vision the sight of the cross[1] shining in heaven. He was amazed at the spectacle, but some holy angels who were standing by exclaimed, "O Constantine! by this, go forth to victory!" And Christ himself appeared to him, and showed him the symbol of the cross, and commanded him to construct one like unto it, and to retain it as his help in battle, as it would insure the victory.

Eusebius, surnamed Pamphilus,[2] affirms that he heard the emperor declare with an oath that as he was reclining about the middle of the day, he and the soldiers who were with him saw in heaven the trophy of the cross composed of light, and encircled by the following words, "By this, go forth to victory." This sign met him by the way, when he was perplexed as to whither he should lead his army. While he was reflecting on what this could mean, night came on; and when he fell asleep, Christ appeared[3] with the sign which he had seen in heaven, and commanded him to construct a representation of the symbol, and to use it as his help in hostile encounters. There was nothing further to be elucidated, for the emperor clearly apprehended the necessity of serving God.

At daybreak, he called together the priests of Christ and questioned them concerning their doctrines. They opened the Sacred Scriptures and expounded the truths relative to Christ, and showed him, from the prophets, how the things which had been predicted had been fulfilled. The sign which had appeared to him was the symbol, they said, of the victory over hell, for Christ came among men, was stretched upon the cross, died, and returned to life the third day. On this account, they said, there was hope that at the close of the present dispensation, there would be a general resurrection of the dead, and entrance upon immortality when those who had led a good life would receive accordingly, and those who had done evil would be punished. Yet, continued they, the means of salvation and of purification from sin are provided, namely, for the uninitiated,[4] initiation according to the canons of the church and, for the initiated, abstinence from renewed transgression. But as few, even among holy men, are capable of complying with this latter condition, another method of purification is set forth, namely, repentance, for God in his love towards man bestows forgiveness on those who have fallen into sin, on their repentance, and the confirmation of their repentance by good works.[5]

NOTES

1. With this chapter, compare the parallel account in Socrates, *Ecclesiastical History,* Book I, Chapter 2.
2. Compare Eusebius's *Life of the Blessed Emperor Constantine,* Book I, Chapter 28.
2. Compare Eusebius's *Life of the Blessed Emperor Constantine,* Book I, Chapter 29.
4. That is, for the unbaptized and catechumens. The baptized were called the "initiated" and "enlightened".
5. *Note to the 2018 edition:* This passage demonstrates that in Sozomen's time, an established rite of penance existed. See Book VII, Chapter 16 of the present volume. See also the entry for the Sacrament of Penance in the *Catholic Encyclopedia* (1913) which has a listing of other Church fathers from this period who mentioned the practice.

CHAPTER IV

CONSTANTINE COMMANDS THE SIGN OF THE CROSS TO BE CARRIED BEFORE HIM IN BATTLE

The emperor, amazed at the prophecies concerning Christ which were expounded to him by the priests, sent for some skilful artisans, and commanded them to remodel the standard called by the Romans *Labarum*,[1] to convert it into a representation of the cross, and to adorn it with gold and precious stones. This warlike trophy was valued beyond all others, for it was always carried before the emperor, and was worshipped by the soldiery.[2] I think that Constantine changed the most honorable symbol of the Roman power into the sign of Christ, chiefly that by the habit of having it always in view, and of worshipping it, the soldiers might be induced to abandon their ancient forms of superstition and to recognize the true God whom the emperor worshipped as their leader, and their help in battle. For this symbol was always borne in front of the household legions and was, at the command of the emperor, carried among the phalanxes in the thickest of the fight by an illustrious band of spearmen, of whom each one in turn took the standard upon his shoulders and paraded it through the ranks. It is said that on one occasion, on an unexpected movement of the hostile forces, the man who held the standard placed it in the hands of another, and fled. When he got beyond the reach of the enemy's weapons, he suddenly received a wound and fell, while the man who had stood by the divine symbol remained unhurt, although many weapons were aimed at him, for the missiles of the enemy, directed by Divine agency, lighted upon the standard and the bearer thereof was preserved in the midst of danger. It is also asserted, that no soldier who bore this standard in battle was ever killed, wounded, or taken prisoner.

NOTES

1. Labarum or Laborum. This was the name by which the standard was known to the Eastern Fathers. Gregory Nazianzen and others derive the term from "Labor." Valesius assents to this derivation, and supports it from the words of Sozomen below, adding "*Laborum* dictum est, quod *laboranti* aciei presidium sit salutare," and referring to *Gretser, de Cruce*, Book II.
2. *Note to the 2018 edition:* For a description of the Labarum, see Eusebius's *Life of the Blessed Emperor Constantine*, Book I, Chapter 31.

CHAPTER V

REFUTATION OF THE ASSERTION THAT CONSTANTINE EMBRACED CHRISTIANITY IN CONSEQUENCE OF THE DEATH OF HIS SON CRISPUS

I am aware that it is reported by the Greeks that Constantine, after slaying some of his nearest relations and particularly after assenting to the murder of his son Crispus, repented of his evil deeds and inquired of Sosipater[1] the philosopher, who was then master of the school of Plotinus, concerning the means of purification from guilt. The philosopher (so the story goes) replied that such moral defilement could admit of no purification. The emperor was grieved at this repulse, but happening to meet with some bishops who told him that he would be cleansed from sin on repentance and on submitting to baptism, he was delighted with their representations and doctrines and became a Christian and the leader of those who were converted to the same faith.

It appears to me that this story was the invention of persons who desired to vilify the Christian religion. Crispus,[2] on whose account it is said Constantine required purification, did not die till the twentieth year of his father's reign. He held the second place in the empire and bore the name of Cæsar, and many laws framed with his sanction in favor of Christianity are still extant. That this was the case can be proved by referring to the dates affixed to these laws, and to the lists of the legislators. It does not appear likely that Sosipater had any intercourse with Constantine, whose government was then centered in the regions near the ocean and the Rhine, for his dispute with Maxentius, the governor of Italy,[3] had created so much dissension in the Roman dominions that it was then no easy matter to dwell in Gaul, in Britain, or in the neighboring countries, in which it is universally admitted, Constantine embraced the religion of the Christians previous to his war with Maxentius and prior to his return to Rome and Italy. And this is evidenced by the dates of the laws which he enacted in favor of religion.

But even granting that Sosipater chanced to meet the emperor, or that he had epistolary correspondence with him, it cannot be imagined the philosopher was ignorant that Hercules, the son of Alcmena, obtained purification at Athens by the celebration of the mysteries of Ceres, after the murder of his children, and of Iphitus,[4] his guest and friend. That the Greeks held that purification from guilt of this nature could be obtained is obvious from the instance I have just alleged, and he is a false calumniator who represents that Sosipater taught the contrary. I cannot admit the possibility of the philosopher's having been ignorant of these facts; for he was at that period esteemed the most learned man in Greece.

NOTES

1. Or Sopater. A philosopher of Apamia in Syria, and an intimate friend of Constantine the Great, who however put him to death upon some pretext.
2. Crispus was put to death by Constantine on account of a false accusation preferred against him by his step-mother Fausta. See Saint Chrysostom, Homily XV, *On Philippians*. Also, Ammianus Marcellinus, *History*, Book XIV, Chapter 11.
3. *Note to the 2018 edition:* That is, Maxentius, son of the previous Augustus of the West, Maximianus, had usurped the imperial power in Italy.
4. See Sophocles *Trachiniae*.

CHAPTER VI

CONSTANTINE THE GREAT CAUSES CHRISTIANITY TO BE PREACHED THROUGHOUT THE WORLD

Under the government of Constantine, the churches flourished and increased in numbers, they were enriched by the benevolence and favor of the emperor, and God preserved them from the persecutions and troubles which they had previously encountered. When the churches were suffering from persecution in other parts of the world, Constantius alone, the father of Constantine, protected the Christians. I know of an extraordinary fact relating to him, which is worthy of being recorded. He wished to test the fidelity of certain Christians, excellent and good men, who were attached to his palace. He called them all together, and told them that if they would sacrifice to idols as well as serve God, they should remain in his service and retain their appointments, but that if they refused compliance with his wishes, they should be sent from the palace, and should scarcely escape his vengeance. When difference of judgment had divided them into two parties, separating those who consented to abandon their religion from those who preferred the honor of God to their present welfare, the emperor determined upon retaining those who had adhered to their faith as his friends and counselors. But he turned away from the others, whom he regarded as unmanly impostors, and sent them from his presence, judging that they who had so readily betrayed their God, could not be faithful to their king. Hence, as Christians were deservedly retained in the service of Constantius, he was not willing that Christianity should be accounted unlawful in the countries beyond the confines of Italy, that is to say, in Gaul, in Britain, or in the region of the Pyrenean mountains as far as the Western Ocean.

When Constantine succeeded to this government, the affairs of the churches became still more prosperous. And when Maxentius, the son of Herculius,[1] was slain, the government of his provinces devolved upon Constantine, and the nations who dwelt by the river Tiber and the Eridanus, the people who were called the aborigines of Padua, those who dwelt by the Aquiline, whither, it is said, the ship of Argos was dragged, and the inhabitants of the coasts of the Tyrrhenian Sea, were permitted the exercise of their religion without molestation.

When the Argonauts fled from Æetes, they returned homewards by a different route, crossed the sea of Scythia, sailed up the mouth of some river, and so gained the shores of Italy, where they built a city, which they called Hemona.[2] The following summer, with the assistance of the people of the country, they dragged their ship, by means of machinery, the distance of four hundred stadia, and so reached the Aquiline, a river which falls into the Eridanus. The Eridanus itself falls into the Italian Sea.

After the battle of Cibalæ,[3] the Greeks and the Macedonians, the inhabitants of the banks of the Danube, of Achaia, and the whole nation of Illyria, became subject to Constantine.

NOTES

1. *Note to the 2018 edition:* That is, the above-mentioned Maximianus. See Chapter V, note 3.
2. Or Hæmus. Compare Pliny, Book III, Chapter 18. It was situated near the Julian Alps, on the confines of Italy and Noricum.
3. The battle in which Licinius was routed by Constantine, AD 314.

CHAPTER VII

CONCERNING THE DISPUTE BETWEEN CONSTANTINE AND LICINIUS, HIS BROTHER-IN-LAW, ABOUT THE CHRISTIANS. DEFEAT AND DEATH OF LICINIUS

After this battle, Licinius, who had previously respected the Christians, withdrew his favor from them, and ill-treated many of the priests who lived under his government. He also persecuted several other persons, but especially the soldiers. He was deeply incensed against the Christians on account of his disagreement with Constantine, and thought to wound him by their sufferings, and besides he suspected that they earnestly desired that Constantine alone should enjoy the sovereign rule. In addition to all this, we may mention that, when on the eve of another war with Constantine, Licinius, in order to prepare his mind for the event of the contest, had recourse to sacrifices and oracles, and that, deceived by promises of power, he returned to the religion of the Greeks. The Greeks themselves, too, relate that about this period he consulted the oracle of Apollo Didymus at Miletus, concerning the result of the war, and received an answer from the demon, couched in the following words of Homer:[1]

> Much, old man, do the youths distress thee, warring against thee!
> Feeble thy strength has become, but thy old age yet shall be hardy.

It has often appeared to me that the Christian religion is supported, and its advancement secured, by the superintendence of Divine Providence. But never was I more fully convinced of this truth, than by the circumstances which occurred at this period, for at the very moment that Licinius was about to persecute all the churches in his dominions, the war in Bithynia broke out which ended in a war between him and Constantine, and in which Constantine was so strengthened by Divine assistance that he was victorious by land and by sea. On the destruction of his fleet and army, Licinius retired to Nicomedia, and resided for some time at Thessalonica as a private individual, but was eventually killed.[2] Such was the end of one who, at the beginning of his reign, had distinguished himself in war and in peace, and who had been honored by receiving the sister of Constantine in marriage.

NOTES

1. *Iliad,* Book X, 132.
2. *Note to the 2018 edition:* The circumstances surrounding the death of Licinius may be found in Socrates, *Ecclesiastical History,* Book I, Chapter 4. For the Pagan point of view, see Zosimus, *History,* Book II.

CHAPTER VIII
CONSTANTINE LEGALIZES THE PROFESSION OF THE CHRISTIAN RELIGION, CONSTRUCTS RELIGIOUS EDIFICES, AND PERFORMS OTHER DEEDS FOR THE PUBLIC WELFARE

As soon as the sole government of the Roman empire was vested in Constantine, he issued a decree[1] commanding all the people of the East to honor the Christian religion, to worship the Divine Being, and to recognize, as God alone, the one true God whose power endureth for ever and ever, for He delighteth to give all good things abundantly to those who zealously embrace the truth, He prospers their undertakings and fulfills their desires, while misfortunes, whether in peace or in war, whether in public or in private life, befall transgressors. Constantine then added, but without vain boasting, that God having accounted him meet and worthy to reign, he had been led from the British seas to the Eastern provinces in order that the Christian religion might be extended, and that the worshippers of God, who had confessed His name and had remained faithful under sufferings, might be advanced to public honors.

After making these statements, he entered upon other details connected with the interests of religion. He decreed that all acts and judgments passed by the persecutors of the church against Christianity should be revoked, and commanded that all those who on account of their confession of Christ had been sent to banishment—either to the isles or elsewhere, contrary to their own inclination—and all those who had been condemned to labor in the mines, the public works, the manufactures, or had been enrolled as public functionaries, should be restored to liberty. He removed the stigma of dishonor from those upon whom it had been cast, and permitted those who had been deprived of high appointments in the army, either to re-assume the command, or to remain in privacy, according to their own choice, and when he recalled them to the enjoyment of their former liberties and honors, he likewise restored their possessions. In the case of those who had been slain, and whose property had been confiscated, he enacted that the inheritance should be transferred to the next of kin, or in default of heirs, to the church belonging to the locality where the estate was situated. And when the inheritance had passed into other hands, and had become either private or national property, he commanded it to be restored. He likewise promised to resort to the fittest and best possible arrangements when the property had been purchased by the exchequer, or had been received therefrom by gift.

These measures, as it has been said, having been enacted by the emperor, and ratified by law, were forthwith carried into execution. Christians were thus placed in almost all the principal posts of the Roman government, the worship of false gods was universally prohibited, and the arts of divination, the dedication of statues, and the celebration of Grecian festivals were interdicted. Many of the most ancient customs observed in the cities fell into disuse and, among the Egyptians, the measure used to indicate the increase of the waters of the Nile, was no longer borne into Grecian temples but into churches. The combats of gladiators were then prohibited among the Romans,[2] and the custom which prevailed among the Phœnicians of Lebanon and Heliopolis of prostituting virgins before marriage was abolished.[3]

As to the houses of prayer, the emperor repaired those which were of sufficient magnitude, enlarged and beautified others, and erected new edifices in places in which no building of the kind had existed previously. He furnished the requisite supplies from the imperial treasury, and wrote to the bishops of the cities and the governors of the provinces, desiring them to contribute whatever they wished, and enjoining submission and obedience to the hierarchy.

The prosperity of religion kept pace with the increased prosperity of the empire. After the war with Licinius, the emperor was successful in battle against foreign nations. He conquered the Sarmatians and the people called Goths, and concluded an advantageous treaty with them. These people dwelt beyond the Danube and, as they were warlike, strong in numbers, and possessed of a large standing army, they kept the other tribes of barbarians in awe, and found antagonists in the Romans alone. It is said that during this war, Constantine perceived clearly, by means of signs and visions, that the special protection of Divine Providence had been extended to him. Hence, when he had vanquished all those who rose up in battle against him, he evinced his thankfulness to Christ by zealous attention to the concerns of religion, and exhorted the governors to recognize the one true faith and way of salvation. He enacted that part of the funds levied from tributary countries should be forwarded by the various cities to the bishops and clergy wherever they might be domiciled, and commanded that the law enjoining this gift should be a statute forever. In order to accustom the soldiers to worship God as he did, he had their weapons marked with the symbol of the cross, and he erected a house of prayer in the palace. When he engaged in war, he caused a tent to be borne before him constructed in the shape of a church, so that in case he or his army might be led into the desert, they might have a sacred edifice in which to praise and worship God and participate in the mysteries.[4] Priests and deacons followed the tent for the purpose of officiating therein according to the law and regulations of the church. From that period the Roman legions, which now were called by their number, provided each its own tent with attendant priests and deacons.

He also enjoined the observance of the day termed the Lord's day,[5] which the Jews call the first day of the week, and which the Greeks dedicate to the sun, as likewise the day before the seventh, and commanded that no judicial or other business should be transacted on those days, but that God should be served with prayers and supplications. He honored the Lord's day because on it Christ arose from the dead, and the day above mentioned because on it He was crucified. He regarded the cross with peculiar reverence on account both of the power which it conveyed to him in war, and also of the divine manner in which the symbol had appeared to him. He abolished the law which had prevailed among the Romans of putting criminals to death by crucifixion. He commanded that this divine symbol[6] should be affixed to his image on coins and pictures, and this fact is evidenced by the relics of this kind which are still in existence. And indeed he strove in everything, particularly in the enactment of laws, to serve God. It appears, too, that he prohibited many flagitious and licentious connexions,[7] which till that period had not been forbidden, and in fact, made so many laws of this kind, that it would, it appears to me, be tedious to recount them, so that I shall now bring this subject to a close. I consider it necessary, however, to mention the laws enacted for the honor and consolidation of religion, as they constitute a considerable portion of ecclesiastical history. I shall therefore proceed to the recital.

NOTES

1. γράμμα δημόσιον. The decree is given at full length by Eusebius. See *Life of the Blessed Emperor Constantine*, Book II, Chapter 24.
2. A custom censured even by some of the heathens. See Cicero, *Tusculan Disputations*. Book II. Compare Lactantius, *Divine Institutes*, Book VI, Chapter 20. This custom was forbidden in the East as early as AD 325.
3. The same custom is mentioned by Herodotus (I. 94) as having prevailed in Lydia.
4. Μυστηρίων, that is to say the sacraments of the Church.
5. Several rescripts of the emperors Theodosius and Justinian ordain that on Sunday the law courts should be closed, as also that theatrical exhibitions should not take place. Compare Eusebius, *Life of the Blessed Emperor Constantine*, Book IV, Chapter 18.
6. Namely, the Cross.
7. He probably alludes to the law of Constantine, "de raptu virginum et viduarum." See *Theodosian Code*, Book IX, Title 24. Constantine was the first who punished the accessaries to a rape, and who disallowed the custom which permitted the ravisher to go unpunished, if he gained the woman's consent afterwards.

CHAPTER IX

CONSTANTINE ENACTS A LAW IN FAVOR OF THE CLERGY AND OF THOSE WHO PRESERVE THEIR VIRGINITY

There was an ancient Roman law, by which those who were unmarried at the age of twenty-five were not admitted to the same privileges as the married.[1] Amongst other clauses in this law, it was specified that they were not to receive any bequests by testament, except[2] from their own relatives, and also, that those who were childless, were to be deprived of half of any property that might be bequeathed to them. The object of this ancient Roman law was to increase the population of Rome and the provinces, which had been much reduced in numbers by the civil wars. The emperor, perceiving that this enactment militated against the interests of those who continued in a state of celibacy and remained childless for the sake of God, and deeming it absurd to attempt the multiplication of the human species by the care and zeal of man—nature always receiving increase or decrease according to the fiat from on high—made a law enjoining that the unmarried and childless should have the same advantages as the married. He even bestowed peculiar privileges on those who embraced a life of continence and virginity, and permitted them, contrary to the usage which prevailed throughout the Roman empire, to make a will before they attained the age of puberty. For he believed that those who devoted themselves to the service of God and the cultivation of philosophy would, in all cases, judge aright. For a similar reason the ancient Romans permitted the vestal virgins to make a will as soon as they attained the age of six years, and the emperor was even more influenced by this example than by his reverence for religion.

Constantine likewise enacted a law in favor of the clergy, permitting judgment to be passed by the bishops when litigants preferred appealing to them rather than to the secular court.[3] He enacted that their decree should be valid, and as far superior to that of other judges as if pronounced by the emperor himself, that the governors and subordinate military officers should see to the execution of these decrees, and that sentence, when passed by them, should be irreversible.

Having arrived at this point of my history, it would not be right to omit all mention of the laws passed in favor of those individuals in the churches who had received their freedom. Owing to the strictness of the laws and the unwillingness of masters, there were many difficulties in the way of the acquisition of freedom, that is to say, of the freedom of the city of Rome. Constantine, therefore, made three laws, enacting that all those individuals whose freedom should be attested by the priests should receive the freedom of Rome. The records of these pious regulations are still extant, it having been the custom to engrave on tablets all laws relating to manumission.

Such were the enactments of Constantine. In everything he sought to promote the honor of religion: and religion was valued, not only for its own sake, but also on account of the virtue of those who then professed it.

NOTES

1. The *Lex Poppœa*. See Tacitus, *Annales*, Book III; Eusebius, *Life of the Blessed Emperor Constantine*, Book IV, Chapter 26.
2. Epiphanius and others omit this word, "except." But, as Lipsius shows, there is good reason to retain it. See *Dictionary of Greek and Roman Antiquities:* Lex Papia.

3. Constantine makes mention of this law in his epistle to the bishops of Numidia. See also Baronius, *Ecclesiastical Annals.* AD 316; Eusebius, *Ecclesiastical History*, Book X, Chapter 7; *Theodosian Code*, Title *de Episcopali Definitione*, leg. 2.

CHAPTER X

CONCERNING THE GREAT CONFESSORS OF THE FAITH WHO FLOURISHED AT THIS PERIOD

During this period of cessation from persecution, many excellent Christians and many who had survived the recent troubles and had witnessed a good confession, adorned the churches. Among these were Hosius,[1] bishop of Cordova, Amphion,[2] bishop of Epiphania in Cilicia, Maximus, who succeeded Macarius in the bishopric of Jerusalem, and Paphnutius,[3] an Egyptian. It is said that by this latter, God wrought many miracles, enabling him to expel demons and to heal divers kinds of sickness. This Paphnutius, and Maximus whom we just mentioned, were among the number of confessors whom Maximinus condemned to the mines, after having deprived them of the right eye, and the use of the left leg.

NOTES

1. For a further account of Hosius, compare Socrates, Book I, Chapters 7 and 13.
2. Amphion is mentioned by Athanasius in his *First Oration against the Arians.*
3. See Socrates, *Ecclesiastical History,* Book I, Chapters 8 and 11.

CHAPTER XI

ACCOUNT OF SAINT SPYRIDION. HIS MODESTY AND TRANQUILLITY

Spyridion,[1] bishop of Trimithon in Cyprus, flourished at this period. His virtues are evidenced by the fame which still surrounds his name. The wonderful works which he wrought by Divine assistance are, it appears, generally known by those who dwell in the same region. I shall not conceal the records concerning him which have come to my knowledge.

He was a peasant, was married, and had children, yet was not on this account deficient in spiritual attainment. It is related that one night some wicked men entered his sheepfold and were in the act of stealing his sheep, when they were suddenly bound, and yet no one bound them. The next day when he went to the fold, he found them there and released them from their invisible bonds. He reproved them for having come as thieves by night to steal the sheep, instead of having asked for them. He felt compassion towards them and, desirous of affording them instruction so as to induce them to lead a better life, he said to them, "Go, and take this ram with you. It is not just that all your labor should be in vain, or that you should return empty-handed after having watched all night." This action is well worthy admiration, but not less so is that which I shall now relate.

An individual confided a deposit to the care of his daughter, who was a virgin, and was named Irene. For greater security she buried it, and it so happened that she died soon after without mentioning the circumstance to any one. The person to whom the deposit belonged came to ask for it. Spyridion knew not what answer to give him, so he searched the whole house for it, but not being able to find it, the man wept, tore his hair, and seemed ready to expire. Spyridion, touched with pity, went to the grave and called the girl by name, and inquired where the deposit was concealed. After obtaining the information desired, he returned, found the treasure in the place that had been signified to him, and gave it to the owner. As I have entered upon this subject, it may not be amiss to mention another incident.

It was a custom with this Spyridion to give a certain portion of his fruits to the poor, and to lend another portion without interest. But neither in giving or receiving did he ever take the fruits in his own hands. He merely pointed out the storehouse, and told those who resorted to him to take as much as they needed, or to restore what they had borrowed. A certain man once came to return what had been lent to him, and Spyridion, as usual, desired him to replace it in the storehouse. The man determined to act unjustly and, imagining that the matter would be concealed, did not liquidate the debt but went away under pretence of having made restoration. This, however, could not be long concealed. After some time the man came back again to borrow and was sent to the storehouse with permission to measure out for himself as much as he required. Finding the storehouse empty, he went to acquaint Spyridion and this latter said to him, "I wonder, O man, how it is that you alone have found the storehouse empty and unsupplied with the articles you require. Reflect whether you do not now stand in need of the things which you did not restore. Were it otherwise, what you seek would not be lacking. Go, trust, and you will find." The man felt the reproof and acknowledged his error.

The firmness of this divine man, and his excellent administration of ecclesiastical affairs, are worthy of admiration. It is said that on one occasion, the bishops of Cyprus met to consult on some particular emergency. Spyridion was present, as likewise Triphyllius,[2] bishop of Ledra, an eloquent and learned man, who had studied the law for many years at Berytus.[3] Having been requested to address the people, Triphyllius had occasion, in the middle of his discourse, to quote the text, "Take up thy bed and walk,"[4] and he substituted the word "couch" for the word "bed".

Spyridion, indignant at this refinement upon the text, exclaimed, "Art thou greater than He who uttered the word 'bed' that thou art ashamed to use His words?" Then, turning from the throne of the priest, he looked towards the people, and said that such learning ought to be used with moderation, lest the pride of eloquence should arise. His age and honorable deeds excited respect, and he ranked high among the presbytery, not only on account of his age, but because he had been long in the priesthood.

The reception which Spyridion gave to strangers will appear from the following incident. When he was about eighty years of age, it happened that a traveller came to visit him at one of those periods of the year when it was his custom to fast, with his household,[5] on alternate days. Perceiving that the stranger was much fatigued, Spyridion desired his daughter to wash his feet and set meat before him. The virgin replying that there was neither bread nor meat in the house, for it would have been superfluous to provide such things at the time of the fast, Spyridion, after having prayed and asked forgiveness, desired her to cook some salt pork which chanced to be in the house. When it was prepared, he sat down to table with the stranger, partook of the meat, and told him to follow his example. But the stranger declining, under the plea of being a Christian, he said to him, "It is for that very reason that you ought not to decline partaking of the meat, for it is taught in the word of God, that to the pure all things are pure."[6] Such are the details which I had to relate concerning Spyridion.

NOTES

1. Compare Socrates, *Ecclesiastical History*, Book I, Chapters 8 and 12.
2. This Triphyllius is mentioned by Jerome (*Ad Magnum, de scriptoribus ecclesiasticis,* Epistle 70) as the author of a commentary on the Canticle, or Song of Solomon.
3. Berytus in Phœnicia was celebrated for its school of law in which, among others, Gregory Thaumaturgus is said to have studied.
4. Matthew 9:6.
5. τῆς τεσσαρακοστῆς ενστάσης. While it was Lent, and probably holy week. See Tertullian, *De Patientia*, Chapter 13, and *De Jejuniis*, Chapter 14.
6. Acts 10:15, 28, and Titus 1:15.

CHAPTER XII

ON THE MANNERS AND CUSTOMS OF THE MONKS. THEIR ORIGIN AND FOUNDERS

AD 324 — Those who at this period had embraced monasticism,[1] manifested the glory of the Church and evidenced the truth of their doctrines by their virtuous line of conduct. Indeed, the most useful thing that has been received by man from God is their philosophy.[2] They neglected many branches of mathematics and the technicalities of dialects because they regarded such studies as superfluous and as a useless expenditure of time, seeing that they contribute nothing toward the better regulation of life and conduct. They applied themselves exclusively to the cultivation of natural and useful science, in order that they might mitigate if not eradicate evil. They invariably refrained from accounting any action or principle as good which occupies a middle place between virtue and vice, for they delighted only in what is good and virtuous. They regarded every man as wicked, who, though he abstain from evil, does not do good. They practiced virtue, not only in word but in deed, and sought not honor of man. They manfully subjugated the passions of the soul, yielding neither to the necessities of nature, nor to the weakness of the body.

Being strengthened by Divine assistance, they lived in ceaseless contemplation of the Creator, night and day worshipping him, and offering up prayers and supplications. Pure in heart and blameless in conduct, they faithfully performed their religious duties, and despised such outward observances as lustrations and instruments of sprinkling, for they believed that sin alone requires purging. They lived above the reach of the external casualties to which we are liable and held, as it were, all things under their control, and were not therefore diverted from the path they had selected by the accidents of life or by the force of necessity. They never revenged themselves when injured, nor complained when suffering from disease or privations, but rather rejoiced in such trials, and endured them with patience and meekness. They accustomed themselves to be content with little, and approximated as nearly to God as is possible to human nature. They regarded this life only as a journey, and were not therefore solicitous about acquiring wealth or amassing more than necessity required. They admired the beauty and simplicity of nature, but their hope was placed in heaven and the blessedness of the future.

Wholly absorbed in the worship of God, they revolted from obscene language, and as they had banished evil practices, so they would not allow such things to be even named. They limited as far as possible the demands of nature, and compelled the body to be satisfied with moderate supplies. They overcame intemperance by temperance, injustice by justice, and falsehood by truth, and attained the happy medium in all things. They dwelt in harmony and fellowship with their neighbors. They provided for their friends and strangers, imparted to those who were in want according to their need and comforted the afflicted.

As they were diligent in all things and zealous in seeking the supreme good, their instructions, though clothed in modesty and prudence and devoid of vain and meretricious eloquence, possessed power, like sovereign medicines, in healing the moral diseases of their audience. They spoke, too, with fear and reverence, and eschewed all strife, raillery, and anger. Indeed, it is but reasonable to suppress all irrational emotions, and to subdue carnal and natural passions. Elias the prophet and John the Baptist were the authors, as some say, of this sublime philosophy.

Philo the Pythagorean[3] relates that in his time the most virtuous of the Hebrews assembled from all parts of the world, and settled in a tract of country situated on a hill near Lake Mareotis for the purpose of living as philosophers. He describes their dwellings, their regulations, and their customs, as similar to those which we now meet with among the monks of Egypt. He says that from the moment they began to apply to the study of philosophy, they gave up their property to their relatives, relinquished business and society, and, quitting the cities, dwelt in fields and in gardens. They had also, he informs us, sacred edifices which were called monasteries in which they dwelt apart and alone, occupied in celebrating the holy mysteries and in worshipping God with psalms and hymns. They never tasted food before sunset, and some only took food every third day or even at longer intervals. Finally, he says that on certain days they lay on the ground and abstained from wine and the flesh of animals, that their food was bread, salt, and hyssop, and their drink, water, and that there were aged virgins among them who, for the sake of philosophy, had refrained from marriage.

In this narrative, Philo seems to describe[4] certain Jews who had embraced Christianity and yet retained the customs of their nation, for no vestiges of this manner of life are to be found elsewhere, and hence I conclude that this philosophy flourished in Egypt from this period. Others, however, assert that this mode of life originated from the persecutions for the sake of religion which arose from time to time, and by which many were compelled to flee to the mountains and deserts and forests, and adopt these customs.

NOTES

1. On the origin and growth of the monastic system, see Socrates, *Ecclesiastical History*, Book IV, Chapter 23. See also "Early Monasticism before Chalcedon," in *The Catholic Encyclopedia* (1911), Vol. 10.
2. The word φιλοσοφεῖν is constantly used by the early Christian historians to signify the practice of asceticism.
3. Valesius would prefer to read "the Platonist" in accordance with the ancient proverb, which says, "either Philo is a Platonist or Plato is a Philonist."
4. Compare Eusebius, *Ecclesiastical History*, Book II, Chapter 17, where he attributes to the Christians what is said by Philo concerning the Therapeutie, as these Jews were called. They were neither ascetic Christians nor yet Essenes.

CHAPTER XIII

ANTONY THE GREAT AND SAINT PAUL

Whether the Egyptians or others are to be regarded as the founders of this philosophy, it is universally admitted that it was carried to perfection by Antony,[1] an ascetic, virtuous, and renowned monk. His fame was so widely spread throughout the deserts of Egypt that the emperor Constantine sought his friendship, entered into epistolary correspondence with him, and urged him to proffer any request that he might desire. He was an Egyptian by birth and belonged to an illustrious family of Coma, a village situated near the town, called by the Egyptians Heraclea. He was but a youth when he lost his parents. He bestowed his paternal inheritance upon his fellow-villagers, sold the rest of his possessions, and distributed the proceeds among the needy. For he was aware that philosophy does not merely consist in the relinquishment of property, but in the proper distribution of it. He obtained the acquaintance of the most eminent men of his time, and strove to imitate all the virtues displayed by others.

Believing that the practice of goodness would become delightful by habit, though arduous at the onset, he entered upon a course of rigid and increasing austerity, and day by day his zeal seemed to augment, just as if he were always re-commencing his undertaking. He subdued the voluptuousness of the body by labor, and restrained the passions of the mind by the aid of the Divine wisdom. His food was bread and salt, his drink water, and he never broke his fast till after sunset. He often remained two or more days without eating. He watched, so to speak, throughout the night, and continued in prayer till day-break. If at any time he indulged in sleep, it was but for a little while on a mat spread upon the ground, but generally he lay upon the ground itself. He rejected the practice of anointing with oil, and of bathing, regarding such habits as likely to relax the body by moisture. And it is said that he never at any time saw himself naked.

He neither possessed nor admired learning, but he valued a good understanding as being prior to learning, and as being the origin and source of it. He was exceedingly meek and philanthropic, prudent and manly, cheerful in conversation and friendly in disputations, even when others used the controverted topics as occasion for strife. He possessed so much skill and sagacity that he restored moderation and stilled altercations at their very commencement, and tempered the ardor of those who conversed with him. Although, on account of his extraordinary virtues, he received the gift of foretelling future events, he never regarded this power as being superior to virtue, nor did he counsel others to seek this gift rashly, for he considered that no one would be punished or rewarded according to his ignorance or knowledge of futurity, for true blessedness consists in the service of God and in obeying his commands. "But," said he, "if any man would know the future, let him seek spiritual purification, for then he will have power to walk in the light and to foresee things that are to happen, for God will reveal the future to him."

He never suffered himself to be idle, but exhorted all those who seemed disposed to lead a good life to diligence in labor, to self-examination and confession of sin before Him who created the day and the night. And when they erred, he urged them to record the transgression in writing that so they might be ashamed of their sins and be fearful lest they should come to the knowledge of others. He zealously defended those who were oppressed and in their cause often resorted to the cities, for many came out to him and compelled him to intercede for them with the rulers and men in power. All the people honored him, listened with avidity to his discourses, and yielded assent to his arguments. But he preferred to remain unknown and concealed in the deserts. When compelled to visit a city, he never failed to return to the deserts as soon as he had accomplished the work he had undertaken. For he said that as fishes are nourished in the water, so the desert is the world prepared for monks. And as fishes die when thrown upon dry land, so monks lose their gravity in the world. His deportment was polite and courteous towards all, and free from the very appearance of pride. I have given this concise account of the manners of Antony, in order that an idea of his philosophy may be formed, by analogy, from the description of his conduct in the desert.[2]

He had many renowned disciples, of whom some flourished in Egypt, and others in Libya, Palestine, Syria, and Arabia. Like their master, they all dwelt in solitude and subjugated themselves, and they instructed others in philosophy and virtue. But it would be difficult to find the disciples of Antony or their successors, for they sought concealment more earnestly than many ambitious men by means of pomp and show now seek popularity and renown.

We must relate, in chronological order, the history of the most celebrated disciples of Antony, and particularly that of Paul, surnamed the Simple. It is said that he dwelt in the country and was married to a beautiful woman, and that having surprised her in the act of adultery, he declared with a smiling and placid countenance, that he would live with her no longer, that he left her with the adulterer, and went immediately to join Antony in the desert. It is further related that he was exceedingly meek and patient, and that being aged and unaccustomed to monastic severity, Antony put his strength to the proof by various trial, and that having given evidence of perfect philosophy, he was sent to live alone as no longer requiring a teacher. And God himself confirmed the testimony of Antony, for Paul manifested his illustrious character by his wonderful works and by his power in expelling demons, in which he even surpassed his teacher.

NOTES

1. Compare Socrates, *Ecclesiastical History,* Book I, Chapter 21.
2. *Note to the 2018 edition:* See Athanasius, *Life of Saint Anthony.*

CHAPTER XIV

ACCOUNT OF SAINT AMMON AND EUTYCHIUS OF OLYMPUS

It was about this period that Ammon[1] the Egyptian embraced philosophy. It is said that he was compelled to marry by his family, but that his wife never knew him carnally, for on the day of their marriage, when they were alone and when he as the bridegroom was leading her as the bride to his bed, he said to her, "Oh woman! Our marriage has indeed taken place, but it is not consummated." And then he showed her from the Holy Scriptures that it is good to remain a virgin, and entreated that they might live apart. She was convinced by his arguments concerning virginity, but was much distressed by the thought of being separated from him and therefore, though occupying a separate bed, he lived with her for eighteen years, during which time he did not neglect the monastic exercises.

At the end of this period the woman, whose emulation had been strongly excited by his virtues, became convinced that it was not just that such a man should on her account live in the domestic sphere, and she considered that it was necessary that each should, for the sake of philosophy, live apart from the other. The husband therefore took his departure, after having thanked God for the counsel of his wife, and said to her, "Do thou retain this house, and I will make another for myself." He retired to a desert place, south of the Mareotic Lake,[2] between Scetis and the mountain called Nitria. And here, during two and twenty years, he devoted himself to philosophy and visited his wife twice every year. This divine man founded monasteries in the regions where he dwelt, and gathered round him many disciples of note whom we shall have occasion to mention hereafter. Many extraordinary events happened to him which have been diligently recorded by the Egyptian monks, for they sought to hand down, in unbroken tradition the record of the virtues of the ancient ascetics. I have here related a few such facts as have come to my knowledge.

Ammon and his disciple Theodore had once occasion to take a long journey, and on the road found it requisite to cross a watercourse called Lycus. Ammon ordered Theodore to pass over backwards, lest they should witness each other's nudity, and as he was likewise ashamed to see himself naked, he was suddenly, and by a divine impulse, seized and carried over, and landed on the opposite bank. When Theodore had crossed the water, he perceived that the clothes and feet of the elder were not wet, and inquired the reason. Not receiving a reply, he expostulated strongly on the subject, and at length Ammon, after stipulating that it should not be mentioned during his lifetime, confessed the fact.

Here follows another miracle of the same nature. Some wicked people having brought to him their son who had been bitten by a mad dog and was nigh unto death, in order that he might heal him, he said to them, "Your son does not require my interposition. Restore to your masters the ox you have stolen, and he will be healed." And the result was even as had been predicted, for the ox was restored and the malady of the child removed.

It is said that when Ammon died, Antony saw his spirit ascending into heaven and surrounded by heavenly beings, singing hymns. Antony regarded this wonderful spectacle with intense amazement, and on being questioned by his companions as to the cause of his evident astonishment, he did not conceal the matter from them. A short time after, certain persons came from Scetis, bringing the intelligence of Amnion's death, and the hour in which they stated this event to have taken place was precisely that which had been indicated by Antony. Thus, as is testified by all good men, each of these holy persons was blessed in a special manner: the one, by being released from this life, the other, by being accounted worthy of witnessing so miraculous a spectacle as that which God showed him, for Antony and Ammon lived at a distance of many days' journey from each other, and the above incident is corroborated by those who were personally acquainted with them both.

I am convinced that it was likewise during this reign that Eutychius[3] embraced philosophy. He fixed his residence in Bithynia, near Olympus. He belonged to the sect of the Novatians,[4] and was a partaker of divine grace. He healed diseases and wrought miracles, and the fame of his virtuous life induced Constantine to seek his intimacy and friendship. It so happened that about this period, a certain person who was suspected of plotting against the emperor, was apprehended near Olympus and imprisoned. Eutychius was besought to intercede on his behalf with the emperor and, in the meantime, to direct that the prisoner's chains might be loosened, lest he should perish beneath their weight. It is related that Eutychius accordingly sent to the officers who held the man in custody, desiring them to loosen the chains, and that on their refusal, he went himself to the prison when the doors, though fastened, opened of their own accord, and the bonds of the prisoner fell off. Eutychius afterwards repaired to the emperor, who was then residing at Byzantium, and easily obtained a pardon, for Constantine esteemed him too highly to refuse his requests.

I have now given in few words the history of the most illustrious professors of the monastic philosophy. If any one desires further or more exact information, he will find it in the numerous works on the subject which have been issued.

NOTES

1. Compare Socrates *Ecclesiastical History*, Book IV, Chapter 23.
2. *Note to the 2018 edition:* A large lake directly south of Alexandria.
3. Or Eutychianus. Compare Socrates *Ecclesiastical History*, Book I, Chapter 13.
4. On the person of Novatus, see Eusebius *Ecclesiastical History*, Book VII, Chapter 8, and Socrates, *Ecclesiastical History*, Book IV, Chapter 28.

CHAPTER XV

THE ARIAN HERESY, ITS ORIGIN, ITS PROGRESS, AND THE CONTENTION WHICH IT OCCASIONED AMONG THE BISHOPS

Although, as we have shown, religion was in a flourishing condition at this period, yet the Church was disturbed by sore contentions. For under the pretext of piety and of seeking the more perfect knowledge of God, certain questions were agitated which had not till then been examined. Arius[1] was the originator of these disputations. He was an elder of the Church at Alexandria in Egypt, and was at first a zealous supporter of truth, yet upholding at the same time the innovations of Melitius. Eventually, however, he abandoned these opinions, and was ordained deacon by Peter, bishop of[2] Alexandria, who afterwards cast him out of the Church because he reprehended the conduct of this prelate in preaching against the Meletians, and in rejecting their baptism.

After the martyrdom of Peter, Arius asked forgiveness of Achillas, and was restored to his office as deacon, and afterwards elevated to the presbytery. Alexander, also, held him in high repute. He was a most expert logician, but perverted his talents to evil purposes, and had the audacity to preach what no one before him had ever suggested, namely, that the Son of God was made out of that which had no prior existence, that there was a period of time in which He existed not, that, as possessing free will, He was capable of virtue or of vice, and that He was created and made. To these, many other similar assertions were added in support of the argument.

Those who heard these doctrines advanced, blamed Alexander for not opposing opinions which seemed at variance with the faith. But this bishop deemed it more advisable to leave each party to the free discussion of doubtful topics, so that by persuasion rather than by force unanimity might be restored. Hence he assembled some of his clergy around him, and sat down as judge to hear the statements of the contending parties. But it happened on this occasion, as is generally the case in a strife of words, that each party claimed the victory. Arius defended the assertions he had advanced against the Son, but the others contended that he was consubstantial and co-eternal with the Father.

The council was convened a second time and the same points contested, but they came to no agreement amongst themselves. During the debate, Alexander seemed to incline first to one party and then to the other.[3] Finally, however, he declared himself in favor of those who affirmed that the Son was consubstantial and co-eternal with the Father, and he commanded Arius to receive this doctrine, and to reject his former opinions. Arius, however, would not be persuaded to compliance, and many of the bishops and clergy considered his statement of doctrine to be correct. Alexander, therefore, ejected him and the clergy who concurred with him in sentiment from the Church. Those of Alexandria who had embraced his opinions were the presbyters Aithalas, Achillas, Carpon, Sarmates, and Arius,[4] and the deacons Euzoius, Macarius, Julius, Minas, and Helladius. Many of the people, likewise, sided with them, some, because they imagined their doctrines to be of God, others, as frequently happens in similar cases, because they believed them to have been ill-treated and unjustly excommunicated.

Such being the state of affairs at Alexandria, the partisans of Arius deemed it prudent to seek the favor of the bishops of other cities. Accordingly, they sent a written statement of their doctrines to them, requesting them that if they considered such sentiments to be of God, they would signify to Alexander that he ought not to molest them, but that if they disapproved of the doctrines, they would do well to declare what opinions were necessary to be held on the points in question. This precaution was of no little advantage to Arius and his partisans, for their tenets became thus universally disseminated, and the questions they had started became matters of debate among all the bishops. Some wrote to Alexander, entreating him not to receive the partisans of Arius into communion unless they repudiated their opinions, while others wrote to urge a contrary line of conduct.

When Alexander perceived that many who were eminent for their virtues, their piety, or their eloquence, held with the party of Arius, and particularly Eusebius bishop of Nicomedia, a man of considerable learning, and held in high repute at the palace, he wrote to the bishops of every church desiring them not to hold communion with them. This measure only served to increase the violence of the controversy and, as might have been expected, the contest was carried on more acrimoniously than before. Eusebius and his partisans had often, though without success, entreated Alexander to continue in communion with them, and they considered themselves so much aggrieved by this measure that they came to a stronger determination than before to support the doctrines of Arius. A synod having been convened in Bithynia, they wrote to all the bishops, desiring them to hold communion with the Arians, as with those making a true confession, and to require Alexander to hold communion with them likewise. As compliance could not be extorted from Alexander, Arius sent messengers to Paulinus bishop of Tyre, to Eusebius Pamphilus, who presided over the church of Cæsarea in Palestine, and to Patrophilus bishop of Scythopolis, soliciting permission for himself and for his adherents, as he had already attained the rank of presbyter, to form the people who were with them into a church. For it was the custom in Alexandria, as it still is in the present day, that all the churches should be under one bishop, but that each presbyter should have his own church, in which to assemble the people.[5] These three bishops, in concurrence with others who were assembled in Palestine, granted the petition of Arius, and permitted him to assemble the people as before, but enjoined submission to Alexander, and commanded Arius to strive incessantly to be restored to peace and communion with him.

NOTES

1. See the parallel account of the rise and growth of Arianism in Socrates, *Ecclesiastical History,* Book I, Chapters 5 to 9.
2. In the *Acta of Peter Martyr*, (which are so ancient that they are quoted by Justinian) it is asserted that Arius was excommunicated on account of his perverse opinions, and not, as Sozomen here says, because he sided with the Meletians. As Valesius remarks, it is somewhat strange that neither Alexander nor Athanasius make any mention of this excommunication of Arius by Peter.
3. Valesius remarks that this statement is not supported by the testimony of any other of the Ecclesiastical writers, and accordingly rejects it.
4. In Theodoret, *Ecclesiastical History*, Book I, Arius alone is said to have been a presbyter, the rest of those mentioned there, according to Theodoret, were deacons.
5. Epiphanius says the same thing of Alexander, but he adds that according to Dionysius Petavius, the same custom prevailed from a very early time at Rome. In support of this assertion he quotes a passage from the epistle of Pope Innocent to Decennius. The passage is curious and valuable, as showing the early origin of the Parochial System.

CHAPTER XVI

CONSTANTINE, HAVING HEARD OF THE STRIFE OF THE BISHOPS, AND THE DIFFERENCE OF OPINION CONCERNING THE PASSOVER, IS GREATLY TROUBLED, AND SENDS HOSIUS, A SPANIARD, BISHOP OF CORDOVA, TO ALEXANDRIA TO SETTLE THESE DISPUTES

After there had been many synods held in Egypt, and the contest had still continued to increase in violence, the report of the dissension reached the palace and Constantine was thereby greatly troubled, for just at this period when religion was beginning to be more generally propagated, many were deterred by the difference in doctrines from embracing Christianity. The emperor openly charged Arius and Alexander with having originated this disturbance, and wrote to rebuke them for having made a controversy public which it was in their power to have concealed, and for having contentiously agitated a question which ought never to have been mooted, or upon which, at least, their opinion ought to have been quietly given. He told them that they ought not to have separated from others on account of difference of sentiment concerning certain points of doctrine, and that though they ought to entertain the same views of Divine Providence, yet that any occasional variation of judgment on minor or doubtful topics ought to be concealed. He exhorted them, therefore, to be of one mind and to refrain from contention, and added that the dissension had grieved him so exceedingly that he had renounced his intention of journeying to the East. It was in this strain that he wrote to Alexander and to Arius, reproving and exhorting them both.

Constantine was also deeply grieved at the diversity of opinion which prevailed concerning the celebration of the Passover, for some of the churches in the East, although they did not secede from communion with the others, kept the festival more according to the manner of the Jews,[1] and thus detracted from its glory. The emperor zealously endeavored to remove both these causes of dissension from the church, and with this view, deputed one who was honored for his faith, his virtuous life, and his steadfast confession of truth to put an end to the strife[2] which existed in Egypt on account of doctrine, and in the East on account of the Passover. This man was Hosius, bishop of Cordova.

NOTES

1. They were called Quartodecimans, because they observed Easter on the 14th day after the new moon. See Socrates, *Ecclesiastical History*, Book V, Chapter 22, and Eusebius, *Ecclesiastical History*, Book V, Chapter 24.
2. For the role of Hosius, see *The Catholic Encyclopedia* (1911), Vol. 7, "Hosius of Cordoba."

CHAPTER XVII

OF THE COUNCIL CONVENED AT NICÆA ON ACCOUNT OF ARIUS

When it was found that the event did not answer the expectations of the emperor, but that on the contrary the breach was widened so that he who had been sent to make peace returned without having accomplished his mission, Constantine convened a synod at Nicæa in Bithynia, and wrote to the most eminent men of the churches in every country, directing them to be there on an appointed day. Of those who occupied the apostolic thrones, the following were assembled at this council: Macarius of Jerusalem, Eustathius who presided over the church of Antioch on the Orontes, and Alexander of Alexandria on Lake Mareotis. Julius,[1] bishop of Rome, was unable to attend on account of extreme old age, but his place was supplied by Vito and Vicentius, presbyters of his church. Many other pious and excellent men of the neighboring provinces were congregated together, of whom some were celebrated for their learning, their eloquence, and their knowledge of literature, sacred and profane, some for the virtuous tenor of their life,[2] and others for the combination of all these qualifications. About three hundred and twenty bishops were present, accompanied by a multitude of presbyters and deacons. There were, likewise, men present who were skilled in the art of disputation and ready to assist in the discussions.[3] And, as was usually the case on such occasions, many priests resorted to the council for the purpose of transacting their own private affairs, for they considered this a favorable opportunity of effecting such alterations as they deemed desirable, and of presenting petitions to the emperor containing complaints against those by whom they considered themselves aggrieved.

As this course was pursued day after day, the emperor set apart one certain day on which all complaints were to be brought before him. When the appointed day arrived, he took the memorials which had been presented to him, and said,

> "All these accusations will be brought forward at the great day of judgment, and will be judged by the Great Judge of all men. As to me, I am but a man, and it would be evil in me to take cognizance of such matters, seeing that the accuser and the accused are priests, and priests ought so to act as never to become amenable to the judgment of others. Imitate, therefore, the divine love and mercy of God, and be ye reconciled to one another. Withdraw your accusations against each other, be ye of one mind, and devote your attention to those subjects connected with the faith on account of which we are assembled."

After having thus urged them to cease from criminating each other, the emperor commanded the memorials to be burnt, and then appointed a day on which to commence the discussion of the questions which had brought them together. But before the appointed day arrived, the bishops assembled together, and having summoned Arius to attend, began to examine the disputed topics, each one amongst them advancing his own opinion. As might have been expected, however, many different questions started out of the investigation. Some of the bishops spoke against the introduction of novelties contrary to the faith which had been delivered to them from the beginning. And those, especially, who had adhered to simplicity of doctrine, argued that the faith of God ought to be received without curious enquiries. Others, however, contended that former opinions ought not to be retained without examination. Many of the bishops and of the inferior clergy attracted the notice of the emperor and the court by these disputations. Athanasius, who was then a deacon of Alexandria, and had accompanied the bishop, Alexander, greatly distinguished himself at this juncture.[4]

NOTES

1. Valesius remarks that this is an error of Sozomen, and that for Julius we must read Sylvester, who was at that time bishop of Rome. Julius did not become a bishop until eleven years later. Cardinal Perronius proposed to read πόλιος (aged) instead of Ἰούλιος. But the word is not found in prose authors.
2. Sozomen here follows Eusebius. See his *Life of the Blessed Emperor Constantine*, Book III, Chapter 9, and compare Socrates, *Ecclesiastical History*, Book I, Chapter 8.
3. Valesius thinks it more probable that they were drawn together for the sake of gratifying their curiosity and quotes in support of his view, Rufinus, Book X, Chapter 3. At the same time he admits that the opinion of Sozomen may be right, and quotes on his side the testimony of Nicephorus.
4. The same testimony to the merit of Athanasius is borne also by Gregory Nazianzen.

CHAPTER XVIII

TWO PHILOSOPHERS ARE CONVERTED TO THE FAITH BY THE SIMPLICITY OF TWO OLD MEN WITH WHOM THEY HELD A DISPUTATION.

While these disputations were being carried on, certain of the Pagan philosophers became desirous of taking part in them, some because they wished for information as to the doctrine that was inculcated, and others because, feeling incensed against the Christians on account of the recent suppression of the Pagan religion, they wished to stigmatize them with engaging in strife about words, and to introduce dissensions among them.

It is related that one of these philosophers, priding himself on his acknowledged superiority of eloquence, began to ridicule the priests, and thereby roused the indignation of a simple old man, highly esteemed as a confessor, who, although unskilled in the arts of reasoning and debating, undertook to oppose him. The less serious of those who knew the confessor, raised a laugh[1] at his expense for engaging in such an undertaking, but the more thoughtful felt anxious lest in opposing so eloquent a man he should only render himself ridiculous. Yet his influence was so great and his reputation so high among them that they could not forbid his engaging in the debate, and he accordingly delivered himself in the following terms:

"In the name of Jesus Christ, O philosopher, hearken to me. There is one God, the Maker of heaven and earth, and of all things visible and invisible. He made all things by the power of the Word, and established them by the holiness of His Spirit. The Word, whom we call the Son of God, seeing that man was sunk in error and living like unto the beasts, pitied him and vouchsafed to be born of a woman, to hold intercourse with men, and to die for them. And He will come again to judge each of us as to the deeds of this present life. We believe these things to be true with all simplicity. Do not, therefore, expend your labor in vain by striving to disprove facts which can only be understood by faith, or by scrutinizing the manner in which these things did or did not come to pass. Answer me, dost thou believe?"

The philosopher, astonished at what had transpired, replied, "I believe." And having thanked the old man for having overcome him in argument, he began to teach the same doctrines to others. He exhorted those who still held his former sentiments, to adopt the views he had embraced, assuring them on oath that he had been impelled to embrace Christianity by a certain inexplicable impulse.

It is said that a similar miracle was performed by Alexander, bishop of

Constantinople. When Constantine returned to Byzantium, certain philosophers came to him to complain of the innovations in religion, and particularly of his having introduced a new form of worship into the empire contrary to that followed by his forefathers and by all who were formerly in power, whether among the Greeks or the Romans. They likewise desired to hold a disputation on the doctrine with Alexander the bishop. And he, although unaccustomed[2] to the art of debating, accepted the challenge at the command of the emperor, for he was a good and virtuous man and was supported by the consciousness of his integrity. When the philosophers were assembled and prepared to engage in the discussion, he requested that one might be chosen as spokesman, while the others were to remain silent. When one of the philosophers began to open the debate, Alexander said to him, "I command thee in the name of Jesus Christ not to speak."

The man was instantaneously silenced. Surely it is a greater miracle that a man, and that man a philosopher, should be struck dumb thus easily, than that a stone wall should be cleft by the power of a word, which miracle I have heard some attribute with pride to Julian, surnamed the Chaldean.[3]

NOTES

1. Valesius remarks that some of the details here are added by Sozomen to the plain story as it is to be found in Ruffinus.
2. Valesius reads here ἀτριβής (*rudis*) in place of the old reading ἀκριβής (*accuratus*), before which, if that reading is to be maintained, the sense requires that we should insert the word μή.
3. He flourished during the age of the Antonines. Suidas attests that his son Julian was so skilled in the magic art, that he called down rain from heaven, when the Roman soldiers were perishing from thirst. It should be observed that a miracle similar to the above is recorded of Attus Nævius by Livy, Book I, Chapter 36.

CHAPTER XIX

THE EMPEROR HARANGUES THE ASSEMBLED SYNOD

The bishops held long consultations, and after summoning Arius before them, inquired diligently into his doctrines, yet at the same time withholding their final decision. When at length the appointed day arrived on which the controversy was to be terminated, they assembled together[1] in the palace because the emperor had signified his intention of taking part in the deliberations. On his entrance, the emperor passed through to the head of the council and seated himself on the throne which had been prepared for him, and then motioned to the members of the synod to be seated, for seats had been arranged on either side along the walls of the palace which was a very large and beautiful edifice.

After they were seated, Eusebius Pamphilus arose and delivered an oration[2] in honor of the emperor, returning thanks to God on his account. When he had ceased speaking, and silence was restored, the emperor delivered himself in the following words:

> "I give thanks to God for all things, but particularly, friends, for being permitted to see you assembled here, for I desired most ardently to gather the priests of Christ into one place. Now, it is my desire that you should be of one mind and hold the same opinions in fellowship of spirit, for dissension in the Church of God is the greatest of evils. I never experienced more poignant sorrow than when I heard that dissension had crept in among you, for such an evil ought to have no existence among you who are the servants of God and the dispensers of peace. On this account it is that I have called you together in a holy synod, and being both your emperor and your fellow-physician I seek from you a favor which is acceptable to our common Lord, and as honorable for me to receive as for you to grant. The favor which I seek is that you examine the causes of division and bring the controversy to a close, and that you thus restore peace and unanimity among yourselves so that I may triumph with you over our enemy the devil, who excited this internal strife because he was provoked to see our external enemies subdued and trampled upon beneath our feet."

The emperor pronounced this discourse in Latin, and the interpretation was supplied by a bystander.

NOTES

1. See Eusebius, *Life of the Blessed Emperor Constantine*, Book III, Chapter 10.
2. Theodoret (*Ecclesiastical History*, Book 1, Chapter 8) places this oration in the mouth of Eustathius, bishop of Antioch.

CHAPTER XX

AFTER GIVING AUDIENCE TO BOTH PARTIES, THE EMPEROR CONDEMNS THE FOLLOWERS OF ARIUS TO EXILE.

The next debate turned upon the doctrinal controversy. The emperor gave patient attention to the speeches of both parties. He applauded those who spoke well, rebuked those who displayed a tendency to altercation and, so far as he was able, addressed himself with kindness to all, for he was almost ignorant of the Greek language.

At the close of the debate, all the priests came to the conclusion that the Son is consubstantial with the Father. At the commencement of the conference there were but seventeen who defended the opinions of Arius, but eventually the majority of these yielded assent to the decision of the council. To this judgment the emperor likewise deferred, for he regarded the unanimity which prevailed in the council to be of Divine appointment, and he ordained that any one who should be rebellious thereto, should be forthwith sent into banishment, as guilty of endeavoring to overthrow the Divine determination. I formerly deemed it necessary to transcribe the confession (or symbol, συβολον) of faith drawn up by the unanimous consent of this council, in order that posterity might possess a public record of the truth. But subsequently, I was persuaded to the contrary by some godly and learned friends, who represented that such matters ought to be kept secret, as being only requisite to be known by disciples and their instructors,[1] and it is probable that this volume will fall into the hands of the unlearned. I have not, however, entirely suppressed the information derived from my authorities, for I would not that my readers should be in total ignorance as to the decrees of the Council.

NOTE

1. μυσται και μυσταγωγοί. These were technical terms borrowed from the ceremonies of Grecian rites. See *Dictionary of Grecian and Roman Antiquities*, under "Eleusinia." The words of Valesius are, "Solebant antiqui, cum sacra suscipere vellent, amicos eligere iisdem sacris jam antea initiatos, qui ipsos initiandos deducerent ad Hierophantem seu Pontificem, qui sacra tradebat."

CHAPTER XXI

THE DECREES OF THE COUNCIL. THE CONDEMNATION OF ARIUS. HIS BOOKS ARE TO BE BURNED. CERTAIN OF THE ARCHIERARCHY DIFFER FROM THE SYNOD. THE PASSOVER.

It ought to be known that the following points were settled by the synod: that the Son is consubstantial with the Father, and that those are to be excommunicated who assert that there was a time in which the Son existed not, and before which he was not, and that he was made from what had no existence, and that he is of another hypostasis and substance from the Father, and that he is subject to change and mutation.

This decision was sanctioned by Eusebius, bishop of Nicomedia; by Theognis, bishop of Nicæa, by Maris, bishop of Chalcedonia, by Patrophilus, bishop of Scythopolis, and by Secundus, bishop of Ptolemais in Egypt.[1] Eusebius Pamphilus, however, at first withheld his assent, but on further examination admitted the justice of the decree. The Council excommunicated Arius and his adherents, and prohibited his entering Alexandria.[2] The words in which his opinions were couched were likewise condemned, as also a work entitled "Thalia," which he had written on the subject. I have not read this book, but have been told it is of a loose character, similar to the odes of Sotades.[3] It ought to be known that although Eusebius, bishop of Nicomedia, and Theognis, bishop of Nicæa, assented to the exposition of faith set forth by the Council, they neither agreed nor subscribed to the deposition of Arius. The emperor sent Arius into exile, and despatched edicts to the bishops and people of every country, denouncing him and his adherents as ungodly, and commanding that their books should be destroyed, in order that no remembrance of him or of the doctrine which he had broached might remain; and the secretion of any of his writings was declared a capital crime.[4]

The emperor wrote letters to every city against Arius and those who had received his doctrines, and commanded Eusebius and Theognis to quit the cities whereof they were bishops; he addressed himself in particular to the churches of Nicomedia and Nicæa, urging them to adhere to the faith which had been set forth by the Council, to elect orthodox bishops, and to let the past fall into oblivion. And he threatened those who should venture to speak well of the exiled bishops, or to adopt their sentiments. In these and in other letters, he expressed resentment against Eusebius, for having sided with the tyrant against him. In accordance with the imperial edicts, Eusebius and Theognis were banished, and Amphion was elected bishop of Nicomedia, and Chrestus of Nicæa. On the termination of the doctrinal controversy, the Council decided that the Paschal feast should be celebrated at the same time in every place.[5]

NOTES

1. Socrates (Book I, Chapter 8) asserts that these five bishops all refused to subscribe the decision of the Council of Nicæa. But the two accounts are easily reconciled, for at first indeed these five bishops withheld their assent from the Nicæan Creed, but were afterwards persuaded to subscribe it See the note on Socrates *in loco*.
2. He was banished into Illyricum.
3. *Note to the 2018 edition:* Sotades was an obscene poet of Alexandria during the reign of Ptolemy Philadelphos ca. 280 BC, known for his poetic attack against the aforementioned king's incestuous marriage to his sister. See Smith: *Dictionary of Greek and Roman Biography and Mythology* (1867), page 888. This same accusation against Arius is also made by Saint Athanasius in his epistle entitled *On the Opinion of Dionysius,* Chapter 6.
4. θάνατον καὶ τιμωριας εἰς κεφαλήν. Valesius says that these two punishments are distinguished here by Sozomen, but he is doubtless mistaken. The figure of speech used is that known to grammarians as Hendiadys.
5. See Eusebius, *Life of the Blessed Emperor Constantine,* Book III, Chapter 14, and Socrates *Ecclesiastical History,* Book I, Chapters 8 and 9.

CHAPTER XXII

ACESIUS, BISHOP OF THE NOVATIANS, IS SUMMONED BY THE EMPEROR TO BE PRESENT AT THE FIRST SYNOD.

It is related that the emperor, under the impulse of an ardent desire to see harmony re-established among Christians, summoned Acesius, bishop of the

Novatians,[1] to the Council, placed before him the exposition of the faith and of the feast, which had received the signature of the bishops, and asked whether he could agree thereto. Acesius answered that their exposition involved no new doctrine, and that he accorded in opinion with the synod, and that he had from the beginning held these sentiments with respect both to the faith and to the feast.

"Why then," said the emperor, "do you keep aloof from communion with others, if you are of one mind with them?"

He replied, that the dissension first broke out under Decius, between Novatius and Cornelius,[2] and that he considered such persons unworthy of communion who, after baptism, had fallen into those sins which the Scriptures declare to be unto death. For that the remission of those sins, he thought, depended on the will of God, and not on the priests.

The emperor replied, by saying, "O Acesius, take a ladder and ascend alone to heaven."[3] By this speech I do not imagine the emperor intended to praise Acesius, but rather to blame him, because being but a man, he fancied himself exempt from sin.

NOTES

1. See above note on Chapter 14.
2. See Eusebius, *Ecclesiastical History*, Book VI, Chapters 43–46.
3. The same story is related by Socrates, *Ecclesiastical History,* Book 10.

CHAPTER XXIII

CANONS APPOINTED BY THE COUNCIL. PAPHNUTIUS, A CERTAIN CONFESSOR OF THE FAITH, RESTRAINS THE COUNCIL FROM FORMING A CANON ENJOINING CELIBACY TO ALL WHO WOULD HAVE THE PRIESTHOOD HONORED.

With the view of reforming the life and conduct of those who were admitted into the churches, the synod enacted several laws which were called canons. Some thought that a law ought to be passed enacting that bishops and presbyters, deacons and subdeacons, should hold no intercourse with the wife they had espoused before they entered the priesthood. But Paphnutius, the confessor, stood up and testified against this proposition. He said that marriage was honorable and chaste, and advised the synod not to frame a law which would be difficult to observe, and which might serve as an occasion of incontinence to them and their wives. And he reminded them that, according to the ancient tradition[1] of the church, those who were unmarried when they entered the communion of sacred orders were required to remain so, but that those who were married were not to put away their wives. Such was the advice of Paphnutius, although he was himself unmarried and, in accordance with it, the synod refrained from enacting the proposed law, but left the matter to the decision of individual judgment. The synod, however, enacted other laws, regulating the government of the church, and these laws may easily be found, as they are in the possession of many individuals.

NOTE

1. Valesius says that we must understand by this tradition, the custom according to which persons once enrolled among the clergy were separated "quoad torum," though not "quoad vinculum matrimonii." He asserts that at this time the clergy all practiced continency, and that therefore in all probability the whole story about Paphnutius is a fiction. This story is also given in Socrates, *Ecclesiastical History,* Book I, Chapter 11.

CHAPTER XXIV

CONCERNING MELITIUS, THE ORDINATIONS MADE BY HIM, AND THE JUST ENACTMENTS OF THE HOLY COUNCIL.

After an investigation had been made into the conduct of Melitius when in Egypt, the synod sentenced him to reside in Lycus, and to retain only the name of bishop, and prohibited him from ordaining any one either in a city or a village. Those who had previously been ordained by him, were permitted by this law to remain in communion and in the ministry, but were to be accounted inferior in point of dignity to other clergy.[1] When by death an appointment became vacant, they were allowed to succeed to it, if deemed worthy by the vote of the multitude, but in this case were to be ordained by the bishop of Alexandria, for they were interdicted from exercising any power or influence in elections. This regulation appeared just to the synod, for Melitius and his followers had manifested great rashness and temerity in administering ordination. The synod also vindicated the honor of Peter, who had been ordained bishop of the church of Alexandria, but who was obliged to flee during the time of persecution, and had since received the crown of martyrdom.

NOTE

1. The Synodical Epistle of the Nicene Fathers speaks rather of bishops than of priests when it forbids any one who had been ordained by Melitius from being appointed to a vacant see, unless elected by the vote of the people and confirmed by the metropolitan of Alexandria. See Socrates, *Ecclesiastical History,* Book I, Chapter 9, and note *in loco.*

CHAPTER XXV

HONOR PAID TO THE BISHOPS BY THE EMPEROR.

At the very time that these decrees were passed by the council, the twentieth anniversary[1] of the reign of Constantine was celebrated: for it was a Roman custom to have a feast on the tenth year of every reign. The emperor, therefore, invited the bishops to the festival, and presented suitable gifts to them. And when they prepared to return home, he called them all together, and exhorted them to be of one mind and at peace among themselves, so that no dissensions might henceforth creep in among them. After many other similar exhortations, he concluded by commanding them, to be diligent in prayer for himself, his children, and the empire, and then bade them farewell.

He wrote to the churches in every city, in order that those who had not been present at the council might be informed of what had transpired. And addressing himself more particularly to the Alexandrians, he urged them to receive unanimously the exposition of faith which had been set forth by the council, and had been proved to be according to the Divine will by the fact that so many bishops, appointed by the Holy Spirit had, after lengthened disputation and investigation, consented to it.

NOTE

1. This feast, called Vicennalia, is mentioned by Eusebius. See *Life of the Blessed Emperor Constantine*, Book III, Chapter 14–16.

BOOK II

CHAPTER I
THE DISCOVERY OF THE CROSS AND OF THE HOLY NAILS.

When the business at Nicæa had been transacted as above related, the priests returned home. The emperor rejoiced greatly at the restoration of unity of opinion in the Church and, desirous of expressing on behalf of himself, his children, and the empire, the gratitude towards God which the unanimity of the bishops inspired, he directed that a house of prayer should be erected at Jerusalem near the place called Calvary.

At the same, time his mother Helena repaired to that city for the purpose of offering up prayer and of visiting the sacred places. Her zeal for Christianity made her anxious to find the wood which had formed the adorable cross. But it was no easy matter to discover either this relic or the Lord's sepulchre, for the Greeks, who in former times had persecuted the church,[1] and who at the first promulgation of Christianity had had recourse to every artifice to exterminate it, had heaped up mounds of earth upon the holy places and, the more effectually to conceal them, had enclosed the place of the resurrection and Mount Calvary within a wall and had moreover ornamented the whole locality and paved it with stone. A temple and statue dedicated to Venus had also been erected on the same spot by these people, for they imagined that those who repaired thither to worship Christ would appear to bow the knee to Venus, and that thus the true cause of offering worship in that place would, in course of time, be forgotten and that as Christians would be unable to frequent the place in safety, the temple and statue would come to be regarded as exclusively appertaining to the Greeks.

At length, however, the secret was discovered and the fraud detected. Some say that the facts were first disclosed by a Hebrew who dwelt in the East, and who derived his information from some documents which had come to him by paternal inheritance. But it seems more accordant with truth to believe that God revealed the fact by means of signs and dreams, for I do not think that human interposition is requisite when God has determined upon the manifestation of hidden things.

When by command of the emperor the place was excavated, the cave[2] whence our Lord arose from the dead was discovered and, at no great distance, three crosses were found and another separate piece of wood on which were inscribed in white letters, in Hebrew, in Greek, and in Latin, the following words: "Jesus of Nazareth, the King of the Jews." These words, as the sacred book of the Gospels relates, were placed by command of Pilate, governor of Judæa, over the head of Christ. There yet, however, remained a difficulty in distinguishing the divine cross from the others, for the inscription had been wrenched from it, and thrown aside, and the cross itself had been cast aside with the others, without any distinction, when the bodies of the crucified were taken down. For according to history, the soldiers found Jesus dead upon the cross, and they took him down and gave him up to be buried while, in order to accelerate the death of the two thieves who were crucified on either hand, they broke their legs and then took down the crosses and flung them out of the way. It was no concern of theirs to deposit the crosses in order, for it was growing late, and, as the men were dead, they cared not to remain to attend to the crosses.

A more divine revelation than could be made by man was therefore necessary in order to distinguish the true cross from the others, and this revelation was given in the following manner. There was a certain lady of rank in Jerusalem who was afflicted with a grievous and incurable disease. Macarius, bishop of Jerusalem, accompanied by the mother of the emperor and her attendants, repaired to her bed-side. After engaging in prayer, Macarius signified by signs to the spectators that the divine cross would be the one which, on being brought in contact with the invalid, should remove the disease. He approached her in turn with each of the crosses, but when two of the crosses were laid on her, it seemed but vanity and mockery to her, for she was at the gates of death. When, however, the third cross was in like manner brought to her, she immediately opened her eyes, regained her strength, and arose. It is said that a dead person was, in the same way, restored to life.

The divine cross having been thus identified, the greater portion of it was deposited in a silver case in which it is still preserved in Jerusalem. But the empress sent part of it to her son Constantine, together with the nails by which the body of Christ had been fastened. Of these, it is related, the emperor had a head-piece and bit made for his horse, according to the prophecy of Zechariah, who referred to this period when he said: "That which shall be upon the bit of the horse shall be holy to the Lord Almighty."[3] These things indeed were formerly known to the sacred prophets, and predicted by them, and at length, in God's own time, were confirmed by wonderful works. Nor does this appear so marvellous when it is remembered that, even among the Greeks, it was confessed that the Sibyl had predicted that thus it should be,

"Oh most blessed tree, on which our Lord was hung."[4]

Our most zealous adversaries cannot deny the truth of this fact, and it is hence evident that a pre-manifestation was made of the wood of the cross, and of the adoration (σέβας) it received.

The above incidents we have related precisely as they were delivered to us by men of great accuracy, by whom the information was derived by succession from father to son. And others have recorded the same events in writing for the benefit of posterity.

NOTES

1. See Socrates, *Ecclesiastical History,* Book I, Chapter 17.
2. Or sepulchre. The Greek word is ἄντρον.
3. Zechariah 14:20.
4. On these oracles the reader may consult with advantage Beveridge's *Codex Canonum Ecclesiæ Universæ,* Chapter 14, and the speech of Constantine "To the Assembly of the Saints" Chapter 18, sometimes appended to his *Life* by Eusebius.

CHAPTER II

CONCERNING HELENA, THE MOTHER OF THE EMPEROR. SHE VISITED JERUSALEM, BUILT TEMPLES IN THAT CITY, AND PERFORMED OTHER GODLY WORKS. HER DEATH.

About this period, the emperor, having determined upon erecting a temple in honor of God, charged the governors to see that the work was executed in the most sumptuous and elaborate manner possible. His mother Helena also erected two temples,[1] the one at Bethlehem near the cave where Christ was born, the other near the top of the Mount of Olives, whence he ascended to heaven. Many other pious acts of hers are on record, among which the following is not the least remarkable. During her residence at Jerusalem, it is related that she assembled the sacred virgins at a feast, ministered to them at supper, presented them with food, poured water on their hands, and performed other similar services customary on such occasions. When she visited the cities of the East, she bestowed gifts on all the churches, enriched those individuals who had been deprived of their possessions, supplied the necessities of the poor, and restored to liberty those who had been long imprisoned, or condemned to exile or the mines. It seems to me that so many holy actions demanded a recompense and, indeed, even in this life, she was raised to the summit of magnificence and splendor. She was proclaimed Augusta, her image was stamped on golden coins, and she was invested by her son with unlimited authority over the imperial treasury. Her death too was glorious, for when at the age of eighty she quitted this life, she left her son and her descendants, (like her of the race of Cæsar) masters of the Roman world. And if there be any advantage in being remembered after death, it is certain that her name will be transmitted to future generations, for two cities are named after her, the one in Bithynia and the other in Palestine.[2] Such is the history of Helena.

NOTES

1. See Eusebius *Life of the Blessed Emperor Constantine,* Book III, Chapters 42, 43.
2. See Procopius *Buildings,* Book V, Chapter 2.

CHAPTER III

TEMPLES BUILT BY CONSTANTINE. THE CITY CALLED BY HIS NAME. THE TEMPLE DEDICATED TO MICHAEL THE ARCHANGEL.

The emperor, always intent on the advancement of religion, erected magnificent temples to God in every place, particularly in metropolises such as Nicomedia in Bithynia, Antioch on the river Orontes, and Byzantium. He greatly improved this latter city, and made it equal to Rome in power and influence. For when he had settled the affairs of the empire according to his own mind and had freed himself from foreign foes, he resolved upon founding a city which should be called by his own name, and should be equal in celebrity to Rome. With this intention he repaired to a plain at the foot of Troy near the Hellespont above the tomb of Ajax, where, it is said, the Achaians intrenched themselves when besieging Troy. And here he laid the plan of a large and beautiful city, and built the gates on an elevated spot of ground, whence they are still visible from the sea to mariners. But when he had advanced thus far, God appeared to him by night, and commanded him to seek another site for his city.

Led by the hand of God, he arrived at Byzantium in Thrace, beyond Chalcedon in Bithynia, and here he was desired to build his city and to render it worthy of the name of Constantine. In obedience to the command of God, he therefore enlarged the city formerly called Byzantium and surrounded it with high walls.[1] He also erected magnificent dwelling-houses, and being aware that the former population was insufficient for so great a city, he peopled it with men of rank and their households whom he summoned thither from Rome and from other countries. He imposed taxes[2] to cover the expenses of building and adorning the city and of supplying its inhabitants with food. He erected all requisite edifices: a hippodrome, fountains, porticoes, and other beautiful embellishments. He named it Constantinople and New Rome, and constituted it the Roman capital for all the inhabitants of the North, the South, the East, and the shores of the Mediterranean, from the cities on the Danube, and from Epidamnus and the Ionian Gulf, to Cyrene and that part of Libya called Bonium.[3] He created another senate, which he endowed with the same honors and privileges as that of Rome, and he sought to render the city which bore his name equal in every respect to that of Rome in Italy. Nor were his wishes thwarted for, by the assistance of God, it became the most populous and wealthy of cities.

I know of no cause to account for this extraordinary aggrandizement, unless it be the piety of the builder and of the inhabitants, and their compassion and liberality towards the poor. The zeal they manifested for Christianity was so great that many of the Jewish inhabitants and most of the Greeks were converted. As this city became the capital of the empire during the period of religious prosperity, it was not polluted by altars, Grecian temples, nor sacrifices, and although Julian authorized the introduction of idolatry for a short space of time, it soon afterwards became extinct. Constantine further honored this new city of Christ by adorning it with numerous and magnificent houses of prayer in which the Deity vouchsafed to bless the efforts of the emperor by giving sensible manifestations of His presence.

According to the general opinion of foreigners and citizens, the most remarkable of these edifices was that built in a place called Hestiis, but since named Michaelius. This place lies to the right of those who navigate the Pontus to Constantinople, and is about thirty-five stadia distant from that city by water, but if you make the circuit of the bay, the distance is seventy stadia and upwards. It is generally believed that Michael, the divine archangel, once appeared at this place and hence its name. And I too can join my testimony to theirs who assert that the power of Michael was manifest in this place. This was evidenced by many wonderful works.[4] For those who had fallen into inevitable peril, those who were oppressed with heavy calamities, or who were suffering from disease and sorrow, there prayed to God and met with immediate deliverance.

I should be prolix were I to give details of these miraculous cures. But I cannot omit mentioning the case of Aquiline, who is an advocate in the same court of justice as that to which we belong,[5] and who is even at the present time residing with us. I shall relate what I saw myself and what I heard from him concerning this occurrence. Being attacked with a severe fever arising from disordered bile, the physicians administered an aperient medicine. This he vomited and, by the effort of vomiting, diffused the bile which tinged his countenance with its own color. He had no power to retain his food and continued a long time in this state—the skill of the physicians was utterly ineffectual. Finding that he was already half dead, he commanded his servant to carry him to the house of prayer, for he said that there he would either die or be freed from his disease. While he was lying there, a Divine Power[6] appeared to him by night and commanded him to dip his foot in a confection made of honey, wine, and pepper. The man did so and was freed from his complaint, although the prescription was contrary to the professional rules of the physicians, a confection of so very hot a nature being considered adverse to a bilious disorder.

I have also heard that Probianus, one of the physicians of the palace, who was suffering greatly from a disease in the feet, likewise met with deliverance from sickness at this place and was accounted worthy of being visited with a Divine and wonderful vision. He had formerly been attached to the Grecian superstitions, but afterwards became a Christian. Yet, while he admitted the probability of the rest of our doctrines, he could not understand how, by the Divine cross, the salvation of all is effected. While his mind was in doubt on this subject, the symbol of the cross⁷ which lay on the altar of this church was pointed out to him in the Divine vision, and he heard a voice openly declaring that as Christ had been crucified on the cross, the necessities of the human race or of individuals whatsoever they might be, could not be met by the ministration of angels or of good men, for that there was no power to help apart from the cross. I have only recorded a few of the incidents which I know to have taken place in this temple: I shall not now recount them all.

NOTES

1. AD 325. Compare Socrates, *Ecclesiastical History,* Book I, Chapter 16.
2. φόροι. Valesius thinks that Sozomen is mistaken as to the first of these taxes.
3. Valesius remarks that on this point too Sozomen is mistaken, for when Constantine transferred the imperial power from Rome to Byzantium, he made no alteration in the limits of the empire. It was his sons who afterwards divided the empire into East and West.
4. Valesius takes ἄλλων as masculine, and would understand it to mean "by many other persons."
5. ἀγορεύοντι. This shows that Sozomen was an advocate in the law courts at the very time of his writing this history.
6. δύναμις.
7. Moveable crosses of silver or gold were always erected on the altars of churches. See Gretser, *de Cruce*, Book II, Chapter 13.

CHAPTER IV

CONSTANTINE THE GREAT ABOLISHES SUPERSTITION AND BUILDS A TEMPLE.

I consider it necessary to detail the proceedings of Constantine in relation to what is called the Oak of Mamre.¹ This place is now called Terebinthus, and is about fifteen stadia distant from Hebron which lies to the south, but is two hundred and fifty stadia distant from Jerusalem. It is recorded that here the Son of God appeared to Abraham, with two angels who had been sent against Sodom, and foretold the birth of his son. Here the inhabitants of the country and of the regions round Palestine, the Phœnicians and the Arabians, assemble annually during the summer season to keep a feast,² and many others, both buyers and sellers, resort thither on account of the fair. Indeed this feast is diligently frequented by all nations: by the Jews, because they boast of their descent from the patriarch Abraham, by the Greeks, because angels there appeared to men, and by Christians, because He who for the salvation of mankind was born of a virgin, there manifested himself to a godly man. This place was moreover honored as the scene of divers religious exercises. Here some prayed to the God of all, some called upon the angels, poured out wine, burnt incense, or offered an ox, or he-goat, a sheep, or a cock, for they were all intent upon offering at this feast, for themselves and their neighbors, the most precious and beautiful sacrifices. And either from honor to the place or from fear of Divine wrath, they all abstained from coming near their wives, although the women made their appearance at the feast, and were then more than ordinarily studious of their deportment and attire. Nor did they act imprudently in any other respect, although the tents were contiguous to each other, and they all lay promiscuously together. The place being under cultivation, contains no houses, with the exception of the buildings around Abraham's oak and well. No one during the time of the feast drew water from that well, for according to Grecian superstition, some placed burning lamps near it, some offered wine and libations, and others gold, myrrh, or incense. Hence, as I suppose, the water was rendered useless by the variety of things cast into it.

Whilst these proceedings were being carried on with usual solemnity by the Greeks, the mother-in-law of Constantine visited the place, and apprised the emperor of what was being done. On receiving this information, be rebuked the bishops of Palestine in no measured terms because they had neglected their duty and had permitted a holy place to be defiled by impure libations and sacrifices, and he expressed his godly indignation in an epistle which he wrote on the subject to Macarius, bishop of Jerusalem, to Eusebius Pamphilus, and to the bishops of Palestine. He commanded these bishops to hold a conference on this subject with the Phœnician bishops, and to issue directions for the demolition of the altar, the destruction of the images by fire, and the erection of a church worthy of so ancient and so holy a place. The emperor finally enjoined that no libations or sacrifices should be offered on the spot, but that it should be exclusively devoted to the worship of God according to the law of the church, and that if any attempt should be made to restore the former rites, the bishops were to inform against the delinquent in order that he might be subjected to the greatest punishment. The governors and priests of Christ strictly enforced the injunctions contained in the emperor's letter.

NOTES

1. See Eusebius, *Life of the Blessed Emperor Constantine*, Book III, Chapters 51–53.
2. See Eusebius, *Life of the Blessed Emperor Constantine*, Book III, Chapters 53, and the note of Valesius *in loco*.

CHAPTER V

CONSTANTINE DESTROYS THE PLACES DEDICATED TO THE IDOLS, AND PERSUADES THE PEOPLE TO EMBRACE CHRISTIANITY.

As many nations and cities throughout the empire retained a feeling of veneration and fear towards their vain idols which led them to disregard the doctrines of the Christians and to cling to their ancient customs and the manners and feasts of their fathers, it appeared necessary to the emperor to teach the governors to suppress their superstitious rites of worship. He thought that this would be easily accomplished if he could get them to despise their temples and the images contained therein. To carry this project into execution, he did not require military aid, for Christian men belonging to the palace went from city to city, bearing letters from the emperor commanding obedience to the decrees. The people were induced to remain passive from the fear that if they resisted these edicts, they, their wives, and their children, would be exposed to evil.

The priests and those who had the charge of the temples, being unsupported by the multitude, brought out from the most secret places of concealment their most precious treasures, and the idols called διοπετη,[1] while recesses known only to the priests, and wherein the people were never admitted, were thrown open to all who desired to enter. Such of the images as were constructed of the precious metals, and whatever else was valuable, were purified by fire and became public property. The brazen images which were skillfully wrought were carried to the city and named after the emperor, and placed there as objects of embellishment, where they may still be seen in public places, as in the Forum, the Hippodrome, and the palace. Amongst them was the statue of Apollo by which the Pythoness divined, and likewise the statues of the Muses from Helicon, the tripods from Delphos, and the much-extolled Pan,[2] which Pausanias the Lacedæmonian and the Grecian cities erected after the war against the Medes.

As to the temples, some were stripped of their doors, others of their roofs, and others were neglected, allowed to fall into ruin, or destroyed. The temple of Æsculapius in Ægis, a city of Cilicia, and that of Venus at Aphaca, near Mount Lebanon and the river Adonis, were uprooted from their foundations. Both of these temples were most highly honored and reverenced by the ancients. In the former, it was said, the demon manifested himself by night, and healed the diseases of the sick. And at Aphaca, it was believed that on a certain prayer being uttered on a given day, a fire like a star descended from the top of Lebanon, and sunk into the neighboring river; this phenomenon they sometimes called Urania, and sometimes Venus.

The efforts of the emperor succeeded to the utmost of his anticipations for, on beholding the objects of their former reverence and fear boldly cast down and stuffed with straw and hay, the people were led to despise what they had previously venerated, and to blame the erroneous opinion of their ancestors. Others, envious at the honor in which Christians were held by the emperor, deemed it necessary to conform to the imperial institutions. Others devoted themselves to an examination of Christianity, and by means of signs, of dreams, or of conferences with monks and bishops, were led to a conviction of its truth.

From this period, nations and citizens spontaneously renounced their former superstitions. A port of Gaza, called Majuma, wherein idolatry and ancient ceremonies had been hitherto upheld, was now distinguished by the alacrity with which its inhabitants suddenly and universally embraced Christianity. The emperor, in honor of their piety, raised their town to the rank of a city, a distinction which it had not formerly enjoyed and, because of its godliness, bestowed upon it the name of Constantia, after one of his children who was more beloved by him than the others. On the same account, also, Constantine in Phœnicia is known to have received its name from the emperor. But it would not be convenient to record every instance of this kind, as the inhabitants of many cities about this time embraced Christianity spontaneously without any edict being issued to that effect by the emperor, overturned the adjacent temples and statues, and erected houses of prayer.

NOTES

1. i.e. "Sent down from heaven." Such were the Palladium of Troy, the Ancile at Rome; and "the image" of Diana "which fell down from Jupiter," mentioned in Acts 19:35.
2. Herodotus (ix. 81) tells us that after the battle at Platæa, 479 BC, Pausanias and the other powers of Greece erected a Tripod in honor of Apollo, but neither he nor any of the Greek historians make any mention of Pan. *Note to the 2018 edition*: The remains of one of the Delphic Platean tripods may be seen to this day at the site of the Hippodrome in Istanbul.

CHAPTER VI

UNDER CONSTANTINE THE NAME OF CHRIST IS SPREAD THROUGHOUT THE WORLD.

The church having been in this manner spread throughout the whole Roman world, religion was introduced even among the barbarians themselves. The tribes on both sides of the Rhine had embraced Christianity, as likewise the Celts and the Gauls who dwelt upon the most distant shores of the ocean. The Goths, too, and the tribes who formerly dwelt on both sides of the Danube, had long been converted to Christianity, and were distinguished by their superiority in manners and customs. All the barbarians had professed to hold the Christian doctrines in honor from the time of the wars between the Romans and foreign tribes under the government of Gallus and the emperors who succeeded him.[1] For when a multitude collected out of various nations passed over from Thrace into Asia, and when other barbarians colonized the boundaries of the Roman empire, many priests of Christ who had been taken captive dwelt among these tribes, and during their residence among them healed the sick, and cleansed those who were possessed of demons by the name of Christ and by calling on the Son of God. Moreover they led a holy and blameless life, and excited envy by their virtues. The barbarians, amazed at the exemplary conduct and wonderful works of these holy men, thought that it would be prudent on their part and pleasing to the Deity if they imitated their example and accordingly, like them, they rendered homage to the Supreme Being. After having been thus practically taught, they received further instruction, were baptized, and admitted into the church.

NOTE

1. It is clear that the Christian faith was very widely spread among the barbarians even at an earlier period than that which is here mentioned. See Justin Martyr's *Dialogue cum Tryphone*, and Tertullian, *Apology*, Chapter 37, and *Against the Jews*, Chapter 7, 8.

CHAPTER VII

HOW THE IBERIANS RECEIVED THE FAITH OF CHRIST.

It is said that during this reign the Iberians,[1] a large and warlike barbarian nation, were converted to Christianity. They dwelt to the north, beyond Armenia. A Christian woman, who had been taken captive, induced them to renounce the religion of their fathers. She was very faithful and godly, and did not, amongst foreigners, remit her accustomed routine of religious duty. To fast, to pray night and day, and to praise God constituted her delight. The barbarians inquired as to the motives of her self-denial. She simply answered, that it was necessary in this way to worship the Son of God, but the name of him who was to be worshipped and the manner of worshipping appeared strange to them. It happened that a boy of the country was taken ill, and his mother, according to the custom of the Iberians, took him from house to house in hope that some one might be found capable of curing the disease and of removing it easily and expeditiously. As no one capable of healing him could be found, the boy was brought to the captive and she said, "As to medicines, I have neither experience nor knowledge nor am I acquainted with the mode of applying ointments or plaisters. But, O woman, I believe that Christ whom I worship, the true and great God, is the Savior of thy child."

Then she prayed for him and freed him from the disease, although just before it was believed that he was about to die. A little while after, the wife of the governor of the nation was, by an incurable disease, brought nigh unto death, yet she too was saved in the same manner. And thus did this captive make known Christ as the Dispenser of health and as the Lord of life, of power, and of all things. The governor's wife, convinced by her own personal experience, believed the words of the captive, held her in much honor, and embraced the Christian religion. The king, astonished at the celerity of the cure and the power of faith, sought an explanation of the occurrence from his wife and commanded that the captive should be rewarded with gifts. "Of gifts," said the queen, "her estimate is very low, whatever may be their value. Nothing is valuable in her eyes, but the services she renders to God. Therefore if we wish to gratify her, or desire to do what is safe and right, let us also worship God who is mighty and a Savior and who, at his will, gives continuance unto kings, casts down the high, renders the illustrious abject, and delivers the oppressed from evil."

The queen continued to argue in this excellent manner, but the sovereign of Iberia remained in doubt and unconvinced, for he was not only prejudiced against the doctrines on account of their novelty, but was also attached to the religion of his fathers. A little while after, he went into the woods with his attendants, on a hunting excursion. All of a sudden thick clouds arose which dispersed themselves through the air and concealed the heavens and the sun. Profound darkness like unto night pervaded the wood. Each of the hunters, alarmed for his own safety, sought refuge in a different direction. The king, while thus wandering alone, thought of Christ, as men are wont to do in times of danger. He determined that if he should be delivered from his present emergency, he would walk before God and worship him. At the very instant that these thoughts were upon his mind, the darkness was dissipated, the air became serene, the rays of the sun penetrated into the wood, and the king went out in safety. He informed his wife of the event that had befallen him, sent for the captive, and commanded her to teach him in what way he ought to worship Christ. After having received her instructions, he called together his subjects and declared to them plainly the divine mercies which had been vouchsafed to himself and to his wife, and although uninitiated, he declared to the rulers the doctrines of Christ.

The whole nation was persuaded to embrace Christianity, the men being convinced by the representations of the king, and the women by those of the queen and the captive. The erection of a church was immediately commenced with the joyful consent of the whole nation. When the external walls were completed, machines were brought to raise up the columns and fix them upon their pedestals. It is related that when the first and second columns had been elevated by these means, great difficulty was found in fixing the third column, neither art nor physical strength being of any avail, although many were assembled to render assistance. When evening came on, the female captive remained alone on the spot and she continued there throughout the night, interceding with God that the erection of the columns might be easily accomplished. The king and all the assistants had taken their departure, for they were distressed at the failure of their attempt. The column was only half raised and one end of it was so imbedded in the earth that it was impossible to move it. It was God's will that by this, as well as by the preceding miracle, the Iberians should be still further confirmed in the truth concerning Himself. Early in the morning when they re-assembled at the church, they beheld a wonderful spectacle which seemed to them as a dream. The column, which before had been immoveable, was now erect and elevated a small space above its proper place. All present were struck with admiration and confessed with one consent that Christ alone is the true God. Whilst they were all looking on, the column descended and became fixed, as by machinery, on its proper foundation. The other columns were then erected with ease, and the Iberians completed the structure with great alacrity.

The church having been thus speedily built, the Iberians, at the recommendation of the captive, sent ambassadors to the emperor Constantine bearing proposals for fellowship and friendship, and requesting that priests might be sent to their nation. On their arrival, the ambassadors related the events that had transpired by which the whole nation had been led to worship Christ. The emperor of the Romans was delighted with the embassy, and after acceding to every request that was proffered, dismissed the ambassadors. Thus did the Iberians receive the knowledge of Christ which they faithfully retain to the present day.

NOTE

1. By the Iberians we are to understand, not the people of Spain (for they had a church among them as early as the time of Irenæus. See *Against Heresies*, Book I, Chapter 3) but the people of that name in Asia. Compare Socrates, *Ecclesiastical History*, Book I, Chapter 20.

CHAPTER VIII
HOW THE ARMENIANS AND PERSIANS EMBRACED CHRISTIANITY.

Subsequently, the Christian religion became known to the neighboring tribes and was very greatly disseminated.[1] The Armenians were the first to embrace Christianity. It is said, that Tiridates, the sovereign of that nation, was converted by means of a miracle which was wrought in his own house and that he issued commands to all the rulers, by a herald, to adopt the same religion.[2] I think that the introduction of Christianity among the Persians[3] was owing to the intercourse which these people held with the Osdrœnians and Armenians. For it is likely that by associating with such divine men they were stimulated to imitate their virtues.

NOTES

1. This paragraph is regarded by Valesius as spurious.
2. Here follows in the Greek text a repetition, word for word, of the first two lines of this chapter, which seems to be superfluous if we do not reject the paragraph above.
3. It is certain from Eusebius (*Ecclesiastical History,* Book III, Chapter 23) that the Christian faith was planted in Persia as early as the Apostolic age.

CHAPTER IX

SAPOR, KING OF PERSIA, IS EXCITED AGAINST THE CHRISTIANS. SYMEON, BISHOP OF PERSIA, AND USTHAZANES, A EUNUCH, SUFFER THE AGONY OF MARTYRDOM.

When in course of time, the Christians increased in number, assembled as churches, and appointed priests and deacons, the Magi, who had from time immemorial acted as priests of the Persian religion, became deeply incensed against them. The Jews who, through envy, are in some way naturally opposed to the Christian religion, were likewise offended. They therefore brought accusations before Sapor, the reigning sovereign, against Symeon who was then archbishop of Seleucia and Ctesiphon, royal cities of Persia, and charged him with being a friend of the Cæsar of the Romans and with communicating the affairs of the Persians to him.

Sapor believed these accusations and at first imposed intolerably oppressive taxes upon the Christians, although he knew that the generality of them had voluntarily embraced poverty. He appointed cruel men to exact these taxes, hoping that by the want of necessaries and the atrocity of the tax-gatherers, they might be compelled to abjure their religion, for this was his aim. Afterwards, however, he commanded that the priests and ministers of God should be slain with the sword. The churches were demolished, their vessels were deposited in the treasury, and Symeon was arrested as a traitor to the kingdom and the religion of the Persians. Thus the Magi, with the co-operation of the Jews, quickly destroyed the houses of prayer. Symeon, on his apprehension, was bound with chains and brought before the king. There he evinced the excellence and firmness of his character, for when Sapor commanded that he should be led away to the torture, he did not fear and would not prostrate himself. The king, greatly exasperated, demanded why he did not prostrate himself as he had done formerly. Symeon replied that formerly he was not led away bound, in order that he might abjure the truth of God, and therefore did not then object to pay the customary respect to royalty. But that on the present occasion it would not be proper for him to do so, for he stood there in defense of godliness and of the one true faith. When he ceased speaking, the king commanded him to worship the sun, promising as an inducement to bestow gifts upon him and to raise him to honor, but on the other hand threatening, in case of noncompliance, to visit him and the whole body of Christians with destruction. When the king found that promises and menaces were alike unavailing, and that Symeon firmly refused to worship the sun or to betray his religion, he remanded him to prison, probably imagining that if kept for a time in bonds, he would change his mind.

When Symeon was being conducted to prison, Usthazanes, an aged eunuch, the foster-father of Sapor and superintendent of the palace who happened to be sitting at the gates of the palace, arose to do him reverence. Symeon reproachfully forbad him in a loud and haughty voice, averted his countenance, and passed by, for the eunuch had been formerly a Christian but had recently yielded to authority and worshipped the sun. This conduct so affected the eunuch, that he wept aloud, laid aside the white garment with which he was robed, and clothed himself as a mourner in black. He then seated himself in front of the palace, crying and groaning, and saying, "Woe is me! What must not await me? For I have denied God, and on this account Symeon, formerly my familiar friend, does not think me worthy of being spoken to, but turns away and hastens from me."

When Sapor heard of what had occurred, he called the eunuch to him and inquired into the cause of his grief and asked him whether any calamity had befallen his family. Usthazanes replied and said, "O king, nothing has occurred to my family but I would rather have suffered any other affliction whatsoever than that which has befallen me. Now I mourn because I am alive and ought to have been dead long ago. Yet I still see the sun which, not voluntarily but to please thee, I professed to worship. Therefore, on both accounts, it is just that I should die, for I have been a betrayer of Christ and a deceiver of thee." He then swore by the Maker of heaven and earth that he would never swerve from his convictions. Sapor, astonished at the wonderful conversion of the eunuch, was still more enraged against the Christians, as if they had effected it by enchantments. Still, he compassionated the old man and strove by alternate gentleness and severity to bring him over to his own sentiments. But finding that his efforts were useless, and that Usthazanes persisted in declaring that he would never have the folly to worship the creature instead of the Creator, he became inflamed with passion and commanded that the eunuch's head should be struck off with a sword.

When the executioners came forward to perform their office, Usthazanes requested them to wait a little that he might communicate something to the king. He then called upon a certain faithful eunuch to convey the following address to Sapor: "From my youth until now I have been well affected, O king, to your house, and have ministered with care and diligence to your father and yourself. I need no witnesses to corroborate my statements, these facts are well established. For all the matters wherein at divers times I have gladly served you, grant me this reward—let it not be imagined by those who are ignorant of the circumstances that I have incurred this punishment by acts of unfaithfulness against the state or by the commission of any other crime, but let it be published and proclaimed abroad by a herald that Usthazanes loses his head for no crime that he has ever committed in the palace, but for being a Christian, and for refusing to obey the king in denying his own God."

The eunuch delivered this message, and Sapor, according to the request of Usthazanes, commanded a herald to make the desired proclamation. The king imagined that others would be easily deterred from embracing Christianity by reflecting that he who sacrificed his aged foster-father and esteemed household servant would assuredly spare no other Christian. Usthazanes, however, believed that as, by his timidity in consenting to worship the sun he had caused many Christians to fear, so now by the diligent proclamation of the cause of his sufferings, many might be edified by learning that he died for the sake of religion and so become imitators of his fortitude.

CHAPTER X
CHRISTIANS SLAIN BY SAPOR IN PERSIA.

In this manner the honorable life[1] of Usthazanes was terminated, and when the intelligence was brought to Symeon in the prison, he offered thanksgiving to God on his account. The following day, which happened to be the sixth day of the week and likewise the day on which, as immediately preceding the festival of the resurrection, the annual memorial of the passion of the Savior is celebrated, the king issued orders for the decapitation of Symeon, for he had been again conducted to the palace from the prison, had reasoned most boldly with Sapor on points of doctrine, and had expressed a determination never to worship either the king or the sun.

On the same day a hundred other prisoners were ordered to be slain. Symeon beheld their execution, and last of all he was put to death. Amongst these victims were bishops, presbyters, and other clergy of different grades. As they were being led out to execution, the chief of the Magi approached them and asked them whether they would preserve their lives by conforming to the religion of the king and by worshipping the sun. As none of them would comply with this condition, they were conducted to the place of execution and the executioners applied themselves to the task of slaying these martyrs. Symeon exhorted them to constancy and reasoned concerning death, and the resurrection, and piety, and showed them from the Sacred Scriptures that a death like theirs is true life, whereas to live and through fear to deny God, is as truly death. He told them, too, that even if no one were to slay them, death would inevitably overtake them, for our death is a natural consequence of our birth, and that after this short and transitory life, an account must be rendered of our actions, after which we enter upon another life wherein virtue receives eternal rewards and vice is visited with endless punishment. He likewise told them that the most glorious of good actions is to die for the cause of God. The martyrs gladly listened to this discourse of Symeon's and went forward with alacrity to meet their death. After the execution of three hundred martyrs, Symeon himself was slain, and Abdechalaas and Ananias, two presbyters of his own church who had been his fellow-prisoners, suffered with him.[2]

NOTES

1. Valesius remarks that his death, rather than his life, is to be regarded as glorious.
2. Some however say that the martyrdom of Symeon and his companions took place in April, AD 349

CHAPTER XI

PUSICIUS, SUPERINTENDANT OF THE ARTISANS OF SAPOR.

Pusicius, the superintendant of the king's artisans, was present at the execution. Perceiving that Ananias trembled as the necessary preparations for his death were being made, he said to him, "Oh, old man, close your eyes and be of good courage, for you will soon behold the light of Christ."

No sooner had he uttered these words than he was arrested and conducted before the king, and as he frankly avowed himself a Christian, and spoke with great boldness concerning the truth of his religion and the innocence of the martyrs, he was condemned to a most extraordinary and cruel death. The executioners pierced the muscles of his neck in such a manner as to extract his tongue. At the same time his daughter who had devoted herself to a life of holy virginity was arraigned and executed. The following year, on the day on which the Passion of Christ was commemorated and when preparations were being made for the celebration of the festival commemorative of his Resurrection from the dead, Sapor issued a most cruel edict throughout Persia, condemning to death all those who should confess themselves to be Christians. And it is said that an immense number of Christians suffered by the sword.

The Magi sought diligently in the cities and villages for those who had concealed themselves, and many voluntarily surrendered themselves, lest they should appear by their silence to deny Christ. Of the Christians who were thus unsparingly sacrificed, many who were attached to the palace were slain, and amongst these was Azadas, a eunuch, who was especially beloved by the king. On hearing of his death Sapor was overwhelmed with grief and put a stop to the indiscriminate slaughter of the Christians, and he directed that the teachers of religion should alone be slain.

CHAPTER XII
MARTYRDOM OF TARBULA, THE SISTER OF SYMEON.

About the same period, the queen was attacked with a disease and Tarbula, the sister of Symeon the bishop, a holy virgin,[1] was arrested, as likewise her sister who was a widow and had abjured a second marriage and her servant who, like her, had devoted herself to a religious life. The cause of their arrest was the calumny of the Jews who reported that they had injured the queen by their enchantments in revenge for the death of Symeon. As invalids easily give credit to the most frightful representations, the queen believed the calumny, and especially because it emanated from the Jews, for she had great confidence in their veracity and in their attachment for herself—she had embraced their sentiments, and lived in the observance of the Jewish rites.

The Magi having seized Tarbula and her companions, condemned them to death and, after having sawn them asunder, fastened them up to posts, advising the queen to pass through the place of execution that the charm might be dissolved and the disease removed. It is said that Tarbula was extremely beautiful and that one of the Magi having become deeply enamored with her, sent some money secretly to her and promised to save her and her companions if she would accede to his desires. But instead of listening to his proposals, she rebuked his licentiousness and joyfully prepared for death, for she preferred to die rather than to lose her virginity.

As it was ordained by the edict of Sapor, which we mentioned above, that the Christians should not be slaughtered indiscriminately, but that the priests and teachers of religion should be slain, the Magi and Archmagi traversed the whole country of Persia in search of the bishops and presbyters. They sought them especially in the country of the Adiabenians, a part of the Persian dominions in which many Christians were located.

NOTE

1. i.e., consecrated to religion.

CHAPTER XIII
MARTYRDOM OF SAINT ACEPSIMUS AND OF HIS COMPANIONS.

About this period they arrested Acepsimus the bishop and many of his clergy. After having taken counsel together, they despoiled the clergy and then dismissed them. James, however, who was one of the presbyters, voluntarily followed Acepsimus, obtained permission from the Magi to share his prison, and joyfully ministered to him and dressed his wounds, for the Magi had cruelly scourged him in order to compel him to worship the sun and on his refusal to do so had remanded him to prison. Two priests, named Aithalas and James, and two deacons, by name Azadanus and Abdiesus, were castigated and imprisoned in the same manner by the Magi on account of their adherence to the doctrines of Christ.

After a long time had elapsed, the great Arch-magi inquired of the king what was his pleasure concerning them, and having received permission to deal with them as he pleased unless they would consent to worship the sun, he made known this decision of Sapor's to the prisoners. They replied that they would never betray the cause of Christ nor worship the sun, and were immediately subjected to the most excruciating tortures. Acepsimus persevered in the manly confession of his faith till death put an end to his torments. Certain Armenians whom the Persians retained as hostages secretly carried away his body and buried it. The other prisoners were severely scourged but did not expire beneath the blows, and as they would not renounce their sentiments, were again consigned to prison. Aithalas was one of those who experienced this treatment. Both his arms were broken when preparations were being made for the scourging, and he afterwards lost the use of his hands so completely that he was obliged to depend upon others to convey the food to his mouth.

Subsequently, a multitude of presbyters, deacons, monks, holy virgins, ministers of the church, and laborers in word and doctrine, terminated their lives by martyrdom. The following are the names of the bishops, so far as I have been able to ascertain: Barbasymes, Paul, Gadiabes, Sabinus, Mareas, Mocius, John, Hormisdas, Papas, James, Romas, Maares, Agas, Bochres, Abdas, Abdiesus, John, Abraham, Agdelas, Sapor, Isaac, and Dausas. The latter had been made prisoner by the Persians, and brought from a place named Zabdæus.[1] He died about this time in defense of the Christian doctrine and Mareabdes, a chorepiscopus and about two hundred and fifty of his clergy, who had also been captured by the Persians, suffered with him.

NOTE

1. Otherwise spelled Zaudæus. It was on the banks of the river Tigris, and had been in the hands of the Romans since the reign of Galerius.

CHAPTER XIV

CONDUCT AND MARTYRDOM OF MILLES THE BISHOP. THE MULTITUDE OF BISHOPS SLAIN IN PERSIA BY SAPOR, BESIDES OBSCURE INDIVIDUALS.

About this period Milles suffered martyrdom. He originally served the Persians in a military capacity, but afterwards abandoned that vocation in order to embrace the apostolical mode of life. It is related that he was ordained bishop over a Persian city where he underwent a variety of sufferings, and that failing in his efforts to convert the inhabitants to Christianity, he uttered imprecations against the city and departed.

Not long after, some of the principal citizens incurred the anger of the king, and an army with three hundred elephants was sent against them. The city was utterly demolished, and corn was sown on its site. Milles, taking with him nothing but the holy Book of the Gospels, repaired to Jerusalem to worship, thence he proceeded to Egypt in order to see the monks. The extraordinary and admirable works which he accomplished are attested by the Syrians, who have written an account of his life and actions.

For my own part, I think that I have said enough of him and of the other martyrs who suffered in Persia during the reign of Sapor. It would be difficult to relate in detail every circumstance respecting them, such as their names, their country, the mode of their martyrdom, and the species of torture to which they were subjected.[1] I shall briefly state that the number of men and women whose names have been ascertained, and who were martyred at this period, has been computed to be upwards of sixteen thousand, while the multitude of martyrs whose names are unknown was so great that the Persians, the Syrians, and the inhabitants of Edessa, have failed in all their efforts to compute the number.

NOTE

1. The ingenuity of the Persians in devising tortures is mentioned by Plutarch in his *Life of Artaxerxes*.

CHAPTER XV

CONSTANTINE WRITES TO SAPOR TO STAY THE PERSECUTION OF THE CHRISTIANS.

Constantine, the Roman emperor, was vividly affected when he heard of the sufferings to which the Christians were exposed in Persia. He desired most anxiously to render them assistance, yet knew not in what way to effect this object. About this time some ambassadors from the Persian king arrived at his court, and after granting their requests and dismissing them, he thought it would be a favorable opportunity to address Sapor in behalf of the Christians in Persia, and wrote to him to that effect:[1]

> "There is nothing in their religion," said he, "of a reprehensible nature. By prayers alone do they offer supplication to God, for he delighteth not in the blood of sacrifices, but taketh pleasure only in a pure soul devoted to virtue and to religion, so that they who believe these things are worthy

of commendation." The emperor then assured Sapor that God would be propitious to him if he treated the Christians with lenity, and adduced his own example and that of Valerian in proof thereof. He had himself, by faith in Christ and by the aid of Divine power, come forth from the shores of the Western Ocean and reduced to obedience the whole of the Roman world, and had terminated many wars against foreigners and usurpers, and yet had never had recourse to sacrifices or divinations, but had merely offered up a holy prayer and carried the symbol of the cross at the head of his army. The reign of Valerian was prosperous so long as he refrained from persecuting the Church. But he afterwards commenced a persecution against the Christians, and was delivered by Divine vengeance into the hands of the Persians who took him prisoner and put him to a cruel death.

It was in this strain that Constantine wrote to Sapor, urging him to protect the professors of religion, for the emperor extended his watchful care over all the Christians of every region whether Roman or foreign.[2]

NOTES

1. The letter of Constantine to which Sozomen here alludes is extant in Eusebius, *Life of the Blessed Emperor Constantine*, Book IV, Chapter 9. But Sozomen is mistaken about its date, as it was written before Sapor had commenced his persecution of the Christians.
2. *Note to the 2018 edition:* Other accounts of this persecution may be found among the Acts of the Persian Martyrs, parts of which are available in English, including Kyle Smith's translation of *The Martyrdom and History of the Blessed Simeon Bar Sabba'e*.

CHAPTER XVI
EUSEBIUS AND THEOGNIS, WHO AT THE COUNCIL OF NICÆA, HAD ASSENTED TO THE WRITINGS OF ARIUS, ARE REINSTATED IN THEIR OWN BISHOPRICS.

AD 328 — Not long after the council of Nicæa, Arius was recalled from exile,[1] but the prohibition to enter Alexandria was unrevoked. It shall be related in the proper place how he strove to obtain permission to return to Egypt. Not long after, Eusebius, bishop of Nicomedia, and Theognis, bishop of Nicæa, regained possession of their bishoprics, after expelling Amphion and Chrestes who had been ordained in their stead. They owed their restoration to a document which they had presented to the bishops, containing a retractation[2] of their sentiments, and couched in the following terms:

"Although we have been condemned without a trial by your piety, we deemed it right to remain silent concerning the judgment passed against

Book II, Chapter XVI

us. But as it would be absurd to remain longer silent, when silence is regarded as a proof of the truth of calumny, we now declare to you that we hold the same faith that you do: that, after a diligent examination of the word 'consubstantial,' we are wholly intent upon preserving peace, and that we are seduced by no heresy. Having proposed for the safety of the church such suggestions[3] as occurred to us, and having certified what we deemed requisite, we signed the confession of faith. We did not certainly sign the anathemas,[4] but this was not because we impugned the confession of faith, but because we did not believe the accused to be what he was represented to us, the letters we had received from him, and the discourses he had delivered in our presence, compelling us to entertain a contrary opinion of him. So far from opposing any of the decrees enacted in your holy synod, we assent to all of them and, by this document, attest our assent thereto.

"And this is not because we are wearied of exile, but because we wish to avert all suspicion of heresy. If you will condescend to admit us into your presence, you will find us in all points of the same sentiments as yourselves, and willing to defer to your decisions. The accused having justified himself and having been recalled from exile, it would be absurd were we by our silence to confirm the reports that calumny had spread against us. We beseech you then, by the love that you bear to Christ, that you make our supplications known to our most godly emperor, and that you immediately direct us to act according to your will."

It was by these means that Eusebius and Theognis, after their change of sentiment, were reinstated in their churches.

NOTES

1. Valesius shows that in this matter Sozomen has followed Socrates (*Ecclesiastical History*, Book I, Chapter 10) in an error, as to the date of the recall of Arius, which he fixes very shortly after the synod of Nicæa.
2. This retractation is given also by Socrates, *Ecclesiastical History*, Book I, Chapter 14.
3. The facts (as we learn from the Epistle of Eusebius of Cæsarea, which is given also by Socrates and Theodoret) are as follows. The bishops who demurred to the term ὁμοούσιον as defined in the Nicene symbol, proposed another form to the synod. But the Nicene fathers rejected this form, and refused to depart from their own definition. Eusebius and his party then signed the catholic and orthodox creed, for fear of the emperor.
4. We are not to suppose from this that a separate signature was appended to the anathemas from that which was affixed to the creed, for they both compose one document. It is probable that they added a note to their subscription to the effect that they did not coincide in the anathemas. See Socrates, *Ecclesiastical History*, Book I, Chapter 9.

CHAPTER XVII

ON THE DEATH OF ALEXANDER, BISHOP OF ALEXANDRIA, ATHANASIUS IS ELECTED IN HIS STEAD. DETAILS CONCERNING HIS YOUTH AND EDUCATION, AND HIS FRIEND ANTONY THE GREAT.

About this period[1] Alexander, bishop of Alexandria, conscious of approaching death, named Athanasius as his successor in accordance, I am convinced, with the Divine will. It is said that Athanasius at first sought to avoid the honor by flight, but that he was afterwards constrained by Alexander to accept the bishopric. This is testified by Apollinarius, the Syrian, in the following terms:

> "In all these matters much disturbance was excited by impiety, but its first effects were felt by the blessed teacher to whom this man was subject as a son would be to his father. Afterwards this holy man himself underwent the same experience, for when appointed to the episcopal succession, he fled to escape the honor, but he was discovered in his place of concealment by the help of God who had revealed to his blessed predecessor that the succession was to devolve upon him. For when Alexander was on the point of death, he called upon Athanasius who was then absent. One who bore the same name and who happened to be present, on hearing him call this way, answered him. But Alexander spoke not to him, but continued calling upon him who was absent. Moreover, the blessed Alexander prophetically exclaimed, 'O Athanasius, thou thinkest to escape, but thou wilt not escape,' meaning that Athanasius would most certainly be called to the conflict."

Such is the account given by Apollinarius respecting Athanasius.

The Arians assert that after the death of Alexander, the respective followers of that bishop and of Melitius held communion together, and fifty-four bishops from Thebes and other parts of Egypt assembled together and agreed by oath to elect a bishop of Alexandria according to their common consent, but that seven[2] of the bishops, in violation of their oath and of the wishes of the other bishops, secretly ordained Athanasius, and that on this account, many of the people and of the Egyptian clergy seceded from communion with him. For my part, I am convinced that it was by Divine appointment that Athanasius succeeded to the bishopric, for he was eloquent and intelligent, and capable of opposing the machinations of his enemies and, in fact, well suited to the times in which he lived. He displayed great aptitude in the exercise of the ecclesiastical functions, and in the instruction of the people and was, so to speak, self-taught in these respects.

Book II, Chapter XVII

It is said, that the following incident occurred to him in his youth. It was the custom of the Alexandrians to celebrate with great pomp an annual festival in honor of one of their bishops named Peter, who had suffered martyrdom. Alexander, who was then bishop, engaged in the celebration of this festival and, after having offered up divine service, he remained on the spot awaiting the arrival of some guests whom he expected to dinner. In the meantime, he chanced to cast his eyes towards the sea and perceived some children playing on the shore and amusing themselves by imitating the ceremonies of the church. At first he considered the amusement as innocent and took pleasure in witnessing it, but on finding that the most secret of the mysteries were among their imitation, he became troubled and communicated the matter to the chief of the clergy. The children were called together and questioned as to the game at which they were playing, and as to what they did and said when engaged in this amusement. At first they refused to reply, but on being further pressed by Alexander, they confessed that Athanasius was their bishop and leader, and that many children who had not been initiated had been baptized by him. Alexander carefully inquired what the bishop of their games was in the habit of saying or doing, and what he taught them. On finding that the exact routine of the church had been accurately observed, he consulted the priests around him on the subject, and decided that it would be unnecessary to rebaptize[3] those who, in their simplicity, had been judged worthy of Divine grace. He therefore merely performed for them such offices as are inseparably connected with priestly ministration. He then took Athanasius and the other children who had playfully acted as presbyters and deacons, to their own relations that they might be brought up for the church and qualified for the exercise of those functions which they had imitated.

Not long after, he took Athanasius into his service and employed him as his secretary. He had been well educated, was versed in grammar and rhetoric, and gave evident proofs of learning and wisdom before his election to the bishopric. But when, on the death of Alexander, the succession devolved upon him, his reputation was greatly increased and was sustained by his own private virtues and by the testimony of the monk, Antony the Great. This monk repaired to him when he requested his presence, visited the cities, accompanied him to the churches, and agreed with him in opinion concerning the Godhead. He evinced unlimited friendship towards him, and avoided the society of his enemies and opponents.

NOTES

1. About five months after the council of Nicæa, according to a statement of Athanasius in his second *Apology*.
2. See the synodical epistle of the bishops of Egypt addressed to all Catholic bishops, as cited by Athanasius in his second *Apology against the Arians*, where he refutes this calumny.

3. See Socrates, *Ecclesiastical History*, Book I, Chapter 15. For a discussion on the dispute over the authenticity of this story, see *Catholic Encyclopedia*, Vol. 2, "St. Athanasius".

CHAPTER XVIII
THE ARIANS AND MELETIANS CONFER CELEBRITY ON ATHANASIUS. CONCERNING EUSEBIUS, AND HIS REQUEST TO ADMIT THE ARIANS TO COMMUNION. CONCERNING THE TERM CONSUBSTANTIAL. CONTEST BETWEEN EUSEBIUS PAMPHILUS AND EUSTATHIUS, BISHOP OF ANTIOCH.

The reputation of Athanasius was, however, increased by the Arians and Meletians, for whatever stratagems they resorted to, they could never succeed in entangling him in their meshes. In the first place, Eusebius wrote to urge him to receive the Arians into communion and threatened, should he refuse to do so, to ill-treat him. But as Athanasius would not yield to his representation, but maintained that those who had devised a heresy in opposition to truth and who had been condemned by the council of Nicæa, ought not to be received into the church, Eusebius contrived to interest the emperor in favor of Arius, and so procured his recall from exile. I shall state a little further on how all these events came to pass.

At this period, the bishops had another dispute among themselves, concerning the precise meaning of the term "consubstantial." Some thought that this term could not be admitted without blasphemy, that it implied the nonexistence of the Son of God, and that it involved the error of Montanus and Sabellius.[1] Those, on the other hand, who defended the term, regarded their opponents as Greeks (that is, Pagans) and considered that their sentiments led to a plurality of gods. Eusebius, surnamed Pamphilus, and Eustathius, bishop of Antioch, took the lead in this dispute. They both confessed the Son of God has an existence (hypostasis) of his own, and yet they contended together as if they had misunderstood each other. Eusthathius accused Eusebius of altering the doctrines ratified by the council of Nicæa, while the latter declared that he approved of all the Nicæan doctrines, and accused Eustathius of cleaving to the heresy of Sabellius.

NOTE

1. For the reason why the names of these two heretics are joined together, see Valesius, notes on Socrates, *Ecclesiastical History,* Book I, Chapter 23.

CHAPTER XIX

SYNOD OF ANTIOCH. UNJUST DEPOSITION OF EUSTATHIUS. EUPHRONIUS ELECTED IN HIS STEAD. CONSTANTINE THE GREAT WRITES TO THE SYNOD AND TO EUSEBIUS PAMPHILUS, WHO REFUSES THE BISHOPRIC OF ANTIOCH.

A synod having been convened at Antioch, Eustathius was deprived of the bishopric of that city. It was most generally believed that he was merely deposed on account of his adherence to the faith of the council of Nicæa, and on account of his having accused Eusebius, Paulinus, bishop of Tyre, and Patrophilus, bishop of Scythopolis, (whose sentiments were adopted by the Eastern priests) of favoring the heresy of Arius. The pretext resorted to for his deposition, however, was that he had defiled the priesthood by unholy deeds. His deposition excited so great a sedition at Antioch, that the people were on the point of taking up arms, and the whole city was in a state of commotion. This greatly injured him in the opinion of the emperor, who regarded him with suspicion as the author of the tumult. The emperor, however, sent an officer of his palace invested with full authority, to calm the populace and put an end to the disturbance without having recourse to violence or severity.

Those who had deposed Eustathius, imagining that their sentiments would be universally received if they could succeed in placing over the church of Antioch one of their own sect who was known to the emperor and held in repute for learning and eloquence, fixed their thoughts upon Eusebius Pamphilus. They wrote to the emperor upon this subject, and stated that Eusebius was greatly beloved by the people. He had, in fact, been sought by all the clergy and laity who were inimical to Eustathius. Eusebius, however, wrote to the emperor to refuse the dignity. The emperor approved of his refusal, for there was an ecclesiastical law prohibiting the removal of a bishop from one bishopric to another. He wrote to Eusebius[1] to express his concurrence in his sentiments, and said that he considered him happy in being deemed worthy to hold the bishopric not only of one single city, but of the world. The emperor also wrote to the people of the church of Antioch concerning oneness of faith, and told them that they ought not to desire the bishops of other regions, even as they ought not to covet the possessions of others. He despatched another epistle on the same subjects to the synod, and commended Eusebius for having refused the bishopric, and having been informed that Euphronius, a presbyter of Cappadocia, and George, of Arethusa, were men of orthodox faith, he commanded the bishops to consecrate one or other of them or whoever they might judge worthy of the honor, and to ordain a bishop over the church of Antioch.

On the receipt of these letters from the emperor, Euphronius was ordained.[2]

I have heard that Eustathius bore this unjust calumny and condemnation with great calmness. He was a man, who, besides his virtues and excellent qualities, was justly admired on account of his extraordinary eloquence, as is evidenced by his works, which are remarkable for classic purity of expression, weighty sentiments, and elegance and clearness of language.[3]

NOTES

1. The letter of the emperor is extant in Eusebius *Life of the Blessed Emperor Constantine*, Book IV, Chapter 7.
2. After the deposition of Eustathius, Paulinus, bishop of Tyre, was translated to the see of Antioch. Dying six months afterwards, he was succeeded by Eulalius, after whom came Euphronius. See Valesius' notes on Socrates, *Ecclesiastical History*, Book I, Chapter 24.
3. *Note to the 2018 edition:* The only full surviving work of Saint Eustathius is a treatise entitled, *On the Witch of Endor and against Origen*. A translation in English is available in Greer and Mitchell: *The "Belly-Myther" of Endor*.

CHAPTER XX

CONCERNING MAXIMUS, WHO SUCCEEDED MACARIUS IN THE BISHOPRIC OF JERUSALEM.

About this time Mark, who had succeeded Silvester and who had held the episcopal sway during a short period, died and Julius was raised to the see of Rome. Maximus succeeded Macarius in the bishopric of Jerusalem. It is said that Macarius had ordained him bishop over the church of Diospolis, but that the members of the church of Jerusalem insisted on his remaining among them. His confession of faith and great virtue had so excited the approbation of the people that they were desirous that he should, on the death of Macarius, succeed to the bishopric.[1]

The dread of offending the people and exciting an insurrection led to the election of another bishop over Diospolis, and Maximus remained in Jerusalem and exercised the priestly functions conjointly with Macarius, and after the death of this latter, he succeeded to the government of the church. It is, however, well known to those who are accurately acquainted with these circumstances, that Macarius concurred with the people in their desire to retain Maximus, for it is said that he regretted[2] the ordination of Maximus, and thought that he should rather have appointed him his own successor, on account of the orthodoxy of his faith and the firmness of his confession, which had so endeared him to the people. He likewise feared that at his death, the adherents of Eusebius and Patrophilus, who had embraced Arianism, would place one of their own sect in his bishopric, for even during his administration they had attempted to introduce some innovations, and tranquillity was not restored until he had excommunicated them.

NOTES

1. The phrase in the text is ὑποψήφιος ην εἰς τὴν ἐπισκοπήν. The nearest translation of the word is perhaps "designate." The same term occurs in Socrates, *Ecclesiastical History,* Book V, Chapter 5.
2. μεταμεληθῆναι. This is the correct meaning of the term, it was restored by Valesius, instead of the old rendering, "was anxious about." It should be observed that several matters here are done contrary to the ancient discipline and canons of the church, by a dispensation. For first, Maximus is translated from Diospolis. Next, a coajutor bishop is assigned to Macarius in his lifetime, as Alexander had been appointed coajutor to Narcissus. (Eusebius, *Ecclesiastical History*, Book VI, Chapter 52). And lastly, Maximus is said to have been consecrated by the bishop of Jerusalem against the will of the metropolitan, in defiance of the seventh canon of the Council of Nicæa, which reserves to the bishops of Jerusalem the rank which they had from early times, saving the authority of the metropolitan, the bishop of Cæsarea.

CHAPTER XXI

THE MELETIANS AND ARIANS AGREE IN SENTIMENT. EUSEBIUS AND THEOGNIS RELAPSE INTO THE ERRORS OF ARIUS.

In the meantime the contention which had arisen among the Egyptians could not be quelled. The heresy of Arius had been positively condemned by the council of Nicæa, while the followers of Melitius had been admitted into communion under the stipulations above stated. When Alexander returned to Egypt, Melitius delivered up to him the churches whose government he had unlawfully usurped, and returned to Lycas. Not long after, finding his end approaching, he nominated John one of his most intimate friends as his successor, contrary to the decree of the Nicæan council, and thus plunged the churches into fresh troubles.

When the Arians perceived that the Meletians were introducing innovations, they also attempted to involve the churches in trouble. For as frequently occurs in similar contests, some applauded the dogmas of Arius, while others contended that those who had been ordained by Melitius ought to govern the churches. These two bodies of sectarians had hitherto been opposed to each other, but, on perceiving that the clergy of the Catholic church were followed by the multitude, they, from motives of jealousy, formed an alliance together, regarding the clergy of Alexandria as their common enemies. Their measures of attack and defense were so long carried on in concert that, in process of time, the Meletians were generally called Arians in Egypt, although they only dissent on questions of supreme rule and church government,[1] while the Arians hold the same opinions concerning God as Arius. But although their sentiments were thus at variance,[2] they had recourse to dissimulation in order to carry on conjointly their schemes against the Catholics.

From this period, however, it seems the Meletians began to examine the contested topics, and were led to receive the Arian doctrines and to hold the same opinions as Arius concerning God. This revived the original controversy concerning Arius, and some of the clergy and laity seceded from communion with the others. The dispute concerning the doctrines of Arius was renewed at Constantinople and other cities and particularly in the provinces of Bithynia and the Hellespont. In short, it is said that Eusebius, bishop of Nicomedia, and Theognis, bishop of Nicæa, bribed the notary to whom the emperor had intrusted the custody of the documents of the Nicæan council, effaced their signatures, and openly taught that the Son is not to be considered consubstantial with the Father.

Eusebius was accused of these irregularities before the emperor, and he replied with great boldness. "If this robe," said he, "had been cut asunder in my presence, I could not affirm the fragments to be all of the same substance." The emperor was much grieved at these disputes, for he had believed that questions of this nature had been finally decided by the council of Nicæa. He more especially regretted that Eusebius and Theognis had received certain Alexandrians into communion,[3] although the synod had recommended them to repent on account of their heterodox opinions, and although he had himself condemned them to banishment from their native land as being the exciters of sedition.[4] It is asserted by some, that it was for the above reasons that the emperor exiled Eusebius and Theognis, but, as I have already stated,[5] I have derived my information from those who are intimately acquainted with these matters.

NOTES

1. Christophorson is mistaken in rendering these words "de Ecclesiarum primatu."
2. ἰδίᾳ τὰ παρ' ἀλλήλων ἀναινόμενοι scil. δόγματα
3. Sozomen has taken this from the epistle of Constantine to the Nicomedians, as given by Theodoret, *Ecclesiastical History,* Book I, Chapter 9.
4. These exciters of sedition, according to Baronius, were the Meletian party, but Valesius is inclined to believe that they were Arians, and he confirms his opinion by referring to the synodical epistle of the bishops of Egypt, as given by Athanasius in his second *Apology against the Arians.*
5. See above, Chapter 16 of this book.

CHAPTER XXII

MACHINATIONS OF THE ARIANS AND MELETIANS AGAINST SAINT ATHANASIUS.

The various calamities which befell Saint Athanasius were primarily occasioned by Eusebius and Theognis. As they possessed great influence over the emperor, they obtained the recall of Arius, with whom they were on terms of concord and friendship, to Alexandria, and at the same time the expulsion of Athanasius, who was opposed to them. They accused him before Constantine of being the author of all the seditions and troubles that agitated the church and of excluding those who were desirous of joining the church, and alleged that unanimity would be restored were he alone to be removed.

The calumnies were substantiated by many bishops and clergy who were with John and who sedulously obtained access to the emperor. They pretended to great orthodoxy and imputed to Athanasius and the bishops of his party all the bloodshed, imprisonments, conflagrations of churches, and deeds of violence and lawlessness which had been perpetrated. But when Athanasius wrote to the emperor and proved the illegality of the ordination of John's adherents, showing that they had altered the decrees of the Nicæan council, that their faith was not sound, and that they persecuted and calumniated the orthodox, Constantine was at a loss to know whom to believe. As he was much chagrined by the mutual and constant accusations of both parties and desired most earnestly the restoration of unanimity of sentiment among the people, he wrote to Athanasius, desiring him to exclude no one from the church and threatening to visit any act of disobedience to this command with instant expulsion from Alexandria. If any one should desire to see this letter of the emperor's, he will here find the portion of it relating to this affair. It is as follows:

> "As you are now acquainted with my will which is that all who desire to enter the church should be permitted to do so, you must not forbid any from entering. For should I hear that any who are willing to join the church have been debarred or hindered therefrom by you, I shall send and depose you by my decree, and shall have you conveyed to some other place."

Athanasius, however, wrote to the emperor and convinced him that the Arians ought not to be received into communion by the Catholic church, and Eusebius, perceiving that his schemes could never be carried into execution while exposed to the opposition of Athanasius, determined to resort to any means in order to get rid of him. But as he could not find any pretext for effecting this design, he promised the Meletians to interest the emperor and those in power in their favor if they would bring an accusation against Athanasius. Accordingly, they first accused him of having obliged the Egyptians to pay a tax on linen tunics, and the accusers affirmed that the tax had been exacted from them. Apis and Macarius, presbyters of the church of Athanasius who then happened to be at court, endeavored to expose the calumny. On being summoned to answer for the offence, Athanasius was further accused of having conspired against the emperor and of having sent, for this purpose, a casket of gold to one Philumen. The emperor detected the calumny, sent Athanasius back to his bishopric, and wrote to the people of Alexandria to testify that their bishop possessed great moderation and orthodoxy, that he had gladly received him, and recognized him to be a man of God, and that, as envy had been the sole cause of his accusation, he had triumphed over his accusers. And having heard that the Arian and Meletian sectarians had excited dissensions in Egypt, the emperor, in the same epistle, conjured the people to look to God, to take heed unto His judgments, to live in peace one with another, and to expel those who excited discord.

Thus the emperor wrote to the people, exhorting them all to oneness of mind and striving to prevent divisions in the church.

CHAPTER XXIII

CALUMNY RESPECTING SAINT ATHANASIUS AND THE HAND OF ARSENIUS.

The Meletians, on the failure of their first attempts, devised other accusations against Athanasius. On the one hand, they charged him with breaking a sacred vase, and on the other, with having slain one Arsenius[1] and with having cut off his arm for the purpose of using it in sorcery. It is said that this Arsenius was one of the clergy,[2] but that having committed some crime, he fled to a place of concealment for fear of being convicted and punished by his bishop.

The enemies of Athanasius thence devised the most odious calumny. They sought Arsenius with great diligence, and having at length discovered the place of his retreat, they showed him great kindness, assured him of their good-will towards him and of his own safety, and conducted him secretly to Prines, a presbyter of a monastery[3] who was one of his friends and of the same sentiments as themselves. After having thus carefully concealed him, they diligently spread the report in the market-places and public assemblies, that he had been slain by Athanasius. They also bribed John, a monk, to corroborate the calumny.

As this evil report was universally circulated, and had even reached the ears of the emperor, Athanasius became apprehensive that it would be difficult to defend his cause before judges whose minds were prejudiced by such false rumors, and resorted to stratagems akin to those of his adversaries. He did everything in his power to prevent truth from being obscured by calumny, but the multitude could not be convinced on account of the non-appearance of Arsenius. Reflecting, therefore, that the suspicion which rested upon him could not be removed except by proving that Arsenius, who was said to be dead, was still alive, he sent a faithful deacon in quest of him. The deacon went to Thebes, and ascertained from some monks that the object of his search had been concealed by Prines. On repairing thither, however, he found that Arsenius was not there, for on the first intelligence of the arrival of the deacon, he had been conveyed to Lower Egypt. The deacon arrested Prines and conducted him to Alexandria, as also Elias, one of his associates who was said to have been the person who conveyed Arsenius elsewhere. He delivered them both to the commander of the Egyptian forces, and they confessed that Arsenius was still alive, that he had been secretly concealed in their house, and that he was then in Egypt.

Athanasius took care that all these facts should be reported to Constantine. The emperor wrote back to him, desiring him to attend to the due performance of the priestly functions, and the maintenance of order and piety among the people, and not to be disquieted by the machinations of the Meletians, it being evident that envy alone was the cause of the false accusations which were circulated against him to the disturbance of the peace of the churches. The emperor added that, for the future, he should not permit the circulation of such reports and that unless the calumniators preserved the peace, he should certainly subject them to the rigor of the laws and let justice have its course, as they had not only unjustly plotted against the innocent, but had also infringed upon the order of the church and religion.

Such was the strain of the emperor's letter to Athanasius, and he further commanded that it should be read aloud before all the people in order that they might all be made acquainted with his intentions. The Meletians were alarmed at these menaces and became more guarded in their conduct. The churches throughout Egypt enjoyed profound peace under the sway of this great bishop, and were daily increased in numbers by the conversion of multitudes of Pagans and heretics.

NOTES

1. See Socrates, *Ecclesiastical History,* Book I, Chapters 27, 29.
2. He was bishop of Hypsele, as Valesius remarks in his notes on Socrates.
3. Valesius sees reason to doubt this fact, and considers that Sozomen has misunderstood the term μονή as it occurs in the apology of Athanasius, whence he derived his story.

CHAPTER XXIV

SOME INDIAN NATIONS ARE CONVERTED TO CHRISTIANITY THROUGH THE INSTRUMENTALITY OF TWO CAPTIVES, FRUMENTIUS AND EDESIUS.

We have heard that about this period some of the most distant of the nations that we call Indian, to whom the preaching of Bartholomew was unknown, were converted[1] to Christianity by Frumentius, a priest.[2] The wonderful circumstances attending the arrival of this priest in India and the cause of his ordination are necessary to be known to show that Christianity is not of man, as is falsely represented by those who are prejudiced against the doctrines of religion.

The most celebrated philosophers among the Greeks[3] took pleasure in exploring unknown cities and regions. Plato, the friend of Socrates, dwelt for a time among the Egyptians in order to acquaint himself with their manners and customs. He likewise sailed to Sicily to examine its craters whence, as from fountains, spontaneously issued streams of fire which by inundating the neighboring regions rendered them so sterile that, as at Sodom, no seed could be sown there nor trees planted. These craters were likewise explored by Empedocles, a man highly celebrated for philosophy among the Greeks, and who has expounded his doctrines in heroic verse. He was engaged in prosecuting inquiries as to the cause and origin of these eruptions, when either because he thought such a mode of death preferable to any other, or because, to say the truth, he knew not wherefore he should seek to terminate his life in this manner, he threw himself into the crater and perished. Democritus of Coos[4] relates that he visited many cities and countries and nations, and that eighty years of his life were spent in travelling through foreign lands. Besides these philosophers, thousands of wise men among the Greeks, ancient and modern, habituated themselves to travel.

Desirous of imitating their example, Merope, a philosopher and native of Tyre in Phœnicia, travelled as far as India. He was accompanied by two youths, named Frumentius and Edesius. They were his relatives and he had the charge of their education. After accomplishing a journey through India, he determined upon returning home and embarked in a vessel which was on the point of sailing for Egypt. It happened that, from want of water or some other necessary, the vessel was obliged to stop at some port, and the Indians rushed upon it, and murdered Merope and the crew. These Indians had just thrown off their alliance with the Romans. They took pity, however, on the youth of the two lads, and conducted them to their king. He appointed the younger one his cup-bearer and, recognizing at once the fidelity and prudence of Frumentius, constituted him his treasurer.

These youths served the king usefully and faithfully during a long course of years, and when he felt his end approaching he rewarded their services by giving them their liberty, with permission to go where they pleased. They were anxious to return to Tyre where their relatives resided, but the king's son and successor being[4] minor, the mother of the young sovereign besought them to remain and take charge of public affairs, until her son reached the years of manhood. They yielded to her entreaties and directed the affairs of the kingdom and of the Indian government. Frumentius was impelled by some Divine impulse, or by the promptings of his own mind and the assistance of God, to inquire whether there were any Christians or Roman merchants in India. Having succeeded in finding the objects of his inquiry, he summoned them into his presence, treated them with great kindness and benevolence, and commanded the erection of houses of prayer, that there worship might be offered and the Roman ecclesiastical routine observed.

When the king's son attained the age of manhood, Frumentius and Edesius besought him and the queen to permit them to resign their appointments and return to the Roman dominions, and they obtained a reluctant assent. Edesius went to Tyre to see his relatives and was soon after advanced to the dignity of presbyter. Frumentius, however, instead of returning to Phœnicia, repaired to Alexandria, for with him patriotism and filial piety were subordinate to religious zeal, conferred with Athanasius, the head of the Alexandrian church, described to him the state of religion in India, and the necessity of appointing a bishop over the Christians located in that country.

Athanasius assembled the clergy of his diocese and consulted with them on the subject. They were all of opinion that Frumentius was peculiarly qualified to hold the office of bishop of India, as it was by him that the name of Christian was first made manifest in that country and that the first seeds of the Word were sown.[5] Frumentius therefore returned to India and, it is said, discharged the priestly functions so admirably that he became an object of universal admiration, and was revered as an apostle. God highly honored him, enabling him to perform many wonderful cures and to work signs and wonders. Such was the origin of the Indian bishopric.

NOTES

1. Compare Socrates, *Ecclesiastical History*, Book I, Chapter 9.
2. These were the Æthiopians, who were called Indi in a loose sense. Pantænus at an earlier time had converted some of them to Christianity, (see Eusebius, *Ecclesiastical History*, Book V, Chapter 10) but having left no successors behind him, Frumentius began the work of conversion again, and so may be called the Apostle of the Indians.
3. Thus Solon was on his travels when he came to the court of Crœsus. See Herodotus, *Histories*, Book I, Chapter 29.
4. Or more properly of Abdera, as Valesius suggests.
5. The region over which Frumentius was appointed bishop was, as nearly as can be ascertained, that which is now called Abyssinia.

CHAPTER XXV

COUNCIL OF TYRE. ILLEGAL DEPOSITION OF SAINT ATHANASIUS.

The malignity of the enemies of Saint Athanasius involved him in fresh troubles, excited the hatred of the emperor against him, and stirred up a multitude of calumniators. Wearied by their importunity, the emperor convened a council at Cæsarea in Palestine. Athanasius was summoned thither but fearing the artifices of Eusebius, bishop of the city, of Eusebius, bishop of Nicomedia, and of their party, he refused to attend, and for thirty months, in spite of all remonstrances, persisted in his refusal. At the end of that period, however, he was compelled to repair to Tyre, where a great number of the bishops of the East were assembled.[1]

They required him to reply to the accusations framed by John and brought against him by Callinicus, a bishop, and a certain Ischurias. These accusations were: that he had broken a vase used in the celebration of the mysteries; that he had thrown down the episcopal chair; that he had often caused Ischurias, although he was a presbyter, to be loaded with chains; and that, by falsely accusing him before Hygenus, governor of Egypt, of casting stones at the statues of the emperor, he had occasioned his being thrown into prison; that he had deposed Callinicus, bishop[2] of the Catholic church at Pelusium, and had debarred him from communion until he could remove certain suspicions concerning his having broken a sacred vase; that he had committed the bishopric of Pelusium to Mark, a deposed presbyter; and that he had placed Callinicus under the custody of soldiers, and had put him to the torture. Other calumnies were brought against him by Euplus, Pachomius, Isaac, Achillas,[3] and Hermeon, bishops of John's party. They all concurred in maintaining that he obtained the episcopal dignity by means of the perjury of certain individuals, it having been decreed that no one should receive ordination who could not clear himself of any crime laid to his charge. They further alleged that having been deceived by him, they had separated themselves from communion with him and that, so far from satisfying their scruples, he had treated them with violence and thrown them into prison.

The accusers then proceeded to renew the calumny concerning Arsenius and, as generally happens in plots of this nature, many of the reputed friends of the accused joined the ranks of his calumniators. A document was then read containing complaints from the people of Alexandria and purporting to convey a refusal to join the ecclesiastical assemblies. Athanasius, having been urged to justify himself, presented himself repeatedly before the tribunal, successfully repelled some of the accusations, and requested permission to delay replying to the others. He was exceedingly perplexed when he reflected on the favor in which his accusers were held by his judges, on the number of witnesses belonging to the sects of Arius and Melitius who appeared against him, and on the indulgence that was manifested towards his accusers after their calumnies had been detected, as for instance, when he was charged with having cut off the arm of Arsenius for purposes of sorcery, and with having seduced a certain female by bribery. Both these charges were proved to be false and absurd. When this female made the deposition before the bishops, Timothy, a presbyter of Alexandria who stood by Athanasius, approached her according to a plan he had secretly concerted and said to her, "Did I then, O woman, violate your chastity?"[4]

She replied, "But didst thou not?" and mentioned the place and attendant circumstances.

He likewise led Arsenius into the midst of them, showed both his hands to the judges, and requested them to make the accusers account for the arm which they had exhibited. For it happened that Arsenius, either acting under Divine inspiration, or grieved at hearing that Athanasius was accused of having slain him, escaped by night from the place of his concealment and arrived at Tyre the day before trial. Both these accusations having been thus summarily dismissed, no mention of the first was made in the Acts of the Council, most probably, I think, because the whole affair was considered too indecorous and absurd for insertion. As to the second, the accusers strove to justify themselves by saying, that a bishop named Plusian[5] had, at the command of Athanasius, burnt the house of Arsenius, fastened him to a column, and scourged him cruelly, and then imprisoned him in a cell. They further stated that Arsenius escaped from the cell through a window and remained for a time in concealment, that as he did not appear, they naturally supposed him to be dead, that the reputation he had acquired by his manly confession of the faith had endeared him to the bishops of John's party, and that they sought for him and applied on his behalf to the magistrates. Athanasius was filled with apprehension when he reflected on these subjects, and began to suspect that his enemies were secretly scheming to effect his ruin.

After several sessions, when the synod was filled with tumult and confusion, and the accusers and a multitude of persons around the tribunal were crying aloud that Athanasius ought to be deposed as a sorcerer and a ruffian and as being utterly unworthy the priesthood, the officers who had been appointed by the emperor to maintain order in the synod compelled the accused to quit the judgment-hall secretly, for they feared that he might be torn to pieces by the mob. On finding that he could not remain in Tyre without peril of his life, and that there was no hope of obtaining justice against his numerous accusers from judges who were inimical to him, he fled to Constantinople.

The synod condemned him during his absence, deposed him from the bishopric, and prohibited his residing at Alexandria lest, they said, he should excite seditions and disturbances. John and all his adherents were restored to communion, as if they had been illegally excommunicated, and were reinstated in the clerical appointments of which they had been deprived. The bishops then gave an account of their proceedings to the emperor, and wrote to the bishops of all regions, enjoining them not to receive Athanasius into communion and not to write to him nor receive letters from him, as they had convicted him in several instances, and had reason to believe from the manner of his flight that he was guilty of many crimes of which they had not taken public cognizance. They likewise declared, in this epistle, that they had been obliged to pass such a condemnation upon him because, when commanded by the emperor the preceding year to repair to the bishops of the East who were assembled at Cæsarea, he disobeyed the injunction, kept the bishops waiting for him, and set at nought the commands of the emperor. They also deposed that when the bishops had assembled at Tyre, he went to that city attended by a large retinue for the purpose of exciting seditions and disturbances in the synod, that when there, he sometimes refused to reply to the charges preferred against him, sometimes insulted the bishops, and at other times would not defer to their decisions. They specified in the same letter, that he was manifestly guilty of having broken a vase used in the celebration of the sacred mysteries, and that this fact was attested by Theognis, bishop of Nicæa, by Maris, bishop of Chalcedonia, by Theodore, bishop of Heraclea, by Valentinus and Ursacius, and by Macedonius, who had been sent to the village in Egypt where the vase was said to have been broken, in order to ascertain the truth.

Thus did the bishops detail successively each point of accusation against Athanasius, with the same art to which sophists resort when they desire to heighten the effect of their calumnies. Many of the clergy, however, who were present at the trial, perceived the injustice of the accusation. It is related that Paphnutius, the confessor,[6] who had taken his place among the synod, arose and took the hand of Maximus, the bishop of Jerusalem, to lead him away, as if those who had made a confession of the faith and had been maimed and blinded for the sake of religion, ought not to remain in an assembly of wicked men.

NOTES

1. For the acts of this synod, see Socrates, *Ecclesiastical History,* Book I, Chapter 28; Theodoret, *Ecclesiastical History,* Book I, Chapter 29.
2. In order to avoid making Sozomen inconsistent with his own statements elsewhere, Valesius proposes to insert ὡς before ἐπίσκοπον which would mean, "conducting himself as bishop."
3. It is thought by Valesius that Achillas and Hermeon were bishops respectively of Cusæ and Cynopolis.
4. It is the opinion of Valesius that this story is taken by Sozomen out of Rufinus.
5. Mention is made of a bishop of this name in the epistle of Arsenius to Athanasius, which is presented in the second Apology of the latter against the Arians.
6. Valesius says that Sozomen has taken this from Rufinus. A certain Paphnutius was an Egyptian bishop, and one of that name is said by Rufinus to have come with Athanasius to the synod of Tyre. He is to be distinguished from another Paphnutius, an anchorite of the Meletian faction, who joined John and Callinicus in accusing Athanasius at Tyre. Valesius thinks that Rufinus has confounded this Paphnutius with Potamo, who was also present at Tyre, and that Sozomen has followed him in his mistake. Compare Socrates, *Ecclesiastical History,* Book I, Chapter 8. *Note to the 2018 edition:* For more on Rufinus, see *The Church History of Rufinus of Aquileia*, translated by Philip R. Amidon.

CHAPTER XXVI
ERECTION OF A TEMPLE BY CONSTANTINE THE GREAT AT GOLGOTHA IN JERUSALEM. ITS DEDICATION.

The temple, called the "Great Martyr,"[1] which was built in the place of the skull at Jerusalem, was completed about the thirtieth year of the reign of Constantine, and Marius, a man employed at the palace in the capacity of a secretary, was forthwith despatched to the bishops who were assembled at Tyre with a letter from the emperor commanding them to repair quickly to Jerusalem in order to consecrate the temple. But before they entered upon this duty, the emperor deemed it necessary that the disputes which prevailed among the bishops who had been convened at Tyre should be adjusted, and that they should cast aside all cause of discord and trouble when they consecrated the temple.

When the bishops arrived at Jerusalem the temple was therefore consecrated, as likewise numerous ornaments and gifts which were sent by the emperor and are still preserved in the sacred edifice. Their magnificence and costliness is such that they cannot be looked upon without exciting wonder. Since that period the anniversary of the consecration has been celebrated with great pomp by the church of Jerusalem. The festival continues eight days, baptism[2] is administered, and people from every region under the sun resort to Jerusalem during this festival and visit the sacred places.

NOTES

1. *Note to the 2018 edition:* Sozomen here refers to the Church of the Holy Sepulchre in Jerusalem, which was dedicated about the year AD 335. The so-called Bordeaux Pilgrim records the following during his visit to the place in AD 333: "At present, by the command of the Emperor Constantine, has been built a basilica, that is to say, a church of wondrous beauty, having at the side reservoirs from which water is raised, and a bath behind in which infants are washed (baptized)." See Stewart: *Itinerary from Bordeaux to Jerusalem.*
2. Literally, μύησις, i.e. initiation.

CHAPTER XXVII
CONCERNING THE PRESBYTER BY WHOM CONSTANTINE WAS PERSUADED TO RECALL ARIUS AND EUZOIUS FROM EXILE. THE WRITTEN CONFESSION OF FAITH PROPOUNDED BY ARIUS, AND THE RECEPTION OF THIS LATTER BY THE SYNOD ASSEMBLED AT JERUSALEM.

The bishops who had embraced the sentiments of Arius found a favorable opportunity of restoring him and Euzoius to communion by convening a council in the city of Jerusalem. They effected their design in the following manner: A certain priest,[1] who was a great admirer of the Arian doctrines, was on terms of intimacy with the emperor's sister. At first he concealed his sentiments, but as he frequently visited and became by degrees more familiar with Constantia, for such was the name of the emperor's sister, he took courage to represent to her that Arius was unjustly exiled from his country, and cast out from the church, through the jealousy and personal enmity of Alexander, bishop of the Alexandrian church. He said that his jealousy had been excited by the esteem which the people manifested towards Arius.

Constantia believed these representations to be true, yet took no steps in opposition to the decrees of the council of Nicæa. Being attacked with a disease which threatened to terminate in death, she besought her brother, who went to visit her, to grant what she was about to ask as her dying request. This request was to receive the above-mentioned priest on terms of intimacy, and to rely upon him as a man of orthodox faith. "For my part," she added, "I am drawing nigh to death, and am no longer interested in the concerns of this life. The only apprehension I now feel arises from dread lest you should incur the wrath of God, and suffer any calamity, or the loss of your empire, since you have been induced to condemn good men to perpetual banishment."

From that period, the emperor received the priest into favor, and after frequently permitting him to converse with him on the same topics on which he had conversed with his sister, deemed it necessary to subject the case of Arius to a fresh examination. It is probable that in forming this decision, the emperor was either influenced by a belief in the credibility of the priest's calumnies, or by the desire of acceding to the wishes of his sister. It was not long before he recalled Arius from exile and demanded of him a written exposition of his faith concerning the Godhead. Arius avoided making use of the new terms which he had previously devised, and couched his sentiments in the must simple phraseology, frequently introducing the words used in Scripture. He declared upon oath that he held the doctrines set forth in this exposition and that there was no other meaning attached to the words than that which met the eye. It was as follows:

> Arius and Euzoius, presbyters, to Constantine, our most religious and best beloved emperor.
>
> According to your pious command, O Sovereign Lord, we here furnish a written statement of our faith, and we protest before God that we, and all those who are with us, believe what is here set forth.
>
> "We believe[2] in one God, the Father Almighty, and in His Son the Lord Jesus Christ, who proceeded from Him before all ages, being God the Word, by whom all things were made, whether things in heaven or things on earth. He took upon Him flesh, suffered and rose again, and

ascended into Heaven, whence he will again come to judge the quick and the dead.

We believe in the Holy Ghost, in the resurrection of the body, in the life to come, in the Kingdom of Heaven, and in one Catholic Church of God, established throughout the earth.

We have received this faith from the Holy Gospels, in which the Lord says to His disciples, "Go forth and teach all nations, baptizing them in the name of the Father, and of the Son, and of the Holy Ghost,"

If we do not believe these truths, and if we do not truly receive the doctrines concerning the Father, the Son, and the Holy Ghost, as they are taught by the whole Catholic Church and by the Sacred Scriptures, let God be our judge, both in this life and in that which is to come.

Wherefore we appeal to your piety, O our best beloved emperor, and beseech you that, as we are enrolled among the members of the clergy, and as we hold the faith and doctrines of the Church and of the Sacred Scriptures, you will effect a reconciliation between us and the Church, which is our Mother, so that useless questions and disputes may be cast aside, and that we and the Church may dwell together in peace, and join together in prayer for the prosperity of your empire and the welfare of your family.

Many considered this declaration of faith as an artful compilation, and as bearing an appearance of opposition to the Arian tenets, while, in reality, it supported them, the terms in which it was couched being so vague that it was susceptible of divers interpretations. The emperor imagined that Arius and Euzoius were of the same sentiments as the bishops of the council of Nicæa, and was delighted at the supposed discovery. He did not, however, attempt to restore them to communion without the sanction and cooperation of those who are, by the law of the church, judges of doctrine. He therefore sent them to the bishops who were then assembled at Jerusalem, and wrote to those bishops, desiring them to examine the declaration of faith submitted by Arius and Euzoius, and so to influence the decision of the synod that, whether they found that their doctrine was orthodox, and that the jealousy of their enemies had been the sole cause of their condemnation, or that, without having reason to blame those who had condemned them, they had subsequently embraced other sentiments, a favorable judgment might, in either case, be accorded them.

Those who had long desired the restoration of Arius to communion were pleased by the opportunity afforded by the emperor's letter for effecting their purpose. They wrote immediately to the emperor himself, to the church of Alexandria, and to the bishops and clergy of Egypt, of Thebes, and of Libya, to beseech them to receive Arius and Euzoius[3] into communion since the emperor bore witness to the orthodoxy of their faith in one of his own epistles, and since the judgment of the emperor had been confirmed by the decree of the synod.

These were the subjects which were zealously discussed by the synod of Jerusalem.

NOTES

1. Compare Socrates, *Ecclesiastical History*, Book I, Chapter 25. *Note to the 2018 edition:* This priest's name is not mentioned in Socrates either. As the incident is not mentioned in the extant works of Athanasius, it is thus considered of doubtful authenticity.
2. The same form is extant in Socrates, *Ecclesiastical History*, Book I, Chapter 26.
3. Concerning the restoration of these persons to the communion of the church, see Valesius, notes on Socrates, *Ecclesiastical History*, Book I, Chapter 33.

CHAPTER XXVIII

LETTER FROM THE EMPEROR CONSTANTINE TO THE SYNOD OF TYRE. EXILE OF SAINT ATHANASIUS THROUGH THE MACHINATIONS OF THE ARIAN FACTION.

Athanasius, after having fled from Tyre, repaired to Constantinople and complained to the emperor Constantine of the injustice of his condemnation and besought him to permit the decrees of the council of Tyre to be submitted to examination in his presence. Constantine regarded this request as reasonable, and wrote in the following terms[1] to the bishops assembled at Tyre:

> I know not what has been enacted in confusion and disorder by your synod, but it appears that from some disturbance or other, decrees which are not in conformity with truth have been enacted, and that your constant disputations among yourselves have prevented you from considering what is pleasing to God. But it will be the work of Divine Providence to terminate these disputes, and to manifest to us whether you have been actuated by a desire to maintain the truth, and whether you have not been misled in your judgment by motives of private friendship or aversion. I therefore command that you all come here to me without delay, in order that we may receive an exact account of your transactions.
>
> I will explain to you the cause of my writing to you in this strain. As I was returning on horseback to that city which bears my name and which I regard as my country, Athanasius, the bishop, presented himself so unexpectedly in the middle of the highway with certain individuals who accompanied him, that I felt exceedingly surprised at beholding him. God who sees all things is my witness that at first I did not know who he was, but that some of my attendants, having ascertained this point and the subject on which he had come to proffer his complaint,

gave me the necessary information. I did not on this occasion grant him an interview. He, however, persevered in requesting an audience, and although I refused him and was on the point of commanding that he should be removed from my presence, he told me with greater boldness than he had previously manifested, that he sought no other favor of me than that I should summon you hither in order that he might, in your presence, complain of the injustice that had been evinced towards him.

As this request appears reasonable and timely, I deemed it right to address you in this strain and to command all of you who were convened at the synod of Tyre to repair to us so that the equity of your decrees may be judged by me, whom you cannot refuse to acknowledge as a faithful servant of God. By my zeal in his service, peace has been established throughout the world, and the name of God is praised among the barbarians[2] who, till now, were in ignorance of the truth. And it is evident that whoever is ignorant of the truth knows not God. Notwithstanding, as is above stated, the barbarians have, through my instrumentality, learnt to know and to worship God, for they perceived that everywhere and on all occasions his protection rested on me, and they reverence God the more deeply because they fear my power. But we who have to announce the mysteries of his clemency (for I will not say that we keep them) we, I say, ought not to do anything that can tend to dissension or hatred or, to speak plainly, to the destruction of the human race.

Come then to us, as I have said, with all diligence and be assured that I shall do everything in my power to preserve the inviolability of the law of God and to expose those enemies of the law who, under the name of holiness, endeavor to introduce various blasphemies.

This letter of the emperor so excited the fears of some of the bishops that they set off on their journey homewards. But Eusebius, bishop of Nicomedia, and his partisans went to the emperor and represented that the synod of Tyre had enacted no decrees against Athanasius but what were founded on justice. They brought forward as witnesses Theognis, Maris, Theodore, Valens, and Ursacius, and deposed that he had broken the sacred vase,[3] and their calumnies were finally triumphant. The emperor, either believing their statements to be true or imagining that unanimity would be restored among the bishops if Athanasius were removed, exiled him to Treves,[4] a city of Gaul, and thither, therefore, he was conducted.

NOTES

1. Compare Socrates, *Ecclesiastical History,* Book I, Chapter 34.
2. He alludes to the Iberians, who have been already mentioned by Sozomen. See above, Book II, Chapter 7.

3. This however is at variance with the account given by Athanasius. See his *Apology against the Arians*, page 132, and the Benedictine *Life of Athanasius*, page 27.
4. Compare Socrates, *Ecclesiastical History* Book I, Chapter 35.

CHAPTER XXIX

ALEXANDER, BISHOP OF CONSTANTINOPLE. HIS REFUSAL TO ADMIT ARIUS INTO COMMUNION. DEATH OF ARIUS.

After the synod of Jerusalem, Arius went to Egypt, but as be could not obtain permission to hold communion with the church of Alexandria, he returned to Constantinople. As all those who had embraced his sentiments and those who were attached to Eusebius, bishop of Nicomedia, had assembled in that city for the purpose of holding a council,[1] Alexander, who was then at the head of the church of Constantinople, used every effort to prevent a council from being convened. But as his endeavors were frustrated, he refused all communion with Arius, affirming that it was neither just nor according to ecclesiastical canons that the decrees of the bishops who had been assembled at Nicæa from every region under the sun should be reversed.

When the partisans of Eusebius perceived that their arguments produced no effect on Alexander, they had recourse to contumely and threatened that unless he would receive Arius into communion on a stated day, he should be expelled from the church and that another should be elected in his place, who would be willing to hold communion with Arius. They then separated, the partisans of Eusebius to await the time they had fixed for carrying their menaces into execution, and Alexander to pray that Eusebius might be prevented from acting as they had said.[2] His chief source of sorrow arose from the fact that the emperor had been led away by the persuasions of his enemies. On the day before the appointed day he prostrated himself before the altar,[3] and continued all the night in prayer to God that his enemies might be prevented from carrying their schemes into execution against him.

On the evening of the same day, Arius, being seized with pain in the stomach, was compelled to repair to the public place set apart for emergencies of this nature. As some time passed away without his coming out, some persons who were waiting for him outside entered and found him dead and still sitting upon the seat.

When his death became known, all people did not view the occurrence under the same aspect. Some believed that he died of disease of the heart, induced by extreme joy at the success which had attended his undertakings, others imagined that this mode of death was inflicted on him in judgment on account of his impiety. Those who held his sentiments were of opinion that his death was brought about by magical arts. It will not be out of place to quote what Athanasius, bishop of

Alexandria, stated on the subject. The following is his narrative.

NOTES

1. Valesius interprets this to mean that they held private meetings in order to agitate the question of holding another council.
2. Compare Socrates, *Ecclesiastical History* Book I, *sub finem*.
3. See Rufinus, *Ecclesiastical History* Book X, Chapter 12.

CHAPTER XXX
ACCOUNT GIVEN BY THE GREAT ATHANASIUS OF THE DEATH OF ARIUS.

Arius, the author of the heresy and the associate of Eusebius, having been summoned before the most blessed Constantine Augustus at the solicitation of the partisans of Eusebius, was desired to give in writing an exposition of his faith. He drew up this document with great artfulness, and like the devil, concealed his impious assertions beneath the simple words of Scripture. The most blessed Constantine said to him, 'If you hold any other doctrines than those which are here set forth, render testimony to the truth.[1] But if you perjure yourself, the Lord will punish you,' and the wretched man swore that he held no sentiments except those specified in the document.

Soon after he went out,[2] and judgment was visited upon him, for he bent forwards and burst in the middle. With all men life terminates in death. We must not blame a man, even if he be an enemy, merely because he died, for it is uncertain whether we shall live till the evening. But the end of Arius was so singular that it seems worthy of some remark. The partisans of Eusebius threatened to reinstate him in the church, and Alexander, bishop of Constantinople, opposed their intention. Arius placed his confidence in the power and menaces of Eusebius. It was Saturday, and he expected the next day to be re-admitted into the church. The dispute ran high. The partisans of Eusebius were loud in their menaces, while Alexander had recourse to prayer. The Lord was the judge and declared himself against the unjust. A little before sunset Arius was compelled by a want of nature to enter the place appointed for such emergencies, and here he lost at once both restoration to communion and his life.

The most blessed Constantine was amazed when he heard of this occurrence and regarded it as the punishment of perjury. It then became evident to every one that the menaces of Eusebius were absolutely futile, and that the expectations of Arius were vain and foolish. It also became manifest that the Arian heresy had met with condemnation from the Savior as well as from the pristine church. Is it not then astonishing that some are still found who seek to exculpate him whom the Lord has condemned, and to defend a heresy of which the author was not permitted by our Lord to be rejoined to the church? We have been duly informed that this was the mode of the death of Arius. It is said that for a long period subsequently, no one would make use of the seat on which he died. Those who were compelled by necessities of nature to visit the public place, always avoided with horror the precise spot on which the impiety of Arius had been visited with judgment. At a later epoch a certain rich and powerful man, who had embraced the Arian tenets, bought the place of the public, and built a house on the spot, in order that the occurrence might fall into oblivion, and that there might be no perpetual memorial of the death of Arius.

NOTES

1. μάτυρα τήν ἀλήθειαν δός, i.e. swear by the truth: a common formula among the early Christians. So Saint Paul in his Epistles frequently exclaims, "I speak in the truth, I lie not." As per Valesius.
2. Athanasius gives an account of the end of Arius in his Epistle to Serapion: but it differs in some slight particulars from that which Sozomen and Socrates have given after Rufinus. Valesius considers that Arius died in a state of excommunication, and that the Arius who was received into communion by the synod at Jerusalem was not the same individual with the heresiarch.

CHAPTER XXXI

EVENTS WHICH TRANSPIRED IN ALEXANDRIA AFTER THE DEATH OF ARIUS. LETTER OF CONSTANTINE THE GREAT.

The death of Arius did not terminate the doctrinal dispute which he had originated. Those who adhered to his sentiments did not cease from plotting against those who maintained opposite opinions. The people of Alexandria loudly complained of the exile of Athanasius and offered up supplications for his return, and Antony, the celebrated monk, wrote frequently to the emperor to entreat him to attach no credit to the insinuations of the Meletians but to reject their accusations as calumnies

Yet the emperor was not convinced by these arguments and wrote to the Alexandrians, accusing them of folly and of disorderly conduct. He commanded the clergy and the holy virgins to remain quiet, and declared that he would not change his mind nor recall Athanasius whom, he said, he regarded as an exciter of sedition justly condemned by the judgment of the church. He replied to Antony by stating that he ought not to overlook the decree of the synod, for even if some few of the bishops, he said, were actuated by ill-will or the desire to oblige others, it scarcely seems credible that so many prudent and excellent bishops could have been impelled by such motives. And, he added, that Athanasius was contumelious and arrogant, and the author of divisions and seditions. The enemies of Athanasius accused him the more especially of these crimes, because they knew that the emperor regarded them with peculiar aversion.

When he heard that the church was split into two factions, of which one supported Athanasius and the other John, he was transported with indignation and exiled John. This John had succeeded Melitius and had, with those who held the same sentiments as himself, been restored to communion and re-established in the clerical functions by the synod of Tyre. His banishment was contrary to the wishes of the enemies of Athanasius, nor could it be revoked by the decrees of the synod of Tyre, for the emperor was inexorable against those who introduced sedition and dissension among the Christians.

CHAPTER XXXII

CONSTANTINE ENACTS A LAW AGAINST ALL HERESIES, AND PROHIBITS THE PEOPLE FROM ASSEMBLING IN ANY PLACE BUT THE CATHOLIC CHURCH, AND THUS THE GREATER NUMBER OF HERESIES DISAPPEAR.

Although the doctrine of Arius was zealously supported by many persons in disputations, a party had not as yet been formed[1] to whom the name of Arians could be applied as a distinctive appellation. For all assembled together as a church and held communion with each other, with the exception of the Novatians, those called Phrygians, the Valentinians, and some few others who adhered to ancient heresies. The emperor, however, enacted a law[2] by which they were forbidden to assemble in their own houses of prayer, in private houses, or in public places, but were compelled to enter into communion with the Catholic church. By means of this law, almost all the heresies, I believe, disappeared.

During the reign of preceding emperors, all those who followed Christ, however they might have differed from each other in opinion, received the same treatment from the Greeks (Pagans), and were persecuted with equal cruelty. These common calamities, to which they were all equally liable, prevented them from prosecuting any close inquiries as to the differences of opinion which existed among themselves. The members of each party assembled themselves together, and however few they might have been in number, did not lose their corporate existence. But after this law was passed they could not assemble in public because it was forbidden, nor could they hold their assemblies in secret, for they were watched by the bishops and clergy of their city. Hence the greater number of these sectarians were led, by fear of consequences, to join themselves to the Catholic church. Those who adhered to their original sentiments did not, at their death, leave any disciples to propagate their heresy, for, owing to the restrictions to which they were subjected, they were prevented from teaching their doctrines.

On account either of the absurdity of the heretical dogmas, or of the utter ignorance of those who devised and taught them, the respective followers of each heresy were, from the beginning, very few in number. The Novatians alone, who had obtained good leaders and who entertained the same opinions respecting the Divinity as the Catholic church, formed a large sect from the beginning and were not decreased in point of numbers by means of this law. The emperor, I believe, relaxed the rigor of the enactment in their favor, for he only desired to strike terror into the minds of his subjects and had no intention of persecuting them. Acesius, who was then the bishop of the Novatians in Constantinople, was much esteemed by the emperor on account of his virtuous life, and it is probable that it was for his sake that the church which he governed met with protection. The Phrygians suffered the same treatment as the other heretics in all the Roman provinces except Phrygia and the neighboring regions, for here they had, since the time of Montanus, existed in great numbers, and they are to the present day to be found in that locality.

About this time the partisans of Eusebius, bishop of Nicomedia, and of Theognis, bishop of Nicæa, began to combat in writing the confession of faith, which had been set forth by the Nicæan council. They did not venture to reject openly the assertion that the Son is consubstantial with the Father because this assertion was maintained by the emperor, but they drew up another formula of belief and signified to the Eastern bishops that, with certain modifications, they had received the Nicæan confession of faith. They thus renewed disputes and the agitation of questions which had almost sunk into oblivion.

NOTES

1. This would seem to be at variance with the assertion of Alexander, in Theodoret, *Ecclesiastical History,* Book I, Chapter 4.
2. This law is extant in Eusebius *Life of the Blessed Emperor Constantine,* Book III, Chapter 64.

CHAPTER XXXIII

MARCELLUS, BISHOP OF ANCYRA. HIS HERESY AND DEPOSITION.

At the same period, Marcellus, bishop of Ancyra in Galatia, was deposed by the bishops assembled at Constantinople because he had introduced some new doctrines whereby he taught that the existence of the Son of God commenced when He was born of Mary and that His reign would have an end. He had, moreover, drawn up a written document wherein these views were propounded.

Basil, a man of great learning and eloquence, was invested by the bishops with the government of the church of Galatia. They also wrote to the churches in the neighboring regions to desire them to search for the copies of the book[1] written by Marcellus and to destroy them, and to lead back those who had embraced his sentiments to the Catholic faith. They stated that the work was too voluminous to admit of their transcribing the whole in their epistle, but that they inserted quotations of certain passages in order to prove that the doctrines which they had condemned were there advocated. Some persons, however, maintained that Marcellus had merely propounded a few questions which had been misconstrued by the adherents of Eusebius and represented to the emperor as formal propositions. Eusebius and his partisans were irritated against Marcellus, because he had not consented to their decrees at the council of Tyre, nor to the regulations which had been made in favor of Arius at Jerusalem, and had likewise refused to attend at the consecration of the church called the Great Martyr in order to avoid communion with them. In their letter to the emperor, they dwelt largely upon this latter circumstance, alleging that it was a personal insult to him to refuse attendance at the consecration of the temple which he had constructed at Jerusalem.

The motive by which Marcellus was induced to write this work was that Asterius, who was a sophist and a native of Cappadocia, had written a treatise in defense of the Arian doctrines, and had read it in various cities, and to the bishops, and likewise at several synods where he had attended. Marcellus undertook to refute his arguments, and while thus engaged, he, either deliberately or unintentionally, fell into the errors of Paul of Samosata. He was afterwards, however, reinstated in his bishopric by the council of Sardis, after having proved that he did not hold the doctrines which had been imputed to him.

NOTE

1. The title of this book is said by Valesius to have been *De Subjectione Filii Dei*.

CHAPTER XXXIV

DEATH OF CONSTANTINE THE GREAT. HE RECEIVES THE RITE OF BAPTISM IN HIS LAST MOMENTS, AND IS BURIED IN THE TEMPLE OF THE HOLY APOSTLES.

The emperor divided the empire among his sons, who were styled Cæsars.[1] To Constantine and Constans he awarded the Western regions, and to Constantius, the Eastern. And, as he was indisposed, and required to have recourse to bathing, he repaired for that purpose to Helenopolis, a city of Bithynia. His malady, however, increased, and he went to Nicomedia, and received the rite of holy baptism[2] in one of the suburbs of that city. After the ceremony he was filled with joy, and returned thanks to God. He then confirmed the division of the empire among his sons, according to his former allotment, and bestowed certain privileges on Old and on New Rome. He placed his testament in the hands of the priest who constantly extolled Arius, and who had been recommended to him as a man of virtuous life by his sister Constantia in her last moments, and commanded him to deliver it to Constantius on his return, for neither Constantius nor the other Cæsars were with their dying father.

After making these arrangements, Constantine survived but a few days. He died in the sixty-fifth year of his age, and the thirty-first of his reign. He was a powerful protector of the Christian religion, and was the first of the emperors who manifested zeal in the extension of the church. He was more successful than any other sovereign in all his undertakings, for he formed no design, I am convinced, without God. He was victorious in his wars against the Goths and Sarmatians and, indeed, in all his military enterprises, and he changed the form of government according to his own mind with so much ease that he created another senate and another capital city to which he gave his own name. He utterly subverted the Grecian religion, which had prevailed for ages among the princes and the people.

After the death of Constantine, his body was placed in a golden coffin, conveyed to Constantinople, and deposited in the palace, and the same honors were rendered to the body by those who were in the palace, as if the emperor had been still alive. On hearing of his father's death, Constantius, who was then in the East, hastened to Constantinople and interred the royal remains with the utmost magnificence, and deposited them in the tomb which had been constructed by order of the deceased in the Church of the Apostles. From this period it became the custom to deposit the remains of subsequent Christian emperors in the same place of interment, and here bishops likewise were buried, for the hierarchial dignity is not only equal in honor[3] to imperial power but in sacred places, even takes the ascendancy.

NOTES

1. With this chapter the reader will do well to compare Eusebius, *Life of the Blessed Emperor Constantine*, Book IV, Chapter 61, etc., and Socrates, *Ecclesiastical History*, Book I, Chapters 39, 40.
2. ἐμυήθη. See above, note on Chapter 26.
3. ὁμότιμος. Valesius remarks that the former of these two assertions may be doubted, since both the sacerdotal and the imperial power have their own separate province and limits. And further, he adds, the reader must be warned that Sozomen here speaks concerning not the authority but the dignity of the priesthood. The former of which does not extend beyond the limits of the church, though the case is otherwise with the sacerdotal dignity which, however, in the opinion of Valesius, falls short of regal dignity.

BOOK III

CHAPTER I
AFTER THE DEATH OF CONSTANTINE THE GREAT THE ADHERENTS OF EUSEBIUS AND THEOGNIS RENEW THE CONTROVERSY CONCERNING THE FAITH ESTABLISHED AT NICÆA.

We have now seen what events transpired in the churches during the reign of Constantine.[1] On his death, the doctrine which had been set forth at Nicæa was subjected to renewed examination. Although this doctrine was not universally approved, no one during the life of Constantine had dared to reject it openly. At his death, however, many renounced this faith, especially those who had previously been suspected of treachery. Eusebius and Theognis, bishops of provinces in Bithynia, did everything in their power to give predominance to the tenets of Arius. They believed that this object would be easily accomplished by retaining Athanasius in exile and by giving the government of the Egyptian churches to a bishop of their own sect. They found an efficient coadjutor in the priest who had obtained from Constantine the recall of Arius. He was held in high esteem by the emperor Constantius, on account of the service he had rendered in delivering to him the testament of his father. He had, in fact, constant liberty of access to the empress, and was on terms of intimacy with the eunuchs of the court.

At this period Eusebius was appointed to superintend the concerns of the royal household, and, being zealously attached to Arianism, he induced the empress and many of the persons belonging to the court to adopt the same sentiments. Hence disputations concerning doctrines again became prevalent, both in public and in private, and mutual revilings and virulent animosities were renewed. This state of things was in accordance with the views of Theognis and his partisans.

NOTE

1. Compare Socrates, *Ecclesiastical History*, Book II, Chapter 2.

CHAPTER II
RETURN OF THE GREAT ATHANASIUS FROM EXILE. LETTER OF CONSTANTINE CÆSAR, SON OF CONSTANTINE THE GREAT. MACHINATIONS OF THE ARIANS AGAINST ATHANASIUS. ACACIUS. WAR BETWEEN CONSTANTINE AND CONSTANS.

At this period Athanasius returned from the West of Gaul to Alexandria. It is said that Constantine intended to have recalled him, and that in his testament he even gave orders to that effect. But as he was prevented by death from performing his intention, his son who bore his name, and who was then commanding in Western Gaul, recalled Athanasius, and wrote a letter on the subject to the people of Alexandria. Having met with a copy of this letter translated from the Latin into Greek, I shall insert it precisely as I found it. It is as follows:

Constantine Caesar, to the people of the Catholic Church of Alexandria.[1]

You cannot, I believe, be unacquainted with the fact that Athanasius, the venerable interpreter of the law, was sent for a time into Gaul lest he should fall a sacrifice to the sanguinary designs of his enemies who sought his destruction. In order to shield him from the dangers which menaced him, he was desired to remain in the country which is under my sway, and means were taken in every city wherein he abode to supply all his wants. But he is endowed with such exalted and extraordinary virtue that by the aid of the grace of God, he sets at nought all the necessities of nature.

Our lord and my father, Constantine Augustus of most blessed memory, intended to have reinstated this bishop in his diocese, and thus to have restored him to your piety. But as he was prevented by death from fulfilling his intention, it devolves upon me, as his heir, to carry his design into execution. Athanasius will inform you in person of the respect which I have manifested towards him. Nor is it surprising that I should have acted as I have done towards him, for I was impelled by the desire of gratifying your wish of seeing him again and by the feeling of esteem which was excited in my mind by the virtue of so holy a man.

May Divine Providence watch over you, my beloved brethren.

In consequence of this letter from the emperor, Athanasius returned from exile and resumed the government of the Egyptian churches. Those who were attached to the Arian doctrines viewed his return with consternation. They excited fresh seditions and had recourse to other machinations against him. The partisans of Eusebius accused him before the emperor of being a seditious person, and of having reversed the decree of exile contrary to the laws of the church and without the consent of the bishops. I shall presently relate in the proper place how, by their intrigues, Athanasius was again expelled from Alexandria.

Eusebius, surnamed Pamphilus, died[2] about this period, and Acacius was appointed to the bishopric of Cæsarea in Palestine. He had been instructed by Eusebius in the interpretation of Holy Writ. He possessed some learning and eloquence and had written several works.

Not long after,[3] the emperor Constantine declared war against his brother Constans and was slain by his own generals. The Roman Empire was divided between the surviving brothers. The East fell to the lot of Constantius, and the West to Constans.

NOTES

1. Compare Socrates, *Ecclesiastical History,* Book II, Chapter 3
2. Compare Socrates, *Ecclesiastical History,* Book II, Chapter 4.
3. Compare Socrates, *Ecclesiastical History,* Book II, Chapter 5.

CHAPTER III

PAUL, BISHOP OF CONSTANTINOPLE. HERESY OF MACEDONIUS.

Alexander died[1] about this time, and Paul obtained the bishopric of Constantinople. The followers of Arius and Macedonius assert that he took possession of this office without the concurrence of Eusebius, bishop of Nicomedia, or of Theodore, bishop of Heraclea in Thrace, upon whom, as being the nearest bishops,[2] the right of conferring ordination devolved. Many, however, maintain, on the testimony of Alexander whom he succeeded, that he was ordained by the bishops who were then assembled at Constantinople. For when Alexander, who was eighty-nine years of age and who had held the episcopal office for twenty-three years, was at the point of death, his clergy asked him whom he wished to succeed him in the government of his church. "If," replied he, "you seek a good man and one who is apt to teach you, have Paul. But if you desire one who is conversant with public affairs, and able to confer with rulers, Macedonius is, in these respects, more qualified than Paul."

The Macedonians themselves admit that this testimony was given by Alexander, but they say that Paul was the more skilled of the two in the transaction of business and the art of eloquence, and that Macedonius was celebrated on account of the purity of his life and conduct. And they accuse Paul of having been addicted to luxury and licentiousness.[3] It appears, however, from their own acknowledgment, that Paul was a man of great eloquence and highly renowned on account of his skill in teaching the church. Events proved that he was not competent to combat the casualties of life or to hold intercourse with those in power. He was never successful in subverting the machinations of his enemies, like those who are adroit in the management of such affairs. Although he was greatly beloved by the people, he suffered severely from the artifices of those who rejected the doctrines established by the council of Nicæa. In the first place, he was expelled from the church of Constantinople, as if some accusation had been established against him.[4] He was then sent into banishment, and finally, it is said, fell a victim to the devices of his enemies and was strangled. But these latter events took place at a subsequent period.

NOTES

1. Compare Socrates, *Ecclesiastical History,* Book II, Chapter 6.
2. Valesius does not acquiesce in the truth of this statement, so far as concerns the bishop of Nicomedia, a city of a different province and the right of ordination belonged only to bishops of the same province. The case may have been different with Heraclea, which was formerly the metropolitan see to Constantinople.
3. ἀδιάφορος βιός literally "an indifferent life." Saint Basil and others of the Christian Fathers use the word in the same sense.
4. He had been originally accused by the presbyter Macedonius. The accusation, according to Theodoret, *Ecclesiastical History,* Book II, Chapter 5, was that of sedition. See Athanasius, *Arian History.*.

CHAPTER IV

A SEDITION WAS EXCITED ON THE ORDINATION OF PAUL.

The ordination of Paul occasioned a great commotion in the church of Constantinople. During the life of Alexander, the Arians did not venture to excite any insurrection, for the people were implicitly obedient to their bishop, and attached to his sway, and moreover, regarded the extraordinary and unexpected death of Arius as a manifest indication of divine wrath drawn down upon him, so to speak, by the prayers and virtues of Alexander. After the death of this bishop, however, the people became divided into two parties, and disputes and contests concerning doctrines were openly carried on.

The adherents of Arius desired the ordination of Macedonius, while those who maintained that the Son is consubstantial with the Father wished to have Paul as their bishop, and this latter party prevailed. After the ordination of Paul, the emperor returned to Constantinople and manifested as much displeasure at what had taken place as if Paul had been unworthy of the bishopric. Through the machinations of the enemies of Paul a synod was convened, and he was expelled from the church. Eusebius, bishop of Nicomedia, was installed in the bishopric of Constantinople.

CHAPTER V
COUNCIL OF ANTIOCH. DEPOSITION OF ATHANASIUS. INSTALLATION OF GREGORY. TWO FORMULARIES OF FAITH.

Soon after these occurrences, the emperor went to Antioch, a city of Syria. Here a large and beautiful church had been founded by the late emperor Constantine, and as the structure had been just completed by his son Constantius, it was deemed a favorable opportunity by the partisans of Eusebius to convene a council. They, therefore, with those from various regions who held their sentiments, met together in Antioch. Their bishops were about ninety-seven in number. Their professed object was the consecration of the new church, but they intended nothing else than the abolition of the decrees of the Nicæan council, and this was fully proved by the sequel. The church of Antioch was then governed by Flacillus,[1] who had succeeded Euphronius. The death of Constantine the Great had taken place about five years prior to this period.

When all the bishops had assembled in the presence of the emperor Constantius, the majority expressed great indignation against Athanasius for having contemned the sacerdotal regulation which they had enacted,[2] and taken possession of the bishopric of Alexandria without first obtaining the sanction of a council. They also deposed that he was the cause of the death of several persons who fell in a sedition excited by his return, and that many others had on the same occasion been arrested and delivered up to the judicial tribunals. By these accusations they contrived to cast odium on Athanasius, and it was decreed that Gregory should be invested with the government of the church of Alexandria.

They then turned to the discussion of doctrinal questions, and found no fault with the decrees of the council of Nicæa. They despatched letters to the bishops of every city in which they declared that, as they were bishops themselves, they had not followed Arius. "For how," said they, "could we have been followers of him, when he was but a presbyter, and we were placed above him?"

They affirmed that they received the faith which had, from the beginning, been handed down by tradition. This they further explained at the bottom of their letter, but without alluding to the substance of the Father or the Son or to the term consubstantial. They resorted, in fact, to such ambiguity of expression, that neither the Arians nor the followers of the decrees of the Nicæan council could call their assertions into question, or affirm that they departed from the doctrines of the Holy Scriptures. They purposely avoided all forms of expression which were rejected by either party, and only made use of those which were universally admitted. They confessed that the Son is with the Father, that he is the only begotten One, and that he is God, and existed before all things, and that he took flesh upon him, and fulfilled the will of his Father. They admitted these and similar truths, but neither affirmed nor denied the doctrine of the Son being co-eternal and consubstantial with the Father. They subsequently disapproved, it appears, of this formulary and issued another which, I think, very nearly resembles that of the council of Nicæa unless, indeed, some secret meaning be attached to the words which is not apparent to me. Although they refrained, I know not from what motive, from saying that the Son is consubstantial with the Father, they confessed that he is immutable, that his Divinity is not susceptible of change, that he is the perfect image of the substance, and counsel, and power, and glory of the Father, and that he is the first-born of every creature. They stated that they had found this formulary of faith, and that it was written by Lucinius,[3] who was martyred in Nicomedia, and who was a man of great celebrity and remarkably conversant with the Sacred Scriptures. I know not whether this statement was really true, or whether they merely advanced it in order to give weight to their own document, by connecting with it the name of an illustrious martyr.

Not only was Eusebius (who, on the expulsion of Paul, had been transferred from the bishopric of Nicomedia to that of Constantinople) present at this council, but likewise Acacius, the successor of Eusebius Pamphilus, Patrophilus, bishop of Scythopolis, Theodore, bishop of Heraclea, formerly called Perinthus, Eudoxius, bishop of Germanicia, who succeeded Macedonius in the government of the Church of Constantinople, and Gregory, who had been appointed bishop of the church of Alexandria. It was universally acknowledged that all these bishops held the same sentiments. Dianius,[4] bishop of Cæsarea in Cappadocia, George, bishop of Laodicea in Syria, and many other metropolitan bishops and primates of renowned churches were also present at this council.

NOTES

1. Πλάκητος. Placitus or Flacillus. See Socrates, *Ecclesiastical History,* Book II, Chapter 8.
2. The canon here alluded to (the twelfth of the council of Nicæa) forbade a priest or deacon, when deposed by a synod, to seek restoration from the emperor, but enjoined him to appeal in such a case to a larger and fuller synod of bishops. There seems to be good ground for believing that this canon was aimed at Athanasius, when he had been restored to Alexandria by a proclamation of the emperor. Hence Saint Chrysostom, on a somewhat similar occasion, declares that the canon quoted above is one of the Arians, and not of the Catholic church. See Socrates, *Ecclesiastical History,* Book VI, Chapter 18.
3. This person was a presbyter of Antioch. This symbol or formulary of faith may be seen in Socrates, *Ecclesiastical History,* Book II, Chapter 10. He was suspected of Arianism, but this imputation has been removed from his name by the learned Bull. See Bull: *Defensio Fidei Nicænæ* Book II, Chapter 13, Number 4.
4. He is also called Dianæus.

CHAPTER VI

EUSEBIUS, SURNAMED EMESIUS. GREGORY ACCEPTS THE BISHOPRIC OF ALEXANDRIA. ATHANASIUS SEEKS REFUGE IN ROME.

Eusebius, surnamed Emesius, likewise attended the council. He sprang from a noble family of Edessa, a city of Osdroëna. According to the custom of his country, he had from his youth upwards been instructed in the knowledge of Sacred Scripture, and was afterwards made acquainted with the learning of the Greeks by the doctors who then frequented his native city. He subsequently acquired a more intimate knowledge of sacred literature, under the guidance of Eusebius Pamphilus and Patrophilus, bishop of Scythopolis. He went to Antioch at the time that Eustathius was deposed on the accusation of Cyrus, and lived with Euphronius, his successor on terms of intimacy. He fled to escape being invested with the priestly dignity, went to Alexandria, and frequented the schools of the philosophers. After acquainting himself with their mode of discipline, he returned to Antioch and dwelt with Flacillus, the successor of Euphronius.

During the time that the council was held in that city, Eusebius, bishop of Constantinople, entreated him to accept the bishopric of Alexandria, for it was thought that by his great reputation for sanctity and consummate eloquence, he would easily supplant Athanasius in the esteem of the Egyptians. He, however, refused the bishopric on the plea that he could otherwise only incur the hatred of the Alexandrians, who would have no other bishop but Athanasius. Gregory was, therefore, appointed bishop of Alexandria, and Eusebius was ordained over the church of Emesa.

A sedition was excited on the inauguration of Eusebius. The people accused him of being addicted to the practice of judicial astronomy, and being obliged to seek safety by flight, he repaired to Laodicea and dwelt with George, bishop of that city, who was his particular friend. He afterwards accompanied this bishop to Antioch, and obtained permission from the bishops Flacillus and Narcissus to return to Emesa. He was much esteemed by the emperor Constantius, and attended him in his military expeditions against the Persians. It is said that God wrought miracles through his instrumentality, as is testified by George of Laodicea who has related many instances of this nature besides those which I have recorded.[1]

But although he was endowed with so many exalted qualities, he could not escape the jealousy of those who are irritated by witnessing the virtues of others. It was insinuated that he had embraced the doctrines of Sabellius. At the same time, however, he voted with the bishops who had been convened at Antioch. It is said that Maximus, bishop of Jerusalem, kept aloof from this council because he repented having unawares consented to the deposition of Athanasius.[2] The bishop of Rome, and the bishops of other parts of Italy, and of the remoter provinces of the empire, also absented themselves from this council.

At the same period of time, the Franks devastated Western Gaul. The provinces of the East, and more particularly Antioch, were visited by a tremendous earthquake. Gregory repaired to Alexandria with a large body of soldiers in order to obtain a safe and undisputed entrance into the city. The Arians also, who were anxious for the expulsion of Athanasius, sided with him. Athanasius, fearful lest the people should be exposed to sufferings on his account,[3] assembled them by night in the church, and when the soldiers came to take possession of the church,[4] prayers having been concluded, he caused a psalm to be sung. During the chaunting of this psalm, the soldiers remained without and quietly awaited its conclusion, and in the meantime Athanasius secretly made his escape and fled to Rome. In this manner Gregory possessed himself of the bishopric of Alexandria. The indignation of the people was aroused, and they burnt the church which bore the name of Dionysius, one of the former bishops of their city.

NOTES

1. *Note to the 2018 edition:* A very similar biography of Eusebius of Emesa may be found in Socrates, *Ecclesiastical History,* Book II, Chapter 25. Socrates mentions that his account is taken directly from the panegyric of Eusebius of Emesa written by George of Laodicea mentioned in this chapter by Sozomen.
2. Compare Socrates, *Ecclesiastical History,* Book I, Chapter 8.
3. Compare Socrates, *Ecclesiastical History,* Book II, Chapter 11.
4. Valesius reminds us that this occurred not on the arrival of Gregory but on his enthronization. Compare Socrates, *Ecclesiastical History,* Book II, Chapter 10.

CHAPTER VII

BISHOPS OF ROME AND OF CONSTANTINOPLE. RESTORATION OF PAUL AFTER THE DEATH OF EUSEBIUS. DEATH OF HERMOGENES, A GENERAL OF THE ARMY.

Thus were the schemes of those who upheld various heresies in opposition to truth successfully carried into execution, and thus did they depose those bishops who strenuously maintained throughout the East the supremacy of the doctrines of the Nicæan council. These heretics had taken possession of the most important bishoprics, such as Alexandria in Egypt, Antioch in Syria, and the capital city of the Hellespont, and they held all the neighboring bishops in subjection.

The bishop of Rome and all the clergy of the West were offended at these proceedings and religiously maintained the faith of the council of Nicæa which they had embraced from the beginning. On the arrival of Athanasius, they received him kindly and proposed to pass judgment on his case. Irritated at this interference, Eusebius wrote to Julius, exhorting him to constitute himself a judge of the decrees that had been enacted against Athanasius by the council of Tyre. But before he had been able to ascertain the sentiments of Julius, and indeed soon after the council of Antioch, Eusebius died.

Immediately upon this event, those citizens of Constantinople who maintained the doctrines of the Nicæan council conducted Paul to the church. At the same time, the adherents of Theognis, bishop of Nicæa, of Theodore, bishop of Heraclea, and others of the same party, aided by the Arians, assembled at Constantinople and ordained Macedonius bishop of Constantinople. This excited a sedition in the city which assumed all the appearance of a war, for the people rose up against each other and many fell in the encounter. The city was filled with tumult so that the emperor, who was then at Antioch, on hearing of what had occurred, was filled with indignation and issued a decree for the expulsion of Paul. Hermogenes, general of the cavalry, endeavored to put this edict of the emperor's into execution, for having been sent to Thrace, he had on the journey to pass by Constantinople, and he thought by means of his army to eject Paul from the church. But the people, instead of yielding, met him with open resistance, and while the soldiers in obedience to the orders they had received were engaged in violent assault on the city, the populace[1] entered the house of Hermogenes, set fire to it, killed him, and attaching to his body a cord, dragged it through the city.

The emperor had no sooner received this intelligence than he took horse to Constantinople in order to punish the people. They, however, went to meet him with tears and supplications, and induced him to desist from his purpose. He deprived them of about half of the corn which his father, Constantine, had granted them annually from the tributes of Egypt, probably from the idea that luxury and great abundance rendered them easily disposed to sedition. He turned all his anger against Paul, and commanded his expulsion from the city. He manifested great displeasure against Macedonius because he had taken part in the murder of the general and of other individuals, and also because he had been ordained without first obtaining his sanction. He, however, returned to Antioch without having either confirmed or dissolved his ordination.

The Arians soon after deposed Gregory, because he had shown little zeal in the support of their doctrines, and had moreover incurred the enmity of the Alexandrians on account of the calamities which had marked the commencement of his authority, especially the conflagration of the church. They elected George, a native of Cappadocia, in his stead.[2] This new bishop was admired on account of his activity and his zeal in support of the Arian dogmas.

NOTES

1. We have adopted here the emendation of Valesius, who reads στρασιῶται for στρατιῶται.
2. Compare Socrates, *Ecclesiastical History,* Book II, Chapter 14.

CHAPTER VIII
ARRIVAL OF THE EASTERN ARCHBISHOPS AT ROME. LETTER OF JULIUS, BISHOP OF ROME. BY MEANS OF THE LETTERS OF JULIUS, PAUL AND ATHANASIUS ARE REINSTATED IN THEIR OWN BISHOPRICS. LETTER FROM THE ARCHBISHOPS OF THE EAST TO JULIUS.

Athanasius, on leaving Alexandria, fled to Rome.[1] Paul, bishop of Constantinople, Marcellus, bishop of Ancyra, and Asclepas, bishop of Gaza, repaired thither at the same time. Asclepas, who was strongly opposed to the Arians, had been accused by them of having thrown down an altar,[2] and Quintian had been appointed in his stead over the church of Gaza. Lucius, also, bishop of Adrianople, who had on some accusation been deposed from his office, was dwelling at this period in Rome.

The Roman bishop, on learning the cause of their condemnation, and on finding that they held the same sentiments as himself and adhered to the Nicæan doctrines, admitted them to communion, and as by the dignity of his seat the charge of watching over the orthodox devolved upon him, he restored them all to their own churches. He wrote to the bishops of the East and rebuked them for having judged these bishops unjustly and for having disturbed the peace of the church by abandoning the Nicæan doctrines. He summoned a few among them to appear before him on an appointed day, in order to account to him for the sentence they had passed, and threatened to bear with them no longer should they introduce any further innovations.

Athanasius and Paul were reinstated in their bishoprics and forwarded the letter of Julius to the bishops of the East. The bishops were highly indignant at this letter, and they assembled together at Antioch and framed a reply to Julius, replete with elegance[3] and the graces of rhetoric, but couched in a tone of irony and defiance. They confessed in this epistle that the church of Rome was entitled to universal honor,[4] because it had been founded by the apostles and had enjoyed the rank of a metropolitan church from the first preaching of religion, although those who first propagated a knowledge of Christian doctrines in this city came from the East. They added that the second place in point of honor ought not to be assigned to them merely on account of the smallness of their city and of their numerical inferiority, for that with respect to zeal and firmness, they surpassed others. They called Julius to account for having admitted Athanasius into communion and expressed their indignation against him for having insulted their synod and abrogated their decrees, and they reprehended his conduct, because, they said, it was opposed to justice and to the canons of the church.

After these complaints and protestations, they proceeded to state, that they were willing to continue on terms of amity and communion with Julius provided that he would sanction the deposition of the bishops whom they had expelled, and the ordination of those whom they had elected in their stead, but that unless he would accede to these terms, they should have recourse to hostility. They added that the bishops who had preceded them in the government of the Eastern churches had offered no opposition to the deposition of Novatian by the church of Rome. They made no allusion in their letter to any deviations they had manifested from the doctrines of the council of Nicæa, but merely stated they had various reasons to allege in justification of the course they had pursued, and that they considered it unnecessary to enter at that time upon any defense of their conduct, as they were suspected of having violated justice in every respect.

NOTES

1. Compare Socrates, *Ecclesiastical History,* Book II, Chapters 15, 16.
2. The same accusation is made against him in the epistle of the Eastern bishops at Sardica.
3. κεκαλλιεπημένην. Compare Athanasius, *Apology against the Arians, Part II,* where Julius complains that the letter of the bishops is written in a proud and arrogant tone, and for the sake of displaying their eloquence (φιλοτιμίας ἐνέκα).
4. Valesius renders φιλοτιμίαν φέρειν, "ambitiose se jactare."

CHAPTER IX

EJECTION OF PAUL AND ATHANASIUS. MACEDONIUS IS INVESTED WITH THE GOVERNMENT OF THE CHURCH OF CONSTANTINOPLE.

After having written in this strain to Julius, the bishops of the East brought accusations against those whom they had deposed before the emperor Constantius. Accordingly, the emperor, who was then at Antioch, wrote to Philip, the prefect[1] of Constantinople, commanding him to reinstate Macedonius in the government of the church and to expel Paul from the city. The prefect, fearing lest the execution of this order should give rise to a sedition among the people, kept the whole matter a profound secret. He repaired to the public bath which is called Zeuxippus, a large and beautiful structure, and having sent for Paul as if he wished to converse with him on some affairs of general interest, showed him on his arrival the edict of the emperor. Paul was immediately and secretly conveyed through the palace, which is contiguous to the bath, to the sea-side and was placed on board a vessel, and conducted to Thessalonica whence, it is said, his ancestors originally came. He was strictly prohibited from approaching the Eastern regions, but was not forbidden to visit Illyria and the remoter provinces.

On quitting the prætorium, Philip, accompanied by Macedonius, proceeded to the church. The people, who had in the meantime been assembling together, quickly filled the church, and the two parties into which they were divided, namely, the Arians and the followers of Paul, respectively strove to take possession of the church. When the prefect and Macedonius arrived at the gates of the church, the soldiers endeavored to force back the people, but as they were so crowded together, it was impossible for them to recede or make way. The soldiers, under the impression that they were met to resist the imperial authority, drew their swords and killed many persons, and several others were slain in the crowd. The edict of the emperor was thus accomplished, and Macedonius reinstated in the government of the church, while Paul, contrary to all previous expectation, was ejected from the church.

Athanasius in the meantime had fled and concealed himself, dreading to be put to death according to the menaces of the emperor Constantius, for the heterodox had made the emperor believe that he was a seditious person, and that he had on his return to the bishopric occasioned the death of several persons. But the anger of the emperor had been chiefly excited by the representation that Athanasius had sold the wheat which the emperor Constantine had bestowed on the poor of Alexandria, and had appropriated the price.

NOTE

1. τῷ ὑπάρχῳ Compare Socrates, *Ecclesiastical History*, Book II, Chapter 16.

CHAPTER X

THE BISHOP OF ROME WRITES TO THE BISHOPS OF THE EAST IN FAVOR OF ATHANASIUS, AND THEY SEND A DEPUTATION TO ROME TO JUSTIFY THEIR PROCEEDINGS. THIS DEPUTATION IS DISMISSED BY CONSTANS CÆSAR.

The bishop of Egypt having sent a declaration in writing that these allegations were false, and Julius having been apprized that Athanasius was far from being in safety in Egypt, sent for him to his own city. He replied at the same time to the letter of the bishops who were convened at Antioch, and accused them of having clandestinely introduced innovations contrary to the edicts of the Nicæan council, and of having violated the laws of the church by neglecting to invite him to join their synod, for there is a sacerdotal canon[1] which declares, that whatever is enacted without the sanction of the bishop of Rome is null and void. He also reproached them for having deviated from justice in all their proceedings against Athanasius, both at Tyre and Mareota, and stated that the decrees enacted at the former city had been annulled on account of the calumny concerning the hand of Arsenius, and at the latter city, on account of the absence of Athanasius. Last of all he reprehended the arrogant style of their epistle.

Julius was induced by all these reasons to undertake the defense of Athanasius and of Paul. The latter had arrived in Italy not long previously, and had complained bitterly of the calamities to which he had been exposed. When Julius perceived that what he had written to those who held the sacerdotal dignity in the East was of no avail, he made the matter known to Constans the emperor. Accordingly, Constans wrote to his brother Constantius requesting him to send some of the bishops of the East, that they might assign a reason for the edicts of deposition which they had passed. Three bishops were selected for this purpose, namely Narcissus, bishop of Irenopolis, in Cilicia; Theodore, bishop of Heraclea, in Thrace; and Mark, bishop of Arethusa, in Syria. On their arrival in Italy, they strove to justify their enactments and to persuade the emperor that the sentence passed by the Eastern synod was just. Being required to produce a statement of their belief, they withheld the formulary they had drawn up at Antioch and presented another which was equally at variance with the doctrines established at the council of Nicæa.

Constans perceived that they had unjustly entrapped the two bishops and had ejected them from communion not, as was stated in the sentence of deposition, on account of immorality of life, but simply on account of differences in doctrine, and he accordingly dismissed the deputation without giving any credit to their representations.

NOTE

1. νόμος ἱεπατικός. Compare Socrates, *Ecclesiastical History*, Book II, Chapter 17. The canon referred to is known as the 6th canon of Nicæa, and the 28th of Chalcedon.

CHAPTER XI

THE LONG FORMULARY AND THE ENACTMENTS ISSUED BY THE COUNCIL OF SARDICA. JULIUS, BISHOP OF ROME, AND HOSIUS, BISHOP OF SPAIN, DEPOSED BY THE BISHOPS OF THE EAST.

Three years afterwards the bishops of the East sent to those of the West a formulary of faith, which on account of its great length and copiousness, has been commonly termed μακρόσιχος ἔκθεσις.[1] In this formulary no allusion is made to the substance of God, and those are excommunicated who maintain that the Son arose out of what had no previous existence, or that he is of another hypostasis and not of God, or that there was a time or an age in which he existed not. Eudoxius, bishop of Germanicia, Martyrius, and Macedonius presented this document, but it was rejected by the Western clergy, who declared that they felt fully satisfied with the doctrines established at Nicæa and were not disposed to inquire further into contested matters.

After the emperor Constans had requested his brother to reinstate Athanasius in his bishopric and had found his application to be unavailing on account of the opposition of heretics who were hostile to this restoration, and when moreover Athanasius and Paul entreated Constans to assemble a council on account of the machinations which had been set on foot against orthodox doctrines, both the emperors were of opinion that the bishops of the East and of the West should be convened on a certain day at Sardica, a city of Illyria. The bishops of the East who had previously assembled at Philippopolis, a city of Thrace, wrote to the bishops of the West who had repaired to Sardica, that they would not join them unless they would eject Athanasius from their assembly and from communion with them, he having, they said, been legally deposed. They afterwards went to Sardica but declared they would not enter the church while those who had been deposed were admitted thither.

The bishops of the West replied that they never had ejected them and that they would not do so now, particularly as Julius, bishop of Rome, after having investigated the case, had not condemned them and as besides, they were present and ready to justify themselves a second time of the offences imputed to them. These declarations, however, were of no avail and served only to increase the mutual dissatisfaction of the two parties. And when at length the time they had appointed for the adjustment of their differences had expired, they assembled separately and issued edicts of condemnation against each other. The Eastern bishops confirmed the sentences they had enacted against Athanasius, Paul, Marcellus, and Asclepas, and deposed Julius, bishop of Rome, because he had been the first to admit those who had been condemned into communion. And Hosius, the confessor, was also deposed, partly for the same reason and partly because he was the friend of Paulinus[2] and Eustathius, bishops of Antioch. Maximus, bishop of Treves, was deposed, because he had been among the first who had received[3] Paul into communion, and had been the cause of his returning to Constantinople, and because he had excluded from communion the Eastern bishops who had repaired to Gaul. Besides the above, they likewise deposed Protogenes, bishop of Sardica, and Gaudentius,[4] the one because he favored Marcellus although he had previously condemned him, and the other because he had adopted a different line of conduct from that of Cyriacus, his predecessor, and had supported many individuals whom the former had deposed. After issuing these sentences, they made known to the bishops of every region that they were not to hold communion with those who were deposed, and that they were not to write to them nor to receive letters from them. They likewise commanded them to believe what was said concerning God in the formulary which they subjoined to their letter, and in which no mention was made of the term "consubstantial," but in which those were excommunicated who said there are three Gods, or that Christ is not God, or that the Father, the Son, and the Holy Ghost form but one and the same Person, or that the Son is unbegotten, or that there was a time or an age in which he existed not.

NOTES

1. *Note to the 2018 edition:* Also termed the "Lengthy Creed". See also Socrates, *Ecclesiastical History*, Book II, Chapter 19.
2. Valerius doubts who this Paulinus was but is inclined to believe him to have been the immediate successor of Philogonius in that see, and to have been soon afterwards expelled.
3. Valesius remarks that these words are taken from the decree of the Eastern bishops at Sardica.
4. He was bishop of Naïsus, in Dacia.

CHAPTER XII

DEPOSITION IN THEIR TURN OF THE EASTERN BISHOPS BY THE BISHOPS OF THE WEST, WHO COMPILE A FORMULARY OF FAITH.

The adherents of Hosius, in the meantime, assembled together and declared that Athanasius was innocent and that unjust machinations had been carried on against him by those who had been convened at Tyre. They likewise attested the innocence of Marcellus, who deposed that he did not hold the opinions which were attributed to him; of Asclepas, who proved by authentic documents that he had been re-established in his diocese by the decree of Eusebius Pamphilus, and of many other bishops; and lastly, of Lucius, whose accusers had fled. They wrote to the people of each of their churches, commanding them to receive and to recognize their bishops. They stated that Gregory had not been appointed by them bishop of Alexandria; nor Basil, bishop of Ancyra; nor Quintian, bishop of Gaza; and that they had not received these men into communion, and did not even account them Christians. They deposed Theodore, bishop of Thrace, Narcissus, bishop of Irenopolis, Acacius, bishop of Cæsarea in Palestine, Menophantes, bishop of Ephesus, Ursacius, bishop of Sigidon in Mæsia, Valens, bishop of Mursa in Pannonia, and George, bishop of Laodicea, although this latter had not attended the synod with the Eastern bishops. They ejected the above-named individuals from the priesthood and from communion because they separated the Son from the substance of the Father and had received those who had been deposed on account of their holding the Arian heresy and had, moreover, promoted them to the highest offices in the service of God.

They afterwards wrote to the bishops of every nation, commanding them to confirm these decrees, and to be of one mind on doctrinal subjects with themselves. They likewise compiled another formulary of faith,[1] which was more copious than that of Nicæa, although the same signification was carefully preserved, and the precise terms, in many cases, retained. Hosius and Protogenes, who held the first rank among the Western bishops assembled at Sardica, fearing lest they should be suspected of making any innovations upon the doctrines of the Nicæan council, wrote[2] to Julius and testified that they were firmly attached to these doctrines, but that they had endeavored to convey their precise signification in more perspicuous language in order that the Arians might not take advantage of the brevity of the original document, and affix some absurd meaning to the words in which it was couched.

When what I have related had been transacted by each party, the synod was dissolved, and the members returned to their respective homes. This synod was held during the consulate of Rufinus and Eusebius, and about eleven years after the death of Constantine. There were about three hundred[3] bishops of cities in the West, and upwards of seventy Eastern bishops, among whom was Ischyrion, who had been appointed bishop of Mareota by the enemies of Athanasius.

NOTES

1. This formulary is extant, appended to the synodal epistle of the council of Chalcedon, in Theodoret, *Ecclesiastical History,* Book II. Baronius, however, maintains that the formulary itself is spurious.
2. This epistle is nowhere extant.
3. This mistake Sozomen has borrowed from Socrates, who in his turn derived it from Athanasius. See Socrates, *Ecclesiastical History,* Book II, Chapter 20, and Valesius' notes *in loco. Note to the 2018 edition:* Athanasius says in his *Apology against the Arians,* that 344 bishops subscribed to the acts of the council. However, in his *History of the Arians,* Book III, Chapter 15, he gives the number who attended the council as 170, more or less.

CHAPTER XIII

AFTER THE COUNCIL, A SEPARATION TAKES PLACE BETWEEN THE EASTERN AND THE WESTERN CHURCHES. THE CHURCH OF THE WEST ADHERES TO THE FAITH OF THE NICÆAN COUNCIL, WHILE THAT OF THE EAST IS DISTURBED BY DOCTRINAL DISPUTES AND DISCUSSIONS.

After this council, the Eastern and the Western churches ceased to maintain the intercourse which usually exists among people of the same faith and refrained from holding communion with each other.[1] The Christians of the West held no further communion with the regions beyond Thrace, nor those of the East with the nations beyond Illyria. This divided state of the churches gave rise, as might be supposed, to dissension and calumny. Although they had previously differed on doctrinal subjects, yet the evil had attained no great height, for they had still held communion together. The church throughout the West adhered to the doctrines of the Fathers, and kept aloof from all contentions and disputations. Although Auxentius, bishop of Milan, and Valens and Ursacius, bishops of Pannonia, had endeavored to introduce Arian doctrines in the West, their efforts had been frustrated by the zeal of the bishop of Rome and of other priests who crushed the heresy in its commencement.

As to the Eastern church, although it had been racked by dissension since the time of the council of Antioch, and although it greatly departed from the Nicæan form of belief, yet I still believe the majority of those who composed it confessed the Son of the substance of the Father. There were some, however, who obstinately rejected the term "consubstantial," because they had refused to admit it at the beginning, and ashamed to defer to the opinion of others or to avow themselves in fault. Others were finally convinced, after long disputation, of the truth of the doctrines concerning God and ever afterwards continued firmly attached to them. Others again, being aware that contentions ought not to arise, adopted the sentiments of their friends or of the more powerful party or were swayed by the various causes which often induce men to embrace what they ought to reject and to dissimulate what they ought boldly to avow. Many others, accounting it absurd to consume their time in altercations about words, quietly adopted the sentiments inculcated by the council of Nicæa. Paul, bishop of Constantinople, Athanasius, bishop of Alexandria, a multitude of monks, Antony the Great, his disciples, and a great number of Egyptians and of other nations within the Roman territories, firmly and openly maintained the doctrines of the Nicæan council throughout the other regions of the East. As I have been led to allude to the monks, I shall briefly mention those who flourished during the reign of Constantius.

NOTE

1. Compare Socrates, *Ecclesiastical History,* Book II, Chapter 22.

CHAPTER XIV

OF THE HOLY MEN WHO FLOURISHED ABOUT THIS TIME IN EGYPT, NAMELY ANTONY, THE TWO MACARIUSES, HERACLIUS, CRONIUS, PAPHNUTIUS, PUTUBASTES, ARSISIUS, SERAPION, PITURION, PACHOMIUS, APOLLONIUS, ANUPHUS, HILARION, AND MANY OTHERS.

I shall commence my recital with Egypt and the two men named Macarius, who were the celebrated chiefs of Scetis and of the neighboring mountain. The one was a native of Egypt, the other was called Politicus, which means a citizen, and was of Alexandrian origin. They were both so wonderfully endowed with divine knowledge and philosophy that the demons regarded them with terror, and they wrought many extraordinary works and miraculous cures. The Egyptian, it is said, restored a dead man to life in order to convince a heretic of the truth of the resurrection from the dead. He lived about ninety years, sixty of which he passed in the deserts. When in his youth he commenced the study of philosophy, he progressed so rapidly that the monks surnamed him "old child" and at the age of forty he was ordained priest.

The other Macarius became a priest at a later period of his life. He was proficient in all the exercises of asceticism, some of which he devised himself. His abstinence was so great that his skin dried up, and the hair of his beard ceased to grow. Pambonius, Heraclius, Cronius, Paphnutius, Putubastes, Arsisius, Serapion the Great, Piturion, who dwelt near Thebes, and Pachomius, the founder of the monks called the Tabennesians,[1] flourished at the same place and period. The attire and customs of this sect differed in some respects from those of other monks. Its members were, however, devoted to virtue. They contemned the things of the earth, excited the soul to heavenly contemplation, and prepared it to quit the body with joy. They were clothed in skins in remembrance of Elias, it appears to me, because they thought that the virtue of the prophet would be thus retained in their memory, and that they would be enabled like him to resist manfully the seductions of pleasure, to be influenced by similar zeal, and be incited to the practice of sobriety by the hope of an equal reward. It is said that the peculiar vestments of these Egyptian monks had reference to some secret connected with their philosophy, and did not differ from those of others without some adequate cause. They wore their tunics without sleeves in order to teach that the hands ought not to be ready to do evil. They wore a covering on their heads called a cowl to show that they ought to live with the same innocence and purity as infants who are nourished with milk and wear a covering of the same form. Their girdle, and a species of scarf,[2] which they wear across the back, shoulders, and arms, admonish them that they ought to be always ready in the service of God. I am aware that other reasons have been assigned for their peculiarity of attire, but what I have said appears to me to be sufficient.

It is said that Pachomius at first dwelt alone in a cave, but that a holy angel appeared to him, and commanded him to assemble some young monks, to instruct them in the practice of philosophy, and to inculcate the laws which were about to be delivered to him. A tablet was then given to him which is still carefully preserved. Upon this tablet were inscribed injunctions by which he was bound to permit every one to eat, to drink, to work, and to fast according to his capabilities of so doing. Those who ate heartily were to be subjected to arduous labor, and the ascetic were to have more easy tasks assigned them. He was commanded to have many cells erected, in each of which three monks were to dwell who were to take their meals at a common refectory in silence and with a veil thrown over the head and face, so that they might not be able to see each other or anything but what was on or under the table. They were not to admit strangers to eat with them, with the exception of travellers to whom they were to show hospitality. Those who desired to live with them were first to undergo a probation of three years, during which time the most laborious and painful tasks were to be imposed upon them. They were to clothe themselves in skins and to wear woollen tiaras adorned with purple nails and linen tunics and girdles. They were to sleep in their tunics and garments of skin, reclining on long chairs closed on each side, which were to serve as couches. On the first and last days of the week they were to approach the altar and partake of the communion of the holy mysteries, and were then to unloose their girdles, and throw off their robes of skin. They were to pray twelve times[3] every day, and as often during the evening, and were to offer up the same number of prayers during the night. At the ninth hour they were to pray thrice, and when about to partake of food they were to sing a psalm before each prayer. The whole congregation was to be divided into twenty-four classes, each of which was to be distinguished by one of the letters of the Greek alphabet. Thus, the name of Iota was given to the most simple, and that of Zeta or of Xi to the most erudite, and the names of the other letters were, according to the same principle, bestowed on the other classes.

These were the laws by which Pachomius ruled his own disciples. He was a man of great philanthropy and piety. He could foresee future events, and was frequently admitted to intercourse with the holy angels. He resided at Tabennis in Thebaïs, and hence the name Tabennesians, used to designate those who lived according to the same rules. They subsequently attained great renown, and in process of time became so numerous that they, numbered upwards of seven thousand men. About thirteen of them dwelt with Pachomius in the island Tabennis. The others were dispersed throughout Egypt and Thebaïs.[4] They all observed one and the same rule of life, and possessed everything in common. They regarded the congregation established in the island Tabennis as their mother, and the rulers of it as their fathers and their princes.

About the same period, Apollonius became celebrated by his profession of monastic philosophy. It is said that from the age of fifteen he devoted himself to philosophy in the solitudes of the deserts, and that when he attained the age of forty, he went, according to a Divine command he then received, to dwell in regions inhabited by men. He likewise dwelt in Thebaïs. He was greatly beloved of God, and was endowed with the power of performing miraculous cures and notable works. He was exact in the observance of duty and instructed others in philosophy with great goodness and kindness. He invariably obtained from God whatever he asked in prayer, but he was so wise that he always proffered prudent requests and such as the Divine Being is ever ready to grant.

I believe that Anuphus the divine lived about this period. I have been informed that from the time of the persecution, when he first avowed his attachment to Christianity, he never uttered a falsehood, nor desired the things of the earth. All his prayers and supplications to God were duly answered, and he was instructed by a holy angel in every virtue. Let, however, what we have said of the Egyptian monks suffice.

The same species of philosophy was about this time cultivated in Palestine, whither it had been transported from Egypt, and Hilarion the divine acquired great celebrity. He was a native of Tanata, a village situated near the town of Gaza, towards the south, and near a torrent which falls into the sea and is known by the same name as the village. When he was studying grammar at Alexandria, he went out into the desert to see Antony, the divine and celebrated monk, and discoursed with him concerning his mode of life and philosophy. A very short time afterwards, he fixed his residence with him, but did not enjoy the quietude he had anticipated on account of the multitudes who flocked around Antony. He, therefore, soon returned to his own country, and finding his parents dead, he distributed his patrimony among his brethren and the poor without reserving anything for himself. He then went to dwell in a desert situated near the sea, and about twenty stadia from his native village. His cell was constructed of planks, broken tiles, and straw, and was of such a height and length that no one could stand in it without bending the head, or lie down in it without drawing back the legs, for in everything he strove to accustom himself to hardship and to the subjugation of sensuality. The practice of temperance was never carried to a greater height than by him. He endured cold and heat, hunger and thirst, and other sufferings, and resisted the desires of the mind and of the body. He was irreproachable in conduct, grave in discourse, and diligent in the study of sacred writ. He was so beloved by God, that even now many diseases are healed and demons expelled at his tomb. It is remarkable that he was first interred[5] in the island of Cyprus, but that his remains are now deposited in Palestine, for it so happened that he died during his residence in Cyprus, and was buried by the inhabitants with great honor and respect. But Hesychius, one of the most renowned of his disciples, stole the body, conveyed it to Palestine, and interred it in his own monastery. From that period an annual festival was celebrated in honor of his memory, for it is the custom in Palestine to bestow this honor on those who have attained renown by their sanctity, such as Aurelius, Antedon, Alexion, a native of Bethagatonia, and Alaphion, a native of Asalia, who, during the reign of Constantius, lived so religiously and so virtuously in the practice of philosophy, that many Pagans were led by their example to embrace Christianity.

Book III, Chapter XIV

About the same period, Julian pursued a course of such rigid austerity at Edessa, that he might be said to live as if he were incorporeal, for he seemed to be freed from flesh and to possess nothing but skin and bones. Ephraim, the Syrian has written an account of his life.[6] God himself confirmed the high opinion which men had formed of him, for he bestowed on him the power of expelling demons and of healing all kinds of diseases, without having recourse to the remedies of the physician, but simply by prayer.

Besides the above, many other ecclesiastical philosophers flourished in the territories of Edessa and of Amida, and in the regions around the mountain Gangalion. Among these were Daniel and Simeon.[7] But I shall now say nothing further of the Syrian monks. I shall at some future time, if God will, describe them more fully.[8] It is said that Eustathius,[9] bishop of Sebaste in Armenia, founded a society of monks in Armenia, Paphlagonia, and Pontus, and imposed upon them a rule of life, containing directions as to what meats they were to partake of or to avoid, what garments they were to wear, and what customs they were to adopt. Some assert that he was the author of the ascetic writings commonly attributed to Basil of Cappadocia. It is said that his great austerity led him into certain extravagancies which were contrary to the laws of the church. Many persons, however, justify him from this accusation, and throw the blame upon some of his disciples who condemned marriage, refused to pray to God in the houses of married persons, despised married priests, fasted on Lord's days, held their assemblies in private houses, contemned those who partook of animal food, clothed themselves in peculiar garments, different from those of others, and introduced many other strange customs and innovations. Many women were deluded by them and left their husbands, but not being able to practice continence, they fell into adultery. Other women, under the pretext of religion, cut off their hair, and arrayed themselves in men's apparel.

The bishops of the neighborhood of Gangris, the metropolis of Paphlagonia, assembled themselves together and declared that all those who imbibed these opinions should be cut off from the Catholic Church unless they would renounce them. It is said that from that time, Eustathius refrained from his former peculiarity of attire and habited himself like other priests, thus proving that he had not been influenced by motives of selfish arrogance but by the desire of attaining to divine asceticism. He was as renowned for the sanctity of his discourse as for the purity of his life. To confess the truth, he was not eloquent, nor had he ever studied the art of eloquence, yet he possessed naturally such strong powers of persuasion that he induced several men and women, who were living in fornication and adultery to enter upon a chaste course of life. It is related that a certain man and woman who, according to the custom of the church, had devoted themselves to a life of virginity, were accused of holding illicit intercourse with each other. Finding that his remonstrances produced no effect upon them, he sighed deeply and said that a woman who had been legally married had on one occasion heard him discourse on the advantage of continence, and was thereby so deeply affected that she voluntarily abstained from legitimate intercourse with her own husband, and that the weakness of his powers of conviction was, on the other hand, attested by the fact, that the parties above mentioned persisted in their illegal course. Such were the men who originated the practice of monastic discipline in the regions above mentioned.

Although the Thracians, the Illyrians, and the other European nations possessed no congregations of monks, yet there were many men devoted to Christian philosophy among them. Of these, Martin, the descendant of a noble family of Sabaria in Pannonia, was the most illustrious. He was originally a noted warrior, and the commander of armies, but accounting the service of God to be a more honorable profession, he embraced a life of philosophy, and retired, in the first place, to Illyria. Here he zealously defended the orthodox doctrines against the attacks of the Arian bishops, and was in consequence persecuted and driven from the country. He then went to Milan, and dwelt alone. He was soon, however, obliged to quit his place of retreat on account of the machinations of Auxentius, bishop of that region, who was opposed to the Nicene faith, and he went to an island called Gallinaria where he remained for some time subsisting solely upon roots. Gallinaria is a small and desert island lying in the Tyrrhenian Sea. Martin was afterwards appointed bishop of Tours.[10] He was so richly endowed with miraculous gifts that he restored a dead man to life and performed other signs as wonderful as those wrought by the apostles.

We have heard that Hilarion, a man noted for the sanctity of his life and conversation, lived about the same time and in the same country. Like Martin, he was obliged to flee from his place of abode on account of his zeal in defense of the faith.

I have now related what I have been able to ascertain concerning the individuals who were celebrated about this period for their piety and philosophy. There were many others who were noted in the church about the same period on account of their great eloquence, and among these the most distinguished were Eusebius, bishop of Emesa; Titus, bishop of Bostra; Serapion, bishop of Thmius; Basil, bishop of Ancyra; Eudoxius, bishop of Germanicia; Acacius, bishop of Cæsarea; and Cyril, bishop of Jerusalem. The numerous and excellent writings which they have bequeathed to posterity demonstrate the truth of what I have asserted.

NOTES

1. So called from the nome of the Thebaïs which was called Tabennesus, according to the analogy of Proconnesus and other terms.

2. ἀναβολεύς. Compare Cassian, *Institutes,* Book I, Chapter 6.
3. δωδεκάκις. Valesius prefers this emendation of Nicephorus. Compare Cassian, *Institutes* Book II, Chapter 4, etc.
4. Cassian speaks of all the monks in the Thebaïs as constituting only one religious house. It is probable that he does so because they were all subject to one rule of life and to one abbot or archimandrite.
5. We have retained the obvious emendation of ἐτάφη for ἐτράφη.
6. Concerning Julian and Ephraim, see below, Book VI, Chapter 34.
7. Valesius considers that this Simeon, or Symeon, is the same person mentioned by Theodoret in his Philotheus.
8. See below, Chapter 16.
9. See Socrates, *Ecclesiastical History,* Book II, Chapter 42. Eustathius is said by Epiphanius and Basil to have died in the Arian heresy.
10. He became bishop of Tours, AD 375, and was afterwards canonized on account of the miracles which were said to have been performed by him.

CHAPTER XV

DIDYMUS THE BLIND, AND ÆTIUS THE HERETIC.

Didymus, an ecclesiastical historian and a professor of sacred literature at Alexandria, flourished about the same period. He was acquainted with every branch of science, and was conversant with poetry and rhetoric, with astronomy and geometry, with arithmetic, and with the various theories of philosophy. He had acquired all this knowledge by the efforts of his own mind, aided by the sense of hearing, for he lost his sight in early childhood. From his youth he manifested an ardent desire to acquire learning, and for this purpose he frequented the schools, where he made such rapid progress that, by means of the sense of hearing alone, he speedily comprehended the most difficult mathematical theorems. It is said that he learnt the letters of the alphabet by means of wooden tablets on which they were sculptured, and which he felt with his fingers, and that he made himself acquainted with syllables and words by the force of attention and memory, and by listening attentively to the sounds. His was a very extraordinary case and many persons resorted to Alexandria for the express purpose of hearing or, at least, of seeing him.

His firmness in defending the doctrines of the Nicæan council was extremely displeasing to the Arians. He carried conviction to the minds of his audience by persuasion rather than by power of reasoning, and submitted his arguments to the investigation of their judgment. He was esteemed and beloved by the members of the Catholic church, by the monks of Egypt, and by Antony the Great. It is related that when Antony left the desert and repaired to Alexandria to give his testimony in favor of the doctrines of Athanasius, he said to Didymus, "It is not a great misfortune, O Didymus, to be deprived of the organs of sight which are possessed by rats, mice, and the lowest animals, but it is a great blessing to possess eyes like angels, whereby you can contemplate the Divine Being and attain to true knowledge."

In Italy and its territories, Eusebius and Hilarion, whom I have already mentioned, acquired great fame by their eloquence and their writings[1] against the heterodox Lucifer, the founder of a heresy which bears his name,[2] also flourished at this period. Ætius[3] was likewise held in high estimation among the heterodox. He was an expert logician, and proficient in the art of disputation. He reasoned so boldly concerning the nature of God, that many persons gave him the name of "Atheist." It is said that he was originally a physician[4] of Antioch in Syria, and that, as he frequently attended meetings of the church for the examination of the Sacred Scriptures, he became acquainted with Gallus, who was then Cæsar, and who honored religion and cherished its professors. It seems likely that, as Ætius obtained the esteem of Cæsar by means of these disputations, he devoted himself the more assiduously to these pursuits, in order to progress in the favor of the emperor. It is said that he was versed in the philosophy of Aristotle, and frequented the schools in which it was taught at Alexandria.

Besides the individuals above specified, there were many others in the churches who were capable of instructing the people, and of reasoning concerning the doctrines of the Holy Scriptures. It would be too great a task to attempt to name them all. Let it not be accounted strange, if I have bestowed commendation upon the leaders of the abovementioned heresies. I admire their eloquence, and their powers of reasoning. I leave their doctrines to be judged by those who are in authority. Judgment does not devolve upon me in my character of historian—I have only to give an account of events as they happened. I have now related what I have heard, concerning those individuals among the Romans and the Greeks who were celebrated for their learning and their eloquence.

NOTES

1. He alludes to the treatises of Hilary against the Arians and Auxentius.
2. That, namely, of the Luciferians. Compare Socrates, *Ecclesiastical History,* Book III, Chapter 9.
3. Compare Socrates, *Ecclesiastical History,* Book II, Chapter 35.
4. The same is asserted by Gregory of Nyssa, in his first book *Contra Eunomium.*

CHAPTER XVI

CONCERNING THE PIETY OF SAINT EPHRAIM.

Ephraim the Syrian[1] was entitled to the highest honors and was the greatest ornament of the church. He was a native of Nisibis, or of the neighboring territory. He devoted his life to monastic philosophy, and although he received no instruction he became, contrary to all expectation, so proficient in the learning and language of the Syrians that he comprehended with ease the most abstruse theorems of philosophy. His style of writing was so replete with splendid oratory and sublimity of thought that he surpassed all the writers of Greece. If the works of these writers were to be translated into Syriac or any other language and divested, as it were, of the beauties of the Greek language, they would retain little of their original elegance and value. The productions of Ephraim have not this disadvantage. They were translated into Greek during his life, and translations are even now being made, and yet they preserve much of their original force and power, so that his works are not less admired when read in Greek than when read in Syriac.

Basil, who was subsequently bishop of the metropolis of Cappadocia, was a great admirer of Ephraim, and was astonished at his erudition. The opinion of Basil, who was the most learned and eloquent man of his age, is a stronger testimony, I think, to the merit of Ephraim, than anything that could be indited in his praise. It is said that he wrote three hundred thousand verses,[2] and that he had many disciples who were zealously attached to his doctrines. The most celebrated of his disciples were Abbas, Zenobius, Abraham, Maras, and Simeon, whom the most learned men of Syria regard as the glory of their country. Paulanas and Aranad are likewise generally included in their number, for they were renowned as men of great eloquence, although reported to have deviated from sound doctrine.

I am not ignorant that there were some very learned men who flourished in Osroene as, for instance, Bardasanes, who originated a heresy designated by his name,[3] and Harmonius his son. It is related that this latter was deeply versed in Grecian erudition, and was the first to compose verses in his vernacular language. Those verses he delivered to the choirs, and even now the Syrians frequently sing, not the precise verses written by Harmonius, but others of the same metre. For as Harmonius was not altogether free from the errors of his father, and entertained various opinions concerning the soul, the generation and destruction of the body, and the doctrine of transmigration, which are taught by the Greek philosophers, he introduced some of these sentiments in the lyrical songs which he composed.

When Ephraim perceived that the Syrians were charmed with the elegant diction and melodious versification of Harmonius, he became apprehensive lest they should imbibe the same opinions, and therefore, although he was ignorant of Grecian learning, he applied himself to the study of the metres of Harmonius, and composed similar poems in accordance with the doctrines of the church, and sacred hymns in praise of holy men. From that period the Syrians sang the odes of Ephraim, according to the method indicated by Harmonius. The execution of this work is alone sufficient to attest the natural endowments of Ephraim. He was as celebrated for the good actions he performed as for the rigid course of discipline he pursued. He was particularly fond of tranquility. He was so serious, and so careful to avoid giving occasion to calumny, that he refrained from looking upon woman. It is related that a female of licentious character, who was either desirous of tempting him or who had been bribed for the purpose, contrived on one occasion to meet him face-to-face and fixed her eyes intently on him. He rebuked her, and commanded her to look down upon the ground.

"Wherefore should I obey your injunction," replied the woman, "for I was born not of the earth, but of you? It would be more just if you were to look down upon the earth whence you sprang, while I look upon you, as I was born of you."

Ephraim, astonished at the language of the woman, recorded the whole transaction in a book which most Syrians regard as one of the best of his productions.

It is also said of him, that, although he was naturally prone to passion, he never exhibited angry feeling towards anyone from the period of his embracing a monastic life. It once happened that after he had, according to custom, been fasting several days, his attendant, in presenting some food to him, let fall the dish on which it was placed. Ephraim, perceiving that he was overwhelmed with shame and terror, said to him, "Take courage. We will go to the food as the food does not come to us." And he immediately seated himself beside the fragments of the dish and ate his supper.

What I am about to relate will suffice to show that he was totally exempt from the love of vainglory. He was appointed bishop of some town and attempts were made to convey him away for the purpose of ordaining him. As soon as he became aware of what was intended, he ran to the marketplace, exhibited himself in an indecorous manner, and ate in public. Those who had come to carry him away to be their bishop, on seeing him in this state, believed that he was out of his mind and departed, and he, meeting with an opportunity for effecting his escape, remained in concealment until another had been ordained in his place.

What I have now said concerning Ephraim must suffice, although his own countrymen relate many other anecdotes of him. Yet his conduct on one occasion shortly before his death, appears to me so worthy of remembrance that I shall record it here. The city of Edessa being severely visited by famine, he quitted the solitary cell in which he dwelt, and rebuked the rich for permitting the poor to die around them, instead of imparting to them of their superfluities. And he represented to them that the wealth which they were treasuring up so carefully would turn to their own condemnation and to the ruin of the soul which is of more value than all the riches of the earth. The rich men, convinced by his arguments, replied, "We are not intent upon hoarding our wealth, but we know of no one to whom we can confide the distribution of our goods, for all are prone to seek after lucre and to betray the trust placed in them."

"What think you of me?" asked Ephraim. On their admitting that they considered him an excellent and just man and worthy of confidence, he offered to undertake the distribution of their alms. As soon as he received their money he had about three hundred beds fitted up in the public galleries, and here he tended those who were ill and suffering from the effects of the famine, whether they were foreigners or natives of the surrounding country. On the cessation of the famine he returned to the cell in which he had previously dwelt, and after the lapse of a few days, he expired. He attained no higher clerical degree than that of deacon, although his attainments in virtue rendered him equal in reputation to those who rose to the highest sacerdotal dignity, while his holy life and erudition made him an object of universal admiration. I have now given some account of the virtue of Ephraim.

It would require a more experienced hand than mine to furnish a full description of his character and that of the other illustrious men who, about the same period, had devoted themselves to a life of philosophy, and it is to be regretted that Ephraim did not enter upon this under-taking. The attempt is beyond my powers, for I possess but little knowledge of these great men or of their exploits. Some of them concealed themselves in the deserts. Others, who lived in populous places, strove to preserve a mean appearance and to seem as if they differed in no respect from the multitude that their virtue might be unknown, and that they might so avoid the praises of others. For as they were intent upon the enjoyment of future blessedness, they desired no other testimony to their virtue than that of God, and sought not outward glory.

NOTES

1. See below, Book VI, Chapter 34.
2. μυριάδας ἔπον. The words ἔπη and στίχοι were constantly used for verses. Thus Origen says that there are nearly 10,000 ἔπη in the Book of Job.
3. Compare Eusebius, *Ecclesiastical History*, Book IV, Chapter 30.

CHAPTER XVII

TRANSACTIONS OF THAT PERIOD, AND PROGRESS OF CHRISTIAN DOCTRINE THROUGH THE JOINT EFFORTS OF EMPERORS AND ARCHBISHOPS.

Those who presided over the churches at this period were noted for purity of life and, as might be expected, the people whom they governed were earnestly attached to the service of Christ. Religion daily progressed and the zeal, virtue, and wonderful works of the priests and of the ecclesiastical philosophers attracted the attention of the Greeks and led them to renounce their superstitions.

The emperors who then occupied the throne were as zealous as was their father in protecting the churches, and they granted honors and privileges to the clergy, their children, and their slaves. They confirmed the laws enacted by their father and enforced new ones, prohibiting the offering of sacrifice and the observance of other Pagan ceremonies. They commanded that all temples, whether in cities or in the country, should be closed. Some of these temples were presented to the churches, when they required either the ground they stood on or the materials for building. The greatest possible care was bestowed upon the houses of prayer. Those which had been defaced by time were repaired, and others were erected in a style of extraordinary magnificence. The church of Edessa is one of the most beautiful and remarkable of these structures.

The Jews were strictly forbidden to purchase a slave belonging to any other heresy than their own. If they transgressed this law, the slave was confiscated[1] to the public, but if they administered to him the Jewish rite of circumcision, the penalties were death and total confiscation of property. For, as the emperors were desirous of promoting by every means the spread of Christianity, they deemed it necessary to prevent the Jews from proselyting those whose ancestors were of another religion, and who were, therefore, carefully reserved for the service of the church. For it was by conversion from the Pagan multitudes that the professors of the Christian religion increased in number.

NOTE

1. δεμόσιον ἐῖναι. The early interpreters understood these words as referring to the Jewish offender, and not to the slave. But the law itself is extant in Book XVI of the *Theodosian Code*. The terms are as follows, "Si aliquis Judæorum, mancipium sectæ alterius seu nationis crediderit comparandum, mancipium fisco protinus vindicetur."

CHAPTER XVIII

CONCERNING THE DOCTRINES HELD BY THE SONS OF CONSTANTINE. DISTINCTION BETWEEN THE TERMS "HOMOUSIAN" AND "HOMŒOUSIAN." CONSTANTIUS IS LED TO ABANDON THE TRUE FAITH.

The emperors had, from the beginning, adopted the same religious ceremonies as had been held by their father, for they both followed the Nicene form of belief. Constans maintained these opinions till his death. Constantius, however, renounced his former sentiments when he discovered that the term "consubstantial" was a subject of debate and attack. Yet he always confessed that the Son is of like substance with the Father. Eusebius, and other holy and learned bishops of the East, made a distinction between the term "consubstantial" (*homousian*) and the expression "of like substance," which latter they designated by the term "*homœousian*"[1] They say that the term "consubstantial" (homousian) properly belongs to corporeal beings, such as men and other animals, trees and plants which are of the same substance as things like unto themselves whereby they are generated. And that the term "homœousian" appertains exclusively to incorporeal beings, such as God and the angels, of each one of whom a conception is formed according to his own peculiar substance. The emperor Constantius was deceived by this distinction, and although I am certain that he retained the same doctrines as those held by his father and brother, yet he adopted a change of phraseology and, instead of using the term "homousian," made use of the term "homœousian." The teachers to whom we have alluded maintained that it was necessary to be thus precise in the use of terms, and that otherwise we should be in danger of conceiving that to be a body which is incorporeal. Many, however, regard this distinction as an absurdity. "For," say they, "the things which are conceived by the mind can be designated only by names derived from things which are seen, and there is no danger in the use of words, provided only that the meaning be clearly understood."

NOTE

1. Compare Socrates, *Ecclesiastical History,* Book II, Chapter 45, and notes.

CHAPTER XIX

FURTHER PARTICULARS CONCERNING THE TERM "CONSUBSTANTIAL." COUNCIL OF ARMINUM.

It is not surprising that the emperor Constantius was induced to adopt the use of the term "homœousian," for it was admitted by many priests who conformed to the doctrines established by the Nicæan council.[1] Many use the two words indifferently, to convey the same meaning. Hence it appears to me that the Arians departed greatly from truth when they affirmed that, after the council of Nicæa, many of the priests, among whom were Eusebius and Theognis, refused to admit that the Son is consubstantial with the Father, and that Constantine was in consequence so indignant, that he condemned them to banishment. They say that it was afterwards revealed to his sister by a vision, during sleep or otherwise, that these bishops held orthodox doctrines and had been unjustly condemned, and that the emperor thereupon recalled them and demanded of them, wherefore they had departed from the Nicene doctrines to which they had formerly subscribed, and that they urged in reply that they had not assented to those doctrines from conviction, but from the fear that if the disputes then existing were prolonged, the emperor, who was then just beginning to embrace Christianity and who was yet unbaptized, might be impelled to return to Paganism and to persecute the church. They assert that Constantine was pleased with this reply and determined upon convening another council, but that being prevented by death from carrying his scheme into execution, the task devolved upon his eldest son, Constantius, to whom he represented that it would avail him nothing to be possessed of imperial power unless he could establish uniformity of worship throughout his empire. And Constantius, they say, at the instigation of his father, convened a council at Ariminum.[2]

This story is easily seen to be a gross fabrication, for the council was convened during the consulate of Hypatius and Eusebius, and twenty-two years after Constantius had, on the death of his father, succeeded to the empire. Now, during this interval of twenty-two years, many councils were held in which debates were carried on concerning the terms "homousian" and "homœousian." No one, it appears, ventured to deny that the Son is of like substance with the Father[3] until Ætius, by starting a contrary opinion, so offended the emperor that in order to arrest the course of the heresy, he commanded the priests to assemble themselves together at Ariminum and at Seleucia. Thus the true cause of this council being convened was not the command of Constantine, but the question agitated by Ætius. And this will become still more apparent by what we shall hereafter relate.

NOTES

1. Compare Socrates, *Ecclesiastical History,* Book II, Chapter 2.
2. Compare Socrates, *Ecclesiastical History,* Book IV, Chapter 16.
3. The text, which was corrupt here, has been much simplified by Valesius, and we have retained his emendations.

CHAPTER XX

RETURN AND RE-INSTALLATION OF ATHANASIUS. ARCHBISHOPS OF ANTIOCH. QUESTION PUT BY CONSTANTIUS TO ATHANASIUS. HYMNS OF PRAISE TO GOD.

When Constans was apprised of what had been enacted at Sardica, he wrote[1] to his brother to request him to restore Paul and Athanasius to their own churches. As Constantius seemed to hesitate, he wrote again and threatened him with war unless he would consent to receive the bishops. Constantius, after conferring on the subject with the bishops of the East, judged that it would be foolish to excite on this account the horrors of civil war. He, therefore, recalled Athanasius from Italy and sent public carriages to convey him on his return homewards, and wrote several letters requesting his speedy return.

Athanasius, who was then residing at Aquilea, on receiving the letters of Constantius, repaired to Rome to take leave of Julius. This latter parted with him with great demonstrations of friendship and gave him a letter addressed to the clergy and people of Alexandria, in which he spoke of him as a wonderful man, deserving of renown by the numerous trials he had undergone, and congratulated the church of Alexandria on the return of so good a priest, and exhorted them to follow his doctrines.

He then proceeded to Antioch in Syria where the emperor was then residing. Leontius presided over the churches of that region for, on the exile of Eustathius, those who held heretical sentiments had seized the government of the church of Antioch. The first bishop they appointed was Euphronius. To him succeeded Flacillus, and afterwards, Stephen. This latter was deposed as being unworthy of the dignity,[2] and Leontius[3] obtained the bishopric. Athanasius avoided him as a heretic and met for worship in a private house with those who were called Eustathians.

Constantius received him with great kindness and benignity, and Athanasius requested to be restored to his church. The emperor, at the instigation of the heterodox, replied as follows: "I am ready to perform all that I promised when I recalled you, but it is just that you should in return grant me a favor, and that is that you yield one of the numerous churches which are under your sway to those who are averse to holding communion with you."

Athanasius replied, "What you have promised, O emperor, is so just and so necessary that I can offer no opposition to it. But as in the city of Antioch there are many of us who eschew communion with the heterodox, I also entreat that one church may be conceded to us, whither we may resort in safety."

As the request of Athanasius appeared reasonable to the emperor, the heterodox deemed it more politic to take no further steps, for they reflected that their peculiar opinions could never gain any ground in Alexandria on account of Athanasius, who was able both to retain those who held the same sentiments as himself and to attract and lead those of contrary opinions and that, moreover, if they gave up one of the churches of Antioch, the Eustathians, who were very numerous, would assemble together and probably introduce innovations without incurring the danger of detaching any of their adherents. Besides, the heterodox perceived that although the government of the churches was in their hands, all the clergy and people did not conform to their doctrines. When they sang hymns to God they were, according to custom, divided into choirs, and at the end of the hymns, each one declared what were his own peculiar sentiments. Some offered praise to "the Father and the Son," regarding them as co-equal in glory. Others glorified "the Father *by*[4] the Son," to denote that they considered the Son to be inferior to the Father. Leontius, the bishop of the opposite faction, who then presided over the church of Antioch, did not dare to prohibit the singing of hymns to God which were in accordance with the Nicene doctrines, for he feared to excite an insurrection of the people. It is related, however, that he once raised his hand to his head, the hairs of which were quite white, and said, "When this snow is dissolved, there will be plenty of mud." By this he intended to signify that after his death, the different modes of singing hymns would give rise to great seditions, and that his successors would not show the same consideration to the people which he had manifested.

NOTES

1. Compare Socrates, *Ecclesiastical History,* Book II, Chapter 23.
2. Compare Athanasius, *History of the Arians*; Theodoret, *Ecclesiastical History,* Book II, Chapters 8, 9; and Socrates, *Ecclesiastical History,* Book II, Chapter 22.
3. Compare Socrates, *Ecclesiastical History,* Book II, Chapter 26.
4. Compare Socrates, *Ecclesiastical History,* Book II, Chapter 21.

CHAPTER XXI

LETTER OF CONSTANTIUS TO THE EGYPTIANS IN BEHALF OF ATHANASIUS. SYNOD OF JERUSALEM.

The emperor, on sending back[1] Athanasius to Egypt, wrote in his favor to the bishops and presbyters of that country and to the people of the church of Alexandria, commended the integrity and virtue of his conduct, and exhorted them to be of one mind and to unite in prayer and service to God under his guidance. He added that if any evil-disposed persons should excite disturbances, they should receive the punishment awarded by the laws for such offences. He also commanded that the former decrees he had enacted against Athanasius, and those who were in communion with him, should be effaced from the public registers and that his clergy should be admitted to the same privileges they had previously enjoyed. And edicts to this effect were despatched to the governors of Egypt and Libya.

Immediately on his arrival in Egypt, Athanasius displaced those priests who were attached to Arianism and placed the government of the church in the hands of those who held his sentiments, and whom he specially exhorted to cleave to the Nicene doctrines. It was said at that time that, when he was travelling through other countries, he effected the same change in churches which were not under his administration when he found the Arians in power. He was certainly accused of having performed the ceremony of ordination in cities where he had no right to do so. But after he was recalled from exile in spite of the machinations of his enemies and was honored with the friendship of the emperor Constantius, he was regarded with greater consideration than before. Many bishops who had previously been at enmity with him, received him into communion, particularly those of Palestine. When he visited these latter, they received him kindly: they held a synod at Jerusalem and Maximus and the others wrote the following letter in his favor.

NOTE

1. Compare Socrates, *Ecclesiastical History,* Book II, Chapter 23.

CHAPTER XXII
EPISTLE WRITTEN BY THE SYNOD OF JERUSALEM IN FAVOR OF ATHANASIUS.

The holy synod assembled at Jerusalem, to the priests, deacons, and people of Egypt, Libya, and Alexandria, our most beloved and cherished brethren, greeting in the Lord.[1]

We can never, beloved, return adequate thanks to God, the Creator of all things, for the wonderful works he has now accomplished, particularly for the blessings he has conferred on your churches by the restoration of Athanasius, your lord and pastor, and our fellow minister. Who could have hoped to have seen this effected? God heard your prayers. He had compassion on His church. He hearkened to your groans and tears, and granted your supplications. You were scattered abroad like sheep without a pastor. The true Shepherd, who from heaven watches over his own flock, restored to you him whom you desired. Behold, we do all things for the peace of the church and are influenced by love like yours. Therefore we received and embraced your pastor and despatch by him this letter of congratulation[2] to you on his return, whereby you may know that we are knit together with you in love for him.

It is right that you should pray for the pious emperors who, having perceived your anxiety for his return and recognized his innocence, restored him to you with great honor. Receive him then joyfully, and offer on his behalf due praises to God, and let us ever rejoice in Him and glorify Him in Christ Jesus our Lord, by whom be glory to the Father throughout all ages, Amen."

NOTES

1. This Epistle is extant in the second Apology of Athanasius against the Arians, page 175.
2. εὐχαρίστιοι εὐχαί.

CHAPTER XXIII

VALENS AND URSACIUS, WHO BELONGED TO THE ARIAN FACTION, CONFESS TO THE BISHOP OF ROME THAT ATHANASIUS HAD BEEN UNJUSTLY DEPOSED.

Such was the letter written by the synod convened in Palestine.[1] Some time after Athanasius had the satisfaction of seeing the injustice of the sentence enacted against him by the council of Tyre publicly recognized. Valens and Ursacius, who had been sent with Theognis and his followers to obtain information in Mareota, as we before mentioned, concerning the chalice which Ischyrion had accused Athanasius of having broken, wrote the following retractation to Julius, bishop of Rome.

> Ursacius and Valens, to Julius the most blessed Lord and Pope.
>
> As, in our former letters to you, we lodged divers insinuations against Athanasius, the bishop, and omitted to comply with the injunctions contained in yours, we now confess to your Reverence[2] in the presence of all the presbyters, our brethren, that all that you have heard concerning the aforesaid Athanasius is utterly false. For this reason, we joyfully enter into communion with him, particularly as you, with your natural benevolence, have granted forgiveness to us for our past error. Moreover, we declare unto you that if the bishops of the East, or even Athanasius himself, should at any time summon us to judgment, we will in no wise appear before them without your consent and sanction. We now and ever shall anathematize, as we formerly did in the memorial which we presented at Milan,[3] the heretic Arius and his followers, who say that there was a time in which the Son existed not and that Christ is from that which had no existence and who deny that Christ was God[4] and the Son of God before all ages. We again protest, in our own handwriting, that we shall ever condemn the aforesaid Arian heresy and its originators.
>
> I, Ursacius, sign this confession with my own signature, as does likewise Valens.[5]

This was the confession which they sent to Julius. It is also necessary to append to it their letter to Athanasius. It is as follows.

NOTES

1. Compare Socrates, *Ecclesiastical History*, Book II, Chapter 24,
2. τῆς σῆς χρηστότητος. Valesius understands them to refer to the letters of Julius to Eusebius and the other adversaries of Athanasius, in which he summoned them to answer for their conduct towards him.

3. There is some doubt among authorities as to whether the synod of Milan was held in AD 347. The present letter Valesius assigns to the year AD 356.
4. The allusion is here to the heresy of Photinus.
5. These events are referred to the year AD 349 by the authors of the Benedictine *Life of Athanasius*.

CHAPTER XXIV

LETTER OF CONCILIATION FROM VALENS AND URSACIUS TO THE GREAT ATHANASIUS. RESTORATION OF THE OTHER EASTERN BISHOPS. EJECTION OF MACEDONIUS AND ACCESSION OF PAUL.

The bishops Ursacius and Valens, to Athanasius our beloved brother in the Lord.

We take the opportunity of the departure of Museus, our brother and fellow presbyter, to write by him to you, O beloved brother, and hope that our letter will find you in good health. You will afford us great encouragement if you will write us a reply to this letter. Know that we are at peace, and in ecclesiastical communion with you.

When Athanasius had returned from the West to Egypt, Paul,[1] Marcellus, Asclepas, and Lucius, who had been recalled by the emperor from exile, were reinstated in their churches. Immediately on the return of Paul to Constantinople, Macedonius retired from public life and held private assemblies. There was a great tumult at Ancyra on the deposition of Basil and the reinstallation of Marcellus. The other bishops were reinstated in their churches without difficulty.

NOTE

1. Valesius observes that this cannot be true of Paul, as no mention is made of his name in the decrees of the council of Sardica, and Theodoret (*Ecclesiastical History*, Book II) expressly states that he was in quiet possession of his see at the time when that council was held.

BOOK IV

CHAPTER I
DEATH OF CONSTANS CÆSAR. OCCURRENCES WHICH TOOK PLACE IN ROME.

Four years after the council of Sardica, Constans was killed in Gaul.[1] Magnentius, who had plotted his death, took possession of his dominions. In the meantime, Vetranio was proclaimed emperor at Sirmium by the Illyrian troops. Nepotian, the son of the late emperor's sister, aided by a body of gladiators, likewise claimed the imperial power and ancient Rome suffered severely from these usurpations. Nepotian, however, was put to death by the soldiers of Magnentius. Constantius, finding himself the sole master of the empire, and invested with the title of emperor, prepared to depose the tyrants.

In the meantime, Athanasius, having arrived in Alexandria, called together the Egyptian bishops and had the enactments confirmed which had been passed at Sardica and in Palestine in his favor.

NOTE

1. Compare Socrates, *Ecclesiastical History,* Book II, Chapter 25.

CHAPTER II
CONSTANTIUS AGAIN EJECTS ATHANASIUS, AND BANISHES THE HOMOUSIANS. DEATH OF PAUL, BISHOP OF CONSTANTINOPLE. MACEDONIUS, HIS USURPATION AND EVIL DEEDS.

The emperor,[1] deceived by the calumnies of the heterodox, changed his mind and in opposition to the decrees of the council of Sardica, exiled the bishops whom he had previously restored. Marcellus was again deposed, and Basil reacquired possession of the bishopric of Ancyra. Lucius was thrown into prison and died there.

Paul was condemned to perpetual banishment and was conveyed to Cucusum in Armenia where he died. I have never, however, been able to ascertain whether or not he died a natural death. It is still reported that he was strangled by the adherents of Macedonius. As soon as he was sent into exile, Macedonius seized the government of his church, and being aided by several orders of monks whom he had incorporated at Constantinople and by many of the neighboring bishops, he commenced, it is said, a persecution against those who held the sentiments of Paul. He ejected them in the first place from the church, and then compelled them to enter into communion with himself. Many perished from wounds received in the struggle. Some were deprived of their possessions, some of the rights of citizenship, and others were branded on the forehead with an iron instrument. The emperor was displeased when he heard of these transactions, and imputed the blame of them to Macedonius and his adherents.[2]

NOTES

1. Namely, Constantius. Compare Socrates, *Ecclesiastical History,* Book II, Chapters 26, 27.
2. The last clause of the chapter, as it stands in the majority of editions, is rejected by Valesius as spurious and interpolated.

CHAPTER III

MARTYRDOM OF THE HOLY MARTYRIUS AND MARCIAN.

The persecution increased in violence and led to deeds of blood. Martyrius and Marcian were among those who were slain. They had been the servants[1] of Paul and were delivered up by Macedonius to the governor as having been guilty of the murder of Hermogenes and of exciting the former sedition against him.[2] Martyrius was a sub-deacon and Marcian a singer and a reader of Holy Scripture. Their tomb is situated opposite to the walls of Constantinople and within the precincts of a house of prayer, which was commenced by John and completed by Sisinius, two bishops of the church of Constantinople. These men, who were so highly honored of God, judged rightly that they would not be deprived of the honors attending martyrdom, for the place where their tomb was erected had been anciently used as a receptacle for the heads of criminals who had been executed and had been in consequence deserted on account of the spectral apparitions which were said to be frequent on the spot. But the spectres were dispersed at their tomb, and many other notable miracles were wrought there. These are the particulars which I have heard concerning Martyrius and Marcian. If what I have related appears to be scarcely credible, it is easy to apply for further information to those who are more accurately acquainted with the circumstances. And, indeed, far more wonderful things are recorded concerning them than those which I have detailed.

NOTE

1. Nicephorus (Book IX, Chapter 20) adds that they were his notaries. The memory of these martyrs is celebrated in the Greek church under the name of the Notaries on the 25th of October.

2. Valesius is of the opinion that the clause expunged by him from the end of the preceding chapter, ought to be inserted here. The terms of it are as follows, "and after this of the deposition of Macedonius himself, when they deprived him of the see of Constantinople.

CHAPTER IV

MILITARY ENTERPRISES OF CONSTANTIUS IN ILLYRIA, AND DETAILS CONCERNING VETRANIO AND MAGNENTIUS. GALLUS RECEIVES THE TITLE OF CÆSAR, AND IS SENT TO THE EAST.

On the expulsion of Athanasius which took place about this period, George persecuted[1] all those throughout Egypt who refused to conform to his sentiments. The emperor marched into Illyria and entered Sirmium whither Vetranio had repaired by appointment. The soldiers[2] who had proclaimed him emperor suddenly changed their mind, and saluted Constantius as sole sovereign and as Augustus. Vetranio, perceiving that he was betrayed, threw himself as a suppliant at the feet of Constantius. Constantius stripped him of the purple and the emblems of the imperial dignity, obliged him to return to private life, liberally provided for his wants out of the public treasury, and told him that at his advanced age he ought to live in quietude, without striving to burden himself with the cares of government.

After terminating these arrangements in favor of Vetranio, Constantius sent a large army into Italy against Magnentius. He then conferred the title of Caesar on his cousin Gallus and sent him into Syria to defend the provinces of the East.

NOTES

1. κακῶς ἐποίει. Sozomen is, however, mistaken as to George, for George had not yet been intruded into the see of Athanasius.
2. Compare Socrates, *Ecclesiastical History*, Book II, Chapters 25, 28.

CHAPTER V

CYRIL SUCCEEDS MAXIMUS IN THE SACERDOTAL OFFICE, AND THE SIGN OF THE CROSS, SURPASSING THE SUN IN SPLENDOR, AGAIN APPEARS IN THE HEAVENS, AND IS VISIBLE DURING SEVERAL DAYS.

At the time that Cyril succeeded Maximus in the government of the church of Jerusalem, the sign of the cross appeared in the heavens.[1] Its radiance was not feeble and divergent like that of comets, but splendid and concentrated. Its length was about fifteen stadia from Calvary to the Mount of Olives, and its breadth was in proportion to its length. So extraordinary a phenomenon excited universal terror. Men, women, and children left their houses, the marketplace, or their respective employments, and ran to the church, where they sang hymns to Christ together, and voluntarily confessed their belief in God.

The intelligence was quickly transmitted throughout our dominions and was conveyed, so to speak, throughout the earth by those who had witnessed the wonderful spectacle at Jerusalem. The emperor was made acquainted with the occurrence, partly by the numerous reports concerning it which were then current, and partly by a letter from Cyril[2] the bishop. It was said that this prodigy was the fulfilment of an ancient prophecy contained in the Holy Scriptures. It was the means of the conversion of many Greeks and Jews to Christianity.

NOTES

1. Compare Socrates, *Ecclesiastical History,* Book II, Chapter 28, and Valesius' notes *in loco.*
2. The letter here alluded to by Sozomen was addressed by Cyril to Constantius, and is extant among his *Works*, page 305, ed. Oxon. 1703. *Note to the 2018 edition:* This letter is available in an English translation in Yarnold: *Cyril of Jerusalem*, page 68.

CHAPTER VI

PHOTINUS, BISHOP OF SIRMIUM, HIS HERESY, AND THE COUNCIL CONVENED AT SIRMIUM IN OPPOSITION THERETO. THREE FORMULARIES OF FAITH.

About this time[1] Photinus, bishop of Sirmium, laid before the emperor, who was then staying at that city, a heresy which he had originated some time previously. His natural ease of utterance and powers of persuasion enabled him to lead many into his own way of thinking. He acknowledged that there was one God Almighty, by whose word all things were created, but would not admit that the generation and existence of the Son was before all ages. On the contrary, he alleged that Christ derived his existence from Mary. As soon as this opinion was divulged, it excited the indignation of the Eastern and of the Western bishops and was rejected as contrary to the faith. And it was equally opposed by those who maintained the doctrines of the Nicene council and by those who favored the tenets of Arius. The emperor also regarded the heresy with aversion and convened a council at Sirmium where he was then residing. Of the Eastern bishops, George, bishop of Alexandria, Basil, bishop of Ancyra, and Mark, bishop of Arethusa, were present at this council. And among the Western bishops were Valens bishop of Mursa, and Hosius the Confessor. This latter, who had attended the council of Nicæa, had not long previously been condemned to banishment through the machinations of the Arians. He was summoned to the council of Sirmium by the command of the emperor, extorted by the Arians, who believed that their party would be strengthened if they could gain over, either by force or persuasion, a man held in universal admiration and esteem as was Hosius.

The period at which the council was convened at Sirmium was the year after the expiration of the consulate of Sergius and Nigrinian, and during this year there were no consuls either in the East or the West, owing to the insurrections excited by the tyrants. Photinus was deposed by this council because he was accused of countenancing the errors of Sabellius and Paul of Samosata. The council then proceeded to draw up three formularies of faith, of which one was written in Greek and the others in Latin. But they did not agree with each other, nor with any other of the former expositions of doctrine either in word or import. It is not said in the Greek formulary that the Son is consubstantial or of like substance with the Father, but it is there declared that those who maintain that the Son had no commencement, or that he proceeded from an expansion of the substance of the Father, or that he is united to the Father without being subject to him, are excommunicated. In one of the Roman formularies, it is forbidden to say of the substance of the Godhead, that the Son is either consubstantial, or of like substance with the Father, as such statements do not occur in the Holy Scriptures, and are beyond the reach of the understanding and knowledge of men. It is said that the Father must be recognized as superior to the Son in honor, in dignity, in divinity, and in the relationship in which he stands as Father, and that it must be confessed that the Son, like all created beings, is subject to the Father, that the Father had no commencement, and that the generation of the Son is unknown to all save the Father.

It is related that when this formulary was completed, the bishops became aware of the errors it contained, and endeavored to withdraw it from the public and to correct it, and that the emperor threatened to punish those who should retain or conceal any of the copies that had been made of it. But having been once published, no efforts were adequate to suppress it altogether.

The third formulary is of the same import as the others. It prohibits the use of the term "substance," and assigns the following reason for the prohibition. "The term 'substance' having been used with too much simplicity by the Fathers and having been a cause of offence to many of the unlearned multitude, we have deemed it right totally to reject the use of it: and we would enjoin the omission of all mention of the term in allusion to the Godhead, for it is nowhere said in the Holy Scriptures, that the Father, Son, and Holy Ghost are of the same substance.[2] But we say, in conformity with the Holy Scriptures, that the Son is like unto the Father."

Such was the decision arrived at in the presence of the emperor concerning the faith. Hosius at first refused to assent to it. Compulsion, however, was resorted to, and being extremely old, he sunk, so to speak, beneath the blows that were inflicted on him and yielded his consent and signature.[3]

The bishops strove to entice Photinus, by the promise of re-establishment in his bishopric, to reject his former sentiments and sign their formulary. But, far from yielding to them, he challenged them to hold a disputation with him. On the day appointed for this purpose, the bishops, therefore, assembled with the judges who had been appointed by the emperor to preside at their meetings, and who, in point of eloquence and dignity, held the first rank in the palace. Basil, bishop of Ancyra, was selected to commence the disputation against Photinus. The conflict lasted a long time, on account of the numerous questions started and the answers given by each party and which were immediately taken down in writing. But finally the victory declared itself in favor of Basil. Photinus was banished, but remained firm in his original sentiments. He wrote many works in Greek and Latin, in which he endeavored to show that all opinions except his own were erroneous.

I have now concluded all that I had to say concerning Photinus and the heresy to which his name was affixed.

NOTES

1. Compare Socrates, *Ecclesiastical History,* Book II, Chapter 29.
2. Valerius remarks that there is a discrepancy between the account given here and as it stands in the treatise of Athanasius *De Synodis*, and in Socrates' narrative of the synod of Ariminum, *Ecclesiastical History,* Book II, Chapter 37.
3. Compare Socrates, *Ecclesiastical History,* Book II, Chapter 13, and notes *in loco*.

CHAPTER VII

DEATH OF THE TYRANTS MAGNENTIUS AND SILVANUS. SEDITION OF THE JEWS IN PALESTINE. GALLUS CÆSAR IS SLAIN.

In the meantime[1] Magnentius made himself master of ancient Rome and put numbers of the senators and of the people to death. Hearing that the troops of Constantius were approaching, he retired into Gaul, and here the two parties had frequent encounters in which sometimes the one and sometimes the other was victorious. At length, however, Magnentius was defeated and fled to Mursa, which is the fortress of Gaul,[2] and here he strove to revive the courage of his soldiers who were much dispirited by their defeat. But although they received Magnentius with the honors usually paid to emperors and rendered him the customary demonstrations of respect, they proclaimed Constantius emperor. Magnentius, concluding from this circumstance that he was not destined by God to hold the reins of empire, endeavored to retreat from the fortress to some distant place. But he was pursued by the troops of Constantius, and being overtaken at a spot called Mount Seleucus, he escaped alone from the encounter and fled to Lugduna. On his arrival there he slew his own mother and his brother, whom he had named Cæsar, and lastly he killed himself. Not long after, Decentius, another of his brothers, put an end to his own existence. Still the public tumults were not quelled, for not long after, Silvanus assumed the supreme authority in Gaul, but he was put to death by the generals of Constantius.

The Jews of Diocæsarea also took up arms and invaded Palestine and the neighboring territories, with the design of shaking off the Roman yoke.[3] On hearing of their insurrection, Gallus Cæsar, who was then at Antioch, sent troops against them, defeated them, and destroyed Diocæsarea. Gallus, intoxicated with success, aspired to the supreme power, and he slew Magnus the treasurer and Domitian, the prefect of the East because they apprized the emperor of his designs. The anger of Constantius was excited, and he summoned him to his presence. Gallus did not dare to refuse obedience and set out on his journey. When, however, he reached the island Havonius, he was killed by the emperor's order.

This event occurred in the third year of his consulate, and in the seventh year of the reign of Constantius.

NOTES

1. Compare Socrates, *Ecclesiastical History,* Book II, Chapter 32.
2. The fortress of Mursa was not in Gaul, but Pannonia. Socrates has made the same mistake as Sozomen. See Spanheim's *Observations on the Emperor Julian's Oration,* Chapter 1, page 230.
3. Compare Socrates, *Ecclesiastical History,* Book II, Chapters 33, 34.

CHAPTER VIII

ARRIVAL OF CONSTANTIUS AT ROME. A COUNCIL HELD IN ITALY. ACCOUNT OF WHAT HAPPENED TO ATHANASIUS THE GREAT THROUGH THE MACHINATIONS OF THE ARIANS.

On the death of the tyrants, Constantius anticipated the restoration of peace and cessation of tumults, and quitted Sirmium in order to return to ancient Rome, and to enjoy the honor of a triumph after his victory over the tyrants. He likewise intended to bring the Eastern and the Western bishops, if possible, to one mind concerning doctrine by convening a council in Italy. Julius died about this period,[1] after having governed the church of Rome during twenty-five years, and Liberius succeeded him.

Those who were opposed to the doctrines of the Nicene council thought this a favorable opportunity to calumniate the bishops whom they had deposed, and to procure their ejection from the church as abettors of false doctrine and as disturbers of the public peace, and to accuse them of having sought during the life of Constans to excite a misunderstanding between the emperors. And it was true, as we related above,[2] that Constans menaced his brother with war unless he would consent to receive the orthodox bishops. Their efforts were principally directed against Athanasius, towards whom they entertained so great an aversion that even when he was protected by Constans and enjoyed the friendship of Constantius, they could not conceal their enmity. Narcissus, bishop of Cilicia, Theodore, bishop of Thrace, Eugenius,[3] bishop of Nicæa, Patrophilus, bishop of Scythopolis, Menophantes, bishop of Ephesus, and other bishops to the number of thirty, assembled themselves in Antioch[4] and wrote a letter to all the bishops of every region, in which they stated that Athanasius had returned to his bishopric in violation of the rules of the church, that he had not justified himself in any council, and that he was only supported by some of his own faction, and they exhorted them not to hold communion with him nor to write to him, but to enter into communion with George who had been ordained to succeed him. Athanasius only contemned these proceedings, but he was about to undergo greater trials than any he had yet experienced.

Immediately on the death of Magnentius, and as soon as Constantius found himself sole master of the Roman empire, he directed all his efforts to induce the bishops of the West to admit[5] that the Son is of like substance with the Father. In carrying out this scheme, however, he did not in the first place resort to compulsion, but endeavored by persuasion to obtain the concurrence of the other bishops in the decrees of the Eastern bishops against Athanasius. For he thought that if he could bring them to be of one mind on this point, it would be easy for him to regulate aright the affairs connected with religion.

NOTES

1. Sozomen is mistaken here, for Pope Julius died AD 352, after having held the pontificate not 25 years, (as Sozomen says) but 15 only.
2. See above, Book III, Chapter 20.
3. For Eugenius, Theogonius is substituted by Epiphanius, though incorrectly. Leontius, bishop of Antioch and George of Laodicea, were also present, according to Valesius.
4. Sozomen is the only historian who makes mention of this synod at Antioch in Syria, and he has placed it a year too early in the opinion of Valesius.
5. συναινεῖν. This word we have adopted into our text at the suggestion of Valesius, instead of the received reading συνεῖναι. It is also quite clear from the whole history of the period that we must read ὁμοιούσιον, and not ὁμοούσιον.

CHAPTER IX

COUNCIL OF MILAN. BANISHMENT OF ATHANASIUS.

The emperor[1] was extremely urgent to convene a council in Milan, yet few of the Eastern bishops repaired thither. Some, it appears, excused themselves from attendance under the plea of illness, others on account of the length and difficulties of the journey. There were, however, upwards of three hundred of the Western bishops at the council. The Eastern bishops insisted that Athanasius should be condemned to banishment and expelled from Alexandria, and the others, either from fear, fraud, or ignorance, assented to the measure. Dionysius, bishop of Alba, the metropolis of Italy, Eusebius, bishop of Vercella in Liguria, Paulinus, bishop of Treves, Rhodanus[2] and Lucifer, were the only bishops who protested against this decision. And they declared that Athanasius ought not to be condemned on such slight pretexts, and that the evil would not cease with his condemnation but that the orthodox doctrines concerning the Godhead would be forthwith attacked and endangered. They represented that the whole measure was a scheme concerted by the emperor and the Arians with the view of suppressing the Nicene faith. Their boldness was punished by an edict of immediate banishment, and Hilarius was exiled with them. The result too plainly showed for what purpose the council of Milan had been convened. For the councils which were held shortly after at Ariminum and Seleucia were evidently designed to change the doctrines established by the Nicene council, as we shall hereafter have occasion to show.

Athanasius, being apprized that plots had been formed against him at court, deemed it prudent not to repair to the emperor himself, as he knew that his life would be thereby endangered. He, however, selected five of the Egyptian bishops, among whom was Serapion, bishop of Thmius, a prelate distinguished by the wonderful sanctity of his life and the power of his eloquence, and sent them with three presbyters of the church to the emperor who was then in the West. They were directed to attempt, if possible, to conciliate the emperor, to reply, if requisite, to the calumnies of the hostile party, and to take such measures as they deemed most advisable for the welfare of Athanasius and of the church.

Shortly after they had embarked on their voyage, Athanasius received some letters from the emperor, summoning him to the palace.[3] Athanasius and all the people of the church were greatly troubled at this command, for they considered that no safety could be enjoyed when acting either in obedience or in disobedience to an emperor of heterodox sentiments. It was, however, determined that he should remain at Alexandria, and the bearer of the letters quitted the city without having effected anything.

The following summer, another messenger from the emperor arrived with the governors of the provinces, and he was charged to urge the departure of Athanasius from the city and to act with hostility against the clergy. When he perceived, however, that the people of the church were full of courage and ready to take up arms, he also departed from the city without accomplishing his mission. Not long after, troops called the Roman legions which were quartered in Egypt and Libya, marched into Alexandria. As it was reported that Athanasius was concealed in the church known by the name "*Theona*" the commander of the troops and Hilarius,[4] whom the emperor had again entrusted with the transaction of this affair, caused the doors of the church to be burst open, and thus effected their entrance,[5] but they did not find Athanasius within the walls, although they sought for him everywhere. It is said that he escaped this and many other perils by the special interposition of God. For just as he had been warned of God and had effected his exit, the soldiers entered the church.

NOTES

1. Compare Socrates, *Ecclesiastical History,* Book II, Chapter 36.
2. Or, as he is sometimes called, Rhodanius. He is thought to have been bishop of Toulouse.
3. William Cave, in his *Lives of the Most Eminent Fathers of the Church, Volume II: Athanasius*, disputes the correctness.
4. He was notary to the emperor Constantius, and was sent by him to expel Athanasius from Alexandria.
5. Compare Socrates, *Ecclesiastical History,* Book II, Chapter 11.

CHAPTER X

DIVERS MACHINATIONS OF THE ARIANS AGAINST ATHANASIUS, AND HIS ESCAPE FROM VARIOUS DANGERS THROUGH DIVINE INTERPOSITION. EVIL DEEDS PERPETRATED BY GEORGE IN EGYPT AFTER THE EXPULSION OF ATHANASIUS.

There is no doubt but that Athanasius was beloved of God and endowed with the gift of foreseeing the future. More wonderful facts than those which we have related might be adduced to prove his intimate acquaintance with futurity. It happened that during the life of Constans, the emperor Constantius was once determined upon ill-treating this holy man, but he made his escape and concealed himself for a long time in a subterraneous place which had been used as a reservoir for water.[1] No one knew where he was concealed except a woman, who had been intrusted with the secret and who waited upon him. As the heterodox, however, were anxiously intent upon taking Athanasius alive, it appears that by means of gifts or promises, they at length succeeded in corrupting the woman. But Athanasius was forewarned by God of her treachery and effected his escape from the place. The woman was punished for having made a false deposition against her masters while they, on their part, fled the country. For it was accounted no venial crime by the heterodox to receive or to conceal Athanasius, but was on the contrary regarded as an act of disobedience against the express commands of the emperor and as a crime against the empire, and was visited as such by the civil tribunals.

Athanasius was saved on another occasion in a similar manner. He was again obliged to flee for his life, and he set sail up the Nile[2] with the design of retreating to the further districts of Egypt, but his enemies received intelligence of his intention and pursued him. Being forewarned of God that he would be pursued, he returned back to Alexandria, the tide being in his favor, whereas his enemies had to steer against the current of the river. He reached Alexandria in safety, and effectually concealed himself in the midst of its dense population.

His success in avoiding these and many other perils led to his being accused of sorcery by the Greek and the heterodox. It is reported that once, as he was passing through the city, a crow was heard to caw and that a number of Pagans who happened to be on the spot, asked him in derision what the crow was saying. He replied, smiling, "It utters the sound *cras*, the meaning of which in the Latin language is 'tomorrow' and it has hereby announced to you that the morrow will not be propitious to you. For it indicates that you will be forbidden by the Roman emperor to celebrate your festival tomorrow." Although this prediction of Athanasius appeared to be absurd, it was fulfilled. For the following day edicts were transmitted to the governors from the emperor, by which it was commanded that the Greeks (Pagans) were not to be permitted to assemble in the temples to perform their usual ceremonies, nor to celebrate their festival, and thus was abolished the most solemn feast which the Pagans had retained. What I have said is sufficient to show that this holy man was endowed with the gift of prophecy.

After Athanasius had escaped in the manner we have described from those who sought to arrest him, his clergy and people remained for some time in possession of the churches, but eventually the governor of Egypt and the commander of the army forcibly ejected all those who maintained the sentiments of Athanasius in order to deliver up the government of the churches to George, whose arrival was then expected. Not long after, he reached the city and the churches were placed under his authority. He ruled by force rather than by priestly moderation, and as he strove to strike terror into the minds of the people, and carried on a cruel persecution against the followers of Athanasius, and, moreover, imprisoned and maimed many men and women, he was accounted a tyrant and became an object of universal hatred. The people were so deeply incensed at his conduct that they rushed into the church and would have torn him to pieces had he not escaped from them, and fled to the emperor. Those who held the sentiments of Athanasius then took possession of the churches. But they did not long retain possession of them. For the commander of the troops, when he returned to Alexandria, restored them to the partisans of George. A secretary of the emperor's was afterwards sent to punish the leaders of the sedition, and he treated many of the citizens with the utmost rigor and cruelty. When George returned, he was more formidable, it appears, than ever and was regarded with greater aversion than before, for he instigated the emperor to the perpetration of many evil deeds, and besides, the monks of Egypt openly declared him to be perfidious and inflated with arrogance. The opinions of these monks were always adopted by the people, and their testimony was universally received because they were noted for their virtue and the philosophical tenor of their lives.

NOTES

1. Valesius remarks that these particulars cannot be relied upon, and that they are probably mere fables taken out of the writings of Rufinus.
2. Compare Socrates, *Ecclesiastical History,* Book III, Chapter 14.

CHAPTER XI

LIBERIUS, BISHOP OF ROME, AND THE CAUSE OF HIS BEING EXILED BY CONSTANTIUS. FELIX, HIS SUCCESSOR.

Although what I have recorded did not occur at the same period of time after the death of Constans to Athanasius and the church of Alexandria, yet I deemed it right, for the sake of greater clearness, to relate all these events in consecutive order. The council of Milan was dissolved without any business having been transacted, and the emperor condemned to banishment all those who had opposed the designs of the enemies of Athanasius. As Constantius wished to establish uniformity of doctrine throughout the church, and to unite the priesthood in the maintenance of the same sentiments, he formed a plan to convene the bishops of every religion to a council, to be held in the West. He was aware of the difficulty of carrying this scheme into execution, arising from the vast extent of land and seas which some of the bishops would have to traverse, yet he did not altogether despair of success. While this project was occupying his mind, and before he prepared to make his triumphal entrance into Rome, he sent for Liberius, the bishop of Rome, and strove to persuade him to conformity of sentiment with priests by whom he was attended, and amongst whom was Eudoxius. As Liberius, however, refused compliance and protested that he would never yield on this point, the emperor banished him to Berœa, in Thrace. It is alleged, that another reason of the banishment of Liberius was, that he would not withdraw from communion with Athanasius, but manfully opposed the emperor who insisted that Athanasius had injured the church, had occasioned the death of his elder brother,[1] and had sown the seeds of enmity between Constans and himself.

As the emperor revived all the decrees which had been enacted against Athanasius by various councils, and particularly by that of Tyre, Liberius told him that no regard ought to be paid to edicts which were issued from motives of hatred, of favor, or of fear. He desired that the bishops of every region should be made to sign the formulary of faith compiled at Nicæa, and that those bishops who had been exiled on account of their adherence to it should be recalled. He suggested that all the bishops should, at their own expense and without being furnished either with money or conveyances by the public, proceed to Alexandria and endeavor to ascertain the truth by inquiries which could be more easily instituted at that city than elsewhere, as the injured and those who had inflicted injury dwelt there. He then exhibited the letter written by Valens and Ursacius to Julius his predecessor in the Roman bishopric in which they solicited his forgiveness and acknowledged that the depositions brought against Athanasius at Mareota were false, and he besought the emperor not to condemn Athanasius during his absence, nor to give credit to enactments which were evidently obtained by the machinations of his enemies. With respect to the alleged injuries which had been inflicted on his brothers, he entreated the emperor not to revenge himself by the hands of priests who had been set apart by God, not for the execution of vengeance but for sanctification and the performance of just and benevolent actions.

The emperor, perceiving that Liberius was not disposed to comply with his mandate, commanded that he should be conveyed to Thrace unless he would change his mind within two days. "To me, emperor," replied Liberius, "deliberation is of no avail. My resolution has long been formed, and I am ready to go forth to exile."

It is said that when he was being conducted to banishment, the emperor sent him five hundred pieces of gold. He, however, refused to receive them and said to the messenger who brought them, "Go, and tell him who sent this gold, to give it to the flatterers and hypocrites[2] who surround him, for their insatiable cupidity plunges them into a state of perpetual want which can never be relieved. Christ, who is, in all respects, like unto his Father, supplies us with food and with all good things."

Liberius having, for the above reasons, been deposed from the government of the Roman church, his bishopric was transferred to Felix,[3] a deacon of the same church. It is said that Felix always continued in adherence to the Nicene faith, and that with respect to his conduct in religious matters, he was blameless. The only thing alleged against him was that, prior to his ordination, he held communion with the heterodox.

When the emperor entered Rome, the people loudly demanded Liberius. After consulting with the bishops who were with him, he replied that he would recall Liberius and restore him to the people, if he would consent to embrace the same sentiments as those held by the priests of the court.

NOTES

1. The interrogation of Liberius by the emperor on this charge is extant in Theodoret, *Ecclesiastical History*, Book II, Chapter 16.
2. He means the Arian bishops.
3. Compare Socrates, *Ecclesiastical History*, Book II, Chapter 37.

CHAPTER XII

ÆTIUS THE SYRIAN, AND EUDOXIUS THE SUCCESSOR OF LEONTIUS IN THE BISHOPRIC OF ANTIOCH. CONCERNING THE TERM "CONSUBSTANTIAL."

About this time,[1] Ætius broached his peculiar opinions concerning the Godhead. He was then deacon of the church of Antioch and had been ordained by Leontius.[2] He maintained, like Arius, that the Son is a created being, that he was created out of nothing, and that he is dissimilar from the Father. As he was extremely addicted to contention, very bold in his assertions on theological subjects, and prone to have recourse to a very subtle mode of argumentation, he was accounted a heretic even by those who held the same sentiments as himself. When he had been, for this reason, excommunicated by the heterodox, he feigned a refusal to hold communion with them because they had unjustly admitted Arius into communion after he had perjured himself by declaring to the emperor Constantine that he maintained the doctrines of the council of Nicæa. Such is the account given of Ætius.

While the emperor was in the West, intelligence arrived of the death of Leontius, bishop of Antioch. Eudoxius requested permission of the emperor to return to Syria, that he might superintend the affairs of that church. On permission being granted, he repaired with all speed to Antioch and installed himself as bishop of that city without the sanction of George, bishop of Laodicea, of Mark, bishop of Arethusa, of the other Syrian bishops or of any other bishops to whom the right of conferring ordination pertained. It was reported that he acted with the concurrence of the emperor and of the eunuchs belonging to the palace who, like Eudoxius, favored the doctrines of Ætius and believed that the Son is dissimilar from the Father. When Eudoxius found himself in possession of the church of Antioch, he ventured to uphold this heresy openly. He assembled in Antioch all those who held the same opinions as himself, among whom were Acacius, bishop of Cæsarea in Palestine, and Uranius, bishop of Tyre, and rejected the terms "of like substance" and "consubstantial" under the pretext that they had been denounced by the Western bishops. Hosius had certainly, with the view of arresting the contention excited by Valens, Ursacius, and Germanius,[3] consented, though by compulsion,[4] with some other bishops at Sirmium to refrain from the use of the terms "consubstantial" and "of like substance" because such terms do not occur in the Holy Scriptures and are beyond the understanding of men,[5] Eudoxius wrote to the bishops as if they all upheld what Hosius had admitted and congratulated Valens and Ursacius and Germanius for having been instrumental in the introduction of orthodox doctrines into the West.

NOTES

1. Compare Socrates, *Ecclesiastical History,* Book II, Chapter 35.
2. So also says Socrates. But Epiphanius asserts that he was ordained by George of Alexandria.
3. Otherwise called Germinius. He was afterwards promoted to the bishopric of Sirmium.
4. See above, Chapter 6, *sub finem.*
5. Athanasius also excuses the lapse of Hosius, on the ground that he acted under compulsion.

CHAPTER XIII

INNOVATIONS OF EUDOXIUS CENSURED IN A LETTER WRITTEN BY GEORGE, BISHOP OF LAODICEA. DEPUTATION FROM THE COUNCIL OF ANCYRA TO CONSTANTIUS.

After Eudoxius had introduced these new doctrines, many members of the church of Antioch who were opposed to them were excommunicated. George, bishop of Laodicea, gave them a letter to take to the bishops who had been invited from the neighboring towns to Ancyra in Galatia by Basil for the purpose of consecrating a church which he had erected. This letter was as follows.

> George, to his most honored lords Macedonius, Basil, Cecropius, and Eugenius, sends greeting in the Lord.
> Nearly the whole city has suffered from the shipwreck of Ætius. The disciples of this wicked man whom you contemned have been encouraged by Eudoxius, and promoted by him to clerical appointments, and Ætius himself has been raised to the highest honor. Go, then, to the assistance of this great city, lest by its shipwreck the whole world should be submerged. Assemble yourselves together and solicit the signatures of other bishops, that Ætius may be ejected from the church of Antioch and that his disciples who have been ordained by Eudoxius may be cut off from the priesthood. If Eudoxius persist in affirming that the Son is dissimilar from the Father and in preferring those who uphold this dogma to those who reject it, the city of Antioch is lost to you.

Such was the strain of George's letter.

The bishops who were assembled at Ancyra clearly perceived by the enactments of Eudoxius at Antioch, that he contemplated the introduction of innovations in doctrine. They apprized the emperor of this fact and besought him that the doctrine established at Sardica, at Sirmium,[1] and at other councils, might be protected and confirmed, and especially the dogma that the Son is of like substance with the Father. In order to proffer this request to the emperor, they sent to him a deputation composed of the following bishops: Basil, bishop of Ancyra, Eustathius, bishop of Sebaste, Eleusius, bishop of Cyzicus, and Leontius who, from being an attendant on the emperor, had been promoted to the priesthood. On their arrival at the palace, they found that Asphalius, a priest of Antioch and a zealot of the Ætian heresy, was on the point of taking his departure after having terminated the business for which he undertook the journey and obtained a letter from the emperor. On receiving, however, the intelligence concerning the heresy conveyed by the deputation from Ancyra, Constantius retracted his decision respecting Eudoxius, withdrew the letter he had confided to Asphalius, and wrote the following one.

NOTE

1. We are not to understand the Catholic council of Sirmium, but one of the Oriental bishops alone, in which Photinus was deposed and in which a formula of faith was drawn up by Mark, bishop of Arethusa, of which formulary Sozomen makes no mention, though it is given by Epiphanius and Hilary.

CHAPTER XIV

LETTER OF THE EMPEROR CONSTANTIUS AGAINST EUDOXIUS AND HIS PARTISANS.

Constantius Augustus the Conqueror, to the holy Church in Antioch.

Eudoxius went to you without our permission, and we by no means regard such persons with favor. If they have recourse to deceit in transactions like this, they give evidence that they mock at God. What can be expected of people who, actuated by insatiable cupidity, go boldly from city to city, hither and thither, with the view of enriching themselves? It is reported that there are among these people certain sophists and impostors, whose very names are scarcely to be tolerated and whose deeds are evil and impious. You all know to what set of people I allude, for you are all acquainted with the doctrines of Ætius and the heresy which he originated. He and his followers have devoted themselves exclusively to the task of corrupting the people and have had the audacity to publish that we approved of their ordination. Such is the report they circulate, but it is not true and indeed far removed from the truth.

Recall to your recollection the words of which we made use when we first made a declaration of our belief, for we confessed that our Savior is the Son of God and of like substance with the Father. But these people who have the audacity to set forth whatever enters their imagination concerning the Godhead, are not far removed from atheism, and they strive moreover to propagate their opinions among others. I am convinced that their iniquitous proceedings will fall back upon their own heads. In the meantime, it is sufficient to eject them from communion and from the synod, for I will not now allude to the chastisements which must hereafter overtake them, unless they will desist from their audacious and furious deeds. How great is the evil they perpetrate when they collect together the leaders of heresies and the most wicked persons and invest them with sacred orders, thereby debasing[1] the priesthood, as if they were empowered to plunder the whole church at will! Who can bear with people who fill the cities with impiety, who sow corruption in the most distant regions, and who delight in nothing but in injuring the righteous?

Now is the time for those who have imbibed the truth to come forward, for the artifices of these evil men have been so accurately detected that it is impossible for them to remain concealed. It is the duty of good men to retain the faith of the Fathers and, so to speak, to augment it without busying themselves with other matters. I earnestly exhort those who have escaped though but recently from the precipice of this heresy, to assent to the decrees of the other bishops.

Thus we see that the heresy usually denominated Anomian, was very likely to have become predominant at this period.

NOTE

1. κιβδηλεύοντας. The metaphor is taken from the debasing of coin with inferior alloy and is very common in classical writers. The word, doubtless, is pointed at Eudoxius, who used to ordain bad and improper persons.

CHAPTER XV

THE EMPEROR CONSTANTIUS REPAIRS TO SIRMIUM, RECALLS LIBERIUS AND RESTORES HIM TO THE CHURCH OF ROME. FELIX IS ASSOCIATED WITH HIM IN THE GOVERNMENT OF THAT CHURCH.

Not long after these events, the emperor returned to Sirmium from Rome, received a deputation from the Western bishops, and recalled Liberius from Berœa. Constantius urged him in the presence of the deputies of the Eastern bishops and of the other priests who were at the court to confess that the Son is not of the same substance as the Father. He was instigated to this measure by Basil, Eustathius, and Eusebius, who possessed great influence over him. They had formed a compilation, in one document,[1] of the decrees enacted at the council of Sirmium against Paul of Samosata and Photinus, to which they subjoined a formulary of faith drawn up at Antioch at the consecration of the church, as if certain persons had, under the pretext of the term "consubstantial," attempted to establish a heresy of their own. Liberius, Athanasius, Alexander, Severianus, and Crescens, bishops of Africa, were induced to assent to this document, as were likewise Ursacius, Germanius, bishop of Sirmium, Valens, bishop of Mursa, and all the other Eastern bishops who were present. They likewise approved of a confession of faith drawn up by Liberius, in which he declared that those who affirm that the Son is not like unto the Father in substance and in all other respects, are excommunicated. For when Eudoxius and his partisans at Antioch, who favored the heresy of Ætius, received the letter of Hosius, they circulated a report that Liberius had renounced the term "consubstantial," and had admitted that the Son is dissimilar from the Father.

After these enactments had been made by the Western bishops, the emperor permitted Liberius to return to Rome. The bishops who were then convened at Sirmium wrote to Felix who governed the Roman church and to the other bishops, desiring them to receive Liberius. They directed that Felix and Liberius should share the apostolical throne and be associated together, without dissension, in the discharge of the ministerial functions, and that whatever illegalities might have occurred in the ordination of the one or the banishment of the other might be buried in oblivion. The people of Rome regarded Liberius as a good man, and esteemed him highly on account of the courage he had evinced in opposing the emperor, so that they had even excited seditions on his account and had gone so far as to shed blood. Felix survived but a short time, and Liberius found himself in sole possession of the church. This event was, no doubt, ordained by God that the seat of Peter might not be dishonored by the occupancy of two bishops,[2] for such an arrangement, being contrary to ecclesiastical law, would certainly have been a source of discord.

NOTES

1. Either the formula adopted at the council of Ancyra, or the new formula of faith which Hilary calls the heresy drawn up at Sirmium. Valesius inclines to the latter opinion. There were in all four synods of Sirmium, they were held in the years 349, 351, 357, 358.
2. *Note to the 2018 edition*: This situation is described variously in the contemporary ancient sources. Compare, among others, Socrates, *Ecclesiastical History*, Book II, Chapter 37; Theodoret, *Ecclesiastical History*, Book II, Chapters 13 and 14; Rufinus, *Church History*, Book 10, Chapter 23; Athanasius, *History of the Arians*, Chapter 5, Sulpitius Severus, *Sacred History*, Book II, Chapter 39, etc.

CHAPTER XVI

THE EMPEROR PURPOSED, ON ACCOUNT OF THE HERESY OF ÆTIUS, TO CONVENE A COUNCIL AT NICOMEDIA, BUT AS AN EARTHQUAKE TOOK PLACE IN THAT CITY, THE COUNCIL WAS FIRST CONVENED AT NICÆA AND AFTERWARDS AT ARIMINUM AND SELEUCIA. ACCOUNT OF ARSACIUS THE CONFESSOR.

Such were the events which transpired at Sirmium. It seemed at this period as if from the fear of displeasing the emperor, the Eastern and Western churches had united in the profession of the same doctrine. The emperor had determined upon convening a council at Nicæa to take into consideration the innovations introduced at Antioch and the heresy of Ætius. As Basil, however, and his party were averse to the council being held in this city because doctrinal questions had previously been agitated there, it was determined to hold the council at Nicomedia in Bithynia, and edicts were issued summoning the most learned and eloquent bishops of every nation to repair thither punctually on an appointed day.

The greater number of these bishops had commenced their journey when it was reported that Nicomedia had been visited by an earthquake, and that the whole city was destroyed.[1] This report prevented the bishops from continuing their journey, for as is usual in such cases, far more was rumored than what had actually occurred. It was reported that Nicæa, Perinthus, and the neighboring cities, even Constantinople, had been involved in the same catastrophe. The orthodox bishops were immoderately grieved at this occurrence, for the enemies of religion took occasion, on the destruction of a magnificent church, to represent to the emperor that a multitude of bishops, men, women, and children, fled to the church in the hope of there finding safety and that they all perished. This report was not true. The earthquake occurred at the second hour of the day, at which hour there was no assembly in the church. The only bishops who were killed were Cecropius, bishop of Nicomedia, and a bishop from the Bosphorus, and they were at a distance from the church when the fatal accident happened. The earthquake occupied but an instant of time, so that the people had not the power, even if they had the wish, to seek safety by flight. At the first shock they were either preserved or they perished on the spot where they were standing.

It is said that this calamity was predicted by Arsacius. He was a Persian and was originally employed in tending the emperor's lions, but during the reign of Licinius he made a noble confession of Christianity and left his former employment. He then went to Nicomedia and led the life of a monastic philosopher within its walls. Here a vision from heaven appeared to him, and he was commanded to quit the city immediately, that he might be saved from the calamity about to happen. He ran with the utmost earnestness to the church and besought the clergy to offer supplications to God that his anger might be turned away. But finding that far from being believed by them, he was regarded with ridicule, he returned to his tower and prostrated himself on the ground in prayer. Just at this moment the earthquake occurred and many perished. Those who were spared fled into the country and the desert. And as in this great and opulent city there were fires on the hearth of every house and in the baths, and in the furnaces of mechanics, it so happened that combustible materials, coming in contact with these fires, excited a general conflagration. The flames spread in all directions until the city became, so to speak, one mass of fire. It being impossible to obtain access to the houses, those who had been saved from the earthquake fled to the citadel. Arsacius was found dead in the tower and prostrated on the ground, in the same posture in which he had begun to pray. It was said that he had supplicated God to permit him to die, because he preferred death to beholding the destruction of a city in which he had first known Christ and practiced monastical philosophy.

As I have been led to speak of this good man, it is well to mention that he was endowed by God with the power of exorcizing[2] demons. A man possessed with a demon once ran through the market-place with a naked sword in his hand. The people fled from him, and the whole city was in confusion. Arsacius went out to meet him and called upon the name of Christ, and at that name the demon was expelled, and the man restored to sanity. Besides the above, Arsacius performed many other actions beyond the power of man. There was a dragon or some other species of reptile which had intrenched itself in a cavity of the roadside and which destroyed those who passed by with its breath. Arsacius went to the spot and engaged in prayer, and the serpent voluntarily crept forth from its hole, dashed its head against the ground, and killed itself. All these details I have obtained from persons who heard them stated by those who had seen Arsacius.

As the bishops were deterred from continuing their journey by the intelligence of the calamity which had occurred at Nicomedia, some awaited the further commands of the emperor, and others declared their opinions concerning the faith in letters which they wrote on the subject. The emperor hesitated as to what measures ought to be adopted and wrote to consult Basil as to whether a council ought to be convened. In his reply, it appears, Basil commended his piety and tried to console him for the destruction of Nicomedia by examples drawn from the Holy Scriptures. He exhorted him, for the sake of religion, not to relinquish his design of convening a council and not to dismiss the priests who had already set forth upon the journey until some business had been transacted. He also suggested that the council might be held at Nicæa instead of Nicomedia, so that the disputed points might be finally decided on the very spot where they had been first called into question. Basil, in writing to this effect, believed that the emperor would be pleased with this proposition, as he had himself originally suggested the propriety of holding the council at Nicæa.

On receiving this epistle from Basil, the emperor commanded that at the commencement of summer, the bishops should assemble together in Nicæa, with the exception of those who were laboring under bodily infirmity, and these latter were to depute priests and deacons to make known their sentiments so that they might consult together on contested points of doctrine and arrive at the same decision. He ordained that ten delegates should be selected from the Western churches, and as many from the Eastern, to take cognizance of the enactments that might be issued and to decide whether they were in accordance with the Holy Scriptures, and also to exercise a general superintendence over the transactions of the council. After further consultation, the emperor enacted that the bishops should remain in their churches, or wherever they might be residing, until it had been decided where the council was to be held and until they received notice to repair thither. He then wrote to Basil and directed him to inquire of the Eastern bishops where they would advise the council to be held, so that a public announcement might be made at the commencement of spring, for the emperor was of opinion that it was not advisable to convene the council at Nicæa, on account of the earthquake which had recently occurred in the province.

Basil wrote to the bishops of every province, urging them to deliberate together and to decide quickly upon the locality in which it would be most expedient to hold the council, and he prefixed a copy of the emperor's letter to his epistle. As is frequently the case in similar circumstances, the bishops were divided in opinion on the subject, and Basil repaired to the emperor who was then at Sirmium. He found several bishops at that city, who had gone thither on their own private affairs, and among them were Mark, bishop of Arethusa, and George, bishop of Alexandria. When, at length, it was decided that the council should be held in Seleucia, a city of Isauria, by the adherents of Valens and by the bishops who were at Sirmium, those who favored the Anomian heresy took occasion to have a formulary of the faith signed by the bishops of the court, which had been prepared for the purpose and in which there was no mention of the term "substance." But while preparations were being zealously made for convening the council, Eudoxius and Acacius, Ursacius and Valens, reflected that while many of the bishops were attached to the Nicene faith and others favored the formulary drawn up at the consecration of the church of Antioch, yet that both parties retained the use of the term "substance," and maintained that the Son was, in every respect, like unto the Father. And being aware that, if both parties assembled together in one place, they would condemn the doctrines of Ætius, as being contrary to their respective creeds, they so contrived matters that the bishops of the West were convened at Ariminum, and those of the East at Seleucia. As it is easier to convince a few than a great many individuals, they conceived that they might possibly lead both parties to favor their sentiments by dealing with them separately or that they might, at any rate, succeed with one, so that their heresy might not incur universal condemnation. Eusebius, a eunuch and attendant of the emperor's, was on terms of friendship with Eudoxius and upheld the same doctrines, and it was by his influence, aided by those who were attached to him, that this measure was carried into execution.

NOTES

1. Compare Socrates, *Ecclesiastical History,* Book II, Chapter 38.
2. καθαίρειν. See Valerius' notes on Eusebius, *Ecclesiastical History,* Book V, Chapter 7.

CHAPTER XVII

PROCEEDINGS OF THE COUNCIL OF ARIMINUM.

The emperor[1] was persuaded that it would not be desirable for the public on account of the expense, nor advantageous to the bishops on account of the length of the journey, to convene them all to the same place for the purpose of holding a council. He therefore wrote to the bishops who were then at Ariminum, as well as to those who were then at Seleucia, and directed them to enter upon an investigation of contested points concerning the faith, and then to turn their attention to the complaints of Cyril, bishop of Jerusalem, and of other bishops who had remonstrated against the injustice of decrees of deposition and banishment which had been issued against them, and to examine the legality of various sentences which had been enacted against other bishops. There were, in fact, several accusations pending against different bishops. George was accused by the Egyptians of rapine and violence. Finally, the emperor commanded that ten deputies should be sent to him from each council to inform him of their respective proceedings.

In accordance with this edict, the bishops assembled at the appointed cities. The synod at Ariminum first commenced proceedings. It consisted of above four hundred members. Those who regarded Athanasius with the greatest enmity, were of opinion that there was nothing further to be decreed against him. When they had entered upon the investigation of doctrinal questions, Valens and Ursacius, supported by Germanius, Auxentius, Caius, and Demophilus, advanced into the middle of the assembly, and demanded that all the formularies of faith which had been previously compiled should be suppressed, and that the formulary which they had but a short time previously set forth in the Latin language at Sirmium should be alone retained. In this formulary, it was taught, according to Scripture, that the Son is like unto the Father. But no mention was made of the substance of God. They declared that this formulary had been approved by the emperor, and that it was incumbent upon the council to adopt it instead of consulting too scrupulously the individual opinions of every member of the council, because too close an investigation of mere words could only lead to dispute and contention. They added, that it was better to establish orthodox doctrines concerning the Godhead, than by aiming at too great a refinement of terms, to introduce the use of neological expressions. By these representations, they designed to denounce the use of the term "consubstantial," because they said it was not found in the Holy Scriptures, and was obscure to the multitude, and instead of this term, they wished to substitute the expression that "the Son is like unto the Father in all things," which is borne out by the Sacred Scriptures.

After they had read their formulary containing the above representations, many of the bishops told them that no new formulary of the faith ought to be set forth, that those which had been previously compiled were quite sufficient for all purposes, and that they were met together for the express purpose of preventing all innovations. These bishops then urged those who had compiled and read the formulary to declare publicly their condemnation of the Arian doctrine, as the cause of all the troubles which had agitated the churches of every region. Ursacius and Valens, Germanius and Auxentius, Demophilus and Caius, having protested against this protestation, the council commanded that the formularies compiled by other parties should be read, and likewise that set forth at Nicæa, so that those formularies which favored divers heresies might be condemned, and those which were in accordance with the Nicene doctrines might be approved, in order that there might be no further ground for dispute and no future necessity for councils, but that a final and efficient decision might be formed. They remarked that it was absurd to compose so many formularies, as if they had but just commenced to become acquainted with the faith, and as if they wished to slight the ancient traditions of the church by which the churches had been governed by themselves and by their predecessors, many of whom had witnessed a good confession and had received the crown of martyrdom.

Such were the arguments adduced by these bishops to prove that no innovations ought to be attempted. As Valens and Ursacius and their partisans refused to be convinced by these arguments, but persisted in advocating the adoption of their own formulary, they were deposed, and it was decided that their formulary should be rejected. It was remarked that the declaration at the commencement of this formulary, of its having been compiled at Sirmium, in the presence of Constantius, "the eternal Augustus," and during the consulate of Eusebius and Hypatius, was an absurdity. Athanasius made the same remark in a letter addressed to one of his friends,[2] and said that it was ridiculous to term Constantius the eternal emperor, and yet to shrink from acknowledging the

Son of God to be eternal. He also ridiculed the date affixed to the formulary, as though condemnation were meant to be thrown on the faith of former ages, as well as on those who had, before that period, been initiated in the faith.

After these events had transpired at Ariminum, Valens and Ursacius, irritated at their deposition, repaired with all haste to the emperor.

NOTES

1. Compare Socrates, *Ecclesiastical History,* Book II, Chapter 37.
2. The remark occurs in his book on the synods of Ariminum and Seleucia.

CHAPTER XVIII

LETTER FROM THE COUNCIL CONVENED AT ARIMINUM TO THE EMPEROR CONSTANTIUS.

The synod selected twenty bishops, and sent them on an embassy to the emperor, with the following letter, which has been translated from Latin into Greek:[1]

> We believe that it is by the will of God, as well as by your pious arrangements, that we have been led from all the cities of the West, to assemble at Ariminum, for the purpose of declaring the faith of the Catholic church, and of detecting those who have set forth heresies in opposition to it. After a close and lengthened investigation, we have come to the conclusion that it is best to preserve the faith which has been handed down from antiquity, and which was preached by the prophets, the evangelists, the apostles, and by our Lord Jesus Christ, the Savior and Protector of your empire. It would have been absurd, as well as illegal, to have introduced any change in the doctrines which were so rightly and so justly propounded by the bishops at Nicæa, with the concurrence of Constantine your father, of glorious memory. These doctrines have been preached to all men, and tend to the utter subversion of the Arian, and indeed of all other heresies. There is great danger in adding to or in taking away from these doctrines, nor can the slightest alteration be made in any one of them, without giving an opportunity to the adversaries to do what they list.
>
> Ursacius and Valens, after having been long suspected of having imbibed the Arian doctrine, were cut off from communion with us.[2] In the hope of being restored to communion, they confessed their error and obtained forgiveness, as their own writings testify. The occasion on which the edict of forgiveness was conceded was at the council of Milan in the presence of the deputies of the Roman church.
>
> The formulary of the faith set forth at Nicæa, having been compiled

Book IV, Chapter XVIII

with the greatest possible care and accuracy in the presence of Constantine, who maintained it throughout his life and at his baptism and when he departed to enjoy the rest and peace of heaven, we judge that it would be absurd to attempt any alteration in it. We hold that it is necessary to retain the doctrines which were professed by so many holy confessors and martyrs, and which they maintained in accordance with the ancient decrees of the church. God has transmitted the knowledge of their faith to the time in which you live, through our Lord Jesus Christ, by whom you reign and rule the world. These wretched men, who can only be regarded as objects of compassion, have had the audacity to publish certain impious doctrines which are in opposition to the truth. After we had received your letters which you charged us to enter upon the investigation of doctrinal questions, the aforesaid disturbers of the church, aided by Germanius, Auxentius, and Caius, laid a new formulary before us replete with pernicious doctrine. When they perceived that this document would inevitably be rejected, they desired to effect some alterations in it. They have but too often been successful in proposing these alterations, but to preserve the church from further trouble arising from this source, we decided that it was requisite to preserve the inviolability of the ancient canons and to eject the aforesaid persons from communion with us. We have, for this reason, sent our deputies to you, and have furnished them with letters declaratory of the sentiments of the council. These deputies have been especially charged by us to maintain the truths which were set forth of old by the Christians of antiquity, and to prove to your Holiness the falsity of the assertion of Valens and Ursacius that a few changes would produce peace in the church. For how can peace be restored by those who destroy peace? They would be more likely to introduce contention and disturbance into Rome and the other cities rather than peace.

We therefore entreat your Clemency to listen to our deputies and to regard them favorably and not to allow the dead to be dishonored by the introduction of alterations and novelties. We pray you to preserve the tradition which we received from our ancestors, who were all wise and prudent and who, we have reason to believe, were led by the Spirit of God. For these innovations not only lead believers to infidelity, but also delude unbelievers. We likewise entreat you to command that the bishops who are now absent from their churches and of whom some are laboring under the infirmities of old age and others under the privations of poverty may be furnished with the means of returning to their own homes in order that the churches may not be longer deprived of their ministry.

Again, we beseech you that nothing be taken away from or added to the faith. Let it remain unchanged even as it has continued from the reign of your father to the present time, so that we may not in future be compelled to leave our churches and undertake long journeys, but that bishops and people may dwell together in peace and be able to devote themselves to prayer and supplication for your own personal welfare and for the continual peace of your empire.

Our deputies will show you the signatures of the bishops, and some of them will offer instruction to your Holiness out of the Sacred Scriptures.

NOTES

1. The letter is extant also in Socrates, *Ecclesiastical History,* Book II, Chapter 37. See the notes of Valesius *in loco*.
2. Ursacius and Valens were first excommunicated AD 342 by a synod held at Rome: four years later they were received back into communion at Milan (346). In the following year (347), having again openly joined the Arian party, they were condemned at Sardica, but they were again received into communion by Pope Julius, bishop of Rome, AD 349.

CHAPTER XIX
CONCERNING THE DEPUTIES OF THE COUNCIL AND THE EMPEROR'S LETTER. MACHINATIONS OF URSACIUS AND VALENS. EXILE OF THE ARCHBISHOPS. CONCERNING THE SYNOD AT NICÆA.

We have now transcribed the letter of the council of Ariminum. Ursacius and Valens, anticipating the arrival of the deputies of the council, read their formulary of faith to the emperor and calumniated the members of the council. The emperor was displeased at the rejection of this formulary, as it had been accepted in his presence at Sirmium, and he therefore treated Ursacius and Valens with honor while, on the other hand, he manifested great contempt towards the deputies and even delayed granting them an audience. At length, however, he wrote to the synod and informed them that an expedition which he was compelled to undertake against the barbarians prevented him from conferring with the deputies, and that he had therefore commanded them to remain at Adrianople until his return, in order that when other business had been dismissed his mind might be at liberty to attend to the representations of the deputies. "For it is right," he said, "to bring to the investigation of Divine subjects, a mind unfettered by other cares." Such was the strain of his letter.

The bishops replied that they could never depart from the decision they had formed, as they had before declared in writing and had charged their deputies to declare, and they besought him to regard them with favor, to give audience to their deputies, and to read their letter. They told him that it must appear grievous to him that so many churches should be deprived of their bishops, and that, if agreeable to him, they would return to their churches before the winter. After writing this letter, which was full of supplications and entreaties, the bishops waited for a time for a reply. But, as no answer was granted them, they afterwards returned to their own cities.

What I have above stated clearly proves, that the bishops who were convened at Ariminum confirmed the decrees which had of old been set forth at Nicæa. Let us now consider how it was that they eventually assented to the formulary of faith compiled by Valens and Ursacius. Various accounts have been given me of this transaction. Some say that the emperor was offended at the bishops having departed from Ariminum without his permission, and allowed Valens and his partisans to govern the churches of the West according to their own will, to set forth their own formulary, to eject those who refused to sign it from the churches, and to ordain others in their place. They say that, taking advantage of this power, Valens compelled some of the bishops to sign the formulary, and that he drove Liberius[1] and many others who refused compliance from their churches. It is further asserted that Valens and his adherents acted in the same manner in Italy and persecuted the bishops of the East in the same manner. As these persecutors were passing through Thrace they stopped, it is said, at Nicæa, a city of that province. They there convened a council and read the formulary of Ariminum which they had translated into the Greek language, and by representing that it had been approved by a general council, they obtained its adoption at Nicæa. They then cunningly denominated[2] it the Nicæan formulary of faith, in order by the resemblance of names, to deceive the simple and cause it to be mistaken for the ancient formulary set forth by the Nicæan council. Such is the account given by some parties.

Others say that the bishops who were convened at the council of Ariminum, were wearied by their detention in that city, as the emperor neither honored them with a reply to their letter, nor granted them permission to return to their own churches, and that at this juncture, those who had espoused the opposite heresy, represented to them that it was not right that divisions should exist between the priests of the whole world for the sake of one word, and that it was only requisite to admit that the Son is like unto the Father in order to put an end to all disputes, for that the bishops of the East would never rest until the term "substance" was rejected. By these representations, it is said, the members of the council were at length persuaded to assent to the formulary which Ursacius had so sedulously pressed upon them.

Ursacius and his partisans, being apprehensive lest the deputies sent by the council to the emperor should declare what firmness was in the first place evinced by the Western bishops and should expose the true cause of the rejection of the term "consubstantial," detained these deputies at Nicæa in Thrace throughout the winter, under the pretext that no public conveyances could be then obtained and that the roads were in a bad state for travelling, and they then induced them, it is said, to translate the formulary they had accepted, from Latin into Greek and to send it to the Eastern bishops. By this means, they anticipated that the formulary would produce the impression they intended without the fraud being detected, for there was no one to testify that the members of the council of Ariminum had not voluntarily rejected the term "substance" from deference to the Eastern bishops, who were averse to the use of that word. But this was evidently a false account, for all the members of the council, with the exception of a few, maintained strenuously that the Son is like unto the Father in substance, and the only differences of opinion existing between them were that some said that the Son is of the same substance as the Father, while others asserted that he is of like substance with the Father. We have now given both the accounts which have been handed down of this transaction.

NOTES

1. This is probably a mistake, for Liberius had been banished and again recalled some time before the council of Rimini.
2. ἐπευφημῆσαι. The word is used in the same sense by Sozomen below, Chapter 22.

CHAPTER XX

EVENTS WHICH TOOK PLACE IN THE EASTERN CHURCHES. MARATHONIUS, ELEUSIUS OF CYZICUS, AND MACEDONIUS EXPEL THOSE WHO MAINTAIN THE TERM "CONSUBSTANTIAL." CONCERNING THE CHURCH OF THE NOVATIANS. THE NOVATIANS ENTER INTO COMMUNION WITH THE ORTHODOX.

While the events I have above related were taking place in Italy, the East was, even before the council of Seleucia, the theater of great disturbances.[1] The adherents of Acacius and Patrophilus, having ejected Maximus, gave the government of the church of Jerusalem to Cyril. Macedonius was, by his severity, the cause of great troubles in Constantinople and the neighboring cities.[2] He was abetted by Eleusius and Marathonius. This latter was originally a deacon in his own church and was a zealous superintendent of the poor and of the monastical dwellings inhabited by each sex, and Macedonius raised him to the bishopric of Nicomedia. Eleusius, who was formerly attached to the military service of the palace, had been ordained bishop of Cyzicus. It is said that Eleusius and Marathonius were both good men, but that they were zealous in persecuting those who maintained that the Son is of the same substance as the

Book IV, Chapter XX

Father, although they never manifested so much cruelty as Macedonius, who not only expelled those who refused to hold communion with him, but imprisoned some and dragged others before the tribunals. In many cases he had recourse to compulsion and extorted compliance to his will. He seized women and children who had not been initiated (i.e., baptized) and initiated them and destroyed many churches in different places, under the pretext that the emperor had commanded the demolition of all houses of prayer in which the Son was recognized to be of the same substance as the Father.

Under this pretext the church of the Novatians at Constantinople, situated in that part of the city called Pelargus, was destroyed. It is related that these heretics performed a courageous action with the aid of the members of the Catholic church, with whom they made common cause. When those who were employed to destroy the church were about to commence the work of demolition, the Novatians assembled themselves together and conveyed the materials to a suburb of the city called Sycea. They quickly achieved this task, for men, women, and children engaged in it and gave their labor as an offering to God. By the exercise of this zeal, the church was soon re-erected and received the name of Anastasia. After the death of Constantius, Julian, his successor, granted to the Novatians the ground which they had previously possessed, and permitted them to rebuild their church. The people joyfully took advantage of this permission and transported the identical materials of the former edifice from Sycea. But this happened at a later period of time than that which we are now reviewing.

At this period a union was nearly effected between the Novatian and Catholic churches, for as they held the same opinions concerning the Godhead and were subjected to a common persecution, the members of both churches assembled and prayed together. The Catholics then possessed no houses of prayer, for the Arians had wrested them from them. It appears too, that from the frequent intercourse between the members of each church, they began to reflect that no solid reason could be adduced for their separation. A reconciliation would certainly have been effected, had not the desire of the multitude been frustrated by the envy of a few individuals who asserted that there was an ancient law prohibiting the union of the churches.

NOTES

1. Compare Socrates, *Ecclesiastical History*, Book II, Chapter 38.
2. In the generally received editions here follow the words ὡς ἤρξατο χειροτονεῖν ὁ Μακάριος, but they are rejected by Valesius as foreign to the text, interrupting the sense, and involving several difficulties.

CHAPTER XXI

PROCEEDINGS OF MACEDONIUS IN MANTINIA. REMOVAL OF THE REMAINS OF CONSTANTINE THE GREAT. JULIAN BECOMES CÆSAR.

About the same time Eleusius demolished the church of the Novatians in Cyzicus.[1] The inhabitants of other parts of Paphlagonia, and particularly of Mantinia, were subjected to similar persecutions. Macedonius, having been apprized that the majority of these people were followers of Novatian and that the ecclesiastical[2] power was not of itself sufficiently strong to expel them, persuaded the emperor to send four cohorts against them. For he imagined that men who are unaccustomed to the use of military weapons would, on the first appearance of armed soldiers, be seized with terror and conform to his sentiments. But it happened otherwise, for the people of Mantinia armed themselves with whatever weapons came first to hand and marched against the military. A sanguinary conflict ensued and many of the Paphlagonians fell, but all the soldiers were slain. Many of the friends of Macedonius blamed him for having occasioned so much bloodshed, and the emperor was displeased, and regarded him with less favor than before.

Inimical feelings were engendered still more strongly by another occurrence. Macedonius contemplated the removal of the remains of the emperor Constantine, as the sepulchre in which they had been deposited was falling into ruin. The people were divided in opinion on this subject: some concurred in the design and others opposed it, deeming it impious to open the sepulchre. Those who maintained the Nicene doctrines were of the latter sentiment and insisted that no indignity should be offered to the body of Constantine, as that emperor had held the same doctrines as themselves. They were besides, I can readily imagine, eager to oppose the projects of Macedonius. However, without further delay, Macedonius caused the coffin to be conveyed to the same church in which the tomb of Acacius the martyr is placed. The people, divided into two factions, the one approving, the other condemning the deed, rushed upon each other in the church and so much carnage ensued that the sacred edifice was filled with blood and slaughtered bodies. The emperor, who was then in the West, was deeply incensed on hearing of this occurrence and he blamed Macedonius as the cause of the indignity offered to his father and of the slaughter of the people.

The emperor was then preparing to return to the East. He conferred the title of Cæsar on his cousin Julian and sent him to Gaul.[3]

NOTES

1. Compare Socrates, *Ecclesiastical History,* Book II, Chapter 38.

2. He means the clergy of the orthodox party.
3. Compare Socrates, *Ecclesiastical History,* Book II, Chapter 34. It should be added that Sozomen is wrong in placing these events subsequent to the council at Rimini.

CHAPTER XXII
COUNCIL OF SELEUCIA.

About the same period the Eastern bishops assembled[1] to the number of about one hundred and sixty in Seleucia, a city of Isauria. This was during the consulate of Eusebius and Hypatius. Leonas, who held one of the most important offices at the palace, repaired to this council at the command of Constantius, as likewise Laurentius, the military governor of the province, to discharge the duties devolving upon them. At the first session of this council, several of the bishops were absent, and among others Patrophilus, bishop of Scythopolis, Macedonius, bishop of Constantinople, and Basil, bishop of Ancyra. They resorted to divers pretexts in justification of their non-attendance. Patrophilus alleged in excuse a complaint in the eyes, and Macedonius pleaded indisposition, but it was suspected they had absented themselves from the fear that various accusations would be brought against them.

As the other bishops refused to enter upon the investigation of disputed points during their absence, Leonas commanded them to proceed at once to the examination of the questions that had been agitated. Then some were of opinion that it was necessary to commence with the discussion of doctrinal topics, while others maintained that inquiries ought to be first instituted into the conduct of those among them against whom accusations had been laid, as had been the case with Cyril, bishop of Jerusalem, Eustathius, bishop of Sebaste, and others. The ambiguity of the emperor's letters, which sometimes prescribed one course and sometimes another, gave rise to this dispute. The contention arising from this source became so fierce that all union was destroyed between them, and they became divided into two parties. However, the advice of those who wished to commence with the examination of doctrine prevailed.

When they proceeded to the investigation of terms, some desired to reject the use of the term "substance" and appealed to the authority of the formulary of faith which had not long previously been compiled by Mark[2] at Sirmium, and had been received by the bishops who were at the court, among whom was Basil,[3] bishop of Ancyra. Many others were anxious for the adoption of the formulary of faith drawn up at the consecration of the church of Antioch. To the first of these parties belonged Eudoxius, Acacius, Patrophilus, George, bishop of Alexandria, Uranius, bishop of Tyre, and thirty-two other bishops. The latter party was supported by George, bishop of Laodicea in Syria, by Eleusius, bishop of Cyzicus, by Sophronius, bishop of Pompeiopolis in Paphlagonia, and by the majority of the prelates. It was suspected, and with reason, that Acacius and his partisans absented themselves on account of the difference between their sentiments and those of the aforesaid bishops and also because they desired to evade the investigation of certain accusations which had been brought against them: for, although they had previously acknowledged in writing to Macedonius, bishop of Constantinople, that the Son is in all respects like unto the Father and of the same substance, yet they had had the hardihood to retract this admission. After prolonged disputations and contention, Silvanus, bishop of Tarsus, declared in a loud and peremptory tone, that no other formulary of faith ought to be received but that which had been set forth at Antioch. As this proposition was repugnant to the followers of Acacius, they withdrew and the other bishops read the formulary of Antioch.

The following day these bishops assembled in the church, closed the doors, and privately confirmed this formulary. Acacius condemned this proceeding and laid the formulary which he advocated before Leonas and Laurentius. Three days afterwards, the same bishops re-assembled and were joined by Macedonius and Basil who had been previously absent. Acacius and his partisans declared that they would take no part in the proceedings of the council until those who had been deposed and accused had quitted the assembly. His demand was complied with, for the bishops of the opposite party were determined that he should have no pretext for dissolving the council, which was evidently his object, in order to prevent the examination of the heresy of Ætius and of the accusations which had been brought against himself and his partisans.

When all the members were assembled, Leonas stated that he held a document which had been handed to him by the partisans of Acacius. It was their formulary of faith with introductory remarks. None of the other bishops knew anything about it, for Leonas, who was of the same sentiments as Acacius, had kept the whole matter a secret. When this document was read, the whole assembly was filled with tumult, for some of the statements it contained were to the effect that, though the emperor had prohibited the introduction of any term into the formularies of faith which was not found in the Sacred Scriptures, yet that bishops who had been deposed, having been brought from various provinces to the assembly with others who had been illegally ordained, the council had been thrown into confusion, and that some of the members had been insulted and others prevented from speaking. It was added that Acacius and his partisans did not reject the formulary which had been compiled at Antioch, although those who had assembled in that city had drawn it up for the express purpose of meeting the difficulty which had just then arisen, but that, as the terms "consubstantial" and "of similar substance" had grieved some individuals and that, as it had been recently asserted that the Son is dissimilar from the Father, it was necessary, on this account, to reject the terms "consubstantial" and "of similar substance" which do not occur in Scripture, to condemn the term "dissimilar," and to confess clearly that the Son is like unto the Father, for he is, as Saint Paul somewhere says, "the image of the invisible God."

These prefatory observations were followed by a formulary which was neither conformable with that of Nicæa nor with that of Antioch, and which was so artfully worded that the followers of Arius and of Ætius could receive it without deviating from their respective creeds. In this formulary, the words used by the bishops of the council of Nicæa in condemnation of the Arian doctrine, were omitted, and the declarations of the council of Antioch concerning the immutability of the Divinity of the Son and concerning his being the perfect image of the substance, the counsel, and the power of the Father, were passed over in silence, and belief was simply expressed in the Father, in the Son, and in the Holy Ghost. And after bestowing some vulgar epithets on a few individuals who had never entered into any doctrinal contention on one side or the other, all those who entertained any other opinions than those set forth in this formulary were declared to be excommunicated. Such were the contents of the document presented by Leonas, and which had been signed by Acacius[4] and by those who had adopted his sentiments.

After it had been read, Sophronius, a bishop of Paphlagonia, exclaimed, "If we daily receive the opinions of individuals as canons of the faith, we shall only fail in arriving at truth." Acacius having retorted that it was not forbidden to compile new formularies, as that of Nicæa had been frequently and greatly altered, Eleusius replied as follows:

"But the council has not met for the purpose of learning what is already known or of accepting any other formulary than that which was set forth by the bishops who assembled at Antioch. And, moreover, we will adhere to this formulary unto death."

The dispute have taken this turn, they entered upon another subject and asked the partisans of Acacius, in what they considered the Son to be like unto the Father. They replied that the Son is similar in will, but not in substance. And the others thereupon insisted that he is similar in substance and convicted Acacius, by a work which he had formerly written, that he had once been of their opinion. Acacius replied that he ought not to be judged from his own writings, and the dispute had continued for some time, when Eleusius, bishop of Cyzicus, spoke as follows:

"It matters little to the council whether Mark or Basil have transgressed in any way, or whether they or the adherents of Acacius have any accusation to bring against each other. Neither does the trouble devolve upon the council of examining whether their formulary be commendable or otherwise. It is enough to maintain the formulary which has been already confirmed at Antioch by ninety-seven priests, and if any one desire to introduce any doctrine which is not contained therein, he ought to be ejected from the church."

Those who were of his sentiments applauded his speech, and the assembly arose and separated. The following day, the partisans of Acacius and of George refused to attend the council, and Leonas, who had now openly declared himself to be of their sentiments, likewise refused, in spite of all entreaties, to repair thither. Those who were deputed to request his attendance found the partisans of Acacius in his house, and he declined their invitation, under the plea that too much discord prevailed in the council, and that he had only been commanded by the emperor to attend the council in case of unanimity among the members. Much time was consumed in this way, and the partisans of Acacius were frequently solicited by the other bishops to attend the assemblies. But they sometimes demanded a special conference in the house of Leonas, and sometimes alleged that they had been commissioned by the emperor to judge those who had been accused, for they would not receive the creed[5] adopted by the other bishops, nor justify themselves of the crimes of which they had been accused. Neither would they examine the case of Cyril, whom they had deposed, and there was no one to compel them to do so. The council, however, eventually deposed George, bishop of Alexandria, Acacius, bishop of Cæsarea, Uranius, bishop of Tyre, Patrophilus, bishop of Scythopolis, Eudoxius, bishop of Antioch, and several other prelates. Many persons were likewise put out of communion until they could vindicate themselves of the crimes imputed to them. The bishops of every church were informed, in writing, of the transactions of the council. Adrian, a presbyter of Antioch, was ordained bishop over that church in room of Eudoxius, but the partisans of Acacius arrested him and delivered him over to Leonas and Laurentius. They committed him into the custody of the soldiers, but afterwards sent him into exile.

We have now given a brief account of the termination of the council of Seleucia. Those who desire more detailed information must seek it in the acts of the council, which have been transcribed by notaries.

NOTES

1. Compare Socrates, *Ecclesiastical History,* Book II, Chapter 39.
2. See above, note on Chapter 13.
3. See above, Chapter 16.
4. Valesius observes that this form of faith, put out by Acacius, is reckoned by Epiphanius in the heresy of the Semiarians, and that he adds the names of the bishops who submitted to it.
5. This is spoken of the party of Acacius so, at least, it is understood by Nicephorus and Valesius.

CHAPTER XXIII
ACACIUS AND ÆTIUS. HOW THE DEPUTIES OF THE TWO COUNCILS OF ARIMINUM AND OF SELEUCIA WERE LED BY THE EMPEROR TO ACCEPT THE SAME DOCTRINES.

Immediately after the above transactions, the adherents of Acacius repaired to the emperor, but the other bishops returned to their respective homes. The ten bishops, who had been unanimously chosen as deputies to the emperor, met on their arrival at the court the ten deputies of the council of Ariminum, and likewise the partisans of Acacius. These latter had gained over to their cause the chief men attached to the palace and, through their influence, had secured the favor of the emperor. It was reported that some of these proselytes had espoused the sentiments of Acacius at some previous period, that some were bribed by means of the wealth belonging to the churches, and that others were seduced by the subtilty of the arguments presented to them and yielded to the power which the Acacians had obtained over their minds.

Acacius was, in fact, no common character. By nature he was gifted with great powers of intellect and eloquence, and he exhibited no want of skill or of address in the accomplishment of his schemes. He was the bishop of a great and illustrious church and could boast of having been the disciple, as well as the successor of Eusebius Pamphilus, in whose literary fame he participated. Endowed with all these advantages, he succeeded with ease in whatever he undertook.

As there were, at this period, ten deputies from each council at Constantinople besides many other bishops who, from various motives, had repaired to the city, Honoratus,[1] whom the emperor before his departure from the East, had constituted chief governor of Constantinople, received directions to examine, in conjunction with some senators, the reports circulated concerning Ætius and his heresy. Constantius, with some of the rulers, eventually undertook the investigation of this case and as it was proved that Ætius had introduced dogmas essentially opposed to the faith, the indignation of the emperor and of the other judges was strongly excited. It is said that the partisans of Acacius at first feigned ignorance of this heresy, for the purpose of inducing the emperor and those around him to take cognizance of it, for they imagined that the eloquence of Ætius would be irresistible, that he would infallibly succeed in convincing his auditory and that his heresy would be triumphant. When, however, the result proved the futility of their expectations, they demanded that the formulary of faith accepted by the council of Ariminum should receive the sanction of the deputies from the council of Seleucia. As these latter protested that they would never renounce the use of the term "substance," the Acacians declared to them upon oath, that they did not hold the Son to be in substance dissimilar from the Father, but that on the contrary they were ready to denounce this opinion as heresy. They added that they esteemed the formulary compiled by the Western bishops at Ariminum the more highly because the word "substance" had been unexpectedly expunged from it because, they said, if this formulary were to be received, there would be no further mention either of the word "substance" or of the term "consubstantial," to which many of the Western priests were, from their reverence for the Nicæan council, peculiarly attached. It was for these reasons that the emperor approved of the formulary, and when he recalled to mind the great number of bishops who had been convened at Ariminum and reflected that there is no error in saying either that "the Son is like unto the Father," or "of the same substance as the Father,"[2] and when he further considered that no difference in signification would ensue if, for terms which do not occur in Scripture, other equivalent and uncontrovertible expressions were to be substituted, (such, for instance, as the word "similar,") he determined upon giving his sanction to the formulary. Such being his own sentiments, he commanded the bishops to accept the formulary.

The next day preparations were made for the pompous ceremony of proclaiming him consul which, according to the Roman custom, took place in the beginning of the month of January, and the whole of that day and part of the ensuing night the emperor spent with the bishops, and at length succeeded in persuading the deputies of the council of Seleucia to receive the formulary of the council of Ariminum.

NOTES

1. Concerning this Honoratus, see the *Fasti* of Hydatius, under the consulship of Eusebius and Hypatius, AD 360.
2. Valesius is of opinion that this passage is probably corrupt. His proposed emendation, however, is far from satisfactory.

CHAPTER XXIV

FORMULARY OF THE COUNCIL OF ARIMINUM APPROVED BY THE ACACIANS. LIST OF THE DEPOSED ARCHBISHOPS, AND THE CAUSES OF THEIR CONDEMNATION.

The partisans of Acacius[1] remained some time at Constantinople, and invited thither several bishops of Bithynia, among whom were Maris, bishop of Chalcedon, and Ulphilas, bishop of the Goths. These prelates having assembled together in number about fifty, they confirmed the formulary read at the council of Ariminum, adding this provision that the terms "substance "and "hypostasis" should never again be used in reference to God. They also declared that all other formularies set forth in times past, as likewise those that might be compiled at any future period, should be condemned. They then deposed Ætius from his office of deacon, because he had written works full of contention, and of a species of vain knowledge opposed to the ecclesiastical vocation, because he had used in writing and in disputation several impious expressions, and because he had been the cause of troubles and seditions in the church. It was alleged by many that they did not depose him willingly, but merely because they wished to remove all suspicion from the mind of the emperor that they favored his doctrines.

Those who held these sentiments took advantage of the resentment with which, for reasons above mentioned, the emperor regarded Macedonius, and they accordingly deposed him, and likewise Eleusius, bishop of Cyzicus, Basil, bishop of Ancyra, Heortasius, bishop of Sardis, and Dracontius, bishop of Pergamus. Although they differed in opinion from these prelates, yet they did not assign dissimilarity of religious sentiment as the cause of their deposition, but merely stated, in general terms, that they had disturbed the peace and violated the laws of the church. They specified, in particular, that when the presbyter Diogenes was travelling from Alexandria to Ancyra, Basil seized his papers, and struck him, they also deposed that Basil had unjustly delivered over many of the clergy from Antioch, from the banks of the Euphrates, and from Cilicia, Galatia, and Asia, to the rulers of the provinces to be exiled and subjected to cruel punishments, so that many had been loaded with chains and compelled to bribe the soldiers who held them in custody not to ill-use them. They added that on one occasion, when the emperor had commanded Ætius and some of his followers to be conducted before Cecropius, that they might answer to him for various accusations laid to their charge, Basil recommended the person who was intrusted with the execution of this edict to act according to the dictates of his own judgment. They said that be wrote directions to Hermogenes,[2] the prefect and governor of Syria, stating who were to be banished, and whither they were to be sent, and that when the exiles were recalled by the emperor, he would not consent to their return but opposed himself to the wishes of the rulers and of the priests.

They further deposed that Basil had excited the clergy of Sirmium against Germanius, and that although he stated in writing that he had admitted Germanius, Valens, and Ursacius into communion, he had placed them as criminals before the tribunal of the African bishops. And that when taxed with this deed, he had denied it and perjured himself, and that when he was afterwards convicted, he strove to screen himself by sophistical reasoning. They added that he had been the cause of contention and of sedition in Illyria, Italy, Africa, and in the Roman church, that he had thrown a servant into prison to compel her to bear false witness against her mistress, that he had baptized a man of loose life who lived in illicit intercourse with a woman and had promoted him to be a deacon, that he had neglected to excommunicate a quack-doctor[3] who had occasioned the death of several persons, and that he and some of the clergy had bound themselves by oath before the holy altar not to bring accusations against each other. This, they said, was an artifice adopted by the clergy to shield themselves from the condemnation they deserved. In short, such were the reasons they specified for the deposition of Basil.

Eustathius, they said, was deposed because, when a presbyter, he had been condemned and put away from the communion of prayers by Eulalius, his own father, who was bishop of Cæsarea in Cappadocia, and also because he had been excommunicated by a council held at Neocæsarea, a city of Pontus and deposed by Eusebius, bishop of Constantinople, for unfaithfulness in the discharge of certain duties that had devolved upon him. He had also been deprived of his bishopric by the council of Gangris on account of his having believed, taught, and acted contrary to sound doctrine. He had been convicted of perjury by the council of Antioch.[4] He had likewise endeavored to reverse the decrees of the bishops convened at Melitina and, although he was guilty of many crimes, had the assurance to aspire to be judge over the others and to stigmatize them as heretics.

They deposed Eleusius because he had raised one Heraclius, a native of Tyre, to be a deacon. This man had been a priest of Hercules at Tyre had been accused of sorcery, and had retired to Cyzicus and feigned conversion to Christianity. And moreover, Eleusius, after having been apprized of these circumstances, had not excommunicated him. He had also rashly ordained certain individuals who had been condemned by Maris, bishop of Chalcedonia, who was present at this council.

Heortasius was deposed because he had been ordained bishop of Sardis without the sanction of the bishops of Lydia. They deposed Dracontius, bishop of Pergamus, because he had previously held another bishopric in Galatia and because, they stated, he had on both occasions been unlawfully ordained.

After these transactions, a second assembly of the council was held, and Silvanus, bishop of Tarsus, Sophronius, bishop of Pompeiopolis in Paphlagonia, Elpidus, bishop of Satalis, and Neonas, bishop of Seleucia in Isauria, were deposed. The reason they assigned for the deposition of Silvanus was, that he had constituted himself the leader of a party and had deceived many in Seleucia and Constantinople. He had, besides, bestowed the bishopric of Castabalis on Theophilus, who had been previously ordained bishop of Eleutheropolis by the bishops of Palestine and who had promised upon oath that he would never accept any other bishopric without their permission.

Sophronius was deposed on account of his avarice and on account of his having sold some of the offerings presented to the church for his own profit, besides, after he had received three commands to appear before the council, he could, at last, be scarcely induced to make his appearance, and then instead of replying to the accusations brought against him, he appealed to other judges.

Neonas was deposed for having resorted to violence in his endeavors to procure the ordination in his own church of Annian, who had been appointed bishop of Antioch,[5] and for having ordained as bishops certain individuals who had previously been *decemviri*,[6] and who were utterly ignorant of the Holy Scriptures and of ecclesiastical canons, and who after their ordination, preferred the enjoyment of their property to that of the priestly dignity, and declared in writing that they would rather take charge of their own possessions than devote themselves exclusively to episcopal duties.

Elpidus was deposed because he had participated in the malpractices of Basil and had occasioned great disorders, and because he had, contrary to the decrees of the council of Melitina, restored to his former rank in the presbytery a man named Eusebius, who had been deposed for having created Nectaria a deaconess after she had been excommunicated on account of perjury, and to confer this honor upon her was clearly contrary to the laws of the church.

NOTES

1. Compare Socrates, *Ecclesiastical History,* Book II, Chapter 41.
2. Further mention is made of this Hermogenes by Ammianus Marcellinus, *History*, Book XIX.
3. περιοδευτήν. Latin "circumforaneum," an empiric.
4. Of this council Valesius remarks, "mihi prorsus ignota est." The council at Melitina, a few lines below, is mentioned by Basil, Epistle 79, *ad Occident.* In this synod, most probably, Eustathius was deposed.
5. Namely, upon the deposition of Eudoxius.
6. *Note to the 2018 edition: Decemviri* is a term used at this point in Roman history to denote leaders of metropolitan senates in various cities throughout the empire. As wealthy political leaders, these men would have been particularly ill-suited to the episcopacy.

CHAPTER XXV

CAUSES OF THE DEPOSITION OF CYRIL, BISHOP OF JERUSALEM. MUTUAL DISSENSIONS AMONG THE BISHOPS. MELETIUS IS ORDAINED BY THE ARIANS, AND SUPPLANTS EUSTATHIUS IN THE BISHOPRIC OF SEBASTE.

Besides the prelates above mentioned, Cyril, bishop of Jerusalem, was deposed[1] because he had admitted Eustathius and Elpidus into communion after they had opposed the decrees enacted by the bishops at Melitina, among whom was Cyril himself, and because he had also received Basil and George, bishop of Laodicea, into communion after their deposition in Palestine. When Cyril was first installed in the bishopric of Jerusalem, he had a dispute with Acacius,[2] bishop of Cæsarea, concerning his right to the title of a Metropolitan which he claimed on the ground of his bishopric being an apostolical see. This dispute excited feelings of enmity between the two bishops, and they mutually accused each other of unsoundness of doctrine concerning the Godhead. In fact, they had both been suspected, the one, that is Acacius, of favoring the heresy of Arius, and the other of siding with those who maintain that the Son is in substance like unto the Father. Acacius being thus inimically disposed towards Cyril and finding himself supported by the bishops of Palestine who were of the same sentiments as himself, contrived to depose Cyril under the following pretext. Jerusalem and the neighboring country was at one time visited with a famine, and the poor appealed in great multitudes to Cyril, as their bishop, for food. As he had no money to purchase the requisite provisions, he sold for this purpose the veil and sacred ornaments of the church. It is said that a man having recognized an offering which he had presented at the altar as forming part of the costume of an actress, made it his business to inquire whence it was procured, and ascertained that a merchant had sold it to the actress, and that the bishop had sold it to the merchant. It was under this pretext, I understand, that Acacius deposed Cyril.

It is said that the Acacians then expelled all the bishops who had been deposed from Constantinople. Ten bishops of their own party who had refused to subscribe to these edicts of deposition were separated from the others and were interdicted from performing the functions of the ministry or ruling their churches until they consented to give their signatures. It was enacted that unless they complied within six months and yielded their assent to all the decrees of the council, they should be deposed, and that the bishops of every province should be summoned to elect other bishops in their stead. Letters were then sent to all the bishops and clergy detailing the transactions of the council and exhorting them to observe and obey his decrees. Soon afterwards a fresh election of bishops took place, in the room of those who had been deposed. Eudoxius took possession of the bishopric of Macedonius, Athanasius was placed over the church of Basil, and Eunomius, who was subsequently the leader of a faction and the originator of a heresy which bears his name, was appointed to the bishopric of Sebaste, instead of Meletius.

NOTES

1. Compare Socrates, *Ecclesiastical History,* Book II, Chapter 40.
2. Acacius grounded his claims as metropolitan over Jerusalem on ancient custom, and the 7th canon of the council of Nicæa, which ordained that Jerusalem should be subject to Cæsarea.

CHAPTER XXVI
DEATH OF MACEDONIUS, BISHOP OF CONSTANTINOPLE. EUDOXIUS AND ACACIUS STRENUOUSLY SEEK THE ABOLITION OF THE FORMULARIES OF FAITH SET FORTH AT NICÆA AND AT ARIMINUM. TROUBLES WHICH THENCE AROSE IN THE CHURCH.

Macedonius,[1] on his expulsion from the church of Constantinople, retired to one of the suburbs of the city where he died. Eudoxius took possession of his church in the tenth year of the consulate of Constantius, and the third of Julian, surnamed Cæsar. It is related that at the consecration of the great church called "Sophia" when he arose to teach the people, he commenced his discourse with the following proposition: The Father is impious, the Son is pious," and that, as these words excited a great commotion among the people, he added, "Be calm. The Father is impious, because he worships no one. The Son is pious, because he worships the Father." This explanation excited laughter among the audience.

Eudoxius and Acacius exerted themselves to the utmost in endeavoring to cause the edicts of the Nicene council to fall into disuse and oblivion. They sent the formulary read at Ariminum, with various alterations and additions of their own, to every province of the empire and procured from the emperor an edict for the banishment of all who should refuse to subscribe to it. But this undertaking, which appeared to them so easy of execution, was the source of the greatest calamities, excited commotions throughout the empire, and entailed upon the church in every region a persecution more grievous than those which it had suffered under the Pagan emperors. For, if this persecution did not occasion such tortures and punishments to the body as preceding ones, it appeared more grievous to all who reflected aright on account of its disgraceful nature, for both the persecutors and the persecuted belonged to the church, and men of the same religion treated their fellows with a degree of cruelty which the ecclesiastical laws prohibit to be manifested towards enemies and strangers.

NOTE

1. Compare Socrates, *Ecclesiastical History,* Book II, Chapter 43.

CHAPTER XXVII

MACEDONIUS, AFTER HIS REJECTION FROM HIS BISHOPRIC, BLASPHEMES AGAINST THE HOLY GHOST. PROPAGATION OF HIS HERESY THROUGH THE INSTRUMENTALITY OF MARATHONIUS AND OTHERS.

When the spirit of innovation becomes regarded with popular favor,[1] it is scarcely possible to arrest its progress. Inflated as it always is with arrogance, it contemns the institutions of the Fathers, and enacts laws of its own. It even despises the theological doctrines of antiquity, and seeks out zealously a new form of religion of its own devising. After Macedonius had been deposed from the church of Constantinople, he renounced the tenets of Acacius and Eudoxius. He began to teach that the Son is God, and that he is in all respects and in substance like unto the Father. But he affirmed that the Holy Ghost is inferior in dignity, and designated him a minister and a servant, and applied to him whatever could, without error, be said of the holy angels.

This doctrine was embraced by Eleusius, Eustathius, and by all the other bishops who had been deposed at Constantinople by the partisans of the opposite heresy. Their example was quickly followed by the people of Constantinople, Thrace, Bithynia, the Hellespont, and of the neighboring provinces. For their manners and mode of life were calculated to produce a great impression on the multitude. They assumed great gravity of demeanor and austerity of life while their style of conversation was pleasing and persuasive. It is said that all these qualifications were united in Marathonius. He originally held a public appointment in the army under the command of the prefects.[2] After amassing some money in this employment, he undertook the superintendence of the hospitals for the relief of the sick and the destitute. Afterwards, at the suggestion of Eustathius, bishop of Sebaste, he embraced an ascetic mode of life, and founded a monastical institution in Constantinople which exists to the present day. He brought so much zeal and wealth to the support of the aforesaid heresy, that the Macedonians were by many termed Marathonians, and it seems to me not without reason, for it appears that without the efforts of Marathonius, the heresy would soon have become extinct. In fact, after the deposition of Macedonius, the Macedonians possessed neither churches nor bishops[3] until the reign of Arcadius. The Arians, who excommunicated and rigorously persecuted all who held different sentiments from themselves, deprived them of all these privileges.

It would be no easy task to enumerate the names of the priests who were at this period ejected from their cities, for I believe that no province of the empire was exempted from these depositions.

NOTES

1. Compare Socrates, *Ecclesiastical History,* Book II, Chapter 45.
2. Valesius says: "Id est, ex numerario officii præfectorum prætorio." Conf. Ammianus Marcellinus, *History,* Book XV, page 84.
3. That is, as Valesius remarks, at Constantinople. Compare Baronius, *Ecclesiastical Annals,* AD 360, Chapter 19.

CHAPTER XXVIII

THE ARIANS, UNDER THE IMPRESSION THAT THE HOLY MELETIUS UPHELD THEIR SENTIMENTS, TRANSLATE HIM FROM SEBASTE TO ANTIOCH. ON HIS PREACHING THE ORTHODOX DOCTRINES, HE IS DEPOSED, AND HIS BISHOPRIC TRANSFERRED TO EUZOIUS.

At the period that Eudoxius obtained the government of the church of Constantinople,[1] there were many aspirants to the bishopric of Antioch and, as is frequently the case under such circumstances, discord and contention divided the clergy and the people of that church. Each party was anxious to commit the government of the church to a bishop of its own persuasion, for interminable disputes concerning doctrine were rampant among them, and they could not agree as to the mode of singing psalms and, as has been before stated, psalms were sung by each individual in conformity with his own peculiar creed. Such being the state of the church of Antioch, the partisans of Eudoxius thought that it would be well to intrust the bishopric of that city to Meletius, then bishop of Sebaste, he being possessed of great and persuasive eloquence, of eminent virtue, and above all, as they imagined, being firmly attached to their tenets. They believed that his fame would attract the inhabitants of Antioch and of the neighboring cities to conform to their heresy, particularly the sectarians called Eustathians who had invariably adhered to the Nicene doctrines. But their expectations were utterly frustrated.

It is said that on his first arrival in Antioch, an immense multitude composed of Arians and of those who were in communion with Paulinus, flocked around him. Some were drawn by curiosity, desiring to know whether his merits were equivalent to the great reputation he enjoyed. Others were anxious to hear what he had to say and to ascertain the nature of his opinions, for a report had been spread abroad, which was afterwards proved to be true, that he maintained the doctrines of the council of Nicæa. In his first discourses, he confined himself to instructing the people in what we call ethics. Afterwards, however, he openly declared that the Son is of the same substance as the Father. It is said that at these words, the archdeacon of the church stretched out his hand and covered the mouth of the preacher, but that he continued to explain his sentiments more clearly by means of his fingers than he could by language. He extended three fingers towards the people, closed them, and then allowed only one finger to remain extended, and thus expressed by signs what he was prevented from uttering. As the archdeacon freed his mouth in order to seize his hand, he unfolded his doctrine with still greater perspicuity than before and exhorted his auditors to adhere to the tenets of the council of Nicæa, assuring them that they would deviate from the truth if they followed any other doctrines. As he persisted in the enunciation of the same sentiments, either by word of mouth, or by means of signs when the archdeacon closed his mouth, the followers of Eustathius testified their joy by loud acclamations, while the Arians gave evident proofs of dissatisfaction.

Eudoxius and his partisans were transported with indignation at this discourse, and contrived by their machinations to expel Meletius from Antioch. Soon afterwards, however, they recalled him, for they fancied that he had renounced his former sentiments and had espoused theirs. As, however, it soon became apparent that his devotion to the Nicene doctrines was firm and unalterable, he was ejected from the church and banished by order of the emperor, and his bishopric was conferred on Euzoius who had formerly been banished with Arius. The followers of Meletius separated themselves from the Arians and held their assemblies apart, for those who had from the beginning, maintained that the Son is consubstantial with the Father, refused to admit them into communion, because Meletius had been ordained by Arian bishops, and because his followers had been baptized by Arian priests. For these reasons, although united by the reception of one creed, they did not hold communion together.

The emperor, having been informed that an insurrection was about to arise in Persia, repaired to Antioch.

NOTE

1. Compare Socrates, *Ecclesiastical History,* Book II, Chapter 44.

CHAPTER XXIX

THE PARTISANS OF ACACIUS EXCITE FRESH COMMOTIONS, STRIVE TO ABOLISH THE TERM "CONSUBSTANTIAL," AND FAVOR THE HERESY OF ARIUS.

The partisans of Acacius were not able to remain in tranquillity, and they therefore assembled in Antioch and condemned the decrees which they had themselves enacted. They erased the term "similar" from the formulary which had been read at Ariminum and at Constantinople and affirmed that in all respects, in substance and in will, the Son is dissimilar from the Father, and that he proceeded from what had no previous existence, even as Arius had taught from the commencement. They were joined by the partisans of Ætius, who had been the first after Arius to venture upon the profession of these opinions, and who had hence obtained the name of atheists. The disciples of Arius were sometimes called Anomians and Exucontians.[1] When those who maintained the Nicene doctrines demanded of the Acacians how they could say that the Son is dissimilar from the Father and that he proceeded out of nothing, when it was affirmed in their own formulary that he is "God of God," they replied that the apostle Paul had declared that "All things are of God,"[2] and that the Son is included in the term "all things" and that it was in this sense and in accordance with the Sacred Scriptures, that the expressions in their formulary were to be understood. Such were the equivocations and sophistry to which they had recourse.

At length, finding that they could advance no efficient argument to justify themselves in the opinion of those who pressed them on this point, they withdrew from the assembly, after the formulary of Constantinople had been read a second time, and returned to their own cities.

NOTES

1. The same statement is made by Athanasius in his book *De Synodis Arimini et Seleuciæ*.
2. 1 Corinthians 11:12.

CHAPTER XXX

GEORGE, BISHOP OF ANTIOCH, AND THE BISHOP OF JERUSALEM. AFTER THE DEPOSITION OF CYRIL, THREE BISHOPS SUCCESSIVELY SUCCEED TO HIS BISHOPRIC. RESTORATION OF CYRIL TO THE CHURCH AT JERUSALEM.

During this period, Athanasius was obliged to remain in concealment,[1] and George returned to Alexandria and commenced a cruel persecution against the Pagans and against the Christians who differed from him in opinion. He compelled both parties to offer worship in the mode he indicated, and where opposition was made he enforced obedience by compulsion. He was hated by the rulers on account of his assumption and arrogance, and the multitude detested him on account of his tyranny and power. The Pagans regarded him with even greater aversion than the Christians, because he prohibited them from offering sacrifices, and from celebrating their ancient festivals, and because he had on one occasion introduced the governor of Egypt[2] and armed soldiery into the city, and despoiled their temples. This was, in fact, as we shall hereafter see, the cause of his death.

On the deposition of Cyril, Herennius obtained the bishopric of Jerusalem.[3] He was succeeded by Heraclius, and to Heraclius succeeded Hilarius, but on the accession of the emperor Theodosius, Cyril was again installed in his bishopric.

NOTES

1. Compare Socrates, *Ecclesiastical History*, Book II, Chapter 28, and Book III, Chapter 2.
2. Namely, Artemius, who was afterwards martyred under Julian.
3. Compare Socrates, ibid. *Ecclesiastical History*, Book IV, Chapter 25. Epiphanius places another Cyril after Herennius.

BOOK V

CHAPTER I
APOSTASY OF JULIAN. DEATH OF THE EMPEROR CONSTANTIUS.

We have now described[1] the transactions which took place in the Eastern churches. About the period we have been passing under review, Julian attacked and conquered the barbarians who dwelt on the banks of the Rhine. Many fell in battle, and the others he took prisoners. As this victory added greatly to his fame, and as his moderation and gentleness had endeared him to the troops, they proclaimed him emperor. Far from seeking to obtain the consent of Constantius to this nomination, he displaced the officers by whom he had been elected, and industriously circulated letters wherein Constantius had solicited the barbarians to enter the Roman territories and aid him against Magnentius. He then suddenly changed his religion and, although he had previously professed Christianity, he declared himself high priest, frequented the Pagan temples, offered sacrifices, and invited his subjects to adopt his own form of worship.

As an invasion by the Persians was expected, and as Constantius had on this account repaired to Syria, Julian conceived that he might easily render himself master of Illyria. He therefore set out on his journey to this province, under pretence that he intended to present an apology to Constantius for having, without his sanction, received the symbols of imperial power. It is said that when he arrived on the borders of Illyria, he found the vines loaded with green grapes, although the time of the vintage was past, and the Pleiades had sunk to the West, and that there fell upon him and his followers a kind of dew, of which each drop bore the sign of the cross. He and those with him regarded the grapes as a favorable omen and attributed the phenomenon of the dew to chance. Others thought that the green grapes signified that Julian would die prematurely after a very short reign, and that the crosses formed by the drops of dew indicated that the Christian religion is from heaven, and that all persons, whoever they may be, ought to receive the sign of the cross. I am, for my own part, convinced that those who regarded these two phenomena as unfavorable omens for Julian were not mistaken, and events proved the accuracy of their opinion.

When Constantius heard that Julian was marching against him at the head of an army, he abandoned his intended expedition against the Persians and departed for Constantinople. But he died on the journey, when he had arrived as far as

Mopsucrenes, which lies near Taurus between Cilicia and Cappadocia. He died in the forty-fifth year of his age, after reigning thirteen years conjointly with Constantine his father, and twenty-five years after the death of that emperor.

Immediately on the decease of Constantius, Julian, who had already made himself master of Thrace, entered Constantinople, and was proclaimed emperor. Pagans assert that diviners and demons had predicted the death of Constantius, and his consequent elevation, before his departure for Galatia, and had advised him to undertake the expedition. This might have been regarded as a true prediction, had not the life of Julian been terminated so shortly afterwards, and when he had only enjoyed the imperial power as in a dream. But it appears to me absurd to believe that after he had heard the death of Constantius predicted and had been warned that it would be his own fate to fall in battle by the hands of the Persians, he should have marched voluntarily to meet his own death, particularly as no advantage could accrue to him and as his name would only be handed down to posterity as that of an inexperienced emperor, utterly unacquainted with the art of war and who, had he lived, would probably have suffered the greater part of the Roman territories to fall under the Persian yoke. This observation, however, is only inserted lest I should be blamed for omitting it. I leave every one to form his own opinion on the subject.

NOTE

1. With this chapter compare Socrates, *Ecclesiastical History,* Book II, last chapter, and Book III, Chapter 1.

CHAPTER II

EDUCATION AND LIFE OF JULIAN, AND HIS ACCESSION TO THE EMPIRE.

Immediately after the death of Constantius, the dread of a persecution arose in the church, and Christians suffered more anguish from the anticipation of this calamity than they would have experienced from its actual occurrence. This state of feeling proceeded from the long peace they had enjoyed, from the remembrance of the cruelties which had been exercised by the tyrants upon their fathers, and from their knowledge of the hatred with which Julian regarded their doctrines. It is said that he renounced the faith of Christ with the utmost profanity and had recourse to sacrifices and sanguinary expiations to efface his baptism and wipe away from himself the sacrament of the church. From that period he employed himself in auguries, and in the celebration of the Pagan rites, both publicly and privately. It is related that one day, as he was inspecting the entrails of a victim, he beheld among them a cross encompassed with a crown. This appearance terrified those who were assisting in the ceremony, for they judged that it indicated the triumph of religion, and the eternal duration of the doctrines of Christianity. They considered that the crown is in itself the symbol of victory, and that as it encircled the cross, and returned as it were into itself without beginning or end, it typified eternity. The chief augur, however, tried to reassure the emperor by insisting that no unfavorable omens were indicated by the appearance of the entrails,[1] but that on the contrary, it might be thence inferred that the Christian sect would be confined within very narrow limits, beyond which all extension would be impossible.

I have also heard, that one day Julian descended into a noted and terrific cavern, either for the purpose of participating in some ceremony or of consulting an oracle, and that by means of machinery, or of enchantment, such frightful spectres appeared before him that, losing all reflection and presence of mind, he thoughtlessly made the sign of the cross, according to the custom of Christians in time of danger. Immediately the spectres disappeared, and the ceremony was arrested. The officiating priest was at first surprised at the disappearance of the spectres, but when apprized of the cause, he declared that it was a profanation and after exhorting the emperor not to fear or to have recourse to anything connected with the Christian religion, he re-commenced the ceremony.

The extravagant attachment which Julian evinced towards the Pagan rites was extremely displeasing to the Christians, more especially on account of his having been himself formerly a Christian. He was born of pious parents, had been baptized in infancy according to the custom of the church, and had been brought up in the knowledge of the Holy Scriptures under the guidance of priests and bishops.[2] He and Gallus were the sons of Constantius, the brother of Constantine the emperor, and of Dalmatius. Dalmatius had a son of the same name, who was declared Cæsar, and was slain by the soldiery after the death of Constantius. His fate would have been shared by Gallus and Julian, who were then orphans, had not Gallus been spared on account of a disease under which he was laboring and which appeared to be hopeless, and Julian on account of his extreme youth, for he was but eight years of age.

After this wonderful preservation, a residence was assigned to the two brothers in a palace called Macella, situated in Cappadocia near Mount Argeus, and not far from Cæsarea. It was a magnificent edifice and adorned with gardens, baths, and fountains. Here they were educated in a manner corresponding to the dignity of their birth. They were taught the sciences and bodily exercises befitting their age and had masters to instruct them in sacred and in profane literature. Such was their progress that they were enrolled among the clergy and permitted to read the ecclesiastical books to the people. Their habits and mode of life indicated no dereliction from piety. They respected the clergy and other good and zealous persons, they repaired regularly to church, and rendered due homage to the tombs of the martyrs. It is said that they undertook to deposit the tomb of Saint Mammas[3] the martyr in a large edifice, and to perform all the labor themselves, and that while they were, in emulation of the martyr, laboring to surpass him in piety, an event occurred which was so astonishing that it would indeed be utterly incredible were it not for the testimony of many who are still among us, and who were eye-witnesses of the transaction. The part of the edifice upon which Gallus labored advanced rapidly, as might have been expected, towards completion. But the portion upon which Julian labored fell into ruin. In one part the stones were detached from the foundations, and in another the foundations themselves were forced from the earth, as if ejected by some secret power. This was universally regarded as a prodigy. The people, however, drew no conclusion from it till subsequent events had manifested its import.

There were a few who, from that moment, doubted the reality of Julian's religion and suspected that he only made an outward profession of religion for fear of displeasing the emperor, and that he concealed his own sentiments because it was not safe to divulge them. It is asserted that he was first led to renounce the religion of his fathers by his intimacy and intercourse with diviners, for when the resentment of Constantius against the two brothers was abated, Gallus went to Asia and took up his residence in Ephesus where the greater part of his property was situated, and Julian repaired to Constantinople and frequented the schools where his natural abilities and great acquirements did not remain concealed. He appeared in public in the garb of a private individual, and was sociable and easy of access. But because he was related to the emperor and was capable of holding the reins of empire, and because many expected him to succeed to the imperial dignity and publicly expressed their wishes to this effect, he was commanded to leave this populous city, and retire to Nicomedia. Here he became acquainted with Maximus, an Ephesian philosopher, who instructed him in philosophy, and inspired him with hatred towards the Christian religion and, moreover, assured him that he would one day attain to empire, whither his own hopes and the wishes of the people already tended. Julian was gratified and cheered in the midst of his adverse circumstances by this announcement and contracted an intimate friendship with Maximus.

As these occurrences reached the ears of Constantius, Julian became apprehensive of receiving ill-treatment, and accordingly shaved himself, and adopted externally the monkish mode of life, while he secretly abandoned himself to Pagan superstitions. When he arrived at the age of manhood, his infatuation for Paganism increased and admiring the art (if there be such an art) of predicting the future, he endeavored to make himself acquainted with it and in his researches had recourse to experiments from which Christians are prohibited. From this period, he manifested great regard towards those who held Pagan sentiments, and after his arrival in Egypt he addicted himself with incredible ardor to superstitious observances.

When Gallus, his brother, who had been surnamed Cæsar, was put to death on account of certain innovations which he designed to introduce into the empire, Julian incurred the suspicion of Constantius, who imagined that he was aiming at the possession of imperial power and therefore put him under the custody of guards. Eusebia, the wife of Constantius, obtained for him permission to retire to Athens, and he accordingly repaired thither and, under pretence of receiving instruction from the philosophers, he consulted diviners concerning his future prospects. Constantius recalled him shortly afterwards, proclaimed him Cæsar, promised him his sister Constantina[4] in marriage, and sent him to Gaul, where the barbarians, whose aid had been implored by Constantius against Magnentius, finding that their services were not required, had fixed their residence. As Julian was very young, generals in whom the chief responsibility was vested were sent with him. But as these generals abandoned themselves to indolence and inaction, Julian assumed the entire conduct of the expedition, used every means to animate the courage of his soldiers, and encouraged them more especially by promising a reward to all who should slay a barbarian. After he had thus secured the affections of the soldiery, he wrote to Constantius, acquainting him with the misconduct of the generals, and when at his request, other generals were sent to take their place, he attacked the barbarians and obtained the victory. They sent to beg for peace and showed the letter in which Constantius had requested them to enter the Roman dominions. But instead of dismissing the ambassador, Julian detained him and, seizing a favorable opportunity for giving battle, he gained another victory.

Some have imagined that Constantius sent Julian on this expedition for the express purpose of exposing him to danger, but this does not appear probable to me. For, as it rested with Constantius alone to nominate him Cæsar, why did he confer that title upon him if he intended to take his life? Or, why did he promise him his sister in marriage, or receive his complaints against the inefficiency of his generals, and send others to displace them? No doubt he was actuated by feelings of regard towards Julian, and by the desire that he should be successful in his expedition. It seems to me that he conferred on him the title of Cæsar from motives of attachment, but that after Julian had without his sanction been proclaimed emperor, he was not averse to exposing him to the perils of the war against the barbarians who had possessed themselves of the banks of the Rhine. And this, I think, resulted from the dread that Julian would seek revenge for the ill-treatment he and his brother Gallus had experienced during their youth, as well as from the apprehension that he would aspire to participation in the government of the empire. But many various opinions are entertained on this subject.

NOTES

1. Valesius observes that this and the following story are recorded also by Gregory Nazianzenus, in his *Invective against Julian*.
2. Julian was brought up at Nicomedia under Eusebius, bishop of that see, who was also nearly related to him by blood. See Ammianus Marcellinus, *History*, Book XVII, page 219.
3. The name of this saint is held in high repute in the Eastern church, but very little is known of the facts of his life. He is said by Gregory Nazianzenus (Oration 43) and by Basil (Homily 26) to have been a shepherd and also a martyr. The miraculous story here related is given also by Gregory Nazianzenus in his third *Oration against Julian*, though he does not mention the martyr's name. It is probable that he suffered about AD 274.
4. Sozomen is mistaken here, as Constantina was married to Gallus Cæsar, the brother of Julian. We ought to read Helena.

CHAPTER III

JULIAN, ON HIS ACCESSION TO THE THRONE, SOUGHT TO SUPPRESS CHRISTIANITY AND TO PROMOTE PAGANISM.

When Julian found himself sole possessor of the empire, he commanded that all the Pagan temples should be re-opened throughout the East, that those which had been neglected should be repaired, that those which had fallen into ruins should be rebuilt, and that the altars should be restored. He assigned money[1] for this purpose. He restored the customs of antiquity and the practice of offering sacrifice. He himself offered libations and sacrifices in the temples, bestowed honors on those who were zealous in the performance of these ceremonies, re-established the priests[2] and ministers[3] of idols in the enjoyment of their former privileges, and exempted them from the payment of public taxes. He revived the pensions formerly granted to those who guarded the temples and commanded them to abstain from certain meats and from whatever the Pagans represented as inimical to purity. He also commanded that the admeasurements of the Nile and the symbols[4] should be conveyed according to ancient usage to the temple of Serapis, instead of being deposited, according to the regulations established by Constantine, in the church.[5] He wrote frequently to the inhabitants of those cities in which the observance of Pagan rites was retained, and urged them to proffer any request that they might desire.

Towards the Christians, on the contrary, he openly manifested his aversion, refusing to honor them with his presence, to give audience to their deputies, or to listen to their complaints. When the inhabitants of Nisibis sent to implore his aid against the Persians, who were on the point of invading the Roman territories, he refused to assist them because they would neither re-open their temples, nor resort to the priests. He would not receive their embassy, and threatened that he would never visit their city until they returned to Paganism.

He likewise accused the inhabitants of Constantius in Palestine of attachment to Christianity, and rendered their city tributary to that of Gaza. Constantius was formerly called Majuma and was used as a harbor for the vessels of Gaza, but on hearing that the majority of its inhabitants were Christians, Constantine conferred on it the name of his own son, and a separate form of government, for he considered that it ought not to be dependent on Gaza, a city addicted to Pagan rites. On the accession of Julian, the citizens of Gaza went to law against those of Constantius. The emperor decided in favor of Gaza and commanded that Constantius should be an appendage to that city, although it was situated at a distance of twenty stadia. It has since been denominated the maritime region of Gaza.

The two cities have now merged into one, under the same magistrates, chiefs,[6] and public regulations. With respect to ecclesiastical concerns, however, they may still be regarded as two cities. They have each their own bishop and their own clergy. They celebrate festivals in honor of their respective martyrs, and in memory of the priests who successively ruled them. And the boundaries by which the jurisdiction of the bishops are divided are still preserved. It happened within our own remembrance that an attempt was made by the bishop of Gaza, on the death of the bishop of Majuma, to unite the clergy of that town with those under his own jurisdiction, and the plea he advanced was that two bishops were not required to rule over one city. The inhabitants of Majuma opposed this scheme, and the council of the province took cognizance of the dispute and ordained another bishop. The council proceeded upon the assumption that it would be unjust to set aside the ecclesiastical privileges of a city which had been deprived of its civil rights by the edict of a Pagan emperor merely on account of its adherence to the laws of the church. But these events occurred at a later period than that now under review.

NOTES

1. φόρους, regular payments: not new taxes.
2. μύσται καὶ ἱερεῖς. The former word, however, is generally used by classical writers for all who were initiated. The term μυσταγωγός would be more accurate. See Valesius' notes on Eusebius, *Life of the Blessed Emperor Constantine,* Book I, Chapter 32.
3. ξοάνων θεραπευταί. Those who clothed the statues of the idols, and other attendants. They were also called ἱεροστολεταί.
4. σύμβολα. There is great doubt as to what is meant by this word here. Valesius takes it as equivalent to idols (εἴδολα). Lowth would render it "charters." Var. Sacr. Par. II, page 395.
5. Compare Socrates, *Ecclesiastical History,* Book I, Chapter 18, and the note of Valesius *in loco.*
6. στρατηγοί, probably the same as the municipal magistrates called *duumviri.*

CHAPTER IV

JULIAN PERSECUTES THE INHABITANTS OF CÆSAREA.
BOLD FIDELITY OF MARIS, BISHOP OF CHALCEDON.

About the same time, the emperor erased Cæsarea, the large and wealthy metropolis of Cappadocia situated near Mount Argeus,[1] from the catalogue of cities and even deprived it of the name of Cæsarea, which had been conferred upon it during the reign of Claudius Cæsar, its former name having been Mazaca.[2] He had long regarded the inhabitants of this city with extreme aversion because they were zealously attached to Christianity, and had formerly destroyed the temple of Apollo and that of Jupiter, the tutelar deity of the city. The temple dedicated to Fortune,[3] the only one remaining in the city, was destroyed after his accession, and on hearing of the deed, his anger against the Christians exceeded all bounds. He also blamed the Pagans, who were few in number but who ought, he said, to have hastened to the temple and to have risked everything in its defense.

He caused all property belonging to the churches of the city and suburbs of Cæsarea to be rigorously sought and carried away: about three hundred pounds of gold, obtained from this source, were conveyed to the public treasury. He also commanded that all the clergy should be enrolled among the troops under the governor of the province, which is accounted the most arduous and least honorable service among the Romans.[4] He ordered the Christian populace to be numbered, women and children inclusive, and imposed taxes upon them as onerous as those to which villages are subjected. He further threatened that unless their temples were speedily re-erected, his wrath would not be appeased but would be visited on the city until none of the Galileans remained in existence, for this was the name which, in derision, he gave to the Christians.

There is no doubt but that his menaces would have been fully executed, had not death intervened. It was not from any feeling of compassion towards the Christians that he treated them at first with greater humanity than had been evinced by former persecutors, but because he had discovered that the Pagans had derived no advantage from their cruelty, while Christianity had been honored by the fortitude of those who died in defense of the faith. It was simply from envy of their glory, that instead of employing fire and the sword against them like former persecutors, and instead of casting them into the sea, or burying them alive in order to compel them to renounce their sentiments, he had recourse to argument and persuasion and sought by these means to seduce them to Paganism. And he expected to gain his ends more easily by abandoning all violent measures and by the manifestation of unexpected benevolence.

It is said that on one occasion, when he was sacrificing in the temple of

Fortune at Constantinople, Maris[5] bishop of Chalcedon, presented himself before him and publicly rebuked him as an irreligious man, an atheist, and an apostate. Julian had nothing in return to reproach him with except his blindness, for his sight was impaired by old age and he was led by a child.

According to his usual custom of uttering blasphemies against Christ, Julian afterwards added in derision, "The Galilean, thy God, will not cure thee."

Maris replied, "I thank God for my blindness, since it prevents me from beholding one who has apostatized from religion."

Julian passed on without giving a reply, for he considered that Paganism would be advanced by the exhibition of greater lenity and mildness towards Christians than could in ordinary circumstances be expected.

NOTES

1. The highest mountain of the country: it lies between Cappadocia and Galatia.
2. Valesius remarks that this was the original Syrian name of the town.
3. τὸ τῆς Τύχης. Scil. ἱερόν. These were called Τύχαια, Tychsea. Gregory Nazianzen, in his first *Oration against Julian*, speaks of the temple dedicated to the genius of this city.
4. There were three kinds of service among the Romans: they were called Palatina, Castrensis, and Cohortalis. The latter ranked as inferior to the other two, and Valesius remarks that it was very profitable. The word δαπανηρὸν must clearly be rendered "arduous," not "expensive."
5. Concerning this Maris, see Socrates, *Ecclesiastical History*, Book III, Chapter 12.

CHAPTER V

JULIAN RESTORES LIBERTY TO THE CHRISTIANS IN ORDER TO EXCITE FURTHER TROUBLES IN THE CHURCH. HIS EVIL TREATMENT OF CHRISTIANS.

It was from these motives that Julian recalled from exile all Christians who, during the reign of Constantius, had been banished on account of their religious sentiments and restored to them their property that had been confiscated. He charged the people not to commit any act of injustice against the Christians, not to insult them, and not to constrain them to offer sacrifice. He commanded that if they should, of their own accord, desire to draw near the altars, they were first to appease the wrath of the demons whom the Pagans regard as capable of averting evil and to purify themselves by the customary course of expiations. He deprived the clergy of the immunities, honors, and revenues which Constantine had conferred,[1] repealed the laws which had been enacted in their favor, and re-enforced their civil liabilities. He even compelled the virgins and widows who on account of their poverty were reckoned among the clergy to refund the provision which had been assigned them from public sources. For, when Constantine adjusted the temporal concerns of the church, he devoted a portion of the taxes raised upon every city to the support of the clergy, and, to insure the stability of this arrangement, he enacted a law which has continued in force from the death of Julian to the present day. These exactions were very cruel and rigorous, as appears by the receipts given by the receivers of the money to those from whom it had been extorted, and which were designed to show that the property received in accordance with the law of Constantine had been refunded. Nothing, however, could diminish the enmity of the emperor against religion. In his hatred against the faith, he seized every opportunity to ruin the church. He deprived it of its property, ornaments, and sacred vessels and condemned those who had demolished temples during the reign of Constantine and Constantius to rebuild them, or to defray the expenses of their re-erection. On this ground, and because they were unable to pay the sums, many of the bishops, clergy, and other Christians, were cruelly tortured and cast into prison.[2]

It may be concluded from what has been said, that if Julian shed less blood than preceding persecutors and that if he devised fewer punishments for the torture of the body, yet that he was equally averse to the church, and equally intent upon injuring it. He certainly recalled the priests who had been banished by Constantius, but he was actuated by the desire of introducing division into the church and of increasing the existing disputes. He also contemplated the condemnation of Constantius, whose memory he thought to render odious to all his subjects by favoring the Pagans who were of the same sentiments as himself and by showing compassion to those Christians who had been unjustly persecuted during the preceding reign. He expelled the eunuchs from the court, because the late emperor had been well-affected towards them. He condemned Eusebius, the governor of the palace, to death from a suspicion he entertained that it was at his suggestion that Gallus his brother had been slain. He recalled Ætius from the region whither Constantius had banished him on account of suspicions which had been excited against him by the friendship formerly existing between him and Gallus, and to him Julian sent letters full of benignity and furnished him with public conveyances to expedite his return. For a similar reason he condemned Eleusius, bishop of Cyzicus, under heavy penalties, to rebuild within two months and at his own expense, a church belonging to the Novatians which he had destroyed. Many other things might be mentioned which he did himself or which, from hatred to his predecessor, he permitted to be done.

NOTES

1. See Eusebius, *Life of the Blessed Emperor Constantine*, Book II, Chapters 36–41.
2. Valesius remarks that they were tortured and imprisoned, not only on this account, but also because they would not deliver up the sacred vessels presented by Constantine to their churches.

CHAPTER VI

ATHANASIUS, AFTER HAVING BEEN SEVEN YEARS CONCEALED IN THE HOUSE OF A HOLY VIRGIN, RE-APPEARS IN PUBLIC, AND ENTERS THE CHURCH OF ALEXANDRIA.

At this period, Athanasius, who had long remained in concealment, having heard of the death of Constantius, appeared by night in the church at Alexandria. His unexpected appearance excited the greatest astonishment. He had escaped falling into the hands of the governor of Egypt who, at the command of the emperor and at the request of the friends of George, had formed plans to arrest him, and had concealed himself in the house of a holy virgin in Alexandria. It is said that she was endowed with such extraordinary beauty, that those who beheld her regarded her as a phenomenon of nature and that men of gravity and reflection kept aloof from her for fear of giving rise to slander or of exciting disadvantageous reports. She possessed in the flower of youth such modesty and such wisdom as would have conferred beauty on an individual who had not received that gift from nature. For it is not true, as some assert, that, "as is the body, so is the soul." On the contrary, the body is the index of the mind and by it our thoughts and affections are reflected and indicated. This is a truth admitted by all who have accurately investigated the subject.

It is related that Athanasius sought refuge in the house of this holy virgin by the revelation of God, who designed to save him in this manner. When I reflect on the result which ensued, I cannot doubt but that all the events were directed by Providence. The friends and relatives of Athanasius would thus have been preserved from danger had search been made for him among them and had they been compelled to swear that he was not concealed with them. There was nothing to excite suspicion of a bishop being concealed in the house of so lovely a virgin. However, she had the courage to receive him and sufficient prudence to preserve his life. She alone ministered to him and supplied him with what nature requires. She washed his feet, brought him food, provided him with the books he wanted, and acted so prudently that during the whole time[1] of his residence with her, none of the inhabitants of Alexandria suspected the place of his retreat.[2]

NOTES

1. Athanasius was in retreat for six or seven years, but Valesius is of opinion that he spent them in the retirement of some Egyptian monastery.
2. The same story is related by Nicephorus, Book VI, Chapter 10. Valesius thinks the remarks of Sozomen here beneath the dignity of an ecclesiastical historian.

CHAPTER VII

VIOLENT DEATH OF GEORGE, THE RESULT OF CERTAIN OCCURRENCES IN THE TEMPLE OF MITHRA. LETTER OF JULIAN ON THE SUBJECT.

After Athanasius had escaped all danger and thus presented himself suddenly in the church, no one knew whence he came. The people of Alexandria, however, rejoiced at his return and restored his churches to him. The Arians, being thus expelled from the churches, were compelled to hold their assemblies in private houses under the guidance of Lucius who had succeeded George as their bishop.

George had been slain a short time previously: for when the magistrates had announced to the public the decease of Constantius and the accession of Julian, the Pagans of Alexandria rose up in sedition. They attacked George with such violence that it was expected he would have been torn to pieces, but they merely, for the time being, committed him to prison. The following day, however, they repaired early in the morning to the prison, killed him, flung the corpse upon a camel, and after exposing it to every insult during the day, burnt it at nightfall. I am not ignorant that the Arians assert that George received this cruel treatment from the followers of Athanasius, but it seems to me more probable that the perpetrators of these deeds were the Pagans. For they had more cause than any other body of men to hate him on account of his having destroyed their temples and their gods, and having, moreover, prohibited them from sacrificing or performing the other rites of their religion according to the custom of their fathers. Besides, the extraordinary influence he had acquired over the emperor rendered him an object of popular odium. For the people, who generally look with suspicion on those in power, regarded him with uncontrollable aversion.

A calamity had also taken place at a spot called Mithra.[1] It was originally a desert, and Constantius had bestowed it on the church of Alexandria. George having given orders to clear the ground in order to erect a house of prayer, an adytum was discovered during the process of digging. In it were idols, and instruments formerly used in Pagan ceremonies which were of a very strange and ludicrous appearance. The Christians caused them to be publicly exhibited, in order to humiliate the Pagans, but this affront was more than the Pagans could bear, and they rushed to attack the Christians after arming themselves with swords, stones, and whatever weapon came first to hand. They slew many of the Christians, and, in derision of their religion, crucified others. This led to the abandonment of the work that had been commenced by the Christians and to the murder of George by the Pagans, as soon as they had heard of the accession of Julian.

This fact is admitted by Julian himself, which would not have been the case had it not been fully established, for he would rather have thrown the blame of the murder on the Christians, whoever they were,[2] than on the Pagans. He expressed great indignation in a letter which he wrote on the subject to the inhabitants of Alexandria,[3] and threatened to take vengeance on them, but he forgave them out of consideration to Serapis, their tutelary divinity, to Alexander their founder, and to Julian his uncle, formerly governor of Egypt and of the Alexandrians. This latter was so bigoted to Paganism and so prejudiced against Christianity that, contrary to the wishes of the emperors, he persecuted the Christians unto death.

NOTES

1. Compare Socrates, *Ecclesiastical History,* Book III, Chapter 2.
2. ὁιουσδήποτε. He means whether they were of the orthodox or heretical party.
3. Compare Socrates, *Ecclesiastical History,* Book III, Chapter 3.

CHAPTER VIII

CONCERNING THEODORE, THE KEEPER OF THE SACRED VASES OF ANTIOCH. HOW JULIAN, THE UNCLE OF THE EMPEROR, HAVING VIOLATED THE SACRED VASES, FALLS A PREY TO WORMS AND CORRUPTION.

Julian, the uncle of the emperor, having determined upon removing the treasures and most precious ornaments of the church of Antioch to the imperial treasury, closed the places of prayer, for all the clergy had fled. One presbyter, by name Theodore, alone remained in the city and it was to him that the charge of these ornaments and treasures had been confided. Julian, the governor of Egypt, commanded him to be slain after he had subjected him to the most cruel tortures, in the vain endeavor to make him reply to his questions and refrain from the confession of his faith. Julian then proceeded to the sacrilege of the sacred vases, which he flung upon the ground and sat upon, at the same time uttering incredible blasphemies against Christ. But his impious course was suddenly arrested, for certain parts of his body were turned into corruption and generated enormous quantities of worms. The physicians confessed that the disease was beyond the reach of their art but, from fear and reverence towards the emperor, they tried all the resources of medicine. They procured the most costly and the fattest birds and applied them to the corrupted part, in the hope that the worms might be thereby attracted to the surface. But this was of no effect for in proportion as some of the worms were thus drawn out, others were generated in the flesh, by which he was ceaselessly devoured until they put an end to his life.[1] Many believed that this disease was an infliction of Divine wrath, visited upon him in consequence of his impiety, and this supposition appears the more probable from the fact, that the treasurer[2] of the emperor, and other of the chief officers of the court who had persecuted the church, died in an extraordinary and dreadful manner, as if Divine wrath had been visited upon them.

NOTES

1. Concerning the death of Julian, the reader will do well to compare Theodoret, *Ecclesiastical History,* Book III, Chapters 8 and 9, and Ammianus Marcellinus, *History,* Book XXIII, Chapter 1.
2. He means Felix, or Helpidius. Compare the account given of their deaths by Theodoret, *Ecclesiastical History,* Book III, Chapter 8 and 9.

CHAPTER IX

MARTYRDOM OF THE SAINTS EUSEBIUS, NESTABIS, AND ZENO IN THE CITY OF GAZA.

As I have advanced thus far in my history and have given an account of the death of George and of Theodore,[1] I deem it right to relate some particulars concerning the death of the three brethren, Eusebius, Nestabis, and Zeno. The inhabitants of Gaza, being inflamed with rage against them, dragged them from their house in which they had concealed themselves and cast them into prison, after having beaten them with unexampled cruelty. They then assembled in the theater, and cried out loudly against them, declaring that they had committed sacrilege in their temple and had used the power with which they were formerly invested to the injury and destruction of Paganism. By these declamations the general excitement was increased to such a pitch that they ran to the prison and with unparalleled fury drew forth their victims and dashed them on the ground. And in this position, sometimes with the face and sometimes with the back upon the ground, the victims were dragged through the streets of the city and were afterwards stoned and beaten. I have been told that even women quitted their work to add to their sufferings by personal inflictions, and that the cooks left their employment to pour boiling water on them and to wound them with their culinary utensils.

When the martyrs had been literally torn to pieces and their brains scattered on the ground, their bodies were dragged out of the city and flung on the spot generally used as a receptacle for the bodies of beasts. Then a large fire was lighted, and their bones mixed with those of asses and camels, so that it might be difficult to distinguish them. But they were not long concealed, for a Christian woman who was an inhabitant though not a native of the city, collected the bones at night by the inspiration of God and conveyed them in a vessel to Zeno, their cousin, even as God had commanded her in a dream. For she was previously unacquainted with Zeno, and he had narrowly escaped being arrested, but he had effected his escape while the people were occupied in the murder of his cousins and had fled to Anthedona, a maritime city about twenty stadia from Gaza, wholly addicted to superstition and idolatry. When the inhabitants of this city discovered that he was a Christian, they beat him violently, and drove him away. He then fled to Gaza and concealed himself, and here the woman found him and gave him the remains. He kept them carefully in his house until the reign of Theodore, when he was ordained bishop and he erected a church beyond the walls of the city and deposited the bones on the altar, near those of Nestor, the Confessor. Nestor had been on terms of intimacy with his cousins, and was seized with them by the people of Gaza, scourged, and imprisoned. But those who dragged him through the city were affected by his personal beauty and struck with compassion, they cast him, before he was quite dead, out of the city. Some persons found him and carried him to the house of Zeno, where he expired during the dressing of his wounds.

When the inhabitants of Gaza began to reflect on the enormity of their crime, they trembled lest the emperor should take vengeance on them. It was reported that the emperor was filled with indignation and had determined upon beheading them, but this report was false and had no foundation but the fears and self-accusations of the criminals. Julian, far from evincing as much anger against them as he had manifested against the Alexandrians on the murder of George, did not even write to rebuke their conduct. On the contrary, he deposed the governor of the province, and represented that clemency alone prevented his being put to death. The crime imputed to him was that of having arrested some of the inhabitants of Gaza who had been guilty of sedition and murder and of having imprisoned them until judgment could be passed upon them in accordance with the laws. "For what right had he," asked the emperor, "to arrest the citizens merely for retaliating on a few Galileans the injuries that had been inflicted by them and by their gods." Thus, it is said, the affair was passed over.

NOTE

1. Nicephorus and Epiphanius call him by the name of Theodoretus.

CHAPTER X

CONCERNING SAINT HILARION AND THE VIRGINS OF HELIOPOLIS. MARTYRDOM OF MARK, BISHOP OF ARETHUSA.

At the same period the inhabitants of Gaza sought for the monk Hilarion. But, aware of their sanguinary designs, he fled to Sicily.[1] Here he employed himself in collecting wood in the deserts and on the mountains, which he carried on his shoulders for sale in the cities, and by these means obtained sufficient food for the support of the body. But as he was at length recognized by a man of quality whom he had dispossessed of a demon,[2] he retired to Dalmatia where, by the power of God, he performed numerous miracles and through prayer repressed an inundation of the sea[3] and restored the waves to their proper bounds. No sooner, however, had these miracles excited the reverence of the people, than he quitted the country in order that he might live unknown, and free from the praises and applauses of men. He sailed for the island of Cyprus, but touched at Paphos, and at the entreaty of the bishop of Cyprus, fixed his residence at a place in that island called Charburis. Here he only escaped martyrdom by flight, for he fled in compliance with the Divine precept which commands us not to expose ourselves to persecution, but that if we fall into the hands of persecutors, to overcome by our own fortitude the violence of our oppressors.

The inhabitants of Gaza and of Alexandria were not the only citizens who exercised such atrocities against the Christians as those I have described. The inhabitants of Heliopolis, near Mount Libanus, and of Arethusa in Syria, perpetrated deeds of still greater cruelty. The former were guilty of an act of barbarity which could scarcely be credited, had it not been corroborated by the testimony of those who witnessed it. They stripped the holy virgins, who had never been looked upon by the multitude, of their garments and exposed them in a state of nudity, as public objects of insult and derision. After numerous other inflictions, they shaved them, ripped them open, and placed inside them the food usually given to pigs, and the animals thus devoured these human entrails in conjunction with their ordinary food. I am convinced that the citizens perpetrated this barbarity against the holy virgins from motives of revenge, on account of the abolition of the ancient custom of yielding up virgins to prostitution, when on the eve of marriage to those to whom they had been betrothed. This custom was prohibited by a law enacted by Constantine, after he had destroyed the temple of Venus at Heliopolis and erected a church upon its ruins.[4]

Mark, bishop of Arethusa, an aged and virtuous prelate, was put to a very cruel death by the inhabitants of that city, who had long entertained inimical feelings against him because he had, during the reign of Constantine, resorted to violence rather than to persuasion in his attempts to lead them from Paganism to Christianity and had demolished a costly and magnificent temple. On the accession of Julian, an edict was issued commanding the bishop either to rebuild the temple or to defray the expenses of its re-erection. Perceiving that the people had risen up against him and reflecting that he had no means to pay for the re-erection of the temple, and that such an act was not lawful for a Christian and still less for a bishop, he fled from the city. On hearing, however, that many were suffering on his account, that some were dragged before the tribunals and others tortured, he returned and offered to suffer whatever the multitude might choose to inflict upon him. The people, instead of admiring this noble deed, conceived that he was actuated by contempt towards them and rushed upon him, dragged him through the streets and covered him with blows. People of each sex and of all ages joined with alacrity and fury in this atrocious proceeding. Some pierced his ears. The young men who frequented the schools made game of him, throwing him from one to the other, and they lacerated him cruelly with their knives. When his whole body was covered with wounds, they anointed him with honey and, placing him in a basket of rushes, raised him up on an eminence. It is said that while he was in this position, and suffering from the attacks of bees and wasps, he told the inhabitants of Arethusa that he was raised up above them, and could look down upon them below him, and that this reminded him of the difference that would exist between them in the life to come. It is also related that the prefect[5] who, although a Pagan, was held in such estimation that his memory is still honored in that country, admired the fortitude of Mark and boldly uttered reproaches against the emperor for allowing himself to be vanquished by an old man, exposed to innumerable tortures, and he added that such proceedings reflected ridicule on the emperor, while the names of the persecuted were at the same time rendered illustrious. Thus did Mark[6] endure all the torments inflicted upon him by the inhabitants of Gaza with such unshaken fortitude, that even the Pagans were struck with admiration.

NOTES

1. Valesius considers that Sozomen is mistaken here, and that Hilarion's refuge was the Oasis in Africa.
2. Compare Jerome, *Life of Hilarion*, Book XXXI.
3. See the *Life of Hilarion* by Jerome.
4. See Eusebius, *Life of the Blessed Emperor Constantine,* Book III, Chapters 56–59.
5. He means Sallustius, who was at this time prætorian prefect.
6. This Mark, as Valesius observes, must be carefully distinguished from another Mark of Arethusa, who was one of the leaders of the Arian faction from the time of Constantine.

CHAPTER XI

MARTYRDOM OF MACEDONIUS, OF THEODULIS, OF TATIAN, OF BUSIRIS, OF BASIL, AND OF EUPSYCHUS.

About the same period,[1] Macedonius, Theodulis, and Tatian, who were Phrygians by birth, courageously endured martyrdom. A temple of Meros, a city of Phrygia, having been re-opened by the governor of the province after it had been closed many years, these martyrs entered therein by night and destroyed the idolatrous images. As other individuals were arrested and were on the point of being punished for the deed, they delivered themselves up and avowed themselves the actors in the transaction. They might have escaped all further punishment by offering sacrifices to idols, but the governor could not persuade them to accept acquittal on these terms. His persuasions being ineffectual, he subjected them to a variety of tortures and finally extended them on a grid-iron beneath which a fire had been lighted. While they were being consumed, they said to the governor, "Amachus (for that was his name), give orders that our bodies may be turned on the fire, if you do not desire to be served with meat cooked only on one side." Thus did they die courageously, in the midst of torments.[2]

It is said that Busiris also obtained renown at Ancyra, a city of Galatia, by his noble confession of the faith. He belonged to the sect denominated Eucrates, and it was reported to the governor of the province that he had ridiculed the Pagans. The governor, in consequence, commanded that he should be put to the torture. Busiris raised his hands to his head so as to leave his sides exposed, and told the governor that it would be useless for the executioners to take the trouble of attaching him to the instrument of torture, as he was ready to receive on his sides as many blows as might be adjudged him. The governor was surprised at this proposition, but his astonishment was increased by what followed, for Busiris remained firm and immoveable, with his hands on his head, while his sides were being torn with nails, according to the governor's direction. Immediately afterwards Busiris was consigned to prison, but was released not long subsequently on the announcement of the death of Julian. He lived till the reign of Theodosius, renounced his former heresy, and joined the Catholic church.

It is said that about this period, Basil, presbyter of the church of Ancyra, and Eupsychus, a native of Cæsarea in Cappadocia, who had but just taken to himself a wife, terminated their lives by martyrdom. I believe that Eupsychus was condemned in consequence of the demolition of the temple of Fortune which, as I have already stated,[3] excited the anger of the emperor against all the inhabitants of Cæsarea. Indeed all the actors in this transaction were condemned, some to death, and others to banishment.

Basil had long manifested great zeal in defense of the faith, and had opposed the Arians during the reign of Constantius. Hence the partisans of Eudoxius had prohibited him from holding public assemblies.[4] On the accession of Julian, however, he travelled hither and thither, publicly and openly exhorting the Christians to cleave to their own doctrines, and to refrain from defiling themselves with Pagan sacrifices and libations. He urged them to account as nothing the honors which the emperor might bestow upon them, such honors being but of short duration, and leading to eternal infamy. His zeal had already rendered him an object of suspicion and of hatred to the Pagans, when one day he chanced to pass by and see them offering sacrifice. He sighed deeply, and uttered a prayer to the effect that no Christian might be suffered to fall into similar delusion. He was seized on the spot and conveyed to the governor of the province. Many tortures were inflicted on him, and in the manly endurance of this anguish, he received the crown of martyrdom.

Although these cruelties were perpetrated contrary to the will of the emperor, yet they serve to prove that his reign was signalized by many martyrdoms. For the sake of clearness, I have related all these occurrences in consecutive order, although the martyrdoms really occurred at different periods.

NOTES

1. Compare Socrates, *Ecclesiastical History,* Book III, Chapter 15.
2. *Note to the 2018 edition:* This story is reminiscent of the martyrdom account of Saint Lawrence in the third century, AD. See Prudentius's *Hymn in Honor of the Passion of the Blessed Martyr Lawrence,* composed about AD 403.
3. See above, Chapter 4.
4. ἐκκλησιάζειν. Valesius remarks that as Eudoxius was at this time bishop of Constantinople, and had jurisdiction over Galatia, he had a right thus to forbid Basil, who was a presbyter of Ancyra in Galatia, to hold assemblies. The word is used in this sense by Sozomen below, Chapter 15, where he distinguishes it from διδάσκειν.

CHAPTER XII
CONCERNING LUCIFER AND EUSEBIUS, BISHOPS OF THE WEST. EUSEBIUS WITH ATHANASIUS THE GREAT AND OTHER BISHOPS HOLD A COUNCIL AT ALEXANDRIA, AND CONFIRM THE FAITH ESTABLISHED AT NICÆA.

After the return of Athanasius from banishment, Lucifer,[1] bishop of Cagliari in Sardinia, and Eusebius, bishop of Vercelli, a city of Liguria in Italy, returned from Thebaïs. They had been condemned by Constantius to perpetual exile in that country. They conferred together concerning the regulation of ecclesiastical affairs. And it was unanimously agreed that Eusebius should repair to Alexandria, and there, in concert with Athanasius, hold a council for the purpose of confirming the Nicene doctrines. Lucifer sent a deacon with Eusebius to take his place in the council and went himself to Antioch, where the church was torn by factions. A schism had been excited by the Arians, then under the guidance of Euzoius, and by the followers of Meletius, who as I have above stated, were at variance even with those who held the same opinions as themselves. As Meletius had not then returned from exile, Lucifer ordained Paulinus bishop.[2]

In the meantime, the bishops of many cities had assembled in Alexandria with Athanasius and Eusebius and had confirmed the Nicene doctrines. They confessed that the Holy Ghost is of the same substance as the Father and the Son, and they made use of the term "Trinity." They declared that the human nature assumed by God the Word is to be regarded as consisting of a perfect soul as well as of a perfect body, even as was taught by the ancient Christian philosophers. As the church had been agitated by questions concerning the terms "substance" and "hypostasis," they decreed, and as I think, wisely, that these terms should not henceforth be lightly used in reference to God, except in refutation of the Sabellian heresy. In discourses of this nature the use of such words was to be permitted, lest from the apparent paucity of terms, there might seem any difficulty in conveying distinctness of idea. These were the decrees passed by the bishops convened at Alexandria. Athanasius read in the council the document he had written in his own justification, detailing the reasons of his flight.

NOTES

1. For an account of the heresy of Lucifer, see above, note on Book III, Chapter 15, and compare Socrates, *Ecclesiastical History,* Book III, Chapter 5, 9.
2. Compare Socrates, *Ecclesiastical History,* Book III, Chapter 6.

CHAPTER XIII
CONCERNING PAULINUS AND MELETIUS, ARCHBISHOPS OF ANTIOCH. DISPUTE BETWEEN EUSEBIUS AND LUCIFER. EUSEBIUS AND HILARIUS DEFEND THE NICENE FAITH.

On the termination of the council, Eusebius repaired to Antioch and found dissension prevailing among the people.[1] Those who were attached to Meletius would not join Paulinus, but held their assemblies apart. Eusebius was much grieved at the state of affairs, for the ordination ought not to have taken place without the unanimous consent of the people, yet from respect towards Lucifer, he did not openly express his dissatisfaction. He refused to hold communion with either party, but promised to redress their respective grievances by means of a council.

While he was thus striving to restore concord and unanimity, Meletius returned from exile and, finding that those who held his sentiments had seceded from the other party, he held meetings with them beyond the walls of the city. Paulinus in the meantime assembled his own party within the city, for his mildness, his virtuous life, and his advanced age, had so far won the respect of Euzoius, the Arian bishop, that instead of being expelled from the city, a church had been assigned him for his own use. Eusebius, on finding all his endeavors for the restoration of concord frustrated, quitted Antioch. Lucifer fancied himself injured by him because he had refused to approve the ordination of Paulinus, and in displeasure, seceded from communion with him. As if purely from the desire of contention, Lucifer then began to cast aspersions on the enactments of the council of Alexandria, and in this way he seems to have originated the heresy which has been distinguished by his name. Those who espoused his cause seceded from the church, but although he was deeply chagrined at the aspect affairs had taken, yet because he had deputed a deacon to accompany Eusebius in lieu of himself, he yielded to the decrees of the council of Alexandria, and conformed to the doctrines of the Catholic church. About this period he repaired to Sardinia.

In the meantime Eusebius traversed the Eastern provinces, restored those who had declined from the faith, and taught them what it was necessary to believe. After passing through Illyria, he went to Italy, and there he met with Hilarius, bishop of Poictiers[2] in Aquitania. Hilarius had returned from exile before Eusebius and had taught the Italians and the Gauls what doctrines they had to receive, and what to reject. He expressed himself with great eloquence in the Latin tongue and wrote many admirable works, it is said, in refutation of the Arian dogmas. Thus did Hilarius and Eusebius maintain the doctrines of the Nicæan council in the regions of the West.

NOTES

1. Compare Socrates, *Ecclesiastical History,* Book III, Chapter 9.
2. Compare Socrates, *Ecclesiastical History,* Book III, Chapter 10.

CHAPTER XIV

DISSENSION BETWEEN THE PARTISANS OF MACEDONIUS AND THOSE OF ACACIUS.

At this period, the adherents of Macedonius, among whom were Eleusius, Eustathius, and Sophronius, who now began to be called Macedonians as constituting a distinct sect, adopted the bold measure, on the death of Constantius, of calling together those of their own sentiments who had been convened at Seleucia and of holding several councils. They condemned the partisans of Acacius and the faith which had been established at Ariminum, and confirmed the doctrines which had been set forth at Antioch and afterwards approved at Seleucia. When interrogated as to the cause of their dispute with the partisans of Acacius, with whom, as being of the same sentiments as themselves, they had formerly held communion, they replied, by the mouth of Sophronius, a bishop of Paphlagonia, that while the Christians in the West maintained the use of the term "consubstantial," the followers of Ætius in the East upheld the dogma of dissimilarity as to substance, that the former party confounded the persons of the Father and of the Son by their use of the term "consubstantial," and that the latter party represented too great a difference as existing between the hypostases of the Father and of the Son, but that they themselves preserved the mean between the two extremes and avoided both errors by religiously maintaining that, in hypothesis, the Son is like unto the Father. It was by such representations as these that the Macedonians vindicated themselves from blame.

CHAPTER XV

ATHANASIUS IS AGAIN BANISHED. CONCERNING ELEUSIUS, BISHOP OF CYZICUS, AND TITUS, BISHOP OF BOSTRA. ANCESTORS OF THE AUTHOR.

The emperor[1] on being informed that Athanasius held meetings in the church of Alexandria, taught the people boldly, and converted many Pagans to Christianity, commanded him under the severest penalties to depart from Alexandria.[2] The pretext made use of for enforcing this edict was that Athanasius, after having been banished by Constantius, had re-assumed his episcopal administration without the sanction of the reigning emperor, for Julian declared that he had never contemplated restoring the bishops who had been exiled by Constantius to their ecclesiastical functions when he recalled them to their native land. On the announcement of the command enjoining his immediate departure, Athanasius said to the Christian multitudes who stood weeping around him, "Be of good courage. It is but a cloud which will speedily be dispersed." He then committed the care of the church to the most zealous of his friends and quitted Alexandria.

About the same period, the inhabitants of Cyzicus sent an embassy to the emperor to lay before him some of their private affairs and particularly to entreat the restoration of the Pagan temples. He applauded their zeal and promised to grant all their requests. He expelled Eleusius, the bishop of their city, because he had destroyed some temples, provided for the support of widows, erected edifices as dwelling-places for holy virgins, and induced many Pagans to abandon their ancient superstition. The emperor prohibited some foreign Christians who had accompanied him from entering the city of Cyzicus from the apprehension, it appears, that they would in conjunction with the Christians within the city excite a sedition on account of religion. There were, in fact, great numbers of artisans engaged in the woollen manufacture and in the coinage of money. They were divided into two bands[3] and had received permission from preceding emperors to dwell with their wives and possessions in Cyzicus, provided that they annually handed over to the public treasury a supply of clothes for the soldiery and of newly-coined money.

Although Julian was anxious to advance, by every means, the Pagan religion, yet he deemed it the height of imprudence to employ force or intimidation against those who refused to sacrifice. Besides, there were so many Christians in every city that it would have been no easy task for the rulers even to number them. He did not even forbid them to assemble together for worship, as he was aware that when freedom of the will is called into question, constraint is utterly useless. He expelled the clergy and bishops from all the cities in order to put an end to these assemblies, imagining that when there would be no longer teaching or administration of the sacraments,[4] religion itself would, in course of time, fall into oblivion. The pretext which he advanced for these proceedings was that the clergy were the leaders of sedition among the people. Under this plea, he expelled Eleusius and his friends from Cyzicus although there was not even a symptom of sedition in that city.

He also publicly called upon the citizens of Bostra[5] to expel Titus, their bishop. It appears that the emperor had threatened to impeach Titus and the other clergy as the authors of any sedition that might arise among the people, and that Titus had thereupon written to him stating that although the Christians were more in number than the Pagans, yet that, in accordance with his exhortations, they were disposed to remain quiet and were not likely to rise up in sedition. Julian, with the view of exciting the enmity of the inhabitants of Bostra against Titus, represented in a letter which he addressed to them that their bishop had advanced a calumny against them by stating that it was in accordance with his exhortations rather than with their own inclination that they refrained from sedition, and Julian exhorted them to expel him from their city as a public enemy.

It appears that the Christians were subjected to similar injustice in other places, sometimes by the command of the emperor, and sometimes by the wrath and impetuosity of the populace. The blame of these transactions may be justly imputed to the emperor, for out of his hatred to the Christian religion, he only visited the perpetrators of such deeds with verbal rebukes, while by his actions, he urged them on in the same course. Hence, although not absolutely persecuted by the emperor, the Christians were obliged to flee from city to city.

My grandfather and many of my ancestors were compelled to flee in this manner. My grandfather was of Pagan parentage, and with his own family and that of Alaphion, had been the first to embrace Christianity in Bethelia, a populous town near Gaza, in which there are temples highly revered by the people of the country on account of their extreme antiquity. The most celebrated of these temples is the Pantheon, built on an artificial eminence commanding a view of the whole town. It is conjectured that the original name given to this temple was in the Syriac language, and that this name was afterwards rendered into Greek and expressed by a word which signifies that the temple is the residence of all the gods. It is said that the above-mentioned families were converted through the instrumentality of the monk Hilarion. Alaphion, it appears, was possessed of a devil, and neither the Pagans nor the Jews could by any of their enchantments deliver him from this affliction. But Hilarion, by simply calling upon the name of Christ, expelled the demon, and Alaphion with his whole family immediately embraced the faith. My grandfather was endowed with great natural ability, which he applied with success to the explanation of the Sacred Scriptures. He had made some attainments in general knowledge and was not ignorant of arithmetic. He was much beloved by the Christians of Ascalon, of Gaza, and of the surrounding country, and was regarded as necessary to religion, on account of his gift in expounding Scripture. No one can speak in adequate terms of the virtues of the other[6] family. The first churches and monasteries erected in that country were founded by members of this family and supported by their liberality and humanity. Some good men belonging to this family have flourished even in our own days, and in my youth I saw some of them, but they were then very aged. I shall have occasion to say more concerning them in the course of my history.[7]

NOTES

1. Compare Socrates, *Ecclesiastical History,* Book III, Chapter 14.
2. The edict of Julian is still extant. It is numbered 26 among his Letters. *Note to the 2018 edition*: This letter is numbered 24 in the Loeb Classical Library translation (1913) and may be found in Volume 3 of the works of Julian.
3. τάγματα. *Classes* vel *ordines.*
4. See above, note on Chapter 11.
5. This edict is extant as the 52nd among the Letters of Julian. *Note to the 2018 edition:* This letter is numbered 41 in the Loeb Classical Library translation (1913) and may be found in Volume 3 of the works of Julian.
6. He probably means that of Alaphion. The reader will observe the notice of Sozomen's family by himself, and compare the memoir prefixed to this volume.
7. He means Salamanes, Phuscon, Malchio, and Crispo, whom he mentions below, Book VI, Chapter 32. See prefatory remarks by Valesius.

CHAPTER XVI

EFFORTS OF JULIAN TO ESTABLISH PAGANISM, AND ABOLISH CHRISTIANITY. HIS EPISTLE TO SOME OF THE PAGAN HIGH PRIESTS.

The emperor was deeply grieved at finding that all his efforts to secure the predominance of Paganism were utterly ineffectual, for although the gates of the temples were kept open, although sacrifices were offered, and the observance of ancient festivals restored in all the cities, yet he was far from being satisfied, for he could plainly foresee that on the withdrawal of his influence, a change in the whole aspect of affairs would speedily take place. He was particularly chagrined on discovering that the wives, children, and servants of many of the Pagan priests had been converted to Christianity. On reflecting that one main support of the Christian religion was the virtuous course of life of its professors, he determined to introduce into the Pagan temples the order and discipline of Christianity, to institute various orders and degrees of ministry, to appoint readers and teachers to give instruction in Pagan doctrines, and to command that prayers should be offered on certain days at stated hours. He, moreover, resolved to found monasteries for the accommodation of men and women who desired to live in philosophical retirement, as likewise hospitals for the relief of strangers and of the poor, and for other philanthropical purposes. He wished to introduce among the Pagans the Christian system of penance for voluntary and involuntary transgressions: but the point of ecclesiastical discipline which he chiefly admired and desired to establish among the Pagans, was the custom of the bishops to give letters of recommendation[1] to those who travelled to foreign lands, wherein they commended them to the hospitality and kindness of other bishops in all places and under all contingencies. In this way did Julian strive to ingraft the customs of Christianity upon Paganism.

But if what I have stated appears to be incredible, I need not go far in search of proofs to corroborate my assertions, for I can produce a letter written by the emperor himself on the subject. He writes as follows:

> To Arsacius, High Priest of Galatia,
>
> Paganism has not yet reached the degree of prosperity that might be desired, owing to the conduct of its votaries. The worship of the gods, however, is conducted on the grandest and most magnificent scale, so far exceeding our very hopes and expectations, that no one could have dared to look for so surprising a change as that which we have witnessed within a very short space of time. But are we to rest satisfied with what has been already effected? Ought we not rather to consider that the progress of Christianity has been principally owing to the humanity evinced by Christians towards strangers, to the reverence they have manifested towards the dead, and to the delusive gravity which they have assumed in their conduct and deportment.
>
> It is requisite that each of us should he diligent in the discharge of duty: I do not refer to you alone, as that would not suffice, but to all the priests of Galatia. You must either put them to shame, or try the power of persuasion, or else deprive them of their sacerdotal offices, if they do not, with their wives, their children, and their servants, join in the service of the gods, or if they permit their wives or their sons to disregard the gods and to prefer impiety to piety. Exhort them not to frequent theaters, not to drink at taverns, and not to engage in any trade, or practice any nefarious art. Honor those who yield to your remonstrances and expel those who disregard them. Establish hospitals in every city, so that strangers from neighboring and foreign countries may reap the benefit of our philanthropy, according to their respective need. I have provided means to meet the necessary expenditure and have issued directions throughout the whole of Galatia, that you should be furnished annually with thirty thousand bushels of corn and sixty thousand measures of wine, of which the fifth part is to be devoted to

the support of the poor who attend upon the priests, and the rest to be distributed among strangers and our own poor. For, while there are no persons in need among the Jews, and while even the impious Galileans provide not only for those of their own party who are in want but also for those who hold with us, it would indeed be disgraceful if we were to allow our own people to suffer from poverty. Teach the Pagans to co-operate in this work of benevolence, and let the first-fruits of the towns be offered to the gods. Habituate them to the exercise of this liberality, by showing them how such conduct is sanctioned by the practice of remote antiquity. For Homer[2] represents Eumæus as saying,

> It never was our guise,
> To slight the poor, or aught humane despise;
> For Jove unfolds our hospitable door,
> 'Tis Jove that sends the stranger and the poor.

Let us not permit others to excel us in piety. Let us not dishonor ourselves, nor the service of the gods by our negligence. If I hear that you act according to my directions, I shall rejoice exceedingly. Do not often visit the governors at their own houses, but write to them frequently. When they enter the city, let no priest go to meet them, and let not the priest accompany them further than the vestibule when they repair to the temple of the gods. Neither let any soldiers march before them on such occasions, but let those follow them who will. As soon as they have entered within the gates of the temple, they are but private individuals. For there it is your duty, as you well know, to preside, according to the divine decree. Those who humbly conform to this law manifest that they possess true religion, whereas those who contemn it are proud and vainglorious. I am ready to render assistance to the inhabitants of Pessena, provided that they will propitiate the mother of the gods, but if they neglect this duty, they will incur my utmost displeasure.

> It is not right for me to show compassion
> Towards those with whom the immortal
>   gods are at enmity.

Convince them, therefore, that if they desire my assistance, they must offer up supplications to the mother of the gods.

NOTES

1. τα συνθήματα. "Literæ Formatæ." On these commendatory letters, see Hunter: *Outlines of Dogmatic Theology*, Volume 1, page 334.
2. *Odyssey*, Ξ. 56.

CHAPTER XVII

JULIAN RESORTS TO ARTIFICE, RATHER THAN TO OPEN VIOLENCE, AGAINST THE CHRISTIANS. THE SIGN OF THE CROSS CEASES TO BE USED AS A STANDARD. THE SOLDIERY INVITED TO OFFER SACRIFICE.

When Julian acted and wrote in the manner aforesaid, he expected that he would, by these means, easily induce his subjects to change their religious opinions. Although he earnestly desired to abolish the Christian religion, yet he refrained from employing violent measures lest he should be accounted tyrannical. He used every means, however, that could possibly be devised to lead his subjects back to Paganism, and he was more especially urgent with the soldiery, whom he sometimes addressed individually, and sometimes through the medium of their officers. To habituate them in all things to the worship of the gods, he restored the ancient form of the standard of the Roman armies which, as we have already stated, Constantine had at the command of God converted into the sign of the cross. Julian also caused to be painted, in juxtaposition with his own figure on the public pictures, a representation either of Jupiter coming out of heaven and presenting to him the symbols of imperial power, a crown or a purple robe, or else of Mars, or of Mercury, with their eyes intently fixed upon him, as if to express their admiration of his eloquence and military skill. He placed the pictures of the gods in juxtaposition with his own, in order that the people might be led to worship them under the pretext of rendering due honor to him, and might thus under the cloak of ancient usages be induced to offer religious homage. He considered that if they would yield obedience on this point, they would be the more ready to obey him on every other occasion, but that if they ventured to refuse obedience, he would have reason to punish them as infringers of the Roman customs and offenders against the emperor and the state. There were but very few (and the law had its course against them) who, seeing through his designs, refused to render the customary homage to his pictures. But the multitude, through ignorance or simplicity, conformed as usual to the ancient regulation, and thoughtlessly paid homage to his image. The emperor derived but little advantage from this artifice, yet he did not cease from his efforts to effect a change in religion.

The next machination to which he had recourse was less subtle and more violent than the former one, and the fortitude of many soldiers attached to the court was thereby tested. When the stated day came round for giving money to the troops, which day generally fell upon the anniversary of some festival among the Romans such as that of the birth of the emperor or the foundation of some royal city, Julian reflected that soldiers are naturally thoughtless and simple, and disposed to be covetous of money, and therefore concluded that it would be a favorable opportunity to seduce them to the worship of the gods. Accordingly, as each soldier approached to receive the money, he was commanded to offer sacrifice, fire and incense having previously been placed for this purpose near the emperor, according to an ancient Roman custom. Some of the soldiers had the courage to refuse to offer sacrifice and receive the gold. Others were so habituated to the observance of the ancient custom, that they conformed to it without imagining that they were committing sin. Others, again, deluded by the luster of the gold, complied with the Pagan rite and suffered themselves to fall into the temptation from which they ought to have fled.

It is related[1] that as some of them who had ignorantly fallen into sin were seated at table and drinking to each other, one among them happened to mention the name of Christ. Another of the guests immediately exclaimed, "It is extraordinary that you should call upon Christ when, but a short time ago, you denied Him for the sake of the emperor's gift by throwing incense into the fire." On hearing this observation, they all became suddenly conscious of the sin they had committed. They rose from table and rushed into the public streets where they screamed and wept, and called upon all men to witness that they were Christians and that they had offered incense unawares and with the hand alone and not with the assent of the judgment. They then presented themselves before the emperor, threw back his gold, and besought him to put them to death, protesting that they would never renounce their sentiments, whatever torments might, in consequence of the sin committed by their hand, be inflicted on the other parts of their body for the sake of Christ. Whatever displeasure the emperor might have felt against them, he refrained from slaying them, lest they should enjoy the honor of martyrdom. He therefore merely deprived them of their military commission and dismissed them from the court.

NOTE

1. Sozomen probably took this story from Gregory Nazianzen's first *Oration against Julian*. Valesius here remarks on the antiquity of the custom of invoking the name of Christ at the commencement of every meal.

CHAPTER XVIII

CHRISTIANS PROHIBITED BY THE EMPEROR FROM STUDYING POLITE LITERATURE. RESISTANCE OF BASIL THE GREAT, GREGORY THE THEOLOGIAN, AND APOLLINARIUS TO THIS DECREE.

Julian entertained the same sentiments as those above described towards all Christians, as he manifested whenever an opportunity was offered. Those who refused the sacrifice to the gods, although perfectly blameless in other respects, were deprived of the rights of citizenship and of the privilege of joining assemblies and of holding public offices. He forbad the children of Christians from frequenting the public schools and from being instructed in the writings of the Greek poets and orators.[1] He entertained great resentment against Apollinarius the Syrian, a man of extraordinary erudition, against Basil and Gregory, natives of Cappadocia, the most celebrated orators of the time, and against other learned and eloquent men, of whom some were attached to the Nicene doctrines and others to the dogmas of Arius. His sole motive for excluding the children of Christian parents from instruction in the learning of the Greeks was because he considered such studies conducive to the acquisition of argumentative and persuasive power.

Apollinarius, therefore, employed his great learning and ingenuity, in which he even surpassed Homer, in the production of a work in heroic verse on the antiquities of the Hebrews from the creation to the reign of Saul. He divided this work into twenty-four parts, to each of which he appended the name of one of the letters of the Greek alphabet. He also wrote comedies in imitation of Menander, tragedies resembling those of Euripides, and odes on the model of Pindar. In short, he produced within a very brief space of time a numerous set of works which, in point of excellence of composition and beauty of diction, may vie with the most celebrated writings of Greece. Were it not for the extreme partiality with which the productions of antiquity are regarded, I doubt not but that the writings of Apollinarius would be held in as much estimation as those of the ancients. The comprehensiveness of his intellect is more especially to be admired, for he excelled in every branch of literature, whereas ancient writers were proficient only in one. He wrote a very remarkable work, entitled *The Truth*,[2] against the emperor and the Pagan philosophers, in which he clearly proved, without any appeal to the authority of Scripture, that they were far from having attained right opinions of God. The emperor, for the purpose of casting ridicule on works of this nature, wrote to the bishops in the following words: "I have read, I have understood, and I have condemned."

To this they sent the following reply: "You have read, but you have not understood, for had you understood, you would not have condemned."

Some have attributed this reply to Basil, bishop of Cappadocia, and perhaps not without reason. But whether dictated by him or by another, it fully displays the magnanimity and learning of the writer.

NOTES

1. Compare the statement of Socrates, *Ecclesiastical History*, Book III, Chapter 16.
2. Apollinaris, bishop of Hierapolis, also wrote a treatise with the same name. See Eusebius, *Ecclesiastical History*, Book IV, Chapter 27.

CHAPTER XIX

WORK WRITTEN BY JULIAN, ENTITLED "AVERSION TO BEARDS." DAPHNE, A SUBURB OF ANTIOCH. TRANSLATION OF THE REMAINS OF BABYLAS, THE PRIESTLY MARTYR.

Julian,[1] having determined upon undertaking a war against Persia, repaired to Antioch in Syria. The people loudly complained that although provisions were very abundant, the price affixed to them was very high. Accordingly the emperor, from liberality, as I believe, towards the people, reduced the price of provisions to so low a scale that the vendors fled the city. A scarcity in consequence ensued for which the people blamed the emperor, and their resentment found vent in ridiculing the length of his beard and the bulls which he had had stamped upon his coins, and they satirically remarked that he upset the world in the same way that his priests, when offering sacrifice, threw down the victims. At first his displeasure was excited, and he threatened to punish them, and prepared to depart for Tarsus. Afterwards, however, he suppressed his feelings of indignation and repaid their ridicule by words alone. He composed a very elegant work under the title of "Aversion to Beards,"[2] which he sent to them. He treated the Christians of the city precisely in the same manner as at other places and endeavored as far as possible, to promote the extension of Paganism.

I shall here recount some of the details connected with the tomb of Babylas, the martyr, and certain occurrences which took place about this period in the temple of Apollo at Daphne. Daphne is a suburb of Antioch, and is planted with cypresses and other trees beneath which all kinds of flowers flourish in their season. The branches of these trees are so thick and interlaced that they may be said to form a roof rather than merely to afford shade, and the rays of the sun can never pierce through them to the soil beneath. The purity and the softness of the air and the great quantity of limpid streams which water the earth, render this spot one of the most delightful places in the world. The Greeks pretend that Daphne, the daughter of the river Ladon, was here changed into a tree which bears her name, while she was fleeing from Arcadia to evade the pursuit of Apollo by whom she was beloved. The passion of Apollo was not diminished, they say, by this transformation. He embraced the tree and made a crown of its leaves. He afterwards often fixed his residence on this spot as being dearer to him than any other place.

Men of grave temperament, however, considered it disgraceful to approach this suburb, for the air and aspect of the place seemed to excite voluptuous feelings. The fable, too, connected with the locality, appeared to add fresh fuel to the ardor of the passions of youth. The example of the gods had so debasing an influence that the young people of this place seemed incapable of being continent themselves, or of enduring the presence of those who were continent. Any one who dwelt at Daphne without a mistress was regarded as callous and ungracious and was shunned accordingly. The Pagans likewise manifested great reverence for this place on account of a statue of Apollo which stood here, as also a magnificent temple, supposed to have been built by Seleucus, the father of Antiochus who gave his name to the city of Antioch. Those who attach credit to fables of this kind, believe that a stream flows from the fountain Castalia which confers the power of predicting the future, and which is similar in its effects to the fountain of Delphi. It is related that Hadrian here received intimation of his future greatness when he was but a private individual, and that he dipped a leaf of the laurel in the water and found written thereon an account of his destiny. When he became emperor, it is said, he commanded the fountain to be closed in order that no one might be enabled to pry into the knowledge of the future. But I leave this subject to those who are more accurately acquainted with mythology than I am.

When Gallus, the brother of Julian, had been declared Cæsar by Constantius, and had fixed his residence at Antioch, his zeal for the Christian religion and his veneration for the memory of the martyrs prompted him to the removal of the abominations which had arisen in Daphne. He considered that the readiest method of effecting this object would be to erect a house of prayer opposite to the temple, and to transfer thither the tomb of Babylas, the martyr, who had with great reputation to himself, presided over the church of Antioch. It is said that from the time of this translation, the demon ceased to utter oracles. This silence was at first attributed to the neglect into which his service was allowed to fall and to the omission of the usual sacrifices, but results proved that it was occasioned solely by the presence of the holy martyr. The silence continued unbroken even after the accession of Julian, although libations, incense, and victims were offered in abundance to the demon. The emperor himself entered the temple for the purpose of consulting the oracle and offering up gifts and sacrifices with entreaties to grant a reply. The demon did not openly admit that the hinderance was occasioned by the tomb of Babylas, the martyr, but he stated that the place was filled with dead bodies and that this prevented the oracle from speaking. Although many interments had taken place at Daphne, the emperor perceived that it was the presence of Babylas, the martyr, alone which had silenced the oracle, and he commanded his tomb to be removed. The Christians, therefore, assembled together and conveyed the relics to the city which was about forty stadia distant, and deposited them in the place where they are still preserved and to which the name of the martyr has been given. It is said that old men and maidens, young men and children, took part in the task of translating the remains, and that they sang psalms as they went along the road, apparently for the purpose of lightening their labor, but in truth because they were transported by zeal for their religion which the emperor opposed. The best singers sang first, and the multitude replied in chorus, and the following was the burden of their song: "Confounded are all they who worship graven images, who boast themselves in idols."

NOTES

1. Compare Socrates, *Ecclesiastical History,* Book III, Chapter 17.
2. *Note to the 2018 edition:* This work is entitled *Misopogon*. It is extant and available in English translation. See Bibliography and Further Reading in the frontmatter of the present volume.

CHAPTER XX

IN CONSEQUENCE OF THE CIRCUMSTANCES ATTENDING THE TRANSLATION OF THESE RELICS, MANY OF THE CHRISTIANS ARE ILL-TREATED. THEODORE THE CONFESSOR. TEMPLE OF APOLLO AT DAPHNE DESTROYED BY FIRE FROM HEAVEN.

The transaction above related[1] excited the indignation of the emperor as much as if an insult had been offered him, and he determined upon punishing the Christians, but Sallust, a prætorian prefect, although a Pagan, tried to dissuade him from this measure. The emperor, however, could not be appeased, and Sallust was compelled to execute his mandate and arrest and imprison many Christians.

One of the first whom he arrested was a young man named Theodore, who was immediately stretched upon the rack. But although his flesh was lacerated by the application of the iron nails, he addressed no supplication to Sallust nor did he implore a diminution of his torments. On the contrary, he seemed as insensible to pain as if he had been merely a spectator of the sufferings of another, and he sang the same psalm which he had joined in singing the day before to show that he did not repent of the act for which he had been condemned. The prefect, struck with admiration at his fortitude, went to the emperor and told him that unless he would desist from the measure he had undertaken, he and his party would be exposed to ridicule, while the Christians would acquire glory and reputation. This representation produced its effect, and the Christians who had been arrested were set at liberty. It is said that Theodore was afterwards asked whether he had been sensible of any pain while on the rack, and that he replied that he had not been entirely free from suffering, but had felt himself greatly refreshed and his torments assuaged by the attentions of a young man who had stood by him, and who had wiped off the perspiration, and supplied him with water. I am convinced that no man, whatever magnanimity he may possess, is capable, without the special assistance of Divine Power, of manifesting such entire indifference about the body.

The body of the martyr Babylas was for the reasons aforesaid removed to Daphne and was subsequently conveyed elsewhere. Soon after it had been taken away, fire suddenly fell upon the temple of Apollo at Daphne. The roof and the statue of the god were burnt, and the naked walls, with the columns on which the portico and the back part of the edifice had rested, alone escaped the conflagration. The Christians believed that the prayers of the martyr had drawn down fire from heaven upon the demon, but the Pagans suspected the Christians of having set fire to the place. This suspicion gained ground, and the priest of Apollo was brought before the tribunal of justice to render up the names of those who had perpetrated the deed. But though bound and subjected to the most cruel tortures, he did not name any one. Hence the Christians were more fully convinced than before, that it was not by the deed of man but by the wrath of God that fire was poured down from heaven upon the temple. Such were the occurrences which then took place.

The emperor, as I conjecture, on hearing that the calamity at Daphne had been occasioned by the martyr Babylas, and on being further informed that the honored remains of martyrs were preserved in several houses of prayer near the temple of Apollo Didymus which is situated close to the city of Miletus, wrote to the governor of Caria, commanding him to destroy with fire all such edifices as were furnished with a roof and an altar, and to throw down from their very foundations the houses of prayer which were incomplete in these respects.

NOTE

1. Compare Socrates, *Ecclesiastical History,* Book III, Chapter 19.

CHAPTER XXI

OF THE STATUE OF CHRIST IN THE CITY OF PANEADES. FOUNTAIN OF EMMAUS IN WHICH CHRIST WASHED HIS FEET. CONCERNING THE TREE WHICH WORSHIPPED CHRIST IN EGYPT.

Among so many remarkable events which occurred during the reign of Julian, I must not omit to mention one which affords a manifest proof of the power of Christ and of the Divine wrath against the emperor. Having heard that at Cæsarea Philippi, otherwise called Paneades, a city of Phœnicia, there was a celebrated statue of Christ which had been erected by a woman whom the Lord had cured of a flow of blood,[1] Julian commanded it to be taken down and a statue of himself erected in its place. But fire from heaven was poured down upon it, the head and breast were broken, and it was transfixed to the ground with the face downwards: it is still to be seen on the spot where it fell, blackened by the effects of the thunder. The statue of Christ was dragged round the city and mutilated by the Pagans, but the Christians recovered the fragments and deposited the statue in the church in which it is still preserved. Eusebius relates that at the base of this statue grew a herb which was unknown to the physicians and empirics but was efficacious in the cure of all disorders. It does not appear a matter of astonishment to me that after God has vouchsafed to dwell with men, he should condescend to bestow benefits upon them.

It appears that innumerable other miracles were wrought, of which accounts have been handed down to the people of the country and with which they only are acquainted. One instance may be cited in proof. There is a city, now called Nicopolis in Palestine, which was formerly only a village and which was mentioned by the holy evangelists[2] under the name of Emmaus. The name of Nicopolis was given to this place by the Romans in consequence of the conquest of Jerusalem and the victory over the Jews.[3] Just beyond the city where three roads meet, is the spot where Christ after his resurrection said farewell to Cleophas and his companions as if he were going to another village, and here is the fountain in which the Savior washed his feet and which has ever since possessed the property of removing every species of disease from man and other animals.

At Hermopolis in Thebaïs is a tree called Persea of which the branches, the leaves, and the least portion of the bark, are said to heal disease when touched by the sick, for it is related by the Egyptians that when Joseph fled with Christ and Mary the holy Mother from the wrath of Herod, they went to Hermopolis, and as they were entering the city, this tree bent down and worshipped Christ. I relate precisely what I have heard from many sources concerning this tree. I think that this phenomenon was a sign of the presence of God in the city, or perhaps as seems most probable, it may have arisen from the fear of the demon who had been worshipped in this large and beautiful tree by the people of the country: for at the presence of Christ, the idols of Egypt were shaken, even in Isaiah[4] the prophet had foretold. On the expulsion of the demon, the tree was permitted to remain as monument of what had occurred and was endued with the property of healing those who believed. The inhabitants of Egypt and of Palestine testify to the truth of these events, which took place among themselves.

NOTES

1. Compare Eusebius, *Ecclesiastical History*, Book VII, Chapter 18.
2. Luke 24:13.
3. This was done in the reign of Hadrian, when Ælia was built on the site of Jerusalem.
4. Isaiah 19:1.

CHAPTER XXII

FROM AVERSION TO THE CHRISTIANS, JULIAN GRANTS PERMISSION TO THE JEWS TO REBUILD THE TEMPLE AT JERUSALEM. THEIR ATTEMPT IS FRUSTRATED BY FIRE FROM HEAVEN, AND BY THE APPEARANCE OF THE SIGN OF THE CROSS ON THEIR GARMENTS.

Though the emperor[1] hated and oppressed the Christians, he manifested benevolence and humanity towards the Jews. He wrote[2] to the Jewish patriarchs and leaders, as well as to the people, requesting them to pray for him, and for the prosperity of the empire. In taking this step he was not actuated, I am convinced, by any respect for their religion, for he was aware that it is, so to speak, the mother of the Christian religion, and he knew that both religions rest upon the authority of the patriarchs and the prophets, but he thought to grieve the Christians by favoring the Jews, who are their most inveterate enemies. He also calculated upon persuading the Jews to embrace Paganism, for they were only acquainted with the mere letter of Scripture and could not, like the Christians and a few of the wisest among their own nation, discern the hidden meaning. Events proved that this was his real motive, for he sent for some of their chiefs and exhorted them to return to the observance of the laws of Moses and the customs of their fathers. On their replying that they were permitted to offer up sacrifices only at the temple of Jerusalem, he commanded them to rebuild the temple and gave them money for that purpose.[3]

The Jews entered upon the undertaking without reflecting that, according to the prediction of the holy prophets, it could not be accomplished. They sought for the most skillful artisans, collected materials, cleared the ground, and entered so earnestly upon the task that even the women carried heaps of earth and sold their ornaments towards defraying the expense. The emperor, the other Pagans, and all the Jews, regarded every other undertaking as secondary in importance to this. Although the Pagans were not well-disposed towards the Jews, yet they assisted them in this enterprise because they reckoned upon its ultimate success and hoped by this means to falsify the prophecies of Christ. Besides this motive, the Jews themselves were impelled by the consideration that the time had arrived for rebuilding their temple. When they had removed the ruins of the former building and had cleared the ground for the purpose of laying the foundations of the new edifice, an earthquake occurred and stones were thrown up from the earth, by which those who were engaged in the work were wounded, as likewise those who were merely looking on. The houses and public porticoes near the site of the temple were thrown down. Many people lost their lives and others were horribly mutilated.

On the cessation of the earthquake, the workmen returned to their task, partly because such was the edict of the emperor and partly because they were themselves interested in the undertaking. Men often, in endeavoring to gratify their own passions, seek what is injurious to them, reject what would be truly advantageous, and are deluded by the idea that nothing is really useful except what is agreeable to them. When once led astray by this error, they are no longer able to act in a manner conducive to their own interests, or to take warning by the calamities which are visited upon them. The Jews, I believe, were just in this state, for instead of regarding this unexpected earthquake as a manifest indication that God was opposed to the re-erection of their temple, they proceeded to re-commence the work. But all parties relate that they had scarcely returned to the undertaking when fire burst from the foundations of the temple and consumed several of the workmen. This fact is fearlessly stated and believed by all, the only discrepancy in the narrative is that some maintain that fire burst from the interior of the temple, as the workmen were striving to force an entrance, while others say that the fire proceeded direct from the bowels of the earth. In whichever way the phenomenon might have occurred, it is equally wonderful.

A more tangible and still more extraordinary prodigy ensued: suddenly the sign of the cross appeared on the garments of the persons engaged in the undertaking. These crosses were disposed like stars and appeared the work of art. Many were hence led to confess that Christ is God and that the rebuilding of the temple was not pleasing to him. Others presented themselves in the church, were baptized, and besought Christ with tears and supplications, to pardon their transgression. If any one does not feel disposed to believe my narrative, let him go and be convinced by those who heard the facts I have related from the eye-witnesses of them, for they are still alive. Let him inquire, also, of the Jews and Pagans who left the work in an incomplete state or who, to speak more accurately, were not able to commence it.

NOTES

1. Compare Socrates, *Ecclesiastical History*, Book III, Chapter 20.
2. The letter is still extant as the 25th Epistle of Julian, but its genuineness has been questioned. Valesius admits it as original. *Note to the 2018 edition:* This letter is numbered 51 in the Loeb Classical Library translation (1913) and may be found in Volume 3 of the works of Julian.
3. This episode, and its subsequent miraculous manifestations, is related in several ancient sources, most notably in Ammianus Marcellinus's *History*, Book XXIII, Chapter 1. See also Brock: *A Letter Attributed to Cyril of Jerusalem on the Rebuilding of the Temple*, as reproduced and translated in the *Bulletin of the School of Oriental and African Studies*, Volume 40, Number 2.

BOOK VI

CHAPTER I
EXPEDITION OF JULIAN AGAINST THE PERSIANS AND HIS MISERABLE END. LETTER WRITTEN BY LIBANUS DESCRIBING HIS DEATH.

I have narrated, in the preceding book, the occurrences which took place in the church during the reign of Julian.[1] This emperor, having determined to carry on the war with Persia, made a rapid transit across the Euphrates in the beginning of spring, and passing by Edessa from hatred to the inhabitants who had long professed Christianity, he went on to Carias where there was a temple of Jupiter in which he offered up sacrifice and prayer. He then selected twenty thousand armed men from among his troops and sent them towards the Tigris in order that they might guard those regions and also be ready to join him in case he should require their assistance. He then wrote to Arsacius, king of Armenia, one of the Roman allies, to bespeak his aid in the war. In this letter, Julian manifested the most unbounded arrogance. He boasted of the high qualities which had, he said, rendered him worthy of the empire and acceptable to the gods. He reviled Constantius, his predecessor, as an effeminate and impious emperor and directed his aspersions against Christianity. He told Arsacius that unless he acted according to his directions, the God in whom he trusted would not be able to defend him from his vengeance.

When he considered that all his arrangements had been duly made, he led his army through Assyria. He took a great many towns and fortresses, either through treachery or by force, and thoughtlessly proceeded onwards without reflecting that he would have to return by the same route. He pillaged every place he approached and destroyed and burnt the granaries and storehouses. As he was journeying up the Euphrates, he arrived at Ctesiphon, a very large city whither the Persian monarchs have now transferred their residence from Babylon. The Tigris flows near the spot. As he was prevented from reaching the city by a part of the land which separated it from the river, he judged that he must either pursue his journey by water or quit his ships and go to Ctesiphon by land, and he interrogated the prisoners on the subject. Having ascertained from them that there was a canal which had been blocked up by the course of time, he caused it to be cleared out and, having thus effected a communication between the Tigris and the Euphrates, he proceeded towards the city, his ships floating along by the side of his army. But the Persians appeared on the banks with a formidable display of troops, of elephants, and of horses, and Julian became conscious that his army was enclosed between two great rivers and was in danger of perishing, either by remaining in its present position or by retreating through the country which he had so utterly devastated that no provisions were attainable. To divert the minds of the soldiers, he proposed horse-races[2] and promised rewards to all who would enter the lists. In the meantime, he commanded the officers to throw the provisions and baggage from the ships, so that the soldiers, being driven to extremity by the want of necessaries, might engage in the conflict with greater courage and ardor.

After supper, he sent for the tribunes and chiefs and commanded the embarkation of the troops. They passed along the Tigris during the night, but their departure was perceived by some of the Persians, who prepared to oppose them. They found a few Persians asleep on the opposite bank, but they were readily overcome. At day-break, the two armies engaged in battle and after much bloodshed on both sides, the Romans returned by the river and encamped near Ctesiphon. The emperor, being no longer desirous of proceeding further, burnt his vessels as he considered that they required too many soldiers to guard them, and he then commenced his retreat along the Tigris which was to his left. The prisoners, who acted as guides to the Romans, led them to a fertile country where they found abundance of provisions.

Soon after, an old man who had resolved to die for the liberty of Persia, allowed himself to be taken prisoner and was brought before the emperor. On being questioned as to the route, he offered to guide the army by the nearest road to the Roman frontiers. He observed that for the space of three or four days' journey, this road would offer many difficulties and impediments and that it would be necessary to carry provisions during that time, as the surrounding country was sterile. The emperor was deceived by the discourse of this wise old man and gave orders to follow the route he indicated. After the lapse of three days, however, it was found that the whole armament had been led astray into a barren and inhospitable region. The old man was put to the torture. But he had exposed himself to death for the sake of his country and was therefore prepared to endure any sufferings that could be inflicted on him.

The Roman troops were now worn out by the length of the journey and the scarcity of provisions, and the Persians chose this moment to attack them. In the heat of the conflict which ensued, a violent wind arose and the sky and the sun were totally concealed by the clouds, while the air was at the same time filled with dust. During the darkness which was thus produced, a horseman riding at full gallop directed his lance against the emperor and wounded him mortally. He then rode from the field, and no one knew whither he went. Some conjectured that he was a Persian. Others, that he was a Saracen. Others assert that he who struck the blow was a Roman soldier who was indignant at the imprudence and temerity which the emperor had manifested in exposing his army to such extreme peril. Libanius[3] the sophist, a native of Syria, the most intimate friend of Julian, expressed himself in the following terms concerning the person who had committed the deed:

> "You desire to know by whom the emperor was slain. I know not his name. We have a proof, however, that the murderer was not one of the enemies: for no one came forward to claim the reward, although the king of Persia caused proclamation to be made by a herald of the honors to be awarded to him who had performed the deed. We are surely beholden to the enemy for not arrogating to themselves the glory of the action, but for leaving it to us to seek the slayer among ourselves. Those who sought his death were those who lived in habitual transgression of the laws, and who had formerly conspired against him, and who therefore perpetrated the deed as soon as they could find an opportunity. They were impelled by the desire of obtaining a greater degree of freedom from all control than they could enjoy under his government, and they were, perhaps, mainly stimulated by their indignation at the attachment of the emperor to the service of the gods, to which they were averse."

NOTES

1. Compare Socrates, *Ecclesiastical History,* Book III, Chapter 21.
2. κέλησιν ἆθλα προσθείς. Valesius observes that the Greek writers use the word κέλης both of the "horse "and the "rider," but that the word is here equivalent to the Latin *Eques*. The Roman order of Equites are spoken of by Polybius as κέλητες and the verb κελητίζειν is used by Homer, *Odyssey,* O., in the sense of leaping down from horseback. See Harpocration in voce ἄμιπποι, and compare the Latin "*Desultor.*"
3. The passage referred to is extant in the funeral oration on the praises of Julian, may be found in King: *Julian the Emperor* (1888). Another oration of the same Libanius, addressed to the emperor Theodosius, is extant according to Valesius.

CHAPTER II

VISIONS OF THE EMPEROR'S DEATH SEEN BY VARIOUS INDIVIDUALS. CALAMITIES WHICH JULIAN ENTAILED UPON THE ROMANS.

In the document above quoted, Libanius clearly states that the emperor fell by the hand of a Christian, and this, probably, was the truth. It is not unlikely that some of the soldiers who then served in the Roman army might have conceived the idea of acting like the ancient slayers of tyrants, who exposed themselves to death in the cause of liberty and fought in defense of their country, their families, and their friends, and whose names are held in universal admiration. Still less is he deserving of blame who, for the sake of God and of religion, performed so bold a deed.[1] But I know nothing further concerning the death of Julian besides what I have narrated. All men, however, concur in receiving the account which has been handed down to us and which evidences his death to have been the result of Divine wrath.

It appears that one of his friends had a vision which I shall now proceed to describe. He had, it is related, travelled into Persia with the intention of joining the emperor. While on the road, he found himself so far from any habitation that he was obliged, on one night, to sleep in a church. He saw during that night either in a dream or a vision, all the apostles and prophets assembled together, and complaining of the injuries which the emperor had inflicted on the church and consulting concerning the best measures to be adopted. After much deliberation, two individuals arose in the midst of the assembly, desired the others to be of good cheer and departed as if to deprive Julian of the imperial power. He who saw this vision did not attempt to pursue his journey, but awaited in horrible suspense the conclusion of the revelation. He laid himself down to sleep again, in the same place, and again he saw the same assembly. The two individuals who had appeared to depart the preceding night to effect their purpose against Julian returned and announced his death to the others.

On the same day, a vision was sent to Didymus, an ecclesiastical philosopher who dwelt at Alexandria and who, being deeply grieved at the apostasy of Julian and his persecution of the churches, fasted and offered up supplications to God continually on this account. From the effects of extreme vigilance and want of food he fell asleep in his chair. Then being, as it were, in an ecstasy, he beheld white horses traversing the air and heard a voice saying to those who were riding thereon, "Go, and tell Didymus that Julian has just been slain and let him arise and eat and communicate this intelligence to Athanasius the bishop." I have been credibly informed that the friend of Julian and the philosopher beheld those things. Results proved that neither of them were far from having witnessed the truth.

But if these instances do not suffice to prove that the death of Julian was the effect of Divine wrath on account of his persecution of the church, let the prediction of one of the ecclesiastics be recalled to mind. When Julian was preparing to enter upon the war against the Persians, he boasted that on the termination of the war, he would treat the Christians with so much severity, that the Son of the Carpenter would be unable to aid them. The ecclesiastic above-mentioned thereupon rejoined that the Son of the Carpenter was then preparing him a coffin.

Book VI, Chapter II

Julian himself was well aware whence the mortal stroke proceeded and what was the cause of its infliction, for when he was wounded, he took some of the blood that flowed from the wound and threw it up into the air, as if he had seen Jesus Christ and intended to throw it at him in order to reproach him with his death. Others say that he was angry with the sun because it had favored the Persians and had not rescued him, although, according to the doctrine of the astronomers, it had presided at his birth, and that it was to express his indignation against this luminary that he took blood in his hand and flung it upwards in the air. I know not whether on the approach of death and while his soul was in the act of being separated from the body, he might have become invested with superhuman powers and so have beheld Christ. Few allusions have been made to this subject, and yet I dare not reject this hypothesis as absolutely false, for God often suffers still more improbable and astonishing events to take place in order to prove that the Christian religion rests not on the wisdom or the power of man.

It is, however, very obvious that throughout the reign of this emperor, God gave manifest tokens of his displeasure and permitted many calamities to befall several of the provinces of the Roman empire. He visited the earth with such fearful earthquakes that the buildings were shaken and no more safety could be found within the houses than in the open air. From what I have heard, I conjecture that it was during the reign of this emperor or, at least, when he occupied the second place in the government, that a great calamity occurred near Alexandria in Egypt, namely, an inundation of the sea of such violence that the land was completely overflowed, and afterwards on the retreat of the waters, boats were found lodged on the roofs of the houses.[2] The anniversary of this inundation, which is regarded as the effect of an earthquake, is still commemorated at Alexandria by a yearly festival.[3] A general illumination is made throughout the city, the rites of religion are celebrated in the most solemn and pompous manner, and the Alexandrians return thanks to God for their deliverance. An excessive drought also occurred during this reign. The plants perished and the air was corrupted and, for want of proper sustenance, men were obliged to have recourse to the food usually eaten by other animals. To the famine succeeded a pestilence, by which many lives were lost. Such was the state of the empire during the administration of Julian.

NOTES

1. The Holy Scriptures, on the contrary, are most severe in their condemnation of the principle here mentioned by implication: and it is scarcely probable that the Greeks would have praised any one who killed his general, after having bound himself to him by the military oath. *Variorum Annot.*
2. Valesius remarks that these inundations occurred two years after the death of Julian, and he

refers to the testimony of Jerome, *Life of Hilarion*, Chapter 33.
3. Called γενέσια, or *Dies Natalia*, though as Valesius remarks, the term ἀνάμνησις would have been more appropriate. See Ammianus Marcellinus, *History*, Book XXVI.

CHAPTER III

ACCESSION OF THE EMPEROR JOVIAN.

After the decease of Julian, the government of the empire was, by the unanimous consent of the troops, tendered to Jovian.[1] He, at first, refused the symbols of imperial power, alleging that he was a Christian, but when the soldiers discovered the cause of his refusal, they loudly proclaimed that they were themselves Christians. The critical condition in which affairs had been left by Julian and the sufferings of the army from famine in an enemy's country, compelled Jovian to conclude a peace with the Persians and to cede to them some territories which had been formerly tributary to the Romans.[2]

Having learned from experience that the impiety of his predecessor had excited the wrath of God and given rise to public calamities, he wrote without delay to the governors of the provinces, directing that the people should assemble together in the churches, that they should serve God with reverence, and that they should receive the Christian faith as the only true religion. He restored to the churches and the clergy, to the widows and the virgins, the same privileges that had been granted by Constantine and his sons and afterwards withdrawn by Julian. He commanded[3] Secundus, who was then a prætorian prefect, to constitute it a capital crime to marry or to carry off any of the holy virgins, or even to regard them with unchaste desires. He enacted this law[4] on account of the wickedness which had prevailed during the reign of Julian, for many men had taken wives from among the holy virgins and, either by force or guile, had completely corrupted them, and thence had proceeded those breaches of morality which always occur when religion is contemned and licentiousness tolerated.

NOTES

1. Compare Socrates, *Ecclesiastical History*, Book III, Chapter 22.
2. Valesius remarks on the error of Christophorson, who rendered this passage as if it referred to tribute, and not to territorial possessions.
3. προσεφώνησε. This was the technical term.
4. This Constitution of Jovian is extant in the *Theodosian Code*, Book IX, Title 25, *De raptu, vel matrimonio sanctimonialium* (The Rape and Marriage of Holy Maidens and Widows). It is worded as follows: "Si quis non dicam rapere, sed vel attentare matrimonii jungendi causa, sacratas virgines vel *invitas* ausus fuerit, capitali sententia ferietur." Sozomen seems to have read *intueri* for *invitas*; but Valesius suggests that the correct reading is probably *viduas*, for widows as well as virgins were found in the cloister. *Note to the 2018 edition:* See Pharr: *The Theodosian Code and Novels*, page 246 for the complete English translation of this law.

CHAPTER IV

TROUBLES AGAIN ARISE IN THE CHURCHES. COUNCIL OF ANTIOCH, IN WHICH THE NICENE FAITH IS CONFIRMED. LETTER OF THE COUNCIL TO JOVIAN.

The rulers of the churches now resumed the agitation of doctrinal questions.[1] They had remained quiet during the reign of Julian when Christianity itself was endangered, and had unanimously offered up their supplications for the favor and protection of God. It is thus that men when attacked by foreign enemies, remain at peace among themselves, but when external troubles are removed, then internal dissensions creep in. This, however, is not a proper place for the citation of the numerous examples which history affords of this fact.

At this period, Basil, bishop of Ancyra, Silvanus, bishop of Tarsus, Sophronius, bishop of Pompeiopolis, and others of their party who regarded the heresy of the Anomians with the utmost aversion and received the term "similar as to substance," instead of the term "consubstantial," wrote to the emperor, and after expressing their thankfulness to God for his accession to the empire, besought him to confirm the decrees issued at Ariminum and Seleucia, and to annul what had been established merely by the zeal and power of certain individuals. They also entreated that if discussion[2] should still prevail in the churches, the bishops from every region might be convened alone[3] in some place indicated by the emperor and not be permitted to assemble elsewhere and issue decrees at variance with each other, as had been done during the reign of Constantius. They added that they had not gone to visit him at his camp because they were fearful of being burdensome to him, but that if he desired to see them, they would gladly repair to him and defray all expenses attendant on the journey themselves.

At this juncture, a council was convened at Antioch in Syria. The form of belief established by the council of Nicæa was confirmed, and it was decided that the Son is incontrovertibly of the same substance as the Father. Meletius, who was then bishop of Antioch, Eusebius, bishop of Samosata, Pelagius, bishop of Laodicea in Syria, Acacius, bishop of Cæsarea in Palestine, Irenius, bishop of Gaza, and Athanasius, bishop of Ancyra, took part in this council. On the termination of the council they acquainted the emperor with the transactions that had taken place by despatching the following letter:

> To the most religious and beloved Lord Jovian Augustus the Conqueror, from the bishops assembled from divers regions, at Antioch.
>
> We know, O emperor, well-beloved of God, that your piety is fully[4] intent upon maintaining peace and concord in the church. Neither are we

ignorant that you have embraced the true and orthodox faith which is the source of all unity. Lest, therefore, we should be reckoned among those who assail these doctrines of truth, we declare and testify that we receive and maintain the form of belief which was anciently set forth by the holy council of Nicæa. Now, although the term 'consubstantial' appears strange to some persons, yet it was safely interpreted by the Fathers and signifies that the Son was begotten of the substance of the Father, and that he is of like substance with the Father. This term does not convey the idea of unbroken generation. Neither does it coincide with the use which the Greeks make of the word 'substance,' but it is calculated to withstand the impious allegation of Arius, that the Son proceeded from what had had no previous existence. The Anomians have still the impudence and rashness to maintain this same audacious dogma, and they thereby most grievously disturb the peace and unanimity of the churches.

We subjoin to this letter a copy of the formulary of faith adopted by the bishops assembled at Nicæa, which we also receive and cherish.

Such were the decisions formed by the bishops convened at Antioch, and they appended to their letter a copy of the Nicene formulary of faith.

NOTES

1. Compare Socrates, *Ecclesiastical History,* Book III, Chapter 25.
2. σχίσματος. We here adopt the reading suggested by Valesius for the original σχήματος, which hardly makes sense.
3. μηδενὸς ἄλλου κοινωνοῦτος. To the exclusion of the inferior clergy and laity.
4. πρώτη, i.e. principally. Or, perhaps, (as Valesius suggests) we may take the word as literally implying that the emperor endeavored to re-establish peace in the church, before he took any measures with reference to the pacification of the state.

CHAPTER V

THE GREAT ATHANASIUS OBTAINS THE FAVOR OF THE EMPEROR, AND IS RE-APPOINTED OVER THE CHURCHES OF EGYPT. VISION OF THE GREAT ANTONY.

At this period, Athanasius, bishop of Alexandria, and some of his friends, deemed it requisite, as the emperor was a Christian, to repair to his court. Accordingly Athanasius went to Antioch and laid such matters before the emperor as he considered expedient. Others, however, say that the emperor sent for him in order to consult him concerning the affairs relative to religion and the true faith. When the business of the church had been transacted, Athanasius began to think of returning. Euzoius, bishop of the Arian heresy in Antioch, endeavored to install Probatius,[1] a eunuch who held the same sentiments as himself, in the bishopric of Alexandria. The whole party of Euzoius conspired with him to effect this design, and Lucius, a citizen of Alexandria who had been ordained priest by George, endeavored to prejudice the emperor against Athanasius, by representing[2] that he had been accused of divers crimes and had been condemned to perpetual banishment by preceding emperors, as the author of the dissensions and troubles of the church. Lucius likewise besought Jovian to appoint another bishop over the church of Alexandria.

The emperor saw through the artifice, attached no credit to the calumny, and dismissed Lucius with suitable admonitions. He also commanded Probatius, and the other eunuchs belonging to his palace whom he regarded as the originators of this contention, to act more advisedly for the future.[3] From that period, Jovian manifested the greatest friendship towards Athanasius and sent him back to Egypt with directions to govern the churches and people of that country as he might think fit. It is also said that he passed commendations on the virtue of the bishop, on the purity of his life, his intellectual endowments, and his great eloquence. Thus, after having been exposed to great opposition, was the Nicene faith fully re-established, but further opposition awaited it within a very short period. For the whole of the prediction of Antony the Monk was not fulfilled by the occurrences which befell the church during the reign of Constantius, part thereof was not accomplished till the reign of Valens. It is said that before the Arians took possession of the churches during the reign of Constantius, Antony had a dream in which he saw mules encompassing the altar and trampling it beneath their feet. On awakening, he predicted that the church would be troubled by the introduction of false and impure doctrines and by the rebellion of the heterodox. The truth of this prediction was evidenced by the events which occurred before and after the period now under review.

NOTES

1. Athanasius does not say that Euzoius studied to get Probatius made bishop of Alexandria on the flight of Athanasius, but only that the Arian party, under cover of the emperor's name, used every effort to get Athanasius expelled and another bishop substituted in his room; and that they were most anxious to bring about the election of Lucius.
2. The accusations made by Lucius against Athanasius are extant in the second volume of that Father's collected works, as Valesius remarks. *Note to the 2018 edition:* The letter referred to here may be found in *Saint Athanasius, Selected Works and Letters* from Schaff and Wace: *A Select Library of Nicene and Post-Nicene Fathers of the Christian Church*, Volume IV, page 568.
3. σωφρονισθῆαι. Valesius, however, renders the term *castigari*, and such is its technical signification in the best writers. See Thucydides, *History of the Peloponnesian War*, Book VI, Chapter 78. Euripides, *Antiope*, 8. It is curious that the word "chastise" in English has the same double meaning.

CHAPTER VI

DEATH OF JOVIAN, ACCESSION OF VALENTINIAN, AND ASSOCIATION OF HIS BROTHER VALENS IN THE GOVERNMENT.

After Jovian had reigned about eight months, he died suddenly at Dadastanis, a town of Bithynia, while on his road to Constantinople. Some say that his death was occasioned by eating too plentiful a supper. Others attribute it to the dampness of the chamber in which he slept, for it was of very recent construction and quantities of coals had been burnt in it during the winter for the purpose of drying the walls.

On the arrival of the troops at Nicæa in Bithynia, they proclaimed Valentinian emperor. He was a good man and capable of holding the reins of the empire. He had not long returned from banishment, for it is said that Julian, immediately on his accession to the empire, erased the name of Valentinian from the Jovian legions, as they were called, and condemned him to perpetual banishment under the pretext that he had failed in his duty of leading out the soldiers under his command against the enemy. The true reason of his condemnation, however, was the following. When Julian was in Gaul, he went one day to a temple to offer incense. Valentinian accompanied him according to an ancient Roman law which still prevails, and which enacted that the Jovians and the Herculeans (that is to say, the legions of soldiers who have received this appellation in honor of Jupiter and of Hercules) should always attend the emperor as his body guard. When they were about to enter the temple, the priest, in accordance with the Pagan custom,[1] sprinkled water upon them with the branch of a tree. A drop fell upon the robe of Valentinian who was a Christian. His indignation arose, and he rebuked the priest with great rudeness. It is even said that he tore off, in the presence of the emperor, the portion of the garment on which the water had fallen and flung it from him. From that moment Julian entertained inimical feelings against him, and soon after banished him to Melitine in Armenia under the plea of misconduct in military affairs: for he would not have religion regarded as the cause of the decree lest Valentinian should be accounted a martyr or a confessor. Julian treated other Christians, as we have already stated, in the same manner, for he perceived that persecution only added to the lustre of their reputation and tended to the consolidation of their religion.

As soon as Jovian succeeded to the throne, Valentinian was recalled from banishment. But the death of the emperor in the meantime took place, and Valentinian, by the unanimous consent of the troops and the chiefs, was appointed his successor. When he was invested with the symbols of imperial power, the soldiers cried out that it was necessary to elect some one to share the burden of government. To this proposition Valentinian made the following reply: "It depended on you alone, O soldiers, to proclaim me emperor. But now that you have elected me, it depends not upon you but upon me to perform what you demand. Remain quiet, as subjects ought to do, and leave me to act as an emperor."

Not long after this refusal to comply with the demand of the soldiery, he repaired to Constantinople and proclaimed his brother emperor. He gave him the East as his share of the government, and reserved to himself the regions along the Western Ocean, from Illyria to the furthest coasts of Libya. Both the brothers were Christians, but they differed in opinion and disposition. Valens, having been baptized by Eudoxius when he officiated as bishop, was zealously attached to the doctrines of Arius and would readily have compelled all mankind by force to yield to them. Valentinian, on the other hand, maintained the faith of the council of Nicæa and favored those who upheld the same sentiments without molesting those who entertained other opinions.

NOTE

1. νόμῳ Ἑλληνικῷ. Compare Herodotus, Book I, Chapter 51. Æschines, 4. 2, and 79. 2. Aristophanes, *Lysistrata*, 1130.

CHAPTER VII

TROUBLES AGAIN ARISE IN THE CHURCHES, AND THE COUNCIL OF LAMPSACUS IS HELD. MELETIUS, BISHOP OF ANTIOCH, AND OTHER ORTHODOX BISHOPS, ARE EJECTED FROM THEIR CHURCHES BY THE ARIANS.

When Valentinian was journeying from Constantinople to Rome,[1] he had to pass through Thrace, and the bishops of the Hellespont and of Bithynia, with others who maintained that the Son is consubstantial[2] with the Father, despatched Hypatian, bishop of Heraclea in Perinthus to meet him and to request permission to assemble themselves together for deliberation on questions of doctrine. When Hypatian had delivered the message with which he was intrusted Valentinian made the following reply: "I am but one of the laity, and have therefore no right to interfere in these transactions. Let the bishops, to whom such matters appertain, assemble where they please."

On receiving this answer, through Hypatian, their deputy, the bishops assembled at Lampsacus. After having conferred together for the space of two months, they annulled all that had been decreed at Constantinople through the machinations of the partisans of Eudoxius and Acacius. They likewise declared null and void the formulary of faith which had been circulated under the false assertion that it was the compilation of the Western bishops and to which the signatures of many bishops had been obtained by the promise that the dogma of dissimilarity as to substance should be condemned—a promise which had never been performed. They decreed that the doctrine of the Son being in substance like unto the Father should have the ascendancy, for they said that it was necessary to resort to the use of the term *"like,"* as indicative of the hypostases of the Godhead. They agreed that the form of belief which had been adopted at Seleucia and set forth at the dedication of the church of Antioch, should be maintained by all the churches. They directed that all the bishops who had been deposed by those who hold that the Son is dissimilar from the Father, should forthwith be reinstated in their churches as having been unjustly ejected. They declared that if any wished to bring accusations against them, they would be permitted to do so but under the penalty of incurring the same punishment as that due to the alleged crime should the accusation prove to be false. The bishops of the province and of the neighboring countries were to preside as judges and to assemble in the church with the witnesses who were to make the depositions.

After making these arrangements, the bishops summoned the partisans of Eudoxius and exhorted them to repentance, but as they would give no heed to these remonstrances, the decrees enacted by the council were sent to all the churches. Judging that Eudoxius would endeavor to persuade the emperor to side with him and would calumniate them, they determined to be beforehand with him and to send an account of their proceedings to the court. Their deputies met the emperor Valens as he was returning to Heraclea from Thrace, where he had been travelling in company with his brother who had gone on to Old Rome. Eudoxius, however, had previously gained over the emperor and his courtiers to his own sentiments so that when the deputies of the council of Lampsacus presented themselves before Valens, he merely exhorted them not to be at variance with Eudoxius. The deputies replied by reminding him of the artifices to which Eudoxius had resorted at Constantinople and of his machinations to annul the decrees of the council of Seleucia, and these representations kindled the wrath of Valens to such a pitch that he condemned the deputies to banishment and made over the churches to the partisans of Eudoxius. He then passed over into Syria, for he feared lest the Persians should break the truce which they had concluded with Jovian for thirty years. On finding, however, that the Persians were not disposed to insurrection, he fixed his residence at Antioch. He sent Meletius into banishment, but spared Paul because he admired the sanctity of his life. Those who were not in communion with Euzoius were either ejected from the churches or fined and punished in some other manner.

NOTES

1. Compare Socrates, *Ecclesiastical History,* Book IV, Chapter 4.
2. Baronius censures Sozomen for holding that the bishops who assembled at Lampsacus were Homoüsians, for placing that synod before AD 364, and for stating that legates from that synod

met Valens at Heraclea. But Valesius shows good reasons for considering that the censure of Baronius is undeserved.

CHAPTER VIII

REVOLT AND EXTRAORDINARY DEATH OF PROCOPIUS. ELEUSIUS, BISHOP OF CYZICUS, AND EUNOMIUS THE HERETIC.

It is probable that a severe persecution might have ensued at this juncture had not Procopius commenced a civil war.[1] As he possessed the chief authority at Constantinople, he soon collected a large army and marched against Valens. The latter quitted Syria, and met Procopius near Nacolia, a city of Phrygia, and captured him alive through the treachery of Agilonius and Gomoarius, two of his generals. Valens put them all to a cruel death, and although he had sworn to show favor to the two generals, he caused them to be sawn asunder. He commanded Procopius to be fastened by the legs to two trees which had been bent together by the application of a great force, so that on the sudden removal of the force, when the trees were left to resume their natural position, the victim was torn in twain.

On the termination of this war, Valens retired to Nicæa and finding himself in possession of profound tranquillity, he again began to molest those who differed from him in opinion concerning the Divine nature. His anger was unbounded against the bishops of the council of Lampsacus, because they had condemned the Arian bishops and the formulary of faith set forth at Ariminum. While under the influence of these resentful feelings, he summoned Eleusius from Syria, and having called together a synod of bishops who held his own sentiments, he endeavored to compel him to assent to their doctrines. Eleusius, at first, manfully refused compliance. But afterwards, from the dread of being ejected from his church and deprived of his property, as was threatened by the emperor, he yielded to the mandate. He soon repented of his weakness and, on his return to Cyzicus, he made a public confession of his fault in the church and urged the people to choose another bishop, for he said that he could not discharge the duties of the priesthood after having denied his own faith. The citizens esteemed and honored Eleusius too highly to proceed to the election of another bishop.

Eudoxius, bishop of the Arians in Constantinople however, ordained Eunomius as bishop of Cyzicus, for he expected that by his great powers of eloquence Eunomius would easily draw the people of Cyzicus over to his own sentiments. On his arrival at that city, he expelled Eleusius, for he was furnished with an imperial edict to that effect, and took possession of the church himself. The followers of Eleusius built a house of prayer without the walls of the city, and here they held their assemblies. I shall soon again have occasion to revert to Eunomius and the heresy which bears his name.

NOTE

1. Compare Socrates, *Ecclesiastical History,* Book IV, Chapters 5–7.

CHAPTER IX

SUFFERINGS OF THOSE WHO MAINTAINED THE NICENE FAITH. AGELIUS, BISHOP OF THE NOVATIANS.

The Christians who adhered to the Nicene doctrines and the followers of the Novatian heresy[1] were treated with equal severity in the city of Constantinople. They were all ultimately expelled from the city, and the churches of the Novatians were closed by order of the emperor. The other party had no churches to be closed, having been deprived of them all during the reign of Constantius. At this period, Agelius, who from the time of Constantius had governed the church of the Novatians at Constantinople, was condemned to banishment. It is said that he was noted for his accurate and implicit observance of the ecclesiastical laws. With respect to his mode of life, he had attained to the highest degree of philosophy, namely, freedom from worldly possessions. This was evidenced by his daily conduct. He had but one coat and always walked barefooted. Not long after his banishment he was recalled and restored to his church through the influence of Marcion, a man of extraordinary virtue and eloquence, who had formerly been enrolled among the troops of the palace but was at this period a presbyter of the Novatians and the teacher of grammar to Anastasia and Carosa,[2] the daughters of the emperor. There are still baths at Constantinople which bear the names of these princesses. It was for the sake of Marcion alone that the privilege abovementioned was conceded to the Novatians.

NOTES

1. Compare Socrates, *Ecclesiastical History,* Book IV, Chapter 9.
2. See the notes of Valesius on Socrates, *Ecclesiastical History,* Book IV, Chapter 8.

CHAPTER X

CONCERNING VALENTINIAN THE YOUNGER AND GRATIAN. PERSECUTION EXCITED BY VALENS. THE HOMOUSIANS, BEING PERSECUTED BY THE ARIANS AND MACEDONIANS, SEND AN EMBASSY TO ROME.[1]

About this period, a son was born to Valentinian in the West, to whom the emperor gave his own name. Not long after, he proclaimed his son Gratian emperor. This prince was born before his father succeeded to the throne.

In the meantime, although hailstones of extraordinary magnitude fell in various places, and although many cities, particularly Nicæa in Bithynia, were shaken by earthquakes, yet Valens the emperor and Eudoxius the bishop, paused not in their career but continued to persecute all Christians who differed from them in opinion. They succeeded to the utmost of their expectations in their machinations against those who adhered to the Nicene doctrines, for throughout many of the more distant provinces and particularly in Thrace, Bithynia, and the Hellespont, these Christians were, during the greater part of the reign of Valens, deprived of their churches and of their priests. Valens and Eudoxius then directed their resentment against the Macedonians, who were more in number than the Christians abovementioned in that reign, and persecuted them without mercy.

The Macedonians, in apprehension of further sufferings, sent deputies to various cities and finally agreed to have recourse to Valentinian and to Liberius, bishop of Rome, rather than conform to the doctrines of Eudoxius and Valens. In prosecution of this design, they selected three of their own number namely, Eustathius, bishop of Sebaste, Silvanus, bishop of Tarsus, and Theophilus, bishop of Castabalis, and sent them to the emperor Valentinian. They likewise intrusted them with a letter addressed to Liberius, bishop of Rome, and to the other bishops of the West, in which they entreated them, as prelates who had undeviatingly adhered to the faith of the apostles and who were peculiarly called upon to watch over the purity of religion, to receive their deputies favorably and to confer with them concerning the re-establishment of order in the church. When the deputies arrived in Italy, they found that the emperor was in Gaul engaged in a war against the barbarians. As they considered that it would be perilous to visit the seat of war in Gaul, they delivered their letter to Liberius.[2] After having conferred with him concerning the objects of their embassy, they condemned Arius and those who held and taught his doctrines. They renounced all heresies opposed to the faith established at Nicæa and received the term "consubstantial" as being a word that conveys the same signification as the expression "like in substance." When they had presented a confession of faith analogous to the above to Liberius, he received them into communion with himself and wrote to the bishops of the East, commending the orthodoxy of their faith, and detailing what had passed in the conference he had held with them. The confession of faith made by Eustathius and his companions was as follows.

NOTES

1. Valesius remarks that the title of this chapter is incorrect, and that it was the Macedonians, and not the orthodox Christians who sent the embassy to Rome.
2. Socrates (*Ecclesiastical History*, Book IV, Chapter 12) places this mission AD 368. But Baronius would place it two or even three years earlier.

CHAPTER XI

THE CONFESSION OF EUSTATHIUS, SILVANUS, AND THEOPHILUS, THE DEPUTIES OF THE MACEDONIANS, TO LIBERIUS, BISHOP OF ROME.

To Liberius, our Lord and Brother and Fellow Minister—Eustathius, Silvanus, and Theophilus, send greeting in the Lord.[1]

The desire of suppressing the absurd dogmas which heretics are perpetually broaching, to the scandal of the Catholic churches, has impelled us to assent to the decrees enacted at Lampsacus, at Smyrna, and at councils in other places, by the orthodox bishops. Having been sent on an embassy to your Holiness, as likewise to all the other bishops of Italy and of the West, we hereby attest and declare that we adhere to the Catholic faith which was established at the holy council of Nicæa, by the blessed Constantine and three hundred and eighteen inspired fathers. This form of belief has ever since remained inviolate, and it most justly admits the term "consubstantial" in testimony against the errors of Arius. We attest, by these our signatures, that we have always held this faith, that we still hold it, and that we shall adhere to it to the last.

We condemn Arius, his impious dogmas, and his disciples. We also condemn the heresies of Patropassius, of Sabellius, of Marcion, of Marcellus, of Paul of Samosata, and all who maintain such doctrines, as well as the doctrines themselves. We anathematize all heresies opposed to the holy faith established by the saintly fathers at Nicæa. We anathematize Arius, and condemn all such decrees as were enacted at Ariminum, in opposition to the faith established by the holy council of Nicæa. We were formerly deluded by the guile and perjury of certain parties and subscribed to these decrees when they were transmitted to Constantinople, from Nicæa, a city of Thrace.

At the conclusion of this document, they subjoined a copy of the entire formulary of Nicæa, and having received from Liberius a written account of all that they had transacted, they embarked on board a ship then sailing from Sicily.

NOTE

1. Compare Socrates, *Ecclesiastical History,* Book IV, Chapter 12.

CHAPTER XII

COUNCILS OF SICILY AND OF TYANE. RENEWED PERSECUTION OF THE ORTHODOX. EXILE AND RETURN OF ATHANASIUS.

A council was convened in Sicily and, after the same doctrines had been confirmed as those set forth in the confession of the deputies, the assembly was dissolved. At the same time, a council was held at Tyane,[1] and Eusebius, bishop of Cæsarea in Cappadocia, Athanasius, bishop of Ancyra, Pelagius, bishop of Laodicea, Zeno, bishop of Tyre, Paul, bishop of Emesa, Otreius,[2] bishop of Melitine, and Gregory, bishop of Nazianzen were present, with many other prelates who, during the reign of Jovian, had assembled at Antioch and determined to maintain the doctrine of the Son being consubstantial with the Father. The letter of Liberius and that addressed to the Western bishops were read at this council. These letters afforded high satisfaction to the members of the council, and they wrote to all the churches, desiring them to peruse the decrees of the Western bishops and the documents written by Liberius and the bishops of Italy, of Africa, of Gaul, and of Sicily which had been intrusted to the deputies of the council of Lampsacus. They urged them to reflect on the great number of prelates by whom these documents had been drawn up and who were far more in number than the members of the council of Ariminum, and exhorted them to be of one mind and to enter into communion with them to signify the same by writing, and finally to assemble together at Tarsus in Cilicia before the end of the spring.

On the approach of the appointed day, when these bishops were accordingly on the point of repairing to Tarsus, about thirty-four of the Asiatic bishops assembled in Caria,[3] commended the design of establishing uniformity of belief in the church, but objected to the term "consubstantial," and insisted that the formularies of faith set forth by the councils of Antioch and Seleucia, and maintained by Lucian the martyr and by many of their predecessors in the midst of great tribulations, ought to obtain the ascendancy over all others. The emperor, at the instigation of Eudoxius, prevented the council from being convened in Cilicia and even prohibited it under severe penalties. He also wrote to the governors of the provinces, commanding them to eject all bishops from their churches who had been banished by Constantine and recalled by Julian.

Those who were at the head of the government of Egypt were anxious to deprive Athanasius of his bishopric and expel him from the city, for according to the edict of the emperor, pecuniary and other punishments were to be visited upon all magistrates and officers who neglected the execution of the mandate. The Christians of the city, however, assembled and besought the governor not to banish Athanasius without further consideration of the terms of the mandate, which merely specified all bishops who had been banished by Constantine and recalled by Julian, and it was manifest that Athanasius was not of this number, inasmuch as he had been recalled by Constantius, and banished by Julian at the very time that all the other bishops had been recalled, and had been finally recalled by Jovian. The governor was by no means convinced by these arguments, but perceiving that Athanasius could only be conveyed away by force, as the people assembled in crowds and as commotion and perturbation prevailed throughout the city, he began to apprehend an insurrection, and therefore wrote to the emperor without making any attempt against the bishop.

Some days afterwards, when the popular excitement had abated, Athanasius secretly quitted the city at dusk and concealed himself. The very same night, the governor of Egypt and the military chiefs took possession of the church in which Athanasius generally dwelt and sought him in every part of the edifice and even on the roof, but in vain, for they had calculated upon seizing the moment when the popular commotion had partially subsided and when the whole city was wrapt in sleep, to execute the mandate of the emperor and to transport Athanasius quietly from the city. The disappearance of Athanasius excited universal astonishment. Some attributed his escape to a special revelation from above, others to the advice of some of his followers. But more than human prudence seems to have been requisite to foresee and to avoid such imminent danger. Some say, that as soon as the people gave indications of being disposed to sedition, he concealed himself among the tombs of his ancestors, being apprehensive lest he should be regarded as the cause of any disturbances that might ensue, and that he afterwards retreated to some other place of concealment.

The emperor Valens soon after granted permission for him to return to his church. It is very doubtful whether in making this concession, Valens acted according to his own inclination. I rather imagine that on reflecting on the esteem in which Athanasius was universally held, he feared to excite the displeasure of the emperor Valentinian who was well known to be attached to the Nicene doctrines, if he proceeded to violent measures against the prelate, or perhaps he might have been apprehensive lest the people who were much attached to their bishop should be impelled to a line of conduct prejudicial to the interests of the empire. I also believe that the Arian bishops did not, on this occasion, plead very vehemently against Athanasius, for they considered that if he were ejected from his church, he would probably repair to the emperor and might possibly succeed in persuading Valens to adopt his own sentiments and in arousing the anger of Valentinian against themselves. They were greatly troubled by the evidences of the virtue and courage of Athanasius, which had been afforded by the events which transpired during the reign of Constantius. He had, in fact, so skillfully evaded the plots of his enemies, that they had been constrained to consent to his re-installation in the government of the churches of Egypt. And yet he could be scarcely induced to return from Italy, although letters had been despatched by Constantius to that effect.

I am convinced that it was solely from these reasons that Athanasius was not expelled from his church like the other bishops who were subjected to as cruel a persecution as was ever inflicted by Pagans. Those who would not change their doctrinal tenets were banished. Their houses of prayer were taken from them and placed in the possession of those who held opposite sentiments. Egypt alone was, during the life of Athanasius, exempted from this persecution.

NOTES

1. This council was held probably AD 367, or early in 368.
2. He is mentioned by Basil the Great in his 316th Epistle.
3. It is probable that we should read here Antioch for Caria, as Valesius suggests. Another synod held at Antioch in Caria is mentioned by Sozomen below, Book VII, Chapter 2.

CHAPTER XIII

DEMOPHILUS ELECTED BISHOP OF CONSTANTINOPLE BY THE ARIANS, AND EVAGRIUS BY THE ORTHODOX. ACCOUNT OF THE PERSECUTION WHICH ENSUED.

About this time the emperor Valens went to Antioch, and during his absence Eudoxius died after having governed the church of Constantinople during the space of eleven years.[1] Demophilus was immediately ordained as his successor by the Arian bishops. The followers of the Nicene doctrines, believing that the course of events was in their power, elected Evagrius as their bishop. He had been ordained by Eustathius, who had formerly governed the church of Antioch in Syria, and who having been recalled from banishment by Jovian, lived in a private manner at Constantinople, and devoted himself to the instruction of those who held his sentiments, exhorting them to perseverance.

The Arians were deeply incensed at this ordination and commenced a violent persecution against those by whom it had been effected. The emperor Valens, who was then at Nicomedia, on being apprized of the occurrences that had taken place in Constantinople since the death of Eudoxius, was fearful lest an insurrection should arise in the city, and therefore sent thither as many troops as he thought requisite to preserve tranquillity. Eustathius was arrested by his command and banished to Bizya,[2] a city of Thrace, and Evagrius was exiled to some other region.

NOTES

1. Compare Socrates, *Ecclesiastical History*, Book IV, Chapters 14, 15.

2. We have adopted Valesius' suggestion here. The town is mentioned by Socrates in the place referred to above.

CHAPTER XIV
EIGHTY ORTHODOX PRIESTS[1] PUT TO DEATH BY VALENS.

The prosperity of the Arians greatly added to their arrogance, and they persecuted unmercifully all Christians whose religions sentiments were opposed to their own.[2] These Christians, being exposed to personal injuries, accusations, and imprisonment, and finding themselves moreover gradually impoverished by the fines and extortions of the Arians, were at length compelled to appeal for redress to the emperor. They deputed to him for this purpose an embassy consisting of eighty ecclesiastics, under the direction of Urbanus, Theodore, and Menedemes. When they arrived at Nicomedia, they presented a memorial of their grievances to the emperor. Although transported with rage, the emperor did not openly manifest any displeasure, but secretly commanded the prefect to slay the whole deputation. But the prefect, being apprehensive that a popular insurrection would be excited if he were to put so many good and religious men to death without any of the forms of justice, pretended that they were to be sent into exile, and under this pretext compelled them to embark on board a ship, to which they assented with the most perfect resignation. When they had sailed to about the center of the bay, which was called Astacenes, the sailors according to the orders they had received, set fire to the vessel and leaped into the boat. A wind arising, the ship was blown along to Dacibiza, a port of Bithynia, but no sooner had it neared the shore, than it was utterly consumed with all the men on board.

NOTES

1. Πρεσβεών. Christophorson renders the word "Legati."
2. Compare Socrates, *Ecclesiastical History,* Book IV, Chapter 16.

CHAPTER XV
DISPUTES BETWEEN EUSEBIUS, BISHOP OF CÆSAREA, AND BASIL THE GREAT, CONCERNING THE CHURCH OF CÆSAREA.

When Valens quitted Nicomedia, he went on to Antioch and in passing through Cappadocia he did all in his power, according to custom, to injure the orthodox, and to deliver up the churches to the Arians. He thought to accomplish his designs the more easily on account of a dispute[1] which was then pending between Basil and Eusebius who governed the church of Cæsarea. This dissension had been the cause of Basil's departing from Pontus, where he lived in retirement with some monks. The people and some of the most powerful and of the wisest men in the city began to regard Eusebius with suspicion, particularly as they considered him the cause of the withdrawal of one who was equally celebrated for his eloquence and his piety, and they accordingly began to meditate a secession from communion with Eusebius. In the meantime, Basil, fearing to be a source of further trouble to the church which was already rent by the dissensions of heretics, remained in retirement at Pontus. The emperor and the Arian bishops who were always attached to his suite, regarded the absence of Basil and the hatred of the people towards Eusebius, as circumstances that would tend greatly to the success of their designs. But their expectations were utterly frustrated. On the first intelligence of the intention of the emperor to pass through Cappadocia, Basil quitted Pontus[2] and returned to Cæsarea, where he effected a reconciliation with Eusebius, and by his eloquence greatly promoted the interests of the church. The projects of Valens were thus defeated, and he returned with his bishops without having accomplished any of his designs.

NOTES

1. Concerning this difference, see Gregory Nazianzen, in his Funeral Oration on the Great Saint Basil, Bishop of Cæsarea in Cappadocia. *Note to the 2018 edition:* This oration may be found in English translation as number 43 in Schaff et al.: *Nicene and Post-Nicene Fathers, Series II, Volume VII: Orations of Gregory Nazianzen.*
2. AD 370. See Socrates, *Ecclesiastical History,* Book IV, Chapter 26.

CHAPTER XVI

BASIL SUCCEEDS EUSEBIUS IN THE BISHOPRIC OF CAPPADOCIA, AND SPEAKS WITH GREAT FREEDOM IN THE PRESENCE OF VALENS.

Some time after, the emperor again visited Cappadocia and found that Eusebius was dead and that the bishopric had been transferred to Basil. He thought of expelling him from this office, but was compelled to abandon his intention. It is said that the night after he had formed his plans, his wife was disturbed by a frightful dream and that his only son, Galates, was about the same time cut off by a rapid disease. The death of this prince was universally attributed to the wrath of God on account of the machinations that had been carried on against Basil. Valens himself was of this opinion, and after the death of his son, offered no further molestation to the bishop. When the prince was sinking under the disease and at the point of death, the emperor sent for Basil and requested him to pray to God for his son's recovery. For as soon as Valens had arrived at Cæsarea, the prefect had sent for Basil and commanded him to embrace the religious sentiments of the emperor, menacing him with death in case of non-compliance. Basil replied that it would be great gain to him to be delivered from the bondage of the body, and that he should consider himself under obligation to whoever would free him from that bondage. The prefect gave him the rest of that day and the approaching night for deliberation and advised him not to rush imprudently into obvious and imminent danger.

"I do not require to deliberate," replied Basil. "My determination will be the same tomorrow as it is today. Never will I worship the creature or recognize the creature as God. Neither will I conform to your religion, nor to that of the emperor. Although your power may be great, and although you have the honor of ruling no inconsiderable a portion of the empire, yet I ought not on these accounts to seek to please men, and at the same time deviate from that Divine faith which neither exile, proscription, nor death have ever impelled me to abjure. Inflictions of this nature have never excited in my mind one pang of sorrow. I possess nothing but a cloak and a few books.[1] I dwell on the earth as a traveller. As to bodily tortures, the weakness of my constitution is such that I should triumph over them on the first application of the rack."

The prefect admired the courage evinced in this bold reply and communicated the circumstance to the emperor. On the festival of the Epiphany, the emperor repaired to the church with the rulers and his guards, presented gifts at the altar, and held a conference with Basil whose wisdom and gravity of deportment strongly excited his admiration. Not long after, however, the calumny of his enemies prevailed, and Basil was condemned to banishment. On the night previous to the execution of the edict, the son of the emperor fell ill with a dangerous and malignant fever. The father prostrated himself on the earth and wept over the calamity, and not knowing what other measures to take toward effecting the recovery of his son, he despatched some of his attendants to Basil whom he feared to summon himself on account of the injustice he had manifested toward him. Immediately on the arrival of Basil, the prince began to rally, so that many maintain that his recovery would have been complete had not some heretics been summoned to pray with Basil for his restoration. It is said that the prefect, likewise, fell ill, but that on his repentance and on prayer being offered to God, he was restored to health. The instances above adduced are quite inadequate to convey an idea of the wonderful endowments of Basil: his austerity of life and astonishing powers of eloquence attracted great celebrity.

NOTE

1. See notes of Valesius on Socrates, *Ecclesiastical History,* Book IV, Chapter 26.

CHAPTER XVII

FRIENDSHIP OF BASIL AND OF GREGORY THE THEOLOGIAN. THEY MAINTAIN THE NICENE DOCTRINES.

Gregory, who it is said was equally noted for the same attainments as Basil,[1] flourished about the same period. They had both studied in their youth at Athens, under Himerius and Proæresius, the most celebrated sophists of the age, and afterwards at Antioch, under Libanius, the Syrian. But as they subsequently conceived a contempt for sophistry and the study of the law, they determined to devote themselves to the practice and study of Christian philosophy according to the canons of the church. After having spent some time in the pursuit of Pagan science, they entered upon the study of the commentaries which Origen and the authors who lived before and after his time have written in explanation of the Sacred Scriptures. They rendered great assistance to those who, like themselves, maintained the Nicene doctrines, and manfully opposed the dogmas of the Arians, proving that these heretics did not rightly understand the data upon which they proceeded, nor even the Commentaries of Origen upon which they mainly depended. These two holy men divided the perils of their undertaking, either by mutual agreement, or as I have been informed, by lot. The cities in the neighborhood of Pontus fell to the lot of Basil, and here he founded numerous monasteries and confirmed the people in the belief of the doctrines which he maintained. After the death of his father, Gregory obtained the bishopric of the small city of Nazianzum,[2] and he was hence obliged to remain for some time at Constantinople and other places. Not long after, he was called by the people to the dignity of the metropolitan see, for there was then neither bishop nor church in Constantinople, and the doctrines of the council of Nicæa were almost extinct.

NOTES

1. See Saint Chrysostom, *de Sacerdotio*, Book I, Chapters 1–7.
2. He had been for some little time coadjutor bishop during his father's lifetime.

CHAPTER XVIII

PERSECUTION OF CHRISTIANS AT ANTIOCH ON THE ORONTES. THE PEOPLE ASSEMBLE NEAR THE CHURCH OF THE APOSTLE THOMAS AT EDESSA.

The emperor went to Antioch and ejected from the churches of that city and of the neighboring towns all those who adhered to the Nicene doctrines.[1] Moreover, he persecuted them with extreme cruelty, putting many of them to death in various ways and causing others to be drowned in the river Orontes. Having heard that there was a magnificent church at Edessa named after the apostle Thomas, he went to see it. On approaching the edifice, he saw the members of the Catholic church assembled for worship without the walls of the city, for they had been deprived of their churches. It is said that the emperor was so indignant with the prefect for permitting these assemblies, that he struck him. Modestus, (for this was the name of the prefect) although he was himself a heretic, secretly warned the people of Edessa not to meet for prayer on the same spot the next day, for he had received orders from the emperor to punish all who resorted thither. But the people, totally disregarding the threat, assembled with more than their customary zeal at the usual place of meeting. Modestus, on being apprized of their proceedings, was undecided as to what measures ought to be adopted and repaired to the place where they had assembled. A woman, leading a child by the hand, forced her way through the ranks of the army, as if bent upon some affair of importance. Modestus remarked her conduct, ordered her to be stopped, and summoned her into his presence to inquire the cause of her anxiety. She replied, that she "was hastening to the spot where the members of the Catholic church were assembled.

"Know you not," replied Modestus, "that the prefect is on his way thither for the purpose of condemning to death all who are found on the spot?"

"I have heard so," replied she, "and this is the very reason of my haste, for I am fearful of arriving too late and thus losing the honor of martyrdom."

The governor having asked her why she took her child with her, she replied, "In order that he may share in the sufferings of the others and participate in the same reward."

Modestus, struck with astonishment at the courage of this woman, went to the emperor, and acquainting him with what had occurred, persuaded him to renounce a design which was neither beneficial nor creditable. Thus was the Christian faith confessed by the whole city of Edessa.

NOTE

1. Compare Socrates, *Ecclesiastical History,* Book IV, Chapter 18.

CHAPTER XIX

DEATH OF THE GREAT ATHANASIUS. HIS BISHOPRIC TRANSFERRED TO LUCIUS THE ARIAN. PETER, THE SUCCESSOR OF ATHANASIUS, SEEKS REFUGE IN ROME.

Athanasius, bishop of Alexandria, died about this period, after having governed the church during the space of forty-six years.[1] The Arians having received early intelligence of his death, Euzoius, bishop of the Arians at Antioch, and Magnus, the chief treasurer, lost no time in seizing and imprisoning Peter whom Athanasius had appointed to succeed him in the bishopric, and they forthwith transferred the government of the church to Lucius. Thence resulted a cruel persecution in Egypt, for as soon as Lucius presented himself in Alexandria and attempted to take possession of the churches, he met with opposition from the people, and the clergy and holy virgins were accused as the originators of the sedition. Some made their escape, as if the city had fallen into the hands of an enemy. Others were seized and imprisoned. Some of the prisoners were afterwards dragged from the dungeons to be torn with iron nails, while others were burnt by means of flaming torches. It seemed wonderful how they could possibly survive the tortures to which they were subjected. Banishment, or even death itself, would have been preferable to such sufferings.

Peter, the bishop, made his escape from prison and embarking on board a ship, proceeded to Rome, the bishop of which church held the same sentiments as himself. Thus the Arians, although not many in number, remained in possession of the churches. At the same time, an edict was issued by the emperor enacting that as many of the followers of the Nicene doctrines should be ejected from Alexandria and the rest of Egypt as might be directed by Lucius. Euzoius, having thus accomplished all his designs, returned to Antioch.

NOTE

1. With this chapter compare the parallel accounts of Socrates, *Ecclesiastical History,* Book IV, Chapter 20, and Theodoret, Ecclesiastical History, Book IV, Chapter 20.

CHAPTER XX

PERSECUTION OF THE EGYPTIAN MONKS AND OF THE DISCIPLES OF SAINT ANTONY. MIRACLES WROUGHT BY THEM.

Lucius went with the governor of Egypt and a band of soldiers against the monks in the desert,[1] for he imagined that if he could overcome their opposition by interrupting the tranquillity which they loved, he would meet with fewer obstacles in drawing over to his party the Christians who inhabited the cities. The monasteries of this country were governed by several individuals of eminent sanctity who were strenuously opposed to the heresy of Arius. The people, who were neither able nor willing to enter upon the investigation of doctrinal questions, received their opinions from them and thought with them, for they were persuaded that men whose virtue was manifested by their deeds were in possession of truth.

We have heard that the leaders of these Egyptian ascetics were two men of the name of Macarius of whom mention has been already made,[2] Pambonius and

Heraclides, and other disciples of Antony. On reflecting that the Arians could never succeed in establishing an ascendancy over the Catholic church unless the monks could be drawn over to their party, Lucius determined to have recourse to force to compel the monks to side with him, all gentler measures having been attended with signal failure. But here again his schemes were frustrated, for the monks were prepared to fall by the sword rather than to swerve from the Nicene doctrines. It is related that at the very time that the soldiers were about to attack them, a man whose limbs were withered and who was unable to stand, was carried to them and that when they had anointed him with oil and commanded him (in the name of Christ whom Lucius persecuted) to arise and go to his house, he was immediately restored to health and strength. This miraculous cure manifested the necessity of adopting the sentiments of those whose prayers were heard and answered by God in opposition to the dogmas of Lucius. But the persecutors of the monks were not led to repentance by this miracle. On the contrary, they arrested these holy men and conveyed them by night to an island of Egypt lying in the midst of swamps and marshes. The inhabitants of this island had never heard of the Christian faith and were devoted to the service of demons. The island contained many temples of great antiquity used for idolatrous purposes. It is said that when the monks landed on the island, the daughter of the priest, who was possessed of a devil, went to meet them. The girl ran screaming towards them, and the people of the island, astonished at her strange conduct, followed in crowds. When she drew near the ship in which were the holy priests, she flung herself upon the ground and exclaimed in a loud voice, "Wherefore are you come to us, O servants of the great God? For we have long dwelt in this island without giving trouble to any one. Unknown to men, we have concealed ourselves here and shut up ourselves within these marshes. If, however, it please you, accept our possessions and fix your abode here. We will quit the island." Macarius and his companions exorcised the demon, and the girl was restored. Her father and all her house, with the inhabitants of the island, immediately embraced Christianity and demolished their temple for the purpose of erecting a church.

On these occurrences being reported at Alexandria, Lucius was overcome by immoderate grief, and fearing lest he should incur the hatred of his own partisans and be accused of warring against God and not against man, he sent secret orders for Macarius and his companions to be re-conveyed to their own dwellings in the wilderness. Thus did Lucius occasion troubles and commotions in Egypt.

About the same period, Didymus the philosopher and several other illustrious men acquired great renown. Struck by their virtue, and by that of the monks, the people followed their doctrines, and opposed those of the partisans of Lucius. The Arians, though not so strong in point of numbers as the other party, grievously persecuted the church of Egypt.

NOTES

1. Compare Socrates, *Ecclesiastical History,* Book IV, Chapter 24.
2. See above, Book III, Chapter 14.

CHAPTER XXI
LIST OF THE PLACES IN WHICH THE NICENE DOCTRINES WERE PREACHED. FAITH MANIFESTED BY THE SCYTHIANS.

Arianism met with similar opposition at the same period in Osroene and Cappadocia. Basil, bishop of Cæsarea, and Gregory, bishop of Nazianzen, were held in high admiration and esteem throughout these regions. Syria and the neighboring provinces, and more especially the city of Antioch, were plunged in confusion and disorder, for the Arians were very numerous in these parts and had possession of the churches. The members of the Catholic church were not, however, few in number. They were called Eustathians and Paulinists, and were under the guidance of Paulinus and Meletius, as has been before stated. It was through their instrumentality that the church of Antioch was preserved from the encroachments of the Arians and enabled to resist the power of Valens and of those who acted under his directions.

Indeed, it appears that all the churches which were governed by men who were firmly attached to the faith did not deviate from the form of doctrine they had originally embraced. It is said that this was the cause of the firmness with which the Scythians adhered to their religion. There are in this country a great number of cities, of towns, and of fortresses. The metropolis is called Tomis. It is a large and opulent city, and lies to the left of the Euxine. According to an ancient custom which still prevails, all the churches of the whole country are under the sway of one bishop.[1] Vetranio ruled over these churches at the period that the emperor visited Tomis. Valens repaired to the church and strove, according to his usual custom, to gain over the bishop to the heresy of Arius, but this latter manfully opposed his arguments, and after a courageous defense of the Nicene doctrines, quitted the emperor and proceeded to another church, whither he was followed by the people. All the citizens had crowded to see the emperor, for they expected that something extraordinary would result from this interview with the bishop. Valens was extremely offended at being left alone in the church with his attendants and in resentment condemned Vetranio to banishment. Not long after, however, he recalled him because, I believe, he apprehended an insurrection, for the Scythians openly deplored the absence of their bishop. He well knew that the Scythians were a courageous nation and that their country possessed many natural advantages which rendered it necessary to the Roman empire, for it served as a barrier to ward off the invasions of the barbarians.

Thus were the designs of the emperor frustrated by Vetranio. The Scythians themselves testify to the virtues of this bishop and to his eminent sanctity of life. The resentment of the emperor at the defeat of his schemes was visited upon all the clergy except those of the Western churches, for Valentinian, who reigned over the Western regions, was attached to the Nicene doctrines, and was imbued with so much reverence for religion that he never imposed any commands upon the priests nor ever attempted to introduce any alteration in ecclesiastical regulations. Whatever might have been his capabilities for guiding the reins of the empire (as, indeed, was evidenced by his deeds) he considered that ecclesiastical matters were beyond the range of his jurisdiction.

NOTE

1. Sozomen repeats this below, Book VII, Chapter 19, where he recounts the various local customs prevailing in the ecclesiastical system.

CHAPTER XXII

DEBATE CONCERNING THE NATURE OF THE HOLY GHOST. IT IS DECIDED THAT HE IS TO BE CONSIDERED CONSUBSTANTIAL WITH THE FATHER AND THE SON.

A question was renewed at this juncture which had previously excited much inquiry,[1] namely—whether the Holy Ghost is or is not to be considered consubstantial with the Father and the Son. Lengthened debates ensued on this subject, similar to those which had been held concerning the nature of God the Word. Those who asserted that the Son is dissimilar from the Father, and those who insisted that he is similar in substance to the Father, came to one common opinion concerning the Holy Ghost, for both parties maintained that the Holy Ghost differs in substance from the other two Persons of the Trinity, and that he is but the Minister, and the third Person of the Trinity in point of dignity and order. Those, on the contrary, who believed that the Son is consubstantial with the Father, believed also that the Spirit is consubstantial with the Father and the Son. This doctrine was zealously maintained in Syria by Apollinarius, bishop of Laodicea, in Egypt by Athanasius[2] the bishop, and in Cappadocia and in Pontus by Basil and Gregory. The bishop of Rome, on hearing that this question was agitated with great acrimony and that the contention seemed daily to increase, wrote to the churches of the East, and urged them to receive the doctrine upheld by the Western clergy, namely—that the three Persons of the Trinity are of the same substance and of equal dignity. The question having been thus decided by the Roman churches, peace was restored and an end was put to the debate.

NOTES

1. Compare Socrates, *Ecclesiastical History*, Book II, Chapter 45.
2. Or, more probably, Peter, for Athanasius was recently dead. But Sozomen (as Valesius remarks) is careless in observing the proper order of time.

CHAPTER XXIII

DEATH OF LIBERIUS, BISHOP OF ROME. HE IS SUCCEEDED BY DAMASUS AND URSINUS. ORTHODOX DOCTRINES PREVAIL THROUGHOUT THE WEST, EXCEPT AT MILAN. SYNOD HELD AT ROME, BY WHICH AUXENTIUS IS DEPOSED.

About this period Liberius died,[1] and Damasus succeeded to the bishopric of Rome. A deacon named Ursinus,[2] having obtained some votes in his favor, caused himself to be clandestinely ordained by some bishops of little note and endeavored to create a division among the people, so as to form separate assemblies. He succeeded in effecting this division, and some of the people followed him while the rest adhered to Damasus. This gave rise to many disputes and to much contention, which at length proceeded to murder and bloodshed. The prefect of Rome was obliged to interfere and to punish many of the clergy and people, and he put an end to the usurpation of Ursinus.

With respect to doctrine, however, no dissension arose either at Rome or in any other of the Western churches. The people unanimously adhered to the form of belief established at Nicæa, and regarded the three Persons of the Trinity as equal in dignity and in power. Auxentius alone differed from the others in opinion. He was then bishop of Milan, and in conjunction with a few partisans, was intent upon the introduction of innovations and the maintenance of the Arian dogma of the dissimilarity of the Son and of the Holy Ghost in opposition to the unanimous decision of the Western priests. The bishops of Gaul and of Venice,[3] having reported that similar attempts to disturb the peace of the church were being made by others, the bishops of several provinces assembled not long after at Rome, and decreed that Auxentius and those who held his sentiments should be excluded from communion. They confirmed the faith established by the council of Nicæa and annulled all the decrees that had been issued at Ariminum contrary to that faith, under the plea that these decrees had not received the assent of the bishop of Rome nor of other bishops, and that they were disapproved by many who had been present at the synod and had assisted in their enactment. That such was the decision really formed by the synod is testified by the epistle[4] addressed by Damasus, the Roman bishop, and the rest of the assembly, to the bishops of Illyria. It is as follows:

Damasus, Valerius,[5] and the other bishops of the holy assembly at Rome, to the dearly beloved brethren the bishops of Illyria, greeting in the Lord.

We believe that you uphold and teach to the people our holy faith, which is founded on the doctrines of the apostles. This faith differs in no respect from that inculcated by the Fathers. Neither is it permitted to the priests of God who are, by the right of their office, the instructors of the wise, to entertain any other sentiment. We have, however, been informed by some of our brethren of Gaul and of Venice, that certain individuals are bent upon the introduction of heresy. All bishops should diligently guard against this evil, lest some of their flock should be led by inexperience and others by simplicity to deviate from our own authorized interpretations. Those who devise strange doctrines ought not to be followed, but the opinions of our fathers ought to be retained, whatever may be the diversity of judgment around us. Hence Auxentius, bishop of Milan, has been condemned and with justice.

It is, therefore, right that all the teachers of the Roman empire should be of one mind and not pollute the faith by divers conflicting doctrines. For, when the evil of heresy first began to develop itself, even as the blasphemy of the Arians is now exhibited, our fathers, to the number of three hundred and eighteen, assembled together at Nicæa, erected a wall of defense against the weapons of the devil, and prepared an antidote to the poison of corrupt doctrine. This antidote consists in the belief that the Father and the Son have one Godhead, one virtue, and one substance (κρῆμα). It is also requisite to believe that the Holy Ghost is of the same hypostasis as the Father and the Son. We have decreed that those who hold any other doctrines are to be excluded from communion with us.

Some have attempted to reverse this useful regulation and adorable decision, but the persons by whom this attempt was made at the council of Ariminum have since, in some measure, atoned for their presumption by confessing that they were deceived by certain specious arguments, which did not appear to them to be contrary to the principles laid down by our fathers at Nicæa. The number of individuals congregated at the council of Ariminum proves nothing in prejudice of orthodox doctrines, for the council was held without the sanction of the bishops of Rome, who ought to have been in the first place consulted, and without the assent either of Vincent, who during a very long series of years enjoyed the episcopal dignity, or of many other bishops who held the same sentiments as those last mentioned. Besides, as has been before stated, those persons who were deceived and induced to deviate from orthodox doctrines, testified their disapprobation of their own proceedings as soon as they made use of their own judgment.

Is it not, therefore, manifest to you that the one true faith is that which was established at Nicæa upon the authority of the apostles and which must ever be retained inviolate, and that all bishops, whether of the East or of the West, who profess the Catholic religion ought to consider it an honor to be in communion with us. We believe that it will not be long before those who maintain other sentiments will be excluded from communion and deprived of the name and dignity of bishop, so that the people who are now oppressed by the yoke of those pernicious and deceitful principles may have liberty to breathe. For it is not in the power of these bishops to undeceive the people inasmuch as they are themselves deceived. Be then of one mind with all the priests of God. We believe that you adhere firmly to the faith, but that we may be more fully assured on this point, convince us of the same by your letters.

NOTES

1. Compare Socrates, *Ecclesiastical History*, Book IV, Chapter 29.
2. Or Ursicius. Concerning his quarrel with Damasus, bishop of Rome, see Baronius, *Ecclesiastical Annals*, AD 367.
3. See the synodical epistle below.
4. This epistle is extant in Theodoret, *Ecclesiastical History*, Book II, Chapter 22. The synod by which it was written was probably held AD 369, and 93 bishops were present at its deliberations.
5. He was bishop of Aquileia.

CHAPTER XXIV

CONCERNING SAINT AMBROSE AND HIS ELEVATION TO AN ARCHBISHOPRIC. THE NOVATIANS OF PHRYGIA AND THE PASSOVER.

The clergy of the West, having thus anticipated the designs of those who sought to introduce innovations among them,[1] carefully continued to preserve the inviolability of the faith which had from the beginning been handed down to them. With the solitary exception of Auxentius and his partisans, there were no individuals among them who entertained heterodox opinions. Auxentius, however, did not live long after this period. At his death, a sedition arose among the people of Milan concerning the appointment of a successor, and the city seemed in danger of a general insurrection. Those who had aspired to the bishopric and been defeated in their expectations, were loud in their menaces, as is usual on such occasions. Ambrose, who was then the governor of the province, being fearful lest further tumult should arise, went to the church and exhorted the people to cease from contention, to re-establish peace and concord, and to respect the laws. Before he had ceased speaking, all his auditors suppressed the angry feelings by which they had been mutually agitated against each other and declared that he who was exhorting them to concord should be their bishop, and receive the rite of baptism, for he had never been baptized. After Ambrose had repeatedly refused the proffered dignity and even quitted the place that it might not be forced upon him, the people still persisted in their choice and declared that the disputes would never be appeased unless he would accede to their wishes, and at length intelligence of these transactions was conveyed to court.[2] It is said that the emperor Valentinian prayed and returned thanks to God that the very man whom he had appointed governor, had been chosen to fill a priestly office. When he was informed of the earnest desires of the people and the refusal of Ambrose, he inferred that events had been so ordered by God for the purpose of restoring peace to the church of Milan and commanded that Ambrose should be ordained as quickly as possible. He was baptized and ordained at the same time, and forthwith proceeded to bring the church under his sway to unanimity of opinion concerning the Divine nature. For while under the guidance of Auxentius, it had been long rent by dissensions on this subject. We shall hereafter have occasion to speak of the conduct of Ambrose after his ordination, and of the admirable and holy manner in which he discharged the functions of the priesthood.[3]

About this period, the Novatians of Phrygia, contrary to their ancient custom, began to celebrate the festival of the Passover (τὸ Πάσχα) on the same day as the Jews. Novatius, the originator of their heresy, refused to receive those who repented of their sins into communion, and it was in this respect alone that he innovated upon established doctrines. But he and those who succeeded him celebrated the feast of the Passover after the vernal equinox, according to the custom of the Roman church. Some Novatian bishops, however, assembled about this time at Pazi, a town of Phrygia, near the source of the river Sangarus, and agreeing not to follow, in this point of discipline, the practice of those who differed in doctrine from them, established a new regulation for their observance. They determined upon keeping the feast of leavened bread, and upon celebrating the Passover on the same days as the Jews. Agelius, the bishop of the Novatians at Constantinople, and the bishops of the Novatians at Nicæa, Nicomedia, and Cotua,[4] a noted town of Phrygia, did not take part in this synod, although they acted as chiefs and presidents, so to speak, in all the meetings and transactions of their sect. Dissension was introduced, which led to the formation of two distinct parties in this sect, as I shall presently require to show.

NOTES

1. Compare Socrates, *Ecclesiastical History,* Book IV, Chapter 30.
2. See below, Book VII, Chapter 8, and the note there given.

3. *Note to the 2018 edition:* See Book VII, Chapter XIII and XXV.
4. Or Cotyæum: It is otherwise called Cosaïum. The town is known as the birth-place of Alexander the Grammarian.

CHAPTER XXV

CONCERNING APOLLINARIUS. FATHER AND SON OF THAT NAME. VITALIUS, THE PRESBYTER. RELAPSE INTO HERESY.

About this period, Apollinarius openly devised a heresy to which his name has since been given.[1] He induced many persons to secede from the church and formed separate assemblies. Vitalius, a presbyter of Antioch and one of the clergy of Meletius, concurred with him in the promulgation of his peculiar opinions. In other respects, Vitalius was blameless in life and conduct and was zealous in watching over those committed to his pastoral superintendence. Hence he was greatly revered by the people. He seceded from communion with Meletius and joined Apollinarius, and presided over those at Antioch who had embraced the same opinions. By the sanctity of his life he attracted a great number of followers, who are still called Vitalians by the citizens of Antioch. It is said he was led to secede from the church from resentment at the contempt that was manifested toward him by Flavian, then one of his fellow presbyters, but who was afterwards raised to the bishopric of Antioch. Flavian having prevented him from holding his customary interview with the bishop, he fancied himself despised and entered into communion with Apollinarius, with whom he contracted a strict friendship.

From that period, the members of this sect have held separate assemblies in various cities under the guidance of their own bishops, and have established laws and regulations contrary to those of the Catholic church. They sang the psalms composed by Apollinarius, for besides his great attainments in other branches of literature, he was a poet and by the beauty of his verses he induced many to adopt his sentiments. He composed verses to be sung by men at convivial meetings and at their daily labor, and by women while engaged at the loom. But, whether his songs were adapted for holidays, festivals, or other occasions, they were all alike to the praise and glory of God.

Damasus, bishop of Rome, and Peter, bishop of Alexandria, were the first to receive information of the rise and progress of this heresy, and they condemned it at a council held at Rome,[2] as contrary to the doctrines of the Catholic church. It is said that it was as much from weakness of mind as from any other cause that Apollinarius deviated from the authorized form of doctrine. For it appears that when Athanasius, bishop of Alexandria, was on his road back to Egypt from the place whither he had been banished by Constantine, he had to pass through Laodicea, and that while in that city he formed an intimacy with Apollinarius, which terminated in the strictest friendship. As, however, the heterodox considered it disgraceful to hold communion with Athanasius, George, the bishop of the Arians in that city, ejected Apollinarius in a very insulting manner from the church under the plea that he had received Athanasius contrary to the canons and holy laws. The bishop did not rest here but reproached him with crimes which he had committed and repented of at a remote period. For when Theodotus, the predecessor of George, governed the church of Laodicea, Epiphanius, the sophist, recited a hymn which he had composed in honor of Bacchus. Apollinarius, who was then a youth and the pupil of Epiphanius, went to hear the recitation accompanied by his father whose name also was Apollinarius and who was a noted grammarian. After the exordium, Epiphanius, according to the custom always observed at the public recitation of hymns, directed the uninitiated and the profane to quit the assembly. But neither Apollinarius the younger nor the elder nor, indeed, any of the Christians who were present left the spot. When Theodotus heard that they had been present during the recitation, he was exceedingly displeased. He, however, pardoned the laymen who had committed this error after they had received a moderate reproof. With respect to Apollinarius, father and son, he convicted them both publicly of their crime and ejected them from the church, for they had belonged to the order of clergy, the father being a presbyter, and the son a reader of the Holy Scriptures. After some time had elapsed, and when the father and son had evinced by tears and fasting a degree of repentance adequate to their transgression, Theodotus restored them to their offices in the church.

When George succeeded to the bishopric, he excommunicated Apollinarius on account of his having, as before stated, received Athanasius into communion. It is said that Apollinarius besought him repeatedly to restore him to communion, but that as he was inexorable, Apollinarius determined from resentment to introduce trouble and dissension in the church by broaching the aforesaid heresy, and that he thought by means of his eloquence to revenge himself on his enemy, by proving that George had deposed one who was more deeply acquainted with the Sacred Scriptures than himself. Thus do the private animosities of the clergy tend to the injury of the church, and the introduction of many heresies in religion! Had George, like Theodotus, received Apollinarius on his repentance into communion, I believe that we should never have heard of the heresy that bears his name. Men are prone, when loaded with opprobrium and contempt, to resort to extreme and contentious measures whereas, when treated with justice, they moderate their natural impetuosity and remain within bounds.

NOTES

1. Compare Socrates, *Ecclesiastical History,* Book IV, Chapter 46.
2. In the year 373, according to Baronius. Valesius, however, considers that it must have been held one year later.

CHAPTER XXVI

EUNOMIUS AND ÆTIUS, THEIR LIFE AND DOCTRINES. OPINIONS FIRST BROACHED BY THEM CONCERNING THE RITE OF BAPTISM.

About this time, Eunomius, who had succeeded Eleusius in the bishopric of Cyzicus and who presided over the Arians,[1] devised another heresy which some have called by his name, but which is sometimes denominated the Anomian heresy. Some assert that Eunomius was the first who ventured to maintain that baptism ought to be performed by immersion and to corrupt in this manner the apostolical tradition which has been carefully handed down to the present day. He introduced, it is said, a mode of discipline contrary to that of the church, and endeavored to disguise the innovation under the cloak of a grave and severe deportment. He was very eloquent and delighted in disputations and conferences. The generality of those who entertain his sentiments have the same predilections. They do not applaud a virtuous course of life and conduct or charity towards the needy unless exhibited by persons of their own sect, so much as skill in disputation and the power of triumphing in debates over the arguments of an opponent. Persons possessed of these accomplishments are accounted religious and virtuous.

Others assert, I believe, with greater appearance of probability that Theophranes, a native of Cappadocia, and Eutychus, both zealous propagators of this heresy, seceded from communion with Eunomius during the succeeding reign and introduced heretical doctrines concerning the rite of baptism. They taught that baptism ought not to be administered in the name of the Trinity but in the name of the death of Christ. It appears that Eunomius broached no new opinion on the subject, but remained from the beginning firmly attached to the sentiments of Arius. After his elevation to the bishopric of Cyzicus, he was accused by his own clergy of introducing innovations upon the established forms of doctrine. Eudoxius, bishop of the Arians at Constantinople, obliged him to undergo a public trial and give an account of his doctrines to the people. Finding, however, no fault in him, Eudoxius exhorted him to return to Cyzicus. Eunomius, however, replied, that he could not remain with people who regarded him with suspicion and, it is said, seized this opportunity[2] to secede from communion, although it seems that in taking this step he was really actuated by the resentment he felt at the refusal which Ætius, his teacher, had met with of being received into communion. Eunomius, it is added, dwelt with Ætius and never deviated from his original sentiments.

Such are the conflicting accounts of various individuals. Some narrate the circumstances in one way and some in another. But whether it was Eunomius, or any other person who first introduced heretical opinions concerning baptism, it seems to me that such innovators, whoever they may have been, were alone in danger, according to their own representation, of quitting this life without having received the rite of holy baptism. For if after having received baptism according to the ancient mode of the church they found it impossible to re-confer it on themselves, it must be admitted that they introduced a practice to which they had not themselves submitted, and thus undertook to administer to others what had never been administered to themselves. Thus, after having laid down certain principles according to their own fancy without any data, they proceeded to bestow upon others what they had not themselves received. The absurdity of this assumption is manifest from their own confession, for they admit that those who have not received the rite of baptism have not the power of administering it. Now, according to their opinion, those who have not received the rite of baptism in conformity with their mode of administration are unbaptized, and they confirm this opinion by their practice, in as much as they re-baptize[3] all those who join their sect although previously baptized by the Catholic church. These varying dogmas are the sources of innumerable troubles, and many are deterred from embracing Christianity by the diversity of opinion which prevails in matters of doctrine.

The dispute daily became stronger and the heresy reached a greater height, for its advocates were not deficient in zeal or eloquence. Indeed, it appears that the greater part of the Catholic church would have been subverted by this heresy, had not Basil and Gregory of Cappadocia strenuously opposed its further progress. With the view of repressing the heresies that had arisen, the emperor Theodosius not long after banished the founders of heretical sects from the populous parts of the empire to the most desert and thinly-populated regions.

But, lest those who read my history should be ignorant of the precise nature of the two heresies to which I have more especially alluded, I think it necessary to state that Ætius, the Syrian, was the originator of the heresy usually attributed to Eunomius, and that like Arius he maintained that the Son is dissimilar from the Father, that he is a created Being, and was created out of what had no previous existence. Those who first adopted these erroneous views were called Ætians. But afterwards, during the reign of Constantius, when, as we have stated, some parties maintained that the Son is consubstantial with the Father, and others that he is like in substance to the Father, and when the council of Ariminum had decreed that the Son is only to be considered like unto the Father, Ætius was condemned to banishment as guilty of impiety and blasphemy against God. For some time subsequently, his heresy seemed to have been suppressed, for neither he nor Eunomius ventured on undertaking its defense. But when Eunomius was raised to the bishopric of Cyzicus, he found it impossible to disguise his sentiments and openly preached the doctrine of Ætius. Hence, as it often happens that the names of the original founders of heretical sects pass into oblivion, the followers of Eunomius were designated by his own name, although he merely renewed the heresy of Ætius and promulgated it with greater boldness than Ætius himself.

NOTES

1. Compare Socrates, *Ecclesiastical History,* Book IV, Chapter 7, and Book V, Chapter 24.
2. Or, rather, "pretext." Compare the parallel account given by Socrates, *Ecclesiastical History,* Book IV, Chapter 12.
3. Valesius observes, that the Eunomians had learnt this practice from the Arians, as their forefathers in heresy, for the Arians, too, were accustomed to re-baptize the Catholics who came over to their party, and even re-ordained the clerics who joined them. In proof of his assertion, Valesius quotes the author of the *Life of Saint Fulgentius*, Marcellinus, Jerome, and other ancient authorities.

CHAPTER XXVII
ACCOUNT GIVEN BY GREGORY THE THEOLOGIAN OF APOLLINARIUS AND EUNOMIUS IN A LETTER TO NECTARIUS. THE HERESY OF EUNOMIUS IS OPPOSED BY THE MONKS OF THAT PERIOD.

It is obvious that Eunomius and Ætius held the same opinions. In several passages of his writings, Eunomius boasts that Ætius was his instructor. Gregory, bishop of Nazianzen, speaks in the following terms of Apollinarius in a letter addressed to Nectarius, bishop of Constantinople:

> Eunomius, who is a constant source of trouble among us, is not content with being a burden to us himself, but would consider himself to blame if he did not strive to drag every one with him to the destruction whither he is hastening. Such conduct, however, may be tolerated in some degree. The most grievous calamity against which the church has now to struggle arises from the audacity of the Apollinarians. I know not how your Holiness could have agreed that they should be as free to hold meetings as we are ourselves. You have been fully instructed, by the grace of God, in the mysteries of our religion, and you are well able to undertake the defense of orthodox doctrine against the attacks of heretics, yet it may not be amiss to inform your Excellency that a book written by Apollinarius has fallen into my hands, replete with more evil assertions than were ever advanced by any other heretic. He declares that the body which the Son of God assumed when he came among us for our redemption was not one which was prepared for Him, but that this carnal nature existed in the Son from the beginning. He substantiates this

evil hypothesis by a misapplication of the following words of Scripture: "No one hath ascended up into heaven except the Son of man, who came down from heaven." He alleges, from this text, that Christ was the Son of man before He descended from heaven, and that when He did descend, He brought with Him His own body, which was eternal. This heretic also refers to the following passage: "The second man is from heaven." He, moreover, maintains that this man who came down from heaven was destitute of mind (νοῦς), but that the Divinity of the only-begotten Son supplied the want of intellect and constituted the third part of the human compound. The body and soul (ψυχὴ) formed two parts, as in other men, and the Word of God held the place of the third part that was wanting.

But this is not the most dangerous of his errors. The most grievous point of the heresy is that he asserts that the only-begotten Son of God, the Judge of all men, the giver of life, and the destroyer of death, is Himself subject to death, that He suffered in His Divine nature, which died with the body, and that it was by the Father raised again from the dead.

It would take too long to recount all the other extravagant doctrines propounded by these heretics. What I have said may, I think, suffice to show the nature of the sentiments maintained by Apollinarius and Eunomius. If any one desire more detailed information, I can only refer him to the works on the subject written by these heretics and by their opponents. I do not profess to understand or to expound these matters. That these heretical doctrines did not finally become predominant is mainly to be attributed to the zeal of the monks of this period, for all the monks of Syria, Cappadocia, and the neighboring provinces, were sincerely attached to the Nicene faith. The eastern regions, however, from Cilicia to Phœnicia, were nearly subverted by the heresy of Apollinarius. The heresy of Eunomius was spread from Cilicia and the mountains of Taurus as far as the Hellespont and Constantinople. These two heretics found it easy to attract to their respective parties the persons among whom they dwelt and those of the neighborhood. But the same fate awaited them that had been experienced by the Arians, for they incurred the full weight of the popular odium and aversion, when it was observed that their sentiments were regarded with suspicion by the monks, whose doctrines were invariably received and followed by the people on account of the virtue exhibited in their actions. In the same way the Egyptians were led by the monks to oppose the Arians.

CHAPTER XXVIII

OF THE HOLY MEN WHO FLOURISHED AT THIS PERIOD IN EGYPT.

As this period was distinguished by many holy men, who devoted themselves to a life of philosophy, it seems requisite to give some account of them.

There was not, it appears, a more celebrated man in Egypt than John. He had received from God the power of discerning the future and the most hidden things as clearly as the ancient prophets, and he had, moreover, the gift of curing the most desperate and inveterate diseases. Another eminent man of this period was Or. He had lived in solitude from his earliest youth, occupying himself continually in singing the praises of God. He subsisted on herbs and roots, and his drink was water when he could find it. In his old age he went, by the command of God, to Thebaïs, where he presided over several monasteries and performed many wonderful works. By means of prayer alone, he expelled devils and healed divers diseases. He knew nothing of letters, but whatever might once engage his attention was never afterwards forgotten.

Ammon, the leader of the monks called Tabennesiotians, dwelt in the same regions, and was followed by about three thousand disciples. Benus and Theonas likewise presided over monasteries, and possessed the gift of foreseeing and of foretelling the future. It is said that, though Theonas was versed in all the learning of the Egyptians, the Greeks, and the Romans, he preserved a profound silence for the space of thirty years. Benus was never seen to manifest any signs of anger, and never heard to swear, or to utter a false, a vain, a rash, or a useless word.

Coprus, Helles, and Elias also flourished at this period. It is said that Coprus had received from God the power of healing sickness and divers diseases and of expelling demons. Helles had, from his youth upwards, pursued a life of monastic asceticism, and he wrought many wonderful works. He could carry fire in his bosom without burning his clothes. He excited the other monks to the practice of virtue by representing that purity of life leads to the acquisition of the power of working miracles. Elias, who dwelt near the city of Antinöus, was at this period about a hundred and ten years of age of which, he said, he had passed seventy years alone in the desert. Notwithstanding his advanced age, he was unremitting in the practice of fasting and asceticism.

Apelles flourished at the same period, and performed numerous miracles in the Egyptian monasteries near the city of Acoris. He worked as a smith at the forge, and one night, when he was engaged at this employment, the devil undertook to tempt him to incontinence by appearing before him in the form of a woman. Apelles, however, seized the iron which was heating in the furnace and burnt the face of the devil, who screamed wildly, and ran away.

Isidore, Serapion, and Dioscorus, who presided over monasteries at this period, were among the most celebrated men of the era. Isidore caused his monastery to be closed, so that no one could obtain egress or ingress, and supplied the wants of those within the walls. Serapion lived in the neighborhood of Arsinoë[1] and had about a thousand monks under his guidance. They lived on the produce of their labor and provided for the poor. During harvest-time, they busied themselves in reaping. They set aside sufficient corn for their own use and furnished grain gratuitously for the other monks. Dioscorus had not more than a hundred disciples. He was a presbyter and applied himself with great diligence to the duties of his ministry. He scrupulously examined those who presented themselves as candidates for participation in the holy mysteries, and excluded those who had not a conscience void of offense.

The presbyter Eulogius was still more scrupulous in the dispensation of the mysteries. It is said that when he was officiating in the priestly office,[2] he could discern what was in the minds of those around him, so that he could clearly detect sin and the secret thoughts of each one of his audience. He excluded from the altar all who had perpetrated crime, or formed evil resolutions, and publicly convicted them of sin, but on their purifying themselves by repentance, he again received them into communion.

NOTES

1. Otherwise called Arsenoë.
2. ἱερώμενον. The present participle, as denoting a person in the act of officiating as a priest: the perfect participle, ἱερωμένον, would denote merely one who had been ordained.

CHAPTER XXIX
CONCERNING THE MONKS OF THEBAÏS.

Apollos flourished about the same period in Thebaïs. He early devoted himself to a life of philosophy, and after having passed forty years in the desert, he shut himself up by the command of God in a cave formed at the foot of a mountain near a very populous district. By his extraordinary miracles, he soon acquired so wide a reputation that many monks placed themselves under his guidance and submitted to his instructions. Timothy, bishop of Alexandria who has written an account of his conduct and of that of the other monks whom I have mentioned, gives a long description of his mode of life and of his miracles.

About two thousand monks dwelt in the neighborhood of Alexandria, some in a district called the Hermitage and others more towards Mareota and Libya. Dorotheus, a native of Thebes, was among the most celebrated of these monks. He spent the day in collecting stones upon the sea-shore which he used in erecting cells for those who were unable to build them. During the night, he employed himself in weaving baskets of palm leaves, and these he sold to obtain the means of subsistence. He ate six ounces of bread with a few vegetables daily and drank nothing but water. Having accustomed himself to this extreme abstinence from his youth, he continued to observe it in old age. He was never seen to recline on a mat or a bed nor even to place his limbs in an easy attitude for sleep. Sometimes, from natural lassitude, his eyes would involuntarily close when he was at his daily labor or his meals and the food would, on those occasions, drop from his mouth. One day, being utterly overcome by lassitude, he fell down on the mat. He was displeased at finding himself in this position and said, in an under-tone of voice, "When angels are persuaded to sleep, then will men of real vigilance and zeal be induced to do likewise." Perhaps he might have said this to himself, or perhaps to the demon who disturbed him in his exercises of devotion. He was once asked why he destroyed his body? "Because it destroys me," was his reply.[1]

Piammon and John presided over two celebrated Egyptian monasteries near Diolchis. They were presbyters, and eminent for the zeal wherewith they discharged the functions of their office. It is said that one day, when Piammon was officiating, he beheld an angel standing near the altar and writing down the names of the monks who were present, while he erased the names of those who were absent. John had received from God such power over disease that he healed the sick and restored the paralytic.

An old man named Benjamin lived about this period in the desert near Scetis. God had bestowed upon him the power of removing diseases by the touch of his hand or by means of a little oil consecrated by prayer. He was attacked by a dropsy and his body was swollen to such a size that it became necessary, in order to carry him from his cell, to enlarge the door. As his malady would not admit of his lying in a recumbent posture, he remained during eight months, seated on some large skins and continued to heal the sick without regretting that his own recovery was not effected. He comforted those who came to visit him and requested them to pray for his soul, adding that he cared little for his body, for it had been of no service to him when in health and could not, now that it was diseased, be of any injury to him.

About the same time, the celebrated Mark, Macarius the younger, Apollonius, and Moses, an Egyptian, dwelt at Scetis. It is said that Mark was, from his youth upwards, distinguished by extreme mildness of disposition and prudence. He committed the Sacred Scriptures to memory, and manifested such eminent piety that Macarius, the priest of the Cells,[2] declared that he had never given to him what priests present to the initiated at the holy altar, but that he had beheld the hand of an angel administering it to him.

Macarius had received from God the power of dispelling demons. A murder which he had unintentionally committed was the original cause of his embracing a life of philosophy. He was a shepherd, and one day led his flock to graze on the banks of Lake Mareotis when, in sport, he slew one of his companions. Fearful of being delivered up to justice, he fled to the desert. Here he concealed himself during three years, and afterwards erected a small dwelling on the spot, in which he dwelt twenty-five years. He was accustomed to say that he owed much to the calamity that had befallen him in early life and even called the unintentional murder he had committed a salutary deed, inasmuch as it had been the cause of his embracing an ascetic and blessed mode of life.

Apollonius, after passing his life in the pursuits of commerce, retired in his old age to Scetis. On reflecting that he was too old to learn a trade or to acquire the art of writing, he purchased, with his own money, a supply of medical drugs and of food suited for the sick, some of which he carried at stated hours to the door of every monastery for the relief of those who were suffering from disease. Such was the mode of life in which he exercised himself, and when he felt death approaching, he delivered his drugs to one whom he exhorted to go and do as he had done.

Moses was originally a slave but was driven from his master's house on account of his perversity. He joined some robbers and became leader of the band. After having perpetrated several murders and other crimes, he embraced a life of asceticism and attained the highest point of philosophical perfection. As the healthful and vigorous habit of body which had been induced by his former avocations acted as a stimulus to his imagination and excited a desire for pleasure, he resorted to every possible means of macerating his body. Thus, he subsisted wholly upon bread, subjected himself to severe labor, and prayed fifty times daily. During six years, he spent all his nights in prayer. He prayed standing without bending his knees or closing his eyes in sleep. He sometimes went during the night to the cells of the monks and secretly filled their pitchers with water, although he had sometimes to go ten, sometimes twenty, and sometimes thirty stadia in quest of the water. Notwithstanding all his efforts to macerate his body, it was long before he could subdue his natural vigor of constitution. Four robbers once broke into the dwelling where he lived alone. He bound them, threw them across his shoulders, and bore them to the church, that the monks who were then assembled might deal with them as they thought fit, for he did not consider himself authorized to punish any one. So sudden a conversion from vice to virtue was never before witnessed, nor such rapid attainments in monastical philosophy. Hence God rendered him an object of dread to the demons and he was ordained presbyter over the monks at Scetis. After a life spent in this manner, he died at the age of seventy-five, leaving behind him numerous eminent disciples.

Paul, Pachomius, Stephen, and Moses, of whom the two latter were Libyans, and Pior, who was an Egyptian, flourished during this reign. Paul dwelt at Ferma, a mountain of Scetis, and presided over five hundred disciples. He did not labor with his hands, neither did he receive alms of any one, except such food as was necessary for his subsistence. He did nothing but pray and daily offered up to God three hundred prayers. He placed three hundred pebbles in his bosom, for fear of omitting any of these prayers, and at the conclusion of each, he took away one of the pebbles. When there were no pebbles remaining, he knew that he had gone through the whole course of his prescribed prayers.

Pachomius also flourished during this period at Scetis. He dwelt in the desert, from youth to extreme old age without ever being seduced by the appetites of the body, the passions of the soul, or the wiles of the devil, to desire any of those things from which the philosopher ought to abstain.

Stephen dwelt at Mareota, near Marmarica. During sixty years, he rigorously practiced all the virtues of asceticism, became noted as a monk, and was admitted into the intimacy of Antony the Great. He was very mild and prudent, and his usual style of conversation was edifying and agreeable, and well calculated to comfort the afflicted, to assuage their sorrows, and to fill them with joy. The same principles supported him under affliction. He was troubled with an incurable ulcer, and surgeons were employed to operate upon the diseased limb. During the operation, Stephen employed himself in weaving palm leaves and exhorted those who were around him not to concern themselves about his sufferings. He told them that God does nothing but for our good and that his affliction would tend to his real welfare, in as much as it would atone for his sins, it being better to be judged in this life than in the life to come.

Moses was celebrated for his meekness, his goodness, and his power of healing diseases and infirmities by prayer.

Pior determined from his youth to devote himself to a life of holy asceticism, and with this view, quitted his father's house after having made a vow that he would never again look upon any one of his relations. After fifty years had expired, one of his sisters heard that he was still alive, and she was so transported with joy at this unexpected intelligence, that she could not rest till she had seen him. The bishop of the place where she resided was so affected by her groans and tears that he wrote to the leaders of the monks of Scetis, desiring them to send Pior to him. The superiors accordingly directed him to repair to the city of his birth, and he could not but obey them, for disobedience was regarded as criminal by the monks of Egypt as well as by other Christians. He went with another monk to the door of his father's house and caused himself to be announced. When he heard the door being opened, he closed his eyes, and calling his sister by name, he said to her, "I am Pior, your brother: look at me as much as you please." His sister was delighted beyond measure at again beholding him, and returned thanks to God. He prayed at the door where he stood, and then returned to the place whence he came. He dug a well and found that the water was bitter, but persevered in the use of it till his death. The height to which he had carried his self-denial was not known till after his death, for several attempted to establish themselves in the place where he had dwelt, but found it impossible to remain there or to endure the inconveniences to which he had been exposed. I am convinced that had it not been for the principles of asceticism which he had espoused, he could easily have rectified the bitterness of the water, for he caused water to flow in a spot where none had existed previously. It is said that some monks, under the guidance of Moses, undertook to dig a well, but failing in their expectation of finding water, they were about to abandon the task when about midday Pior joined them. He first embraced them, and then rebuked their want of faith. He then descended into the pit they had excavated and after engaging in prayer, struck the ground thrice with a rod. A spring of water soon after rose to the surface and filled the whole excavation. After prayer, Pior departed, and though the monks urged him to break his fast with them, he refused, alleging that he had not been sent to them for that purpose but merely in order to perform the act he had effected.

NOTES

1. Valesius thinks that there is good reason for believing that Sozomen got this story at second-hand, not from Palladius (who relates it differently), but from an inferior annalist of his own time.
2. κελλιών. Valesius, however, is inclined to regard the word as a proper name, and he identifies it with a place called Cellia, mentioned by Sozomen below, Chapter 31.

CHAPTER XXX

MONKS OF SCETIS.

At this period, many of the disciples of Antony the Great still flourished in the solitude of Scetis. Origen, who was then far advanced in life, Didymus, Cronius, who was about one hundred and ten years of age, Arsisius the Great, Putubastes, Arsio, and Serapion had all been contemporary with Antony the Great. They had grown old in the exercises of asceticism, and were at this period presiding over the monasteries.

There were some holy men among them who were not so far advanced in age, but who were celebrated for their great and excellent qualities, among these were Ammon, Eusebius, and Dioscorus. They were brothers but on account of their height of stature, were called the "Great Brothers." It is said that Ammon attained the height of philosophy and overcame the love of ease and pleasure. He was very studious and had read the works of Origen, of Didymus, and of

Book VI, Chapter XXX

other ecclesiastical writers.[1] From his youth to the day of his death he never tasted anything with the exception of bread that had been prepared by means of fire. He was once chosen to be ordained bishop, and after urging every argument that could be devised in rejection of the honor, but in vain, he cut off one of his ears, and said to those who were besieging him with their importunities, "Henceforward I am excluded from ordination, for the ecclesiastical canons require that the person of a priest should be perfect." Those who had been sent for him accordingly departed but, on ascertaining that the church does not observe the Jewish law in requiring a priest to be perfect in all his members but merely requires him to be irreprehensible in point of morals, they returned to Ammon and endeavored to take him by force. He protested to them that if they attempted any violence against him, he would cut out his tongue, and terrified at this menace, they immediately took their departure. Ammon was ever after surnamed Parstides.

Some time afterwards, during the ensuing reign, the wise Evagrius formed an intimacy with him. Evagrius was a very learned man, powerful in thought and in word, and skillful in discerning the first appearances of virtue and of vice and in urging others to imitate the one and to eschew the other. His eloquence is fully attested by the works he has left behind him. With respect to his moral character, it appears that he was totally free from all pride or superciliousness, so that he was not elated when just commendations were awarded him, nor displeased when unjust reproaches were brought against him. He was a native of Iberia[2] near the Euxine. He had studied philosophy and the Sacred Scriptures under Gregory, bishop of Nazianzen, and had filled the office of archdeacon in the church of Gregory at Constantinople. He was handsome in person, and careful in his mode of attire, and hence, an acquaintanceship he had formed with a certain lady excited the jealousy of her husband, who determined upon slaying him. While the assassins were waiting for an opportunity to take his life, God vouchsafed to show him a vision which was the means of saving him. It appeared to him that he had been arrested in the act of committing some crime and that he was chained hand and foot. As he was being led before the magistrates, to receive the sentence of condemnation, a man who held in his hand the book of the Holy Gospels addressed him and swore to rescue him, provided he would promise to quit the city. Evagrius touched the book,[3] and gave the required promise. Immediately his chains appeared to fall off and he awoke. Having received this timely intimation of danger, he was enabled to evade it. He resolved upon devoting himself to a life of asceticism and proceeded from Constantinople to Jerusalem. Some time after, he went to visit the ascetics of Scetis, with whom he eventually fixed his abode.[4]

NOTES

1. Nicephorus understands Sozomen here to refer to Evagrius. But Valesius shows the absurdity of this supposition by a comparison of dates.
2. This place is also called Ibora by Constantine Porphyrogenitus. Uranius, bishop of Ibora, was among the bishops who subscribed to the council of Chalcedon, and another bishop of the same see was present at the council of Constantinople.
3. The custom of swearing upon the Holy Scriptures is very ancient. Allusion is made to it by Gregory Nazianzen, Epistle 219, and in his Iambic verses, entitled "Contra sæpè jurantes," as also by Tertullian, *On Idolatry,* Chapter 23.
4. Sozomen is probably mistaken as to his chronology here, as it is certain that Evagrius adopted the monastic life in the reign of Theodosius.

CHAPTER XXXI

CONCERNING THE MONASTERIES OF NITRIA. MONASTERIES CALLED CELLS.

Nitria,[1] inhabited by a great number of persons devoted to a life of philosophy, derives its name from its vicinity to a village in which nitre is found. It contains about fifty monasteries built tolerably near to each other, some of which are inhabited by monks who live together in society and others by monks who have adopted a solitary mode of existence. More in the interior of the desert, about seventy stadia from this locality, is a region called the cells,[2] throughout which numerous little dwellings are dispersed hither and thither, but at such a distance that those who dwell in them can neither see nor hear each other. They assemble together on the first and last days of each week, and if any monk happen to be absent, it is immediately concluded that he is ill or has been attacked by some disease, and all the other monks visit him alternately and carry to him such remedies as are suited to his case.

Except on these occasions, they seldom converse together unless, indeed, there be one among them capable of communicating further knowledge concerning God and the salvation of the soul. Those who dwell in the cells are those who have attained the summit of philosophy, and who are therefore able to regulate their own conduct, to live alone, and to seek nothing but quietude. This is what I had briefly to state concerning Scetis and its ascetic inhabitants. I should be justly reproached with prolixity were I to enter into further details concerning their mode of life, their labors, their customs, their exercises, their abstinence, and other regulations which they adapted to their respective circumstances and ages.

Rinocorurus was also celebrated at this period, on account of the holy men who were born and who flourished there. I have heard that the most eminent among them were Melas, the bishop of the country, Denis, who presided over a monastery situated to the north of the city, and Solon, the brother and successor of Melas. When the decree for the ejection of all bishops opposed to Arianism was issued, the officers appointed to execute the mandate found Melas engaged in trimming the lights of the church and clad in an old cloak soiled with oil, fastened by a girdle. When they asked him for the bishop, he replied that he was within and that he would conduct them to him. As they were fatigued with their journey, he led them to the episcopal dwelling, made them sit down to table, and placed before them such things as he had. After the repast, he supplied them with water to wash their hands, and then told them who he was. Amazed at his conduct, they confessed the mission on which they had arrived, but from respect to him, gave him full liberty to go wherever he would. He, however, replied that he would not shrink from the sufferings to which the other bishops who maintained the same sentiments as himself were exposed, and that he was ready to go into exile. He had been accustomed from his youth upwards to the practice of all the virtues of asceticism.

Solon quitted the pursuits of commerce to embrace a monastic life, a measure which tended greatly to his welfare. For under the instruction of his brother and other ascetics, he progressed rapidly in piety towards God and in charity towards his neighbor. The church of Rinocorurus having been thus, from the beginning, under the guidance of such exemplary bishops, never afterwards swerved from their precepts and can still boast of many eminent men. The clergy of this church dwell in one house, sit at the same table, and have everything in common.

NOTES

1. A town of Egypt, in the Mareotic nome.
2. See above, note on Chapter 29.

CHAPTER XXXII
MONKS OF PALESTINE.

Many monastical institutions flourished in Palestine. In narrating the events of the reign of Constantius, I had occasion to mention several of the illustrious individuals who dwelt in these monasteries. Many of their associates attained the summit of philosophical perfection and added luster to the reputation of the monasteries to which they belonged, and among them Hesycas, a companion of Hilarion, and Epiphanius, afterwards bishop of Salamis in Cyprus, deserve to be particularly noticed.

Hesycas devoted himself to a life of philosophy in the same locality where his master had formerly resided, and Epiphanius fixed his abode near the village of Besauduc which was his birth-place, in the government of Eleutheropolis. Having been instructed from his youth by the most celebrated ascetics of Egypt with whom he resided many years, Epiphanius became celebrated both in Egypt and Palestine by his attainments in monastic philosophy and was chosen by the inhabitants of Cyprus to fill the metropolitan see of their island. This important office tended to increase the reputation which his virtues had acquired, and the admiration of strangers and of the inhabitants of the country was soon attracted by the exemplary manner in which he discharged the episcopal duties. Before he went to Cyprus, he resided for some time, during the reign of Valens, in Palestine.[1]

At the same period, Salamanes, Phuscon, Malchius, and Crispus, four brethren who were distinguished by their high attainments in ascetic philosophy, dwelt in seclusion near Bethlehem, a town of Gaza. They were of noble origin, and had been instructed in philosophy by Hilarion. It is related that the brothers were once journeying homewards, when Malchius was suddenly snatched away and became invisible. Soon afterwards, however, he re-appeared and continued the journey with his brothers. He did not long survive this occurrence, but died in the flower of his youth. In point of philosophy, virtue, and piety, he was equal to men of the most advanced age.

Ammonius lived at a distance of ten stadia from those last mentioned. He dwelt near Capharcobra, the place of his birth, a town of Gaza. He was very exact in the discharge of duty and sincerely devoted to the practice of asceticism.

I think that Silvanus, a native of Palestine to whom, on account of his virtue, an angel was once seen to minister, dwelt about the same time in Egypt. At one period, he fixed his residence on Mount Sinai, and afterwards founded at Geraris near the great torrent a very extensive establishment for holy men, over which the excellent Zachariah subsequently presided.

NOTE

1. Or Malachias, otherwise Malachion. He is mentioned by Theodoret in his *Philotheus*.

CHAPTER XXXIII

MONKS OF SYRIA.

Passing thence to Syria and Persia, we shall find that the monks of these countries emulated those of Egypt in zeal and austerity. Battheus, Eusebius, Barges, Halas, Abbo, Lazarus, who attained the episcopal dignity, Abdaleus, Zeno, and Heliodorus flourished in Nisibis near the mountain called Sigoro. When they first entered upon the ascetic mode of life, they were denominated shepherds because they had no houses, ate neither bread nor meat, and drank no wine, but dwelt constantly on the mountains, and passed their time in praising God by prayers and hymns according to the canons of the church. At the usual hours of meals, they each took a sickle and cut some grass on the mountains, and this served for their repast. Such was their course of life. Eusebius voluntarily shut himself up in a cell near Carræ. Protogenes dwelt in the same locality and subsequently succeeded to the bishopric of the celebrated Vitus [1] whom God caused repeatedly to appear in a vision before Constantine, after charging the emperor to follow faithfully the injunctions of the man who should be shown him. Aones dwelt at Phadana near the spot where Jacob, the grandson of Abraham, on his journey from Palestine, met the damsel whom he afterwards married, and where he rolled away the stone that her flock might drink of the water of the well. It is said that Aones was the first who introduced the ascetic mode of life in Syria, just as ascetic philosophy was first introduced by Antony in Egypt.

NOTE

1. He was bishop of Carræ under Valens.

CHAPTER XXXIV

MONKS OF EDESSA, MONKS OF GALATIA AND CAPPADOCIA.

Gaddanas and Azizius dwelt with Aones and emulated his virtues. Ephraim the Syrian, who was an historian and has been noticed[1] in our recital of events under the reign of Constantius, acquired great renown by his devotion to ascetic philosophy in the neighborhood of Edessa, and the same may be said of Julian. Barses and Eulogius were both, at a later period than that to which we are referring, ordained bishops, but not over any particular church, for the title was merely an honorary one conferred on them on account of their purity of life, and they were ordained in their own monasteries. Lazarus, to whom we have already alluded, was ordained bishop in the same manner.

Such were the most celebrated philosophers of asceticism who flourished in Syria, Persia, and the neighboring countries so far, at least, as I have been able to ascertain. Their invariable course of life, so to speak, consisted in diligent attention to the state of the soul, which by means of fasting, prayer, and offering up praise to God, they kept in constant preparation to quit the things of this world. They devoted the greater part of their time to these holy exercises, and they despised worldly possessions, temporal affairs, and the ease and adornment of the body. Some of the monks carried their self-denial to an extraordinary height. Battheus, for instance, by long abstinence from food, had worms generated between his teeth. Halas, again, did not taste bread till he was seventy years of age, and Heliodorus passed many nights without yielding to sleep, and only partook of food one day in seven.

Although Cœle-syria and Upper Syria, with the exception of the city of Antioch, did not receive the Christian religion till a comparatively later period, they produced several individuals who devoted themselves to ecclesiastical philosophy, and whose conduct appeared the more heroic from their having to encounter the enmity and malice of their fellow-countrymen. For they did not repel the injuries with which they were assailed by having recourse to violence or to the law, the only opposition which they tendered was the patience with which they submitted to these sufferings. Such was the course pursued by Valentian, who according to some accounts, was born at Edessa, but according to others, at Arethusa. Another individual of the same name, distinguished himself by similar conduct, as likewise Theodore of Tittis in Apamea, Marosas, a native of Nechilis, Bassus, Bassones, and Paul. This latter was a native of the village of Telmison. He founded several monastic institutions, the most extensive and most celebrated was at a place called Jugates. Here, after a long and honorable life, he died and was interred.

Some of the ascetic philosophers have survived to our own days. Indeed, most of those to whom allusion has been made, enjoyed a very long term of existence, and I am convinced that God added to the length of their days for the express purpose of furthering the interests of religion. They were instrumental in converting nearly the whole Syrian nation, and many of the Persians and Saracens from Paganism. They also induced many individuals to follow their example and embrace the monastic mode of life.

It appears reasonable to suppose that there were many monks in Galatia, Cappadocia, and the neighboring provinces, for Christianity was embraced at an early period by the inhabitants of these regions. The monks of these countries, however, dwelt together in cities and villages, for they did not habituate themselves, like other monks, to live in deserts. The severity of the winters would probably render such a course almost impracticable in these regions. Leontius and Prassides were, I understand, the most celebrated of these monks. The former was bishop of Ancyra, and the latter, a man of very advanced age, performed the episcopal functions in several villages. Prassides also presided over a hospital of great celebrity, founded by Basil, bishop of Cæsarea, whose name it still retains.

NOTE

1. See above, Book III, Chapters 14, 16.

CHAPTER XXXV

THE WOODEN TRIPOD ON WHICH WERE INDICATED THE FIRST LETTERS COMPOSING THE NAME OF HIM WHO WAS TO SUCCEED TO THE THRONE. DESTRUCTION OF THE PAGAN PHILOSOPHERS.

Such is the information which I have been enabled to collect concerning the ecclesiastical philosophers.[1] As to the Pagan philosophers, they were nearly all exterminated about the period to which we have been referring. Some among them who were reputed to excel in philosophy, and who viewed with extreme displeasure the progress of the Christian religion, were desirous of ascertaining who would be the successor of Valens on the throne of the Roman empire and resorted to magical arts for the purpose of attaining this insight into futurity. After various incantations, they constructed a tripod of laurel wood and uttered certain magical words over it, so that the letters of the alphabet might appear upon the tripod and indicate the name of the future emperor. Theodore, who held a distinguished appointment at court and who was a Pagan, was the individual whom they most desired to see on the imperial throne, and the first letters of his name so far as the letter "D" appeared on the tripod and deceived the philosophers. They hence expected that Theodore would be the future emperor, but their hopes were utterly frustrated, for their proceedings were detected by Valens and he was as deeply incensed as if a conspiracy had been formed against himself. He ordered all the parties concerned in the construction of the tripod to be arrested, commanded them to be burned alive, and caused Theodore himself to be beheaded. The indignation of the emperor was, in fact, so unbounded, that the most famous philosophers of the time were slain in consequence of what had occurred and even those who were not philosophers, but who wore garments similar to those of the philosophers,[2] were sacrificed to his resentment. Hence, these garments were disused, lest they should lead to the imputation of magic and sorcery.

I believe that all sensible persons will not blame the cruelty and impetuosity of the emperor more than the rashness of the philosophers in entering upon so unphilosophical an undertaking. The emperor, absurdly supposing that he could put his successor to death,[3] spared neither those who had performed the incantations, nor those who bore the name that had been indicated, for he sacrificed even those whose names commenced with nearly the same letters as those that had appeared on the tripod. The philosophers, on the other hand, acted as if the deposition and restoration of emperors had depended solely on them, for if the imperial succession was to be considered dependent on the arrangement of the stars, what was requisite but to await the accession of the future emperor, whoever he might be? Or if the succession was regarded as dependent on the will of God, what right had man to interfere with His decrees? Can man penetrate the secret counsels of God? Or can man, whatever may be his wisdom, make a better choice than God? If it were merely from rash curiosity to discern the things of futurity, that these philosophers were induced to violate the laws of the Roman empire that had subsisted ever since the legislation of the Pagan sacrifices, their motives and conduct differed widely from those of Socrates. For, when unjustly condemned to drink poison, he refused to save himself by violating the laws of his country, nor would he escape from prison although it was in his power to do so.

NOTES

1. Compare Socrates, *Ecclesiastical History*, Book IV, Chapter 19.
2. These were called κροκωτά or κροσσωτά. See Hesychius *sub voce*. The flowing robe of the philosophers is frequently alluded to in the Greek and Latin classical writers as approximating to the long dress of women.
3. Sozomen probably alludes here to the celebrated saying of Diocletian, "Successorem suum nullus occidit" (No one kills his successor).

CHAPTER XXXVI

EXPEDITION AGAINST THE SARMATIANS. DEATH OF THE EMPEROR VALENTINIAN IN GAUL. VALENTINIAN THE YOUNGER. PERSECUTION OF THE PRIESTS. ORATION OF THE PHILOSOPHER THEMISTIUS.

Such subjects as the above, however, are best left to the examination and decision of individual judgment.

The Sarmatians[1] having invaded the Western provinces of the empire, Valentinian levied an army to oppose them. As soon, however, as they heard of the number and strength of the troops raised against them, they sent an embassy to solicit peace. When the ambassadors were ushered into the presence of Valentinian, he asked them whether all the Sarmatians were similar to them. On their replying that the principal men of the nation had been selected to form the embassy, the emperor exclaimed in great fury, that he regarded it as an especial misfortune that the territories under his sway should be exposed to the incursions of a barbarous nation like the Sarmatians, who had even presumed to take up arms against the Romans! He spoke in this strain for some time in a very high pitch of voice, and his rage was so violent and so unbounded, that at length he burst simultaneously a blood-vessel and an artery. He lost, in consequence, a great quantity of blood, and expired soon after in a fortress of Gaul.[2] He was about fifty-four years of age and had during thirteen years guided the reins of government with great wisdom and skill. Six days after his death, his youngest son who bore the same name as himself, was proclaimed emperor by the soldiers, and soon afterwards Valens and Gratian formally assented to this election, although they were at first irritated at the soldiers having adopted such a measure without their sanction.

During this period, Valens had fixed his residence at Antioch in Syria, and carried on a most cruel and unmerciful persecution against all who differed from him in opinion concerning the Divine nature.[3] The philosopher Themistius pronounced an oration in his presence, in which he took occasion to show that the diversity of opinion existing concerning ecclesiastical doctrines ought not to be regarded with surprise, inasmuch as still greater diversity of opinion leading to perpetual disputes and contentions, was prevalent among the Pagans, and he further insisted that God might be well pleased to permit this diversity of opinion concerning his own nature, because the inscrutability of this subject, and the deficiency of all accurate knowledge concerning it tend to afford exalted ideas of the Divine nature.

NOTES

1. Compare Socrates, *Ecclesiastical History,* Book IV, Chapter 31.
2. It was in Pannonia, as is clear from the narrative of Ammianus Marcellinus, *History*, Book XXX, Chapter 6.
3. Compare Socrates, *Ecclesiastical History,* Book IV, Chapter 32.

CHAPTER XXXVII

CONCERNING THE BARBARIANS BEYOND THE DANUBE, AND THEIR CONVERSION TO CHRISTIANITY. ULPHILAS AND ATHANARICUS. CAUSE OF ARIANISM BEING EMBRACED BY THE GOTHS.

The oration of Themistius had some effect in mitigating the resentment of the emperor, and the persecution became in consequence less cruel and violent than before. The priests, however, were not restored to favor, and they would have felt the full weight of the emperor's indignation, had not the state of public affairs diverted his attention from the concerns of the church. For the Goths who inhabited the regions beyond the Danube and held several barbarian nations under their sway, having been vanquished and driven from their country by the Huns, marched towards the Roman territories.

The Huns, it is said, were unknown to the Thracians of the Danube and the Goths before this period, for though they dwelt in a neighboring region, a lake of vast extent formed a boundary between them and the inhabitants on each side of the lake respectively imagined that their own country was situated at the extremity of the earth and that there was nothing beyond them but the sea and water. It so happened, however, that an ox tormented by insects, plunged into the lake and was pursued by the herdsman, who perceiving for the first time that the opposite bank was inhabited, made known the circumstance to his countrymen. Some, however, relate that a stag pursued by hunters, showed them the way to cross the lake by fording it at a place where the water was not deep. On arriving at the opposite bank, the hunters were struck with the beauty of the country, the abundance of its produce, and the serenity of the air, and they reported what they had seen to their king.

The Huns then made an attempt to attack the Goths with a few soldiers, but they afterwards raised a powerful army, conquered the Goths, and took possession of their whole country. The vanquished nation, being pursued by their enemies, fled towards the Roman territories. They crossed the river and despatched an embassy to the emperor, assuring him of their co-operation in any warfare in which he might engage, provided that he would assign a portion of land for them to inhabit. Ulphilas, the bishop of the nation, was the chief of the embassy. The object of his embassy was fully accomplished, and the Goths were permitted to take up their abode in Thrace. Soon after, contentions broke out among them which led to their division into two parties, one of which was headed by Athanaric, and the other by Phritigernes. They took up arms against each other, and Phritigernes was vanquished and implored assistance of the Romans. The emperor having commanded the troops in Thrace to assist him, a second battle was fought, and Athanaric and his party were put to flight. In acknowledgment of the timely succor afforded by Valens, and in proof of his fidelity to the Romans, Phritigernes embraced the religion of the emperor and persuaded the barbarians over whom he ruled to follow his example.

It does not, however, appear to me that this is the only reason that can be advanced to account for the Goths having retained, even to the present day, the tenets of Arianism. Ulphilas, their bishop, originally held no opinions at variance with those of the Catholic church. For though he took part, as I am convinced from thoughtlessness, at the council of Constantinople in conjunction with Eudoxius and Acacius, yet he did not swerve from the doctrines of the Nicene council.[1] He afterwards, it appears, returned to Constantinople and entered into disputations on doctrinal topics with the chiefs of the Arian faction, and they promised to lay his requests before the emperor and forward the object of his embassy if he would conform to their opinions. Compelled by the urgency of the occasion or possibly induced by a conviction of the truth of their sentiments concerning the Divine nature, Ulphilas entered into communion with the Arians and separated himself and his whole nation from all connection with the Catholic church. For as he had instructed the Goths in the elements of religion and the practice of morality and gentleness, they placed the most implicit confidence in his directions, and were firmly convinced that he could neither do nor say anything that was evil. He had, in fact, given many signal proofs of the greatness of his virtue. He had exposed himself to innumerable perils in defense of the faith during the period that the aforesaid barbarians were abandoned to Paganism. He taught them the use of letters and translated the Sacred Scriptures into their own language. It was on this account that the nations on the banks of the Danube followed the tenets of Arius.

At the same period, there were many of the subjects of Phritigernes who testified to Christ and were martyred. Athanaric also resented the change in religion that had been effected by Ulphilas, and irritated because his subjects had abandoned the superstition of their fathers, he imposed cruel punishments on many individuals. Some he put to death after they had been dragged before tribunals and had nobly confessed the faith, and others were slain without being permitted to utter a single word in their own defense. It is said that the officers appointed by Athanaric to execute his cruel mandates, caused a statue to be constructed which they placed on a chariot and had it conveyed to the tents of those who were suspected of having embraced Christianity, and who were therefore commanded to worship the statue and offer sacrifice. If they refused to do so, they were burnt alive in their tents. But I have heard that an outrage of still greater atrocity was perpetrated at this period. Men, women, and children, who were compelled to offer sacrifice, fled from their tents and sought refuge in a church, whither also they carried the infants at the breast. The Pagans set fire to the church and consumed it with all who were therein.

The Goths were not long in making peace among themselves and they then began to ravage Thrace and to pillage the cities and villages. Valens was soon convinced of the utter failure of his experiment, for he had calculated that the Goths would always be useful to the empire and formidable to its enemies, and had therefore neglected the reinforcement of the Roman legions. He had taken gold from the cities and villages under his dominion, instead of the usual complement of men for the military service. On his expectation being thus frustrated, he quitted Antioch and hastened to Constantinople. Hence the persecution which he had been carrying on against Christians differing in opinion from himself was arrested. Euzoius, bishop of the Arians, died and was succeeded by Theodore.

NOTES

1. Christophorson wrongly understood Sozomen to mean here that Eudoxius and Acacius were among the bishops present at the council of Nicæa. But Acacius was not made bishop till many years later. Sozomen here says that Ulphilas at first strictly adhered to the Nicene faith, but that during the reign of Constantius he was imprudently led to join in the synod at Constantinople with Eudoxius and Acacius, (AD 359) but that he still kept up outward communion with the orthodox bishops, and at length, on the accession of Valens, upon coming to Constantinople as representative of the Goths, he went openly over to the side of the Arians.

CHAPTER XXXVIII

CONCERNING MAVIA, QUEEN OF THE SARACENS.
WAR AND SUBSEQUENT PEACE BETWEEN THE SARACENS
AND ROME. DETAILS CONCERNING THE ISHMAELITES
AND THE SARACENS, AND THEIR CONVERSION TO CHRISTIANITY.

About this period the king of the Saracens died,[1] and the peace which had previously existed between that nation and the Romans was dissolved. Mavia,[2] the widow of the late monarch, finding herself at the head of the government, led her troops into Phœnicia and Palestine as far as the regions of Egypt lying to the left of those who sail towards the source of the Nile, and which are generally denominated Arabia. This war was by no means a contemptible one, although conducted by a woman. The Romans, it is said, considered it so arduous and so perilous, that the general of the Phœnician troops applied for assistance to the general of the cavalry and infantry of the East. This latter ridiculed the summons and undertook to give battle alone. He accordingly attacked Mavia, who commanded her own troops in person, and he met with so signal a defeat, that it was with difficulty he saved his life. This rescue was solely effected by the intervention of the general of the troops of Palestine and Phœnicia. Perceiving the extremity of the danger, this general deemed it unnecessary to obey the orders he had received to keep aloof from the combat. He therefore rushed upon the barbarians and then, while retreating, discharged volleys of arrows upon them, in order to enable the Romans to make good their escape. This occurrence is still held in remembrance among the people of the country and is celebrated in songs by the Saracens.

As the war was still pursued with vigor, the Romans found it necessary to send an embassy to Mavia to solicit peace. It is said that she refused to comply with the request of the embassy, unless consent were given for the ordination of a certain man named Moses, who dwelt in solitude in a neighboring desert, as bishop over her subjects. This Moses was a man of virtuous life and capable of performing the most wonderful miracles. On these conditions being announced to the emperor, the chiefs of the army were commanded to seize Moses and conduct him to Lucius. The monk exclaimed, in the presence of the rulers and the assembled people, "I am not worthy of the honor of bearing the name of bishop. But if, notwithstanding my unworthiness, God destines me to this office, I take him to witness who created the heavens and the earth, that I will not be ordained by the imposition of the hands of Lucius, which are defiled with the blood of the saints."

Lucius immediately rejoined, "If you are unacquainted with the nature of my creed, you do wrong in judging me before you are in possession of all the circumstances of the case. If you have been prejudiced by the calumnies that have been circulated against me, at least allow me to declare to you what are my sentiments, and do you be the judge of them."

"Your creed is already well known to me," replied Moses, "and its nature is testified by bishops, priests, and deacons, of whom some have been sent into exile and others condemned to the mines. It is clear that your sentiments are opposed to the faith of Christ, and to all orthodox doctrines concerning the Godhead."[3]

Having again protested, upon oath that he would not receive ordination at the hands of Lucius, the Roman rulers conducted him to the bishops who were then in exile. After receiving ordination from them, he went to exercise the functions of his office among the Saracens. He concluded a peace with the Romans and converted many of the Saracens to the faith.

It appears that the Saracens were descended from Ishmael, the son of Abraham and were, in consequence, originally denominated Ishmaelites. As their mother Hagar was a slave, they afterwards, to conceal the opprobrium of their origin, assumed the name of Saracens as if they were descended from Sarah the wife of Abraham. Such being their origin, they practice circumcision like the Jews, refrain from the use of pork, and observe many other Jewish rites and customs. If, indeed, they deviate in any respect from the observances of that nation, it must be ascribed to the lapse of time and to their intercourse with neighboring nations. Moses, who lived many centuries after Abraham, only legislated for those whom he led out of Egypt. The inhabitants of the neighboring countries, being strongly addicted to superstition,[4] probably soon corrupted the laws imposed upon them by their forefather Ishmael. These laws, though not set down in writing, were the only ones known to the ancient Hebrews before the promulgation of the written laws of Moses. These people certainly served the same gods as the neighboring nations, recognized them by the same appellations, and rendered them the same species of homage, and this clearly evidences their departure from the laws of their forefathers. It appears probable that in the lapse of time their ancient customs fell to oblivion, and that they gradually learnt to follow the practices of other nations. Some of their tribe afterwards happening to come in contact with the Jews, gathered from them the facts of their true origin and returned to the observance of the Hebrew customs and laws. Indeed, there are some among them, even at the present day, who regulate their lives according to the Jewish precepts.

Some of the Saracens were converted to Christianity not long before the accession of Valens. Their conversion appears to have been the result of their intercourse with the priests who dwelt among them and with the monks who dwelt in the neighboring deserts and who were distinguished by their purity of life and by their miraculous gifts. It is said that a whole tribe and Zocomus their chief, were converted to Christianity and baptized about this period, under the following circumstances. Zocomus was childless and went to a certain monk of great celebrity to complain to him of this calamity, for among the Saracens and, I believe, other barbarian nations, it was accounted of great importance to have children. The monk desired Zocomus to be of good cheer, engaged in prayer on his behalf, and sent him away with the promise that if he would believe in Christ, he would have a son. When this promise was accomplished by God and when a son was born to him, Zocomus was baptized and all his subjects with him. From that period this tribe was peculiarly fortunate and became strong in point of number, and formidable to the Persians as well as to the other Saracens.

Such are the details that I have been enabled to collect concerning the conversion of the Saracens and their first bishops.

NOTES

1. Compare Socrates, *Ecclesiastical History,* Book IV, Chapter 36.
2. Otherwise called Mania, though she is termed Mavia by Socrates, Nicephorus, Epiphanius, and all writers before Rufinus from whom, in the opinion of Valesius, Sozomen borrowed this account. See Theodoret, *Ecclesiastical History,* Book IV, Chapter 23, and Rufinus, Book II, Chapter 6.
3. See above, Book II, Chapter 46.
4. ὡς ἄγαν δεισωδαίμονες ὄντες. Compare Acts 17:22, and Xenophon, *Cyropædia,* Book III, Chapter 3:58.

CHAPTER XXXIX

PETER, HAVING RETURNED FROM ROME, SUPERSEDES LUCIUS IN THE GOVERNMENT OF THE CHURCHES OF EGYPT. EXPEDITION OF VALENS AGAINST THE SCYTHIANS.

Those in every city who maintained the Nicene doctrine now began to take courage, and more particularly the inhabitants of Alexandria. Peter had returned thither with a letter from Damascus confirmatory of the tenets of Nicæa and of his own ordination, and he was installed in the government of the churches in the place of Lucius, who retired to Constantinople. The emperor Valens was so distracted by other affairs, that he had no leisure to attend to these transactions. He had no sooner arrived at Constantinople than he incurred the suspicion and hatred of the people. The barbarians were pillaging Thrace and were even advancing to the very gates of Constantinople, and yet the emperor made no effort to repress their incursions. Hence he became an object of popular indignation and was even regarded as the cause of the inroads of the enemy. At length, when he was present at the sports of the Hippodrome, the people openly and loudly accused him of neglecting the affairs of the state and demanded arms that they might fight in their own defense. Valens, offended at these reproaches, immediately undertook an expedition against the barbarians, but he threatened to punish the insolence of the people on his return and also to take vengeance on them for having formerly supported the tyrant Procopius.

CHAPTER XL

SAINT ISAAC, THE MONK, PREDICTS THE DEATH OF VALENS. VALENS IS DEFEATED. HIS DEATH.

When Valens was on the point of departing from Constantinople, Isaac, a monk of great virtue who feared no danger in the cause of God, presented himself before him and addressed him in the following words: "Give back, O emperor, to the orthodox and to those who maintain the Nicene doctrines, the churches of which you have deprived them and the victory will be yours."

The emperor was offended at this act of boldness and commanded that Isaac should be arrested and kept in chains until his return when he meant to bring him to justice for his temerity. Isaac, however, replied, "You will not return unless you restore the churches." And so, in fact, it came to pass.

Valens marched at the head of his troops in pursuit of the Goths, through Thrace, as far as Adrianople. Here he found the barbarians encamped in a very advantageous position, and yet he had the rashness to attack them before he had ranged his own legions in proper order.[1] His cavalry was dispersed, his infantry compelled to retreat, and he himself escaped with difficulty with a few of his attendants and sought refuge and concealment in a small house or tower. The barbarians were in full pursuit and went beyond the tower, not suspecting that he had selected it for his place of concealment. As the last detachment of the barbarians was passing by the tower, the attendants of the emperor let fly a volley of arrows, which immediately led to the conjecture that Valens was concealed within the building. The barbarians loudly shouted this intelligence to their companions who were in advance of them, and thus the news was conveyed till it reached the detachments which were foremost in the pursuit. They returned and encompassed the tower. They collected vast quantities of wood from the country around which they piled up against the tower, and finally set fire to the mass. A wind which then happened to arise favored the progress of the conflagration; and in a short period the tower, with all that it contained, including the emperor and his attendants, was utterly destroyed.

Valens was fifty years of age. He had reigned thirteen years conjointly with his brother, and three by himself.

NOTES

1. *Note to the 2018 edition:* This is the decisive Battle of Adrianople which took place on August 9, AD 378. A very detailed description of this catastrophic Roman defeat at the hands of the Goths may be found in Ammianus Marcellinus, *History*, Book XXXI, Chapter 12.

BOOK VII

CHAPTER I
MAVIA ASSISTS THE ROMANS AGAINST THE BARBARIANS. GRATIAN LEAVES TO EVERYONE FULL LIBERTY OF OPINION.

Such was the fate of Valens. The barbarians,[1] flushed with victory, overran Thrace and advanced to the gates of Constantinople. In this emergency, a few Saracens sent by Mavia were of great service. Dominica, the widow of Valens, furnished money out of the public treasury, and some of the people, after hastily arming themselves, attacked the barbarians and drove them from the city.

Gratian, who at this period reigned conjointly with his brother over the whole Roman empire, disapproved of the late persecution that had been carried on to check the diversity in religious creeds and recalled all those who had been banished on account of their religion. He also enacted a law by which it was decreed that every individual should be freely permitted the exercise of his own religion and should be allowed to hold assemblies, with the exception of the Manichæans and the followers of Photinus and Eunomius.

NOTE

1. Compare Socrates, *Ecclesiastical History,* Book V, Chapters 1, 2.

CHAPTER II
THEODOSIUS IS ASSOCIATED WITH GRATIAN IN THE GOVERNMENT OF THE EMPIRE. ARIANISM PREVAILS THROUGHOUT THE EASTERN CHURCHES EXCEPT THAT OF JERUSALEM. COUNCIL OF ANTIOCH.[1]

On reflecting that while it was indispensably requisite to check the incursions of the barbarians of the Danube in Thrace and Illyria, his presence was equally necessary in Gaul to repel the inroads of the Alemanni,[2] Gratian associated Theodosius with himself at Sirmich in the government of the empire. Theodosius belonged to an illustrious family of the Pyrenees in Spain and had acquired so much renown in war, that before he was raised to the imperial power, he was universally considered capable of guiding the reins of the empire.

At this period all the churches of the East, with the exception of that of Jerusalem, were in the hands of the Arians. The Macedonians differed but little in opinion from those who maintained the doctrines of Nicæa and held intercourse and communion with them in all the cities, and this had been more especially the case with the Macedonians of Constantinople, ever since their reconciliation with Liberius. But after the enactment of Gratian's law by which every sect was permitted the full exercise of its own form of religion, the Macedonians re-took possession of the churches from which they had been ejected by Valens. They assembled together at Antioch in Caria[3] and protested that the Son is not to be declared "consubstantial" with the Father, but only like unto him in substance. From that period, many of the Macedonians seceded from the others and held separate assemblies, while others, condemning this schismatic spirit, united themselves still more closely with the followers of the Nicene doctrines.

Many of the bishops who had been banished by Valens and who were recalled about this period in consequence of the law of Gratian, manifested no ambition to be restored to the highest offices in the church. On the contrary, they urged the Arian bishops to retain the posts they occupied and not to rend the church by their love of contention and of personal promotion, or disturb the unity which had been established by God and the apostles. Eulalius, bishop of Amasia in Pontus, was one of those who pursued this course of conduct. It is said that when he returned from exile, he found that his church had passed into the hands of an Arian bishop and that scarcely fifty inhabitants of the city had submitted to the control of this new bishop. Eulalius, desiring the restoration of concord above all other considerations, offered to take part with the Arian bishop in the government of the church and expressly agreed to allow him the precedence. But as the Arian would not comply with this proposition, it was not long before he found himself deserted by the few who had followed him and who went over to the other party.

NOTES

1. With this chapter compare the parallel account given in Socrates, *Ecclesiastical History*, Book V, Chapter 3.
2. This people dwelt near Belgæ and on the east of the river Rhine. Their name has remained as an appellation of Germany itself.
3. See above, Book IV, Chapter 12, and note.

CHAPTER III

CONCERNING SAINT MELETIUS AND PAULINUS, BISHOPS OF ANTIOCH. THEIR OATH RESPECTING THE BISHOPRIC.

In consequence of this law, Meletius returned about this period to Antioch in Syria, and his presence gave rise to great contentions.[1] Paulinus, whom Valens from veneration for his piety had not ventured to banish, was still alive. The partisans of Meletius, therefore, proposed his association with Paulinus in the government of the church. This was opposed by the followers of Paulinus, who condemned the ordination of Meletius because it had been conferred by Arian bishops. The other party, however, possessing the advantage in point of strength, placed Meletius over a church in the suburbs of the city. The mutual animosity of the two parties increased and sedition would doubtless have been the consequence had not means been devised for the restoration of concord. Flavian and five of the clergy who were in expectation of eventually being elected to the episcopal dignity, promised that they would not accept this office during the life of Paulinus and Meletius, and that in the event of the decease of either of these great men, the other should succeed to the bishopric. On their ratifying this promise with oaths, unanimity was restored among the people, and no further dissension remained except among a small party of Luciferians who contended that Meletius had been ordained by heretics. On the termination of this contest, Meletius proceeded to Constantinople where some bishops had assembled together to deliberate on the necessity of translating Gregory from the bishopric of Nazianzen to that of this city.

NOTE

1. Compare Socrates, *Ecclesiastical History*, Book V, Chapter 5.

CHAPTER IV

REIGN OF THEODOSIUS THE GREAT. HE IS BAPTIZED BY ASCHOLIUS, BISHOP OF THESSALONICA.

As Gaul was about this period infested by the incursions of the Alemanni,[1] Gratian returned to his Western dominions, which he had reserved for himself[2] and his brother, when he bestowed the government of Illyria and of the Eastern provinces upon Theodosius. He succeeded in repelling these barbarians, and Theodosius was equally successful against the tribes from the banks of the Danube. He defeated them, compelled them to sue for peace, and after accepting hostages from them, proceeded to Thessalonica. He fell ill while in this city, and after receiving instructions in the rudiments of religion from Ascholius the bishop, he was baptized and was soon after restored to health.

The parents of Theodosius were Christians and were attached to the Nicene doctrines. Hence he took pleasure in the ministrations of Ascholius who maintained the same doctrines and was endowed with every priestly virtue and qualification.[3] He also rejoiced at finding that the Arian heresy had not been received in Illyria.[4] He inquired concerning the religious sentiments which were prevalent in the other provinces and ascertained that, as far as Macedonia,[5] one form of belief was universally predominant, which was that the same homage ought to be rendered to God the Word and to the Holy Ghost as to God the Father, but that towards the East and particularly at Constantinople, the people were divided into many different sects. Reflecting that it would he better to propound his own religious views to his subjects than to enforce the reception of any creed by mere compulsion, Theodosius enacted a law at Thessalonica which he caused to be published at Constantinople, that it might be thence transmitted to the remotest cities of his dominions. He made known by this law his intention of leading all his subjects to the reception of that faith which Peter, the chief of the apostles, had from the beginning preached to the Romans and which was professed by Damasus, bishop of Rome, and by Peter, bishop of Alexandria. He enacted[6] that the title of "Catholic Church" should be exclusively confined to those who rendered equal homage to the Three Persons of the Trinity, and that those individuals who entertained opposite opinions should be treated as heretics, regarded with contempt, and delivered over to punishment.

NOTES

1. Compare Socrates, *Ecclesiastical History,* Book V, Chapter 6.
2. The ancient annotators remark that Gaul, Britain, and Spain fell to the lot of Gratian, while his brother Valentinian took Italy, Illyricum, and Africa. See Zosimus, Book IV, page 746. Sozomen is therefore mistaken in connecting Illyria with the name of Gratian.
3. The original Greek is here hopelessly corrupt. We have followed the opinion of Valesius in our text.
4. The same testimony is given by Basil, Epistle 324, *ad Valerianum.*
5. This is also asserted in the synodical epistle put forth by the council of Aquileia.
6. This edict is extant in the *Theodosian Code,* under the title "*de Fide Catholica.*"

CHAPTER V
GREGORY THE THEOLOGIAN RECEIVES FROM THEODOSIUS THE GOVERNMENT OF THE CHURCHES. EXPULSION OF DEMOPHILUS AND OF ALL WHO DENY THAT THE SON IS CONSUBSTANTIAL WITH THE FATHER.

Soon after the enactment of this law, Theodosius went to Constantinople. The Arians, under the guidance of Demophilus, still retained possession of the churches. Gregory of Nazianzen presided over those who maintain the "consubstantiality" of the Holy Trinity and assembled them together in a dwelling which had been altered into the form of a house of prayer, and which subsequently became one of the most remarkable in the city by the magnificence of its decorations and the special revelations which were there vouchsafed of the grace of God. For the power of God was there manifested by dreams, by visions, and by miraculous cures of divers diseases. These miracles were usually attributed to the instrumentality of Mary the Holy Virgin, the Mother of God. The name of Anastasia was given to this church because, as I believe, the Nicene doctrines which were, so to speak, buried beneath the errors of heterodoxy at Constantinople, were here brought to light and maintained by Gregory. Others ascribe the origin of this appellation to the miracle, and relate that one day when the people were met together for worship in this edifice, a pregnant woman fell from the highest gallery, and was found dead on the spot, but that at the prayer of the whole congregation, she was restored to life and she and the infant were saved. On account of this wonderful occurrence, the place, as some assert, obtained its name.

The emperor sent to command Demophilus[1] to conform to the doctrines of Nicæa and to lead the people to embrace the same sentiments, or else to deliver up the government of the churches. Demophilus assembled the people, acquainted them with the imperial edict, and informed them that it was his intention to hold an assembly the next day without the walls of the city in accordance, he said, with the Divine law which commands us when we are persecuted in one city to "flee unto another."[2] From that day he always assembled without the city with Lucius who was formerly the bishop of the Arians at Alexandria and who, after having been expelled, as above related, from that city, had fixed his residence at Constantinople.

When Demophilus and his followers had quitted the church, the emperor entered therein and engaged in prayer, and from that period those who maintained the consubstantiality of the Holy Trinity held possession of the houses of prayer. These events occurred in the fifth year of the consulate of Gratian, and in the first of that of Theodosius and after the churches had been during forty years[3] in the hands of the Arians.

NOTES

1. See Socrates, *Ecclesiastical History,* Book IV, Chapter 7.
2. Matthew 10:23.
3. *Viz.* from AD 339.

CHAPTER VI

INTRIGUES OF THE ARIANS. ELOQUENCE OF EUNOMIUS. BOLDNESS OF SAINT AMPHILOCHIUS.

The Arians, who were still very strong in point of numbers and who, through the protection formerly granted by Constantius and Valens, were still permitted to hold their assemblies and discourse publicly concerning God and the Divine nature, now determined upon making an attempt to gain over the emperor to their party, through the intervention of individuals of their sect who held appointments at court, and they entertained hopes of succeeding in this project as well as they had succeeded in the case of Constantius. These machinations excited great terror among the members of the Catholic church, but the chief cause of their apprehension was the eloquence of Eunomius. It appears that during the reign of Valens, Eunomius had some dispute with the clergy of Cyzicus and had in consequence seceded from the Arians and retired to Bithynia near Constantinople. Here multitudes resorted to him, some with the design of testing his principles, and others merely from the desire of listening to his discourses. His reputation reached the ears of the emperor who would gladly have held a conference with him,[1] but the empress Flacilla[2] studiously prevented any interview from taking place between them, for she was strenuously attached to the Nicene doctrines and feared lest Eunomius might, by his powers of disputation, induce a change in the sentiments of the emperor.

In the meantime, while these intrigues were being carried on by each party, it is said that the bishops then residing in Constantinople went to the emperor to render him the customary salutations. An old bishop who presided over a city of little note[3] and who was simple and unworldly yet well instructed in Divine subjects, formed one of this party. He went through precisely the same forms as the others in reverentially saluting the emperor. But instead of rendering equal honor to the prince who was seated beside his father, the old priest approached him, patted him familiarly, and called him his dear child. The emperor was deeply incensed at this indignity being offered to his son and commanded that the old man should be thrust from his presence. While being led away, however, the old bishop turned round and exclaimed, "Reflect, O emperor, on the wrath of the Heavenly Father against those who do not honor his Son as himself, and who have the audacity to assert that the Son is inferior to the Father." The emperor felt the force of this observation, recalled the priest, apologized to him for what had occurred, and confessed that he had spoken the truth. The emperor was henceforward less disposed to hold intercourse with heretics, and he enacted a law by which he prohibited, under the severest penalties, all public disputes, assemblies, or disputations concerning the Divine substance and nature.

NOTES

1. Valesius sees good reason for doubting the truth of this assertion. He thinks that the credulity of Sozomen led to his being imposed upon by one of the partisans of Eunomius.
2. She was the first and not the second wife of Theodosius, and the mother of Arcadius and Honorius. Her funeral panegyric was delivered by Gregory of Nyssa, among whose works it is still extant.
3. Nicephorus says that the old man was Amphilochius, bishop of Iconium, but this city can hardly be said to be one "of little note."

CHAPTER VII

CONCERNING THE SECOND HOLY GENERAL COUNCIL, AND THE PLACE AND THE CAUSE OF ITS CONVENTION. ABDICATION OF GREGORY THE THEOLOGIAN.

AD 381 — The emperor soon after convened a council of orthodox bishops for the purpose of confirming the decrees of Nicæa and of electing a bishop to the vacant see of Constantinople.[1] He likewise summoned the Macedonians to this assembly, for as their doctrines differed but little from those of the Catholic church, he judged that it would be easy to effect a reunion with them. About a hundred and fifty bishops who maintained the consubstantiality of the Holy Trinity were present at this council,[2] as likewise thirty-six of the Macedonian bishops, chiefly from the cities of the Hellespont, of whom the principal were Eleusius, bishop of Cyzicus, and Marcian, bishop of Lampsacus. The other party was under the guidance of Timothy, who had succeeded his brother Peter as bishop of Alexandria, of Meletius, bishop of Antioch, who had repaired to Constantinople a short time previously, on account of the election of Gregory, and of Cyril, bishop of Jerusalem, who had, at this period, renounced the tenets of the Macedonians. Ascholius, bishop of Thessalonica, Diodorus, bishop of Tarsus, and Acacius, bishop of Berœa, were also present at the council. These latter unanimously maintained the decrees of Nicæa and urged Eleusius and his partisans to conform to these sentiments, reminding them, at the same time, of the embassy they had formerly deputed to Liberius, and of the confession they had conveyed to him through the medium of Eustathius, Silvanus, and Theophilus. The Macedonians, however, declared openly that they would never admit the Son to be of the same substance as the Father, whatever confession they might formerly have made to Liberius, and immediately withdrew. They then wrote to those of their own sect in every city, exhorting them not to conform to the doctrines of Nicæa.

The bishops who remained at Constantinople now turned their attention to the election of a prelate to the see of that city. It is said that the emperor, from profound admiration of the sanctity and eloquence of Gregory, judged that he was worthy of this high dignity and that from reverence of his virtue, the greater number of the bishops were of the same opinion. Gregory at first consented to accept the bishopric of the city but afterwards, on ascertaining that some of the bishops,[3] particularly those of Egypt, objected to the election, he withdrew his consent.

For my own part, I confess that in reviewing these circumstances, I know not how to express adequate admiration of this great man. His eloquence did not inspire him with pride, nor did vainglory lead him to desire to retain an office upon which he had entered at a very perilous juncture. He surrendered his appointment to the bishops when it was required of him as readily as if it had been merely a deposit committed to his charge, and never complained of the labors to which he had been exposed or of the dangers he had incurred in the suppression of heresies. Had he retained possession of the bishopric of Constantinople, it would have been no detriment to the interests of any individual, as another bishop had been appointed in his stead at Nazianzen. But the council, in strict obedience to the laws of the fathers and the canons of the church, withdrew from him, with his own acquiescence, the deposit which had been confided to him without making an exception in favor of so eminent a man.

The emperor and the priests therefore proceeded to the election of another bishop which they regarded as the most important affair then requiring attention, and the emperor was urgent that diligent investigations might be instituted so that the most able and exemplary individual might be intrusted with the archbishopric of the great and royal city. The council, however, was divided in sentiment, for each of the members desired to see one of his own friends ordained over the church.

NOTES

1. Compare Socrates, *Ecclesiastical History,* Book V, Chapter 8.
2. For a parallel account of this council, see Socrates, *Ecclesiastical History,* Book V, Chapter 8.
3. Namely, Maximus and his party, who had irregularly elected the latter into the see of Constantinople.

CHAPTER VIII

ELECTION OF NECTARIUS TO THE BISHOPRIC OF CONSTANTINOPLE. HIS BIRTH-PLACE AND EDUCATION.

A certain man of Tarsus in Cilicia of the order of senator was at this period residing at Constantinople.[1] Being about to return to his own country, he called upon Diodorus, bishop of Tarsus, to inquire whether he had any letters to send by him. Diodorus was fully intent upon the election of a bishop, which was the subject then engrossing universal attention. He had no sooner seen Nectarius, than struck by the dignity of his appearance and the suavity of his manners, he judged him to be worthy of the bishopric and secretly desired that he might be elected to it. He conducted him, as if upon some other business, to the bishop of Antioch, and requested him to use his influence to procure his election. The bishop of Antioch derided this request, for the names of the most eminent men had already been proposed for consideration. He, however, called Nectarius to him and desired him to remain for a short time with him.

Book VII, Chapter VIII

Some time after, the emperor commanded the bishops to draw up a list of the names of those whom they desired to ordain to the bishopric, reserving to himself the right of nominating any one of those whose names were thus submitted to him. All the bishops complied with this mandate and among the others, the bishop of Antioch wrote down the names of those whom he proposed as candidates for the bishopric, and at the end of his list, from consideration for Diodorus, he inserted the name of Nectarius. The emperor read the list, stopped at the name of Nectarius on which he placed his finger, and seemed for some time lost in reflection. Then he again read the list, and finally nominated Nectarius. This nomination excited great astonishment, and all the people were anxious to ascertain whence Nectarius came, and who and what he was. When they heard that he had not been baptized, their amazement was increased at the decision of the emperor. I believe that Diodorus himself was not aware that Nectarius had not been baptized, for had he been acquainted with this fact, it is probable that he would not have ventured to seek his election to the bishopric. It appears reasonable to suppose that on perceiving that Nectarius was of advanced age, he took it for granted that he had been baptized long previously. But these events did not take place without the interposition of God.[2] For when the emperor was informed that Nectarius had not been baptized, he did not alter his decision, although strongly opposed by the bishops.

When at last consent had been given to the imperial mandate, Nectarius was baptized and while yet clad in his white robes, was proclaimed bishop of Constantinople by the unanimous voice of the synod. Many have conjectured that the emperor was led to make this election by a Divine revelation. I shall not pause to inquire whether this conjecture be true or false, but I feel convinced when I reflect on the extraordinary circumstances attending this ordination, that all the events were brought about by the interposition of Divine Providence, and that it was by the will of God that so mild and virtuous and exemplary a man was elevated to the priesthood. Such are the details which I have been able to ascertain concerning the ordination of Nectarius.

NOTES

1. Compare Socrates, *Ecclesiastical History,* Book V, Chapter 8.
2. Sozomen has already mentioned (Book VI, Chapter 24) that Ambrose, while yet a catechumen, was elected by the suffrages of the people to the archbishopric of Milan, contrary to the 80th of the Apostolical Canons, and in defiance of the 2nd Canon of Nicæa. This happened, however, doubtless by the special intervention of God, as also in the case of Nectarius.

CHAPTER IX

DECREES OF THE SECOND GENERAL COUNCIL. MAXIMUS, THE CYNICAL PHILOSOPHER.

After these transactions, Nectarius and the other priests assembled together and decreed that the faith established by the council of Nicæa should remain inviolate and that all heresies should be condemned, that the churches should be governed according to the ancient canons, that each bishop should remain in his own church, and not go elsewhere under any light pretext, or perform ordinations in which he had no right to interfere, as had frequently been the case in the Catholic church during the times of persecution. They likewise decreed that the affairs of each church should be subjected to the investigation and control of a council of the province and that the bishop of Constantinople should rank next in point of precedence to the bishop of Rome as occupying the bishopric of New Rome,[1] for Constantinople was not only favored with this appellation, but was also in the enjoyment of many privileges—such as a senate of its own and the division of the citizens into ranks and orders. It was also governed by its own magistrates, and possessed contracts,[2] laws, and immunities similar to those of Rome in Italy.

The council also decreed that Maximus was not a bishop, and that those individuals whom he had ordained were not of the order of the clergy, and that all that had been done by him or in his name was null and void. Maximus was a native of Alexandria and by profession a cynical philosopher. He was zealously attached to the Nicene doctrines and had been secretly ordained bishop of Constantinople by bishops from Egypt.[3]

Such were the decrees of the council. They were confirmed by the emperor, who enacted that the faith established at Nicæa should be preserved inviolate and that the churches should be placed in the hands of those who acknowledged one God in three Persons of equal honor, and of equal power, namely—the Father, the Son, and the Holy Ghost.[4] To designate them still more precisely, the emperor declared that he referred to those who held communion with Nectarius at Constantinople, with Timothy bishop of Alexandria in Egypt, with Diodorus bishop of Tarsus, with Pelagius bishop of Laodicea in the East, and with Amphilochius bishop of Iconium in Asia; to those in Pontus and Bithynia who held communion with Helladius bishop of Cæsarea in Cappadocia, with Gregory bishop of Nyssa, and with Otreius bishop of Melitine, and to the inhabitants of Thrace and Scythia, who held communion with Terence bishop of Tomis, and with Martyrius bishop of Marcianopolis. The emperor was personally acquainted with all these bishops, and had ascertained that they governed their respective churches wisely and piously. After these transactions, the council was dissolved and each of the bishops returned homewards.

NOTES

1. Compare Socrates, *Ecclesiastical History,* Book V, Chapter 8, with Valesius' note *in loco*. The canon, which was the 28th of Chalcedon, ran as follows: "We following in all things the decision of the holy Fathers....do also determine and decree the same things respecting the privileges of the Most Holy City Constantinople, new Rome. For the Fathers properly gave the primacy to the throne of the elder Rome." Baronius, it should be added, considered this canon spurious.
2. συμβολαῖα. This is the emendation of Valesius for the received version σύμβολα, the sense of which is very obscure.
3. On this uncanonical ordination of Maximus, see Baronius, *Ecclesiastical Annals,* AD 379.
4. See above note on Chapter 4.

CHAPTER X

CONCERNING MARTYRIUS OF CILICIA. TRANSLATION OF THE REMAINS OF SAINT PAUL THE CONFESSOR, AND MELETIUS, BISHOP OF ANTIOCH.

Nectarius made himself acquainted with the routine of sacerdotal ceremonies under the instruction of Cyriacus, bishop of Adana, whom he had requested Diodorus, bishop of Tarsus, to leave with him for a short period. Nectarius also retained several other Cilicians with him, amongst whom was Martyrius his physician, who had been a witness of the regularities of his youth. Nectarius was desirous of ordaining him deacon, but Martyrius refused the honor under the plea of his own unworthiness and called upon Nectarius himself to witness as to the course of his past life. To this Nectarius replied as follows: "Although I am now a priest, do you not know that my past career was a more guilty one than yours, inasmuch as you were but an instrument in my numerous transgressions?"

"But you, O blessed one," replied Martyrius, "were cleansed by baptism, and were then accounted worthy of the priesthood. Both these ordinances are appointed by the Divine law for purification from sin,[1] and it seems to me that you now differ in no respect from a new-born infant. But I received long ago the holy rite of baptism and lived subsequently as if I had not received it."

It was under this plea that he excused himself from receiving ordination, and it appeared to me to be so valid and commendable, that I have given the whole transaction a place in my history.

The emperor Theodosius, on being informed of various events connected with Paul, formerly bishop of Constantinople, caused his remains to be removed to the church erected by Macedonius his enemy. This church is a spacious and magnificent edifice and is still distinguished by the name of Paul. Hence, many persons who are ignorant of the facts of the case, particularly women and the mass of the people, imagine that Paul the apostle is interred therein. The remains of Meletius were at the same time conveyed to Antioch and deposited near the tomb of Babylas the martyr. It is said that by the command of the emperor, the relics were received with honor in every city through which they had to be conveyed during the journey to Antioch and that psalms were sung on the occasion, a practice which was quite contrary to the usual Roman customs.

NOTE

1. ἀμφότερα δὲ καθάρσια. Valesius remarks as follows on this passage. "The sacrament of Orders has not the same power to wash away sins as belongs to that of Baptism. To receive the grace of the latter sacrament, faith only is necessary, as Christ says, 'He that believeth and is baptized shall be saved.' (Mark 16:16.) But holy orders do not confer remission of sins. So, if any one is ordained in a state of sin, he receives the indelible character of the priesthood, but not the grace, because his sins are a barrier. But if, after ordination, his sins are remitted in the sacrament of Penance, the character impressed upon him works grace, as the *obex* is removed. In this sense Holy Orders may be called καθάρσια τῶν ἁμαρτημάτων."

CHAPTER XI

ORDINATION OF FLAVIAN AS BISHOP OF ANTIOCH, AND SUBSEQUENT OCCURRENCES.

After the pompous interment of the remains of Meletius, Flavian was ordained in his stead, and that too in direct violation of the oath he had taken, for Paulinus was still alive.[1] This gave rise to fresh troubles in the church of Antioch. Many persons refused to hold communion with Flavian, and assembled together apart with Paulinus. Even priests differed among themselves on this subject. The bishops of Egypt, of Arabia and of Cyprus, were indignant at the injustice that had been manifested towards Paulinus. On the other hand, the bishops of Syria, of Palestine, of Phœnicia, and of the greater part of Armenia, Cappadocia, Galatia, and Pontus, sided with Flavian. The bishop of Rome and all the Western priests, regarded the conduct of Flavian with the utmost displeasure. They addressed the customary epistles, called synodical, to Paulinus as bishop of Antioch and took no notice of Flavian. They also withdrew from communion with Diodorus, bishop of Tarsus, and Acacius, bishop of Berœa, because they had ordained Flavian.[2] To take further cognizance of the affair, the Western bishops and the emperor Gratian wrote to the bishops of the East, and summoned them to attend a council in the West.

NOTES

1. Compare Socrates, *Ecclesiastical History*, Book V, Chapter 9, and 17.
2. The Western bishops condemned not only Diodorus and Flavian, because they had ordained Flavian while Paulinus was still surviving, but also Nectarius, because he had been privy to the proceeding.

CHAPTER XII
PROJECT OF THEODOSIUS TO UNITE ALL THE DIFFERENT FORMS OF RELIGION INTO ONE. AGELIUS AND SISINIUS. THE NOVATIANS. THOSE WHO REJECT THE TERM "CONSUBSTANTIAL" ARE EJECTED FROM THE CHURCHES.

Although all the houses of prayer were at this period in the possession of the Catholic church, yet the Arians continued to be a constant source of trouble and contention.[1] The emperor Theodosius therefore, soon after the council above mentioned, again summoned together the leaders of the different sects in order that they might either bring others to their own state of conviction on disputed topics or be convinced themselves. For he imagined that all would be brought to oneness of opinion if a free discussion were entered upon concerning ambiguous points of doctrine.

The council, therefore, was convened. This occurred in the year of the second consulate of Merobandes and the first of Saturninus, and at the same period that Arcadius was associated with his father in the government of the empire. Theodosius sent for Nectarius, consulted with him concerning the synod, and commanded him to introduce the discussion of all questions which had given rise to heresies, so that one faith might be established throughout the church of Christ.

When Nectarius returned home, feeling anxious about the affair confided to him, he made known the mandate of the emperor to Agelius, the bishop of the Novatians, who held the same religious sentiments as himself. Agelius was a man of virtuous and exemplary life but was unaccustomed to discussions and disputations. He therefore recommended the services of one of his readers, by name Sisinius, who afterwards succeeded him as bishop. Sisinius possessed great powers of intellect and of eloquence. He was deeply versed in the knowledge of Scripture and was well acquainted with profane and with ecclesiastical literature. He proposed that all disputation with the heterodox, as being a fruitful source of contention and animosity, should be avoided but recommended that inquiries should rather be instituted as to whether the heretics admitted the testimony of the teachers and expositors of Scripture who lived before the church was rent by division. "If they reject the testimony of these great men," said he, "they will be condemned by their own followers, but if they admit their authority as being adequate to resolve ambiguous points of doctrine, we will produce their works." For Sisinius was well aware that as the ancients recognized the Son to be eternal like the Father, they had never presumed to assert that he had had a beginning.

This suggestion received the approbation of Nectarius, and afterwards of the emperor, and investigations were set on foot as to the opinions entertained by heretics concerning the ancient interpreters of Scripture. As it was found that the heretics professed to hold these early writers in great admiration, the emperor asked them whether they would defer to their authority on controverted topics, and test their own doctrines by the sentiments propounded in their works. This proposition excited great contention among the leaders of the various heretical sects, but it was withdrawn by the emperor, when he perceived that the heretics were divided in opinion concerning the doctrines and books of the ancients, and that each sect was mainly intent on the defense of its own peculiar dogmas. He blamed their proceedings and commanded each party to draw up a written exposition of its own creed.

On the day appointed for the presentation of these documents, Nectarius and Agelius appeared at the palace as representatives of those who maintain the consubstantiality of the Holy Trinity. Demophilus, the Arian bishop, came forward as the deputy of the Arians. Eunomius represented the Eunomians. And Eleusius, bishop of Cyzicus, appeared for the sectarians denominated Macedonians. The emperor, after receiving their formularies, expressed himself in favor of that one alone in which the consubstantiality of the Trinity was recognized and destroyed the others. The interests of the Novatians were not affected by this transaction, for they held the same doctrines as the Catholic church concerning the Divine nature.

The members of the other sects were indignant with the bishops for having entered into unwise disputations in the presence of the emperor. Many renounced their former opinions and embraced the authorized form of religion. The emperor enacted a law prohibiting heretics from holding assemblies, from giving public instructions in religion, and from conferring ordination.[2] Some of the heterodox were expelled from the cities and villages, while others were disgraced[3] and deprived of the privileges enjoyed by other subjects of the empire. Great as were the punishments adjudged by the laws against heretics, they were not always carried into execution, for the emperor had no desire to persecute his subjects. He only desired to enforce uniformity of religion through the medium of intimidation. Those who voluntarily renounced heretical opinions received great commendation from him.

NOTES

1. Compare Socrates, *Ecclesiastical History,* Book V, Chapter 10.
2. Sozomen alludes to the 6th, 7th, and following edicts of the *Theodosian Code.*
3. ἀτίμους. He alludes to the Manichaeans, who were made incapable of even executing a will.

CHAPTER XIII

TYRANNY OF MAXIMUS. CONCERNING THE EMPRESS JUSTINA AND SAINT AMBROSIUS. DEATH OF THE EMPEROR GRATIAN.

As the emperor Gratian was at this period occupied with a war against the Germans,[1] Maximus quitted Britain with the design of usurping the imperial power. Valentinian was then residing in Italy, but as he was a minor, the affairs of state were transacted by Probus, a prætorian prefect, who had formerly been consul.

Justina, the mother of the emperor, having espoused the Arian heresy, persecuted Ambrose, bishop of Milan, and disquieted the churches by her efforts to introduce alterations in the Nicene doctrines and to obtain the predominance of the form of belief set forth at Ariminum.[2] She was incensed against Ambrose because he strenuously opposed her attempts at innovation, and she represented to her son that he had insulted her. Valentinian believed this calumny and determining to avenge the supposed wrongs of his mother, he sent a party of soldiers against the church. On their reaching the edifice, they forced their way into the interior, arrested Ambrose, and were about to lead him into exile, when the people assembled in crowds and evinced a resolution to die rather than submit to the banishment of their bishop. Justina was still further incensed at this occurrence, and with a view of enforcing her project by law, she sent for Benevolus, one of the legal secretaries and commanded him to draw up as quickly as possible an edict confirmatory of the decrees of Ariminum. Benevolus,[3] being firmly attached to the Catholic church, refused to write the document, and the empress tried to bribe him by promises of honors and promotion. He still, however, refused compliance and, tearing off his belt, he threw it at the feet of Justina and declared that he would neither retain his present office nor accept promotion as the reward of impiety. As he remained firm in his refusal, others were intrusted with the compilation of the document. By this law, all were prohibited from holding assemblies except those who conformed to the doctrines set forth at Ariminum and ratified at Constantinople, and it was enacted that death should be the punishment of those who should violate this decree.

While Justina was planning the means of carrying this cruel law into execution, intelligence was brought of the murder of Gratian through the treachery of Andragathos, the general of Maximus. Andragathos obtained possession of the chariot of the empress and sent word to the emperor that his consort was travelling towards his camp. Gratian, who was but recently married and was exceedingly attached to the empress, hastened across the river and in his anxiety to meet her, fell into the hands of Andragathos and was put to death. He was in the twenty-fourth year of his age, and had reigned fifteen years.

This calamity diverted the thoughts of Justina from her angry altercation with Ambrose.

Maximus in the meantime raised a large army of Britons, Gauls, Celts, and other nations, and marched into Italy. The pretext which he advanced for this measure was, that he desired to prevent the introduction of innovations in the ancient form of religion and of ecclesiastical discipline, but he was, in reality, actuated by the desire of dispelling any suspicion that might have been excited as to his aspiring to tyranny. He wished it to appear that it was not by force but by the sanction of the laws and the consent of the people that he had been invested with the imperial power. Valentinian, who was compelled by the exigencies of the times to recognize him as emperor, soon after fled with his mother Justina and Probus, the prætorian prefect, to Thessalonica.

NOTES

1. Compare Socrates, *Ecclesiastical History,* Book V, Chapter 11.
2. See Socrates, *ubi supra* Valesius remarks that Valentinian allowed the Arian party to assemble in the churches. He quotes the *Theodosian Code* under the title *de Fide Catholica.*
3. Socrates, as Valesius remarks, has borrowed much of what follows from the 11th book of Rufinus' *Ecclesiastical History.* Sozomen is, however, mistaken here in his chronology, the events which he mentions as happening before the death of Gratian, not having occurred till AD 386

CHAPTER XIV

BIRTH OF HONORIUS. THEODOSIUS LEAVES ARCADIUS AT CONSTANTINOPLE AND PROCEEDS TO ITALY. SUCCESSION OF THE NOVATIAN AND OTHER PATRIARCHS. AUDACITY OF THE ARIANS. TRIUMPH OF THEODOSIUS.

While Theodosius was making preparations for a war against Maximus, his son Honorius was born.[1] On the completion of these warlike preparations, he left his son Arcadius to govern at Constantinople and proceeded to Thessalonica, where he saw Valentinian. He refused either to dismiss or to give audience to the embassy sent by Maximus, but continued his journey at the head of his troops towards Italy.

About this period, Agelius, bishop of the Novatians at Constantinople, feeling his end approaching nominated Sisinius, one of the presbyters of his church, as his successor. The people, however, murmured that the preference had not rather been given to Marcian who was noted on account of his piety, and Agelius therefore ordained him and addressed the people who were assembled in the church in the following words: "After me you shall have Marcian for your bishop, and after him, Sisinius." Agelius died soon after he had uttered these words: he had governed his church forty years with the greatest approbation of his own party, and some assert that during the times of Pagan persecution, he had openly confessed the name of Christ.

Not long after, Timothy and Cyril died. Theophilus succeeded to the bishopric of Alexandria, and John to that of Jerusalem. Demophilus, bishop of the Arians at Constantinople, likewise died and was succeeded by Marinus, but he was superseded by Dorotheus who soon after arrived from Antioch in Syria, and who was considered by his sect to be better qualified for the office than Marinus.

Theodosius having in the meantime entered Italy, various conflicting reports were spread as to the success of his arms. It was rumored among the Arians that the greater part of his army had been cut to pieces in battle, and that he himself had been captured by the tyrant, and assuming this report to be true, these sectarians ran to the house of Nectarius and set it on fire from indignation at the power which the bishop had obtained over the churches. The emperor, however, was completely successful in this war, for the soldiers of Maximus, impelled by fear or treachery, slew the tyrant. Andragathos, the murderer of Gratian, no sooner heard of the death of Maximus, than he leaped into the river with his armor and perished. The war having been thus terminated and the death of Gratian avenged,[2] Theodosius, accompanied by Valentinian, entered Rome in triumph and restored order in the churches in Italy, for the empress Justina was dead.

NOTES

1. Compare Socrates, *Ecclesiastical History,* Book V, Chapter 12–14.
2. Namely, in the war itself. Valesius says: "Neque enim bello jam finito, Theodosius Gratianum ultus est; sed in ipso bello cædem Gratiani vindicavit, sumpto de Maximo Gratiani interfectore supplicio."

CHAPTER XV

FLAVIAN AND EVAGRIUS, BISHOPS OF ANTIOCH. DEMOLITION OF IDOLATROUS TEMPLES.

Paulinus,[1] bishop of Antioch, died about this period, and those who had assembled with him persisted in their aversion to Flavian, although his religious sentiments were precisely the same as their own because he had violated the oath he had formerly made to Meletius. They, therefore, elected Evagrius as their bishop. Evagrius did not long survive this appointment, and although Flavian prevented the election of another bishop, those who had seceded from communion with him still continued to hold their assemblies apart.

About this period, the bishop of Alexandria to whom the temple of Bacchus had, at his own request, been granted by the emperor, converted the edifice into a Christian church. The statues were removed, the most secret recesses of the temple explored, and in order to cast contumely on the Pagan mysteries, the most absurd and indecorous objects appertaining thereto that had been concealed within the temple were exposed to the public gaze. The Pagans, amazed at so unexpected an exhibition, could not suffer it in silence, but conspired together to attack the Christians. They slew many of the Christians, wounded others, and seized the temple of Serapis, a large and beautiful structure seated on an eminence. This they converted into a temporary citadel, and here they conveyed their prisoners, put them to the torture, and compelled them to offer sacrifice. Those who refused compliance were crucified, had their legs broken, or were put to death in some cruel manner.

When the sedition had lasted some time and had attained a fearful height, the rulers with Romanus, the general of the Egyptian troops, and Evagrius, the Alexandrian prefect,[2] hastened to the spot and urged the people to obey the laws, to lay down their arms, and to give up the temple of Serapis. As their efforts, however, to reduce the people to submission were utterly in vain, they made known what had transpired to the emperor. Those who had shut themselves up in the temple of Serapis were averse to yield from fear of the punishment that they knew would await their audacious proceedings, and they were further instigated to revolt by the inflammatory discourses of a man named Olympius attired in the garments of a philosopher, who told them that they ought to die rather than neglect the gods of their fathers. Perceiving that they were greatly intimidated by the destruction of the idolatrous statues, he assured them that such a circumstance did not warrant their renouncing their religion, for that the statues were composed of corruptible materials, subject to decay, whereas the powers which had dwelt within them had flown to heaven. By such representations as these, he retained the multitude with him in the temple of Serapis.

When the emperor was informed of these occurrences, he declared that the Christians who had been slain were blessed inasmuch as they had been admitted to the honor of martyrdom and had suffered in defense of the faith. He offered free pardon[3] to those who had slain them, hoping that by this act of clemency they would be the more readily induced to embrace Christianity, and he commanded the demolition of the temples which had been the cause of the sedition. It is said that when this edict was read in public, the Christians uttered loud shouts of joy because the emperor laid the odium of what had occurred upon the Pagans. The people who were guarding the temple of Serapis were so terrified at hearing these shouts that they took to flight, and the Christians immediately obtained possession of the spot which they have retained ever since.

I have been informed that on the night preceding this occurrence, Olympius heard the voice of one singing hallelujah in the temple of Serapis.[4] The doors were shut and as he could see no one but could only hear the voice of the singer, he at once understood what the sign signified, and unknown to any one he quitted the temple and embarked for Italy. It is said that when the temple was being demolished, some stones were found on which were hieroglyphic characters in the form of a cross which, on being submitted to the inspection of the learned, were interpreted as signifying the life to come.[5] These characters led to the conversion of several of the Pagans, as did likewise other inscriptions found in the same place and which contained predictions of the destruction of the temple. It was thus that the temple of Serapis was converted into a church. It received the name of the emperor Arcadius.

There were still Pagans in many cities who contended zealously in behalf of their temples, as for instance, the inhabitants of Petræa and of Areopolis[6] in Arabia, of Raphi and Gaza in Palestine, of Hieropolis in Phœnicia, and of Apamea on the river Axius in Syria. I have been informed that the inhabitants of the last-named city often armed the men of Galilee, and the peasants of Lebanon, in defense of their temples, and that they even carried their audacity to such a height, as to slay a bishop named Marcellus. This bishop had commanded the demolition of all the temples in the city and neighboring villages, under the supposition that more efficient means of deterring the people from the observance of their ancient superstitions could not be devised. Having heard that there was a very spacious temple at Aulone, a district of Apamea, he repaired thither with a body of soldiers and gladiators. He stationed himself at a distance from the scene of conflict, beyond the reach of the arrows, for he was afflicted with the gout and was unable either to fight or to effect an escape in case of defeat. Whilst the soldiers and gladiators were engaged in the assault against the temple, some Pagans, discovering that he was alone, hastened to the place where he was awaiting the issue of the combat, seized him, and burnt him alive. The perpetrators of this deed were not then known, but in course of time, they were detected, and the sons of Marcellus determined upon avenging his death. The council of the province, however, prohibited them from executing this design and declared that it was not just that the relatives or friends of Marcellus should seek to avenge his death, when they should rather return thanks to God for having accounted him worthy to die in such a cause.

NOTES

1. Compare Socrates, *Ecclesiastical History,* Book V, Chapter 15, 16.
2. ὕπαρχος. He held the office of Præfectus Augustalis, AD 391, and also that of Romanus Comes rei familiaris in the same year, as we learn from the *Theodosian Code,* Lex XI, *de Paganis,* etc.
3. The opinion of Saint Augustine (Epistle 158, *ad Marcellinus*) is here quoted by Valesius, "lest the sufferings of the servants of God, which ought to be held in esteem in the church, be denied by the blood of their enemies." See also below, the death of Marcellus of Apamea.

4. It is to be observed that Sozomen reports this story only on hearsay.
5. See Socrates, *Ecclesiastical History,* Book V, Chapter 17, and Rufinus, *Ecclesiastical History,* Book XI, Chapter 29.
6. Or, in the opinion of Valesius, Aëropolis, which place is mentioned by Eusebius as a town of Arabia.

CHAPTER XVI

IN WHAT MANNER AND FROM WHAT CAUSE THE FUNCTIONS OF THE PRESBYTER, APPOINTED TO PRESIDE OVER THE IMPOSITION OF PENANCE, WERE ABOLISHED. DISSERTATION ON THE MODE OF IMPOSING PENANCE.

Nectarius, about this period, abolished the office of the presbyter whose duty it was to preside over the imposition of penance, and this is the first instance of the suppression of this office in the church.[1] This example was followed by the bishops of every region. Various accounts have been given of the nature, the origin, and the cause of the abolition of this office. I shall state my own views on the subject. Impeccability is a Divine attribute and belongs not to human nature, therefore God has decreed that pardon should be extended to the patient, even after many transgressions. As in supplicating for pardon,[2] it is requisite to confess the sin, it seems probable that the priests, from the beginning considered it irksome to make this confession in public before the whole assembly of the people. They therefore appointed a presbyter of the utmost sanctity and the most undoubted prudence, to act on these occasions. The penitents went to him, and confessed their transgressions, and it was his office to indicate the kind of penance adapted to each sin, and then, when satisfaction had been made, to pronounce absolution.

As the custom of doing penance never gained ground among the Novatians, regulations of this nature were, of course, unnecessary among them, but the custom prevailed among all other religious sects and exists even to the present day. It is observed with great rigor by the Western churches,[3] particularly at Rome where there is a place appropriated to the reception of penitents, where they stand and mourn until the completion of the solemn services, from which they are excluded, then they cast themselves with groans and lamentations prostrate on the ground. The bishop conducts the ceremony, sheds tears, and prostrates himself in like manner,[4] and all the people burst into tears and groan aloud. Afterwards, the bishop rises from the ground and raises up the others. He offers up prayer on behalf of the penitents and then dismisses them. Each of the penitents subjects himself in private to voluntary suffering, either by fastings, by abstaining from the bath or from divers kinds of meats, or by other prescribed means, until a certain period appointed by the bishop. When this time arrives, he is made free from the consequences of his sin and is permitted to resume his place in the assemblies of the church. The Roman priests have carefully observed this custom from the beginning to the present time.

At Constantinople, a presbyter was always appointed to preside over the penitents, until a lady of illustrious birth made a deposition to the effect that when she resorted as a penitent to the presbyter to fast and offer supplications to God, and tarried for that purpose in the church, a rape had been committed on her person by the deacon. Great displeasure was manifested by the people when this occurrence was made known to them on account of the discredit that would result to the church, and the priests in particular were thereby greatly scandalized. Nectarius, after much hesitation as to what means ought to be adopted, deposed the deacon, and at the advice of certain persons who urged the necessity of leaving each individual to examine himself before participating in the sacred mysteries, he abolished the office of the presbyter presiding over penance.

From that period, therefore, the performance of penance fell into disuse and it seems to me, that extreme laxity of principle was thus substituted for the severity and rigor of antiquity. Under the ancient system, I think, offenses were of rarer occurrence, for people were deterred from their commission by the dread of confessing them and of exposing them to the scrutiny of a severe judge. I believe it was from similar considerations that the emperor Theodosius, who was always zealous in promoting the glory of the church, issued a law,[5] enacting that women should not be admitted into the ministry unless they had had children and were upwards of sixty years of age according to the precept of the apostle Paul.[6] By this law it was also decreed that women who had shaved their heads should be ejected from the churches and that the bishop by whom such women were admitted should be deposed.

NOTES

1. Compare Socrates, *Ecclesiastical History,* Book V, Chapter 19.
2. ἐν τῷ παραιτεῖσθαι. Christophorson renders these words, "in order to obtain pardon," but, as Valesius observes, this must be incorrect. The passage is doubtless corrupt: we have endeavored to give the simplest meaning.
3. Hence it is inferred that it was Sozomen's opinion that it was customary in the West to have a presbyter appointed by the bishop as Pœnitentiarius: but it is remarkable that no mention is made of such an ecclesiastical officer in the early councils of the church, or in the canons which they promulgated.
4. This (observes Valesius) was the ancient custom of the Roman church, that the bishop, in conducting the ceremony of absolution, should prostrate himself upon the ground in the presence of the penitents, and a second time when he reconciled them. This is supported by the ancient "Ordo Romanus," which, though of more recent date than the days of Sozomen, preserves many vestiges of an earlier antiquity.
5. See Lex 27 in the *Theodosian Code,* entitled *de Episcopis et Clericis.*
6. 1 Timothy 5:9. Compare Justinian *Novellae* 123, Chapter 13.

CHAPTER XVII

BANISHMENT OF EUNOMIUS BY THEODOSIUS THE GREAT. HERESIES OF HIS SUCCESSOR, THEOPHRONIUS, OF EUTYCHUS, AND OF DOROTHEUS. DIVISIONS AMONG THE ARIANS.

Such subjects as the above, however, are best left to the decision of individual judgment.

The emperor, about this period, condemned Eunomius to banishment.[1] This heretic had fixed his residence in the suburbs of Constantinople[2] and held frequent assemblies in private houses, where he read his own writings. He induced many to embrace his sentiments, so that the sectarians who were named after him, became very numerous. He died not long after his banishment and was interred at Dacora, his birth-place, a village of Cappadocia situated near Mount Argeus in the territory of Cæsarea.

Theophronius, who was also a native of Cappadocia and who had been his disciple, continued to promulgate his doctrines. Having given some attention to the writings of Aristotle, he composed an appendix to them which he entitled "Exercises for the Mind." But he afterwards engaged, I have understood, in many unprofitable disputations and soon ceased to confine himself to the doctrines of his master. Under the assumption of being deeply versed in the terms of Scripture, he attempted to prove that though God is acquainted with the present, the past, and the future, his knowledge on these subjects is not the same in degree and is subject to some kind of mutation. As this hypothesis appeared positively absurd to the Eunomians, they excommunicated him from their church, and he constituted himself the leader of a new sect called after his own name, Theophronians.

Not long after, Eutychus, one of the Eunomians, originated another sect at Constantinople to which his own name was given. For the question having been proposed, as to whether the Son of God is or is not acquainted with the day and hour of the last judgment, the words of the evangelist were quoted in which it is stated that the day and hour are known only to the Father. Eutychus, however, contended that this knowledge belongs also to the Son, inasmuch as he has received all things from the Father. The Eunomian bishops having condemned this opinion, he seceded from communion with them and went to join Eunomius in his place of banishment. A deacon and some other individuals who had been despatched from Constantinople to accuse Eutychus and, if necessary, to oppose him, arrived first at the place of destination. When Eunomius was made acquainted with the object of their journey, he expressed himself in favor of the sentiments propounded by Eutychus, and on his arrival prayed with him, although it was not customary to pray with any one who travels unprovided with letters written in secret characters attesting his being in communion. Eunomius died soon after this contention, and the Eunomian bishop at Constantinople refused to receive Eutychus into communion from envy and jealousy at the part he had enacted in the late controversy, more especially as he held no rank among the clergy. Eutychus, therefore, formed those who had espoused his sentiments into a separate sect. Many assert that he and Theophronius were the first who propounded the peculiar views entertained by the Eunomians concerning the rite of baptism. The above is a brief account of such details as I have been able to ascertain concerning the disputes of the Eunomians. I should be prolix were I to enter into further particulars, and indeed the subject would be by no means an easy one to me.

The following question was, in the meantime, agitated among the Arians of Constantinople. Prior to the existence of the Son (whom they regard as having proceeded out of nothing) is God to be termed the Father? Dorotheus, who had been summoned from Antioch to rule over them in the place of Marinus, was of opinion that God could not have been called the Father prior to the existence of the Son, because the name of Father has a necessary connexion with that of Son. Marinus, on the other hand, maintained that the Father was the Father even when the Son existed not, and he advanced this opinion either from conviction, or else from the desire of contention, and from jealousy at the preference that had been shown to Dorotheus. The Arians were thus divided into two parties. Dorotheus and his followers retained possession of the houses of prayer, while Marinus and those who seceded with him erected new edifices in which to hold their assemblies. The names of Psathyrians and of Goths were given to the partisans of Marinus, Psathyrians because Theoctistes, a certain vendor of cakes (ψαθυροπώλης), was a zealous advocate of their opinions, and Goths because their sentiments were approved by Selinus, bishop of that nation. All these barbarians followed the instructions of Selinus, who had formerly been the secretary of Ulphilas, and had succeeded him as bishop. He was capable of preaching, not only in the vernacular, but also in the Greek language.

Soon after, a contest for precedency arose between Marinus and Agasius whom Marinus himself had ordained over the Arians at Ephesus, and in the quarrel which ensued, the Goths took the part of Agasius. It is said that many of the Arian clergy of that city were so much irritated at the ambition displayed by these two bishops that they seceded from them and joined the Catholic church. Such was the origin of the division of the Arians into two factions—a division which still subsists—so that in every city they have separate places of meeting. The Arians of Constantinople, however, after a separation of thirty-five years, were reconciled to each other by Plinthas, formerly a consul,[3] general of the cavalry and infantry, a man possessed of great influence at court. To prevent the revival of the former dissension among them, the question which had been the cause of the division was forbidden to be mooted.

NOTES

1. Compare Socrates, *Ecclesiastical History,* Book V, Chapters 10, 20, 23, 24.
2. Or, rather, at Chalcedon.
3. He held the consulate AD 418 or 419.

CHAPTER XVIII
ANOTHER HERESY ORIGINATED BY THE NOVATIANS. DIGRESSION CONCERNING THE FESTIVAL OF EASTER.

A division arose during the same reign among the Novatians,[1] concerning the celebration of the festival of Easter, and from this dispute originated another, called the Sabbatian. Sabbatius who, with Theoctistes and Macarius, had been ordained presbyter by Marcian, adopted the opinion of the priests who had been converted at Pazacoma during the reign of Valens and maintained that the feast of the Passover (Easter) ought to be celebrated by Christians in the same manner and on the same day as by the Jews. He seceded from communion for the purpose of exercising greater austerity, for he professed to adopt a very austere mode of life. He also declared that one motive of his secession was that many persons who participated in the mysteries appeared to him to be unworthy of the honor. When, however, his design of introducing innovations was detected, Marcian expressed his regret at having ordained him and, it is said, was often heard to exclaim that he would rather have laid his hands upon thorns than upon the head of Sabbatius. Perceiving that the people of his diocese were being rent into two factions, Marcian summoned all the bishops of his own persuasion to Sangara, a town of Bithynia near the sea-shore not far from the city of Helenopolis. When Sabbatius appeared before them, they inquired into the grievances which had been the cause of his secession, and as he merely complained of the diversity of customs prevailing in regard to the observance of the Paschal feast, they inferred that he advanced this complaint as a pretext to disguise his real motives, and suspecting that he was mainly actuated by the ambition of obtaining a bishopric, they made him declare upon oath that he would never accept the episcopal office. When he had taken the required oath, all the members of the assembly declared themselves of opinion that the difference prevailing in the mode of celebrating the Paschal feast ought by no means to be made an occasion of schism or cessation from communion, and they decided that each individual should be at liberty to observe the feast according to his own judgment. They enacted a decree on the subject, which they styled the "Indifferent (ἀδιάφορος) Decree." Such were the transactions of the assembly at Sangara.

Book VII, Chapter XVIII

From that period, Sabbatius adhered to the usages of the Jews, and as the Christians did not observe the paschal feast on the same day as the Jews, he was a day in advance of them. He fasted according to custom and celebrated the feast with the usual ceremonies by himself. He passed the Saturday from the evening to the appointed time in watching and in offering up the prescribed prayers, and on the following day he assembled with the multitude and partook of the mysteries. This mode of observing the feast was at first unnoticed by the people, but as in process of time it began to attract observation and to become more generally known, he found a great many imitators, particularly in Phrygia and Galatia. Eventually, he openly seceded from communion and became the bishop of those who had espoused his sentiments, as we shall have occasion to show in the proper place.

I am, for my own part, astonished that Sabbatius and his followers attempted to introduce this innovation. The ancient Hebrews, as is related by Eusebius[2] on the testimony of Philo, Josephus, Aristobulus, and several others, celebrated the Passover after the vernal equinox, when the sun is in the first sign of the Zodiac, called by the Greeks, the Ram, and when the moon is in the opposite quarter of the heavens, and in the fourteenth day of her age. Even the Novatians themselves, who have studied the subject with some accuracy, declare that the founder of their sect and his first disciples did not follow this custom, which was introduced for the first time by those who assembled at Pazacoma, and that at Rome the members of this sect still observe the same practice as the Romans who have never deviated from their original usage in this particular, the custom having been handed down to them by the holy apostles Peter and Paul. Further, the Samaritans, who are scrupulous observers of the laws of Moses, never celebrate this festival till the first-fruits have reached maturity. It is hence called the Feast of First-Fruits and cannot, therefore, necessarily have been observed till after the vernal equinox. Hence arises my astonishment that those who profess to adopt the Jewish custom in the celebration of this feast, do not conform to the ancient practice of the Jews.

With the exception of the people above mentioned, and the Quartodecimani of Asia, all other sects, I believe, celebrate the Passover in the same manner as the Romans and the Egyptians. The Quartodecimani are so called because they observe this festival, like the Jews, on the fourteenth day of the moon. The Novatians observe the day of the resurrection. They follow the custom of the Jews and the Quartodecimani, except when the fourteenth day of the moon falls upon the first day of the Sabbath, in which case they celebrate the feast so many days after the Jews as there are intervening days between the fourteenth day of the moon and the following Lord's day.

The Montanists, who are called Pepuzites and Phrygians, celebrate the

Passover according to a mode of their own devising. They blame those who regulate the time of observing the feast according to the course of the moon, and affirm that it is right to attend exclusively to the revolutions of the sun. They reckon each month to consist of thirty days[3] and account the day after the vernal equinox as the first day of the year, which according to the Roman method of computation, would be called the ninth day before the calends of April. It was on this day, they say, that the two great luminaries appointed for the indication of times and of years were created. This they prove by the fact that every eight years the sun and the moon meet together in the same point of the heavens. The moon's cycle of eight years is accomplished in ninety-nine months, and in two thousand nine hundred and twenty-two days, and during that time there are eight revolutions made by the sun, each comprising three hundred and sixty-five days and the fourth part of a day. For they compute the day of the creation of the sun, mentioned in Sacred Writ, to have been the fourteenth day of the moon, occurring after the ninth day before the calends of the month of April and answering to the eighth day prior to the ides of the same month. They always celebrate the Passover on this day,[4] when it falls on the day of the resurrection. Otherwise, they celebrate it on the following Lord's day. For it is written, according to their assertion, that the feast may be held on any day between the fourteenth and the twenty-first.

NOTES

1. Compare Socrates, *Ecclesiastical History,* Book V, Chapters 21, 22.
2. See Eusebius, *Ecclesiastical History,* Book VII, Chapter 32.
3. Usher, in his learned treatise "de anno solari Macedonum et Asianorum," Chapter 2, asserts that Sozomen is mistaken here.
4. Valesius points out that Usher has good reason for doubting the assertion of Sozomen in this point also: and in his own support he quotes Tertullian, *De Jejuniis,* Chapter 14, to which we must refer the reader.

CHAPTER XIX

DISSERTATION ON THE VARIOUS CUSTOMS PREVALENT AMONG DIFFERENT CHURCHES AND NATIONS.

We have now described the various usages that prevailed in the celebration of the Passover.[1] It appears to me that Victor, bishop of Rome, and Polycarp, bishop of Smyrna, came to a very wise decision on the controversy that had arisen among them.[2] For as the bishops of the West considered it right to adhere to the tradition handed down to them by Peter and by Paul and as, on the other hand, the Asiatic bishops persisted in following the rules laid down by John the evangelist, they unanimously agreed to continue in the observance of the festival according to their respective customs without abstaining from communion with each other.

They very justly reflected that it would be absurd to render a mere point of discipline a ground of schism between those who were bound to each other by the profession of the same faith.

Different customs prevail in many churches where the same doctrines are received. There are, for instance, many cities in Syria which possess but one bishop between them, whereas in other nations, a bishop is appointed even over a village, as I have myself observed in Arabia and in Cyprus and among the Novatians and Montanists of Phrygia. Again, there are but seven deacons at Rome, answering precisely to the number ordained by the apostles, of whom Stephen was the first martyr, whereas in other churches, the number of deacons is unlimited. At Rome, hallelujah[3] is sung once annually,[4] namely, on the first day of the festival of the Passover, so that it is a common thing among the Romans to swear by the fact of hearing or singing this hymn. In this city, the people are not taught by the bishop, nor by any one in the church.[5] At Alexandria, the bishop alone teaches the people and it is said that this custom has prevailed there ever since the days of Arius who, though but a presbyter, broached a new doctrine. Another custom also prevails at Alexandria, which I have never witnessed nor heard of elsewhere, and this is that when the Gospel is read, the bishop does not rise from his seat. The archdeacon alone reads the Gospel in this city, whereas in some places it is read by the deacons, and in others only by the presbyters, while in many churches, it is read on stated days by the bishops, as for instance at Constantinople on the first day of the festival of the resurrection.[6]

In some churches, the interval called Quadragesima which occurs before this festival and is devoted by the people to fasting, is made to consist of six weeks, and this is the case in Illyria, and the Western regions, in Libya, throughout Egypt, and in Palestine, whereas it is made to comprise seven weeks at Constantinople, and in the neighboring provinces as far as Phœnicia. In some churches, the people fast three alternate weeks during the space of six or seven weeks, whereas in others they fast continuously during the three weeks immediately preceding the festival. Some people, as the Montanists, only fast two weeks.

Assemblies are not held in all churches on the same day or upon the same occasions. The people of Constantinople and of several other cities assemble together on the sabbath as well as on the next day, which custom is never observed at Rome or at Alexandria. There are several cities and villages in Egypt where, contrary to the usages established elsewhere, the people meet together on sabbath evenings, and although they have dined previously, partake of the mysteries.

The same prayers and psalms are not recited, nor the same passages read on the same occasions in all churches. Thus the book entitled "The Apocalypse of Peter," which was considered spurious by the ancients, is still read in some of the churches of Palestine on the day of preparation, when the people observe a fast in memory of the passion of the Savior. So the work entitled "The Apocalypse of the Apostle Paul," though rejected by the ancients, is still esteemed by most of the monks. Some persons affirm that the book was found during this reign by Divine revelation in a marble box buried beneath the soil in the house of Paul at Tarsus in Cilicia. I have been informed that this report is false by a presbyter of Tarsus, a man of very advanced age, as is indicated by his grey hairs. He says that the rumor was probably devised by heretics. What have said upon this subject must now suffice.[7]

Many other customs are still to be observed in cities and villages, and those who have been brought up in their observance would, from respect to the great men who instituted and perpetuated these customs, consider it wrong to abolish them. Similar motives must be attributed to those who observe different practices in the celebration of the feast, which has led us into this long digression.

NOTES

1. With this chapter the reader will do well to compare Socrates, *Ecclesiastical History*, Book V, Chapter 22.
2. *Note to the 2018 edition:* For more information on this controversy, see the entry in the *Catholic Encyclopedia* (1909) under "Easter controversy" by Herbert Thurston.
3. See Augustine on Psalms 106 and 148.
4. Baronius, *Ecclesiastical Annals*, AD 384, condemns this assertion as untrue, but Valesius considers his arguments insufficient.
5. It is probable that sermons, homilies, or discourses were not delivered at this early date. Those of Popes Leo and Gregory were more recent, and Valesius considers that they were the earliest that were ever preached in Rome. He remarks that the verb διδάσκειν is used technically concerning this kind of teaching.
6. Nicephorus (Book XII, Chapter 34) declares that this custom lasted down to his own day, and that it was practiced also on the 1st of January, as well as at Easter.
7. *Note to the 2018 edition:* Translations of the *Apocalypse of Peter* and the *Apocalypse of Paul* may be found in James: *The New Testament Apocrypha*, originally translated and published in 1924, and reprinted in 2004. For a summary of these and similar works, see the entry in the *Catholic Encyclopedia* (1907) under "apocrypha" by George Reid.

CHAPTER XX

EXTENSION OF THE CHRISTIAN RELIGION. DEMOLITION OF TEMPLES. INUNDATION OF THE NILE.

The dissensions among heretics contributed greatly to the extension of the church, which was daily increased by the accession of malcontents from the heretics and of converts from the Pagan multitudes. The emperor having observed that the practice of idolatry had been greatly promoted by the facility of constant ingress and egress to and from the temple, directed the entrances of all temples to be closed, and eventually he commanded the total demolition of these edifices. When the Pagans found themselves deprived of their own houses of prayer, they began to frequent our churches, for they did not dare to offer sacrifices in secret, there being a law prohibiting the practice under the penalty of death and of confiscation of property.

It is said that the river of Egypt did not overflow its banks this year at the proper season, and that the Egyptians angrily ascribed this circumstance to the laws that had been enacted prohibiting sacrifices from being offered to it. The governor of the province, apprehensive lest the general discontent should terminate in sedition, sent a message to the emperor on the subject. But the emperor, far from attaching more importance to the temporary fertility produced by the Nile than to the fidelity he owed to God and the interests of religion, replied as follows: "Let the river cease to flow, if enchantments are requisite to insure the regularity of its course, or if it delights in sacrifices, or if blood must be mingled with the waters that derive their source from the paradise of God."

Soon afterwards, the Nile overflowed its banks with such violence, that the highest eminences were submerged. The fears of drought and scarcity that had prevailed throughout Egypt, were now converted into dread lest the city of Alexandria and part of Libya should be destroyed by the inundation. The Pagans of Alexandria, irritated at this unexpected occurrence, exclaimed in derision at the public theaters that the river, like an old man or fool, could not moderate its proceedings. Many of the Egyptians were hence induced to abandon the superstitions of their forefathers and embrace Christianity.

CHAPTER XXI

DISCOVERY OF THE HEAD OF THE PRECURSOR OF OUR LORD.

About this period, the head of John the Baptist which Herodias had asked of Herod the tetrarch, was removed to Constantinople.[1] It is said that it was discovered by some monks of the Macedonian persuasion, who originally dwelt at Constantinople and afterwards fixed their abode in Cilicia. Mardonius, the first eunuch of the palace, made known this discovery at court during the preceding reign, and Valens commanded that the relic should be removed to Constantinople. The officers appointed to convey it thither, placed it in a public chariot and proceeded with it as far as Pantichium, a district in the territory of Chalcedonia. Here the mules of the chariot suddenly stopped, and neither the application of the lash nor any of the other means that were devised, could induce them to advance further. So extraordinary an event was considered by all—and even by the emperor himself—to be of God, and the holy head was therefore deposited at Cosila, a village in the neighborhood which belonged to Mardonius.

Soon after, the emperor Theodosius, impelled by an impulse from God or from the prophet, repaired to the village. He determined upon removing the remains of the Baptist, and it is said met with no opposition except from a holy virgin who had been intrusted with the care of the relic. He laid aside all authority and force, and after many entreaties, extorted a reluctant consent from her to remove the head, for she bore in mind what had occurred at the period when Valens commanded its removal. The emperor placed it, with the box in which it was encased, in his purple robe and conveyed it to a place called Hebdoma in the suburbs of Constantinople, where he erected a spacious and magnificent church. The woman who had been appointed to the charge of the relic could not be persuaded by the emperor to renounce her religious sentiments, although he had recourse to entreaty and promises, for she was, it appears, a Macedonian.

A presbyter of the same sect named Vincent, who also took charge of the remains of the prophet and performed the sacerdotal functions over it,[2] followed the religious opinions of the emperor, and entered into communion with the Catholic church. He had taken an oath, as the Macedonians affirm, never to swerve from the doctrines of his religion, but he afterwards openly declared that if the Baptist would follow the emperor, he also would enter into communion with him. He was a Persian and had left his country in company with a relative named Abdus during the reign of Constantius in order to avoid the persecution which the Christians were then suffering in Persia. On his arrival in the Roman territories, he was placed in the ranks of the clergy and appointed a presbyter. Abdus married and rendered great services to the church. He left a son, named Auxentius, who was noted for his piety, his benevolence, the sanctity of his life, and the greatness of his attainments in Grecian and ecclesiastical literature. He was modest and retiring in deportment, although admitted to familiarity with the emperor and the courtiers, and possessed of a very illustrious appointment. His memory is still revered by the monks and ascetics who were well acquainted with him.

The woman who had been intrusted with the relic remained during the rest of her life at Cosila. She was greatly distinguished by her piety and wisdom and instructed many holy virgins, and I have been assured that even at the present day, their virtue reflects honor on their instructress.

NOTES

1. Valesius is far from satisfied as to the truth of this story. It rests, as he observes, on the statement of a certain Archimandite, named Marcellus, and there is a discrepancy as to the time at which it occurred.
2. Valesius here observes on the antiquity of the custom of placing the relics of saints and martyrs beneath the altars of churches.

CHAPTER XXII

DEATH OF VALENTINIAN. TYRANNY OF EUGENIUS.
PROPHECY OF JOHN, A MONK OF THEBAÏS.

While Theodosius was thus occupied in the wise and peaceful government of his subjects and in the service of God, intelligence was brought that Valentinian had been strangled.[1] Some say that he was put to death by the eunuchs at the solicitation of Arbogastes, a military chief, and of certain courtiers who were displeased because the young prince had begun to walk in the footsteps of his father and had adopted a system of government of which they disapproved. Others assert, however, that Valentinian committed the fatal deed with his own hands, because he found himself impeded from the gratification of the impetuous passions of his age by the authority of those around him, who did not permit him to act according to the dictates of his own will. It is said that he was handsome in person and of a good disposition and that, had he lived to the age of manhood, he would have shown himself worthy of holding the reins of empire and would have surpassed his father in magnanimity and justice. But though endowed with these promising qualities, he died in the manner above related.

A certain man named Eugenius, who was by no means sincere in his profession of Christianity, aspired to sovereignty and seized the symbols of imperial power. It is thought that his ambition was excited by the predictions of individuals who professed to foresee the future by the examination of the entrails of animals and the course of the stars. Men of the highest rank among the Romans were addicted to these superstitions. Flavian, then a prætorian prefect—a learned and an able man—was noted for being conversant with every means of a foretelling the future.[2] He persuaded Eugenius to take up arms by assuring him that he was destined to the throne, that his warlike undertakings would be crowned with victory, and that the Christian religion would be abolished. Deceived by these flattering representations, Eugenius raised an army and took possession of the Julian Alps, an elevated and precipitous range of mountains among which was a very narrow passage leading into Italy.

Theodosius was perplexed as to whether he ought to wait the issue of the war, or whether it would be better in the first place to attack Eugenius, and in this dilemma he determined to consult John, a monk of Thebaïs, who as I have before stated, was celebrated for his knowledge of the future. He, therefore, sent Eutropius, a eunuch of tried fidelity, to Egypt, with orders to bring John, if possible, to court, but in case of his refusal, to question him on the results of the war. The monk could not be persuaded to go to the emperor, but he sent word by Eutropius that the war would terminate in favor of Theodosius and that the tyrant would be slain, but that after the victory, Theodosius himself would die in Italy. The truth of both these predictions was confirmed by events.

NOTES

1. Socrates, *Ecclesiastical History,* Book V, Chapter 25.
2. Valesius observes that Sozomen has borrowed this story from Rufinus, *Ecclesiastical History,* Book XI, Chapter 33.

CHAPTER XXIII

EXACTION OF TRIBUTE IN ANTIOCH. DEMOLITION OF THE STATUES OF THE EMPEROR. EMBASSY HEADED BY FLAVIAN THE ARCHBISHOP.

The continuance of the war having compelled the rulers to impose fresh taxes on the people, a sedition was excited at Antioch in Syria.[1] The statues of the emperor and of the empress were thrown down and dragged through the city, and as is usual on such occasions, the enraged multitude uttered every insulting epithet that passion could suggest. The emperor, determining to avenge this insult by the death of the principal conspirators, the whole city was filled with terror at the announcement of his intended vengeance. The rage of the citizens had subsided and had given place to repentance, and as if already subjected to the threatened punishment, they abandoned themselves to grief and lamentation and sang psalms of supplication to God to turn away the anger of the emperor.

They deputed Flavian their bishop on an embassy to Theodosius, but on his arrival, finding that the resentment of the emperor at what had occurred was unabated, he had recourse to the following artifice. He caused some young men to sing the psalms of supplication and contrition at the table of the emperor, which the inhabitants of Antioch had composed in reference to their condition. It is said that the compassion of the emperor was excited, his wrath was subdued, and as his heart yearned over the city, he shed tears on the cup which he held in his hand. It is reported that on the night before the sedition occurred, a spectre was seen in the form of a woman of prodigious height and terrible aspect pacing through the city with a whip in her hand, similar to that which is used in goading on the beasts brought forward at the public theaters. It might have been inferred that the sedition was excited by the agency of some evil and malicious demon. There is no doubt but that much bloodshed would have ensued, had not the wrath of the emperor been stayed by his respect for the entreaties of a bishop.

NOTE

1. Sozomen, as Valesius observes, is wrong in the date which he assigns to this sedition. Theodoret, however, (*Ecclesiastical History,* Book V, Chapter 20) agrees with him. Baronius shows that it occurred AD 388.

CHAPTER XXIV
VICTORY OF THEODOSIUS OVER EUGENIUS.

When he had completed his preparations for war, Theodosius declared his younger son Honorius emperor, and leaving him to reign at Constantinople conjointly with Arcadius who had previously been appointed emperor, he departed to the West from the East at the head of his troops. His army consisted not only of Roman soldiers but of bands of barbarians from the banks of the Danube. It is said that on his arrival at Constantinople, he went to the church which he had erected at Hebdoma in honor of John the Baptist and in his name prayed that success might attend the Roman arms, and besought the Baptist himself to aid him. After offering up these prayers he proceeded towards Italy and crossed the Alps.

On descending from the heights of these mountains, he perceived a plain before him, covered with infantry and cavalry and became at the same time aware that some of the enemy's troops were lying in ambush behind him among the recesses of the mountains. The advance guard of his army attacked the infantry stationed in the plain, and a desperate and very doubtful conflict ensued. At this juncture, the troops in ambuscade appeared on the point of attacking the army behind, and seeing that all chances of escape would thus be cut off and that his position was one of imminent peril and beyond the intervention of human aid, the emperor prostrated himself on the ground and besought with tears the assistance of God. His request was instantly granted, for the officers of the troops stationed in ambush sent to offer him their services as his allies provided that he would assign them honorable posts in his army. As he had neither paper nor ink within reach, he took up some tablets and wrote on them the high appointments he would confer upon them, provided that they would fulfill their promise to him. Under these conditions, they ranged themselves under the imperial standard.

Even after this reinforcement, the issue of the combat still remained uncertain, when a wind of unheard-of violence suddenly arose and blew right in the face of the enemy. Their darts were blown back upon themselves, and their bucklers were wrenched from them and rolled in the dust. Standing thus exposed in a defenseless condition to the weapons of the Romans, many of them perished, while the few who attempted to effect an escape were soon captured. Eugenius threw himself at the feet of the emperor and implored him to spare his life, but while in the act of offering up these entreaties, a soldier struck off his head. Arbogastes fled after the battle and fell by his own hands. It is said that while the battle was being fought, a demoniac presented himself in the temple of Hebdoma where the emperor had engaged in prayer and insulted John the Baptist, taunting him with having had his head cut off, and shouted the following words: "You conquer me and lay snares for my army." The persons who happened to be on the spot and who were waiting impatiently to learn the issue of the war, wrote an account of this extraordinary circumstance on the day that it occurred and afterwards ascertained that it was the same day as that on which the battle had been fought. Such is the history of these transactions.

CHAPTER XXV

INTREPID BEARING OF SAINT AMBROSE IN THE PRESENCE OF THE EMPEROR. MASSACRE AT THESSALONICA.

After the death of Eugenius, the emperor went to Milan and repaired toward the church to pray within its walls. When he drew near the gates of the edifice, he was met by Ambrose, the bishop of the city, who took hold of him by his purple robe and said to him in the presence of the multitude, "Stand back! A man defiled by sin and with hands imbrued in blood unjustly shed is not worthy, without repentance, to enter within these sacred precincts or partake of the holy mysteries."

The emperor, struck with admiration at the boldness of the bishop, began to reflect on his own conduct, and with much contrition retraced his steps. The crime alluded to had been committed under the following circumstances. A charioteer had made a declaration of obscene passion to Buthericus,[1] a military chief of Illyria, and had in consequence been committed to prison. Some time after, some magnificent races were to be held at the hippodrome and the populace of Thessalonica demanded the release of the prisoner, considering him necessary to the celebration of the games. As their request was not attended to, they rose up in sedition and slew Buthericus. On hearing of this deed, the wrath of the emperor was excited to a fearful height, and he commanded that a certain number of the citizens should be put to death. The whole city was deluged with blood unjustly shed, for strangers who had but just arrived there on their journey to other lands were sacrificed with the others.

There were many cases of suffering well worthy of commiseration, of which the following is an instance. A merchant offered himself to be slain as a substitute for his two sons who had both been selected as victims and promised the soldiers to give them all the gold he possessed on condition of their effecting the exchange. They could not but compassionate his misfortune and consented to take him as a substitute for one of his sons, but declared that they did not dare to let off both the young men, as that would render the appointed number of the slain incomplete. The father gazed on his sons and wept bitterly, and loving them both equally, he could not make choice between them. He was still standing irresolute and utterly unable to decide, when they were both slain before his eyes. I have also been informed that a faithful slave voluntarily offered to die instead of his master, who was being led to the place of execution.

Book VII, Chapter XXV

It appears that it was for these and other acts of cruelty that Ambrose rebuked the emperor, forbad him to enter the church, and excommunicated him. Theodosius publicly confessed his sin in the church, and during the time set apart for penance, refrained from wearing his imperial ornaments as being inconsistent with a season of mourning. He also enacted a law[2] prohibiting the officers intrusted with the execution of the imperial mandates from inflicting the punishment of death till thirty days after the mandate had been issued, in order that the wrath of the emperor might have time to be appeased and that room might be made for the exercise of mercy and repentance.

Ambrose, no doubt, performed many other actions worthy of his priestly office which are known only to the inhabitants of the country. Among the illustrious deeds that are attributed to him, I have been made acquainted with the following. It was the custom for the emperor to take a seat in assemblies of the church within the palisades of the altar so that he sat apart from the rest of the people. Ambrose, considering that this custom had originated either from subserviency or from want of discipline, caused the emperor to be seated without the trellis work of the altar, so that he sat in front of the people and behind the priests.[3] The emperor Theodosius approved of this wise alteration, as did likewise his successors, and we are told that it has been ever since scrupulously observed.

I think it necessary to mention another magnanimous action performed by this bishop. A Pagan of distinction insulted Gratian, affirming that he was unworthy of his father, and he was in consequence condemned to death. As he was being led out to execution, Ambrose went to the palace to implore a pardon. Gratian was then engaged in witnessing a private exhibition of horse-racing, for it was frequently the practice of the emperors to engage in these diversions at times that the public were excluded. The officers at the gates of the palace would not therefore interrupt him by informing him that Ambrose solicited an interview. On finding this to be the case, the bishop went to the circus, and entering with the persons who took charge of the animals, he made his way up to the emperor and would not leave him till he had obtained a pardon for the man who had been condemned to death.

Ambrose was very diligent in the observance of the canons of the church and in maintaining discipline among his clergy. I have selected the above two incidents from among the records of his numerous magnanimous deeds in order to show with what intrepidity he addressed those in power when the service of God was in question.

NOTES

1. Sozomen is mistaken here. See Baronius, *Ecclesiastical Annals,* AD 390.
2. See Baronius, *Ecclesiastical Annals,* AD 390.
3. Compare Theodoret, *Ecclesiastical History,* Book V, Chapter 18.

CHAPTER XXVI

SAINT DONATUS, BISHOP OF EURŒA, AND THEOTIMUS, ARCHBISHOP OF SCYTHIA.

There were at this period many other bishops in various parts of the empire highly celebrated for their sanctity and high qualifications, of whom Donatus, bishop of Eurœa[1] in Epirus, deserves to be particularly instanced. The inhabitants of the country relate many extraordinary miracles which he performed, of which the most remarkable seems to have been the destruction of a dragon of enormous size. It had stationed itself on the high road, at a place called Chamaigephyra, and devoured sheep, goats, oxen, horses, and men. Donatus attacked it unarmed, without sword, lance, or javelin. It raised its head and was about to dart upon him, when Donatus made the sign of the cross with his finger in the air and spat upon the dragon. The saliva entered its mouth, and it immediately expired. As it lay extended on the earth, it did not appear inferior in size to the noted serpent of India.[2] I have been informed that the people of the country yoked eight pair of oxen to transport the body to a neighboring field, where they burnt it, that it might not during the process of decomposition corrupt the air and generate disease. The tomb of this bishop is deposited in a magnificent house of prayer which bears his name. It is situated near a stream of water which God caused to rise from the ground in answer to his prayer in an arid spot where no water had previously existed. For it is said that one day when on a journey, he had to pass through this locality, and perceiving that his companions were suffering from thirst, he moved the soil with his hand and engaged in prayer. Before his prayer was concluded, a spring of water arose from the ground which has never since been dried up. The inhabitants of Isoria, a village in the territory of Eurœa, bear testimony to the truth of this narration.

The church of Tomis, and indeed all the churches of Scythia, were at this period under the government of Theotimus. He had been brought up in the practice of philosophical asceticism, and his virtues had so won the admiration of the Huns, who dwelt on the banks of the Danube, that they called him the god of the Romans. It is said that one day, when travelling towards their country, he perceived at a distance some of these barbarous tribes advancing towards Tomis. His attendants burst forth into lamentations, and gave themselves up for lost, but he merely descended from horseback and prayed. The consequence was that the barbarians passed by without seeing him, his attendants, or the horses. As these tribes frequently devastated Scythia by their predatory incursions, he tried to subdue the ferocity of their disposition by presenting them with food and gifts. One of the barbarians hence concluded that he was a man of wealth, and determining to take him prisoner, leaned upon his shield, as was his custom when parleying with his enemies, and raised up his right hand in order to throw a rope which he firmly grasped over the bishop, for he intended to drag him away to his own country. But his arm, while extended in this position, became fixed and perfectly immoveable, until his companions had implored Theotimus to intercede with God for the removal of the invisible bonds. It is said that Theotimus always retained the long hair which he wore when he first devoted himself to the practice of philosophy. He was very temperate, had no stated hours for his repasts, but ate and drank when compelled to do so by the calls of hunger and of thirst. I consider it to be the part of a philosopher to yield to the demands of these appetites from necessity, and not from the love of sensual gratification.

NOTE

1. We have emended the proper name according to the suggestion of Valesius.
2. *Note to the 2018 edition:* This "noted serpent of India" may refer to Ælian's description of great serpents that devour elephants in India. See *On Animals*, Book 6, Chapter 21.

CHAPTER XXVII
PARTICULAR ACCOUNT OF SAINT EPIPHANIUS, BISHOP OF CYPRUS.

Epiphanius was at this period at the head of the metropolitan church of Cyprus.[1] He was celebrated not only for his virtues and miraculous deeds during life, but also for the honor that was rendered to him by God after his death, for it is said that demons were expelled and diseases healed at his tomb. Many wonderful actions are attributed to him, of which the following is one of the most remarkable that has come to our knowledge. He was extremely liberal towards those who had suffered from shipwreck or any other calamity, and after expending the whole of his own patrimony in the relief of such cases, he applied the treasures of the church to the same purpose. These treasures had been greatly increased by the donations of pious men of various provinces who had been induced by their admiration of Eusebius to intrust him with the distribution of their alms during their lives or to bequeath their property to him for this purpose at their death. It is said that on one occasion, the treasurer, who was a godly man, discovered that the revenues of the church had been nearly drained, and so little remained in the treasury that he considered it his duty to rebuke the bishop for his extensive liberality. Epiphanius, however, having notwithstanding these remonstrances given away the small sum that had remained, a stranger went to the treasurer and placed in his hands a bag filled with gold. As it is very seldom that such liberality is practiced in secret, the whole transaction was regarded as the work of God.

I shall now relate another miracle that is attributed to Epiphanius. I have heard that a similar action has been related of Gregory, formerly bishop of

Neocæsarea, and I see no reason to doubt the veracity of the account, but it does not disprove the authenticity of the miracle attributed to Epiphanius. Peter the apostle was not the only man who raised another from the dead. John the evangelist wrought a similar miracle at Ephesus, as did likewise the daughters of Philip at Hierapolis. Similar actions have been performed in different ages by the men of God. The miracle which I wish to instance is the following. Two beggars, having ascertained when Epiphanius would pass that way, agreed to extract a larger donation than usual from him by having recourse to stratagem. As soon as the bishop was seen approaching, one of the beggars flung himself on the ground and simulated death. The other uttered loud lamentations, deploring the loss of his companion and his own inability to procure him the rite of sepulture. Epiphanius prayed to God that the deceased might rest in peace. He gave the survivor sufficient money for the interment and said to him, "Take measures, my son, for the burial of your companion and weep no more. He cannot now arise from the dead—the calamity was inevitable. Therefore you ought to bear it with resignation." Saying these words, the bishop departed from the spot.

As soon as there was no one in sight, the beggar, who had addressed Epiphanius, touched the other with his foot as he lay extended on the ground and said to him, "You have well performed your part. Arise now, for through your labor we have a good provision for today."

He, however, returned no answer to this address, and as he appeared incapable of speech or motion, the other beggar ran after Epiphanius, wept, and tore his hair, confessed the deception that had been practiced, and besought him to restore the dead man to life. Epiphanius merely exhorted him to submit with patience to the catastrophe and sent him away. God did not raise the dead beggar to life because, I feel persuaded, it was his design to show that those who practice deception on his servants are accounted as guilty of the fraud as if it had been perpetrated against him who sees all and who hears all.

NOTE

1. Compare Socrates, *Ecclesiastical History,* Book VI, Chapter 14.

CHAPTER XXVIII

VIRTUES OF ACACIUS, BISHOP OF BERŒA, OF ZENO, AND OF AJAX.

Acacius, who was at this period bishop of Berœa in Syria, rendered himself very conspicuous by his virtues. Many wonderful actions are ascribed to him. He was from his youth brought up to the profession of ascetic monasticism and was rigid in observing all the regulations of this mode of life. When he was raised to the bishopric, he kept his house open at all hours of the day so that the citizens and strangers were always free to enter, even when he was at meals or at repose. This course of conduct is, in my opinion, very admirable. It might have emanated from his perfect confidence in his own rectitude, or possibly he might have been led to seek the presence of others in order to be always on his guard against those infirmities to which all men are liable, and perhaps from fear lest he should be unawares tempted to any action inconsistent with his profession.

Zeno and Ajax, two celebrated brothers, flourished about the same period. They devoted themselves to a life of monasticism, but did not fix their abode in the desert but at Gaza, a maritime city in the territory of Majuma. They both defended the truth of their religion with invincible intrepidity, and confessed themselves to be Christians so repeatedly in the presence of the Pagans that they were subjected to the most cruel treatment. It is said that Ajax married a very lovely woman and after he had known her thrice, had three sons and that subsequently he held no further intercourse with her but persevered in the exercises of asceticism. He brought up two of his sons to the monastic profession, and the third he permitted to marry. He governed the church of Botelion with great wisdom and piety.

Zeno, who had from his youth renounced the world and marriage, persevered in steadfast adherence to the service of God. It is said, and I myself am witness of the truth of the assertion, that when he was bishop of Majuma, he was never absent, morning or evening or any other period, from the public worship of God unless attacked by some malady, and yet he was at this period nearly a hundred years of age. After his elevation to the episcopal dignity, he did not relax in any of the exercises of monasticism, but by pursuing his trade of weaving linen, continued to earn the means of supplying his own wants and of providing for the poor. He never deviated from this course of conduct till the close of his life, although he attained, as I before said, a very advanced age and although he presided over the richest and greatest church of the province.

I have advanced the examples of these bishops to show the high attainments possessed by those who ruled over the church at this period. It would be difficult to enumerate all the bishops who were distinguished in this manner. The majority of them were endowed with extraordinary virtues, and God bore testimony to this fact by granting their prayers and by working miracles on their behalf.

CHAPTER XXIX

DISCOVERY OF THE REMAINS OF THE PROPHETS HABAKKUK AND MICAH. DEATH OF THE EMPEROR THEODOSIUS THE GREAT.

While the church was under the sway of these eminent men, the clergy and people were excited to the imitation of their virtues. Nor was the church of this era distinguished only by these illustrious examples of piety, for the relics of the proto-prophets[1] Habakkuk and Micah were brought to light about the same period. God made known the place where these relics were deposited in a dream to Zebennus, bishop of Eleutheropolis. The relics of Habakkuk were found at Cela, a city formerly called Ceila. The tomb of Micah was discovered at a distance of ten stadia from Cela, at a place called Beratsatia.[2] This tomb was ignorantly styled by the people of the country, "the tomb of the faithful," or, in their language, Nephsameemana. Such were the events which occurred during the reign of Theodosius to the honor and glory of the Christian religion.

After conquering Eugenius,[3] Theodosius remained for some time at Milan and here he was attacked with a serious malady. He recalled to mind the prediction of the monk John and conjectured that his sickness was unto death. He sent in haste for his son Honorius from Constantinople, and after his arrival found himself a little better so that he was able to be present at the sports of the Hippodrome. After dinner, however, he grew worse and sent to desire his son to preside at the games. He died on the following night. This event happened during the consulate of the brothers Olybrius and Probinus.

NOTES

1. They were not actually the earliest, though among the earliest, of the prophets. Jonah and Joel were the two πρωτοπροφῆται.
2. Or, simply, Bera.
3. Compare Socrates, *Ecclesiastical History,* Book V, Chapter 26.

BOOK VIII

CHAPTER I
SUCCESSORS OF THEODOSIUS THE GREAT.
RUFINUS, THE PRÆTORIAN PREFECT, IS SLAIN. PRIMATES
OF THE PRINCIPAL CITIES. DISPUTES AMONG THE HERETICS.
ACCOUNT OF SISINIUS, BISHOP OF THE NOVATIANS.

Such was the death of Theodosius who had contributed so efficiently to the aggrandizement of the church. He expired in the sixtieth year of his age and the sixteenth of his reign. He left his two sons as his successors. Arcadius the elder reigned in the East, and Honorius in the West. They both held the same religious sentiments as their father.

Damasus was dead and at this period, Siricius had succeeded him as bishop of Rome. Nectarius presided over the church of Constantinople, Theophilus over the church of Alexandria, Flavian over the church of Antioch, and John over that of Jerusalem. Armenia and the Eastern provinces were at this time overrun by the Huns. Rufinus,[1] prefect of the East, was suspected of having clandestinely invited them to devastate the Roman territories[2] in furtherance of his own ambitious designs, for he was said to aspire to tyranny. This suspicion led to his being soon after slain, for on the return of the troops from the conquest of Eugenius, the emperor Arcadius, according to custom, went forth from Constantinople to meet them and the soldiers took this opportunity to massacre Rufinus. These circumstances tended greatly to the extension of religion. The emperors attributed to the piety of their father the ease with which the tyrant had been vanquished and the insidious and ambitious schemes of Rufinus arrested, and they confirmed all the laws which had been enacted by their predecessors in favor of religion and bestowed upon the church fresh tokens of their own zeal and devotion.[3] Their subjects profited by their example, so that even the Pagans were converted without difficulty to Christianity and the heretics united themselves to the Catholic church.

Owing to the disputes which had arisen among the Arians and Eunomians, and to which I have already alluded, these sectarians daily diminished in number. Many of them, on reflecting on the diversity of sentiments which prevailed among those of their own persuasion, judged that the truth of God could not be present with them, and went over to those who held the same faith as the emperors.

The interests of the Macedonians of Constantinople were materially affected by their possessing no bishop, for ever since they had been deprived of their churches by Eudoxius under the reign of Constantius, they had been governed only by presbyters. The Novatians, on the other hand, although they had been agitated by the controversy concerning the Passover which had been renewed by Sabbatius, had been allowed to remain in quiet possession of most of their churches and had not been molested by any of the laws enacted against other heretics because they maintained that the Three Persons of the Trinity are of the same substance. The virtue of their bishops also tended greatly to the maintenance of union and concord among them. After the death of Agelius, they were governed by Marcian, a bishop of eminent piety, and on his decease[4] the bishopric devolved upon Sisinius,[5] a very eloquent man well versed in the doctrines of philosophy and of Scripture and so expert in disputation that even Eunomius, who made a practice of discussing controverted topics, often refused to hold disputes with him. His course of life was exemplary and above the reach of calumny, yet he indulged in luxury and even in superfluities, so that those who knew him not, were incredulous as to whether he could remain temperate in the midst of so much abundance. He possessed so much kindness of disposition and suavity of manner that he was highly esteemed by the bishops of the Catholic church, by the rulers, and by the learned.

His jests were replete with good nature, and he could bear ridicule without manifesting the least resentment. He was very prompt and witty in his rejoinders. Being once asked wherefore, as he was a bishop, he bathed twice daily, he replied, "Because I do not bathe thrice." On another occasion, being ridiculed by a member of the Catholic church because he dressed in white, he asked where it was commanded that he should dress in black, and as the other hesitated for a reply, he continued, "You can give no argument in support of your position, but I refer you to Solomon, the wisest of men, who says, 'Let your garments be always white.' Moreover Christ is described in the Gospel as having appeared in white, and Moses and Elias manifested themselves to the apostles in robes of white."

It appears to me that the following reply was also very ingenious. Leontius, bishop of Ancyra in Galatia, repaired to Constantinople after he had deprived the Novatians in his province of their churches. Sisinius went to him to request that the churches might be restored, but far from yielding compliance, he reviled the Novatians and said that they were not worthy of holding assemblies because, by abolishing the observance of penance, they intercepted the mercy of God. To this Sisinius replied: "No one does penance as I do." Leontius asked him in what way he did penance. "In coming to see you," retorted Sisinius.

Many other witty speeches are attributed to him, and he is even said to have written several works with some elegance. But his discourses obtained greater applause than his writings, for the intonation of his voice, the expression of his countenance, and all his attitudes, produced extraordinary effects upon his audience. This brief description may serve to convey some idea of the disposition and mode of life of this great man.

NOTES

1. Socrates, *Ecclesiastical History*, Book V, Chapter 1.
2. Valesius observes that Claudianus, in his 2nd book against Rufinus, has mentioned that the Huns were called in by the latter for the purpose of laying waste the Eastern provinces. Jerome also mentions the same invasion of the Huns, and says that it took place in the consulship of Arcadius III and Honorius II (AD 394).
3. Concerning the laws passed by Arcadius in support of the Catholic faith at the beginning of his reign, see Baronius, *Ecclesiastical Annals*, Volume V.
4. Marcian is said to have died the 5th day of the Calends of December AD 395.
5. Compare Socrates, *Ecclesiastical History*, Book VI, Chapter 22.

CHAPTER II

CONDUCT AND WISDOM OF THE GREAT JOHN CHRYSOSTOM. HIS PROMOTION TO THE BISHOPRIC OF CONSTANTINOPLE.

Nectarius died about this period,[1] and lengthened debates were held on the ordination of a successor. Great division of opinion prevailed on this subject. There was, however, at Antioch on the Orontes, a certain presbyter named John, a man of noble birth and of exemplary life and possessed of such wonderful powers of eloquence and persuasion, that he was declared by Libanius the Syrian to surpass all the orators of the age. When this sophist was on his death-bed, he was asked by his friends, who should take his place. "It would have been John," replied he, "had not the Christians taken him from us."

Many of those who heard the discourses of John in the church were thereby excited to the love of virtue and to the reception of his own religious sentiments.[2] But it was chiefly by the bright example of his private virtues that John inspired his auditors with emulation. He produced conviction the more readily[3] because he did not resort to rhetorical artifices but expounded the Sacred Scriptures with truth and sincerity. Arguments which are corroborated by actions always commend themselves as worthy of belief, but when a preacher's deeds will not bear investigation, his words, even when he is anxious to declare the truth, are regarded as contradictory. John taught both by precept and example, for while, on the one hand, his course of life was virtuous and austere, on the other hand, he possessed considerable eloquence and persuasiveness of diction. His natural abilities were excellent, and he improved them by studying under the best masters. He learnt rhetoric from Libanius and philosophy from Andragathius. It was expected that he would have embraced the legal profession, but he devoted himself to the study of the Sacred Scriptures and to a life of ecclesiastical philosophy under the guidance of Carterius and Diodorus, two celebrated presidents of monastic assemblies. Diodorus was afterwards bishop of Tarsus, and I have been informed, wrote several works in which he explained the words of Scripture according to their literal meaning without having recourse to allegory. John did not receive the instructions of these men by himself, but persuaded Theodore and Maximus who had studied with him under Libanius to accompany him. Maximus afterwards became bishop of Seleucia in Isauria, and Theodore, bishop of Mopsuestia in Cilicia.

Theodore was a learned man, well conversant with sacred and profane literature. After studying the ecclesiastical laws and frequenting the society of holy men, he was filled with admiration of the ascetic mode of life and devoted himself to it. Afterwards, however, he changed his purpose and resumed his former course of life, and to justify his conduct, cited many examples from ancient history with which he was well acquainted. On hearing of the steps he had taken, John addressed a most divine epistle[4] to him which contained thoughts and expressions apparently transcending all productions of the human mind. Upon receiving this letter, Theodore gave up his possessions, renounced his intention of marrying, and in accordance with the remonstrances of John, returned to the profession of monasticism. This seems to me a remarkable instance of the power of John's eloquence, for he readily forced conviction on the mind of one who was himself habituated to persuade and convince others.

By the same eloquence, John attracted the admiration of the people while he strenuously expatiated against sin and testified the same indignation against all acts of injustice as if they had been perpetrated against himself. This boldness pleased the people but grieved the wealthy and the powerful, who were guilty of most of the vices which he denounced.

Being, then, held in such high estimation by those who knew him personally and by those who were acquainted with him through the reports of others, John was adjudged worthy, in word and in deed by all the subjects of the Roman empire, to preside over the church of Constantinople. The clergy and people were unanimous in electing him. Their choice was approved by the emperor. Messengers were despatched for John, and to confer greater solemnity on his ordination, a council was convened. When the edict of the emperor reached Asterius, the general of the East, he sent to desire John to repair to him as if he had need of him. On his arrival, he made him get into his chariot and conveyed him to Pagras, where he delivered him to the officers whom the emperor had sent in quest of him. Asterius acted very prudently in sending for John before the citizens of Antioch knew what was about to transpire for they would probably have excited a sedition and have inflicted injury on others, or subjected themselves to acts of violence rather than have suffered John to be taken from them.

When John had arrived at Constantinople and when the priests were assembled together, Theophilus[5] opposed his ordination and proposed as a candidate in his stead a presbyter of his church named Isidore, who took charge of strangers and of the poor at Alexandria. I have been informed by persons who were acquainted with Isidore, that from his youth upwards he led a life of virtue and asceticism near Scetis. Others say that he had gained the friendship of Theophilus by assisting him in a very perilous undertaking. For it is reported that during the war against Maximus, Theophilus intrusted Isidore with gifts and letters respectfully addressed to the emperor and to Maximus and sent him to Rome,[6] desiring him to remain there until the termination of the war when he was to deliver the gifts, with the letters, to whoever might prove the victor. Isidore acted according to his instructions, but the artifice was detected and fearful of being arrested, he fled to Alexandria. Theophilus from that period evinced much attachment toward him, and with a view of recompensing his services, strove to raise him to the bishopric of Constantinople. But whether there was really any truth in this report, or whether Theophilus was solely influenced by a sense of the merit of Isidore in proposing him for election, it is certain that he eventually yielded to the wishes of the other bishops and nominated John. He was induced to accede to the ordination of John from fear of the menaces of Eutropius, who held a situation in the palace and who threatened, unless he would vote with the other bishops, to call him to account at the synod for his conduct, for many accusations had been proffered against him.

NOTES

1. Compare Socrates, *Ecclesiastical History,* Book VI, Chapters 2, 3.
2. Some of the disciples of Libanius who had the habit of attending to the public instructions of John in the church, were converted by him to the faith of Christ.
3. Valesius here remarks that Sozomen says that John by his teaching in the church restored his listeners to virtue, and the right and orthodox faith. He inspired them with a love of virtue by the example of his own life and conversation: he persuaded them to come back to the true faith, not by his eloquence, but by his pure and faithful interpretation of the Holy Books. Such is the sense of the passage, though perhaps the words have been altered.
4. This letter of Chrysostom still exists in Volume IV of the works of that father. *Note to the 2018 edition*: A translation in English may be found in Volume 9 of the *Select Library of Nicene and Post-Nicene Fathers*, edited by Philip Schaff, 1908.
5. Socrates also, in Book VI of his *Ecclesiastical History*, attests that Theophilus was present at the ordination of John Chrysostom.
6. Valesius says that Isidore had been sent to Theophilus of Alexandria for the purpose of delivering a pacific or communicatory letter, written to Theophilus by Flavian, to Anastasius, bishop of Rome (AD 398).

CHAPTER III

PROMOTION OF JOHN TO THE BISHOPRIC. HE RE-ESTABLISHES DISCIPLINE IN THE CHURCHES. DEPUTATION TO ROME.

As soon as John was raised to the episcopal dignity, he devoted his attention to the reformation of the lives of his clergy and to the regulation of their pursuits and conduct. He even ejected some of the clergy from the church. He was naturally disposed to reprehend the misconduct of others and to feel excessive indignation against those who acted unjustly, and these characteristics gained strength after his elevation to the bishopric, for when power was placed in his hands, he became more zealous than ever in testifying his anger and resentment against sin. He did not confine his efforts to the reformation of his own church, but sought to rectify abuses throughout the world. He strove to put an end to the dissension which had arisen concerning Paulinus between the Western and Egyptian bishops and the bishops of the East and requested the assistance of Theophilus in effecting the reconciliation of Flavian with the bishop of Rome. Theophilus agreed to cooperate with him in the restoration of concord, and Acacius, bishop of Berœa, and Isidore whom Theophilus had proposed as a candidate for ordination instead of John, were sent on an embassy to Rome. They soon effected the object of their journey and returned to Egypt. Acacius repaired to Syria bearing conciliatory letters concerning Flavian from the bishops of Egypt and of the West.

By these means, unity was restored among the churches after a long period of mutual animosity and division. The people at Antioch who were called Eustathians continued, indeed, for some time to hold separate assemblies, although they possessed no bishop. Evagrius, the successor of Paulinus, did not, as we have stated, long survive him and unanimity was the more easily re-established from there being no one to keep up the division. The laity, as is customary with the populace, gradually went over to those who assembled together under the guidance of Flavian, and thus in course of time unity was restored among them.

CHAPTER IV

ENTERPRISE OF GAÏNAS, THE GOTH. EVILS WHICH HE PERPETRATED.

A barbarian named Gaïnas,[1] who had taken refuge among the Romans and who had risen from the lowest ranks of the army to military command, formed a design to usurp the throne of the Roman empire. With this view, he invited his countrymen, the Goths, to invade the Roman territories and promoted several of them who were his particular friends to the highest posts of the army.[2] Tirbigildes,

Book VIII, Chapter IV

a relative of his who commanded a large body of troops in Phrygia, commenced an insurrection and all persons of judgment rightly inferred that he was acting in concert with Gaïnas. Under the pretext of resenting the devastation of many of the Phrygian cities which had been committed to his superintendence, Gaïnas hastened into that province, but on his arrival he threw aside the mask he had assumed and openly pillaged some cities, and prepared to take possession of others. He then proceeded to Bithynia, and threatened to attack Chalcedonia.

The cities of the East, of Asia, and of the countries bordering on the Euxine, being thus menaced with imminent danger, the emperor and his counselors judged that it would not be safe at so critical a juncture to give battle to the insurgents without having previously made due preparations, and sent to Gaïnas to offer him whatever he might demand. He requested that two consuls named Saturninus and Aurelian, whom he suspected of being inimical to him, should be delivered up to him, and when they were in his power, he pardoned them. He afterwards held a conference with the emperor near Chalcedonia, in the house of prayer in which the tomb of Saint Euphemius the martyr is deposited, and after he and the emperor had mutually bound themselves by vows of friendship to each other, he threw down his arms and repaired to Constantinople where, by an imperial edict, he was appointed general of the infantry and cavalry. Prosperity so far beyond his deserts was more than he could bear with moderation, and as contrary to all expectation he had succeeded so wonderfully in his former enterprise, he determined to undermine the peace of the Catholic church. He was a Christian and, like the rest of the Goths, had espoused the Arian heresy.[3] Urged either by the solicitations of his party or by the suggestions of his own ambition, he applied to the emperor to place one of the churches of the city in the hands of the Arians. He represented that it was neither just nor proper that while he was at the head of the Roman troops, he should be compelled to retire without the walls of the city when he wished to engage in prayer.

John did not remain inactive when made acquainted with these proceedings. He assembled all the bishops who were then residing in the city and went with them to the palace. He spoke at great length in the presence of the emperor and of Gaïnas, reproached the latter with being a stranger and a fugitive, and reminded him that his life had been saved by the father of the emperor to whom he had sworn fidelity, as likewise to his children, to the Romans, and to the laws which he was striving to violate. Then, addressing himself to the emperor, John exhorted him to maintain the laws which had been established against heretics and told him that it would be better to be deprived of the empire than to betray the house of God into the hands of the impious. Thus did John boldly contend in defense of the church that was under his care.

Gaïnas, however, regardless of his oaths, attacked the city. His enterprise was pre-announced by the appearance of a comet directly over the city. This comet was of extraordinary magnitude, larger, indeed, than any that had previously been seen. Gaïnas intended to seize first upon the stores of the silversmiths, and to appropriate their enormous wealth. The silversmiths, however, received timely notice of his designs and concealed the precious commodities,[4] which were usually kept exposed to the view of the public. Gaïnas then sent some of the barbarians by night to set fire to the palace, but fear fell upon them and they returned without executing the mandate. For when they drew near the edifice, they fancied that they saw before them a multitude of armed men of immense stature and they returned to inform Gaïnas that fresh troops had just arrived. Gaïnas disbelieved their report, for he was confident that no troops had entered the city. As, however, other individuals whom he despatched to the palace for the same purpose on the following night, returned with the same report, he went out himself to be an eye-witness of the extraordinary spectacle.

Imagining that the army before him consisted of soldiers who had been withdrawn from other cities, and that these troops protected the city and palace by day and concealed themselves by night, Gaïnas feigned to be possessed of a demon, and under the pretext of offering up prayer, went to the church which the father of the emperor had erected in honor of John the Baptist, at Hebdoma. Some of the Goths remained in Constantinople and others accompanied Gaïnas, having first clandestinely provided themselves with weapons of war which they placed in their chariots. The soldiers who guarded the gates of the city stopped the chariots and forbad them to carry away arms. The Goths, thereupon, slew the guards and the city was immediately filled with as much confusion and uproar as if it had suddenly fallen under the power of an enemy.

A timely thought, however, occurred to the emperor at this perilous juncture, which was to declare Gaïnas a public enemy and to command that all the Goths within the city should be slain. No sooner was this mandate issued than the soldiers rushed upon the Goths and slew the greater number of them. They then set fire to the church which belonged to that people and in which those who had escaped the sword had taken refuge. As the doors were closed, the barbarians could not effect an exit[5] and they all perished.

On hearing of this calamity, Gaïnas passed through Thrace and proceeded towards the Chersonesus, intending to cross the Hellespont and to subdue some of the Eastern provinces. His expectations proved as futile, however, on this occasion as before, and the Romans were again aided by the intervention of Divine power on their behalf. The emperor sent naval and military forces against the insurgents under the command of Fravitas who, although a barbarian by birth, was a good man and an able general. The Goths, having no ships, imprudently attempted to cross the Hellespont on rafts, which when the wind arose, were dashed to pieces against the Roman vessels. The greater part of the barbarians and their horses were drowned, but many were slain by the military. Gaïnas, however, with a few of his followers, escaped, but not long after when making their way through Thrace, they fell in with another detachment of the Roman army, and Gaïnas with all his barbarians perished. Such was the termination of the life and daring schemes of Gaïnas.

Fravitas had rendered himself very conspicuous in this war and was therefore appointed consul.[6] During his consulate and that of Vincent, a son was born to the emperor. The young prince was named after his grandfather and, at the commencement of the next consulate, was proclaimed Augustus.

NOTES

1. Compare Socrates, *Ecclesiastical History*, Book VI, Chapter 6.
2. Christophorson explains "συνταγματάρχας" by "officers of the armies," but Valesius thinks better to translate it by "chiefs." Sozomen uses the same word in the sense of "tribune," above, Book VI, Chapter 6.
3. According to Valesius, the words "Οἳ τὰ Ἀρείου φρονοῦσι" seem not to be the words of Sozomenus, but to have been added by somebody as an interpretation, and ought therefore to be thrown back to the margin.
4. "Τὸν πρόχιερον πλοῦτον" mean "gems, gold and silver vases, and all precious household goods," according to the interpretation of Valesius.
5. By the words "Οἷς οὐκέτι φυγεῖν ἐξεγένετο" is meant either that those who were in that church could not go out because the doors were shut, or that, not being able to escape with Gaïnas because the gates of the town were closed, they had taken refuge in that church. This last interpretation Valesius thinks the right one.
6. Fravitas was consul (AD 401) with Vincentius.

CHAPTER V

PUBLIC DISCOURSES OF JOHN. CONCERNING THE MACEDONIAN WOMAN, AND THE CONVERSION OF BREAD INTO STONE.

John governed the church of Constantinople with exemplary prudence and induced many of the Pagans and of the heretics to unite themselves with him. Crowds of people daily resorted to him, some for the purpose of being edified by listening to his discourses, and others with the intention of tempting him. He, however, pleased and attracted all classes and led them to embrace the same religious sentiments as himself. As the people pressed around him, and so far from feeling any weariness, crowded to hear him in such numbers as even to molest each other, he placed himself in the midst of them at the desk (βῆμα) of the readers, and having taken a seat, taught the multitude.

It seems to me, that this is a suitable place in my history for the insertion of the account of a miracle which was performed during the life of John. A certain man of the sect of the Macedonians, who was married and lived with his wife, chanced to hear John discoursing concerning the Divine nature. He was convinced by the argument he heard advanced and strove to persuade his wife to embrace the same sentiments. Her previous habits of mind and the conversation of other women deterred her from complying with his wishes, and when he found that all his efforts to convince her were futile, he told her that unless she would be of one mind with him on Divine subjects, she should not continue to live with him. The woman, therefore, promised to do as she was required, but at the same time, she made known the matter to one of her servant maids in whose fidelity she confided and used her as an instrument in deceiving her husband. At the time of the celebration of the mysteries (the initiated will understand what I mean) this woman kept what was given to her, and held down her head as if engaged in prayer. Her servant, who was standing behind her, placed in her hand a bit of bread which she had brought with her, but as soon as she had placed it between her teeth, it was converted into stone. Astonished at what had occurred, and fearful lest any further calamity should befall her, she ran to the bishop and informed him of what had happened. She showed him the stone, which bore the marks of her teeth. It was composed of some unknown substance, and was of a very strange and peculiar color. She implored forgiveness with tears, and continued ever after to hold the same religious tenets as her husband. If any person should consider this narrative incredible, he can inspect the stone in question, for it is still preserved in the treasury of the church of Constantinople.

CHAPTER VI

PROCEEDINGS OF JOHN IN ASIA AND PHRYGIA. HERACLIDES, BISHOP OF EPHESUS, AND GERONTIUS, BISHOP OF NICOMEDIA.

John, having been informed that many of the bishops of Asia and of the neighboring churches were unworthy of their office and that they sold the priesthood for money or bestowed that dignity as a matter of private favor, repaired to Ephesus and deposed thirteen bishops of Lycia, Phrygia, and Asia, and elected others in their stead. The bishop of Ephesus was dead,[1] and he therefore ordained Heraclides[2] over that church. Heraclides was a native of Cyprus and was one of the deacons under John. He had formerly joined the monks at Scetis, and had been the disciple of Evagrius.

John also deposed Gerontius, bishop of Nicomedia. This latter was a deacon under Ambrose of the church of Milan. He declared, either with an intention to deceive others or because he had been himself deceived by some illusion of the devil, that he had seized a quadruped resembling an ass (ὀνοσκελίς)[3] by night, had cut off its head, and flung it into a grinding-house. Ambrose regarded this mode of discourse as utterly unworthy of a servant of God and commanded Gerontius to remain in seclusion until he had expiated his fault by repentance. Gerontius, however, was a very skillful physician. He was eloquent and persuasive and knew well how to gain friends. He therefore ridiculed the command of Ambrose and repaired to Constantinople. In a short time, he obtained the friendship of the most powerful men at court, and not long after, was elevated to the bishopric of Nicomedia. He was ordained by Helladius,[4] bishop of Cæsarea in Cappadocia, who performed this office the more readily for him because he had been instrumental, through his interest at court, in obtaining a high appointment in the army for his son. When Ambrose heard of this ordination, he wrote to Nectarius, bishop of Constantinople, desiring him to eject Gerontius from the priesthood and not to permit the discipline of the church to be violated by such gross abuses. However desirous Nectarius might have been to obey this injunction, he could never succeed in carrying it into effect owing to the determined resistance of the people of Nicomedia.

John deposed Gerontius and ordained Pansophius who had formerly been preceptor to the wife of the emperor and who, though a man of decided piety and of a mild and gentle disposition, was not liked by the Nicomedians. They arose in sedition and declaimed publicly and privately on the charity and beneficence of Gerontius and on the benefits which all classes, rich and poor, had enjoyed from his skill in medicine and, as is usual when we applaud those we love, they ascribed many other virtues to him. They went about the streets of Nicomedia and Constantinople as if some earthquake or pestilence or other visitation of Divine wrath had occurred, and sang psalms and offered supplications that they might have Gerontius for their bishop. They were at length compelled to yield to necessity and parted most reluctantly with Gerontius, receiving in his stead a bishop whom they regarded with fear and aversion. The bishops who had been deposed and all their followers declaimed against John and alleged that he had violated the laws of the church and set aside ordinations which had been legally conferred, and in the excess of their resentment, they condemned deeds which were worthy of commendation. Among other matters, they reproached him with the proceedings that had been taken against Eutropius.

NOTES

1. Compare Socrates, *Ecclesiastical History,* Book VI, Chapter 11.
2. Socrates, in Book VI, Chapter 10, says that this Heraclides was the deacon of Chrysostom.
3. The Gentiles gave this name to a certain spectre, because it had the legs and feet of a young ass. By the ancient Greeks it was called ἔμουσα (see Aristophanes *Ranæ*, 1. 293). This spectre usually presented itself to travellers, as we learn from Harpocrates.
4. Valesius says that he does not see why it is that Helladius, bishop of Cæsarea, ordained Gerontius bishop of Nicomedia. It can be alleged that the bishop of Cæsarea claimed the ordination of the bishop of Nicomedia, as being primate of the diocese of Pontus.

CHAPTER VII

CONCERNING EUTROPIUS, CHIEF OF THE EUNUCHS, AND THE LAW ENACTED BY HIM. MURMURS AGAINST JOHN.

Eutropius was originally the chief of the eunuchs, and was the first and only person of that rank who attained the consular and patrician dignity.[1] When he was raised to power, he thought not of the future nor of the instability of human affairs but caused those who sought an asylum in churches to be thrust out. He treated Pentadia, the wife of Timasius, in this manner. Timasius was a general in the army, possessed of considerable influence. But Eutropius procured an edict for his banishment[2] to Pasis in Egypt, under the pretext that he aspired to tyranny. I have been informed that Timasius fell a victim to thirst or the cruelty of his enemies and was found dead among the sands of the desert. Eutropius issued a law enacting that no one should seek refuge in churches and that the asylums should be violated if any one should attempt to avail himself of them. He was, however, the first to transgress this law, for not long after its enactment, he offended the empress and immediately left the palace and fled to the church. While he was lying beneath[3] the altar, John pronounced a discourse in which he reprehended the pride of power and directed the attention of the people to the instability of human greatness. The enemies of John hence took occasion to cast reproach on him, because he had rebuked instead of compassionating one who was suffering under the calamities of adverse fortune. Eutropius soon after paid the penalty of his impiety and was beheaded, and the law which he had enacted was effaced from the public inscriptions. The wrath of God having been thus promptly visited on the injustice that had been perpetrated, prosperity was restored to the church and the people of Constantinople were hence more sedulous than before in attendance at the singing of the morning and the evening hymns.

NOTES

1. Πατρὸς βασιλεώς. The Patricians were called the Fathers of the Emperor—a title first given to them by Constantine.
2. This happened AD 395, or, according to Valesius, 396.
3. ὑπὸ τὴν ἱερὰν τράπεζαν. Compare the passage relating to Alexander in Socrates, *Ecclesiastical History*, Book I, Chapter 36, where the same phrase is used.

CHAPTER VIII

HYMNS AGAINST ARIANISM INTRODUCED BY JOHN. EFFECTS OF HIS PUBLIC MINISTRATIONS.

The Arians, having been deprived of their churches in Constantinople during the reign of Theodosius, held their assemblies without the walls of the city.[1] They

Book VIII, Chapter VIII

assembled by night in the public porticoes and sung in parts certain hymns[2] which they had composed in vindication of their own tenets and at the break of day, marched in procession singing these hymns to the places in which they held their assemblies. They proceeded in this manner on all solemn festivals and on the first and last[3] days of the week. The sentiments propounded in these hymns were such as were likely to engender disputes as, for instance, the following: "Where are those who say that the Three Persons constitute one Power?" Other similar acrimonious observations were interspersed throughout their compositions.

John was fearful lest any of his own people should be led astray by witnessing these exhibitions, and therefore commanded them to sing hymns in the same manner. The orthodox, being more numerous and more wealthy than the Arians, soon surpassed them in the pomp and splendor of their processions, for they had silver crosses and lighted torches borne before them. The eunuch of the empress was appointed to regulate these processions, to pay the cost of whatever might be required, and to prepare hymns adapted to be sung on these occasions.

Hence the Arians, impelled either by jealousy or revenge, attacked the members of the Catholic church. Much bloodshed ensued on both sides. Briso (for this was the name of the eunuch) was wounded on the forehead by a stone that was cast at him. The resentment of the emperor was kindled, and he put a stop to the Arian assemblies. Having commenced the custom of singing hymns in the manner and from the cause above stated, the members of the Catholic church did not discontinue the practice but have retained it to the present day. The institution of these processions, and the faithfulness of his ministrations in the church endeared John to the people, but he was hated by the clergy and the powerful on account of his boldness and candor, for he never failed to rebuke the clergy when he detected them in acts of injustice, nor to exhort the powerful to return to the practice of virtue when they abused their wealth, committed impiety, or yielded to voluptuousness.[4]

NOTES

1. Compare Socrates, *Ecclesiastical History*, Book VI, Chapter 8.
2. ἀκροτελεύτια. Literally, "endings of verses." Sozomen understands the Arian doxologies mentioned by Socrates (see Valesius' notes on his *Ecclesiastical History*, Book II, Chapter 21) subjoined to Arian hymns. Valesius thinks it more probable that they were added at the end of the Psalms of David.
3. That is, on the Sunday, or Lord's day, and on the Saturday, or Jewish sabbath. The Sunday is always called the first day of the week by Christian writers. See note on Socrates, *Ecclesiastical History*, Book I, Chapter 38.
4. For an account of the birth and early education of Saint John Chrysostom, see Socrates, *Ecclesiastical History*, Book VI, Chapter 3.

CHAPTER IX

SERAPION THE ARCHDEACON AND SAINT OLYMPIAS. COMPLAINTS OF THE CLERGY AGAINST JOHN.

The enmity of the clergy against John was greatly increased by Serapion, his archdeacon, a man naturally prone to anger and always ready to insult his opponents.[1] The feelings of hostility were further fostered by the counsel which Olympias received from John. Olympias was a widow of illustrious birth, zealously attached to the exercises of monastic philosophy, and notwithstanding her youth, Nectarius had ordained her deaconess.[2] John, perceiving that she bestowed her goods liberally on whoever asked her for them and that she despised everything but the service of God, said to her: "I applaud your intentions but would have you know that those who aspire to the perfection of virtue ought to distribute their wealth with prudence. You, however, have been bestowing wealth on the wealthy, which is as useless as if you had cast it in the sea. Know you not that you have, for the sake of God, devoted all your possessions to the relief of the poor. You ought, therefore, to regard your wealth as belonging to your Master and to remember that you will have to account for its distribution. If you will be persuaded by me, you will in future regulate your donations according to the wants of those who solicit relief. You will thus be enabled to extend the sphere of your benevolence, and your zeal and charity will be accepted by God."

John had several disputes with many of the monks, particularly with Isaac. He commended those who in conformity with the rules of their profession, remained in quietude in their monasteries. He protected them from all injustice and supplied all their wants.[3] But the monks who made their appearance in cities were severely censured by him and declared to be the disgrace of monasticism. He hence incurred the hatred of the clergy and of many of the monks who represented him as a hard, passionate, morose, and arrogant man. They therefore attempted to bring his life into public disrepute by stating confidently as if it were the truth that he would eat with no one, and that he refused every invitation that was offered him. I know of no pretext that could have given rise to this assertion except that, as I have been assured by a man of undoubted veracity, John had, by rigorous asceticism, rendered himself liable to pain in the head and stomach and was thus prevented from being present at some of the most solemn festivals. Hence, however, originated the greatest accusation that was ever devised against him.

NOTES

1. Compare Socrates, *Ecclesiastical History,* Book VI, Chapter 4.
2. It is to be observed, remarks Valesius, that she was ordained at an age earlier than was

generally allowed, and also that she was ordained by Nectarius, and that each of these points were contrary to the canons of the church. See Council of Chalcedon, canon 15, and Nicene, canon 19, and compare Rufinus, *Ecclesiastical History,* Book X, Chapter 6, Saint Clement, *Apostolic Constitutions,* Book III, Chapter 15.
3. Sozomen here speaks of the monks of Constantinople and its neighborhood, where monasteries abounded. See above, Book IV, Chapter 2.

CHAPTER X

SEVERIAN, BISHOP OF GABALES, AND ANTIOCHUS, BISHOP OF PTOLEMAIS. DISPUTE BETWEEN SERAPION AND SEVERIAN. RECONCILIATION EFFECTED BY THE EMPRESS.

John likewise incurred the enmity of the empress through the machinations of Severian, bishop of Gabales in Syria. Severian and Antiochus, bishop of Ptolemais in Syria, were both learned men and well qualified to teach the people. Antiochus had so fine a voice and delivery that by some persons he was surnamed Chrysostom. Severian, on the other hand, had a harsh and provincial accent, but in point of general knowledge and acquaintance with Scripture, he was considered superior to Antiochus.

It appears that Antiochus was the first to visit Constantinople. He gained great applause by his eloquence, amassed some property, and then returned to his own city. Severian followed his example and went to Constantinople. He formed an intimacy with John, secured the admiration of the public by his ministrations in the church, and even attracted the notice of the emperor and empress. When John went to Asia, he commended the church to his care, for he was so far deceived by the adulation of Severian, as to imagine him his friend. Severian, however, thought only of gratifying his auditors and of pleasing the people by his eloquence. When John was apprized that this was the course he was pursuing, he was highly incensed against him, and his resentment was further kindled, it is said, by the representations of Serapion. After the return of John from Asia, Serapion happened to see Severian passing, but instead of rising to salute him, he kept his seat in order to show his utter contempt for the man. Severian was offended by this manifestation of disrespect, and exclaimed, "If Serapion die a Christian, then Christ was not incarnate."

Serapion reported these words and John, in consequence, expelled Severian from the city as a blasphemer, for witnesses were brought forward to attest that the above words had been really uttered by him. Some of the friends of Serapion even went so far as to suppress part of the speech of Severian, and to affirm that he had declared that Christ was not incarnate. John also rebuked Severian, by asking whether, if Serapion should not die among the clergy, it would follow that Christ had not been incarnate.

As soon as the wife of the emperor was informed of what had occurred by the friends of Severian, she immediately sent for him from Chalcedonia. John, notwithstanding all her remonstrances, positively refused to hold any intercourse with him until the empress placed her son Theodosius on his knees[1] in the church of the Apostles, and then John yielded a reluctant consent to receive Severian into favor. Such are the accounts which I have received of these transactions.

NOTE

1. Adjuring him by her son.

CHAPTER XI

QUESTION AGITATED IN EGYPT AS TO WHETHER GOD HAS A CORPOREAL FORM. THEOPHILUS, BISHOP OF ALEXANDRIA. BOOKS OF ORIGEN.

A question was at this period agitated in Egypt, which had been propounded a short time previously, namely, whether it is right to believe that God possesses a corporeal nature.[1] Owing to a too liberal and simple mode of interpreting Scripture, most of the monks of that part of the world supposed that God possesses eyes, a face and hands, and other members of the bodily organization. This position, however, was denied by those who searched into the hidden meaning of the words of Scripture, and they maintained that those who denied the incorporeality of God were guilty of blasphemy. This latter opinion was espoused by Theophilus and preached by him in the church and in the epistle[2] which, according to custom, he wrote respecting the celebration of the Passover. He took occasion to state that God is to be regarded as incorporeal and as bearing no resemblance to the human form.

When it was signified to the Egyptian monks that Theophilus had broached these sentiments, they went to Alexandria, assembled the people together, excited a tumult, and determined upon slaying the bishop as an impious man. Theophilus, however, presented himself to the insurgents and said to them, "When I look upon you, it is as if I beheld the face of God."

This address mollified their resentment, and they replied: "Wherefore, then, if you really hold orthodox doctrines, do you not denounce the books of Origen, which set forth doctrine of an opposite tendency?"

"Such has long been my intention," replied he, "and I shall do as you advise, for I blame as much as you do all those who follow the doctrines of Origen."

By these means he deluded the monks, and quelled the sedition.

NOTES

1. Compare Socrates, *Ecclesiastical History,* Book VI, Chapter 7.
2. This epistle is no longer extant.

CHAPTER XII

ENMITY OF THEOPHILUS AGAINST FOUR BROTHERS, CALLED "THE GREAT."

The controversy would most likely have been terminated had it not been renewed by Theophilus himself from inimical feelings against Ammon, Dioscorus, Eusebius, and Euthymius who were called "the great."[1] They were brothers, and as we have before stated, rendered themselves very conspicuous among the ascetics at Scetis. They were at one period beloved by Theophilus above all the other monks of Egypt. He sought their society and frequently dwelt with them. He even conferred on Dioscorus the bishopric of Hermopolis. But from the time of his attempt to ordain Isidore as successor to Nectarius in the bishopric of Constantinople, he had regarded them with hatred.

Some[2] say that a woman belonging to the Manichæan sect, having been converted to the faith of the Catholic church, Theophilus rebuked the arch-presbyter (towards whom he had other reasons for entertaining resentful feelings) because he had admitted her to participate in the sacred mysteries before she had abjured her former heresy. Peter, for this was the name of the arch-presbyter, maintained that he had received the woman into communion according to the laws of the church and at the consent of Theophilus, and referred to Isidore as a witness to the truth of what he deposed. Isidore happened to be then at Rome, but on his return he testified that the assertions of Peter were true. Theophilus resented this avowal, and ejected both him and Peter from the church.

Such is the account given by some persons of the transaction. I have, however, heard it alleged by a man of undoubted veracity who was very intimate with the monks above-mentioned, that the enmity of Theophilus towards Isidore originated from two causes. One of these causes was identical with that specified by Peter the presbyter, namely, that he had refused to attest the existence of a testament in which the inheritance was entailed on the sister of Theophilus. The other cause alleged by this individual was that Isidore refused to give up certain monies that had been confided to him for the relief of the poor, and which Theophilus wished to appropriate to the erection of churches, and told his bishop that it would be far better to apply the money to the relief of the bodies of the sick, which are the temples of God, than to the building of edifices.

But from whatever cause the enmity of Theophilus might have originated, Isidore, immediately after his excommunication, joined his former companions, the monks at Scetis. Ammon, with a few others, then repaired to Theophilus and entreated him to restore Isidore to communion. Theophilus readily promised to do as they requested, but as time passed away and his promise still remained unfulfilled, they again repaired to him, renewed their entreaties, and pressed him to be faithful to his engagement. Instead of complying, Theophilus thrust one of the monks into prison, for the purpose of intimidating the others. Ammon and all the monks then went to the prison, into which they were readily admitted by the jailer who imagined that they had come to bring provisions to the prisoner, but having once obtained admission, they refused to leave the prison. When Theophilus heard of their voluntary confinement, he sent to desire them to come to him. They replied that he ought to take them out of prison himself, for it was not just after having been subjected to public indignity that they should be privately released from confinement. At length, however, they yielded and went to him. Theophilus apologized for what had occurred and dismissed them as if he had no further intention of molesting them. But he retained in secret the utmost resentment against them and studied the most efficient means of injuring them. He was in doubt, however, as to how he could ill-treat them, as they had no possessions and despised everything but wisdom, until it occurred to him to disturb the peace of their retirement. From his former intercourse with them he had gathered that they blamed those who believe that God has a human form, and that they adhered to the opinions of Origen. He therefore seized this pretext to set all the other monks, who maintained contrary doctrines, at variance with them.[3] A furious dispute ensued among the monks, for instead of resorting to argument and striving to convince each other of the truth, they mutually insulted each other and gave the name of Origenists to those who maintained the incorporeality of the Deity, while those who held the opposite opinion were called Anthropomorphists.

NOTES

1. Compare Socrates, *Ecclesiastical History,* Book VI, Chapters 7, 9.
2. He probably alludes to Socrates (see above) or to those authors whence Socrates borrowed his information.
3. Socrates gives the same account, but like Sozomen, he suppresses the reason: *viz.* that Theophilus had convened an episcopal synod at Alexandria and had condemned Ammonius and his brethren as followers of Origen.

CHAPTER XIII

THE MONKS REPAIR TO JOHN.
HOSTILITY OF THEOPHILUS AGAINST JOHN.

Dioscorus, Ammon, and the other monks, having discovered the machinations of Theophilus, retired to Jerusalem and thence proceeded to Scythopolis because this latter region abounded in palm trees, and the wood of these trees was wrought into various articles by the monks. Dioscorus and Ammon were accompanied hither by about eighty other monks.

In the meantime, Theophilus sent messengers to Constantinople to prefer complaints against them, and to oppose any petitions that they might lay before the emperor. On being informed of this fact, Ammon and the monks embarked for Constantinople and took Isidore with them, and they requested that their cause might be tried in the presence of the emperor and of the bishop, for they imagined that the well-known boldness of John would be of assistance to them at this juncture. John, although he received them with kindness and treated them with honor and did not forbid them to pray in the church, refused to admit them to participation in the mysteries until their cause had been decided. He wrote to Theophilus, desiring him to receive them back into communion, as their sentiments concerning the Divine nature were orthodox, requesting him if he regarded their orthodoxy as doubtful to send someone to act as their accuser. Theophilus returned no reply to this epistle.

Some time subsequently, Ammon and his companions presented themselves before the wife of the emperor, and complained of the machinations of Theophilus against them. As she was well acquainted with the facts of the case, she stopped her chariot, inclined her head forward, and said to them, "Pray for the emperor, for me, for our children, and for the empire. For my part, I shall shortly cause a council to be convened to which Theophilus shall be summoned." A false report having been spread abroad in Alexandria that John had received Dioscorus and his companions into communion and had afforded them every aid and encouragement in his power, Theophilus began to reflect upon what measures it would be possible to adopt in order to eject John from the church.

CHAPTER XIV

PERVERSITY OF THEOPHILUS. ARRIVAL OF SAINT EPIPHANIUS AT CONSTANTINOPLE. HE EXCITES THE PEOPLE OF THAT CITY AGAINST JOHN.

Theophilus kept his designs against John as secret as possible and wrote to the bishops of every city, condemning the books of Origen.[1] It also occurred to him that it would be advantageous to enlist Epiphanius, bishop of Salamis in Cyprus, on his side because the eminent virtues of this prelate had secured him universal admiration, and he therefore formed a friendship with him, although he had formerly blamed[2] him for asserting that God possessed a human form. As if repentant of having ever entertained any other sentiment, Theophilus wrote to Epiphanius to acquaint him that he now held the same opinions as himself, and to condemn the works of Origen, whence he had drawn his former hypothesis. Epiphanius had long regarded the writings of Origen with peculiar aversion, and was therefore easily led to attach credit to the epistle of Theophilus. He soon after assembled the bishops of Cyprus together and prohibited the perusal of the books of Origen. He also wrote to the other bishops, and among others to the bishop of Constantinople, exhorting them to issue similar prohibitions. Theophilus, perceiving that there could be no danger in following the example of Epiphanius, whose exalted virtues were universally appreciated and reverenced, assembled the bishops of his province and enacted a similar decree.

John, on the other hand, paid little attention to the letters of Epiphanius and Theophilus. Those among the powerful and the clergy who were opposed to him perceived that the designs of Theophilus tended to his ejection from the bishopric and therefore endeavored to procure the convention of a council in Constantinople in order to carry this measure into execution. Theophilus exerted himself to the utmost in convening this council. He commanded the bishops of Egypt to repair by sea to Constantinople. He wrote to request Epiphanius and the other Eastern bishops to proceed to that city with as little delay as possible, and he himself set off on the journey thither by land. Epiphanius was the first to sail from Cyprus. He landed at Hebdoma, a suburb of Constantinople, and after having prayed in the church erected at that place, he proceeded to enter the city. In order to do him honor, John went out with all his clergy to meet him. Epiphanius, however, evinced clearly by his conduct that he believed the disadvantageous report that had been spread against John, for he would not remain in his house and avoided all intercourse with him. He also privately assembled all the bishops who were in Constantinople and showed them the decrees that he had issued against the works of Origen. Some of the bishops approved of these decrees, while others objected to them. Theotimus, bishop of Scythia, strongly opposed the proceedings of Epiphanius and told him that it was not right to cast insult on the memory of one who had long been numbered with the dead, nor to call into question the conclusion to which the ancients had arrived on the subject. While discoursing in this strain, he drew forth a work of Origen's which he had brought with him, and after reading aloud a passage conducive to the edification of the church, he remarked that those who condemned such sentiments were guilty of manifest absurdity and that while they were ridiculing the words of the author, they were evidently in danger of being tempted to ridicule the subjects themselves upon which he wrote.

John manifested great respect towards Epiphanius and invited him to join in the meetings of his church and to dwell with him. But Epiphanius declared that he would neither reside with John, nor pray with him, unless he would denounce the works of Origen and expel Dioscorus and his companions from the city. Not considering it just to act in the manner proposed until judgment had been passed on the case, John tried to postpone the adoption of further measures to some future time. In the meantime his enemies met together and arranged that on the day when the people would be assembled in the Church of the Apostles, Epiphanius should publicly pronounce condemnation on the works of Origen and on Dioscorus and his companions as the partisans of this writer, and also denounce the bishop of the city as the abettor of Dioscorus. By this means, it was hoped, that the affections of the people would be alienated from their bishop. The following day, when Epiphanius was about to enter the church in order to carry his design into execution, he was stopped by Serapion at the command of John, who had received intimation of the plot. Serapion proved to Epiphanius that while the project he had devised was unjust in itself, it could be of no personal advantage to him, for that if it should excite a popular insurrection, he would be regarded as responsible for the outrages that might follow. By these arguments Epiphanius was induced to relinquish his designs.

NOTES

1. Compare Socrates, *Ecclesiastical History,* Book VI, Chapter 10.
2. See Valesius's notes on Socrates mentioned above.

CHAPTER XV

THE SON OF THE EMPRESS AND THE HOLY EPIPHANIUS. CONFERENCE BETWEEN THE "GREAT BROTHERS" AND EPIPHANIUS, AND THE RETURN OF THIS LATTER TO CYPRUS. EPIPHANIUS AND JOHN.

About this time, the son of the empress was attacked by a dangerous illness and the mother, apprehensive of consequences, sent to implore Epiphanius to pray for him. Epiphanius returned for answer that her son would recover provided that she would avoid all intercourse with the heretic Dioscorus and his companions. To this message the empress replied as follows: "If it be the will of God to take my son, his will be done. The Lord who gave me my child, can take him back again. You have not power to raise the dead, otherwise your archdeacon would not have died." She alluded to Chrispio, the archdeacon, who had died a short time previously. He was brother to Phuscon and Salamanes, monks whom I had occasion to mention[1] when detailing the history of events under the reign of Valens.

Ammon and his companions went to Epiphanius at the permission of the empress. Epiphanius inquired who they were and Ammon replied, "We are, O father, the Great Brothers: allow us to ask whether you have read any of our works or those of our disciples." On Epiphanius replying that he had not seen them, he continued, "How is it then that you condemn us as heretics, when you have no proof as to what sentiments we may hold?" Epiphanius said that he had formed his judgment by the reports he had heard on the subject, and Ammon replied, "We have pursued a very different line of conduct from yours. We have conversed with your disciples, and read your works, and among others, that entitled 'The Anchor.' When we have met with persons who have ridiculed your opinions and asserted that your writings are replete with heresy, we have defended you as our father. Ought you then to condemn upon mere report and without any substantial proofs those who have so zealously defended your sentiments and spoken well of you?"

Epiphanius was affected by this discourse and dismissed them. Soon after, he embarked for Cyprus,[2] either because he recognized the futility of his journey to Constantinople or because, as there is reason to believe, God had revealed to him his approaching death, for he died while on his voyage back to Cyprus. It is reported that he said to the bishops who had accompanied him to the place of embarkation, "I leave you the city, the palace, and the stage, for I shall shortly depart." I have been informed by several persons that John predicted that Epiphanius would die at sea, and that this latter predicted the deposition of John. For it appears that when the dispute between them was at its height, Epiphanius said to John, "I hope you will not die a bishop," and that John replied, "I hope you will never return to your bishopric."

NOTES

1. See above, Book VI, Chapter 32.
2. Compare Socrates, *Ecclesiastical History,* Book VI, Chapter 14.

CHAPTER XVI

DISPUTE BETWEEN THE EMPRESS AND JOHN. ARRIVAL OF THEOPHILUS FROM EGYPT. CYRINUS, BISHOP OF CHALCEDONIA.

After the departure of Epiphanius, John, when preaching in the church as usual, chanced to inveigh against the vices to which females are more peculiarly prone.[1] The people imagined that his strictures were expressly directed against the wife of the emperor. The enemies of the bishop did not fail to report his discourse in this sense to the empress and she conceiving herself to have been insulted, complained to the emperor and urged the necessity for the presence of Theophilus and the immediate convocation of a council. Severian, bishop of Gabales, who still entertained great resentment against John, strenuously supported these measures. I am not in possession of sufficient data to determine whether there was any truth in the current report that John delivered the discourse abovementioned with express allusion to the empress, because he suspected her of having excited Epiphanius against him.

Theophilus arrived soon after at Chalcedonia in Bithynia and was followed thither by many bishops. Some of the bishops joined him in compliance with his own invitation, and others in obedience to the commands of the emperor. The bishops whom John had deposed in Asia, repaired to Chalcedonia with the utmost alacrity, as likewise all those who cherished any feeling of hostility against him. On the arrival of the ships which Theophilus expected from Egypt, the enemies of John met to deliberate on the means of carrying on their designs against him, and at this assembly Cyrinus, bishop of Chalcedonia, who was an Egyptian and a relative of Theophilus and who had besides some private motives of resentment against John, burst forth into bitter invectives against him. His injustice, however, was speedily followed by judgment, for Maruthas, a native of Mesopotamia who had accompanied the bishops, happened to tread on his foot, and Cyrinus suffered so severely from this accident that he was unable to repair with the other bishops to Constantinople, although his aid was necessary to the execution of the designs that had been formed against John. The wound assumed so alarming an appearance, that the surgeons were obliged to perform several operations on the leg, and at length mortification took place, and spread over the whole body, and even extended to the other foot. He expired soon afterwards in great agony.

NOTE

1. Compare Socrates, *Ecclesiastical History,* Book VI, Chapter 15.

CHAPTER XVII

COUNCIL HELD BY THEOPHILUS AND THE ENEMIES OF JOHN. JOHN IS SUMMONED TO ATTEND, BUT ON HIS REFUSAL, IS DEPOSED BY THEOPHILUS.

When Theophilus entered Constantinople, none of the clergy went out to meet him, for his enmity against John had become publicly known.[1] Some sailors from Alexandria, however, who chanced to be on shore received him with great acclamations of joy. Passing by the church he proceeded direct to the palace, where a lodging had been prepared for his accommodation. He soon perceived that many people of the city were strongly prejudiced against John and ready to bring accusations against him, and taking his measures accordingly, he repaired to a place called "The Oak," in the suburbs of Chalcedonia. This place now bears the name of Rufinus,[2] for he was a consul and erected here a magnificent palace and a church in honor of the apostles Peter and Paul, and appointed a congregation of monks to perform the clerical duties in the church.[3]

When Theophilus and the other bishops met for deliberation in this place, he judged it expedient to make no further allusion to the works of Origen and tried to extort some expression of contrition from the monks of Scetis by assuring them that the past should be buried in oblivion. His partisans zealously seconded his efforts and told them that they must ask Theophilus to pardon their conduct, and as all the members of the assembly concurred in this request, the monks were troubled, and believing that it was necessary to do what they were desired by so many bishops, they used the words which it was their custom to use even when injured and declared that they asked forgiveness. Theophilus willingly received them into favor and restored them to communion, and all further investigation of their conduct was abandoned.

I feel convinced that this matter would not have been so quickly settled had Dioscorus, Ammon, and the other monks been present. But Dioscorus had died some time previously and had been interred in the church dedicated to Saint Mocius the martyr. Ammon, also, had been taken ill at the very time that preparations were being made for the convocation of the council, and although he insisted upon repairing to "The Oak," yet his malady was thereby greatly increased. He died soon after his journey and was buried with great pomp. Theophilus, it is said, shed tears on hearing of his death and declared that although he had been the cause of much perplexity, there was not a monk to be found of more exalted character than Ammon. It must, however, be admitted that the death of this monk tended much to promote the success of the designs of Theophilus.

The members of the council summoned all the clergy of Constantinople to appear before them, and threatened to depose those who did not obey the summons. They cited John to appear and answer to the accusations laid to his charge, as likewise Serapion, Tigris a presbyter, and Paul a reader. John acquainted them, through the medium of Demetrius bishop of Pessena, and of some of the other clergy who were his friends, that he did not desire to screen his conduct from investigation, and that he was ready, if the names of his accusers and the subject of his accusations were made known to him, to justify his proceedings before a larger council than that which was then assembled but, he added, that he was not so imprudent as to subject himself to the judgment of his enemies.

The bishops testified so much indignation at the non-compliance of John, that some of the clergy whom he had sent to the council were intimidated and did not return to him. Demetrius, and those who preferred his interests to all other considerations, quitted the council, and returned to him. The same day, a courier and a secretary were despatched by the emperor to command John to repair to the bishops, and to urge the bishops to decide his cause without further delay. After John had been cited four times, and had appealed to a general council, no other accusation could be substantiated against him, except his refusal to obey the summons of the council, and upon this ground, he was deposed.

NOTES

1. Compare Socrates, *Ecclesiastical History*, Book VI, Chapter 15.
2. *Note to the 2018 edition:* Sozomen here refers to the Rufiniane, a palace which was at this time imperial property, but would later become the estate of Justinian's general, Belisarius. See Bury: *History of the Later Roman Empire*, Volume I, page 111, and Volume II, page 58 and associated footnote.
3. This practice, in course of time, became very general. See Possidius, *Life of Saint Augustine*.

CHAPTER XVIII

SEDITION OF THE PEOPLE AGAINST THEOPHILUS AND THE MEMBERS OF HIS COUNCIL. RE-INSTALLATION OF JOHN IN THE BISHOPRIC.

The people of Constantinople were made acquainted with the decree of the council towards the evening, and they immediately rose up in sedition.[1] At the break of day they ran to the church and shouted that a large council ought to be convened to take cognizance of the matter, and they prevented the officers who had been sent by the emperor to convey John into banishment from carrying the edict into execution. John, apprehensive lest another accusation should be preferred against him under the pretext that he had disobeyed the mandate of the emperor or excited an insurrection among the people, secretly made his escape from the church at noon, three days after his deposition. When the people became aware that he had gone into exile, the sedition assumed a more formidable aspect than before, and many insulting speeches were uttered against the emperor and the council and particularly against Theophilus and Severian, who were regarded as the originators of the plot. Severian happened to be teaching in the church at the very time that these occurrences were taking place, and he took occasion to commend the sentence that had been enacted against John and stated that even supposing him guiltless of other crimes, John deserved to be deposed on account of his pride, because while God willingly forgives all other sins, he resists the proud.

This discourse excited the anger of the people to such a pitch, that their impetuosity could no longer be repressed. They ran to the churches, to the market-places, and even to the palace of the emperor, and with loud vociferations demanded the restoration of their bishop. The empress was, at length, overcome by their vehemence and importunity, and she persuaded the emperor to yield to the wishes of the people. She sent a eunuch, named Brison, in whom she placed the utmost confidence, to bring back John without delay from Prenetes, a small city of Bithynia, wither he had been banished and protested that she had taken no part in the machinations that had been carried on against him, but had on the contrary, always respected him as a priest and an administrator of baptism[2] to her children.

When John, on the journey homeward, reached the suburbs belonging to the empress, he stopped near Anaplus, and refused to re-enter the city until the injustice of his deposition had been recognized by the larger synod of bishops. But as this refusal tended to augment the popular excitement and led to many public declamations against the emperor and the empress, he allowed himself to be persuaded to enter the city. The people went forth to meet him, bearing lighted torches, and singing psalms in honor of his return. They conducted him to the church, and although he at first objected to enter the edifice until the sentence enacted against him had been revoked, yet they compelled him to take the episcopal seat and to bestow the benediction of peace, as usual, upon the people. He then delivered an extemporaneous discourse in which, by a pleasing figure of speech, he declared that Theophilus had meditated an injury against his church, even as the king of Egypt had contemplated the violation of Sarah, the wife of the patriarch Abraham, which is recorded in the books of the Hebrews. He then proceeded to commend the zeal of the people and to extol the emperor and the empress, and his praises of these august personages so excited the admiration of his auditors that the discourse was interrupted by their acclamations.

NOTES

1. Compare Socrates, *Ecclesiastical History,* Book VI, Chapter 16.
2. μυσταγωγός. Others regard the word as equivalent to tutor; others, to catechist. But, as Valesius remarks, the meaning of the term is settled by the use of μυσταγωγεῖν in Chapter 21, below, in the sense of "baptize."

CHAPTER XIX

PERVERSITY OF THEOPHILUS. ENMITY BETWEEN THE EGYPTIANS AND THE CITIZENS OF CONSTANTINOPLE. DEPARTURE OF THEOPHILUS. NILAMMON THE ASCETIC.

Although Theophilus would fain have brought an accusation against John[1] under the plea that he had unlawfully reinstated himself in his bishopric, yet he was deterred from doing so by the fear of offending the emperor, who had been compelled to recall John as the means of suppressing the popular insurrection. Theophilus, however, received an accusation against Heraclides during the absence of the accused, in the hope of thereby authorizing the sentence of condemnation which had been issued against John. But the friends of Heraclides interposed and declared that it was unjust and contrary to ecclesiastical law to condemn one who was absent. Theophilus and his partisans maintained the opposite side of the question. The people of Alexandria and of Egypt sided with them and were opposed by the citizens of Constantinople.

The strife between the two parties became so vehement that bloodshed ensued. Many were wounded and others slain in the contest. Severian and all the bishops at Constantinople who did not support the cause of John became apprehensive for their personal safety and quitted the city in haste. Theophilus, also, fled the city at the commencement of the winter and in company with Isaac the monk, sailed for Alexandria. A wind arose which drove the vessel to Gera,[2] a small city about fifty stadia from Pelusium. The bishop of this city died, and the inhabitants, I have been informed, elected Nilammon to preside over their church. He was a good man and had attained the summit of monastic philosophy. He dwelt without the city in a cell, of which the door was built up with stones. He refused to accept the dignity of the priesthood, and Theophilus therefore visited him in person to exhort him to receive ordination at his hands. Nilammon repeatedly refused the honor, but as Theophilus would take no refusal, he said to him, "Tomorrow, my father, you shall act as you please. Today it is requisite that I should arrange my affairs."

Theophilus repaired on the following day to the cell of the monk and commanded the door to be opened, but Nilammon exclaimed, "Let us first engage in prayer." Theophilus complied and began to pray. Nilammon likewise prayed within his cell, and in the act of prayer he expired. Theophilus, and those who were with him without the cell, knew nothing at the time of what had occurred, but when the greater part of the day had passed away, and the name of Nilammon had been loudly reiterated without his returning any answer, the stones were removed from the door and the monk was found dead. He was interred with great solemnity, a tomb was erected to his honor, and a house of prayer built on the spot, and the day of his death is still commemorated. Thus died Nilammon, if it can be called death to quit this life for another rather than accept a bishopric of which, with extraordinary modesty, he considered himself unworthy.

After his return to Constantinople, John appeared to be more than ever beloved by the people. Sixty bishops assembled together in that city, and annulled all the decrees of the council of the Oak. They confirmed John in the possession of the bishopric and enacted that he should officiate as a priest, confer ordination, and perform all the duties of the church usually devolving on the bishop. At this time, Serapion was appointed bishop of Heraclea in Thrace.

NOTES

1. Compare Socrates, *Ecclesiastical History,* Book VI, Chapter 17.
2. This city is mentioned in the 4th Act of the Council of Chalcedon.

CHAPTER XX

THE STATUE OF THE EMPRESS. PUBLIC TEACHING OF JOHN. CONVOCATION OF ANOTHER SYNOD AGAINST JOHN. HIS DEPOSITION.

Not long after these occurrences, the silver statue of the empress which is still to be seen to the south of the church opposite the grand council-chamber, was placed upon a column of porphyry,[1] and the event was celebrated by loud acclamations, dancing, games, and other manifestations of public rejoicing, usually observed on the erection of the statues of the emperors. In a public discourse to the people, John declared that these proceedings reflected dishonor on the church. This remark recalled former grievances to the recollection of the empress and irritated her so exceedingly that she determined to procure the convocation of another council. Instead of striving to conciliate her, John added fuel to her indignation by openly declaiming against her in the church, and it was at this period that he pronounced the memorable discourse commencing with the words, "Herodias is again enraged. Again she dances. Again she demands the head of John in a basin."

Several bishops arrived soon after at Constantinople, and amongst them were Leontius, bishop of Ancyra, and Acacius, bishop of Berœa. The festival of our Lord's Nativity was then at hand and the emperor, instead of repairing to the church as usual, sent to acquaint John that he could not hold communion with him until he had cleared himself of the crimes whereof he was accused. John replied that he was ready to prove his innocence, and this so intimidated his accusers that they did not dare to appear against him or proffer the accusations. The judges decided that having been once deposed, he ought not to be admitted to a second trial. Without taking cognizance of any other ground of accusation, they therefore called him to account for having taken possession of the bishopric of Constantinople after having been deposed by one council and before he had been reinstated by another. In his defense, he appealed to the decision of the bishops who had, subsequently to the council of the Oak, held communion with him. The judges waved this argument under the plea that those who had held communion with John were inferior, in point of number, to those who had deposed him,[2] and that a canon was in force by which he stood condemned. Under this pretext, they therefore deposed him, although the law in question had been enacted by heretics, for the Arians, after having taken advantage of various calumnies to expel Athanasius from the church of Alexandria, enacted this law from the apprehension that their machinations against him and the cause and manner of his deposition, might at some future time be subjected to investigation.

NOTES

1. Compare Socrates, *Ecclesiastical History,* Book VI, Chapter 10.
2. The exact number is debated. According to one account they were 36, according to another, 45.

CHAPTER XXI

CALAMITIES SUFFERED BY THE PEOPLE AFTER THE EXPULSION OF JOHN. MACHINATIONS AGAINST HIS LIFE.

After his deposition, John held no more assemblies in the church, but quietly remained in the episcopal dwelling-house. At the termination of the season of Quadrigesima, on the holy night on which the people were gathered together to commemorate the resurrection of Christ, the celebration of the baptismal mysteries[1] was suddenly interrupted by the unexpected entrance of some soldiers and the enemies of John. The baptistry was filled with tumult and disorder. The women wept and lamented and the children screamed. The priests and the deacons were beaten and were forcibly ejected from the church in the priestly garments in which they had been officiating. They were charged with the commission of such disorderly acts as can be readily conceived by those who have been admitted to the mysteries, but which I consider it requisite to pass over in silence, lest my work should fall into the hands of the uninitiated.

The next day the church was, in consequence of this outrage, abandoned, and the people assembled at some public baths of vast extent called the baths of Constantius[2] to celebrate the Passover under the guidance of bishops and presbyters who espoused the cause of John. They were, however, driven hence and then assembled on a spot without the walls of the city which the emperor Constantine had caused to be cleared and enclosed with woods for the purpose of celebrating there the games of the hippodrome. From that period, the people held separate assemblies, sometimes in that locality and sometimes in another, and they hence obtained the name of Johnites.

About this time, a man who was either possessed of a devil or who feigned to have one was seized with a poignard on his person which he had concealed with the intention of assassinating John. He was dragged by the people before the magistrate, but John sent some bishops to free him from custody before he had been questioned by torture. Some time afterwards, a slave of Elpidus the presbyter who was an avowed enemy of the deacon,[3] was seen running as swiftly as possible towards the episcopal residence. A passer-by endeavored to stop him in order to ascertain the cause of so much haste, but instead of answering him, the slave plunged his poignard into him. Another person who happened to be standing by and who cried out at seeing the other wounded, was also wounded in a similar way by the slave, as was likewise a third bystander. All the people in the neighborhood, on seeing what had occurred, shouted that the slave ought to be arrested, and as he tried to escape, they pursued him. A man, who just then came out from the baths, strove to stop him and was so grievously wounded that he fell down dead on the spot. At length, the people contrived to encircle the slave. They seized him and conveyed him to the palace of the emperor, declaring that he had intended to have assassinated John and that the crime ought to be visited with punishment. The magistrate allayed the fury of the people by putting the delinquent into custody and by assuring them that justice should have its course against him.

NOTES

1. μυσταγωγοῦντες. See above, note on Chapter 18. Some commentators have wrongly interpreted the term as referring to the holy Eucharist.
2. See Socrates, *Ecclesiastical History,* Book IV, Chapter 8. And Palladius, *Dialogue of Palladius Concerning the Life of Saint John Chrysostom* [1921], page 80.
3. Namely, the deacon of John Chrysostom.

CHAPTER XXII

UNLAWFUL EXPULSION OF JOHN FROM HIS BISHOPRIC. CONFLAGRATION OF THE CHURCH BY FIRE FROM HEAVEN. EXILE OF JOHN TO CUCUSUM.

From this period the most zealous of the people alternately guarded the house of John by night and by day.[1] The bishops who had condemned him complained of this conduct as a manifest violation of the laws of the church, declared that they could answer for the justice of the sentence that had been enacted against him, and asserted that tranquillity would never be restored among the people until he had been expelled the city. A messenger having conveyed to him a mandate from the emperor enjoining his immediate departure, John obeyed and escaped from the city unnoticed by those who had been appointed to guard him. He made no other remark than that in being sent into banishment without a legal trial or any of the forms of the law, he was treated more severely than murderers, sorcerers, and adulterers. He was conveyed in a bark to Bithynia and thence continued his journey.

Some of his enemies were apprehensive lest the people, on hearing of his departure, should pursue him and bring him back by force, and therefore commanded the gates of the church to be closed. When the people who were in the public places of the city heard of what had occurred, great confusion ensued, for some ran to the seashore, and others fled hither and thither and awaited in great terror the calamities consequent on sedition and the vengeance of the emperor. Those who were within the city pressed towards the doors, and by thus obstructing the entrance, rendered it impossible to force open the doors. While they were endeavoring to effect an exit, and while efforts were being made by another party without the edifice to break open the doors by means of stones, the church was suddenly discovered to be on fire. The flames extended to the grand council-chamber which is situated towards the south. The two parties mutually accused each other of incendiarism. The enemies of John asserted that his partisans had been guilty of the deed from revenge, on account of the sentence that had been passed against him by the council. These latter, on the other hand, maintained that they had been calumniated, and that the crime was perpetrated by their enemies with the intention of burning them in the church. In the meantime, while the conflagration was spreading on all sides, the officers who held John in custody conveyed him to Cucusum, a city of Armenia, which the emperor had appointed as the place of his detention. Other officers were commissioned to arrest all bishops and priests who had favored the cause of John and to imprison them in Chalcedonia. Those citizens who were suspected of attachment to John were sought out and cast into prison and compelled to pronounce anathema against him.

NOTE

1. Compare Socrates, *Ecclesiastical History,* Book XI, Chapter 18.

CHAPTER XXIII
ARSACIUS APPOINTED TO SUPPLANT JOHN IN THE BISHOPRIC. PERSECUTION OF THE FOLLOWERS OF JOHN.

Arsacius, brother of Nectarius the predecessor of John, was not long afterwards ordained over the church of Constantinople.[1] He was of a very mild disposition and possessed of great piety, but the reputation he had acquired as a presbyter was diminished by the conduct of some of the clergy to whom he delegated his power and who did what they pleased in his name, for their evil deeds were imputed to him. Nothing, however, operated so much to his disadvantage as the persecution that was carried on against the followers of John. They refused to hold communion or even to join in prayer with him because the enemies of John were associated with him, and as they persisted, as we have before stated, in meeting together in the further parts of the city, he complained to the emperor of their conduct. The tribune was commanded to attack them with a body of soldiers, and by means of clubs and stones he soon dispersed them. The most distinguished among them in point of rank, and those who were most zealous in their adherence to John, were cast into prison. The soldiers, as is usual on such occasions, went beyond their orders and stripped the women of their ornaments, their golden girdles, their earrings, and their jewels. Although the whole city was thus filled with trouble and lamentation, the affection of the people for John still remained the same, and they refrained from appearing in public. Many of them absented themselves from the marketplace and public baths, while others, not considering themselves safe in their own houses, fled the city.

Among the zealous men and excellent women who adopted this latter measure was Nicarete, a lady of Bithynia. She belonged to a very illustrious family, and was celebrated on account of her perpetual virginity and her virtuous life. She excelled all women that we have ever seen in modesty and circumspection, and throughout her life she invariably preferred the service of God to all earthly considerations. She bore with invincible fortitude the calamities which befell her. She saw herself unjustly despoiled of the greater part of her ample patrimony without manifesting any indignation and managed the little that remained to her with so much economy that although she was advanced in age, she contrived to supply all the wants of her household and to contribute largely to the relief of the poor. To great charity she added so much ingenuity that she was able to compound medicines for the poor who were suffering from sickness, and she frequently succeeded in curing patients who had derived no benefit from the skill of the physicians. To sum all in a few words, we have never known a religious woman endowed with so much modesty, gravity, and virtue, but her great qualifications were concealed by her humility. She would not accept of the office of deaconess, nor of instructress of the virgins consecrated to the service of the church,[2] because she accounted herself unworthy, although the honor was pressed upon her by John.

After the popular insurrection had been quelled, the prefect of the city appeared in public, as if to inquire into the cause of the conflagration and to bring the perpetrators of the deed to punishment, but being a Pagan, he exulted in the destruction of the church and ridiculed the calamity.

NOTES

1. Compare Socrates, *Ecclesiastical History,* Book VI, Chapter 19.
2. These differed from the regular "monachæ," or nuns. They had a separate place in the churches, and communicated apart from the others. They were called "*ecclesiasticæ,*" says Valesius, "*quod ascripte essent albo seu matriculo ecclesiae.*"

CHAPTER XXIV

EUTROPIUS THE READER, AND THE BLESSED OLYMPIAS, AND THE PRESBYTER TIGRIS ARE PERSECUTED ON ACCOUNT OF THEIR ATTACHMENT TO JOHN.

Eutropius, a reader,[1] was required to name the persons who had set fire to the church, but although he was scourged severely, although his sides and cheeks were torn with iron nails, and although lighted torches were applied to the most sensitive parts of his body, no confession could be extorted from him, notwithstanding his youth and delicacy of constitution. After having been subjected to these tortures, he was cast into a dungeon where he soon afterwards expired.

A dream of Sisinius concerning Eutropius seems worthy of insertion in this history. Sisinius, the bishop of the Novatians, saw in his sleep a man, tall of stature and handsome in person, standing near the altar of the church which the Novatians erected to the honor of Stephen the proto-martyr. The man complained of the rarity of goodness among men and said that he had been searching throughout the city and had found but one who was good, and that one was Eutropius. Astonished at what he had seen, Sisinius made known the dream to the most faithful of the presbyters of his church and commanded him to seek Eutropius wherever he might be. The presbyter rightly conjectured that this Eutropius could be no other than he who had been so barbarously tortured by the prefect and went from prison to prison in quest of him. At length he found him and made known to him the dream of the bishop and besought him with tears to pray for him. Such are the details we possess concerning Eutropius.

Great fortitude was evinced in the midst of these calamities by Olympias, the deaconess. Being dragged before the tribunal and interrogated by the prefect as to her motives in setting fire to the church, she replied, "My past life ought to avert all suspicion from me, for I have devoted my large property to the reconstruction and embellishment of the temples of God."

The prefect alleged that he was well acquainted with her past course of life. "Then," continued she, "you ought to appear as our accuser instead of sitting as our judge." As the accusation against her was wholly unsubstantiated by proofs, and as the prefect found that he had no ground on which he could justly blame her, he adopted another tone, and as if desirous of advising her, represented to her and the other ladies that it was absurd in them to secede from communion with their bishop and thereby to entail trouble upon themselves. They all deferred to the advice of the prefect with the exception of Olympias, who said to him, "It is not just that after having been publicly calumniated without having had anything proved against me, I should be obliged to clear myself of charges totally unconnected with the accusation in question. Let me rather take counsel concerning the original accusation that has been preferred against me. For even if you resort to unlawful compulsion, I will not hold communion with those from whom I ought to secede, nor consent to anything that is contrary to the principles of piety."

The prefect, finding that he could not prevail upon her to hold communion with Arsacius, dismissed her that she might consult the advocates. On another occasion, however, he again sent for her and condemned her to pay a heavy fine, for he imagined that by this means she would be compelled to change her mind. But she totally disregarded the loss of her property and quitted Constantinople for Cyzicus.

Tigris, a presbyter, was about the same period stripped of his clothes, scourged on the back, bound hand and foot, and stretched on the rack. He was a foreigner and a eunuch but not by birth. He was originally a slave in the house of a man of rank and on account of his faithful services had obtained his freedom. He was afterwards ordained as presbyter and was distinguished by his moderation and meekness of disposition, and by his charity towards strangers and the poor. Such were the events which took place in Constantinople.

Siricius died after having governed the church of Rome fifteen years. Anastasius held the same bishopric three years and then died and was succeeded by Innocent. Flavian, who refused to consent to the deposition of John, was also dead, and Porphyry, being appointed to succeed him in the bishopric of Antioch, signed the condemnation of John. Many seceded on this account from communion with him, and hence a cruel persecution was commenced against them in Syria. Those who were in power at court procured a law in favor of Arsacius, Porphyry, and Theophilus, bishop of Alexandria, by which it was enacted[2] that the orthodox were to assemble together in churches only, and that if they seceded from communion with the above-mentioned bishops, they were to be exiled.

NOTES

1. The ἀναγνῶσται were sometimes called "Psaltæ" and "Lectores."
2. This law is extant in the *Theodosian Code*, Book 16, Title *de his qui de religione contendunt*. See Baronius, *Ecclesiastical Annals*, AD 404, Chapter 54, etc.

CHAPTER XXV

TROUBLES IN THE CHURCH FOLLOWED BY DISTURBANCES IN THE STATE. STILICHO, THE GENERAL OF HONORIUS.

About this period[1] the dissensions by which the church was agitated were followed, as is frequently the case, by commotions in the state. The Huns crossed the Danube and devastated Thrace. A band of robbers from Isauria ravaged cities and villages as far as Caria and Phœnicia. Stilicho, the most powerful general of his time, commanded the troops of Honorius and had under his sway the flower of the Roman and of the barbarian soldiery. Conceiving feelings of enmity against the rulers who held office under Arcadius, he determined to sow the seeds of dissension between the two empires. He caused Alaric, the leader of the

Goths, to be appointed by Honorius to the command of the Roman troops and sent him into[2] Illyria, whither also he despatched Jovian, the prætorian prefect, and promised to join them there with military forces in order to add that province to the dominions of Honorius. Alaric marched at the head of his troops from the barbarous regions bordering on Dalmatia and Pannonia to Epirus, and after passing some time in waiting the arrival of Stilicho, returned to Italy. Stilicho was prevented from fulfilling his agreement of joining Alaric by some letters which were transmitted to him from Honorius.

NOTES

1. With this chapter compare the parallel account given by Zosimus, *History*, Book V, page 802, etc.
2. This passage has been wrongly rendered by commentators. We have followed the emendation of Valesius, who quotes in his support the passage of Sozomen above, Book IV, Chapter 9.

CHAPTER XXVI

TWO EPISTLES FROM INNOCENT, THE POPE OF ROME, OF WHICH ONE WAS ADDRESSED TO JOHN CHRYSOSTOM, AND THE OTHER TO THE CLERGY OF CONSTANTINOPLE.

Innocent, bishop of Rome,[1] was extremely indignant when apprized of the measures that had been adopted against John and condemned the whole proceedings. He then turned his attention to the convocation of an œcumenical council and wrote to John and to the clergy of Constantinople. Subjoined are the two letters, precisely as I found them, translated from the Latin into Greek.

Innocent, to the beloved brother John.

Although one conscious of his own innocence ought to expect every blessing and to look for the mercy of God, yet it seems well to us to write to you by Cyriacus, the deacon, and to exhort you to patience lest the contumely cast upon you should have more power in subduing your courage than the testimony of a good conscience in encouraging you to hope. It is not requisite to remind you, who are the teacher and pastor of so great a people, that God often tries the best of men and puts their patience to the severest tests, and that they are firmly supported under the most adverse occurrences that can befall them by the approving voice of conscience. He who does not triumph over calamity by patience, is necessarily regarded with suspicion, for either his trust is not firm in God or his own conscience condemns him. A good man may be sorely tried but he cannot be overcome, for he is preserved and guarded by the truths of Holy Scripture. The Holy Bible, which we expound to the people, affords abundant examples of the afflictions to which the saints have been invariably subjected and shows that they did not receive their crowns till they had passed with patience through the severest trials.

Take courage, then, O honored brother, from the testimony of your conscience, for virtue affords support in calamity. When you have been purified by affliction, you will enter into the haven of peace in the presence of Christ our Lord."

Innocent, the bishop, to the Presbyters, Deacons, and all the Clergy, and to the people of Constantinople under the episcopal guidance of John. Peace be unto you, beloved brethren.

From the letters that you forwarded to me through Germanus the presbyter and Cassius the deacon, I have been made acquainted with the scenes of evil that have been enacted before your eyes and have learnt how great has been the trial of faith among you. In such circumstances there is no remedy but patience. Our God will shortly put an end to such sufferings, and they will eventually tend to your profit. But I read with much pleasure several remarks at the commencement of your letter on the necessity of patience in affliction and find that you have there anticipated the consolation which we ought to have conveyed to you in our letter. Our Lord gives to his servants the power of procuring consolation for themselves in tribulation by the reflection that like afflictions were endured by the saints. And even we ourselves derive comfort from your letters, for we are not insensible to your sufferings, but suffer with you.

Who, indeed, can endure to witness the disorders introduced by those who were bound to preserve peace and concord? But far from maintaining peace, they expel guiltless bishops from their own churches. John, our brother and fellow-minister and your bishop has been the first to suffer this unjust treatment without being allowed to speak in his own defense. No accusation was brought against him, nor was anything permitted to be advanced in his justification. What proceedings could be more contrary to reason than to give, without the formality of investigation or the shadow of justice, successors to living priests? Those who by such iniquitous measures have been appointed to their bishoprics, cannot surely be held in estimation in the church. Our fathers never acted in any way that could authorize so audacious a step but, on the contrary, prohibited it by enacting that no one should ever be ordained during the lifetime of a bishop as his successor.[2] It is not possible that by so illegal an ordination a bishop can be excluded from his office, or that the dignity can be transferred to the person unjustly appointed to supplant him.

Book VIII, Chapter XXVI

With respect to the observance of canons, we declare that those established at Nicæa are alone[3] entitled to the obedience of the Catholic church. If any individuals should attempt to introduce other canons at variance with those of Nicæa, and the compilation of heretics, such canons ought to be rejected by the Catholic church, for it is not lawful to add the inventions of heretics[4] to the Catholic canons. Attempts are always being made by adversaries to subvert the objects aimed at by the fathers of Nicæa. We say, then, that the canons we have censured are not only to be disregarded, but to be condemned with the dogmas of heretics and schismatics, even as they have been already condemned at the council of Sardica by the bishops who were our predecessors. For it would be better, O honored brethren, to condemn laudable enactments, than to establish any decrees that are contrary to the canons.

What measures ought we to adopt under these adverse circumstances? It is necessary, as we have before said, to convene a council. There are no other means of arresting the fury of the tempest. Until a council can be assembled, it will be well to await the manifestation of the will of the Great God and of our Lord Christ. We shall thus behold the cessation of all the woes which have been excited by the malice of the devil and which have served as trials for our faith. If we remain firm in the faith, there is nothing that we ought not to expect from our Lord. We are constantly watching for the opportunity of convening an œcumenical council, whereby in accordance with the will of God, an end may be put to trouble and dissension. Let us, then, wait till this can be accomplished, and being supported by patience, let us trust in the goodness of God for the restoration of order.

We had previously been made acquainted with all that you have related concerning your trials by our fellow-bishops, Demetrius, Cyriacus, Eleusius, and Paladius,[5] who visited Rome at different periods, and while they were with us, we carefully inquired into all the details of the case.

NOTES

1. He succeeded to the papal chair AD 402. Chrysostom appealed to him on being ejected from his see and was restored by him.
2. Innocent probably here alludes to the 8th canon of the council of Nicæa.
3. Hence it is clear that the Roman church, at the commencement of the fifth century, had received only the Nicene canons, of course with those of Sardica added by way of appendix. The same church also at this time held only to the Nicene creed as sufficient.
4. This is not to be understood as if all of those who put together the Antiochian canons were heretics, but only that some of them were such. Pope Julius bears witness to this effect in his epistle to the oriental bishops quoted by Athanasius in his Second *Apology against the Arians*.

5. These four bishops were among those afterwards sent on an embassy to the emperor Arcadius by Pope Innocent. See below, Chapter 28.

CHAPTER XXVII

DEATH OF THE EMPRESS EUDOXIA. DEATH OF ARSACIUS. HISTORY OF ATTICUS THE PATRIARCH.

From these two letters of Innocent, the opinion which he entertained of John may readily be inferred.

About the same period some hailstones of extraordinary magnitude fell at Constantinople and in the suburbs of the city.[1] Four days afterwards, the wife of the emperor died. These occurrences were by many regarded as indications of Divine wrath on account of the persecution that had been carried on against John. For Cyrinus, bishop of Chalcedonia, one of his principal calumniators, had not long previously terminated his life in the midst of great bodily agony arising from the accident that had occurred to his foot, and the consequent necessary amputation of the leg.

Arsacius, too, died after he had presided but a very short period over the church of Constantinople. Many candidates were proposed as successors to his bishopric, and four months after his decease, Atticus, a presbyter of the clergy of Constantinople and one of the enemies of John, was ordained over the church. He was a native of Sebaste in Armenia. He had been instructed from his youth in the principle of monastic philosophy by some monks of the Macedonian sect. These monks, who then enjoyed a very high reputation at Sebaste, had been the disciples of Eustathius, to whom allusion has been already made as an exemplary bishop and a president of monastic establishments. When Atticus attained the age of manhood, he embraced the tenets of the Catholic church. He possessed more natural gifts than literary attainments, evinced considerable aptitude for the management of affairs, and was as skillful in carrying on intrigues as in evading the machinations of others. He was of a very engaging disposition, and was generally beloved. The discourses which he delivered in the church did not rise above mediocrity, and although not totally devoid of erudition, were not accounted by his auditors of sufficient value to be preserved in writing. When he had leisure and opportunity, he studied the writings of ancient authors, but he made little display of acquaintance with their works in conversation or disputation, and was not, therefore, considered a learned man. It is said that he manifested much zeal in behalf of those who entertained the same sentiments as himself, and that he rendered himself formidable to his opponents. But while he inspired them with dread, he never failed to treat them with lenity. Such is the information which we have gathered concerning this bishop.

John acquired great celebrity even in the place of his exile. He possessed ample pecuniary resources, and being besides liberally supplied with money by Olympias the deaconess, and others, he purchased the liberty of many captives in Isauria and restored them to their families. He also administered to the necessities of many who were in want, and by his kind words comforted those who did not stand in need of money. He was hence exceedingly beloved, not only in Armenia where he dwelt, but by all the people of the neighboring countries and the inhabitants of Antioch and of the other parts of Syria, and of Cilicia frequently sought his society.

NOTE

1. Compare Socrates, *Ecclesiastical History,* Book VI, Chapters 19, 20.

CHAPTER XXVIII

EFFORTS OF INNOCENT, BISHOP OF ROME, TO CONVENE A COUNCIL AND PROCURE THE RECALL OF JOHN. DEATH OF JOHN CHRYSOSTOM.

Innocent, bishop of Rome, was very anxious, as appears by his letters, to procure the recall of John.[1] He sent five bishops and two presbyters with the bishops[2] who had not returned from the East, to the emperors Honorius and Arcadius to request the convocation of a council and solicit them to name the time and place. The enemies of John at Constantinople brought the embassy into disrepute by their calumnies and caused the ambassadors to be ignominiously dismissed under the pretext that indignity had been offered to the emperor of the East. John was at the same time condemned by an imperial edict to a remoter place of banishment, and soldiers were sent to conduct him to Pityuntum, the spot appointed by the emperor. It is said that during this journey, Basilicus the martyr appeared to him at Comana in Armenia, and apprized him of the time of his death. Being attacked with pain in the head and being unable to bear the heat of the sun, he could not prosecute his journey but closed his life in this town.

NOTES

1. Compare Socrates, *Ecclesiastical History,* Book VI, Chapter 21.
2. See above, note on Chapter 26.

BOOK IX

CHAPTER I
DEATH OF ARCADIUS. ACCESSION OF THEODOSIUS THE YOUNGER. PIETY, VIRTUE, VIRGINITY, AND GOOD WORKS OF THE PRINCESS PULCHERIA.

Such are the details that have been transmitted concerning John. Not long after his death and three years after the elevation of Atticus to the bishopric of Constantinople and during the consulate of Bassus and Philip, Arcadius died. He left Theodosius his son,[1] who was still an infant, as his successor to the empire. He also left three daughters of tender age, named Pulcheria, Arcadia, and Marina.

It appears to me that it was the design of God to show by the events of this period that piety alone suffices for the safety and prosperity of princes, and that without piety, armies, a powerful empire, and political resources are of no avail. He who alone regulates the affairs of the universe, foresaw that the young emperor would be distinguished by his piety, and therefore caused his education to be conducted by his sister Pulcheria. This princess was but fifteen years of age, but was endowed with astonishing wisdom and prudence. She devoted her virginity to God and instructed her sisters to do likewise. To avoid all cause of scandal and opportunity for intrigue, she permitted no man to enter her palace. In confirmation of her resolution, she took God, the priests, and all the subjects of the Roman empire as witnesses of her self-dedication, and presented a table, elaborately adorned with gold and precious stones, to the church of Constantinople, in token of the life of virginity to which she and her sisters had devoted themselves, and a suitable inscription was carved on the table.

She superintended with extraordinary wisdom the transactions of the Roman government, concerted her measures well, and allowed no delay to take place in their execution. She was able to write and to converse with perfect accuracy in the Greek and Latin languages. She caused all affairs to be transacted in the name of her brother, and devoted great attention to furnishing him with such information as was suitable to his years. She employed masters to instruct him in horsemanship and the use of arms, and in literature and science. But he was taught how to maintain a deportment befitting an emperor by his sister. She showed him how to gather up his robes and how to take a seat, and taught him to refrain from ill-timed laughter, to assume a mild or a formidable aspect as the occasion might require, and to inquire with urbanity into the cases of those who came before him with petitions. But she chiefly strove to imbue his mind with piety and with the love of prayer. She taught him to frequent the church regularly, and to be zealous in contributing to the embellishment of houses of prayer, and she inspired him with reverence for priests and other good men and for those who, in accordance with the law of Christianity, had devoted themselves to philosophical asceticism.

Many troubles which would have been excited in the church at this period by the influence of erroneous opinions, were averted by her zeal and vigilance. It is mainly owing to her prudence, as we shall have occasion to show in the afterpart of this history, that we are at the present time preserved from new heresies. It would take a long time to describe the magnificent houses of prayer which she erected, the hospitals for the relief of the poor and of strangers which she founded, and the monastical establishments which she endowed. If any one should doubt my statements, and desire to inquire into their truth, he will discover that I have been guilty neither of falsehood nor of partiality, if he will examine the registers kept by the treasurers of the princess. If these proofs suffice not to convince him of the truth, let him believe the testimony vouchsafed by God himself, for he heard and answered her prayers, and on many occasions bestowed on her the knowledge of future events. Such indications of Divine love are not conferred upon men unless they have merited them by their good works. But I must pass over in silence the manifestations of Divine favor that were granted to the sister of the emperor, lest I should be condemned as a mere panegyrist. One incident relating to her is, however, so connected with my history, that I shall now proceed to detail it, although it did not occur till a period subsequent to that which we are now reviewing.

NOTE

1. Compare Socrates, *Ecclesiastical History,* Book VI, Chapter 23.

CHAPTER II

DISCOVERY OF THE REMAINS OF FORTY HOLY MARTYRS.

A woman by name Eusebia, who was a deaconess of the Macedonian sect, had a house and garden without the walls of Constantinople, in which she kept the holy remains of forty soldiers[1] who had suffered martyrdom under Licinius, at Sebaste in Armenia. When she felt death approaching, she bequeathed the aforesaid property to some orthodox monks and bound them by oath to place the relics of the martyrs in her coffin above her head, without apprizing anyone of the circumstance. The monks fulfilled their promise, but in order to render due honor to the martyrs and at the same time to keep the affair a secret, they formed a subterranean house of prayer beneath the spot where they had interred Eusebia. Above this chapel they erected a small edifice, with the flooring so contrived as to furnish a secret means of access to the relics of the martyrs, which were preserved beneath.

Soon after, Cæsar, a man of high rank, who had formerly been consul and prefect, lost his wife and caused her to be interred near the tomb of Eusebia, for the two ladies had been knit together by the most tender friendship, and had been of one mind on all doctrinal and religious subjects. Cæsar was hence induced to purchase the whole of the adjacent spot of ground, for he desired to erect a sepulchre for himself close to that of his wife. After having disposed of the property, the monks went elsewhere without divulging the concealment of the holy relics. Cæsar ordered the building to be demolished, and the ground to be cleared in order to erect a magnificent temple in honor of Thrysus the martyr on the spot. It appears probable that God permitted the demolition of this building in order that the discovery of the relics of the martyrs, after so long a period of concealment, might be regarded as a marvellous and auspicious event and as a proof of the Divine favor towards the discoverer.

The discoverer was, in fact, no other than Pulcheria the sister of the emperor. Thrysus, the martyr, appeared to her three times and revealed to her that the relics of the martyrs were concealed beneath the earth and commanded that they should be deposited near his tomb, in order that the same honor might be rendered to them that was rendered to him. The forty martyrs themselves also appeared to her arrayed in shining robes and made the same communication to her. But the occurrence seemed too marvellous to be credible, for the aged of the clergy of that region, after having prosecuted numerous inquiries, had always failed in gathering any information concerning the relics of the martyrs. At length, when all further researches had been abandoned as futile Polychronius, a certain presbyter who had formerly been a servant in the household of Cæsar, was reminded by God that the locality in question had once been inhabited by monks. He therefore went to the clergy of the Macedonian sect to inquire concerning them. All the monks were dead with the exception of one, who seemed to have been preserved in life for the express purpose of pointing out the spot where the relics of the holy martyrs were concealed. Polychronius questioned him closely on the subject, and finding that on account of the promise made to Eusebia his answers were reserved and unintelligible, he made known to him the revelation that had been vouchsafed to Pulcheria, and her consequent anxiety for further information. The monk then confessed that he remembered that in his youth when he was first entering on the course of monastic discipline under the instructions of the superiors of the monastery, the relics of the martyrs had been deposited near the tomb of Eusebia, but that the subsequent lapse of time and the changes which had been carried on in that locality, deprived him of the power of recalling to his recollection whether the relics had been deposited beneath the church or in any other spot. "I remember," replied Polychronius, "that I was present at the interment of the wife of Cæsar and, as well as I can judge from the relative situation of the high road, I infer that she must have been buried beneath the pulpit[2] where the desk of the readers now stands."

"Then," exclaimed the monk, "it must be near the remains of Cæsar's wife that the tomb of Eusebia must be sought, for the two ladies lived on terms of the closest friendship and intimacy and mutually agreed to be interred beside each other."

When it was intimated to the princess that the holy relics were deposited underground, she[3] commanded the work of disinterment to be forthwith commenced. On removing the earth near the pulpit of the church, the coffin of Cæsar's wife was discovered according to the conjecture of Polychronius. At a short distance they found a pavement of bricks placed transversely, and a marble tomb of equal dimensions, in which was the coffin of Eusebia, and close by was an elegant oratory constructed of white and purple marble. The upper part of the tomb was in the form of an altar, and at the summit where the relics were deposited, a small orifice[4] was visible. A man attached to the palace who happened to be standing by, thrust a cane which he held in his hand into the orifice, and on withdrawing the cane the most delightful fragrance was diffused around, which inspired the workmen and bystanders with fresh confidence. When the coffin was opened, the remains of Eusebia were found, and near her head was discovered the coffer, firmly bound on each side with bars of iron and lead. A small aperture at the top of the coffer clearly revealed the fact of the relics being concealed within.

As soon as the discovery was announced, the princess and the bishop ran to the church of the martyr[5] and sent for smiths to unfasten the iron bars and open the coffer. A great many perfumes were found within, and among the perfumes were two silver caskets containing the holy relics. The princess returned thanks to God for the discovery of the relics, and for having accounted her worthy of being the discoverer. She then caused the relics to be deposited in a most splendid vase and placed with the utmost pomp and ceremony beside the remains of Saint Thrysus. I myself was present at this gorgeous spectacle, and others who were present can also bear testimony to the grandeur of the festival, for it occurred at no great distance of time, but during the period that Proculus governed the church of Constantinople.

NOTES

1. The names of the Forty Martyrs (for such is the name under which they are commemorated) maybe seen in Theodore Ruinart, *Acta Primorum Martyrum Sincera et Selecta*, page 581, and in the *Lives* of the Bollandists. They suffered martyrdom under Licinius at Sebaste in Armenia, about AD 320. The finest homily on the Forty Martyrs extant is that by Saint Basil.
2. ἀμβών. "Latini pulpitum vocant, quod medium est inter altare et capsum ecclesiae." The term is derived from the Greek word ἀναβαίνειν, ascendere. Valesius remarks that only priests and martyrs and founders of churches were usually buried within the choir near the altar, the laity being buried outside the city in cemeteries.
3. It would have been sacrilege, as Valesius remarks, to have attempted to do this without her command.
4. τρύπημα μικρόν. Probably for the purpose of letting down handkerchiefs, etc., to touch the remains of the deceased.
5. Called in Greek μαρτύριον, and in Latin *confessio*.

CHAPTER III

THE VIRTUES AND PIETY OF PULCHERIA AND OF HER SISTERS.

It is said that God on many occasions revealed future events to Pulcheria and conferred on her and on her sisters many special indications of favor. They all pursue the same mode of life. They are sedulous in their attendance in the house of prayer and evince great charity towards strangers and the poor. These sisters generally take their meals and walks together and pass their days and their nights together in singing the praises of God. Like other exemplary women, they employ themselves in weaving and in similar occupations. Although of royal birth and educated in palaces, they avoid idleness as unworthy of the life of virginity to which they have devoted themselves. The favor of God has been, for their sakes, manifested towards their family and the state and the emperor in proportion, as he has grown in years, has increased in power, while all seditions and wars undertaking against him have spontaneously come to nought.

CHAPTER IV

TRUCE WITH PERSIA. HONORIUS AND STILICHO. TRANSACTIONS IN ROME AND DALMATIA.[1]

Although the Persians had prepared to take up arms, they were induced to conclude a truce with the Romans for a hundred years.

Stilicho, the general of the troops of Honorius, was suspected of having conspired to raise his son Eucherius to the throne of the Eastern empire, and was in consequence slain by the army at Ravenna. He had, at a former period, conceived bitter feelings of enmity against the chiefs of the troops of Arcadius, and was hence impelled to sow the seeds of division between the two empires. He caused Alaric, the leader of the Goths, to be invested with the command of the troops of Honorius and advised him to seize Illyria and, at the same time, he appointed Jovian prefect[2] of that province and sent him thither, promising to join him shortly with some Roman legions and to take possession of Illyria in the name of Honorius. Alaric quitted the barbarous region bordering on Dalmatia and Pannonia where he had been dwelling, and marched at the head of his soldiery to Epirus. After remaining for some time in that country, he retreated to Italy without having accomplished anything.

After the death of Arcadius, Honorius projected a journey to Constantinople for the purpose of appointing ministers in whose fidelity confidence might be placed, and who might be trusted to watch over the security and maintain the power of his nephew. But when Honorius was on the very point of setting out on this journey, Stilicho dissuaded him from his design by proving to him that his presence was requisite in Italy to repress the schemes of Constantine, who sought to possess himself of the sovereign power at Arles. Stilicho then took one of the Roman standards, obtained some letters from the emperor with which he set out at the head of four legions to carry on war in the East. But a report having been spread that he had conspired against the emperor and had formed a scheme in conjunction with those in power to raise his son[3] to the throne, the troops rose up in sedition and slew the prætorian prefect[4] of Italy and of Gaul, the military commanders, and the chief officers of the court. Stilicho himself was slain by the soldiers at Ravenna. He had attained almost absolute power, and all men, so to speak, whether Romans or barbarians, were under his control. Thus perished Stilicho on a suspicion of having conspired against the emperors. Eucherius, his son, was slain with him.

NOTES

1. *Note to the 2018 edition:* Here begins a shift in Sozomen's focus from Eastern ecclesiastical affairs to the evolving Western political crisis. It is posited by Rohrbacher in *The Historians of Late Antiquity* that Sozomen's main source for this section is the *History* of Olympiodorus of Thebes. As the work of Olympiodorus exists today only in scattered fragments, this section of political history in Sozomen is therefore particularly valuable.
2. See Cassiodorus, *Historia Ecclesiastica Tripartita,* Book X, 24.
3. Zosimus says the same, *History,* Book V, page 808.
4. His name was Longianus.

CHAPTER V

NUMEROUS NATIONS TAKE UP ARMS AGAINST THE ROMANS, OF WHOM SOME ARE, THROUGH THE PROVIDENCE OF GOD, DISPERSED, AND OTHERS BROUGHT TO TERMS OF AMITY.

It happened about the same time that the Huns who were encamped in Thrace suddenly took to flight, although they had neither been attacked nor pursued.

Uldis, the leader of some barbarous tribes who dwell near the Danube, crossed that river at the head of a large army and encamped on the frontiers of Thrace. He took possession of a city of Mœsia, called Castra Martis, and thence made incursions in Thrace and insolently refused to enter into terms of alliance with the Romans. The prefect of the Thracian cohorts made propositions of peace to him, but he replied by pointing to the sun and declaring that it would be easy to him, if he desired to do so, to subjugate every region of the earth that is enlightened by that luminary. But while Uldis was uttering menaces of this description and even threatening to impose a tribute on the Romans, God gave manifest proofs of special favor towards the emperor. For shortly afterwards, the immediate attendants and chief officers of Uldis were discussing the Roman form of government, the philanthropy of the emperor, and his promptitude in rewarding merit, when they suddenly formed the resolution of ranging themselves under the Roman banners. Finding himself thus abandoned, Uldis escaped with difficulty to the opposite bank of the river. Many of his troops were slain, and among others, a barbarous tribe called the Sciri. This tribe had previously been very strong in point of numbers, but being pursued and overtaken when vainly endeavoring to effect an escape, many of its members were cut to pieces and others were taken prisoners and conveyed in chains to Constantinople. The governors were of opinion that if allowed to remain together, they would probably combine and create a sedition. Some of them were, therefore, sold at a low price, while others were given away as slaves upon condition that they should never be permitted to return to Constantinople, or to Europe, but be conveyed across the sea. I have seen several of these slaves employed in cultivating the earth in Bithynia, near Mount Olympus.

CHAPTER VI

ALARIC, KING OF THE GOTHS. SIEGE OF ROME.

Thus was the Eastern empire preserved from the evils of war[1] and governed with consummate prudence contrary to all expectations, for the emperor was still in extreme youth.

In the meantime, the Western empire fell a prey to disorders and to the domination of tyrants. After the death of Stilicho, Alaric, king of the Goths, sent an embassy to Honorius to treat of peace, but as his terms were rejected, he laid siege to Rome, and by posting a large army of barbarians on the banks of the Tiber, he effectually prevented the transmission of all provisions from the port to the city. After the siege had lasted some time, and fearful ravages had been made in the city by famine and pestilence, many of the slaves and most of the foreigners within the walls went forth to Alaric. Those among the senators who still adhered to Pagan superstition proposed to offer sacrifice in the Capitol and the other temples, and certain Etrurians, who were summoned by the prefect of the city promised to launch thunder and lightning and disperse the barbarians. They boasted of having performed a similar exploit at Narni,[2] a city of Tuscany. Events, however, proved the futility of these propositions.[3]

All persons of sense were aware that the calamities which this siege entailed upon the Romans were indications of Divine wrath sent to chastise them for their luxury, their debauchery, and their manifold acts of injustice towards each other as well as towards strangers. It is said that when Alaric was marching against Rome, a monk of Italy besought him to spare the city and not to become the author of so many calamities. Alaric, in reply, assured him that he did not feel disposed to commence the siege, but found himself compelled by some hidden and irresistible impulse to accomplish the enterprise. While he was besieging the city, the inhabitants presented many gifts to him as inducements to abandon the undertaking and promised to persuade the emperor to enter into a treaty of peace with him.

NOTES

1. Compare Socrates, *Ecclesiastical History,* Book VII, Chapter 10.
2. Otherwise called Nevia and Larnia.
3. *Note to the 2018 edition:* Modern scholars believe that Sozomen took this mention of the pagan adherents from the *History* of Olympiodorus. It is also believed that the more detailed account of this event contained in Zosimus also derives from Olympiodorus. See Zosimus's *History*, Book V, and Dunn: "Innocent, Alaric, and Honorius: Church and State in Early Fifth-Century Rome," in Luckensmeyer: *Studies of Religion and Politics in the Early Christian Centuries*, page 250.

CHAPTER VII

DEPUTATION SENT TO ALARIC BY INNOCENT, BISHOP OF ROME. JOVIUS, PREFECT OF ITALY. EMBASSY DESPATCHED TO THE EMPEROR.

Although ambassadors were despatched to treat of peace, the enemies of Alaric at the court of the emperor sedulously guarded against the conclusion of any treaty with him. But as an embassy was sent to him by Innocent, bishop of Rome, and as an imperial edict reached him about the same time, summoning him to appear before the emperor, Alaric repaired to the city of Ariminum, which is two hundred and ten stadia distant from Ravenna. He encamped beyond the walls of the city and Jovius, the prætorian prefect of Italy, held a conference with him and conveyed his demands to the emperor, one of which was that he might be appointed to the generalship of the cavalry and infantry. The emperor gave full power to Jovius to grant Alaric as much money and corn as he might desire, but firmly refused to confer the military dignity to which he aspired.

Jovius waited in the camp of Alaric the return of the messenger who had been despatched to the emperor, and had the imprudence to cause the imperial reply to be read aloud in the presence of all the barbarians. On finding that the appointment he had demanded was denied him, Alaric ordered the trumpets to be sounded, and marched towards Rome. Jovius, apprehensive of being suspected of siding with Alaric, committed a still greater act of imprudence by taking an oath on the safety of the emperor and compelling the principal officers to swear that they would never consent to any terms of peace with Alaric. The barbarian chief, however, soon after changed his mind and sent word he did not desire any post of rank or dignity, but was willing to act as an ally of the Romans, provided that they would grant him a certain quantity of corn and some territory of secondary importance to them, in which he might establish himself.[1]

NOTES

1. *Note to the 2018 edition:* The account of this embassy of Pope Innocent I to the western emperor Honorius appears to be unique to Sozomen. See Dunn: "Innocent, Alaric, and Honorius: Church and State in Early Fifth-Century Rome," in Luckensmeyer: *Studies of Religion and Politics in the Early Christian Centuries*, page 257.

CHAPTER VIII

REBELLION OF ATTALUS, AND HOW HE EVENTUALLY CRAVES FORGIVENESS AT THE FEET OF HONORIUS.

After having sent some bishops as ambassadors on two different occasions to treat on this subject but without effect, Alaric returned to Rome, raised the siege, took possession of the port, and compelled the inhabitants of Rome to recognize Attalus, then prefect of the city, as their sovereign.[1] The other officers of rank were then distributed. Alaric was appointed general of the cavalry and infantry, and Ataulphus, his brother-in-law, was raised to the command of the force called the domestic cavalry. Attalus assembled the senators, and addressed them in a long and elaborate discourse, in which he promised to restore the ancient honors of the senate, and also to bring Egypt and the other Eastern provinces under the sway of Italy. Such was the vanity of a man who was not destined to bear the name of sovereign during the space of a single year. He was deceived by the representations of some diviners who assured him that he would be able to conquer Africa without striking a single blow. Under the influence of this false impression, he neglected the advice of Alaric, who urged him to send a moderate supply of troops to Carthage to slay the officers of Honorius, in case of their attempting any resistance. He also refused to follow the counsels of John, whom he had raised to military command and who advised him to intrust Constans, on his proposed departure for Africa, with an edict[1] drawn up in the name of Honorius, by which Heraclean might be dispossessed of the command of the troops in Africa. Had this artifice been adopted, it would probably have proved successful, for the designs of Attalus were unknown in Africa. But as soon as Constans had set sail for Carthage, Attalus, who labored under the delusive idea that Africa would, according to the assurances of the diviners, soon acknowledge his authority, marched at the head of his army towards Ravenna.[2]

When it was announced that Attalus had reached Ariminum with an army, composed partly of Roman and partly of barbarian troops, Honorius wrote to him to acknowledge him as emperor and deputed the highest officers of his court to wait upon him and offer him a share in the government. Attalus, however, refused to share the imperial power with another, and sent word that Honorius might choose an island or spot of ground in any region for his residence, and that he might retain in this retirement the outward honors of sovereignty. The affairs of Honorius were reduced to so critical a condition that ships were kept in readiness to convey him to the Eastern court that he might implore aid of his nephew, when an army of four thousand men arrived unexpectedly during the night at Ravenna from the East. Honorius caused the walls of the city to be guarded by this reinforcement, for he distrusted the troops of Italy, and believed them to be inclined to treachery.

In the meantime, Heraclean had put Constans to death, and had ranged troops along the shores and ports of Africa to put a stop to all traffic with Rome. The Romans were in consequence exposed to the horrors of famine, and in this extremity they sent to request assistance of Attalus. Being at a loss what measures to adopt, he returned to Rome to consult the senate. The famine was so grievous that chestnuts were used to supply the place of corn, and many persons were suspected of having partaken of human flesh. Alaric advised that five hundred barbarians should be sent into Africa against Heraclean, but the senators and Attalus objected to intrust an expedition of this nature to them. It then became evident to Alaric that God disapproved of Attalus, and finding that it would be futile to make any further attempts to maintain his power, he entered into negotiations with Honorius to deprive him of his sovereignty. All the parties concerned assembled together without the walls of the city, and Attalus threw aside the symbols of imperial power. His officers stripped themselves of their girdles, and they all joined together in imploring forgiveness of Honorius for the past. He granted them permission to retain their rank and honors. Attalus retired with his son to Alaric, for he thought his life would not be in safety if he continued to dwell among the Romans.[3]

NOTES

1. Compare Socrates, *Ecclesiastical History,* Book VII, Chapter 10.
2. γράμμα. Valesius would render it by "preceptum."
3. *Note to the 2018 edition:* Compare also Zosimus, *History,* Book VI.

CHAPTER IX

PRESUMPTUOUS EXPECTATIONS ENTERTAINED BY THE PAGANS AND ARIANS CONCERNING ATTALUS. ALARIC, BY A STRATAGEM, OBTAINS POSSESSION OF ROME.

The failure which had attended the designs of Attalus was a source of deep displeasure to the Pagans and the Christians of the Arian denomination. The Pagans had inferred from the known predilections and early education of Attalus that he would openly maintain their superstitions and restore their ancient temples, their festivals, and their altars. The Arians imagined that as soon as he found himself firmly established in the possession of power, Attalus would reinstate them in the supremacy over the churches which they had enjoyed during the reigns of Constantius and of Valens, for he had been baptized by Sigesarius,[1] bishop of the Goths, to the great satisfaction of Alaric and the Arian party.

Soon after, Alaric stationed himself among the Alps,[2] at a distance of about sixty stadia from Ravenna, and held a conference with the emperor concerning the conclusion of a peace. Saros, a barbarian by birth, imagining that any treaty formed between the Romans and the Goths would militate against his own private interests, rushed upon Alaric with an army only three hundred strong, but composed of chosen and valiant men. Many of the Goths fell in this encounter and impelled by rage and terror, Alaric retraced his steps and returned to Rome, and the city was betrayed into his hands. He permitted his followers to seize the wealth of the citizens and to plunder the houses, but from respect towards the apostle Peter, he prohibited the desecration of the large and beautiful church erected around his tomb. This prohibition was the only cause which prevented the entire demolition of Rome, for many had taken refuge within the church, and being permitted to escape with their lives, they undertook to rebuild their city.[3]

NOTES

1. He is mentioned by Olympiodorus as having endeavored in vain to rescue the sons of the king of the Goths from death.
2. Another reading is "Classen," meaning the port of Ravenna, which was called Classis, but the distance does not agree.
3. *Note to the 2018 edition:* Zosimus provides a sparse account of the sack of Rome in his *History,* Book VI. This was probably derived from Olympiodorus. Procopius, writing over a century later, offers a few additional details. See *History of the Wars,* Book III, Chapter 2.

CHAPTER X
VIRTUE OF A ROMAN LADY.

It is obvious that the capture of so great a city as Rome must have been attended with many remarkable circumstances. I shall therefore now proceed to the narration of such events as seem worthy of a place in ecclesiastical history.

I shall recount a pious action performed by a barbarian and record the fortitude and chastity of a Roman lady. The barbarian and the lady were both Christians, but belonged to different sects, the former being an Arian and the latter a zealous follower of the Nicene doctrines. The lady was very beautiful, and the barbarian above-mentioned, who was a young man and a soldier in the army of Alaric, was dazzled by her extreme loveliness and attempted to offer her violence. As she, however, exerted all her strength and resisted his designs, he drew his sword and threatened to slay her but he was restrained by the passion which he entertained towards her, and merely inflicted a slight wound on her neck. The blood flowed in abundance, and the lady meekly waited to receive her deathblow, for she preferred death to the violation of her chastity and duty towards her husband. The barbarian redoubled his efforts, but finding that they availed nothing, he was at length struck with wonder and admiration at her chastity. He conducted her to the church of Peter the Apostle and gave six pieces of gold to the officers who were guarding the church, commanding them to take care of her and to restore her in safety to her husband.

CHAPTER XI
MANY INSTANCES OF REBELLION AND USURPATION OCCUR IN THE WEST. THE FAVOR OF GOD MANIFESTED TOWARDS HONORIUS BY THE DEFEAT AND DEATH OF THE TYRANTS.

During this period, many persons rebelled against Honorius and seized the imperial authority in the West, but some of these tyrants were permitted to destroy each other, while others most unexpectedly fell under the power of the Roman arms, and in every case it was evidenced that the Divine favor rested in an especial manner upon Honorius.

The soldiers in Britain[1] were the first to rise up in sedition and they proclaimed Mark as tyrant. Afterwards, however, they slew Mark and proclaimed Gratian. Within four months subsequently they killed Gratian and elected Constantine in his place, imagining that on account of his name, he would be able to reduce the empire under his authority, and for no other reason than this, several other persons of the same name were advanced to power. Constantine passed over from Britain to Boulogne,[2] a maritime city of Gaul, and after inducing all the troops in Gaul and Aquitaine to espouse his cause, he reduced to obedience the inhabitants of the regions extending to the mountains which divide Italy from Gaul, and which the Romans have named the Cottian Alps. He then sent his eldest son, Constans, whom he had already nominated Cæsar and whom he afterwards proclaimed emperor, into Spain. Constans, after making himself master of this province and appointing governors over it, commanded that Didymus and Verinian, relatives of Honorius, should be loaded with chains and brought before him. Didymus and Verinian had long been on unfriendly terms, but a reconciliation was effected between them when they found themselves menaced by the same danger. They combined their forces, which consisted chiefly of armed peasants and slaves, committed some acts of hostility in Lusitania, attacked the troops that had been sent against them by the tyrant, and slew a great number of them.

NOTES

1. Zosimus, Book VI, page 824, relates the story in the same way. He is confirmed by the Venerable Bede, *Ecclesiastical History*, Book I, who says, "In the year of our Lord's Incarnation 407, Honorius, the younger son of Theodosius and the 44th from Augustus, being emperor two years before the invasion of Rome by Alaric, king of the Goths, when the nations of the Alani, Suevi, Vandals, and many others with them, having defeated the Franks and crossed the Rhine, ravaged all Gaul, Gratianus Municeps was set up as tyrant and killed. In his place, Constantine, one of the meanest soldiers, only for his name's sake and without any worth to recommend him, was chosen emperor. As soon as he had taken upon him the command, he passed over into France."
2. βουβονία, though others read βονωνία, Bononia.

CHAPTER XII

THEODOSIOLUS AND LAGODIUS. THE VANDALS AND SUEVI. DEATH OF ALANICUS. RETREAT OF THE TYRANTS CONSTANTINE AND CONSTANS.

The troops of Constans were shortly afterwards strengthened by reinforcements, and Didymus and Verinian, with their wives, were taken prisoners, and were eventually put to death. Their brothers Theodosiolus and Lagodius fled the country and sought refuge elsewhere. The former escaped to Italy and put himself under the protection of the emperor Honorius. The latter fled to the East, and sought safety at the court of Theodosius. After these transactions, Constans returned to his father, but on leaving the country, he established forts along the frontiers, which he garrisoned with his own soldiers, for he feared to adopt the ancient custom of intrusting the Spaniards with the defense of their native land. This precaution was probably the cause of the ruin of the country, for when Constantine was deprived of his power, the Vandals, Suevi, and Alans seized the mountain passes, took possession of many forts and cities in Spain and Gaul, and arrested the chief officers of the tyrant.

In the meantime Constantine, who was still confident of ultimate success, caused his son Constans to be proclaimed emperor and determined to possess himself of Italy. With this view, he crossed the Cottian Alps and entered Verona,[1] a city of Liguria. He was on the point of crossing the Po, when he was compelled to retrace his steps by the intelligence which was then conveyed to him of the death of Alanicus. This Alanicus was the commander of the troops of Honorius, and being suspected of conspiring to place the Western empire under the domination of Constantine, he was slain when returning from a procession in which according to custom it was his office to march in advance of the emperor. Immediately after this occurrence, the emperor descended from horse-back and publicly returned thanks to God for having delivered him from one who had openly conspired against him. Constantine fled to Arles, and Constans his son hastened from Spain, and sought refuge in the same city.

On the decline of the power of Constantine, the Vandals, Suevi, and Alans took forcible possession of the rich and fertile region of the Pyrenees. They easily dispossessed the soldiers whom Constans had left to guard the frontier, and effected an entrance into Spain.

NOTE

1. Λιβέρωνα. We have followed here the opinion of Valesius.

CHAPTER XIII

CONCERNING GERONTIUS, MAXIMUS, AND THE TROOPS OF HONORIUS. DEFEAT OF GERONTIUS. HE AND HIS WIFE PERISH TOGETHER.

Gerontius, from being the most efficient of the generals of Constantine, became his enemy, and believing that Maximus, his intimate friend, was well qualified to hold the reins of power, he invested him with the imperial purple and conveyed him to Tarracon. Gerontius then marched against Constantine and put Constans to death at Vienna.

As soon as Constantine heard of the usurpation of Maximus, he sent one of his generals named Edovicus beyond the Rhine, to levy an army of Franks and Alemanni, and he sent his son Constans to guard Vienna and the neighboring towns. Gerontius then laid siege to Arles, but some troops of Honorius marched to its relief under the command of Constantius, the father of that Valentinian who subsequently became emperor of Rome. Gerontius retreated precipitately with a few soldiers, for the greater number of his troops deserted to the army of Constantius. The Spanish soldiery conceived an utter contempt against Gerontius on account of his cowardly retreat, and took counsel how to slay him. They attacked his house during the night, but he with one Alanus, his friend, and a few slaves, ascended to the top of the house and did such execution with their arrows that no less than three hundred of the soldiers fell. When the stock of arrows was exhausted, the slaves made their escape from the house, and Gerontius might easily have followed their example had not his affection for Nunchia, his wife, detained him by her side. At day-break the next day, the soldiers deprived him of all hope of saving his life by setting fire to the house, and he cut off the head of Alanus in compliance with his entreaties. His wife then besought him with groans and tears to perform the same office for her rather than permit her to fall into the hands of another, and he complied with her last request. Thus died one who manifested a degree of courage worthy of her religion, for she was a Christian and her death deserves to be held in remembrance. Gerontius then struck himself thrice with his sword, but not succeeding in wounding himself mortally, he drew forth his poignard which he wore at his side, and plunged it into his heart.[1]

NOTE

1. *Note to the 2018 edition:* Compare the account in the epitome of Olympiodorus which may be found in *The Library of Photius*, page 138.

CHAPTER XIV
DEFEAT AND DEATH OF EDOVICUS.

Although the city of Arles was closely besieged, Constantine refused to surrender because he was in expectation of the arrival of the reinforcements for which he had despatched Edovicus. The besiegers were seized with terror when they heard of his return and, after some deliberation, they hastened to cross the river Rhone. Constantius, who commanded the infantry, quietly awaited the approach of the enemy, while Ulphilas, his general, remained in ambush with his cavalry. When the troops of the enemy attacked Constantius and commenced the conflict, Ulphilas, at a given signal, rushed upon them from behind and soon threw them in disorder. Some tried to escape, some were slain, while others threw down their arms, and entreated for life and pardon. Edovicus mounted his horse, and fled to the lands of one Ecdicius, to whom he had formerly rendered some important service, and whom he therefore imagined to be his friend. Ecdicius, however, struck off his head and presented it to the generals of Honorius in hope of receiving some great reward. Constantius exclaimed, as he received the head, that the public were obliged to Ecdicius for the victory of Ulphilas.[1] He commanded, however, that Ecdicius should be dismissed from the army, for he disdained to retain in his service a man capable of enacting so dishonorable a part against his guest and his former friend. Thus Ecdicius reaped no advantage from the murderous deed which he had perpetrated.

NOTE

1. For, as Valesius remarks, if Ulphilas had not routed the forces of Edovicus, Ecdicius would never have been able to cut off his head.

CHAPTER XV

CONSTANTINE THROWS ASIDE THE EMBLEMS OF IMPERIAL POWER, AND IS ORDAINED AS PRESBYTER. HIS DEATH. DEATH OF THE OTHER TYRANTS WHO HAD CONSPIRED AGAINST HONORIUS.

After this victory, the troops of Honorius again laid siege to Arles. When Constantine heard of the death of Edovicus, he cast aside his purple robe and imperial ornaments and repaired to the church, where he caused himself to be ordained as presbyter. The besieged surrendered and opened the gates of their city, and their lives were spared. From that period the whole province returned to its allegiance to Honorius, and has since been governed by the rulers of his appointment. Constantine with his son Julian was sent into Italy, but he was waylaid and killed. Not long afterwards, Jovius and Maximus, the tyrants above-mentioned, Saros,[1] and many others who had conspired against Honorius, were slain.

NOTE

1. He was a Goth, and had been on the side of Honorius against Alaric, but afterwards in anger he abandoned the cause of Honorius, and espoused the cause of Jovius.

CHAPTER XVI

FAVOR OF GOD MANIFESTED TOWARDS THE EMPEROR HONORIUS. DEATH OF HONORIUS. HIS SUCCESSORS. PEACE ESTABLISHED THROUGHOUT THE WORLD.

This is not the proper place to enter into details concerning the deaths of the tyrants, but I considered it necessary to allude to the circumstance in order to show that to insure the stability of imperial power, it is sufficient for an emperor to serve God with reverence, which was the course pursued by Honorius. Galla Placidia, who was born of the same father as himself, dwelt with him and likewise distinguished herself by real zeal in the maintenance of religion and of the churches. After Constantius, who was a brave and able general, had conquered the tyrant Constantine, the emperor rewarded him by giving him his sister in marriage and admitting him to a share in the government. Constantius did not long survive the promotion.[1] He died soon after and left two children, Valentinian, who succeeded Honorius, and Honoria.

A profound peace reigned at this period throughout the Eastern empire, and notwithstanding the extreme youth of the emperor, the affairs of government were, contrary to all expectation, conducted with great wisdom. It seems as if God openly manifested his favor towards the emperor, not only by causing all wars and seditions to cease, but also by permitting the discovery of the remains of many persons who had rendered themselves celebrated by their piety. Among other relics, those of Zechariah, the ancient prophet, and of Stephen, who was ordained deacon by the apostles, were discovered, and it seems incumbent upon me to describe the mode in which these holy remains were unexpectedly brought to light.

NOTE

1. Compare Socrates, *Ecclesiastical History,* Book VII, Chapter 22.

CHAPTER XVII
DISCOVERY OF THE REMAINS OF ZECHARIAH THE PROPHET, AND OF STEPHEN THE PROTO-MARTYR.

I shall first speak of the relics of the prophet. Caphar-Zechariah is a village of the territory of Eleutheropolis, a city of Palestine. The land of this district was cultivated by Calemerus, a man who was faithful to the proprietor of the soil, but morose and even unjust towards his neighbors. Although he possessed these defects of character, the prophet appeared to him in a dream, pointed out to him a particular garden, and said to him, "Go, dig in that garden at the distance of two cubits from the hedge which divides it from the road leading to the city of Bithereman. You will there find two coffins, a wooden one enclosed in one of lead. Beside the coffins you will see a crystal vase full of water, and two serpents of moderate size, but tame, and perfectly innoxious."

Calemerus followed the directions of the prophet, and zealously applied to the task. When he found the holy coffins, the one enclosed within the other, as had been described to him, the prophet appeared to him, clad in a white robe, which makes me think that he was a priest. At the foot of the coffin was the body of a child, apparently of royal birth, for on its head was a golden crown, its feet were encased in golden sandals, and it was arrayed in a costly robe. The wise men and priests of the time were greatly perplexed about this child, for they could ascertain no particulars concerning its birth or parentage, or the reason of its having been interred in this place. It is said that Zechariah, the superior of a monastery at Geraris, found an ancient document written in Hebrew, which had not been received among the canonical books. In this document it was stated, that when Zechariah the prophet had been put to death by Joash, king of Judah, the family of the monarch was visited by a dire calamity, for on the seventh day after the death of the prophet, one of the sons of Joash whom he tenderly loved, suddenly and unexpectedly expired. Judging that this affliction was a special manifestation of Divine wrath, the king ordered his son to be interred at the feet of the prophet as a kind of atonement for the crime. Such are the particulars which I have ascertained on the subject.

Although so long a space of time had elapsed since the interment of the prophet, his body was found in a state of perfect preservation. His hair was closely shorn, his nose was straight, his beard of a moderate length, his head short, his eyes rather sunken, and overshadowed by thick eye-brows.[1]

NOTE

1. *Note to the 2018 edition*: Thus ends the extant text of Sozomen's *History*. It will be noted that Sozomen's promised description of the finding of the relics of Saint Stephen the Proto-martyr is missing from this chapter. Based on Valesius's comment in the introduction, the work was meant to extend to AD 439. It is therefore assumed that the extant work is merely a large fragment and the remainder is either lost or was never completed.

INDEX

Abbas, disciple of Saint Ephraim the Syrian 113
Abbo, a monk in Syria 254
Abdaleus, a monk in Syria 254
Abdas, bishop and martyr of Persia 58
Abdiesus, deacon in Persia 58
Abdus, a Persian Christian exile 296
Abraham, bishop and martyr of Persia 58
Abraham, disciple of Saint Ephraim the Syrian 113
Abraham the patriarch 3, 6, 46, 255, 263, 332
Acacians, a heretical sect 159, 164, 169
Acacius, Arian bishop of Cæssarea in Palestine 91, 94, 103, 110, 138, 145, 152, 155–159, 164–166, 168, 191, 213, 217, 260, 261
Acacius, a martyr 154
Acacius, bishop of Berœa 273, 278, 304, 312, 334
Acepsimus, martyr, bishop in Persia 57–58
Acesius, bishop of the Novatians 36–37, 86
Achaia 12
Achillas, Arian presbyter 27–28
Achillas, a bishop 74, 76
Adana 277
Adiabenians 57
Adonis River 48
Adrian, presbyter of Antioch 158
Adrianople 98, 150, 265
Æetes, king of Colchis 12
Ægis 48
Æsculapius, pagan god 48
Ætius, Arian bishop 111–112, 118, 138–140, 142–143, 145, 156–157, 159, 161, 168, 180, 191, 241–243
Africa 142, 161, 187, 223, 270, 355, 356
Africanus, Sextus Julius 5
Agas, bishop and martyr of Persia 58
Agasius, a heretical bishop 289
Agdelas, bishop and martyr of Persia 58
Agelius, Novatian bishop at Constantinople 220, 238, 279–280, 282, 308
Aithalas, Arian presbyter 28
Aithalas, priest in Persia 58
Ajax 44
Ajax, bishop of Botelion 305
Alanicus, a general 360
Alans 359–360
Alanus, friend of Gerontius 361
Alaphion of Asalia xix–xx, 108, 193–194,
Alaric, king of the Goths xii, 340–341, 351–359, 362

Alevadæ xxv
Alemanni 267, 269, 360
Alexander, a bishop in Africa 142
Alexander, bishop of Constantinople 82–83, 86, 91–92
Alexander, Patriarch of Alexandria 7, 27–33, 62–63, 67, 78
Alexander the Grammarian 239
Alexander the Great xxvii, 183
Alexandria xvii, 7, 26–28, 30–31, 35–36, 38, 60, 62, 67–70, 73–75, 79, 82–84, 90, 91, 93–96, 98, 100, 103, 105, 108, 111–112, 119–121, 125, 128, 133, 134–137, 139, 145, 155, 158, 161, 169, 181–183, 186, 189–192, 210–211, 214–215, 230–232, 239, 246, 264, 270–271, 273, 276, 283, 293, 295, 307, 311, 322, 324–325, 329, 332–334, 340
Alexion of Bethagatonia, a holy man 108
Alps 12, 297, 299, 357, 359–360
Ambrose, bishop of Milan 237–238, 275, 281–282, 300, 301, 316–317
Ammon, abbot of the Tabennesiotians 245
Ammon, one of the four "great brothers" 250–251, 323–325, 327, 330
Ammonius, a monk in Palestine 254, 324
Ammon the Egyptian 25–26
Amphilochius, bishop of Iconium 272, 276
Amphion, bishop of Epiphania in Cilicia 18
Amphion, bishop of Nicomedia 36, 60
Anastasius, pope of Rome 311, 340
Ancyra 86, 98, 103, 110, 123, 125, 128, 130, 139, 140, 142, 155, 161, 188–189, 213, 223, 256, 308, 334
Andragathius, a philosopher 309
Andragathos, a usurping general 281, 283
angels 6, 8, 46–47, 106–108, 111, 117, 166, 247, 254
Annian 163
Anomians, heretical sect 141, 145, 169, 241
Antedon, a holy man of Palestine 108
Anthedona 185
Anthropomorphists 324
Antioch xxi, 7–8, 30, 34, 44, 64–66, 93–102, 105, 112, 119, 131–132, 138–143, 145, 155–158, 161–163, 167–168, 183, 189–191, 200–201, 213–214, 218, 223, 225–226, 229, 231, 233, 239, 255, 259, 261, 268, 273–275, 277–278, 283, 289, 298, 307, 309, 310, 312, 340, 345
Antiochus, bishop of Ptolemais in Syria 321

Antiochus, founder of Antioch 201
Antony the Great of Egypt 22, 24–26, 63, 84, 108, 111, 215, 232, 249, 250, 255
Anuphus, a monk in Egypt 108
Aones, a monk in Syria 255
Apamea 256, 285
Apelles, a holy man in Egypt 245
Aphaca 48
Apis, presbyter in Alexandria 69
Apocalypse of Peter 293–294
Apollinarius, heretical bishop of Laodicea 62, 199, 234, 239–240, 243, 244
Apollo, pagan god 13, 48–49, 178, 200–201, 203
Apollonius, a monk at Scetis 247–248
Apollonius, a monk in Egypt 107
Apollos, an anchorite at Thebaïs 246
Aquilea 118
Aquiline, advocate 45
Aquiline River 12, 45
Aquitaine 359
Aquitania 191
Arabia 24, 262, 278, 285–286, 293
Aranad, disciple of Saint Ephraim the Syrian 113
Arbogastes, a barbarian general 297, 299
Arcadia 200
Arcadia, daughter of the emperor Arcadius 347
Arcadius, emperor xxviii, 166, 272, 279, 282, 285, 299, 307, 309, 340, 344–345, 347, 351–352
Areopolis 285
Arethusa 65, 101, 128, 138, 140, 145, 186–187, 256
Argeus, Mount 173, 178, 288
Arianism 7, 29, 66, 89, 94, 120, 233, 253, 260
Ariminum 118, 130, 133, 146, 148, 150–152, 159, 160, 165, 168, 191, 213, 219, 222–223, 235–236, 242, 281, 354, 356
Aristobulus 291
Arius, the heresiarch 27–31, 33–36, 60–61, 64–65, 67–68, 74, 77–79, 82–85, 87–89, 91–93, 122, 128, 138, 157, 164, 168–169, 199, 214, 217, 221, 222, 231, 233, 241–242, 261, 293
Arles 352, 360–362
Armenia xx, 50, 109, 125, 207, 216, 278, 307, 337, 344–345, 348, 351
Armenians 52, 58
Arsacius, a holy man of Nicomedia 143–144
Arsacius, bishop of Constantinople 337, 340, 344
Arsacius, king of Armenia 207
Arsacius, pagan high priest of Galatia 195
Arsenius, bishop of Hypsele 70–71, 74–76, 101
Arsinoë 246
Arsisius, a monk at Scetis 106, 250
Asalia 108
Ascalon xix, xxiii, 194
Ascholius, bishop of Thessalonica 269, 273
Asclepas, bishop of Gaza 98, 102–103, 123
Asia 50, 52, 161, 174, 276, 291, 313, 316, 321, 329

Asphalius, Ætian priest of Antioch 140
Assyria 207
Astacenes, bay 226
Asterius, an Arian philosopher 87
Asterius, general of the East 310
Ataulphus, brother-in-law of Alaric 355
Athanaric, Gothic warlord 260–261
Athanasius, bishop of Ancyra 213, 223
Athanasius the Great, Patriarch of Alexandria 18, 24, 29, 31, 36, 62–64, 68–71, 73–76, 80–82, 84–85, 89–105, 111, 118–123, 125, 127, 130, 132–137, 139, 142, 146–147, 164, 169, 181–182, 189–190, 192, 210, 214–215, 223–225, 230–231, 235, 239–240, 334, 343
Athens 11, 175, 229
Attalus, prefect of Rome and usurper 355–357
Atticus, bishop of Constantinople 344, 347
Augustus Caesar 3
Aulone 285
Aurelian, a consul 313
Aurelius 108
Aurelius, a holy man of Palestine 108
Auxentius, Arian bishop of Milan 105, 110, 112, 146–147, 149, 235–238
Auxentius, son of Abdus 296
Axius River 285
Azadanus, deacon in Persia 58
Azadas, martyr, eunuch in the Persian court 56
Azizius, a monk of Palestine 255

Babylas, a martyr 200–203, 278
Bacchus, pagan god 240, 283
baptism 10, 27, 37, 149, 172, 238, 241–242, 277, 289
Barbasymes, bishop and martyr of Persia 58
Bardasanes, heretic of Osroene 113
Barges, a monk in Syria 254
Barses, a bishop 255
Bartholomew the Apostle 71
Basil the Great, bishop of Cæsarea in Cappadocia 92, 109, 111, 123, 176, 225–229, 233–234, 242, 256, 270, 351
Basil, bishop of Ancyra 87, 103, 110, 113, 125, 128, 130, 139, 141, 143–145, 155–157, 161–164, 199, 213
Basil, presbyter of Ancyra 188–189
Basilicus, a martyr 345
Bassones, a monk 256
Bassus, a consul 347
Bassus, a monk 256
Battheus, a monk in Syria 254–255
Benevolus 281
Benevolus, a legal secretary 281
Benjamin, an anchorite near Scetis 247
Benus, abbot in Egypt 245
Beratsatia 306

INDEX

Berœa 7, 136, 141, 304, 312
Berytus xx, xxiii, 19, 20,
Besauduc 253
Bethagatonia 108
Bethelia xii, xix, 193
Bithynia xxvi, 13, 26, 28, 30, 44, 68, 87, 89, 143, 160, 166, 216–217, 221, 226, 272, 276, 290, 313, 328, 331, 336, 338, 353
Bizya 225
Bochres, bishop and martyr of Persia 58
Bonium 44
Bosphorus 143
Bostra 110, 193
Boulogne 358
Britain 11–12, 270, 281, 358
Britons 282
Busiris 188
Buthericus, master of soldiers in Illyria 300
Byzantium 26, 33, 44, 46

Cæsar, a consul and prefect 349
Cæsarea in Cappadocia 94, 162, 173, 178, 188, 223, 226–227, 233, 256, 276, 288, 317
Cæsarea in Palestine 28, 67, 73, 75, 91, 103, 110, 138, 158, 164, 213
Cæsarea Philippi 203
Cagliari 189
Caius, Arian bishop 146–147, 149
Calemerus, a farmer near Eleutheropolis 363
Callinicus, a bishop 74, 76
Caphar-Zechariah 363
Capharcobra 254
Cappadocia 65, 87, 94, 97, 109, 113, 162, 172–173, 178–179, 188, 199, 223, 226–227, 233–234, 241–242, 244, 256, 276, 278, 288, 317
Caria 203, 223, 225, 340
Carpon, Arian presbyter 28
Carræ 255
Carterius, an abbot 310
Carthage 355–356
Cassius, a deacon 342
Castabalis 162, 221
Castalia, a fountain at Antioch 201
Castra Martis 353
Catholics 67, 153, 243
Cecropius, bishop of Nicomedia 139, 143, 161
Cela (*also Ceila*) 306
Celts 49, 282
Chalcedon (*also Chalcedonia*) 22, 44, 101, 104, 160, 162, 179, 252, 277, 290, 295, 321, 328–329, 333, 337, 344
Chamaigephyra 302
Charburis 186
Chersonesus 314
Chrestus, bishop of Nicæa 36, 60
Chrispio, an archdeacon 327

Cibalæ, Battle of 12
Cilicia 18, 48, 101, 132, 161, 172, 223, 244, 274, 294–295, 310, 345
Claudius I, emperor 178
Clement 7
Cleophas, disciple of Jesus 204
Cœle-syria 255
Coma 23
Comana 345
Constans I, emperor 87, 91, 101, 102, 116, 118, 125, 131–132, 134, 136
Constans II, son of Constantine III 355–356, 359–360
Constantia, sister of Constantine 78, 88
Constantina, sister of Constantius II 175–176
Constantia (*formerly Majuma, port of Gaza*) 49
Constantine II 87, 90–91
Constantine III, usurper in Gaul 352, 358–362
Constantine I the Great, emperor xvi, xxi, xxvii, 7–18, 22, 26, 29–30, 33, 38, 42–47, 49, 52, 59–60, 68–69, 71, 77–78, 80, 83, 88–90, 93, 97, 100, 104, 117–118, 138, 148–149, 154, 172–173, 176–177, 179–180, 186–187, 197, 222–224, 239, 255, 318, 335
Constantinople xii, xix, xx, xxiii. 33, 44–45, 68, 75, 80, 82–83, 86, 88, 91–92, 94–99, 102, 105, 123, 126–127, 143, 152–153, 155–156, 159–160, 162, 164–169, 171–172, 174, 179, 189, 216–220, 222, 225, 229, 238, 241, 243–244, 251–252, 260–261, 264–265, 267–277, 281–283, 287–289, 293, 295–296, 299, 306–308, 310–311, 313–318, 321, 323, 325–326, 328–334, 337, 340–342, 344–345, 347–348, 350, 352–353
Constantius, brother of Constantine I 173
Constantius I Chlorus, emperor 11–12
Constantius II, emperor 87–89, 91, 93, 95, 99–101, 105, 108, 116–120, 125–128, 130–132, 134, 136, 140, 141, 147, 153, 155, 159, 165, 171–177, 179–182, 188, 189, 191–192, 201, 207, 213, 215, 220, 224–225, 242, 253, 255, 261, 271–272, 296, 308, 357
Constantius III, emperor 360–363
consubstantial 27, 34–35, 61, 64, 68, 86, 92–94, 103, 105, 116–117, 129, 138, 141–142, 147, 152, 156–157, 160, 168, 191, 213–214, 221–223, 234, 242, 268
Coprus, a holy man in Egypt 245
Cosila 295–296
Cottian Alps 359–360
Cotua 238
Crescens, a bishop in Africa 142
Cretans xxv
Crispus, monk in Palestine 254
Crispus, son of Constantine I xxvii, 7, 10–11
Cronius, a monk at Scetis 106, 250
Ctesiphon 53, 207–208

367

Cucusum 125, 337
Cyprus xx, 18–19, 108, 186, 253–254, 278, 293, 303, 316, 325, 326, 328
Cyrene 44
Cyriacus, a deacon 341
Cyriacus, bishop of Adana 277, 343
Cyriacus of Naissus 102
Cyril, patriarch of Jerusalem 8, 110, 127–128, 146, 152, 155, 158, 163–164, 169, 206, 273, 283
Cyrinus, bishop of Chalcedon 329, 344
Cyrus of Beroea 95
Cyzicus 139, 152, 154–155, 157, 161–162, 180, 192–193, 219, 241–242, 272–273, 280, 340

Dacibiza 226
Dacora 288
Dadastanis 216
Dalmatia 186, 341, 352
Dalmatius, half-brother of Constantine I 173
Dalmatius, nephew of Constantine I 173
Damascus 264
Damasus I, pope of Rome 235, 236–237, 239, 270, 307
Daniel, a holy man in Syria 109
Danube River 12, 15, 44, 49, 259, 261, 267, 269, 299, 302, 340, 353
Daphne, suburb of Antioch xxi, 200–201, 203
Dausas, bishop and martyr of Persia 58
David, king of Israel xxvi
Decentius, brother of the usurper Magnentius 130
Delphi 201
Delphos 48
Demetrius, bishop of Pessena 330, 343
Democritus of Coos 72
demons 13, 18, 24, 48, 50, 106, 108–109, 144, 172, 179, 186, 193, 201, 203–204, 232, 245, 247–248, 298, 303, 314
Demophilus, Arian bishop of Constantinople 146–147, 225, 271, 273, 280, 283
Denis, an abbot in Rinocorurus 252
Dianius, bishop of Cæsarea in Cappadocia 94
Didymus, a monk at Scetis 250
Didymus, relative of the emperor Honorius in Spain 359
Didymus (*Apollo*), pagan god 13, 203
Didymus a monk at Scetis 250
Didymus the Blind 111, 210, 232
Diocæsarea 131
Diodorus, bishop of Tarsus 273–278, 310
Diogenes, a presbyter 161
Dionysius, bishop of Alba in Italy 133
Dionysius, patriarch of Alexandria 96
Dionysius, tyrant of Sicily xxv
Dioscorus, an abbot in Egypt 246
Dioscorus, one of the four "great brothers" 250, 323–327, 330

Dominica, empress 267
Domitian, prefect of the east 131
Donatus, bishop of Eurœa 302
Dorotheus, Arian bishop of Constantinople 283, 289
Dorotheus, a monk at Thebes in Egypt 246
Dracontius, bishop of Pergamus 161–162
dragon 144, 302

earthquake 96, 143–145, 205–206, 211, 317
Ecdicius, a Roman nobleman 361–362
Edesius, a presbyter in Tyre 72–73
Edessa 59, 95, 109, 114, 116, 207, 230, 255–256
Edovicus 360–362
Egypt xii, xx, 7, 22, 24, 27, 29–30, 35, 38, 59–60, 62–63, 67–68, 70–72, 74, 76, 79, 82, 96–97, 100, 105, 107–108, 111, 120–121, 123, 127, 133–135, 175, 181, 183, 204, 211, 215, 223–225, 231–232, 234, 239, 245, 249, 253–255, 262–263, 273, 276, 278, 293, 295, 297, 312, 318, 322–323, 326, 329, 332, 355
Eleusius, Macedonian bishop of Cyzicus 139, 152, 154–155, 157, 161–162, 166, 180, 191–193, 219, 241, 273, 280, 343
Eleutheropolis 162, 253, 306, 363
Elias, an anchorite in Egypt 245
Elias, associate of Arsenius in Egypt 70
Elias the Prophet 21, 106, 308
Elpidus, a presbyter 335
Elpidus, bishop of Satalis 162–163
Emesa 95–96, 110, 223
Emmaus 204
Empedocles, a philosopher 72
Ephesus 103, 132, 174, 289, 304, 316
Ephraim the Syrian, Saint 109, 111–115, 255
Epidamnus 44
Epiphanius, bishop of Salamis in Cyprus 253, 303, 304, 325–328
Epiphanius, the sophist 240
Epirus 302, 341, 352
Eridanus River 12
Etrurians 354
Eucherius, son of Stilicho 351–352
Eucrates 188
Eudoxius, Arian bishop of Germanicia, Antioch and Constantinople 94, 101, 110, 136, 138–142, 145–146, 155, 158, 163–168, 188–189, 217–219, 221, 223, 225, 241, 260–261, 308
Eugenius, bishop of Nicæa 132, 139
Eugenius, usurper 297, 299–300, 306–307
Eulalius, bishop of Amasia in Pontus 268
Eulalius, bishop of Cæsarea in Cappadocia 162
Eulogius, a bishop 255
Eulogius, a presbyter in Egypt 246
Eumæus 196
Eunomians, heretical sect 243, 280, 288–289, 307

INDEX

Eunomius, Arian bishop of Cyzicus 164, 219, 241, 242–244, 267, 272, 280, 288–289, 308
Euphrates River 161, 207–208
Euphronius. bishop of Antioch 65–66, 93, 95, 119
Euplus, a bishop 74
Eupsychus of Cæsarea in Cappadocia, martyr 188
Euripides, Greek playwright 199, 215
Eurœa 302
Eusebia, Macedonian deaconess 348–350
Eusebia, wife of Constantius II 175
Eusebius, a eunuch in the court of Constantius II 146
Eusebius, a presbyter 163
Eusebius, bishop of Cæsarea in Cappadocia 223, 226–227
Eusebius, bishop of Emesa 95–96, 110
Eusebius, bishop of Nicomedia 28, 35–36, 60–61, 64–66, 68–69, 73, 81–83, 86–87, 89, 91–97, 116, 117, 122, 141, 162, 176
Eusebius, bishop of Samosata 213
Eusebius, bishop of Vercelli 112, 133, 189–191
Eusebius, consul in AD 348 104
Eusebius, consul in AD 360 118, 147, 155, 160
Eusebius, governor of the palace 180
Eusebius, monk in Syria 254–255
Eusebius, one of the four "great brothers" 250, 323
Eusebius of Gaza, martyr 184
Eusebius Pamphilus, bishop of Cæsarea in Palestine 5, 7, 8, 28, 33, 35, 47, 64–65, 73, 91, 94–95, 103, 159, 204, 303
Eustathius, bishop of Antioch 7, 30, 34, 64–66, 95, 102, 111, 119, 141, 162–163, 166, 168, 191, 225
Eustathius, bishop of Sebaste 109, 139, 155, 166, 221–222, 273, 344
Euthymius, one of the four "great brothers" 323
Eutropius, a reader 338–339
Eutropius, head eunuch of the palace 297, 311, 317–318
Eutychius of Olympus 26
Eutychus, a heresiarch 241, 288–289
Euxine Sea (*also the Black Sea*) 233, 251, 313
Euzoius, Arian bishop of Antioch 28, 77–79, 168, 189–190, 214–215, 218, 231, 261
Evagrius, bishop of Antioch 283, 312
Evagrius, bishop of Constantinople 225
Evagrius, prefect of Alexandria 284
Evagrius Ponticus, a monk at Scetis 251–252, 316
Exucontians, heretical sect 169

Felix II, pope of Rome 137, 142
Flacillus, bishop of Antioch 93–95, 119
Flavian, bishop of Antioch 239, 269, 278, 283, 298, 307, 311–312, 340
Flavian, prætorian prefect 297
Fortune, pagan goddess 178–179, 188
Franks 96, 359–360

Fravitas, an imperial general 314–315
Frumentius, a bishop in India 71–73

Gabales 321, 328
Gaddanas, a monk of Palestine 255
Gadiabes, bishop and martyr of Persia 58
Gaïnas, a usurper 312–315
Galates, son of the emperor Valens 227
Galatia 86–87, 139, 161–162, 172, 179, 188–189, 195, 255–256, 278, 291, 308
Galilee 285
Galla Placidia, daughter of the emperor Theodosius I 362
Gallinaria 110
Gallus, Cæsar under Constantius II 49, 112, 127, 131, 173–176, 180, 201
Gangris 109, 162
Gaudentius, bishop of Naïsus in Dacia 102
Gaul 11, 12, 81, 90, 96, 102, 125, 130–131, 154, 175, 216, 221, 223, 235–236, 258, 267, 269–270, 352, 358–359
Gauls 49, 191, 282
Gaza xii, xix, xx, xxiii, 49, 98, 103, 108, 177, 184–187, 193, 194, 213, 254, 285, 305
George, Arian patriarch of Alexandria 97, 127–128, 132, 135, 139, 145–146, 155, 158, 169, 181–182, 184–185, 215
George, bishop of Arethusa 65
George, bishop of Laodicea 94–95, 103, 138–139, 155, 163, 240
Gera 333
Geraris 254, 364
Germanicia 94, 101, 110
Germanius, Arian bishop of Sirmium 138, 142, 146–147, 149, 161
Germanus, a presbyter 342
Gerontius, bishop of Nicomedia 316–317
Gerontius, usurper 360–361
gladiators 15, 125, 285
Golgatha 77
Goths xii, 15, 49, 88, 160, 259–261, 265, 312–314, 341, 351, 353, 357, 359
Goths, a heretical sect 289
Gratian, a usurper in Britain 358
Gratian, emperor xxviii, 220, 259, 267–271, 278, 281–283, 301
Greeks 4–5, 8, 10–13, 15, 33, 41–42, 45–47, 64, 72, 85, 95, 112, 115, 128, 135, 199, 200, 211, 214, 245, 291, 317
Gregory, Arian bishop of Alexandria 93–97, 103
Gregory of Nazianzum, bishop of Constantinople 10, 31, 176, 179, 198, 223, 227, 229, 233–234, 243, 251–252, 269–271, 273
Gregory of Nyssa 112, 199, 242, 272, 276
Gregory Thaumaturgus, bishop of Neocæsarea 20, 303

369

Habakkuk the prophet 306
Hadrian, emperor 201, 204
Hagar, concubine of Abraham the patriarch 263
Halas, a monk in Syria 254–255
Harmonius, son of Bardasanes, heretic in Osroene 113
Havonius, island 131
Hebdoma 296, 299, 314, 326
Hebrews (*see also, Jews*) 3, 4, 22, 199, 263, 291, 332
Hebron 46
Hegesippus 5
Helena, mother of Constantine the Great 41, 43–44
Helenopolis 87, 290
Helicon 48
Heliodorus, a monk near Nisibis 254–255
Heliopolis 15, 186
Helladius, Arian deacon 28
Helladius, bishop of Cæsarea in Cappadocia 276, 317
Helles, a holy man in Egypt 245
Hellespont 44, 68, 96, 166, 217, 221, 244, 273, 314
Hemona xxi, 12
Heortasius, bishop of Sardis 161–162
Heraclea, a town in Egypt 23
Heraclea a city in Pontus xxvi
Heraclea, a town in Thrace 76, 91–92, 94, 97, 101, 217–218, 333
Heraclean, master of soldiers in Africa 356
Heraclides, a holy man in Egypt 232
Heraclides, bishop of Ephesus 316, 317, 332
Heraclius, a deacon in Tyre 162
Heraclius, a holy man of Egypt 106
Heraclius, patriarch of Jerusalem 169
Herculeans, Roman legionaries 216
Hercules, pagan god 11, 162, 216
Herennius, patriarch of Jerusalem 169–170
Hermeon, a bishop 74, 76
Hermogenes, general of the cavalry 97, 126
Hermogenes, prefect and governor of Syria 161, 163
Hermopolis 204
Herodias, wife of Herod Antipas 295, 334
Herod Antipas, tetrarch of Galilee 295
Herod the Great, king of Judea 3, 204
Hestiis 45
Hesycas, a monk in Palestine 253
Hesychius, disiciple of Saint Hilarion 108, 258
Hieropolis 285
Hilarion, a holy man 110
Hilarion, saint xix, xx, xxiii, 108, 112, 185, 187, 193, 253–254,
Hilarius, bishop of Poictiers 133, 191
Hilarius, notary to the emperor Constantius II 134
Hilarius, patriarch of Jerusalem 169
Himerius, a sophist 229

Hippodrome 48–49, 264, 306
Homer xxv, 13, 196, 199, 209
homœousian 117–118
homousian 116–118
Honoratus, governor of Constantinople 159–160
Honoria, daughter of the emperor Honorius 363
Honorius, emperor xxviii, 272, 282, 299, 306–307, 309, 340–341, 345, 351–356, 358–363
Hormisdas, bishop and martyr of Persia 58
Hosius, bishop of Cordova 18, 30, 102–104, 128–129, 138–139, 142
Huns 259–260, 302, 307, 309, 340, 352, 375
Hygenus, governor of Egypt 74
Hypatian, bishop of Heraclea in Perinthus 217
Hypatius, consul in AD 360 118, 147, 155, 160
hypostasis 35, 64, 101, 160, 190, 236

Iberians of Asia 50, 52, 81
Iberia in Asia 51, 251
idols 12, 48, 176–177, 182, 188, 202, 204
Illyria 12, 100, 102, 104, 110, 127, 161, 171, 191, 217, 235, 236, 267, 269–270, 293, 300, 341, 352
Illyrians 8, 110
India 71–73, 302, 303
Indians 72–73
Innocent, pope of Rome xvi, 29, 340–345, 354, 355
Irenius, bishop of Gaza 213
Irenopolis 101, 103
Isaac, a monk 320, 333
Isaac, bishop 74
Isaac, bishop and martyr in Persia 58
Isaac, saint, a monk 265
Isaac the patriach 3
Isauria 145, 155, 162, 310, 340, 345
Ischurias, a presbyter 74
Ischyrion, bishop of Mareota 104, 122
Ishmael, son of Abraham the patriarch 263
Isidore, an abbot in Egypt 246, 311, 312, 323, 325
Isoria 302
Italy xii, 11–12, 44, 96, 101, 112, 118, 127, 131, 133, 151–152, 161, 189, 191, 221–223, 225, 270, 276, 281–283, 285, 297–299, 341, 352, 354–356, 359–360, 362

Jacob, the patriarch 3, 6, 255
James, priest in Persia 57, 58
Jerusalem xv, xvi, xviii, 7, 18, 30, 41–43, 46–47, 59, 66–67, 76–77, 79–80, 82, 84, 87, 95, 110, 121, 127–128, 146, 152, 155, 163–164, 169, 204–206, 251, 267, 273, 283, 307, 324
Jews (*see also Hebrews*) xix, 3–4, 15, 22, 30, 42, 46, 50, 53, 57, 116, 128, 131, 193, 196, 204–206, 238, 263, 290–291
Joash, king of Judah 364
John, an abbot in Diolchis in Egypt 247
John, a monk 70, 74–75

INDEX

John, a monk of Thebaïs 245, 297, 306
John, bishop and martyr of Persia 58
John, follower of Meletius of Lycopolis 67, 69, 75, 76, 85
John, military commander under Attalus 355
John, patriarch of Jerusalem 283, 307
John Chrysostom, Saint 126, 309–322, 325–338, 340–342, 344–345, 347
John the Baptist 21, 295–296, 299
John the Evangelist 292, 304
Josephus 3
Jovian, emperor xxvii, 212–213, 215–216, 218, 223–225
Jovian, prætorian prefect 341, 352
Jovians, Roman legionaries 216
Jovius, prætorian prefect of Italy 354–355, 362
Jugates 256
Julian, a monk of Edessa 109, 111, 255
Julian, son of Constantine III 362
Julian, uncle of Julian the Apostate 183–184
Julian Alps 12, 297
Julian the Apostate, emperor xxvii, 45, 153–154, 165, 170–183, 185–186, 188, 192–195, 197–198, 200–201, 203, 206–213, 216, 223–224
Julian the Chaldean 33
Julius, Arian deacon 28
Julius, pope of Rome 30–31, 66, 97–102, 104, 118, 122, 131–132, 137, 150, 343
Jupiter, pagan god 49, 178, 196–197, 207, 216
Justina, empress 281–283

Labarum 9–10
Ladon River 200
Lagodius, relative of the emperor Honorius 359
Lampsacus 217–219, 222–223, 273
Laodicea 94–96, 103, 132, 138–139, 155, 163, 213, 223, 234, 239, 240, 276
Laurentius, military governor in Isauria 155–156, 158
Lazarus, a bishop in Syria 254–255
Lebanon 15, 48, 285
Leonas, palace official under Constantius II 155–158
Leontius, Arian bishop of Antioch 119, 132, 138–139
Leontius, bishop of Ancyra 256, 308, 334
Libanius the Sophist 209, 229, 309–311
Libanus, mountain 186
Liberius, pope of Rome 131, 136–137, 141–142, 152, 221–223, 235, 268, 273
Libya 7, 24, 44, 79, 120–121, 133, 217, 246, 293, 295
Licinius xxi, xxiii, 5, 7–8, 12–13, 15, 143, 348, 351
Liguria 133, 189, 360
Lucifer, bishop of Cagliari 112, 133, 189–190
Lucius, Arian bishop 182, 271

Lucius, Arian bishop of Alexandria 215, 231–232, 262–264
Lucius, bishop of Adrianople 98, 103, 123, 125
Lugduna 130
Lusitania 359
Lydia 16, 162

Maares, bishop and martyr of Persia 58
Macarius, Arian deacon 28
Macarius, a monk of Scetis 105, 231–232, 247
Macarius, a presbyter 290
Macarius, a presbyter in Alexandria 69
Macarius, bishop of Jerusalem 7, 18, 30, 42, 47, 66–67
Macarius Politicus, priest in Egypt 106
Macarius the Younger, Monk at Scetis 247
Macedonia 269
Macedonians xxvii, 8, 12
Macedonians, heretical sect (*see also Marathonians*) 91, 166, 191, 221, 267, 268, 273, 280, 296, 308, 315
Macedonius, Arian bishop of Constantinople 91–92, 94, 97, 99–101, 123, 125–127, 139, 152–156, 161, 164–166, 191, 277
Macedonius, a martyr 187
Macedonius, a presbyter 76, 92
Macella, a palace 173
Mæsia 103
Magi 53, 55–58
Magnentius, usurper 125, 127, 130, 132, 171, 175
Magnus, treasurer at Alexandria 231
Magnus, treasurer of the east 131
Majuma xx, 49, 177, 305
Malchius, a monk in Palestine 254
Mammas, Saint 174
Manichæans 267, 323
Mantinia 154
Maras, disciple of Saint Ephraim the Syrian 113
Marathonians, heretical sect (*see also Macedonians*) 166
Marathonius, heretical bishop of Nicomedia 152, 166
Marcellus, heretical bishop of Ancyra 86–87, 98, 102–103, 123, 125, 222
Marcellus, martyr, bishop of Apamea in Syria 285
Marcian, bishop of Lampsacus 273
Marcian, Novatian bishop 282, 290, 308–309
Marcian, singer and reader at Constantinople, a martyr 126
Marcion, a Novatian 220
Marcion, heretic 222
Mardonius, a palace eunuch 295
Mareabdes, bishop and martyr in Persia 58
Mareas, bishop and martyr of Persia 58
Mareota 100, 104, 122, 137, 246, 249
Mareotis, lake 22, 30, 248

371

Marina, daughter of the emperor Arcadius 347
Marinus, Arian bishop 283, 289
Maris, bishop of Chalcedonia 35, 76, 81, 160, 162, 179
Marius, a secretary in the palace 77
Mark, a monk at Scetis 247
Mark, a tyrant in Britain 358
Mark, bishop of Arethusa 101, 128, 138, 140, 145, 157, 186, 187
Mark, bishop of Pelusium 74
Mark, Pope of Rome 66
Marosas, a monk of Nechilis 256
Mars, pagan god 197
Martin of Tours, Saint 110
Martyrius, a sub-deacon in Constantinople 101, 126
Martyrius, bishop of Marcianopolis 276
Martyrius of Cilicia 277
Maruthas, bishop of Martyropolis 329
Mary, the Blessed Mother of Jesus 86, 128, 204, 271
Mavia, queen of the Saracens 262, 264, 267
Maxentius 8, 11, 12
Maximianus Herculius, emperor 12
Maximinus Daia, emperor 18
Maximus, bishop of Jerusalem 18, 66–67, 76, 95, 121, 127, 152
Maximus, bishop of Seleucia 310
Maximus, bishop of Treves 102
Maximus, friend of the usurper Gerontius 360, 362
Maximus, philosopher from Ephesus 174
Maximus, usurper in Britain 281–283, 311
Maximus of Alexandria, improperly ordained bishop of Constantinople 276
Mazaca (*also Cæsarea in Cappadocia*) 178
Melas, bishop of Rinocorurus 252–253
Meletius, bishop of Antioch 164, 167–168, 189, 190, 213, 218, 233, 239, 268–269, 273, 277–278, 283
Melitina 162–163
Melitine 216, 223, 276
Melitius, heretical bishop of Lycopolis 27, 38, 62, 67, 74, 85
Menander, Greek playwright 199
Menedemes, an orthodox cleric 226
Menophantes, bishop of Ephesus 103, 132
Mercury, pagan god 197
Merobandes, a consul 279
Merope of Tyre, a philosopher 72
Meros 187
Micah the prophet 306
Michaelius 45
Milan 105, 110, 122–123, 132, 133, 136, 148, 150, 235–238, 275, 281, 300, 306, 316
Miletus 13, 203
Milles, bishop and martyr in Persia 58–59
Minas, Arian deacon 28

Mocius, bishop and martyr of Persia 58, 330
Modestus, prefect at Edessa 230
Mœsia 353
monks xx, 20, 22, 24–25, 49, 58–59, 70, 105–106, 108–111, 125, 135–136, 226, 231–232, 243–250, 252, 254–256, 263, 294–296, 316, 320–325, 327, 329–330, 344, 348–349
Montanists, a heretical sect 291, 293
Montanus, heretic 64, 86
Mopsucrenes 172
Mopsuestia 310
Moses, a bishop among the Saracens 262–263
Moses the Black, a monk at Scetis 247–248
Moses the Libyan, a monk of Thebaïs 248–250
Moses the Prophet 205, 263, 291, 308
Mursia 103
Museus, a presbyter 123

Narcissus, bishop of Irenopolis in Cilicia 67, 95, 101, 103, 132
Narni 354
Nazianzen 10, 31, 179, 223, 227, 233, 243, 251, 252, 269–270, 274
Nectaria, a deaconess 163
Nectarius, bishop of Constantinople 243, 274–280, 283, 286–287, 307, 309, 317, 320–321, 323, 337
Neonas, bishop of Seleucia in Isauria 162–163
Nephsameemana 306
Nepotian, usurper 125
Nestabis of Gaza, martyr 184
Nestor of Gaza, confessor 185
Nicæa 7, 30, 35–36, 41, 60–61, 63–65, 67–68, 76, 78–79, 82, 86, 89, 92–94, 96–97, 99, 101–102, 104–105, 117, 128, 132, 136, 138, 143–145, 147–148, 151–152, 157, 164, 167–168, 213–214, 216–217, 219, 221–222, 229, 235–238, 261, 264, 268, 271, 273, 275–276, 343
Nicarete, a woman of Bithynia 338
Nicomedia 13, 28, 35–36, 44, 60, 68, 73, 81–82, 86–87, 91–92, 94, 143–144, 152, 174, 176, 225–226, 238, 316–317
Nigrinian, consul AD 350 129
Nilammon, a monk near Pelusium 333
Nile 15, 134, 176, 262, 295
Nisibis 112, 176, 254
Nitria 25, 252
Novatians 26, 37, 85–86, 153–154, 180, 220, 238, 279–280, 282, 286, 290–291, 293, 308, 339
Novatius, heretiarch 37, 238
Nunchia, wife of Gerontius 361

Oak of Mamre 46
Olybrius, a consul 306
Olympias, deaconess in Constantinople 320, 339, 345
Olympius, a pagan philosopher in Alexandria 284

Olympus, mountain 26, 353
Oppianus, a poet xxv
Origen, a monk at Scetis 250
Origenists 324
Origen of Alexandria 66, 115, 229, 250, 322, 324–327, 329
Orontes River 7, 30, 44, 230, 309
Osdroëna xx, 95
Osdrœnians 52
Osroene 113, 233
Otreius, bishop of Melitine 223, 276

Pachomius, a bishop 74
Pachomius, a monk at Scetis 248–249
Pachomius, founder of the Tabennesians 106–107
Padua 12
Pagan xxiii, 13, 32, 116, 165, 171, 172–174, 176–177, 182, 187–188, 192–194, 198–199, 202, 216, 229, 257–258, 283–284, 294, 301, 338, 354
Paganism 117, 174, 176, 178–179, 183–184, 186, 194–195, 197, 200, 205, 256, 261
Pagras 310
Paladius, a bishop 343
Palestine xv, xix, xx, xxiii, 24, 28, 44, 46–47, 73, 91, 103, 108, 120, 122, 125, 131, 138, 162–164, 176, 204, 213, 253–255, 262, 278, 285, 293–294, 363
Pambonius, a holy man in Egypt 106, 231
Pan, pagan god 48–49
Paneades (*also Cæsarea Philippi*) 203
Pannonia 103, 105, 110, 131, 259, 341, 352
Pansophius, bishop of Nicomedia 317
Pantheon, temple at Bethelia xix, 193
Pantichium 295
Papas, bishop and martyr of Persia 58
Paphlagonia 109, 154–155, 157, 162, 191
Paphnutius, a holy man in Egypt 37–38, 76, 106
Paphnutius the Confessor 18, 76
Parstides (*See also Ammon, one of the "great brothers"*) 251
Pasis 318
Passover 30, 238, 290–293, 308, 335
Patropassius, heretic 222
Patrophilus, Bishop of Scythopolis 28, 35, 65–66, 94–95, 132, 152, 155, 158
Paul, abbot at Ferma 248–249
Paul, a monk in Telmison 256
Paul, a reader in Constantinople 330
Paul, bishop and martyr in Persia 58
Paul, bishop of Constantinople 87, 91–92, 94, 97–102, 105, 118, 123, 125–126, 218, 277
Paul, bishop of Emesa 223
Paulanas, disciple of Saint Ephraim the Syrian 113
Paulinus, bishop of Antioch 103, 167, 189–190, 233, 268–269, 278, 283, 312
Paulinus, bishop of Treves 133

Paulinus, bishop of Tyre 28, 65–66
Paul of Samosata 129, 141, 222
Paul of Tarsus, saint 84, 157, 169, 277, 287, 291–292, 294, 329
Paul the Simple 24
Pazacoma 290–291
Pazi 238
Pelagius, bishop of Laodicea in Syria 213, 223, 276
Pentadia, wife of the general Timasius 318
Pepuzites, a heretical sect (*see also Montanists*) 291
Pergamus 161, 162
Perinthus (*former name of the city of Heraclea*) 94, 143, 217
Persea, a type of tree 204
Persians 6, 53, 58–60, 95, 171–172, 176, 207–208, 210–212, 218, 256, 264, 351
Pessena 196, 330
Peter, patriarch of Alexandria 27–38, 231, 235, 239, 264, 270, 273
Peter, patriarch of Alexandria, martyr 63
Peter the Apostle 142, 270, 291–292, 304, 329, 357, 358
Peter the archpresbyter 323
Petræa 285
Phadana 255
Philip, consul 347
Philip, king of Macedon xxv, xxvii
Philip, prefect of Constantinople 99–100
Philip, the Apostle 304
Philo 22, 291
Philumen 69
Phœnicia xx, 20, 49, 72–73, 203, 244, 262, 278, 285, 293, 340
Photinus, heretical bishop of Sirmium 123, 128–130, 140–141, 267
Phritigernes, Gothic warlord 260–261
Phrygia 86, 187, 219, 238, 291, 293, 313, 316
Phrygians 187
Phrygians, a heretical sect 85–86, 291
Phuscon, a monk in Palestine 254, 327
Piammon, an abbot in Diolchis in Egypt 247
Pilate, governor of Judea 42
Pindar, Greek poet 199
Pior, an anchorite at Scetis 249–250
Piturion, a holy man near Thebes in Egypt 106
Pityuntum 345
Plato, the philosopher xxv, 22, 71
Plinthas, an Arian consul 289
Plusian 75
Poictiers 191
Polycarp, bishop of Smyrna 292
Polychronius, a presbyter 349–350
Pompeiopolis 155, 162, 213
Pontus xx, xxvi, 45, 109, 162, 226–227, 229, 234, 268, 276, 278, 317
Porphyry, bishop of Antioch 340

Prassides 256
Prassides, a monk in Galatia 256
Prines, a presbyter 70
Proæresius, a sophist 229
Probatius, a eunuch of the palace 215
Probianus, physician 45
Probinus, a consul 306
Probus 281–282
Probus, prætorian prefect 281
Procopius, usurper 219, 265
Proculus, bishop of Constantinople 350
Protogenes, bishop of Carræ 255
Protogenes, bishop of Sardica 102, 104
Psathyrians, a heretical sect 289
Ptolemais in Egypt 35
Ptolemais in Syria 321
Pulcheria, empress xii, 347, 349, 351
Pusicius, martyr in Persia 56
Putubastes, a monk at Scetis 106, 250
Pyrenees 267, 360
Pythoness 48

Quadragesima (*also Lent*) 293
Quartodecimani, a heretical sect 291
Quintian, bishop of Gaza 98, 103

Raphi 285
Ravenna 351–352, 354, 356–357
Rhine River 11, 49, 171, 175, 268, 359–360
Rhodanus, bishop of Toulouse 133
Rhone River 361
Rinocorurus 252–253
Romanus, bishop of Antioch 7–8
Romanus, general of the Egyptian garrison 284–285
Romas, bishop and martyr of Persia 58
Rome 7, 11, 17, 29–31, 44, 46, 49, 66, 88, 96, 98, 99–100, 102, 105, 118, 122, 125, 130–131, 136–137, 141–142, 149–150, 217–218, 221, 231, 234–237, 239, 264, 270, 276–278, 283, 286, 291–294, 307, 311–312, 323, 340–341, 343, 345, 353–360
Rufinus, a consul 104
Rufinus, prætorian prefect of the east 307, 329

Sabbatius, a heretic 290–291, 308
Sabellius, heretic 64, 95, 129, 222
Sabinus, bishop and martyr of Persia 58
Sacred Scriptures xix, 3, 5, 8, 55, 79, 94, 112, 147, 150, 156, 169, 193, 229, 240, 247, 251, 261, 309–310
Salamanes, a monk in Palestine xix–xx, 194, 254, 327
Salamis in Cyprus 253, 325
Sallust, prætorian prefect 202
Sangara 290
Sangarus River 238
Sapor, bishop and martyr of Persia 58
Sapor, king of Persia 53–57, 59–60
Sarah, wife of Abraham the Patriarch 263, 332
Sardica 99, 102–104, 118, 123, 125, 139, 150, 343
Sardinia 189, 191
Sardis 87, 161, 162
Sarmates, Arian presbyter 28
Sarmatians 15, 88, 258
Saros, a Gothic general 357, 362
Satalis 162
Saturninus, a consul 279, 313
Saul, king of Israel 199
Scetis 25–26, 105, 247–252, 311, 316, 323, 329
Sciri, a barbarian tribe 353
Scythians 233, 234
Scythopolis 28, 35, 65, 94–95, 132, 155, 158, 324
Sebaste 109, 139, 155, 164, 166–167, 221, 344, 348, 351
Secundus, bishop of Ptolemais in Egypt 35
Secundus, prætorian prefect 212
Seleucia 53, 118, 133, 145–146, 148, 152, 155, 158, 159–160, 162, 191, 213, 218, 223, 310
Seleucus, father of Antiochus 201
Seleucus, Mount 130
Selinus, bishop of the Goths 289
Serapion, abbot in Egypt 84, 106, 246, 250
Serapion, bishop of Heraclea in Thrace 320–321, 327, 330, 333
Serapion, bishop of Thmius 110, 133
Serapis, pagan god 176, 183, 284–285
Sergius, consul AD 350 129
Severian, bishop of Gabales 321–322, 328, 331, 333
Severianus, a bishop in Africa 142
Severus, Septimius, emperor xxv
sibyl 42
Sicily 72, 185, 222–223
Sigesarius, bishop of the Goths 357
Sigoro, mountain 254
Silvanus, a monk in Palestine 254
Silvanus, bishop of Tarsus 156, 162, 213, 221–222, 273
Silvanus, usurper in Gaul 131
Silvester, Pope 7, 66
Simeon, a disciple of Saint Ephraim 113
Simeon, a holy man in Syria 109, 111
Simonides xxv
Sinai, mountain 254
Siricius 307, 340
Sirmich 267
Sirmium 125, 127–129, 131, 138–142, 143, 145–147, 150, 155, 161
Sisinius, bishop of Constantinople 126
Sisinius, bishop of the Novatians 279, 282, 308, 339
Socrates, the philosopher xxv, 71
Sodom 6, 46, 72
Solomon, king of Israel xxvi

INDEX

Solon, abbot at Rinocorurus 252–253
Sophia, the great church in Constantinople 165
Sophronius, bishop of Pompeiopolis in Paphlagonia 155, 157, 162, 191, 213
Sosipater the Philosopher 11
Sotades, a poet 35, 36
Spain 52, 267, 270, 359–360
Spyridion, bishop of Trimithon 18–20
Stephen, a monk of Mareota 248–249
Stephen, bishop of Antioch 119
Stephen the Protomartyr 293, 339, 363–364
Stilicho, master of soldiers 340–341, 351–353
Suevi 359–360
Sycea 153
Symeon, archbishop of Seleucia and Ctesiphon 53–57, 111
Syria xx, 11, 24, 93–94, 96, 101, 112–113, 119, 127, 132, 138, 155, 161, 171, 186, 200, 209, 213, 218–219, 225, 233–234, 244, 254–255, 259, 268, 278, 283, 285, 293, 298, 304, 312, 321, 340, 345
Syriac language 113, 193
Syrians 59, 112–114

Tabennesians 106, 107
Tabennis 107
Tarbula, martyr in Persia 57
Tarsus 156, 162, 200, 213, 221, 223, 273, 274, 276–278, 294, 310
Taurus mountains 172, 244
Terebinthus 46
Terence, bishop of Tomis 276
Thalia, a work by Arius 35
Thebaïs 107, 110–111, 189, 204, 245–246, 297
Thebes 62, 70, 79, 106, 246
Themistius, a philosopher 259
Theoctistes, a heretic 289–290
Theodore, an orthodox cleric 226
Theodore, Arian bishop at Antioch 261
Theodore, a confessor 202
Theodore, a pagan at the imperial court 257
Theodore, bishop of Heraclea 76, 81, 91, 94, 97, 101, 103, 132, 185
Theodore, bishop of Mopsuestia 310
Theodore, disciple of Ammon 25
Theodore, keeper of the sacred vases in Antioch 183–184
Theodore of Tittis, a monk 256
Theodosian Code xvii, 16, 18, 116, 212, 270, 280, 282, 285, 287, 340
Theodosiolus, relative of the emperor Honorius 359
Theodosius I, emperor xxi, xxiii, xxviii, 16, 169, 188, 209, 242, 252, 267, 269–272, 277, 279, 282–283, 287, 296–299, 301, 306–307, 318, 359
Theodosius II, emperor xxv, 322, 347, 359
Theodotus, bishop of Laodicea 240
Theodulis, martyr 187

Theognis, Arian bishop of Nicæa 35–36, 60–61, 68, 76, 81, 86, 89, 97, 117, 122
Theona, a church in Alexandria 133
Theonas, abbot in Egypt 245
Theophilus, Macedonian bishop of Castabalis 162, 221–222, 273
Theophilus, patriarch of Alexandria 283, 307, 311–312, 322–326, 328–333, 340
Theophronians, a heretical sect 288
Theophronius, a heresiarch 288–289
Theopompus, Greek historian xxv
Theotimus, bishop of Scythia 302–303, 326
Thessalonica 13, 99, 269–270, 273, 282, 300
Thmius 110, 133
Thrace 44, 50, 91, 97, 101–104, 132, 136–137, 151–152, 166, 172, 217, 218, 221–222, 225, 260–261, 264–265, 267, 276, 314–315, 333, 340, 352–353
Thracians 110, 259
Thrysus, a martyr 349–350
Tiber River 12, 353
Tigris, a presbyter 330, 340
Tigris River 58, 207–208, 340
Timasius, a general 318
Timothy, a presbyter of Alexandria 74
Timothy, bishop of Alexandria 246, 273, 276, 283
Tirbigildes, a usurping general 312
Tiridates 52
Titus, bishop of Bostra 110, 193
Tomis 233, 276, 302
Treves 81, 102, 133
Trinity 189, 234–235, 241, 270–271, 273, 280, 308
Triphyllius, bishop of Ledra 19–20
Troy 44, 49
Tuscany 354
Tyane 223
Tyre 28, 65–66, 72–73, 75–77, 80–81, 85, 87, 97, 100, 103, 122, 136, 138, 155, 158, 162, 223
Tyrrhenian Sea 12, 110

Uldis, a Hun chieftan 353
Ulphilas, bishop of the Goths 160, 260–261, 289
Ulphilas, general under Constantius III 361–362
Uranius, bishop of Tyre 138, 155, 158
Urbanus, an orthodox cleric 226
Ursacius, Arian bishop of Sigidon 76, 81, 103, 105, 122–123, 137–138, 142, 145–151, 161
Ursinus, anti-pope in Rome 235
Usthazanes, martyr, a eunuch in the Persian court 54–55

Valens, Arian bishop of Mursa 81, 103, 105, 122–123, 128, 137–138, 142, 145–151, 161
Valens, emperor xix, xxvii, 215, 217, –219, 221, 224–227, 233, 254–255, 257, 259–261, 263–265, 267–268, 271–272, 290, 295–296, 327, 357

375

Valentian, a monk 256
Valentinians, a heretical sect 85
Valentinian I, emperor xxvii, 216–217, 220–221, 224, 234, 238, 258
Valentinian II, emperor xxviii, 270, 281–283, 297
Valentinian III, emperor 360, 363
Valentinus 76
Valerian, emperor 60
Valerius, bishop of Aquileia 236
Vandals 359–360
Venice 235–236
Venus, pagan goddess 41, 48, 186
Vercelli 189
Verinian, relative of the emperor Honorius 359
Verona 360
Vetranio, bishop of the Scythians 233–234
Vetranio, usurper 125, 127
Vicentius 30
Vicentius, presbyter from Rome 30
Victor, pope of Rome 292

Vienna 360
Vincent, a bishop 236
Vincent, a consul 315
Vincent, a Macedonian presbyter 296
Vitalians 239
Vitalius, heretical presbyter of Antioch 239
Vito, presbyter from Rome 30
Vitus, bishop of Carræ 255

Zabdæus 58
Zebennus, bishop of Eleutheropolis 306
Zechariah the Prophet 42–43, 363–364
Zeno, a monk near Nisibis 254
Zeno, bishop of Gaza 305
Zeno, bishop of Tyre 223
Zenobius, disciple of Saint Ephraim the Syrian 113
Zeno of Gaza, martyr xx, 184, 185
Zeuxippus, baths of 99
Zocomus, Saracen chief 263–264

Also available in the Christian Roman Empire Series

Volume 1. *The Life of Belisarius*
    by Lord Mahon

Volume 2. *The Gothic History of Jordanes:*
In English Version with an Introduction and a Commentary
    Translated by Charles Christopher Mierow

Volume 3. *The Book of the Popes (Liber Pontificalis):*
To the Pontificate of Gregory I
    Translated by Louise Ropes Loomis

Volume 4. *The Chronicle of John, Bishop of Nikiu:*
Translated from Zotenberg's Ethiopic Text
    Translated by R. H. Charles

Volume 5. *The Ecclesiastical Annals of Evagrius:*
A History of the Church from AD 431 to AD 594
    by Edward Walford

Volume 6. *The Life of Saint Augustine:*
A Translation of the Sancti Augustini Vita *by Possidius, Bishop of Calama*
    by Herbert T. Weiskotten

Volume 7. *The Life of Saint Simeon Stylites:*
A Translation of the Syriac in Bedjan's Acta Martyrum et Sanctorum
    by Rev. Frederick Lent

Volume 8. *The Life of the Blessed Emperor Constantine:*
In Four Books from 306 to 337 AD
    by Eusebius Pamphilus

Volume 9. *The Dialogues of Saint Gregory the Great*
    edited by Edmund G. Gardner

Volume 10. *The Complete Works of Saint Cyprian of Carthage*
    edited by Phillip Campbell

Volume 11. *The Fragmentary History of Priscus:*
Attila, the Huns and the Roman Empire, AD 430-476
    translated with an introduction by John Given

For more information on this series, see our website at:
http://www.evolpub.com/CRE/CREseries.html

www.ingramcontent.com/pod-product-compliance
Lightning Source LLC
Chambersburg PA
CBHW030733250426
43671CB00034B/85